MLS
$ 29.60
Po 73587
11-29-00

Ethics and World Religions

Cross-Cultural Case Studies

REGINA WENTZEL WOLFE
CHRISTINE E. GUDORF
Editors

ORBIS BOOKS
Maryknoll, New York 10545

The Catholic Foreign Mission Society of America (Maryknoll) recruits and trains people for overseas missionary service. Through Orbis Books, Maryknoll aims to foster the international dialogue that is essential to mission. The books published, however, reflect the opinions of their authors and are not meant to represent the official position of the society. To obtain more information about Maryknoll and Orbis Books, please visit our website at www. maryknoll.org.

Published by Orbis Books, Maryknoll, NY 10545-0308
Manufactured in the United States of America

Library of Congress Cataloging-in-Publication Data

Ethics and world religions : cross-cultural case studies / Regina Wentzel Wolfe, Christine E. Gudorf, editors.
    p. m.
   Includes bibliographical references.
   ISBN 1-57075-240-0 (pbk.)
   1. Religious ethics—Case studies. 2. Ethical problems.
I. Wolfe, Regina Wentzel.   II. Gudorf, Christine E.
BJ1188.E825   1999
291.5—dc21
                                      99-17423
                                          CIP

Contents

PART II
RELIGION AND THE STATE

PART III

RELIGION, ECONOMICS, AND ECOLOGY

Introduction

Many social analysts have described our present historical period as postmodern, due to the increasing convergence of trends that move in a direction distinctively different from, even counter to, the central trends of the previous modern period. Just as modernity began earlier in some places than others, postmodernity is well advanced in some parts of the world and barely noticeable in others. But the trends of postmodernity[1] seem undeniable and, to many, inexorable. The differences between the modern and the postmodern periods have serious implications for the religions of the world and contribute to a need for approaching ethics in the way that this book does: through a focus on cases, or real-life situations, treated from a multitude of specific religious perspectives and traditions.

This book is addressed to an English-speaking, predominately American audience which is thus culturally Western and Christian influenced if not actually Christian. We have tried to allow other religions of the world to speak for themselves in the commentaries. Originally we intended to obtain responses only from scholars who were also native practitioners of the various religions. Though we frequently succeeded in this goal, we were sometimes unable to locate or to elicit agreement from such scholars. The religious and academic realms do not yet fully reflect the diversity of postmodernity. Our demand—regrettable and modernist—for commentaries in English within a specific time period, our request that authors anticipate and correct, insofar as possible, the most common misconceptions of Western readers regarding aspects of the cases, the varied nature of religious expertise in some non-Western religions, and the failure of some authors to produce the agreed upon commentaries together narrowed the size of the pool of potential authors and led us sometimes to broaden our criteria. Nevertheless, we feel confident that we have obtained the best possible range of diversity and representation.

Representation of diversity is itself a distinctly postmodern concern. The modern world was structured in terms of new technologies that both allowed increased travel and contact between different peoples and transformed the way people made their living. The industrial revolution, the European voyages of discovery, and European colonization of Australia, the Americas, and large parts of Asia and Africa were all major movements initiating the modern period. Social philosophy developed during the modern period into what we now call sociology, whose purpose was to put together grand narratives which laid out the basic structures and mechanisms of change in human societies in much the same way as the various natural sciences did for nature. The bedrock assumption of this social philosophy was that humanity was one, and therefore, that there was one universal, true theory of human society. As modern social theory took shape, it assumed that history was unilinear and progressive and that modern Western society represented the epitome of human civilization, the inevitable direction of other less advanced societies.

Within this modern world the West slowly began to recognize cross-cultural differences and to become familiar with the history, culture, and accomplishments of other peoples. But because European religious and cultural experience was the lens through which other peoples were seen by the West, knowledge of diverse cultures was not seen as important in its own right but only as instrumentally important for transforming those cultures in a European direction. Similarly, in societies of immigrants such as the United States, acculturation of non-Western and even non-Anglo Europeans to European Anglo culture was a priority. Though separation of church and state was grounded in the Constitution and laws of the United States, it did not prevent the privileging of majority Christian culture in the United States in hundreds of practical ways, from holidays to drug laws.

As westerners became increasingly aware of other religions during the modern period, they began to abandon their historic dichotomy of Christians and pagans—with Jews as a stubborn, problematic intermediate group—and began to make distinctions among non-Christian religions. By late modernity Western interest in and study of most of the religions of the world had moved beyond the xenophobic assignment of pejorative labels but was by no means nonjudgmental. The most common scheme was to divide known religions into "indigenous" and "world" religions, while recognizing a hybrid, syncretic category which included Sikhs, Baha'is, Afro-Caribbean religions such as Vodou, Santeria, and Macumba, and Christian/Native American varieties. The world religions—Christianity, Judaism, Islam, Buddhism, and Hinduism—were singled out for special attention, while indigenous religions were disparagingly dismissed as primitive. The method for teaching the world religions began with sacred texts, their history, and commandments, and then moved to the great figures, organizations, and events in the history of the religion. The method was deductive; the emphasis was on the basic principles from which all particular practices could be deduced.

When identifying the beginning of the postmodern period, most political analysts focus on the 1960s, when the grand narratives—with their universalist assumptions about human nature, society, and history—were increasingly being challenged. The world saw the end of colonialism and the rise of a multitude of new voices and new groups speaking for themselves, disputing the colonialist interpretations of their cultures, religions, directions, and aspirations. In the United States as well, the 1960s were characterized by the rise of new voices from American peoples of color—Africans, Hispanics, Natives, and Asians—as well as from women and young people across racial and ethnic groups. Pluralism of voices and interpretations often became the rule, and as groups represented themselves in the public arena, the degree of social diversity quickly became too great to be subsumed under any one grand narrative. Pundits proclaimed the end of theory.

The late sixties also saw the rise of economic postmodernity in the form of global capitalism. Capital became more mobile and shifted—in the form of industrial jobs—from high wage to low wage areas of the world. The United States, and much of Western Europe, began to recognize a "postindustrial" age as industry shifted to Korea, Indonesia, Taiwan, Mexico, Brazil, and other locales. Since then such nations have been dealing with the political and social dilemmas of modernity—industrialization, urbanization, democratization, labor unrest, and the growth of state bureaucracy to meet escalating demand for social services—at the same time that they are engaged in economic competition within a postmodern global division of labor. In our cases, the global capitalism of postmodernity forms a major part of the background in "The Successful *Sarariiman*," "For the Good of the Children," "What Model of Development?" and "An Unlikely Donor."

Poor societies today are under assault not only from postmodern economic trends but also from the ideas and practices of modernity, as seen in the business practices in "A Conflict of Interest," the attitudes of the international medical committee in "An Issue of Murder?" and the historical background in "Fighting for a Homeland." While the economies of indigenous peoples are still struggling to shift from exporting raw materials to modern industrial production, the global capitalist economy has already shifted from an emphasis on production to an emphasis on consumption, which has made industrial production much less profitable. The high profit end of the division of labor is increasingly not at the production end but at the consumption end, and especially in financial services, information systems, and design.

Not only are poor societies under pressure from the economic changes which affect diverse aspects of people's everyday lives, but the economic emphasis on consumption has been accompanied by globalization of information media such that Western products, lifestyles, and attitudes are increasingly presented in all cultures of the world as desirable, though often in conflict with traditional culture. Many of the cases in this book reflect a clash between traditional (religious) values and culture and a trend toward late modern/postmodern Western monoculture, a clash that sometimes has national settings as in "A Question of Compromise" and "A Conflict of Interest" and at other times has international settings as in "A Tangle of Laws," "A Spectrum of Violence," "Marriage Is for Life," and "A Matter of Veils."

The structure of this book reflects postmodernity's rejection of a deductive method of presenting religions by focusing on sacred texts, creeds, or codes. It focuses instead on how a wide variety of religions respond to a variety of practical, real-life dilemmas. Furthermore, this focus on real-life dilemmas is not usually a focus on dilemmas unique and internal to a specific religion. Instead, virtually all the cases presented here involve contact between different religious and cultural systems; in some of the cases such contact is the primary problem, while in others it is the background for other dilemmas. This is the reality of the postmodern world: there are no homogenous societies anymore. To reflect the diversity of our world, real-life stories from all over the world were selected and developed into cases with names (and sometimes countries and ethnicities) changed to ensure privacy. Each case is followed not by a single response that definitively interprets the case but by two responses each from different religious perspectives, perspectives that often disagree on what the primary issues are as well as how they should be treated.

This text not only insists that we present and seriously consider the broad range of religious and cultural diversity present in our world. It also insists that great diversity neither precludes the possibility of societies reaching internal agreement on basic values and standards of behavior nor prevents real possibilities of dialogue about values and standards between societies. The moral behavior of real people across cultural and religious borders illustrates the ability of people to make moral decisions that demonstrate responsibility for self and others.

The case study approach—based on real-life people and situations—takes the postmodernist critique of modernism seriously without fully accepting the totality of the critique. Our approach accepts what Seyla Benhabib calls a "weak version" of postmodernism, but rejects a "strong version" as incompatible not only with traditional religious teaching on human freedom and responsibility but also with the actual behavior of most human beings faced with moral dilemmas.[2]

Understanding Religion

To recognize and appreciate both the similarities and the differences that exist in the many religious perspectives represented in the commentaries found in the text, a basic framework for understanding religion in general is important. Religious historian Martin Marty's extensive research has identified some primary characteristics or elements which identify a religion. First, religion focuses on an ultimate concern. Second, there is a preference for myth and symbolic language. Third, rites and events are sacralized. A fourth common element is the "meta-story" or large-scale narrative drama, such as is found in the Hindu scriptures. Fifth, religion has a moral or ethical dimension. Though this is not always presented in a structured systematic way, some behavioral correlates are usually present. Finally, there is a tendency toward formation of community, or in noncommunal religions, there is a tendency toward spirituality.[3]

Though not every religion will manifest all of these elements, the majority of the elements will be observable. Likewise, different religions will place different emphasis on one or more of the elements. For example, those speaking from an Islamic or Orthodox Jewish tradition often place heavy emphasis on conformity to ethical codes or behavioral correlates and will make authoritative or universalist claims, while others, for example, most Buddhists, will not.

The very focus on ethics reflects a Western bias to this comparative project. Commentators were asked to illustrate how different religious/cultural systems, and different cultural populations within religions, approach ethical problems and to describe the religious resources and the inherited processes for resolving ethical questions within the religious tradition from which they speak. However, to focus on ethics is not necessarily representative of non-Western thought and religions, which often place particular emphasis not on actions but on states of being.

Despite the attempt to select and frame issues so that ethical conflict is recognizable to Americans, for some readers the perspectives taken will be unfamiliar and difficult to understand. There may not be many points of convergence with those aspects of religion with which the reader is familiar. What is important to recall is that ethics is more than a set of rules governing actions. A rich, thick reading of the dilemmas presented in the text will require a holistic approach that acknowledges both the complexities of the issue and the variety of directions from which it can be approached as well as the sometime equivocal responses to it. Often those who come from Eastern cultures are more willing to accept ambiguity and are comfortable with it. For them the categorical claims of some traditions may be challenging and may require that they move beyond such claims in order to understand the perspective being presented. Those from Western cultures, particularly those whose roots are in the Anglo-Saxon tradition, might find ambiguity in some of the responses uncomfortable. Their challenge will be to suspend judgment and learn to be comfortable with the unfamiliar and the ambiguous.

Indigenous Religions

Indigenous religions are religions that are not distinct from, but are rather coextensive with, a particular people's cultural expression, geographical origins and location. In indigenous religions, subsistence activities—farming, hunting, fishing, gathering—tend to be strongly reflected in religious practice; much of religious ritual often revolves around protecting the group's subsistence by honoring or appealing to divine figures who control weather, animal populations, and/or various related forms of magical power. The underlying assumption in indigenous religions is that humans are part of the cycle of nature and dependent on it. This assumption is one reason indigenous religions are often characterized as holistic. The lives of their members are not compartmentalized; rather the spiritual dimension permeates subsistence activities, social organization, and family life—as each of these areas penetrates all the rest. Most indigenous religions are found in relatively nonspecialized societies, where the roles and activities of members are similar. Indigenous religions are often nonliterate in the sense of not being oriented to written texts, though they may have extensive oral literature.

Indigenous religions do not travel easily, even though indigenous peoples have migrated and do migrate. The Native American Apache, for example, migrated from Canada to the American Southwest during the last 800–900 years, and the Navajo to their eventual home in Arizona/New Mexico only in the nineteenth century. Yet the religious way of life for both Apache and

Navajo is grounded in specific territory with specific landmarks and historic sites; changes in territory are disruptive and require difficult accommodation. One is able to practice only small isolated parts of these religions as an individual apart from the tribe and the tribal land. Religious ritual links the tribe, the land, and the tribal god(s), who are not usually understood as universal divine figures but rather as the god(s) of this people, who gave and watch over this land, though many native religions do have a concept of an overarching superior god-figure. Often migrations of peoples with indigenous religions lead to the new syncretic religions. The Yoruban people, for example, in "What Model of Development?" greatly influenced the syncretic religious practices of the various Afro-Caribbean peoples of French, Spanish, Portuguese, and English language groups—vodou, santeria, candoble, macumba—because so many of the original captured and transported Africans in the Caribbean were from Yorubaland.

All religion is syncretic in that religious communities, both consciously and unconsciously, adopt beliefs and practices from other groups with whom they come into contact. To speak of syncretic religions is not meant to deny historical syncretism in other religions. Indigenous religions have sometimes adopted practices and beliefs from each other. Archeologists and anthropologists have a great deal of evidence that indigenous peoples throughout history have been influenced by their neighbors both voluntarily and under coercion. They not only learned techniques of domesticating particular crops and animals from neighbors and adopted and adapted special ceremonies, rituals, and even deities from neighbors, but often saw other religious cultures imposed on their own, even before the period of modern colonialism.

In the modern period many indigenous societies have either disappeared or been pushed by modern societies into the most inaccessible and/or undesirable territory. In addition, they have often been forced to accept foreign religious, economic, and political practices which further weaken their ability to withstand the pressures of assimilation. In his commentary on "An Issue of Murder?" Diego Irarrázaval describes the result of this type of syncretism. The Christian Aymaran commentary represents this type of syncretism, which arose within native resistance to attempts of Spanish colonial powers to substitute European Christianity for the traditional Aymaran culture which connected the people to the spirits of the mountains. In much of the world today it is difficult to locate indigenous religions that have not been impacted in discernable ways by Christian, Muslim, Buddhist, or other religious missionaries. In Africa and the Americas, anthropologists collecting native myths over the last century have repeatedly found varying levels of penetration of Christian, and in Africa often Muslim, symbolism and teaching within myths understood by the people to be entirely native.[4]

Other more self-conscious and systematic types of syncretism are also possible. The Baha'i religion is an example of a relatively new religion which incorporates many elements of more than one earlier religion. The Baha'i founder, Baha'u'llah, accepted all the world religions as having a common truth and as flawed only by failures to recognize the single foundation of divine religions. Baha'i worship, therefore, makes use of traditional texts and teachings of many different religions. While few religions are born in such self-conscious syncretism, most religions have some elements of syncretism. Christianity, for example, adapted Jesus' version of first century Judaism first to the Greco-Roman world and later to Indo-European religious tribal culture.

From Indigenous to World Religions

Some religions began as indigenous religions but came to share many characteristics of what we call world religions. Judaism is perhaps the primary example, with Hinduism another, of a world religion that began as an indigenous religion and still reveals some indigenous characteristics, though it has spread around the world. Indigenous characteristics of Judaism include its special ties to the land of Israel, its general lack of proselytization, and its reliance on descent. On the other hand, monotheism in Judaism developed early and allowed the Jews of the diaspora to worship their God anywhere. The historical focus of Jewish religious reflection is shared by most world religions, while indigenous religions tend to be more structured around the cycles of nature in their home territory.

Judaism traces itself back to a covenant between God and a nomadic herder in Mesopotamia named Abraham. That covenant, in which Abraham pledged his loyalty and obedience to God in return for God's promise of protection, land, and progeny, was later followed by a second covenant between God and the descendants of Abraham. God sent Moses to lead Abraham's descendants out of slavery in Egypt. As a part of the Mosaic covenant, God gave the Israelite people the Law, a set of 613 commandments expressing God's will as to how they should live. The foundation and symbol of that Law was the Ten Commandments, carved in stone and given to Moses on Mt. Sinai.

After Moses died, the Israelites settled in Canaan, eventually establishing a monarchy. The sacred texts of ancient Judaism are the Torah, the Prophets, and the Writings, which together make up the Hebrew Scriptures. Ancient Judaism ended with the destruction of Solomon's Temple in Jerusalem by the Romans in 70 CE and was replaced by rabbinic Judaism, which substituted prayer for animal sacrifice. After the destruction of the Temple, religious leadership shifted from priests to teachers (rabbis), experts in the study of the Talmud, the collection of rabbinic writings from the first centuries of the Common Era.

The final chapter in the diaspora, the dispersion of the Jewish people to other lands, took place between the destruction of the Temple in 70 CE and the Roman destruction of Judea in 135 CE. Jews became concentrated in Europe and elsewhere as minorities and survived through the policy of separation dictated by the Law. Jewish communities were separate from the surrounding communities in terms of diet, dress, worship, and self-governance, and they forbade intermarriage. The Christian majorities in European nations also enforced separation as part of their persecution of Jews. The uniformity of traditional Judaism endured in Europe until the modern period, when, beginning with the French Revolution, religion (Christianity) was first separated from citizenship, raising the possibility of equal citizenship for Jews. The second half of the nineteenth century saw civil discrimination—as distinct from social discrimination—against Jews end in nation after nation. Some Jews saw the possibility of social and economic assimilation into European society as requiring a reform of Judaism. A new type of Judaism called itself Reform and abandoned those elements of traditional Judaism which enforced separation—the dietary law, dress regulations, the use of Hebrew, and many others—in the name of equal participation in the modern world. The rise of Reform caused the end of uniformity in traditional Judaism in ghetto after European ghetto, prompting the majority of rabbis to support the formation of Orthodox Judaism, which opposed dropping any traditional element that could still be practiced. Later, Conservatism arose as a middle ground between Reform and Orthodoxy, and still later Reconstructionism arose alongside Reform. Today Judaism exists in Orthodox, Conservative, Reform, and in the United States, Reconstruction forms, with Orthodoxy retaining the most of traditional practice and the greatest degree of separatism, as well as the smallest numbers.

From Reform Movement to New Religion

This book contains more commentaries from the Christian perspective than any other, for a number of historical and geographical reasons. Christianity is one of the largest religions in terms of numbers, but not the largest. Christianity developed among the followers of a Jewish teacher, Jesus of Nazareth, who was put to death in Jerusalem in the first half of the first century by the Romans in conjunction with the Jewish authorities. In his teaching Jesus announced the inbreaking of the Kingdom of God. He aimed at internal reform of the Judaism of his day through compassion and service. Opposing fatalism, Jesus emphasized hope in God's forgiving love, which drew to him the poor, the marginalized, and powerless groups of his society. Jesus' resurrection three days after his death and his series of appearances to followers became the basis for their proclamation of Jesus as the Messiah, who would return in glory to complete the victory over sin and death that his resurrection created. The sacred texts of Christianity include both the Hebrew Scriptures (called the Old Testament) and the New Testament, which includes the four gospels recounting the life, death, and resurrection of Jesus, a history of the early church, a number of letters from missionary apostles, and a visionary account of the final Apocalypse.

As the cult of Jesus spread around the Mediterranean in the first and second centuries, its followers became steadily less Jewish and more Greek. Over the next millennium Christianity became more and more European, and less and less Semitic, in its theology and worldview as well as its geography. In fact, by the fourth century when Christianity became the official religion of the Roman Empire, Christianity had begun to take on many organizational aspects of the Roman Empire, as seen in its legal framework and the formulation and trappings of episcopal and papal office.

The Great Schism of 1054 between the eastern and western halves of the Roman Empire created the first of the major Christian divisions remaining today, that between Orthodox and Catholic Christianity. Orthodoxy divided along the lines of the patriarchs (Greek and Russian, for example), while in the West the papacy retained control of all the Latin (Roman) Christians as well as many small eastern groups. Division came to the West in the sixteenth century with the Protestant Reformation, in which a series of religious reformers, including Martin Luther, John Calvin, Huldrake Zwingli, and the King of England, Henry (Tudor) VIII, led large groups, even whole nations, in separation from the papacy in Rome over issues of corruption in the church and individual religious agency. Many of the resulting Protestant denominations became national churches, with more or less connection to other national churches with the same historical roots. Within Protestantism the process of division continued long after the sixteenth century, not only over theology and church polity, but also over moral and political issues such as war and slavery.

Christianity has been the dominant religion of the modern period because it was the dominant religion in the West during the period of Western colonization of much of the world. A number of world religions have spread in conjunction with empires, such as Buddhism under King Asoka, Christianity under the Roman Empire, and Islam through military conquest in Arabia and North Africa and trade in sub-Saharan Africa and Asia. The expansion of Christianity through colonial conquest during the centuries leading into the modern period served to legitimize colonial economic and political structures in much of the world. Religious studies scholars and historians continue to debate whether there is any intrinsic connection between Christianity and capitalism, or Christianity and modernity.[5] The German sociologist Max Weber, for example, linked the more ascetic strains of Protestantism, especially the Reformed tradition with its teaching of predestination, with the spirit of capitalism.[6] Connections between Christianity and modernity, however, are somewhat easier to make. For example, the early transition in Christianity from a Judaic to a Greek context caused a soteriological shift, which, when combined with the adoption of virginity and celibacy as paths to freedom from the restrictions of patriarchal family life,[7] set the stage for the development of religious individualism in Christianity. This was a development which flowered fully in the Enlightenment and the scientific revolution and later helped to erode traditional, more communal, society during the social transitions of the industrial revolution and the rural to urban migrations which accompanied it. European colonial conquest carried Christian missionaries along with, and often as carriers of, modern philosophy, science, and nation states.

Different versions of Christianity had different histories and impacts in different parts of the world. Catholic Christianity came to Latin America with the conquistadores, but Protestant Christianity arrived later. Protestantism was carried largely by the English and Americans who supported colonial revolutions against Spain and Portugal in the interest of breaking those nations' trade monopolies with Latin America. Protestant Christianity presented itself in Enlightenment terms, as the religion of liberalism and progress. A multiplicity of patterns developed, including a variety of syncretic versions of particular indigenous American traditions with particular Christian traditions such as Aymaran Catholicism.

In other parts of the world, Christianity also developed various local inculturations. Latin American Catholics differ from Indian Catholics and Italian Catholics and Korean Catholics, but all of them share common core beliefs, even though Korean Catholics may share as many, or even more, aspects of their particular faith practice with Korean Presbyterians than with French Catholics. And these same Korean Catholics may share some of their religious worldview with Korean shamanic practitioners. In Africa, there are African Methodist, Catholic, Anglican, and other Christian churches in which aspects of Christian ritual and theology reflect tribal traditions, but the congregation is organizationally linked to other churches of the same denomination around the world. But there are also the independent churches of Africa, a fast-growing phenomenon in which aspects of Christianity have been adapted to largely African religious thought and practice by charismatic local leaders who have started their own churches, independent of European/American Christian churches.

In this text we make no attempt to represent all the various Christian denominations. Some of the Christian commentaries take a general Christian perspective, and at certain points identify differences between Christian groups, while others clearly represent a Catholic, an Orthodox, or a specific Protestant perspective, and yet others represent a particular syncretic version of Christianity and another tradition. The underlying intention is to present the diversity within Christian religious reality today.

Prophecy from the Deserts

A similar diversity exists in Islam which, over the centuries, has spread from the deserts of Arabia throughout the world. It was founded in the early seventh century by the prophet Muhammad who received a vision telling him he was Allah's messenger; for the rest of his life he received revelations from Allah, which were later gathered into the Qur'an. The monotheism of Islam is intimately connected to a humanism which is egalitarian at its core and is reflected in its insistence on economic and social justice. Thus, in common with other religions, the focus of Islamic teachings is both personal and social.

The Five Pillars of Islam focus on the personal dimension of being a faithful Muslim. The first and overarching pillar is the fundamental creedal statement of Islam: There is no God but Allah, and Muhammad is his Messenger. This makes clear the uncompromising monotheism of Islam. The remaining pillars focus on the personal responsibilities of faithful followers. They are to pray five times daily, to give alms to the poor, to observe the holy month of Ramadan, and, if at all possible, to go on pilgrimage to Mecca at least once.

The social teachings of Islam are contained in the Qur'an, which Allah dictated to Muhammad. These sacred scriptures are at the heart of Islamic life. These teachings provide clearly articulated laws that govern all aspects of the lives of believers including social, political, economic, and familial relationships. In considering the issue of child labor, Mohamed Adam El-Sheikh's commentary on "For the Good of the Children," provides an excellent example of the specificity which is found in *shari'a*—Islamic law.

While followers share a fundamental belief system summarized in the Five Pillars of Islam and accept the body of normative social teachings based in the Qur'an and elaborated in the *shari'a*, the lived expression of the faith is not monolithic. The most basic division has its roots in an early disagreement over who was the legitimate successor to the prophet Muhammad; this disagreement among the followers of Islam resulted in the distinction between Shi'i and Sunni Muslims. As in other faith traditions, Islam also has its mystics. Known as Sufis, these are individuals who seek, through various ascetic and meditative practices, to come to deeper experience and communion with God. As are mystics in other religions, so too the mystics of Islam are decidedly a minority. Sufis have periodically been regarded either with reverence for their holiness or suspicion by those who understand the Qur'an as an unambiguous and completely reliable path to salvation.

While the Muslim community understands the Qur'an as divine and immutable, there is some debate as to the status of the *shari'a*. Some traditionalists understand *shari'a* as also divine and immutable, while others regard it as the specific application of divine law to historical situations. In Sunni Islam, the bases for *shari'a* include, besides the Qur'an, *sunna* (the practices and traditions of the prophet Muhammad), *qiyas* (analogy), and *ijma'* (consensus). The four different Sunni schools of jurisprudence have different approaches to these sources for *shari'a*. Al-Shafi'i and Abu Hanifa, who lived in Egypt and Iraq, respectively, used *qiyas* and *ijma'* more liberally than did Ahmad Ibn Hanbal and Malik, who lived in Baghdad and Medina, respectively, and thus shared the general social ethos of the Qur'an and the *hadith* (reports of Muhammad's sayings and deeds). When Islam spread into new territory, new situations and questions arose which had not been anticipated in the Qur'an and the *hadith*. Among Shi'i Muslims it is clear that jurisprudence is based only on the Qur'an and the pronouncements of Muhammad as reported by the imams, male descendants of the Prophet's daughter Hazrat Fatima and her husband Ali. However, there are major divisions among Shi'i over who were rightfully appointed imams.

As with other religious traditions, particularly Judaism and Christianity, a range of responses and attitudes to contemporary issues and problems can be found in Islam. These run the spectrum from fundamentalist to liberal and often reflect differing degrees of openness to economic, social, political, and cultural attitudes deemed to be external to Islam. An example of these differences as they relate to understandings of the modern nation-state is found in the comments of Ismail Abdalla in his response to "Fighting for a Homeland."

Some of the images most associated with Islam by casual Western observers, such as female circumcision and veiled women, are as much or more reflections of cultural and social traditions than of religious law. They point to the spread of Islam throughout the world and the numerous cultures and societies that have accepted it. The complexities of these issues are examined by Marcia Hermansen in her response to "A Question of Compromise" which focuses on female circumcision and by Bahar Davary in her response to "A Matter of Veils."

An Ancient Framework for Living

Hinduism, a complex blend of many traditions, permeates the life of a follower, making it difficult to separate religious beliefs from the cultural and social setting. The roots of Hinduism are in a very ancient oral tradition, the Vedas, first composed in the twelfth century BCE. The Vedas, known as *sruti* (scripture), are considered to be the primary revelation. These differ from *smriti* ("newer" literature), the secondary revelation that includes the great epics of the people of ancient India and of Rama, the incarnation of the god Vishnu. *Smriti* also includes the law books which provide a basis for discerning needed corrections in society and explanations of ritual and meditative practices which pervade and govern Hindu life with its emphasis on maintaining a balance between the sacred and the profane, or the pure and the impure.

The many gods of Hinduism, whose stories are recounted in the *smriti*, reflect a belief that there are many paths to god and/or *moksa* (spiritual freedom or liberation), with none being deemed better than another. Various mediators—physical representations of the god(s), temples, sacred groves, or human mediums—enable followers to come in contact with the sacred in myriad ways. The three Hindu responses found in this text point to the richness and variety of the Hindu way of life. Despite this variety and openness, the whole of life is conceived in a rather structured way that correlates the four purposes of life and the four stages of life with the caste system and its four groups, which Christopher Chapple describes in his response to "A Conflict of Interest." Finding a way to *moksa* and, thus, ending *samsara* (the cycle of reincarnation) is seen as the ultimate, though not only, purpose in life. The Hindu is also concerned with three other purposes in life: pleasure, success, and duty, each of which assists in coming to religious fulfillment.

There is a recognition that people strive for pleasure, but it is understood that this must be undertaken in a sensible manner. Achievement of long-term pleasure may demand sacrificing more immediate pleasures. Thus, striving for pleasure should not be understood as a call for immediate gratification. There is also a recognition that people seek worldly success. Attaining success provides people with a sense of self-worth and dignity while enabling them to meet their basic needs and to participate in the larger society.

However, success in and of itself is understood to be limited, because it focuses on the finite here and now and does not provide true satisfaction or sate some ultimate desire. As they move along the path to *moksa*, individuals will move beyond pleasure and success which tend to focus on the self, and they will focus on the community and the duties that attend membership in it.

These duties, which are many and varied, are for the most part determined by one's station in life (*asrama*). Originally the institution of *asrama* was restricted to Brahman males who would take up the occupation of student and engage in the tasks of gaining knowledge of the tradition and of attending to the development of character. Having embarked on this path, the Brahman boy could, if he desired, choose to remain a student in his teacher's house all of his life rather than move on to the householder stage with its attendant responsibilities to family and community. This second stage of life centered on the human desire for pleasure, success, and duty. Here the focus was on marriage and family, vocation, and civic or community responsibilities. When familial and civic duties had been discharged, it was possible to retire from worldly obligations and move to the third stage of life with its focus on the inner life in preparation for the final stage—the search for the true self which results in the ability to transcend the finite and so come to *moksa*.

This classical model of *asrama* or the stages of life was in part an effort to reconcile the ascetic tradition with the householder tradition of the Brahman class and is a result of what is called "Sanskritization," the process by which popular religion was influenced by the Brahmanical tradition. "Advancement" to the next stage was not simply a matter of course or in any sense linear. In the first place, not all castes were allowed to study the tradition. In the second place, the vast majority of the population existed outside of the structured society of classical Hinduism which has, however, greatly influenced everyday life with its consequent cultural and societal expectations.

In the fourfold structure of the caste system only members of the three highest castes—Brahmins, Kshatriyas, and Vaishya—are deemed fit to study the tradition. This is because members of these three castes are *dvija*—twice born—and, therefore, have the potential to come to the infinite. *Atmans* (individual souls) are independent of the bodies that they inhabit. The *atman* progresses through various bodies. Only when the *atman* comes into a human body does it become aware of itself. This self-awareness brings with it freedom as well as responsibility.

This freedom and responsibility is governed by the law of *karma* that encompasses the moral universe through which the *atman* passes. *Karma* is not analogous to the Western concept of a set of ethical principles. Rather *karma* is a principle which holds that individuals determine their own being through the actions of their past and present lives. Thus, the path of a particular journey is determined by the individual's desires and actions as he or she moves through various incarnations. At base the goal is to lead a holy life (*varnasramadharma*) in preparation for *moksa*—spiritual freedom.

The *atman* may have many reincarnations before finally attaining *moksa*. There is not one correct path through these stages. As noted above, Hinduism recognizes that different people will follow different ways, that is, that there are different spiritual paths, all of which have the holy life as their end. It is important to recognize, however, that each of these paths requires order and balance in a person's life, particularly in his or her relationships. Reflecting the richness and variety of human life, Hindus are clear that the paths may vary, yet the ultimate goal of each person's journey is the same, as is each person's ability to determine the trajectory and length of that journey through the choices he or she makes. Despite this openness to other approaches to the sacred, Hinduism is intertwined with culture and society. The traditional social structures of India with which Hinduism is inexorably bound sometimes lead to conflicts between generations and within families of those who have either emigrated from India or been raised or educated in foreign cultures.

The Path to Awakening

Buddhism, which has some roots in Hinduism, is often difficult for the Western mind to comprehend. It has elaborate and highly systematized doctrine, shaped by the teachings of the Buddha which have been passed on through oral traditions as well as in sacred texts. There are many varieties of Buddhism yet each shares a common starting point—the life and teachings of Siddhartha Gautama, the Buddha.

Gautama Buddha, who lived in the sixth century BCE, rejected what he viewed as distortions and abuses within Hinduism. This included his rejection of the caste system which placed power and authority with the Brahmins, his rejection of the highly ritualistic, sacrificial practices, and his rejection of the fatalistic attitude of the Hinduism of his day which was resigned to a Brahmanic interpretation of dharma. The Dharma (teaching) of Gautama Buddha is based in the Four Noble Truths: that life is *dukkha* (suffering); that the cause of *dukkha* is *tanha* (insatiable craving); that there is a relief or liberation from suffering, *nirvana*; and that there is a path of liberation, The Eightfold Noble Path. It is this path that leads to *nirvana*, the state of Enlightenment that transcends the limitations of this world through complete Awakening to the nature of reality.

The Eightfold Path is a practical guide to Enlightenment that calls for right understanding, right thought, right speech, right behavior, right livelihood, right effort, right mindfulness, and right contemplation. It is rather linear in terms of progression. Buddhists say that the attainment of meditative concentration depends on one's ethical life, and the attainment of wisdom penetrating the nature of reality depends on the attainment of meditative concentration. It is not linear in the sense that one can train in all three aspects simultaneously, but their attainment is not simultaneous. The three categories of practices of the Eightfold Path are: (1) *sila* (ethical discipline) which is concerned with right speech, right behavior, and right livelihood;

(2) *samadhi* (meditative concentration) which includes right effort, right mindfulness, and right contemplation; and (3) *prajna* (wisdom) which pertains to the right view, seeing the reality as it is.

Though the teaching of the Four Noble Truths is characteristic of all Buddhist schools, various sects and traditions within Buddhism emphasize different aspects of the Eightfold Path that leads to Enlightenment. In order to gain even a minimal understanding of the impact of this difference in emphasis it will be helpful to look briefly at the three main divisions of Buddhism: Theravada (Sravakayana) Buddhism, Mahayana Buddhism, and Vajrayana Buddhism.

Theravada Buddhism emphasizes that only those who lead a monastic life can attain arhatship. It understands progress along the path to Enlightenment to be an individual endeavor. Each person is solely responsible for his or her own progress. Others, including the Buddha, are simply models to be emulated. Theravada Buddhism understands the primary characteristic of Enlightenment to be wisdom, specifically the insight into the Four Noble Truths. An important aspect of the Fourth Noble Truth, the path, is to practice Four Divine Abidings, *Brahmaviharas: metta* (loving kindness), which calls for unconditional love of all beings including one's own self; *karuna* (compassion), which calls for empathy with another rather than sympathy for another; *mudita* (sympathetic joy), which is an expression of sincere joy for another's success; and *upekkha* (equanimity), which calls for an even-handed attitude toward all. The ideal person is the arhat, who through his or her own merit has achieved freedom from suffering. The *nirvana* of arhats is not the same as the *nirvana* of Buddha. In this tradition, seeking Enlightenment is a full-time occupation.

Mahayana Buddhism holds that progress toward Enlightenment is not possible without a community of sentient beings who provide one with the opportunity to practice compassion. Its followers, unlike those of Theravada Buddhism, are assisted on the path by bodhisattvas, those who have not entered *nirvana* in favor of assisting others until the time when all sentient beings—animals, spirits, and so forth—will have reached Enlightenment. In the Mahayana tradition the monastic life is not indispensable for attaining Enlightenment. Laypersons, through their prayers and bodhisattva practices, with help from the buddhas and bodhisattvas, can cultivate the virtues and attain Enlightenment. Followers of this tradition place great emphasis on the virtues, particularly compassion, because it is the expression of wisdom in action. These two, compassion and wisdom, are viewed as two wings of Enlightenment. Pure Land Buddhism, which Richard Payne represents in his commentary on "The Successful *Sarariiman*," and Zen Buddhism are two of the more familiar schools of Mahayana Buddhism, dominant in East Asia. Both have considerable followings in the West, appealing as they do to the postmodern search for meaning.

The emphasis of Vajrayana Buddhism is on esoteric interpenetration of the world which recognizes the interrelatedness and nonduality of all things. What distinguishes this tradition from other Buddhist traditions is not the ultimate goal of Enlightenment but the practices which enable one to attain *nirvana* in one lifetime. Rather than attempting to reject passion and worldly things as the Theravada Buddhists do, followers of the Vajrayana tradition use them to their advantage. For example, sensual pleasures become aids on the path to Enlightenment rather than distractions from the path to Enlightenment.

It is important to remember that all of the traditions share the same goal as well as the same basic teachings. Among those teachings not yet mentioned but of some relevance to the discussions in this text are the five ethical guidelines for right behavior: abstinence from killing; abstinence from stealing; abstinence from lying; abstinence from engaging in sexual misconduct; and abstinence from intoxicants. The rules of conduct are not given as commandments but rather as guidelines as to the things to be avoided. These are the basic five elements of moral conduct, equally applicable to monastics and laypersons. Monastics usually have more than 200 precepts, whereas laypersons have significantly fewer. Yet, as Vesna Wallace indicates in her commentary, both interpretive and evaluative applications of them in determining the ethical quality of any given action can differ among Buddhist perspectives. As is obvious to anyone familiar with Judaism, Christianity, or Islam, such specification of rules of moral conduct and the evaluative application of them are not unique to Buddhism. Rather, they point to a more fundamental human search for the good, a search in which humans have been engaged throughout the ages. The heritage of Buddhist tradition is lived out in a rich diversity among its followers, a trait not uncommon to other religious traditions.

Working with Cases

The cases found in this volume represent true-to-life situations and are presented as an avenue for readers to reflect on ethical issues from a variety of religious and cultural perspectives. Given the nature of this book readers will be challenged to engage the material on many different levels. They will be asked to examine the cases both from their own perspectives and from the perspectives of others. As with any case study, readers should be prepared to identify the problem or problems that are found in each case and to provide some indication of why they believe these to be ethical issues and dilemmas. In addition, readers should be prepared to say whether their perceptions of what the ethical issues and dilemmas are differ from or are similar to the issues and dilemmas identified by the various commentators. In part, this is a question of determining whether the questions that a specific case raises are universal in character or whether they are particular to one or more religious tradition/s or culture/s.

These case studies and their accompanying commentaries also provide readers with a basic introduction to major world religions. Readers should give careful consideration to the commentaries themselves in order to gain a better insight into the way that individuals from a particular religious tradition identify and respond to ethical issues and dilemmas. For example, by carefully studying each of the commentaries written from a Christian perspective, readers will be able to identify commonly held beliefs and understandings among Christians. At the same time, readers will see that differences exist and that not all Christians have the same response to moral dilemmas. One of the challenges facing readers will be to consider what counts as appropriate responses to these moral distinctions within particular religious traditions.

A similar challenge is presented when considering the cases from an interfaith perspective. Again, the task is to examine each perspective carefully, to determine where similarities and differences exist, and to identify reasons for those similarities and differences. Understanding the context and setting of each case is important in this endeavor. The commentaries will provide some discussion of cultural, social, economic, or other factors important to the case; but readers should recognize that a willingness to be open to different attitudes and approaches to human dilemmas will enhance their ability to grasp both the import of these factors for the people and situations in the cases and the implications that these factors have for possible resolutions to the problem or problems presented in the cases. Again, readers will be challenged to respond to distinctions and differences in the approaches to and resolutions of the issues present in the cases.

As they consider their own reactions to these differences, readers might want to consider four possible responses to the challenge of moral distinctions that John Mahoney has identified.[1] One possible response is to ignore the challenge. Those who respond in this way usually deny both the complexities that exist in the situation and the existence of real conflicts in moral values. In part, this is a result of a tendency to assume shared values whether or not they actually exist.

A second response is to reject the challenge of moral distinctions by denying the existence of shared values. Those who adopt this position contend that there is no moral understanding upon which distinctions can be analyzed. Often those who fall into this category are unable to distinguish the "difference between moral chaos and moral pluralism" because the validity of equally legitimate responses to complex moral dilemmas is not recognized.[1] They are unwilling to acknowledge legitimate diversity, the existence of conflicting moral values, or the possibility that some values simply cannot be realized in particular situations. Thus, they often understand themselves as keepers of the one set of values, the one right answer which they hold has been rejected by the broader society. What for others is legitimate pluralism and diversity which might present more than one adequate response and, therefore, which might require compromise is for them moral chaos or anarchy.

A third response is to view moral distinctions as indicators of adequate or appropriate responses to moral decision making. Here individuals understand moral distinctions to be the result of allowing circumstances to qualify a moral principle generally accepted as valid. They recognize the existence of ambiguity and are willing to qualify and nuance their positions. William

P. George, in his commentary on "Fighting for a Homeland," provides an example of this response in his discussion of the Roman Catholic tradition's understanding of the concept of premoral evil.

Finally, there are those who accept moral distinctions though they do not understand them to be static and absolute but rather are willing to modify or refine them as necessary. This group of individuals is willing to recognize and accept ambiguity. In addition, they recognize and accept ethical pluralism and diversity. Thus, they are willing to acknowledge that there may be more than one adequate resolution to a particular ethical issue or dilemma, though they do not blindly accept any or every response. Readers who find themselves in this group will be concerned with assessing the adequacy of proposed resolutions in an effort to determine the compatibility of the responses. In some instances more than one way to resolve the case may exist. Some of these resolutions may be more or less adequate than others, while there may be cases where two or more equally suitable resolutions exist. It is important that readers be able to understand the reasons put forth in support of various resolutions if any judgment or assessment of the adequacy of the resolution or resolutions is to be made.

Such assessment requires careful and critical analysis of the cases in order to identify the reasons for differences. Understanding the reasons for difference will assist in distinguishing instances where there are no fundamental differences from instances where the differences are radical and potentially irresolvable. As Cynthia Crysdale has shown, there are different ways of accounting for and responding to differences.[10]

Sometimes differences are a result of individuals' being at different developmental stages and do not reflect fundamental differences. These differences will be resolved over time as individuals grow and develop. In other instances differences are a result of judgments based on different lived experiences and/or different data. In these instances, familiarity with the lived experience of others and access to the same data is necessary in order to determine whether or not fundamental differences exist.

When addressing issues of fact or "judgments of truth," readers should ensure that they have sought "sufficient evidence to affirm a particular possibility as true."[11] This means that they must ask all the relevant questions: who? what? where? why? when? and how? Thus, for example, in considering the subject of child labor presented in "For the Good of the Children," they will be able to judge the veracity of Maria's claim that forcing children "to stretch or otherwise accommodate themselves to equipment that is oversized for them . . . can hamper their muscle and bone development leaving them more susceptible to neurological complications when they get older."

Readers will also have to engage in judgments of value. Here it is important to recognize the possibility of personal or cultural bias coloring one's judgments. While perspectives might differ because they are rooted in particular worldviews and lived experiences, it is important to recognize that they reflect judgments of truth or fact. That is, they are based in a reality rather than being reflections of bias or prejudice which are rooted in ignorance.

To fully enter into the task of comparing their perspectives with the perspectives of the commentators, readers will have to do the hard work of distinguishing between their own biases and prejudices and legitimate perspectives that arise from different lived experiences. This means that they must be aware of the potential for self-deception and rationalization. This will require a certain level of maturity and a willingness to ask themselves penetrating questions and examine their own positions and assumptions. The same willingness to engage in serious inquiry will be needed to distinguish between biases and prejudices found in the wider community and legitimate cultural and societal perspectives. In addition to considering all the relevant questions, this will require an openness to other perspectives and the challenges that they bring to one's own views, an openness to engaging in honest dialogue with others, an openness to the possibility of error, and an openness to the possibility of change. Thus, for example, in attempting to find an adequate resolution to Takeo Mashimoto's dilemma in "The Successful *Sarariiman*," readers should try to understand the cultural context in which Takeo finds himself in order to determine the degree to which it impacts an adequate resolution to his dilemma.

This book challenges readers to examine their own perspectives and biases. At the same time, however, readers should critically analyze the various responses offered to the cases under consideration. Thus, the questions they put to themselves should also be put to the commentators in a manner that fosters greater understanding of the perspectives of others with their underlying worldviews and values which find expression in their religious traditions and give rise to their responses to ethical issues and problems with which they are confronted.

Notes

1. Postmodernity is to be distinguished from postmodernism, which is an interpretation of and response to the material postmodern world.

2. Benhabib's critique of postmodernism was from the perspective of feminism, which she understands in terms of a historical political project. But the argument works similarly well for any religion with both a critical perspective on social reality and a historical task stemming from that critical perspective. See Seyla Benhabib, *Situating the Self: Gender, Community and Postmodernism in Contemporary Ethics* (New York: Routledge, 1992).

3. Martin Marty, "What Role Should Religion Have in Public Life?" The Public Religion Project Symposium (Minneapolis, MN, 28 April 1998). See also Martin Marty and R. Scott Appleby, eds., *Religion, Ethnicity, and Self-Identity: Nations in Turmoil* (Hanover, NH: University Press of New England, 1997), 10–12.

4. See, for example, the Native American and African myths in Barbara C. Sproul, *Primal Myths: Creating the World* (New York: Harper and Row, 1979).

5. See, for example, Anthony Giddens, *Capitalism and Modern Social Theory* (Cambridge, England: Cambridge University Press, 1971), 119–132.

6. Max Weber, *The Protestant Ethic and the Spirit of Capitalism* (New York: Charles Scribner's Sons, 1958).

7. Peter Brown, *The Body and Society: Men, Women and Sexual Renunciation in Early Christianity* (New York: Columbia University Press, 1988).

8. John Mahoney, "The Challenge of Moral Distinctions," *Theological Studies* 53 (1992). Though he is writing from a Roman Catholic perspective, the responses he identifies can be applied more broadly.

9. Mahoney, "The Challenge," 670.

10. Cynthia Crysdale, "Horizons that Differ: Women and Men, the Flight from Understanding," *Cross Currents* 44, no. 3 (1994).

11. Crysdale, "Horizons," 352.

PART I

RELIGION, FAMILY, AND CULTURE

CHAPTER 1

A Question of Compromise

A CASE STUDY by Christine E. Gudorf

"Husband, we must talk," Awa pronounced solemnly as she placed a plate of dinner before her husband, Joseph. Joseph was a truck driver driving between their village outside Kaolack, Senegal, and the cities of Banjul and Dar Salamay in The Gambia. He had just returned from a week-long trip.

"What is it, Awa—can't you handle whatever it is? I don't like the tone of your voice," responded Joseph tiredly.

"Your mother was here again while you were gone, demanding to know why I haven't arranged the womanhood ceremonies for the girls, and telling them stories of the treats and special status that follow. She keeps warning them that they will never get husbands, that they will be shunned, without the ceremony. You must stop her, Joseph," insisted Awa.

"So, she has been doing the same for five years. Why must I stop her now?" asked Joseph as he bit into a leaf-wrapped mixture of rice and chicken.

"Because Fatima asked if she could spend a few weeks with her grandmother. I was afraid your mother would arrange the ceremony, so I refused. But Fatima angrily repeated what your mother had told her, that I couldn't be a proper wife or mother and would never have sons because I had not been properly circumcised, but had had only the 'imitation' rite. Joseph, I want to move away from your mother."

"Now you're being silly, Awa. My mother will complain but not interfere. You know she is just baiting you—she has never liked that I married a Serer woman instead of a local Wolof, or that your bride price was so high because of your education. She knows that I will honor my betrothal promise to you that the girls will not go to the circumciser. We don't need to move—where would we go? You know I cannot leave the job—it is one of the best, especially now that I am the senior driver on my route. Kaolack is one end of my route—it makes no sense to live anywhere else in Senegal. Your family is spread between Dakar and Yoff, and both are too far away from my route. All my family and our friends are here. Now that's an end to it. I didn't come home to hear complaints and demands. My mother has always said I was a fool to agree in your marriage contract not to take a second wife. But what man could stand the complaints of two wives?" he concluded as he rose from his chair and headed for a nap on his bed.

A week later Awa was marketing with her friend Assitan, who had come with Awa to Kaolack from Dakar twelve years before when the two had taken positions as the first female teachers in the Muslim elementary school. Assitan had also married a local Wolof man, an artist who did Senegalese reverse-glass painting and was becoming well known to galleries in Dakar and Banjul as well as in Kaolack.

"Awa," Assitan urged after hearing Awa's account of her talk with Joseph, "don't worry about Joseph. The man is not going to pursue *talaq* [divorce pronounced by the husband]. He is the only driver for his company who is known for celibacy on his route, and according to you that is not because he is not interested in sex. He is only trying to appease his mother a little to preserve peace—he is not going to either break his betrothal promises or divorce you. Speak to the girls. They are nine and eleven now, and old enough to object to the ceremony themselves if they learn what it is and how it will affect them. When they were little you were afraid to scare them, but now if Fatima is asking for the ceremony you need to give her all the information about it. You can be sure your mother-in-law doesn't. Joseph is trying to stay neutral between you and his mother while honoring his promise—you need the girls themselves to support your decision."

The next afternoon Awa called both of the girls into the kitchen and presented each with large piles of fresh vegetables to be cleaned and prepared. "I need to talk with you both. You are growing up, and all too soon you will be deciding whether your own daughters should be whole or crippled," she said. Fatima's face took on a sulky look of resistance as she realized the subject at hand, but Hadija looked questioningly at her mother.

"When I was a girl in Dakar," Awa began, "my mother and my father argued over whether I was to have the womanhood ceremony. My mother and both my grandmothers insisted that I had to have it. They argued just as you have heard—that the genitals of a girl who did not have the cutting of the ceremony grew long and deformed until they hit her knees, that she had the parts of a man, and could not bring forth a son, and that even the girl babies she bore died from touching her male parts in birth." Both the girls nodded that they had heard the consequences of foregoing the ceremony.

"But my father had been influenced by his French teachers in the university. He believed that the cutting of the ceremony was physical mutilation, and that it was contrary to the instructions of the Messenger of Allah not to excise any organ. He told me that his favorite sister had been sent to the circumciser when she was nine, and she died a week later. His mother had attributed the death to evil spirits, but my father said it was infection from the ceremony." Both Fatima and Hadija had completely stopped their work to listen, but Awa continued to chop the vegetables.

"Finally they compromised, and I was circumcised by a doctor, with anesthesia so I did not scream with the pain, and only a small piece of skin was cut off, the covering over the clitoris. My mother and grandmothers were not fully satisfied, for they believed that the entire clitoris should be cut out, so my husband would not fear my being tempted to adultery by sexual desire, but they thought this was better than nothing. They could at least report to the neighborhood that I had been circumcised and was therefore marriageable, though they feared that no husband would be satisfied with the modest results." Awa smiled to herself, remembering how Joseph had remarked on many private occasions that he was more than satisfied with the modesty of the results. Once on a visit to her family in Dakar when he and her father had relaxed in the garden after a big meal, Joseph had even insisted on thanking her father for his resistance to the full ceremony.

Fatima insisted, "If you were anesthetized anyway, why not have it all cut off so you would be purely female and not deformed? Where was your faith, your religious submission?"

Awa explained that she disagreed that this was a matter of religious submission, however much the grandmothers and the circumcisers insisted that it was. Most Muslims did not practice any form of female circumcision. The Muslims of Saudi Arabia, Iraq, Iran, Kuwait, Pakistan—none of these had ever practiced it. In Africa, some places like Sudan called the most drastic and dangerous form of circumcision (genital infibulation) *sunna*, the Muslim word for tradition, while in Egypt and other places the type called *sunna* was much more moderate, at most clitoridectomy, often only the removal of the clitorial hood.

"If you lived in Sudan," Awa continued, "or even in some villages in Senegal, Mali, or Burkina Faso, circumcision would involve a bunch of women holding you down and gagging you while some dirty-fingered old woman uses a knife that has just cut other girls to cut off the inner lips of your vulva, then the outer lips, then the entire clitoris, and then sticks a straw in your urethra and sews together the sides of your crotch around the straw. If you survive, you will walk differently, more slowly and carefully, all your life, for all the skin will be scar tissue, and tight. It will take you much longer to empty your bladder, for the opening in the scar tissue is so small. Your menses will last longer for the same reason, and you will have infections and bad smells, for it will be impossible to clean that collection space on the inside of the scar tissue. When you marry it may take days, even a week or more for your husband to "open" you, and you will scream with pain. The scar tissue will tear in childbirth and have to be sewn up again after each birth. And whether you are infibulated [sewn up] or not, any circumcision which cuts out the clitoris will leave you very little or no ability to enjoy sexual pleasure with your husband. Sex will be a duty you will come to resent; the inability to share pleasure will be an obstacle driving you apart."

When she finished, both the girls were in tears. Fatima choked out, "Kiti went home to her mother's village to have the ceremony last year, and afterward she hasn't played soccer anymore at school. This is why, isn't it? She said that her mother said she was too mature for children's games now, but I could tell it wasn't just what her mother said—she was different. She walks slowly, and she never laughs." Awa thought to herself how young Fatima still was, that she was more interested in the ability to play soccer than painful, dangerous childbirth or being forever barred from sexual pleasure with a husband.

Awa and her daughters discussed the stories of female circumcisions in the surrounding villages, the occasional death, the changes in health and demeanor. She also mentioned the variety of customs within Islam regarding the treatment of women. "You know that none of the Senegalese Muslims seclude their women, but the Hausa of Nigeria do. The Serer women have more freedom and economic independence in Senegal than the Wolof, and the Wolof women have much more than the Tukelor. And all of these are Muslim. What do you think Allah cares more about—whether you are a healthy mother, a good worker, and good wife, or whether you are secluded, or veiled, or allow your husband three other wives?" Then she dismissed them, urging them to think about what they wanted for themselves and their daughters.

A month later the stakes were raised when a group of local Islamic clerics decreed the necessity of female circumcision, and Joseph's mother was back, demanding compliance. Both the girls were confused and tense. Awa explained to Joseph, "They are afraid. They have asked your mother what exactly the circumciser will do, and she has told them they do not need to know, that the circumciser is the expert, and will do whatever is decreed by tradition for the faithful. That leaves them more afraid of the pain and possible debility. On the other hand, they are afraid of being different from the other girls, of being excluded and scorned. They cannot live like this for month after month."

That evening Joseph came back from his trucking office where he had picked up the loading orders for his trip beginning the next morning. "Sit down, Awa," Joseph ordered. "My supervisor called me into his office when I got to the dock. He said he had heard that I was no longer a good Muslim, and that he was unwilling to let me be a bad influence on the other drivers. He was talking about us not having the girls circumcised! My job could be at stake. He was clearly applying pressure. I don't know if he could fire me. Probably not for that, because the owners aren't even Muslim and wouldn't care anyway. But he wouldn't have to say this was the reason if he wanted to fire me—he could just 'suspect' me of pilfering cargo, and I would be let go."

The practical side of Awa knew that they could not allow this job to be taken away. Jobs, especially well paying ones, were simply too scarce. But she was angry. "Are you saying you will retract your betrothal promise to me?" she demanded furiously.

"Can't you see that we have to bend in this situation for the good of the whole family? What good is it for the girls if they are saved from the circumcision and then they get sick from malnutrition, or are too poor to marry?" Joseph responded. "I don't want to send them to the circumciser either, but can't we arrange something like your father did for you? It did not cripple you in any way, as we both know. We could take a holiday to Dakar and find a doctor there to do it."

Awa stalked out of the room without answering, and Joseph left for Banjul the next morning. Over the next few days she kept the girls close to her in the house and refused them permission to go out without her, which made them cranky. But she was firm. All the while she was thinking about Joseph's suggestion. The evening of his return they spoke of the problem in quiet whispers so the girls would not overhear.

"I have thought and thought about what you said. And I understand that it is the practical thing to do. But it seems to me a capitulation to superstition. A generation ago my family had to resort to this, to agree to a minor mutilation in order to prevent a major mutilation. What progress has been made in our country in a generation? Mutilation of the body of innocents is wrong, however small the degree. All the reasons for the mutilation are simply superstitions without a shred of truth. The lips of my vulva do not hang to my knees, and I could hardly have gotten pregnant more quickly than I did with Fatima. And we both know from science that it is the male who determines the sex of a child, not the female. Furthermore, Mohammed neither invented nor decreed any form of female circumcision. The only *hadith* that has a possibility of truth is the one that maintains that he allowed a minor form of circumcision in which there is no excision of the clitoris, to replace the more severe forms. So how can it be good to 'compromise' with this mutilating practice?"

Joseph hesitated and then responded gently, "Would it not be good for everyone if we could find a way that satisfied my mother and my supervisor, made the girls feel accepted by the neighbors and yet safe from pain and mutilation, and also satisfied the needs we feel to be both modern and yet submissive to Allah's will in all things? Perhaps we could talk to some of the other parents and get some support for a more modern circumcision that would be less dangerous. If there were a group of girls getting the modified circumcision our girls would feel better, and we would have some help in facing down my mother. I could talk to Anwar, one of the other drivers who has an uncircumcised daughter a little younger than ours. And you could talk to that nurse from the clinic that you met at the last meeting of your *dahira* [village association]. Perhaps even my mother could be brought around. What do you say?"

AN ISLAMIC RESPONSE by Marcia K. Hermansen

Most Muslims would be surprised to hear of the practice of female circumcision and to find it associated, in particular, with their religion. At the same time, it cannot be denied that in certain Muslim societies, particularly but not exclusively in African ones, it is common, and religious teachings often are cited as condoning it. Therefore, it is appropriate to enter into the parameters of this case study and to formulate a response from a Muslim perspective.

Islam, like other religious traditions, is confronted today with changing attitudes, social transformations, and other aspects of shifting authoritative knowledge which challenge both scholars and laypersons to reevaluate interpretations of its major sources. This process of reevaluation is unavoidable and takes a range of forms grounded in varying concepts of the meaning of the revelatory event and of its relevance for succeeding ages.

Islam is a legalistic religion, not in the sense of neglecting the spiritual side of religion but in the sense of implicating all human activities under the scope of divine ordinances. According to Islamic belief, the final, complete, divine statement is the Qur'an, revealed to the Prophet Muhammad as the exact word of God. The Qur'an states that the Prophet is "the best example" for humans. Thus, the records of his pronouncements and behaviors were preserved over succeeding generations and became known as the *hadith*. The corpus of Islamic law, known as the *shari'a*, is derived by Muslim scholars from these documents. Cases and issues not dealt with explicitly in these sources may be addressed though processes of analogy and reasoning or even more broadly according to principles such as the preservation of a person's life, honor, property, and so on, known as the goals of the *shari'a*.

For the individual "ordinary" Muslim, determining the ruling of the *shari'a* on a specific action is usually left to the authorities. Within majority, Sunni Islam this authority is somewhat diffuse. Muslims follow four different schools of law which developed over time following the core teachings of the *imams*, brilliant legal scholars of the past. These four schools also came to have a roughly geographical provenance. They are the Hanafi school, which predominates in West Asia, Afghanistan, India, and Pakistan; the Shafi'i school, found in Egypt, North Africa, most areas of the Arab Middle East, Indonesia, and Malaysia; the Maliki school, found in the Maghrib and West Africa; and the Hanbali school, found in Saudi Arabia and the Gulf States.[1] Those Muslims who lack the necessary competence and authority for interpreting legal injunctions may ask a scholar (*alim, mufti*) for a legal opinion (*fatwa*) of the status of the case according to the *shari'a* injunctions. In the course of the *fatwa*, the action is usually stipulated as falling under one of five categories: obligatory, recommended, neutral, undesirable, or forbidden. This opinion carries a certain moral force in that the questioner should adhere to the opinion if his or her conscience determines that the authority consulted was reliable and has interpreted the law accurately. The individual Sunni Muslim is, however, free to consult other authorities on the same question and to choose among their rulings. In fact, this option is rarely taken, given the weight of traditional authority and the fact that most Muslims follow the practice of their peer group.

In the ethical case at hand, regarding the necessity of performing some kind of cutting of the female genitalia, there exists no Qur'anic pronouncement concerning its desirability or indicating its being practiced in the Prophet's community. For certain Muslim scholars today, usually considered to be liberals or "Modernists," this would be sufficient argument for omitting the practice. According to such opinions, even certain actions allowable according to the Qur'an, such as polygamy, might be undesirable or even disallowed today on the basis of historical understandings of the context in which they were revealed. For example, the Qur'an 4:3 enjoins a man to marry two, three, or even four wives only if he felt that he could be just to them all, materially and emotionally, which could be seen as tantamount to banning the practice. Similarly, the practice of slavery is envisioned in the Islamic revelation, while most scholars today believe that the intent of the Qur'an was the eventual abolition of this practice due to the text's frequent injunctions to deal with slaves justly and to liberate them.

The sayings (*hadith*) and actions of the prophet Muhammad also carry strong legal force according to the majority of Muslim scholars, and it is from here that those advocating female circumcision, known as *khifad* or *khitan*, draw their textual legitimacy. In fact, there are only three reports which touch on the topic, and none of them directly commands it.

They are as follows:

1. It is said that Prophet Muhammad addressed a woman who had been performing female circumcisions stating, "Umm Atiyya, restrict yourself to a minimum and do not cut too much, it is more pleasant in appearance and pleasing to the husband."
2. "Circumcision is a Sunna for men and a mark of respect (*makrama*) for women."[2]
3. "If the two circumcised organs meet, then the greater ablution (a full bath) is obligatory before one can perform the ritual prayers."[3]

While this third *hadith* is taken to be authentic and is found in most authoritative Sunni collections of Prophetic reports, some scholars contend that the use of "two circumcised organs" is a particularity of Arabic grammar. In this usage the dual form of the noun gives more prominence to the male organ and accordingly does not stipulate that the female organ was also circumcised.[4] It is also clear that the concern of this *hadith* is with ritual purity and not with circumcision.

The arguments concerning female circumcision in countries where it is practiced, such as Egypt, generally take the following two sides. On the one hand, medical professionals, liberals, feminists, and some religious scholars argue against the practice on the basis that:

a. It is not declared obligatory on Muslims either in the Qur'an or the *sunna*.
b. The *hadith* which refer to it are weak in terms of the traditional criteria for evaluating such sources.
c. Medical evidence available today indicates a strong possibility of negative physiological or psychological consequences to women who have undergone this practice. Because preventing such "harms" is one of the broader goals of the Islamic law, this "harmful" practice should now be abandoned.

On the other hand, some religious authorities and even some medical professionals have argued to the contrary, holding that this practice remains recommended for Muslim women because:

a. It has been favorably mentioned in the *hadith* and was not condemned by them.
b. It has a salutary effect in calming women's temperament and preventing them from excessive lust which might lead to promiscuous behavior.
c. It increases a male's sexual pleasure during intercourse and prevents urine and menstrual blood from collecting in the clitoral area.
d. There is no reliable medical or scientific evidence that it is harmful to women.[5]

The various legal schools (*madhhabs*) took varying positions on the topic of female circumcision and this, along with pre-Islamic customs, explains the geographical dispersion of the practice. For example, the Shafi'i school declares it *wajib* (a requirement) for both males and females. The Malikis say it is a *sunna* (practice of the Prophet which should be imitated) for males and desirable in the case of females. Among Hanafis and Hanbalis it seems to have less approval, although some scholars have declared it to be a sign of respect.[6]

To confine the basis for such a decision to its classification under one of the five categories of actions in Islamic law according to a formal *fatwa* seems to be excessively limiting the scope of ethical reasoning in Islam. Beyond such legalistic categorizations of actions, Muslim thinkers have explored concepts such as the reason behind the *shari'a* injunctions. The search for this reason is known as seeking the *'illa* (rationale) and involves a personal struggle with the circumstances behind the original case and the use of reason. Through this process, if it could be determined that the reasons for female circumcision being practiced in the Prophet's community no longer remained in force or that such actions were incidental and contained no beneficial purpose, this practice would cease its claim to legal desirability.

Addressing the ethical issues involved more broadly, asserting the role of human conscience and rational ability in the face of the opposing position that every legitimately Islamic opinion must have a textual indication in revelation raises issues that were debated in classical Muslim theology.[7] Within Sunni Islamic tradition, the proponents of more literalist interpretations were victorious, to the extent that it was claimed that "good" and "bad" were unknowable by human reason acting on its own and that only revelation could serve as a source for making ethical judgments.[8] Fortunately the tradition in practice was much more complex and adaptable.[9] During the past century, however, conservative tendencies and the extended role of *fatwas* in brokering theological and political disputes have tended to inculcate the perception on the part of both Muslims and non-Muslims that in Islam *shari'a* rulings and *fatwas* are the only source for deriving theological and ethical positions.[10] This occurs at the expense of reading the Qur'an as a guide for moral reasoning and for undertaking that reasoning.

Living in a Muslim society where her peers practice female circumcision in the name of Islam, Awa's ethical decisions must be taken within a range of complex allegiances. Values such as family harmony, respect and acceptance by one's peers, and being "honorable" have a strong impact on decision making.

In traditional societies, authority carries great weight and its coercive power is strong. The majority of the male religious scholars in her region would likely find the practice supported in their tradition of Maliki *fiqh* (process of jurisprudence), and they would be unlikely to support a prohibition. At best, they might rule the practice to be discretionary.

The title of the piece, "compromise," evokes the ethical dilemma faced by Awa for whom resisting the performance of this operation has become a matter of conscience. She believes that it is wrong and for this reason is willing to go against all kinds of family and social pressures to resist it. Beyond the physical harm which it might occasion, she fears the message which will be communicated to her daughters even by submitting to a token form of excision, a message that there is something wrong, unclean, and undesirable about their female sexuality. In favor of compromise, one may cite the fact that it is the strategy of gradually reducing the intensity of the ritual, for example from the more invasive procedures of genital infibulation known as "Pharoanic circumcision" to the lesser (*sunna*) one[11] which is being advocated in some African societies. On the other hand, some activists in the societies where the practice is still current have argued that medicalization, that is, putting the ritual into the hands of nurses and doctors, would lend further legitimacy to the custom and make its ultimate eradication more difficult.

It is also a challenge to Awa's faith when the people surrounding her declare actions which she finds repugnant and reprehensible religiously necessary or recommended. Her common sense experience as a woman is being negated by men with very uneven medical and psychological expertise. Can she remain a believer in a system which is unjust, which seems arbitrary and designed to keep women in their place, somewhere behind males?

Some Muslim women in this situation have taken hope in the fact that an increase in the level of education for females in Muslim societies is bound to bring positive changes in their status and role in decision and policy making. In Islamic law, there is technically no bar to a female obtaining the necessary knowledge to become an interpreter of the law. The Prophet's wife, Ayesha, was considered one of the seven of his companions with the most legal acumen. Social conventions have tended to prevent females from pursuing this rank, but as in other religions today, both more general and specific increases in religious education have allowed females to have a voice in interpreting and questioning the male perspectives of the past. Up until now, it has been primarily male religious scholars who blatantly denied any harm in the practice of female circumcision and perceived any criticism as a challenge to the authority of the religion.

Awa's resistance to the practice is further undermined in her own community by the political legacy of Western colonialism. The accusation that

she is selling out her religious and cultural values and is contaminated by
"Western" ideas means that she has to "fight on two fronts." On the one
front she is struggling to improve women's rights, on the other, she wants to
be included in asserting her nation's cultural integrity, authenticity, and independence. In this case the two goals seem to be at odds. In reality, eliminat-
ing such cultural practices is unlikely as long as the economic and social
factors undergirding them remain in place.[12] At the same time, pressures alter-
ing traditional concepts of female status, including female sexuality, deeply
challenge and threaten centuries of male domination, and provoke as well a
reexamination of the tabooed area of male sexuality.[13]

The debate over female circumcision has provoked a broader discussion
of the limits of cultural relativism and whether setting universal standards
for human rights constitutes an imposition of Western categories on all other
societies. Awa would certainly agree with those who argue that certain rights
are universal, such as rights to the integrity of the person and the highest
attainable level of physical and mental health.

At the same time, one should note that while Westerners have been quick
to label practices such as female circumcision cruel and barbaric, it is clear
that parents in societies where it is practiced believe that they are doing the
best for their daughters. Ingrained ideas make it more difficult to resist the
practice and the cost of resisting may be high, not only in terms of community disapproval but also in future loss to the daughters in terms of their mar-
riageability and status. Awa can take some confidence from the fact that she
was able to make a happy marriage despite her family's rejection of the tradition. Her own society is one where the practice is far from universal,[14]
unlike some communities where alternative models are not readily available.

In the end, Awa may opt to have the token form of the operation performed on her daughters. She might make efforts to reframe the experience
in terms of positively valuing her daughters' womanhood. For instance, she
might create some new and positive traditions for her daughters such as gift
exchanges, keeping in mind that initiation rites in many tribal societies do
involve some type of bodily marking or trial as an entry into adulthood. In
Malaysia, for instance, where female circumcision is seen as a symbolic rite
of passage into the Muslim community, the procedure consists of a token
pinprick performed on infant girls. It is often an occasion for female family
members and friends to gather and celebrate. Females in this society tend to
have a positive view of the practice and are offended by the idea that Western
feminists find it demeaning and barbaric.

In the long term, Awa may also decide to work more aggressively within
her community towards eventual elimination of any physical procedure, con-
tending that her use of medical professionals was not in the spirit of condoning the practice but, rather, was a temporary necessity in the interests of
her daughters' physical well being. Numerous activist groups are now working within the context of African societies, among Muslim and non-Muslim
populations, focusing on making more information available to religious specialists, government policy makers, and the general public concerning the

negative health consequences of female circumcision. They are struggling to find solutions in the context of indigenous cultural values and changing understanding of women's roles. Hopefully, Awa can enlist her husband's support in working with his circle of friends so that women in her community will find increased support among their brothers, fathers, and husbands for ending the practice.

Notes

1. Shi'i Muslims follow their own legal schools.

2. Found in the *hadith* compilations of Ahmad ibn Hanbal and al-Baihaqqi. For a detailed discussion of why these *hadiths* are considered weak or of doubtful authenticity, see Muhammad Lutfi al-Sabbagh, *Islamic Ruling on Male and Female Circumcision* (Alexandria, Egypt: World Health Organization, 1996), 19–20.

3. Cited in the *hadith* collections of al-Bukhari, Muslim, al-Tirmidhi, Malik, and ibn Majah.

4. Muhammad Salim al-Awwa, "Female Circumcision: Neither a Sunna, nor a Sign of Respect" in al-Sabbagh, *Islamic Ruling*, 38.

5. For citations of a number of such opinions by Egyptian scholars, see Abu Bakr 'Abd al-Raziq, *al-khitan: ra'i al-din wa-l-ilm fi khitan al-aulad wa-l banat* (Cairo, Egypt: Dar al-I'tisam, 1989), 75–94.

6. al-Raziq, *al-khitan*, 75. It is unclear whether the reference is to respect for the husband or a woman's self-respect.

7. On this debate, see Wael B. Hallaq, *A History of Islamic Legal Theories* (Cambridge, MA: Harvard University Press, 1997), 135–36, and George F. Hourani, *Reason and Tradition in Islamic Ethics* (Cambridge, England: Cambridge University Press, 1985).

8. Most apparent in the theological debates between the more literalist Asharite school versus the Mu'tazilite theologians who supported increased scope for human reason.

9. Richard Bulliet, "The Individual in Islamic Society," in *Religious Diversity and Human Rights*, ed. Irene Bloom, J. Paul Martin, and Wayne L. Proudfoot (New York: Columbia University Press, 1996), 175–91. This article highlights Muslim diversity in social praxis and the element of individual choice in choosing authoritative guidance.

10. Farid Ishaq, *Islam and Pluralism: An Islamic Perspective on Interreligious Solidarity against Oppression* (Oxford: Oneworld, 1997). On the rise of the role of *fatwas* in recent times, see Muhammad Khalid Masud, Brinkley Messick, and David S. Powers, eds., *Islamic Legal Interpretations: Muftis and their Fatwas* (Cambridge, MA: Harvard University Press, 1996).

11. This milder form is sometimes known as *sunna* circumcision. This designation is problematic according to opponents of the practice because it continues to legitimize the practice as being Islamic.

12. Ellen Gruenbaum, "Women's Rights and Cultural Self-Determination in the Female Genital Mutilation Controversy," *Anthropology Newsletter*, May 1995:14–15.

13. Nadia Wassef, "Masculinities and Mutilations: Female Genital Mutilation in Egypt," *Middle East Women's Studies Review* 13, no. 2 (1998):1–4.

14. Statistics estimate only 20–45 percent of Senegalese women have been circumcised.

A JEWISH RESPONSE by Mary Gendler

"A Question of Compromise" raises fascinating and difficult ethical questions which I will address from within a "Jewish framework." As is true with most religions, this Jewish framework is multifaceted and sometimes even fractured. At one pole are the "orthodox," or traditional, Jews who follow laws and customs classically codified in the Shulhan Aruch, the sixteenth-century Code of Jewish Law of Joseph Karo, and at the other pole are the "reform" and "feminist" Jews who want to adapt the religion to current customs, beliefs, and practices while remaining true to its central teachings. Of course, there is a full spectrum of gradations, with the "conservative" movement falling between these two poles.

The situation is further complicated because of the dispersal of our people in the first century CE and the resulting diaspora which saw us settling in all the continents of the world—in countries and cultures as diverse as India, Ethiopia, Morocco, Russia, Germany, Argentina, and the United States. Insofar as it is inevitable that most people living in a particular culture will be influenced by it, no matter what their religious beliefs and practices, a "Jewish" response to a problem such as the one raised in this case study is bound to be various and complex, even though the central teachings of Judaism are common to all Jews.

Before proceeding further, I feel it important to say that I am responding as a North American liberal, feminist Jewish woman of Ashkenazic (European) background. Other Jews, from different countries and cultures, and from more traditional religious backgrounds, would undoubtedly respond somewhat differently. Also, there is a certain danger inherent in persons from one religion and culture presuming to comment on the customs and beliefs of those from another. I do so here with some trepidation and ultimate respect for the diversity of points of view within the Islamic community as well as with full awareness that I speak for only one of many perspectives within Judaism itself.

How does an individual arrive at a personal decision on matters of religious practice within a community? The factors influencing the decision are several. The specific teachings and practices of the religious tradition itself may be the first determinant, but along with these come other influences as well. Personal temperament and inclinations surely play some part, as does the general cultural atmosphere within the wider society, which influences both how we see things and how we behave. No religion, no culture, remains static. The question is how to bring about change when individual beliefs begin to clash with cultural and traditional religious norms.

The case study illustrates a number of dialectics and tensions which arise within most societies and religions and give rise to complex ethical questions and issues. I have chosen five categories which illustrate these tensions:

- individual rights vs. group norms
- innovation/change vs. tradition
- individual conscience vs. submission to religious authority
- science vs. superstition
- normative tradition vs. local customs

In the story Awa and Joseph's mother represent the two polarities, while Joseph finds himself caught between the two women. Awa insists that the custom of female circumcision is based on superstitions: that the genitals of the girl will grow long and deformed; that she will have the parts of a man; that she will not be able to bear sons; and that girl babies will die from touching her male parts at birth. Awa and her father have been influenced by the French and modern science. Indeed, she invokes the scientific method when she points out that none of the above dire predictions was true for her even though she did not have the full ceremony. She seems ready to brave the social ostracism that can come with breaking group norms and gives weight to her own beliefs and knowledge rather than simply accepting or submitting to the local religious hierarchy. Awa wants radical, immediate change. Like the Prophets in Jewish tradition, she roundly condemns a practice she believes is wrong and seeks, at a minimum, to protect herself and her own daughters from it.

Joseph's mother, on the other hand, simply follows custom and local authority. In response to the children's question about what the circumciser will do, she tells them they don't need to know, that the circumciser is the expert. She herself seems neither to question the practice nor to believe that there is anything wrong with it. She worries about the girls' exclusion from the community and is convinced that they will be shunned and never get husbands without the ceremony.

Joseph advocates a compromise solution. He proposes that they try to interest others in their community in having a partial circumcision ceremony—removing only the hood of the clitoris under anesthesia—a procedure far less dangerous and brutal. Awa sees his suggestion as a capitulation to superstition. Joseph sees it as a way to restore harmony and to begin to convert the community to a new practice without making a move so radical that others will totally reject it and them. A further refinement of Joseph's plan might entail a public declaration of what the families who are having only the partial ceremony are doing and why. Such a declaration might prove to be a catalyst for broader community discussion of the issue and, perhaps, result in greater support for change. We are left to decide for ourselves what we feel is the best solution.

A Jewish Response

How would Jews go about responding to this problem? I propose to answer this in two ways: (1) by referring to a number of sometimes conflicting ethical principles within the Jewish tradition; and (2) by discussing a similar but opposite concern within the Jewish community about male and female circumcision.

Ethical Principles

At the personal level, the principle of *pikuach nefesh*—care of the body—is important in Judaism. "Man as child of God has first of all duties in regard to his own self . . . and is in duty bound to preserve his life (*Talmud Berahot* 32b, after Deuteronomy 4:9; Sifra, *Ahare Mot*, xiii) and his health (*Talmud Baba Kama* 91b; *Talmud Shabbat* 82a)."[1] Sexual pleasure is a desideratum as is the parity of sexual pleasure between the sexes.[2] Female circumcision as described in this case study could easily be seen as contradicting these duties and desiderata.

At the communal level there is a tradition dating back to the Prophets obliging the individual to condemn what is "wrong," even if it goes against local practices. Believing as she does that the custom of female circumcision is based on superstition and is harmful to girls, Awa would be doing wrong not to speak out on this publicly according to the following principle articulated in the Talmud.

> If one could have influenced his/her household and failed to speak out, one is implicated in household misdeeds. In the case of one's city, the same holds true: could one have influenced by speaking out but instead maintained silence, she/he is implicated in communal misdeeds. . . . [B]y acquiescence through silence one bears responsibility. Yet further, to the ends of the earth itself, this responsibility extends: that ever we attempt, by clear and forthright speech and action, to prevent that from happening which ought not to happen. (*Talmud Shabbat* 54b–55a)

On the other hand, the great sage Hillel taught, "Separate not yourself from the community."[3] In addition, a proverb counseled, "If you have entered a city conform to its laws."[4] *Klal Yisrael*—Jewish unity, community unity—and *sh'lom bayit*—household harmony, peace within the family—are of great importance within Judaism. How far one should go in compromising one's own personal ethics and beliefs to maintain community and household harmony is not easy to resolve. This tension—the pull exerted between standing up for what one believes on the one hand, and the compromises that are sometimes entailed in order to be part of a peaceful household and harmonious community on the other—is best encapsulated in Rabbi Hillel's famous maxim: "If I am not for myself, who is for me? If I am for myself alone, what am I? And if not now, when?"[5]

Jewish Concerns about Circumcision

Within Judaism, there have also been concerns about circumcision, with both similarities to and differences from the concerns cited in the case study. A brief discussion of how these concerns have been dealt with might help illuminate how Jews approach a similar issue within their own community.

The commandment to circumcise all males occurs early in the Torah and clearly carries strong spiritual overtones. "Every male among you shall be circumcised. And ye shall be circumcised in the flesh of your foreskin, and it shall be a token of a covenant betwixt Me and you. And he that is eight days old shall be circumcised among you, every male throughout your generations" (Gen 17:11–12). The covenant of circumcision, *brit milah*, thus became the visible, living sign of covenant with the deity, and the ritual came to be the sign of God's unique relationship to Israel. "The promise that Abraham's seed should inherit the land of Canaan was bound up together with this covenant. The punishment for failure to observe this command was *karet*, to be 'cut off' from one's kind ([Gen] 21:4), understood by the rabbis to mean 'excision at the hand of heaven from the community.'"[6]

The importance of circumcision within Judaism cannot be exaggerated. Nevertheless, the ritual has been challenged in the past century, leading to some serious turmoil and upset within the community. In 1843 the Reform (liberal) movement in Germany proposed the abolition of circumcision for the following five reasons:

(1) It was commanded to Abraham and not to Moses. It is not distinctive of Israel since it is also practiced by the descendants of Ishmael; (2) It is mentioned only once in the Mosaic law; it is not repeated in Deuteronomy; (3) Moses did not circumcise his own son; (4) The generation of the desert was not circumcised; (5) There is no initiation of daughters into Judaism.[7]

Orthodox and Conservative Jews, aghast at the suggestion that the sacred rite would be tampered with, cited the scriptural commandments, Torah, and custom as reasons not to abolish the rite. Their claim that male circumcision represented the very heart of Judaism meant that the controversy threatened to tear apart the community. Eventually most Reform Jews, torn between their misgivings about a ritual they consider repugnant and their desire to remain part of *Klal Yisrael*, have opted, finally, to circumcise their boy babies, albeit sometimes with misgivings and reluctance. Yet the controversy is still very much alive today. The *Jewish Advocate*, a widely distributed Boston-based Jewish journal, recently ran an article entitled "New Findings Related to Circumcision Stir an Old Controversy."[8] The article not only discusses the issue of new developments in science for uses of the foreskins of circumcised babies and the ethics of so doing, but it also describes the concerns of Ronald Goldman, a psychologist who claims that circumcision not only causes significant psychological damage to the child, but also conflicts with Jewish laws and values.[9]

It should be said, however, that the concerns about mutilation and even psychological damage regarding male circumcision are of a different order than those involving the young girls in Africa. For example, in contrast to female circumcision, where reduction of sexual pleasure is one of the goals, no one has argued that the sexual pleasure for the male is impaired by removal of the foreskin of the penis. In addition, a credible scientific argument has been mounted which holds that the practice of circumcising males is actually beneficial and that removal of the foreskin makes the penis easier to keep clean, which leads to fewer infections. In contrast, the case study, through Awa's voice, cites examples of serious physical impediments that can follow female circumcision: difficulties with urination and menstruation, physical disability, and even death.

The most enduring legacy of the uproar about male circumcision in the Jewish community was its focus on the inequalities toward women within Judaism. Although there is some evidence that female circumcision may have been practiced by the Jews in the earliest times, there is no hard proof that it ever existed, and if it did, the practice died out long ago. The custom among traditional Ashkenazi Jews from Eastern Europe of women cutting off their hair when they marry so they will not be attractive to other men might well be a carryover from female circumcision.[10]

Although there are few in the American Jewish community who would advocate the kind of ritual to which these young girls in Africa are subjected, Jewish women do face the problem of marginalization and, at times, even exclusion from the heart of religious ritual practice because women are de facto excluded from carrying the covenant in their flesh. For all its barbarity, female circumcision within Judaism can create a certain communal and religious standing for women, albeit at the cost of their physical well being and full sexual functioning. The question for liberal and feminist Jews has not been how to protect women from genital mutilation but has been how to include women in the covenant of the flesh without mutilation.

Some Jewish feminists have offered radical solutions. I, myself, proposed a ritual hymenotomy to be performed on the eighth day as an equivalent ceremony to male circumcision.[11] The proposal was based on my belief that much of the power of circumcision lies in its being a blood rite focused on the male reproductive organ. I argued that nothing short of a closely equivalent ritual would carry the same awesome—if also somewhat repugnant—power. At the same time, I was careful to propose an act that would not do violence to the body of the young girl—a hymenotomy being simply rupturing the membrane, which occurs naturally at the time of first intercourse. There is evidence that "artificial defloration," a potentially liberating operation for girls, was a widespread, ancient rite predating even male circumcision.[12] The differences between this practice and the cutting off of the vulva and clitoris are enormous. Although my proposal provoked strong reactions and few followers, even among liberals and feminists, its radical nature did help to awaken the community which, however, has chosen to follow a more moderate path.

New rituals, primarily "naming ceremonies," have been developed in which family and friends gather either at home or in the synagogue to bless and welcome baby girls into *Klal Yisrael*. This has become a widely observed practice, even within the more conservative sector of the community.

Although they do not evoke the primitive blood elements of physical circumcision, the ceremonies do have the value of bringing the community together to honor the advent of this girl-child into their midst.

Conclusions

Where, then, does all this leave us? And where does it leave Awa, Joseph, and their daughters? Ultimately we must all make our own decisions and choices. With regard to the case study, I must confess that I personally have mixed feelings. Emotionally I fully agree with Awa and feel that female circumcision as practiced in her society is cruel, barbaric, and wrong. As a twentieth—almost twenty-first—century Jewish feminist living in America the choice would be an easy one for me both in terms of the Jewish values described above and the values of my surrounding culture, particularly the belief in the sanctity of the individual. It is important, however, to view the situation not only from my own privileged vantage point but also from that of Awa and Joseph. When I look at it from that lens, I find myself, albeit quite reluctantly, wondering if, ultimately, Joseph's "compromise" represents the wiser approach in their situation.

We have to think about the ultimate aim of our actions. If Awa's goal here is primarily to protest what is wrong and to protect her loved ones from harm, then of course her position is correct. She is right, at one level, that any compromise entails a capitulation to superstition. However, as with my proposal, Awa is likely to have few followers, and she risks total community exclusion for herself and her family as well as the possibility of great economic insecurity if her husband loses his job. Joseph's proposal has the virtue of protecting the girls from the worst of the circumcision ritual while maintaining the possibility of creating change within the community. If through striking this middle path they are able to combine Awa's goal of protesting a practice she believes is wrong while convincing the community gradually to change, then they will have fulfilled all of the ethical principles through whose lenses I have focused here: *pikuach nefesh*—care of the body; the *prophetic tradition*—speaking out against what one feels to be wrong; *sh'lom bayit*—maintenance of household harmony; and *Klal Yisrael*—not separating oneself from the community.

Yet it is also important to postulate what could happen if Awa sticks to her principles and holds Joseph to his promise of not having their girls circumcised, even partially. In so doing, Awa would be following in the footsteps of the Jewish prophets who often spoke unwelcome and unwanted truths. Perhaps the community reaction would not be as severe as Joseph fears; perhaps the actions of the family would attract supporters, and a faster change in the community would be precipitated; and perhaps, finally, Awa would rather suffer the ostracism and trials rather than subject her daughters to what she feels is a barbaric custom. It takes great courage to challenge a deep-seated tradition, especially in a traditional culture. Ultimately, it is those within who must make the choice.

Notes

1. *Jewish Encyclopedia*, (New York: KTAV Publishing House, 1906), 5:249.
2. "The Mitzvah of Marital Sex," and "The Legitimacy of Sexual Pleasure," in David M. Feldman, ed., *Birth Control in Jewish Law* (New York: New York University Press, 1968).
3. *Mishnah Aboth*, 11:5. Also found as "Pirkei Abot," *Ethics of the Fathers*, in all traditional Jewish prayer books.
4. *Midrash Genesis Rabbah*, 48:14, in Abraham Cohen, *Everyman's Talmud* (New York: E. P. Dutton, 1949).
5. *Mishnah Abot*, 1:15 in *Jewish Encyclopedia*, 1906 ed., 5:249.
6. *Encyclopaedia Judaica* (Jerusalem: Keter Publishing, 1972) 5:567.
7. *Encyclopaedia Judaica*, 1972 ed., 5:571.
8. "New Findings Related to Circumcision Stir an Old Controversy," *Jewish Advocate*, February 1998: 13–19.
9. Ronald Goldman, *Questioning Circumcision: A Jewish Perspective* (Boston: Vanguard, 1997).
10. This is the author's interpretation.
11. Mary Gendler, "Sarah's Seed," *Response*, no. 24 (Winter 1974/75).
12. Robert Briffault, *The Mothers*, vol. 3, 1st ed. (London: George Allen and Unwin, 1927), 319.

Bibliography and Suggested Reading

Briffault, Robert. *The Mothers*. Vol. 3. 1st ed. London: George Allen and Unwin, 1927.

Bulliet, Richard. "The Individual in Islamic Society." In *Religious Diversity and Human Rights*, ed. Irene Bloom, J. Paul Martin, and Wayne L. Proudfoot. New York: Columbia University Press, 1996.

Cairo Family Planning Association. *Facts about Female Circumcision*. Cairo: Cairo Family Planning Association, March 1991.

Callaway, Barbara, and Lucy Creevy. *The Heritage of Islam: Women, Religion and Politics in West Africa*. Boulder, CO: Lynne Reinner Publishers, 1994.

Cohen, Abraham. *Everyman's Talmud*. New York: E. P. Dutton, 1949.

Dorkenoo, Efua, and Scilla Elworthy. *Female Genital Mutilation: Proposals for Change*. London: Minority Rights Group International, 1992.

Feldman, David M. In *Birth Control in Jewish Law*. New York: New York University Press, 1968. See chap. 4, "The Mitzvah of Marital Sex," and chap. 5, "The Legitimacy of Sexual Pleasure."

Gendler, Mary. "Sarah's Seed." *Response*, no. 24 (Winter 1974/75).

Goldman, Ronald. *Questioning Circumcision: A Jewish Perspective*. Boston, MA: Vanguard, 1997.

Greenberg, Blu. "Women and Judaism." In *Contemporary Jewish Religious Thought*, ed. Arthur A. Cohen and Paul Mendes-Flohr. Washington, DC: Bnai Brith International Commission on Continuing Jewish Education, 1987.

Gruenbaum, Ellen. "Women's Rights and Cultural Self-Determination in the Female Genital Mutilation Controversy." *Anthropology Newsletter* (May 1995).

Gudorf, Christine E. "Gender and Culture in the Globalization of Bioethics." *St. Louis University Public Law Review* 25, no. 2 (1996): 331–52.

Hallaq, Wael B. *A History of Islamic Legal Theories*. Cambridge, MA: Harvard University Press, 1997.

Hosken, Fran. *The Hosken Report: Sexual/Genital Mutilation of Females.* 4th ed. Lexington, MA: Women's International Network, 1994.

Hourani, George F. *Reason and Tradition in Islamic Ethics.* Cambridge, England: Cambridge University Press, 1985.

Ishaq, Farid. *Islam and Pluralism: An Islamic Perspective on Interreligious Solidarity against Oppression.* Oxford: Oneworld, 1997.

Lightfoot-Klein, Hanny. *Prisoners of Ritual: An Odyssey into Female Genital Circumcision in Africa.* New York: Harrington Park Press, 1989.

Masud, Muhammad Khalid, Brinkley Messick, and David S. Powers, eds. *Islamic Legal Interpretations: Muftis and their Fatwas.* Cambridge, MA: Harvard University Press, 1996.

"New Findings Related to Circumcision Stir an Old Controversy." *Jewish Advocate.* February 1998:13–19.

al-Raziq, Abu Bakr 'Abd. *Al-khitan: ra'i al-din wa-l-ilm fi khitan al-aulad wa-l banat* (Circumcision: Religious and Scientific Opinion on Male and Female Circumcision). Cairo, Egypt: Dar al-I'tisam, 1989.

al-Sabbagh, Muhammad Lutfi. *Islamic Ruling on Male and Female Circumcision.* Alexandria, Egypt: World Health Organization, 1996.

Walker, Alice, and Pratibha Parmar. *Warrior Marks: Female Genital Mutilation and the Sexual Blinding of Women.* New York: Harcourt Brace, 1993.

Wassef, Nadia. "Masculinities and Mutilations: Female Genital Mutilation in Egypt." *Middle East Women's Studies Review* 13, no. 2 (1998).

CHAPTER 2

Sex and the Single Person

A CASE STUDY by Christine E. Gudorf

Connie filled the last of the ten wine glasses, and Wes passed them around as the five couples spread out and relaxed on the couches and the floor of Greg and Connie's home. It was Friday night, one of their twice-monthly get-togethers eagerly anticipated by all of them. Originally formed after a weekend retreat for couples in their church, the group had now been meeting for two years.

"Who's in charge of the agenda for tonight?" asked Bob, a local executive with United Way.

"Me," Solange replied, "but I need to change the topic because something came up. Remember we had said we wanted to talk about difficulties in personal and communal prayer? Well, Marty and I need some help with an issue more pressing. Okay?"

"If it's important, of course," volunteered Jack.

"I'm glad to hear that from you, Jack, because you and Beth have the least personal stake in this—your children aren't even teenagers yet."

"Oh, no, it's the teenagers again," groaned Bob in a mocking voice. "What has Dan done now—or don't I want to know?"

Marty put it baldly, "This morning Solange went downstairs to put in a load of wash. She went in Dan's room to get his laundry basket and found him and Denise asleep in his bed."

Greg, the jokester of the bunch, said, "That must have been uncomfortable in that narrow little bed of his. It would be hard to get a good night's sleep so crowded."

"Is Denise the same girl he brought to the picnic at church last month?" Beth asked, and received a nod from Solange.

Amy, a grade school teacher and the mother of another eighteen-year-old son, demanded in a horrified voice, "What did you do?"

"I backed out, shut the door, made sure the other boys didn't go down in the basement, and told Marty," responded Solange.

"And then what?" Amy and Beth asked together.

"We waited until they got up and Dan drove Denise home, and then confronted him," Marty explained.

"But what did you say to him?"

"That's what we want to talk about—what we both said and what we should have said," pronounced Marty solemnly. "Not only did we give two different messages that may contradict each other, but they may both be less than we should have said."

"So tell us what you said," insisted Amy.

Marty gestured to Solange that she should begin. "Well, Marty told him to come into the study, and told him that we knew Denise had spent the night. Then Marty told him that he should be ashamed of himself for the example he set his brothers, who could have walked in at any time. Dan pointed out that there was no lock on his door, so Marty told him to install one that afternoon. I told him that I was angry at him, as well as feeling disappointed and insulted."

Marty broke in, "I had no idea where she was going when she said she felt insulted."

"Well, I did feel insulted. Here was my son, who I had thought I had raised to respect women as equals, and I find this." Solange held up her hand to stop anticipated protests from the group and continued, "The problem for me was not primarily premarital sex, but casual sex, even sexual manipulation. He could care less about Denise. She is a convenience for him. She calls him and he doesn't return her calls. He asks her over and then doesn't look up from the ball game on TV to greet her. In fact, he doesn't even speak to her 'til there's a commercial, and then usually to tell her to get him a Coke or pretzels, as if she were his slave. She's grateful for every crumb of affection that falls her way, and she swallows her anger when he fails to show up for a date because he decided at the last minute to play pool with the guys. I constantly feel like apologizing for him to her and telling her to dump him for her own good. And then he has sex with her, with a seventeen-year-old girl! Which was, of course, one of the things Marty, being a lawyer, also jumped on him for—that she was underage, and that could get him arrested for statutory rape if her mother found out where she spent the night and objected."

"Is that all the two of you said?" demanded Amy.

"I told him that I was angry because he had no business defiling sex by having it with someone who was as important to him as an ashtray or a beer. I told him I thought we had given him better example and teaching than that: that sex was for sharing with someone that you love, that it was an experience of grace and gift, and that from my perspective, he had degraded both Denise and sex itself for a little casual pleasure."

"Solange was really on a roll for a while. She told him that it was like cutting up the Bayeux tapestry to use for toilet paper or using Michelangelo's *David* for a birdbath or making Picasso's *Guernica* a bulletin board," volunteered Marty appreciatively.

"I told him he had no business in an exclusive relationship with any girl because he wasn't willing to keep his commitments within such a relationship—he wasn't even willing to extend her the common courtesies he gives all his male buddies who come to the house, like greeting them when they arrive, returning their phone calls, and keeping appointments with them," concluded Solange.

"So what's the problem? That sounds like a great answer to me," responded Bob. Amy, Jack, and Beth nodded their heads in agreement.

Wes and Arlene were the oldest couple in the group and also the only African-Americans. He worked in commercial real-estate management and she directed a nonprofit agency that built low-income housing. They now entered the conversation for the first time.

"And if he had treated Denise better, would it have been OK to find them in bed together?" Wes wanted to know.

Arlene added, "Are you afraid that's the impression you left him with?"

Marty responded, "Yes, that's what Solange is afraid of. I don't have much of a problem with it, but I think she does. I don't understand it, either. You know, we waited for the whole three years that we dated until we married to have sex, but we both agreed later that had we been born five years later, so that we would have been more influenced by the sixties, we almost certainly would not have felt we had to wait all that time. We regarded ourselves as engaged the last two years before we married, even before it was announced. I don't think it is wrong for engaged couples to have sex, and I can't really believe that she does, either."

Arlene hesitantly offered, "We went through a lot of this with our boys. We treated all of them the same, but they sure took different messages from us about sex. Our oldest son, David, had three children with three different women before he was twenty-five, and he wasn't married to any of them. Finding strange women in our house was one reason why we finally kicked him out of the house when he was only back from Vietnam six months. Now he and his wife haven't had any children and they've been married six years! Our second son dated a little—not sleeping around—and then married. The hard thing for us in Mike's marriage was that he married a white girl. Though we love Becca now, and their three kids are great, it was hard to take at the time. But other than marrying white, Mike was conservative—about sex like everything else. He believes in rules—that's why he does so well in the Navy. Ted is another story. He doesn't have much interest in dating or women at all." (Some but not all of the group knew that Arlene and Wes's youngest son was gay and had only recently come out to them.)

"One of the problems we have," Wes added, "is that we think we should treat David's children as our grandchildren, too, but he and his wife don't want us to, because it creates friction in their marriage, and gives these other women, none of whom are married, ties to him. He keeps telling us that if we really believe that sex outside marriage is wrong, then we shouldn't support it by keeping up relationships with these kids. But isn't that making the kids pay for David's mistakes? What David wants us to do would make things easier on us, too, because the mothers not only appreciate our taking out the kids and remembering them on birthdays and Christmas, but they appeal to us to get David to pay child support or to visit and call the kids more—and that puts us in the middle."

"That's a whole other issue we brought up," Solange said. "Dan and Denise only use condoms sometimes, he says. He says he can't always afford them."

"Or," Marty broke in with irritation, "he actually bragged that sometimes they used the two or three they had brought with them and didn't have any more!"

"So I went out and got him a large supply, left the box on his bed, and told him that rather than have him do without, I will buy them myself," admitted Solange. "And this is the other part of my worry. I know that it makes no sense to give him condoms and then tell him I expect him not to have sex until he finds himself in a committed relationship. But I don't know what else to do. He's almost nineteen, and the chances are he won't marry for five or more years. Have you looked at the number of young people getting herpes, genital warts, and AIDS? These kids are risking getting incurable sexual diseases that can kill or cripple their children, and, in the case of AIDS, kill the parents, too. And they do it every time they have sex. Dan wasn't Denise's first, but she is so young, and her mother is usually so careful that she was probably relatively safe for him—I hope he was as safe for her! But the girls he dates are going to get older as he does, and so the number of people they have had sexual contact with will increase, and so the risk of contracting STDs [sexually transmitted disease] goes up."

Amy spoke up. "I don't even want to think about it. James is still bemoaning the fact that he is so shy he rarely gets up the nerve to ask a girl out, so I don't think we need to worry about him just yet, even if he is eighteen. But Nancy is seventeen, has no problems with shyness, dates constantly, and could also get pregnant. I don't want to raise my children's children, but we all know people who are doing it. Just think of the Adams, the Jenkins, or the Sigenthalers at church. And I know in my heart of hearts that is what I'd do before supporting abortion or adoption."

"You know," Jack suggested, "it just struck me that no one here has mentioned the church or faith as having a role in the decision making around sex and parenting. Isn't it a useful resource?"

"Well, I guess we could avoid all these problems if we locked up our daughters in our homes and didn't allow them out without a parent and then married them off at menarche like in the biblical stories," Beth teased. "Is that what you are suggesting for our daughters, Jack?"

Jack grinned, "Well, it sounds like it would solve a lot of problems. But really, does the biblical blindness to the equality and dignity of women mean that it has nothing to say about sex that is valuable? Do I just think that it must because I am an ignorant math teacher?"

Part of the group looked to Wes, who was a deacon in the church, and the rest to Solange, who taught religion at their church's grade school. Wes nodded to Solange, saying, "This one is yours."

Solange began, "I think this is the issue that is tying the churches in knots today. The Bible's assumptions about the value and place of women color every aspect of its teachings on sexuality and marriage. The Bible accepts the practice of giving and taking women in marriage without their consent and takes for granted the selling of women and girls into prostitution. Adultery is understood as an offense against the husband's ownership, and fornication and rape are both understood as offenses against a father's economic interest in and responsibility for the daughter. Today we can say adultery and rape are forbidden because adultery violates the fidelity that a husband and a wife promise each other, and rape is wrong because it violates a woman's right to control the sexual activity of her body. But fornication violates no promise, involves no bodily violation. What biblical reason can you think of for banning nonmarital sex, so long as it is respectful of the dignity of the other, and responsible—contraceptive and STD-protected? The Bible didn't feel that it had to make arguments against fornication, because methods of having sex without procreation were few, uncertain, and largely unknown; sex had to be confined to marriage so that children would have a father to support them, because women had no sources of income apart from men. Modern contraception has changed that. But we don't want to go back to saying that sex is wrong for the unmarried because it is only for making babies, do we? Aren't we all agreed that contraception is okay in marriage, even that most sex needs to be contraceptive, that we need to have fewer babies without lowering the frequency of mutually pleasurable sexual sharing?"

"This is dangerous stuff," Bob replied. "Like Jack, I am really uncomfortable saying the Bible doesn't have any legitimate prohibitions on premarital sex. Surely there must be some!"

"I've been thinking," said Wes, "and I can't think of any place where the Bible gives reasons for banning fornication. It just takes for granted that it's wrong because it violates the rules about who owns and cares for women and children. Nothing in the commandments, nothing in the gospels. There could be some indirect references, like St. Paul's condemnations of *porneia*, but that translates better into filth or sexual nastiness than to fornication. The Mosaic law has some references to sex between the unmarried, but the ones that come to mind are about rape, or rape and incest, and in them, sure enough, the victim is understood to be the father or family of the victim."

Amy stared around, surprised. "Are you telling me that when it comes down to it, unless we are fundamentalists and blindly follow the rules and attitudes of the Bible, all we can tell our children about sex before marriage is that if they use condoms they can have sex with any consenting person with whom they share an ongoing relationship—which for them means whoever they are going with at the moment?"

Marty answered, "That's what we have been talking about. Solange wants to insist that some level of commitment beyond that is necessary, and I don't see how parents or society in general could enforce such a standard. Dan will just insist that he loves every girl he sleeps with, and so long as he has serial instead of simultaneous affairs, how could we dispute him? He may even truly think this pale thing he feels for Denise is real love."

Beth suggested, "I think maybe Christians have to do the hard thing and give up on finding a rule hidden somewhere in the Bible that will fix our problem. It seems to me that we need to focus on where the Spirit is in our lives and what it is telling us. How does the love, justice, and community of the gospel message of Jesus get communicated in sexual experience, and how does it get violated in sexual experience? I am impatient with all this stress on feeling, as if one's individual emotions are our only guides as to how to live. Jesus didn't promise us all love and flowers; he called us to act lovingly toward each other and said that if we all do, we will have a community that shares the love of God with each other. That's why Solange was right to tell Dan that he doesn't love Denise; if he did he would treat her lovingly and not like a used tissue."

Jack blurted out, "Our kids are only eight and ten, but you make me scared to death. We are telling our kids that when they grow up they will marry and have kids. When Jill asked about sounds coming from our bedroom while we were making love, we told her that when she grew up and got married, she, too, would feel great pleasure from loving her husband. I don't want to tell her that the first time she feels infatuated in junior high she can find out for herself what makes Mom moan with pleasure. But I don't want her to feel guilty if she anticipates her wedding by a few weeks, either. We did, and I think that is normal and acceptable. What do we do?"

Turning to Greg, Connie remarked, "I wish we had this talk a few years ago! We might have been able to save Ann from that disastrous relationship with Alan if we had talked more of the power in sex. We could have warned her to be more careful before she got so hurt, risking herself on someone she wasn't sure of."

"You know," Greg added, "our real problem was that we fell in love so young that our only experience of sex has been in the safety of marriage, and I think we just assumed that when we talked to the kids about sex. I'll bet that's even more true for you two," he commented, pointing to Marty and Solange. "You are so open about sex being good and pleasurable and so clear about how your sexual intimacy supports you in times of trouble and tension. You probably didn't convey to Dan any sense of danger, any awareness that people can use sex to wound or use another. He probably saw it as a way of building a relationship like his parents'."

Beth looked at her watch and jumped up, announcing "The sitter threatened to quit if we were late one more time. We've got to go."

Connie suggested, "I haven't said much because I haven't sorted out all my thoughts. Can we all think some more about it and come back in two weeks with concrete suggestions about what we think we should tell our children, or in some cases, our grandchildren, about sexual behavior?"

All quickly agreed, and the group moved into goodbye hugs. As the last of the taillights receded in the distance, Greg turned to Connie and asked, "Do you really think that we can find an answer that satisfies our concerns for our kids' moral and religious character as well as our concern for their life and health?"

A BLACK MISSIONARY BAPTIST RESPONSE
by Gregory Pope

Introduction

The Black Missionary Baptist Churches (BMBC), which make up the National Baptist Convention, are independent organizations. There are no bishops, councils, or books of discipline in the BMBC. Although there are thousands of BMBC, each church is autonomous. Each church conducts its own business: offering motions, debating, forming committees, voting, hiring preachers, and adopting doctrine and dogma. The main authorities of the BMBC are the Bible, the tradition of the Fathers, and the local pastor.

The Bible is the "book of authority" in the BMBC—and not just any version of the Bible, but the King James Version, which is believed to be the authoritative English translation. The Baptist Covenant says, "we believe that the Bible is the inspired word of God. . . ." And in many of the BMBC, this inspiration is seen as a kind of dictation from God.

Within the BMBC, the tradition of the Fathers is the ethics that were handed down from the progenitors. These laws were taught to their posterity and passed on to the present. Many times these ethical laws are not found in the Bible, but they are just as binding. These laws are to the BMBC what the oral law was to the Pharisaic Jew.

The local pastor is the leader of the BMBC. He is many times referred to as the shepherd of the flock. This is a perfect metaphor of the relationship between the pastor and his congregation. The congregation sees itself as helpless, defenseless sheep in need of a shepherd. The pastor is seen as that shepherd who leads them beside still waters and in green pastures. In other words, the congregation has a kind of trusting respect for the pastor. Next to God and the Bible, the pastor is the authoritative figure.

It is this tradition out of which my commentary on "Sex and the Single Person" arises. But before I proceed, I need to qualify my argument from the tradition of the BMBC. Although I am speaking for many BMBC, given the absence of a set of laws and enforcement procedures, there are always some divergent views: not all would agree.

The Old Testament

As Solange has said, the Bible is blind to the equality and dignity of women. In the Old Testament, women are seen as the property of men. They are sold to their husbands by their fathers, stripped of their identities, and made subservient to their husbands. It seems that their self-worth is based in nothing more than bringing their husbands sexual pleasure and bearing their children. There is a verse in Genesis which seems to corroborate this: "Unto the woman he said, I will greatly multiply thy sorrow and thy conception; in sorrow thou shalt bring forth children; and thy desire shall be to thy husband, and he shall rule over thee" (Gen 3:16).

Men have used this verse to keep women subjugated and pregnant. My grandfather, who was a Baptist preacher, used it. He did not like my grandmother working outside the home. Therefore, he would quote this verse to try to convince her to quit her job. He would say, "God cursed the man with work (from the sweat of your brow you shall eat bread), but he cursed the woman with pain during childbirth and submission to her husband. Therefore, God did not intend for the woman to work because he would have said so; he intended for her to obey her husband and have plenty of children." Although this may sound strange, the patriarchal world of the Bible held pretty much the same view. It saw women as the property of men. And under this cloak, women have been stripped of their body-rights and dignity.

The Bible is full of stories with the patriarchal view that women are the property of men. The following are simply two examples:

And Dinah the daughter of Leah, which she bare unto Jacob, went out to see the daughters of the land. And when Shechem the son of Hamor the Hivite, prince of the country, saw her, he took her, and lay with her, and defiled her. And his soul clave unto Dinah the daughter of Jacob, and he loved the damsel, and spake kindly unto the damsel. And Shechem spake unto his father Hamor, saying, Get me this damsel to wife. And Jacob heard that he had defiled Dinah his daughter: now his sons were with his cattle in the field: and Jacob held his peace until they were come. And Hamor the father of Shechem went out unto Jacob to commune with him. And the sons of Jacob came out of the field when they heard it: and the men were grieved, and they were very wroth, because he had wrought folly in Israel in lying with Jacob's daughter; which thing ought not to be done. (Gen 34:1–7)[1]

Now as they were making their hearts merry, behold, the men of the city, certain sons of Belial, beset the house round about, and beat at the door, and spake to the master of the house, the old man, saying, Bring forth the man that came into thine house, that we may know him. And the man, the master of the house, went out unto them, and said unto them, Nay, my brethren, nay, I pray you, do not so wickedly; seeing that this man is come into mine house, do not this folly. Behold, here is my daughter a maiden, and his concubine; them I will bring out now, and humble ye them, and do with them what seemeth good unto you: but unto this man do not so vile a thing. But the men would not hearken to him; so the man took his concubine, and brought her forth unto them; and they knew her, and abused her all the night until the morning: and when the day began to spring, they let her go. (Judg 19:22–25)[2]

After reading the stories about the rape of Dinah and the Levite's concubine, there can be little doubt that the injury in Israel was to be avenged in order that God's justice prevail. But as Marie Fortune has argued, the primary message that is conveyed in these stories is that women were property whose welfare was not important in itself, for nothing was done to redress their loss.[3] There are other stories which corroborate Fortune's argument: the rape of Tamar (2 Sam 13) and the sacrifice of Jephthah's daughter (Judg 11).

The Black Missionary Baptist Churches and the Old Testament

The BMBC is very Old Testament focused in its approach. Because of the method of oral transmission that was used by the slaves, the preachers of the BMBC found it easier to preach the stories found in the Old Testament. Also, the congregation found it easier to understand and remember those stories. It is the Old Testament stories that continue to influence and shape the lives of the members of the BMBC and that are used to develop ethical values.

In the view of the BMBC, Denise, by having sex with Dan, is compromising one of the greatest possessions of a woman, virginity. *Webster's Dictionary* defines the term "virgin" as one who has not experienced sexual intercourse. This definition is both acceptable and universal. But the Old Testament tends to integrate this definition with chastity or moral purity. It seems, in the eyes of both the Old Testament and BMBC, that for women "holiness" before marriage is associated with being a virgin. In the Book of Leviticus the priest was commanded by God to take a wife who was a virgin: "Widow, or a divorced woman, or profane, or an harlot, these shall he not take: but he shall take a virgin of his own people to wife" (Lev 21:14). The priests were men who offered sacrifices unto the Lord, and the commandment was that they must be holy. This commandment restricted their activities. They could not indulge in uncleanness. Among this list of unclean things was a woman who was not a virgin. This is a clear indication that holiness was associated with being a virgin.

Second, according to the BMBC, the Old Testament seems to indicate that virginity has some great value: "Who can find a virtuous woman? For her price is far above rubies" (Prov 31:10). This verse of scripture is usually understood to be referring to the woman's ability as a homemaker. But the verse "Many daughters have done virtuously, but thou excellest them all" (Prov 31:29), points to something else. The virtue of this woman is in her reverence of God: "Favor is deceitful, and beauty is vain: but a woman that feareth the Lord, she shall be praised" (Prov 31:30). This reverence of God, according to the BMBC, is associated with her virginity before marriage.

Third, virginity is one element that should consummate a marriage:

> If any man takes a wife, and goes in to her, and then scorns her, and charges her with shameful things and gives her an evil reputation, and says, I took this woman, and when I came to her, I did not find in her the tokens of a virgin, then the father of the young woman, and her mother, shall get and bring out the tokens of her virginity to the elders of the city in the gate; And her father shall say to the elders, I gave my

daughter to this man as wife, and he hates and spurns her. And, lo, he has made shameful charges against her, saying, I found not in your daughter the evidences of her virginity; and yet these are the tokens of my daughter's virginity. And they shall spread the garment before the elders of the city. And the elders of that city shall take the man and rebuke and whip him; And they shall fine him 100 shekels of silver, and give them to the father of the young woman, because he has brought an evil name upon a virgin of Israel; and she shall be his wife; he may not divorce her all his days. (Deut. 22:13–19, amplified version)

There was a custom among the Jews where the midwives would check the sheets after the first sexual encounter between newlyweds. These midwives would be looking for bloodstains, which resulted from the breaking of the woman's hymen. If they found blood, then this was a sign of the woman's virginity and the marriage was consummated. But if blood was not found, then the woman was considered unchaste and severe punishment was measured out: "But if it is true that the evidences of virginity were not found in the young woman, Then they shall bring her to her father's house, and the men of her city shall stone her to death . . . (Deut. 22:20–21, amplified version). This punishment was for having sex before she was married, an act that was criminal.

Because the BMBC is Old Testament focused in its approach, the above scriptures have affected its views of and teachings on unmarried women. The BMBC teaches that women who are not married should not engage in sexual intercourse. The belief is that somehow this will affect their relationships with their future husbands. The men are taught to view unmarried women who are sexually active as "loose" women. Although the BMBC would not revoke the marriage license of a man who marries a woman who is not a virgin, the man who marries a woman who is a virgin is praised, his wife is respected, and their children are highly accepted in the church community. Therefore, because of the benefits that come along with marrying a virgin, upon the first sexual encounter with his wife the husband looks for the bloodstain on the sheet.

The New Testament on Fornication

"Now the body is not for fornication, but for the Lord; and the Lord for the body." (1 Cor 6:13)

Because Wes has understood the Greek word *"porneia"* used in this verse to mean sexual uncleanness and not fornication, he concluded that the Bible does not give direct reasons for banning fornication. It is true that *porneia* has to do with filth and sexual nastiness, and this is not the case with Dan and Denise. They are both single, monogamous, and consensual sexual partners. They are decent people coming from Christian homes. This is not a case of filth and sexual nastiness. And there are no Biblical stories that explicitly speak to this case.

The BMBC uses the King James translation of the Bible which, unlike more modern translations, uses the word "fornication" for the Greek term "*porneia.*" The BMBC does not take into consideration arguments about translation or original context. The ancient scriptures in the King James Version are read as a contemporary document. In other words, the Bible says fornication is wrong and that is just what it means. Therefore, there is no need to study the historical context or culture from which the term derived or other uses of the Greek words in the original text. The text is taken to be literal. The BMBC is clear: no fornication means no sex outside of the bonds of marriage.

According to *Webster's Dictionary*, fornication is illicit sexual intercourse, illicit meaning unlawful intercourse. It is a fact that Dan is breaking the law because Denise is only seventeen years old. Marty is right; Dan could be arrested for statutory rape. This is clearly a case of unlawful intercourse. And this relationship could be condemned on this basis. But what about when Denise turns eighteen years old, will sex still be illegal? No, she will be an adult. The argument could be made that they should wait, but that in itself does not prohibit sex before marriage.

The Bible, according to the BMBC, gives a different twist to unlawful sex: "Marriage is honourable in all, and the bed undefiled: but whoremonger and adulterers God will judge" (Heb 13:4). This verse seems to convey the idea that honorable or lawful sex cannot take place outside of wedlock. The sexual act between the unmarried is an offense and will be judged by God.

The Apostle Paul added insult to injury when he opted for celibacy over against marriage. He said, "It is good for a man not to touch a woman. Nevertheless to avoid fornication, let every man have his own wife, and let every woman have her own husband" (1 Cor 7:1–2). And then Paul further drives this wedge of sexual prohibition between the unmarried: "But to the unmarried people and to the widows, I declare that it is well-good, advantageous, expedient, and wholesome for them to remain [single] even as I do. But if they have not self-control (restraint of their passions), they should marry. For it is better to marry than to be aflame (with passion and tortured continually with ungratified desire)" (1 Cor 7:8–9, amplified version). Paul seems to indicate in these verses that it is either marriage or abstinence. Any sexual impulse should be satisfied only in marriage. Therefore, both Dan and Denise are breaking the law of God, even after Denise turns eighteen years old, because any sexual relationship outside the bond of marriage is fornication, and thus unlawful. And if they must continue to have sexual intercourse, then they are commanded by scripture to get married.

Men's Sexual Obligation

Solange is right; Dan needs to respect Denise. Denise has given him her most precious jewel, vulnerability, and she has received little in return. Because of her love for him and need to be with him, she gave herself to him to be used as a sexual object—after all, isn't that the only time he pays her any real attention? If Dan really cares for Denise, he would help to prepare her for the future. He would teach her by example how she should expect to be treated by a man—open the door for her, pull out the chair for her, listen to her, and so forth. But if he does not love her or plan to marry her, then he should not take advantage of her. It appears that Denise is only an object to Dan. With this type of treatment, Dan can scar Denise for life. The words of Tamar to her brother Amnon are most appropriate; after Amnon had raped Tamar, he ordered his servant to send her away, but Tamar said, "this great evil of sending me away is worse than what you did to me" (2 Sam 13:16). Tamar was crying out for respect, and this is what Dan owes Denise, respect.

Parental Responsibility, the Black Missionary Baptist Churches, and the Old Testament

Parents are responsible for bringing up their children in the admonition and fear of God. By this I mean parents are to use the necessary means to rear good children. Regardless of what psychologists say, in the BMBC, the rod is generally the means for raising good children. There are several scriptures that seem to corroborate this action:

> He that spareth his rod hateth his son; but he that loveth him chasteneth him betimes. (Prov 13:24)

> Foolishness is bound in the heart of a child; but the rod of correction will drive it far from him. (Prov 22:15)

> Withhold not instruction from the child: for if thou beatest him with the rod, he shall not die. Thou shalt beat him with the rod, and shalt deliver his soul from hell. (Prov 23:13–14)

The BMBC holds the view that the child cannot collaborate with parents because the parents have more experience. Therefore, there is no compromising with the child; the child should be compelled, by the use of corporal punishment if necessary, to do the right thing. I remember one day talking back to my mother. She said to me, "Son, I brought you into this world and I will take you out of this world." Needless to say, I never tried that again. This, according to the BMBC, is good parenting.

Parents are held responsible by the church community for their children's actions. Their children can bring either shame or honor to the family's name. I remember one day an old lady was excluded from the church circle because her son had been convicted of murder. It was obvious to me that the old lady did not have anything to do with the action of her son. She had done the best she could in raising him. But the church community shied away from her as if they held her responsible for her son's action. This was because they expected her to raise a Christian son. This boy brought dishonor to his family's Christian name. This attitude is not foreign to the Bible. There are several scriptures supporting it:

Train up a child in the way he should go; and when he is old, he will not depart from it. (Prov 22:6)

Let thine ear now be attentive, and thine eyes open, that thou mayest hear the prayer of thy servant, which I pray before thee now, day and night, for the children of Israel thy servants, and confess the sins of the children of Israel, which we have sinned against thee; both I and my father's house have sinned. (Neh 1:6)

Keeping mercy for thousands, forgiving iniquity and transgression and sin, and that will by no means clear the guilty; visiting the iniquity of the fathers upon the children, and upon the children's children, unto the third and to the fourth generation. (Ex 34:7)

And his sons went and feasted in their houses, every one his day; and sent and called for their three sisters to eat and to drink with them. And it was so, when the days of their feasting were gone about, that Job sent and sanctified them, and rose up early in the morning, and offered burnt offerings according to the number of them all; for Job said, It may be that my sons have sinned, and cursed God in their hearts. (Job 1:4–5)

These scriptures seem to give the impression that the parents should be held responsible for the child's actions and welfare. This view of parental responsibility is a popular view among the BMBC.

Disciplinary Action within the Black Missionary Baptist Churches

Normally persons are not arbitrarily excluded from the church community based on rumor or unfounded prejudice. There is a process for face-to-face confrontation as commanded in the New Testament:

Moreover if thy brother shall trespass against thee, go and tell him his fault between thee and him alone; if he shall hear thee, thou hast gained thy brother. But if he will not hear thee, then take with thee one or two more, that in the mouth of two or three witnesses every word may be established. And if he shall neglect to hear them, tell it unto the church; but if he neglect to hear the church, let him be unto thee as an heathen man and a publican. (Matt 18:15–17)

In 1 Timothy the following process of rebuking, not tolerating sin, is recommended: "Them that sin rebuke before all, that others also may fear" (1 Tim 5:20). And St. Paul makes the argument for exclusion from the church community specifically with regard to fornicators:

I wrote unto you in an epistle not to company with fornicators: Yet not altogether with the fornicators of this world, or with the covetous, or extortioners, or with idolaters; for then must ye needs go out of the world. But now I have written unto you not to keep company, if any man that is called a brother be a fornicator, or covetous, or an idolater, or a railer, or a drunkard, or an extortioner; with such an one no not to eat. For what have I to do to judge them also that are without? Do not ye judge them that are within? But them that are without God judgeth. Therefore put away from among yourselves that wicked person. (1 Cor 5:9–13)

The BMBC developed its rules of discipline from the above scriptures. It follows these scriptures almost to the letter. When a brother or sister has sinned, the first step is personal confrontation. If the person repents, the fault is forgotten. But if the person does not repent, the second step is to inform one or two others about the fault. The two or three people then go and confront the person. But if the person does not repent, the third step is to take him or her before the church. The person will be rebuked openly, lose his or her position in the church, and be demoted to the status of heathen or publican. But if the person still does not repent, the fourth step is to put him or her out of the church. This is the discipline that Dan and Denise would have faced in the BMBC. But with repentance and reform of one's behavior, former sinners are accepted and often compassionately welcomed into the community.

Conclusion: The Pastor's Role

The pastor plays a key role in the BMBC. As I have already stated, he is the shepherd of the congregation. He provides the inspiration, insight, and information that are necessary for the daily lives of his sheep, the members. The sheep look to him for answers to the questions about life: What shall I do? Why is this happening? How am I going to make it? Many times members will be heard to say things like, "The lawyer told me one thing, but I went to Reverend to see what he thought about it." There is this kind of trusting relationship between the pastor and his people.

The pastor is the bearer of tradition. He takes on the temperament of the church. If he is to have a smooth administration, he must learn the traditions of his congregation and follow it. Many times these traditions influence pastoral decisions. For instance, a pastor friend of mine once refused to perform a wedding ceremony because the couple wanted to sing a love song. Love songs were considered worldly and sinful by his congregation. Therefore, if the pastor wanted to remain respectable, he could not perform that wedding, especially in the church.

The pastor is the bearer of the word of God. This is the secret to the pastor's authority. He does not speak like men; he speaks the words of God. Therefore, the pastor must know the stories of the Bible. Although his opinion does matter, a word from the Bible is always better. Often members will say, "Our Pastor don't give you his opinion; he gives you the Word."

In this case, the role of the pastor would be as follows. First, the pastor would counsel Dan and Denise. Second, if they do not repent, he would speak to them again, taking along one or two others—usually deacons—with him to help persuade them. Third, if they still do not repent, he is to rebuke them before the church and demote them. Fourth, if they persist in refusing to repent, he is to put them out of the church and counsel them from the outside in hopes of restoring them. This is the disciplinary process of the BMBC.

Notes

1. Genesis, chapter 34, should be read in its entirety in order to understand the argument.
2. Judges, chapter 19, should be read in its entirety in order to understand the argument.
3. Cited in Christine E. Gudorf, *Body, Sex, and Pleasure* (Cleveland, OH: The Pilgrim Press, 1994), 9.

A CONSERVATIVE JEWISH RESPONSE
by Adam Silverman

The case study dealing with the parents' discovery of the eighteen-year-old son in bed with his under-eighteen-year-old girlfriend raises some serious, intriguing, and unprecedented ethical questions. The reasons for the last descriptive category are exactly as the character Beth states in the case: that all premarital sexual problems could have been averted if "we married (our daughters) off at menarche like in the biblical stories." As recently as fifty to sixty years ago the questions raised in the case study would have been largely academic exercises in moral, ethical, and legal logic and reasoning for most members of major religious movements throughout the world. While it is true that most women have not been married off at menarche in the United States and most of Western Europe for more than a century, the mores and constraints of society before the sixties' sexual revolution held the number of instances of premarital sex, especially among minors, down to a small number. Now, however, in our contemporary, postsexual-revolution social milieu, the question of sex before marriage and its implications for law, ethics, and morals is a major question that has to be answered in regards to the daily lives of the practitioners of religion in contemporary society.

What, then, *is* the Jewish response and how does Judaism's seemingly all-embracing code of legal and ethical practice, the *halakha*, deal with the question of premarital sexual relations? Amazingly enough, while there is a fair amount written by the sages about the issue, there is no actual commandment in the Torah and no prohibition in the legal code that apply to premarital sexual relations between consenting adults.[1] This assertion, so tantalizingly and provocatively presented by Eugene Borowitz, seems to be a contradiction. As Solange asserts, the Bible seems to "accept the practice of giving and taking women in marriage without their consent, and takes for granted the selling of women into prostitution. Adultery is understood as an offense against the husband's ownership, and fornication and rape are both understood as offenses against a father's interest in and responsibility for the daughter."

It is with Solange's assertion that our inquiry as to what Judaism has had to say about the issue of premarital sex must begin. All of the situations that Solange mentions are in fact dealt with through the Mosaic code. The Torah does forbid a wide range of sexual misconduct. However, in each case there is a claim upon at least one of the parties involved: they are either engaged to be, or already are, married, are members of a family, or are members who can bring into the family a payment as a dowry or bride price. Also it seems fairly certain that while Solange's assertion—that many of these biblical proscriptions about sex and male/female relations being of a fiduciary nature seem to make women and girls a form of chattel—is correct in practice, in the many centuries since the Jewish law was written women and girls have not always been viewed that way by the Jews who were attempting to make sense of the rules and apply them to daily life. The first two laws that bear on this question of premarital sex are from Exodus and Deuteronomy, respectively.

In Exodus the Torah states that if a man seduces an unbetrothed virgin, then he must pay the girl's bride price to her father and make her his wife. If the father refuses to give the girl over to him for any reason, then the seducer must still pay the bride price for a virgin (Ex 22:15–16). The rule from Deuteronomy closely follows the one from Exodus. If an unengaged virgin is raped by a man, and they are discovered, the rapist shall pay fifty silver shekels to her father, marry her, and because the initial contact was of a violatory nature, never divorce her (Deut 22:28–29). The formulation of these two laws is similar; the main difference is that the former involves what appears to be consensual sexual behavior, while the latter is one of force. Leaving aside the issue of discovery in the second law,[2] both of these laws indicate that the father must be compensated in regards to the value of his unbetrothed and virginal daughter. Notice that the key conditional descriptive words here are "unbetrothed," "virginal," and "girl." This raises the question of what happens in either case if the young woman is either pledged, not a virgin, or no longer a girl?

The latter two descriptive terms, "virginity" and "girlness," need to be considered first. Roland de Vaux, the archeologist and biblical scholar, laments that the Bible gives no information as to when girls were betrothed or married and that the only real assertion about unmarried sexual relations concerns a priest's daughter who has been caught for prostitution.[3] What then, in the *halakhic* tradition, constitutes a girl? The earliest attempts to quantify and qualify this issue are from the Talmud, where the rabbis equate the stages of female development with those of a fig: unripe, ripening, and ripe. Unripe is her childhood, ripening is her maidenhood, and ripe is maturity. In the first two stages the father has the legal right to her produce and to overturn decisions that she might make. Upon reaching the third stage the woman is freed from her father's authority (Niddah 5:7–8). Adding to this, several of the rabbis attempt to explain and identify the mature stage of female development:

> Rab Jose the Galilean said, "When a wrinkle appears under the breast."
> Rab Akiva said, "When the breasts hang down." Rab Ben Azzai said,
> "When the ring around the nipple darkens." Rab Jose said, "When the
> breasts are so developed that, should a hand be placed on the tip of a
> nipple, it sink; and only slowly rises again." (Niddah 5:7–8)

In a portion of the text preceding this passage the rabbis make a three-way distinction, with a woman falling within the first stages being subject to her father's rules and authority, while a woman in the last category is a legal entity under herself. Eventually they tried to tie the signs of physical maturation to chronological age. A female under twelve, *yeldah* (girl) or *tinoket* (minor), is solely under her father's direction, from twelve to twelve and a half the status changes to that of a *naarah*, a young woman or maiden who has some special responsibilities of her own apart from her father, and at twelve and a half she becomes a mature woman, *bogeret*, who is competent to act for herself.[4] Arranging betrothals and marriages was usually done during the middle stage, while the daughter was no longer a child but also not yet a woman. It may be that the father's action of arranging a marriage for his daughter while she was undergoing her maturation may have been a way to deal with the anxiety created by her change from girl to woman. The act of pledging her in marriage may have been a very low-level liminality-containing lifecourse ritual.

It is fairly clear that the laws of Exodus and Deuteronomy apply to women who have not reached maturation, are still virgins, and/or are betrothed. This would seem to indicate that, at least in theory, the mature woman would be free not only to arrange her own affairs, including marriage, but also to engage in whatever relations that she chooses, barring those that are prohibited. As stated, this interpretation is theoretical and probably had little practical meaning or application until the modern period. Even today many devout Jews, the Orthodox, arrange betrothals for their children, and some of the Orthodox denominations even prohibit physical contact between males and females outside of familial bonds unless they are married.[5] Is it possible in today's modern and contemporary society to draw a Jewish sexual ethic from the distinctions made by these rules? The answer is no. These rules do not directly address the issue at hand: consensual, premarital sexual relations. To find the answer it is necessary to continue looking through the Judaic tradition.

In the Talmud (Sanhedrin 76:a–b) there is a discussion of the necessity of marrying off one's daughter before she reaches the *bogeret* state in order not to violate the law that says one should not make one's daughter a whore (Lev

19:29). Much of this argument is tied to when to marry her and to whom to marry her. It appears that by the Middle Ages these rules had been adapted to the betrothal by mid to late puberty and marriage by the mid to late teens. Borowitz asserts that during the time period of the betrothal, the engaged were involved in a semi-marriage because the laws interpreted the pledged woman having sexual relations with any man other than her fiancée as adultery.[6] While this law, which considered an engaged woman's sexual relations with someone other than her fiancée adultery, was expanded and used to prohibit and prevent all premarital sexual relations for most of Judaic history, it does raise an interesting question: can the engaged woman have consensual premarital sex with the husband-to-be?

It seems fairly clear from a search of the rabbinic literature that the preeminent sexual concern of the community was not the limiting of consensual premarital sex—a minor nuisance at most—but rather controlling against adultery and prostitution. In Sanhedrin 75a there appears a lengthy technical discussion that bears on the question of premarital sex. The sages, in discussing the desire of a man for a particular woman, conclude that rather then even suggest that he marry the object of his desire he should be left to die from his desire. This conclusion is based on the belief of Rab Isaac that since the Temple was destroyed, sexual relations of the moral do not have the same passion and pleasure as those of the immoral. Rab Isaac bases this on the passage from Proverbs 9:17 about the sweetness of stolen waters and the pleasure of secretly partaking in bread. Yet even this Talmudic ruling is not definitive in regards to the questions raised by the case, unless Solange and Marty intend to let their son die from his desire. In order to supplement the dearth of direct legislation regarding premarital sexual relations, the rabbis worked around the problem by emphasizing the importance and sanctity of marriage and of the role of sex within it.

It is not until the Maimonides *Mishneh Torah*, composed in the twelfth century, that a fully developed legal prohibition of premarital intercourse is found. Rabbi Moshe ben Maimon (Rambam)[7] asserts that there are four commandments, two positive and two negative, in regards to marriage. They are: (1) one should marry a woman by means of betrothal; (2) one should be fruitful and multiply; (3) a woman should not surrender herself without a *ketubah* (marriage) contract and a betrothal so as not to be a harlot; and (4) one should not withhold from a designated Hebrew maidservant her food, raiment, and conjugal rights (applicable to other women as well).[8] The Rambam makes it quite clear that women who engage in intercourse without a *ketubah* and a betrothal are making themselves into prostitutes. Maimonides seems to bring solidity to an issue that had none. He bases his four commandments on Deuteronomy 24:1—to take a wife; Genesis 1:28—to be fruitful and multiply; Deuteronomy 23:18—there shall be no prostitute daughters of Israel; and Exodus 21:10—her food, raiment, and conjugal rights should not be diminished. The result is that where there was no concrete basis for an ethic about premarital sex before Maimonides, there is definitely one after him. The only point that seems to have caused any conflict was in regards to the last point over the maidservant or concubine. Several other rabbis disagreed with the Rambam's formulation on this, and, as a result, many later rulings disagreed with him on this one matter. Because the dispute involved concubinage, which was a reality in the biblical period and in Rambam's social milieu, but was not relevant to other medieval Jewish communities, or in our own time, this fourth provision was set aside by later tradition. However, the later tradition found Maimonides's first three rulings sufficient to formulate a Jewish sexual ethic which prohibited premarital sexual relations.

They are prohibited because a man must lawfully wed, a woman should not/must not surrender herself outside of the valid marriage, a husband cannot keep back from her food, apparel, or conjugal rights, and from those conjugal rights a husband must be fruitful and multiply. This last part is also interesting because while the sages realize that in order for a man to fulfill this commandment he must have a woman's, presumably his wife's, help, they say that this commandment only applies to men. The reason for this is because there is always an inherent risk in pregnancy and childbirth for the woman, she can never be commanded to be fruitful and multiply as this could put her in jeopardy.[9] Traditional Judaism's stance in regards to the substantive portion of the case is that Solange and Marty, if they were adhering to traditional Judaism, should have told their son that what he was doing was a violation of the *halakhic* code of behavior, explained what this meant if he was not sure, and told him that he either needed to end the sexual relationship or, if he was unwilling to do so, marry his girlfriend in order to continue it. None of these options sounds either very appealing or helpful in the situation, which is why Orthodox Judaism has created a social system that from around the time of puberty limits physical contact between unmarried males and females, and why, even though they are much more liberal in regards to male/female contact, Conservative and Reform Judaism still consider marriage to be a necessity for the fulfillment of the command to be fruitful and multiply.

In regards to the other substantive question in the case, that of the mixed message sent by Solange and Marty urging their son to use contraception, in this case condoms, to prohibit sexually transmitted disease and protect against unwanted pregnancy, Judaism is quite clear: contraceptive action taken by the male partner is forbidden. It is forbidden because it violates the commandment to be fruitful and multiply, and, until the arrival of the femidom, because the man must wear the condom, this form of contraception is expressly forbidden.[10] The Jewish legal code does permit four methods of contraception:[11] the safe period, twisting movements by the woman after intercourse, oral contraceptives, and an absorbent device.[12] Each of these must be performed by the woman as she cannot be forced into fulfilling the command to be fruitful and multiply. The Jewish position on limiting population growth is again tied to the command over procreation. Having one male and one female child is generally understood as the minimum for fulfilling the requirement,[13] and the use of contraception by the wife to prevent further children is considered legitimate, but not necessary.

One would think that because Judaism has such an exhaustive code of legal and ethical practice that it would be possible to find a clear, cut-and-dried solution to Solange and Marty's ethical conundrum. It is evident, however, that because there is no specific prohibition against premarital intercourse in the Torah, that Judaism has a dearth of answers on the subject. While it is true that from the twelfth century onwards the codification given by Maimonides in his *Mishneh Torah* clarifies the issue greatly, he could not have foreseen the changes in society that would allow for a situation to develop that would cause Solange and Marty so much anguish. Furthermore, it is not entirely certain that the Orthodox Jewish approach to preventing the problem from occurring—strict regulation of contact between young men and young women—is the best solution to the problem. The Orthodox Jewish community thus creates a situation in which no ethic on premarital sex need be applied because it is hard to imagine, though not unthinkable, that a breach of the strictly scrutinized social mores of the Orthodox community would occur.

Moreover, it is also clear that Maimonides had to stitch his legal arguments placing sex solely within the marriage together using different pieces of Judaic cloth. The *halakhic* garment for a sexual ethic, which he helped to fashion as a result of his codification of the Torah, had to be pulled together from different parts of the Law because the Law itself is silent on the question as to whether consensual sex between consenting adults is acceptable or unacceptable.

The Judaic position in regards to sexual matters is largely based on Maimonides's work. The Rambam takes four laws and, weaving them into his *halakhic* codification, created a standard for practice, which in turn created the ethic. The ethic that results from Maimonides's jurisprudence reinforces the already central role of marriage in the Jewish tradition. The central role of marriage in Judaism is designed to accomplish a number of things. Among them is to aid in the perpetuation of religious practice, of national identity, and of cultural norms and standards and to aid in the protection of women. The protection of women comes largely through interpretation and codification of the Law in such a way as to reinforce traditional roles for women. These roles—mother, homemaker, and transmitter of cultural and national identity—have changed as a result of modernity and contemporary society. In many, if not most, Jewish households, the wife/mother now faces many new responsibilities that often emanate from outside of Jewish society and law. Often a balance has to be struck between the traditional *halakhic* requirements and economic need and personal desire for a career. The problem that many Jewish women, as well as many Jewish couples, now face is that laws which were originally intended to safeguard women now seem to carry the potential to hinder them by prohibiting them from accepting and participating in many of the challenges of contemporary life.

Notes

1. Eugene Borowitz, *Choosing a Sex Ethic: A Jewish Inquiry* (New York: Schocken Books, 1969), 31. This author was as shocked by this assertion as the assertion seems to be shocking; however, after examination of as much of the source material that could be found, I have to agree with Borowitz that there is no commandment or prohibition directly aimed at preventing premarital sexual relations between consenting adults.

2. This issue is tied up in lengthy *halakhic* discourse regarding either making unverifiable or untrue charges against another in regards to a crime that can have a capital punishment. The penalty for bearing false witness in regards to a capital charge is to be charged as if one has attempted murder. The reasoning is that one has pursued the life of another through the legal system.

3. Roland de Vaux, *Ancient Israel* (New York: McGraw Hill, 1961), 26, 29, 32, 37.

4. In a footnote to his text, Borowitz conveys that the sages were convinced that as a woman matured the signs of her virginity disappeared, and therefore, if a father wanted to get the bride price for a virgin he had to set the betrothal at the right time (Borowitz, *Choosing a Sex Ethic*, 138).

5. I had an Orthodox professor who once related the story that upon completion of his rabbinical training and law degree he was seen by a fellow student holding hands with a woman in a park. The student reported him to the head of the institution, who called him on it only to be chagrined when he found out that the couple were married and, therefore, allowed to have contact.

6. Borowitz, *Choosing a Sex Ethic*, 38.

7. Rabbi Moses ben Maimon, the twelfth-century scholar and physician, can be referred to by either his full name, by "Maimonides" (roughly meaning "the man named Maimon"), or by the abbreviation "Rambam" (for Rabbi Moshe ben Maimon).

8. Moses ben Maimon, *Mishneh Torah: The Book of Women*, trans. Isaac Klein (New Haven, CT: Yale University Press, 1972), 4–5.

9. David S. Shapiro, "Be Fruitful and Multiply," in *Jewish Bioethics*, ed. Fred Rosner and J. David Bleich (Brooklyn, NY: Hebrew Publishing Company, 1979), 64–67.

10. Fred Rosner, "Contraception in Jewish Law," in *Jewish Bioethics*, 91.

11. I was unable to find anything newer than the early nineties on this matter and can, therefore, not offer any information on whether or not the femidom is or is not *halakicly* acceptable.

12. Rosner, "Contraception in Jewish Law," 70–71.

13. Shapiro, "Be Fruitful and Multiply," 70–71.

Bibliography and Suggested Reading

Borowitz, Eugene. *Choosing a Sex Ethic: A Jewish Inquiry*. New York: Schocken Books, 1969.

Brown, Joanne Carlson, and Carole R. Bohn. *Christianity, Patriarchy, and Abuse: A Feminist Critique*. Cleveland, OH: Pilgrim Press, 1989.

Brown, Peter. *Body and Society*. New York: Columbia University Press, 1988.

Gudorf, Christine E. *Body, Sex, and Pleasure*. Cleveland, OH: Pilgrim Press, 1994.

Heyward, Carter. *Touching Our Strengths: The Erotic as Power and the Love of God*. San Francisco: Harper and Row, 1989.

Maimon, Moses ben. *Mishneh Torah: The Book of Women.* Trans. Isaac Klein. New Haven, CT: Yale University Press, 1972.

Nelson, James B. *Between Two Gardens: Reflections on Sexuality and Religious Experience.* Cleveland, OH: Pilgrim Press, 1983.

Nelson, James B., and Sandra P. Longfellow. *Sexuality and the Sacred: Sources for Theological Reflection.* Louisville, KY: Westminster John Knox, 1994.

Shapiro, David S. "Be Fruitful and Multiply." In *Jewish Bioethics,* ed. Fred Rosner and J. David Bleich. Brooklyn, NY: Hebrew Publishing Company, 1979.

de Vaux, Roland. *Ancient Israel.* New York: McGraw Hill, 1961.

CHAPTER 3

A Tangle of Laws

A CASE STUDY by Adam Silverman and Christine E. Gudorf

"I'll speak with Rabbi Fink this very afternoon and call you after Shabbat," promised Rabbi Jacob Iskowitz to the depressed-looking man leaving his office. The rabbi stood at his office door shaking his head with sympathy for Yonaton Friedman as he departed. "It's almost ten years now that he has been alone. We have got to find some way," he muttered to himself as he walked down the hall to find Rabbi Yuri Fink.

"Good, you're free. Do you have a little time?" asked Rabbi Iskowitz. At Rabbi Fink's nod, Rabbi Iskowitz explained, "I have just had another visit from Yonaton Friedman, the poor man. We need to discuss again what we can do for him. I know that until Rabbi Ben Amir recovers from his accident we can't do anything official, but if you and I can agree, he will certainly support us." Rabbi Iskowitz referred to the fact that Rabbi Fink tended to the liberal end of the *Bet Din*, their three-judge tribunal, Rabbi Iskowitz to the conservative end, and Rabbi Ben Amir was the moderate who often occupied the middle ground. The *Bet Din* has civil authority in some areas of Jewish law, including marriage and divorce, as well as religious authority.

"Fine. Remind me of the case. The name seems very familiar," agreed Rabbi Fink.

"Yes, it should be familiar. It's a divorce case. The man first came to us ten years ago, after his wife took the three children and returned to the United States. The *moredet* [rebellious woman] wanted to live in the United States, and when he insisted they stay in Israel, she took off while he was on a business trip. She notified the United States Department of Immigration that he had only married her to get United States citizenship, so they have a flag on his name and a pick-up order out on him if he enters the country. She got a civil divorce in the United States, which he could not attend in order to either contest the divorce or demand custody or visitation with the children. More than that," Rabbi Iskowitz continued pointedly, "the woman refuses to accept a *get* [a Jewish divorce decree], even when we tried to deliver one officially through a *shaliakh liqabalah* [messenger of receipt]. If he goes to the States he will be picked up at the airport, arrested, and deported. Without her acceptance of the *get*, he is still married to her under both Israeli law and Jewish religious law and cannot marry again. More than that, he has not seen his children in ten years." Rabbi Iskowitz shook his head in disgust.

"How did these two marry in the first place?" asked Rabbi Fink.

"Ruth Friedman was an American from UCLA doing her junior year abroad in Israel—would that she had never come!" exclaimed Rabbi Iskowitz. "They were students together here, and when she went back to complete her degree they wrote and spoke on the telephone. When he visited the States for her graduation, they got engaged, and some months later he went to the United States to marry. He agreed to work there the first few years. He worked as an engineer and got dual citizenship (United States and Israeli); she worked as a teacher. Their first child was born in the States. After a few years they moved back to Israel to live; their younger two children are *sabras* [native-born Israelis]. But a dispute over where they should live developed, and finally they spoke of divorce. He went away for a month of army reserve training. After his calls the first week or so went unanswered, he worried. When he returned the family was gone. She would not speak to him when he called her family, and by the time he wound up his affairs in Tel Aviv to follow them to the United States, she had already reported him to Immigration and Naturalization Service [INS] officials as if he were some criminal to be deported. He could not contest the civil divorce because he did not know for some months that she had filed for divorce; he was too busy trying to convince the INS that his citizenship was legitimate, that they were depriving him of his children. But nothing worked."

"Did we have American rabbis talk to Ruth Friedman?" asked Rabbi Fink. "Perhaps they could make her see her obligations, and at least persuade her to accept the *get*."

"Yes, we have, but she doesn't seem to care about a *get*," Rabbi Iskowitz replied. "In the States she could remarry civilly based on her civil divorce, though she has not in ten years, and she doesn't seem to care about her religious status. Yonaton has little to bargain with. She wants to keep him from his children. He feels that she fears she will lose them to him, that they will live here and not in the United States. As if Israel were not the place for Jews to live!"

"So Yonaton Friedman is a male *agunah* [bound one], hum?" asked Rabbi Fink rhetorically, referring to a group of Jewish women who could not obtain divorce. They remained bound because under Jewish and Israeli law, only men could initiate the *get*, though to be final, the *get* must be accepted by the wife. Women whose husbands had disappeared or were presumed dead (as in war), as well as women whose husbands simply refused to initiate a *get*, were stuck in a no-man's-land between singleness and marriage. Rabbi Fink had strongly supported the political activism of organizations that represented the *agunah*. Their activism had recently led Israel to pass a new law designed to improve the situation of these women who were *agunot* (bound). Under the new law the husbands identified by the rabbinical courts as preventing the *agunah* from getting divorces could be denied certain civil rights: to vote in elections, to run for office, to work in civil service, to sign checks, and to obtain drivers' licenses. The law was designed to persuade them to free their wives. But none of the provisions of these laws had any persuasive power outside of Israel, and Yonaton Friedman's problem was that he was operating within Israeli law, while his wife was using United States civil law.

"What does Mr. Friedman want the court to do?" asked Rabbi Fink. "It sounds as if we have exhausted our remedies for him."

"He has read about the new law on the *agunah*, and thought that if the courts were now involved in more activism on their behalf, perhaps we could represent him with the American court system. The divorce is not the main problem. You know as well as I that we can get 100 rabbis to sign off on a *get* so that the poor man can remarry. I don't think anyone will disagree that this is an extraordinary case that justifies using the remedy for exceptional cases. This is my answer—to tell him we can enable him to marry and that he should marry a good Israeli and have a new family."

"I have no problem with that so far as it goes," said Rabbi Fink.

"Good," responded Rabbi Iskowitz. "We can begin that process as soon as Rabbi Ben Amir returns, perhaps by the end of next week. I will call Yonaton after Shabbat." Rabbi Iskowitz walked back to his office, gathered up his things, and left to prepare for Shabbat.

Rabbi Fink called his wife, Rahel, to tell her that he was on the way home and then also left the court building. When he arrived home he went into the kitchen where his wife was still preparing the Shabbat dinner. She asked if he could finish setting the table, and as he did, he told her of the Friedman case. Rahel paused as he told her what had been decided.

"I've heard you explain many times, Yuri, that our law was given to a distinct people to govern all aspects of life and that it was presumed to be, and was, efficient so long as our people either lived in their own land or in separate communities in other lands. But pluralism in Israel and the world and movement back and forth between the pluralist groups present problems. This is a great example, hmm? This woman sounds as cruel and vindictive as Jezebel—or that man who spent nineteen years in jail in Jerusalem for contempt of the rabbinical court because he continued to refuse to grant his wife a *get*. But this wife is not being made to suffer for her mean spirit—in fact, she is actually gaining, because she need not take any risks of sharing the children or of them perhaps choosing to live here. That seems wrong. Isn't there anything that you can do?" Rahel asked.

"Not that I can see. But I was thinking that next month I go to speak at that rabbinical school in the States. Perhaps I will ask some of the rabbis there and see if there is anything to be done about the citizenship and custody issue. The separation of state and religion in America causes Americans to ignore the fact that our rabbinical courts are also state courts with regard to marriage and divorce, so our decisions do not always have the status of those of other national courts. But perhaps those who understand the American system better can give us good advice. I'll call one of the rabbis in Queens and see if they can arrange for me to get some advice," decided Rabbi Fink.

A month later Rabbi Fink emerged from his El-Al jet. As he walked with his fellow passengers toward customs and immigration he wondered whether Rabbi Weir, his contact in New York, would be on time. Half an hour later, as he exited the customs hall he saw Rabbi Weir and smiled. They greeted each other and headed for the exit. As they walked, Rabbi Weir filled him in on the schedule for his six-day visit. He would be speaking to and meeting with a number of groups of rabbis who wanted to know about everything in Israel from the latest in the rabbinical courts to his slant on the current divisions in Israeli politics. Rabbi Weir added, "I have put together a little *chavurah* [purposeful informal gathering] Wednesday morning on that immigration problem of yours. I knew a person or two myself, but called around to get other names. It's a mix of legal experts. I hope it will be helpful."

Rabbi Fink thanked him, " I am very grateful. It would be impossible to be less helpful than we have been for this man."

At the Wednesday meeting Rabbi Fink was introduced to five lawyers, judges, and professors of law who listened respectfully to his description of the Friedman case. The response was at first rather general.

"We have some of the same problems, of course," said one lawyer whose last name he had forgotten. "Here the issue is a little different, because Jews need first a civil divorce and then a *get* in order to remarry. Some husbands tell the wives that if the wife wants him to give her a *get* so she could remarry, she has to agree to whatever he wants in the civil divorce—usually very unfavorable financial settlements or, sometimes, custody arrangements. Women don't have the same power, because if they refuse to accept a *get*, some of the orthodox rabbis tell the husbands to go ahead and remarry, that the law technically allows men to have more than one wife. But women must have the *get* to remarry, or they and their children by a second marriage are cut off."

A judge from Brooklyn added, "Yes, we had a few very notorious cases. One husband wanted the wife's family to deed over almost a million dollars in shares in the family business in addition to his share of the joint assets in return for a *get*. The family let the story go public, but nothing embarrassed the husband into dropping the demand."

Another attorney insisted, "But why is this so surprising? We see this kind of bargaining among all groups in divorces. There are friendly divorces, and there are divorces ruled by vengeance or greed. This kind of bargaining over the right to remarry is no worse than the bargaining that goes on over child custody, is it?"

At this point, the retired federal judge remarked, "That takes us to Rabbi Fink's issue. Are there any suggestions about how Mr. Friedman should proceed? It seems to me that if he can afford an immigration attorney here, it should not be difficult for Mr. Friedman to gain entry to the States."

Mr. Feldstein, an attorney from Queens, agreed. "I would agree to represent him at least to check out the situation and see if he needs an immigration attorney. He does not want to—and seems to never have wanted to—live in the United States for himself but did so only as an accommodation to his wife, and that not permanently. That may be all he has to convince INS about. The wife has said he married her to get citizenship; INS's initial suspicion will be that he wants to use the children as an excuse to come into the country and stay. Unless they have some other suspicions, it should not be too difficult for him to receive permission to come into the United States to visit his children or to sue for visitation rights."

The judge, who had a reputation for scholarship within the Conservative community of New York, suggested, "So Rabbi Fink will put the husband in touch with Mr. Feldstein, and he can see what needs to be done to begin the resolution of this situation. But I have a concern. It occurred to me in the controversy around the *get* law that when we do things like we are gathered here to do—try to resolve a sticky case that falls between two or more sets of laws—that we weaken all of them in some way, especially the Jewish law. We feel compelled to do this out of compassion for people such as this husband, who has been deprived of his children for ten years. But there is a problem, and it is bigger than the charges of favoritism we heard so often around the *get* law."

Mr. Feldstein explained to Rabbi Fink, who was puzzled by this reference to favoritism, "In the 1980s the New York legislature passed a law that made it a condition of civil divorce that plaintiffs must pledge to help their spouses to overcome all obstacles to remarriage. There were a lot of problems with the law—it did not help when Jewish women were the divorce plaintiffs. But the biggest problem was that many legal scholars consider it to be unconstitutional, in that it was aimed at solving what was basically a religious problem of one religious group."

The judge continued, "It is a dangerous situation for any people when their law becomes impotent, when to resolve situations they must go outside the law to other authorities, or when flouting the law brings no penalties. We see the dangers in allowing civil law to be flouted with impunity in this nation. Why should criminals learn respect for the law when they can be convicted of serious crimes five and ten times without seeing a prison door, when the police do not even arrest juveniles for crimes like car theft because the court system is too clogged even to hear the case? We see this problem of disrespect for religious law in a different, but equally disturbing, way. In traditional Jewish communities not only did the rabbis have the power to enforce their decrees, but also the moral suasion of the community supported them. To defy the rabbis meant to be completely ostracized. Today there are whole communities of Jews [Reform] who do not even require a *get* in order to remarry. So why bother with one? Only the civil law becomes important, not the religious law. This relates to the dilemma of the Jewish community over intermarriage. Should we strictly adhere to the religious law and shun those who marry outside the faith? Or do we accept intermarriage and the resulting decline in the numbers of our children and grandchildren who are raised as Jews? Assimilation is death to Judaism and the Jewish community. But is the only alternative to assimilation an unbending traditionalism that virtually ignores 300 years of modernity?"

Rabbi Fink replied, "I am not sure that there are not many distinctions that belong within this argument, though the general framework is, as you can imagine, one that we in the rabbinical courts in Israel debate regularly. But we in Israel are in a somewhat different situation, because even the traditionalists among us are open to some new interpretations of the law as necessary. After all, being a nation again has required a great many changes in the administration of the same law under which the community lived for previous centuries. We have our worries about assimilation, too, but they are not so pressing. It seems to me that for Jews in the United States, they can either be observant Jews under the Jewish law, or they can be simply Americans. Whereas in Israel, many feel that they can be religious or not, but they will still be Jews in a Jewish culture. I do not agree with this, but there is no doubt that this is the position of secular Israelis."

Nathan Perlman, a constitutional lawyer who had not yet spoken, now asked, "What does that mean for American Jews? That we can either live in Orthodox communities here or we need to come to Israel? And in Israel, are all Israelis really Jews? What does this say about Arabs in Israel, if citizenship carries Jewishness? Is there really any escape from the question His Honor posed to Rabbi Fink? Can a law which took separatism as the cornerstone of Jewish identity provide for justice within the Jewish community and with the wider society and still preserve Jewish identity and community? This is not only a Jewish question, though it is more pressing for Jews because historic anti-Semitism has tended to make Jewish identity total identity, while gentiles often have distinct racial, religious, and national identities. Other religions have these same problems with intermarriage, with maintaining religious observance, with dying out. Look at liberal Protestantism here in the States or Catholicism in northern Europe."

The little group of six looked at each other solemnly, without words. It was late, and they were about to break. But the same questions hovered in all their minds. The old judge spoke. "My grandfather was a rabbi who died in the camps. He and his generation would never have believed that freedom could pose a greater danger to the faith than persecution. When the faith community and the lived community are not coextensive, religion becomes redundant. Is separatism the only answer?"

A CONSERVATIVE JEWISH RESPONSE
by Adam Silverman

The case study "A Tangle of Laws" presents three major questions in regards to Judaism and divorce: (1) in what circumstances does Judaism allow divorce, (2) how does Judaism deal with the problem of intransigence on the part of one of the parties to the divorce, and (3) what is the Jewish position on child support? This commentary will address each of these three related issues from a traditional Jewish perspective.

The Jewish concept of divorce, often referred to as the giving of a *get*,[1] while not approached lightly is grounded in the Judaic legal code (*halakhah*). In fact, Maimonides (Rambam) in his *Mishneh Torah* asserts that the bases for divorce are the commandments of Deuteronomy 24:1 and 24:4, which are, respectively: "that he writes for her a writ of divorce" and "her former husband, who sent her away, may not take her again to be his wife."[2] These two basic laws cover the how but do not do much to illuminate the why of divorce. The Judaic code outlines a number of reasons—for both men and women—for which a *get* can be issued. In the case of the husband there are nine instances in which he can compel his wife into a divorce. They are:

(1) the wife changes her religion or knowingly transgresses the Judaic law or leads her husband into doing so, (2) the wife commits adultery or the husband brings two witnesses who provide convincing evidence that she did, (3) the wife is guilty of continuous indecent behavior—immodest dress or action that brings shame upon the husband, (4) the wife grossly and publicly assaults her husband or father-in-law, (5) the wife refuses conjugal relations for the course of a whole year, (6) the wife suffers from a disability or illness that precludes marital relations, (7) the wife is barren after ten years of marriage, (8) the wife unjustifiably refuses to move to another house in the same country where the standard of living is not lower, and (9) the wife refuses to settle with him in the Land of Israel.[3]

The wife, however, has twenty instances for which she may seek a divorce:

(1) the husband changes his religion or forces her to violate the laws of Judaism, (2) the husband is morally dissolute or commits adultery, (3) the husband suffers from a major physical defect, (4) the wife finds him repugnant, (5) the husband refuses marital relations with her, (6) the husband insists on having marital relations while clothed, (7) the husband becomes weakened or debilitated so that marital relations are not possible for more than six months, (8) the wife claims her husband is impotent—even if he denies it, (9) the wife wants children and the husband is infertile, (10) the husband is malodorous, (11) the husband engages in a disgusting trade, (12) the husband is always angry and quarrelsome—regularly expelling her from their home, (13) the husband habitually beats his wife, (14) the husband refuses to support his wife, (15) the husband keeps her from regularly visiting her parents, (16) the husband prevents her from attending a wedding or making a condolence call, (17) the husband insists that they reside with his parents—even if she insists that they are unpleasant to her, (18) the husband prevents her from adorning herself, (19) the wife wants to move from an unpleasant neighborhood to a better one and the husband refuses unreasonably, and (20) the wife wishes to move to the Land of Israel and the husband refuses.[4]

It is clear from the list that three of the items on the list for the wife are related to the husband's failure to fulfill his duties to his wife according to their *ketubah* (marriage contract) as codified by Maimonides. These responsibilities, detailed in the response to the issue of premarital sex found in the previous chapter, as well as the husband's failure to live up to his responsibilities towards his wife as outlined in the marriage contract, form a core around which the marriage could break down and necessitate a divorce.

From a perusal of both the husband's and the wife's lists it is apparent that centuries ago Judaism seems to have created a concept of no-fault divorce. No-fault divorce is a recent American legal concept that many states employ in order to make divorce "quick and easy." Often when one seeks a no-fault divorce, the advice of legal counsel is that all they must do is testify at the hearing that the marriage has broken down due to one of a number of reasons. These reasons include, but are not limited to, no love, no sex, and adultery.[5] It is important to realize that Judaism's version of no-fault divorce predates the Western legal notion by many centuries. This is significant in that Western legal systems, including that of the United States, have been grounded in the legal traditions that developed throughout Christendom where divorce was generally forbidden. The recent creation of no-fault divorce by the American legal system was a significant break with the past when divorce was rare and hard to come by. The rarity of and stringent rules for divorce reflect the Christian ethical notion, as put forward in the New Testament, that divorce should not be permitted. The Jewish concept of divorce as a necessary evil that may have to happen is significantly different than that of Christianity.

The Agunah *or* Chained Woman

It is clear that the woman has many more options for requesting a divorce. There is, however, a catch—the husband is not required to grant the issuance of the divorce,[6] even should the wife request one. Rabbenu Gershom, a medieval rabbinical authority, did attempt to even the playing field between husband and wife by recognizing that the wife had to consent to a husband's compulsion of a divorce. This raises an important and tragic question: what happens if either the husband refuses to issue a *get* or if the wife refuses to accept one? The latter—an instance that mirrors our case—seems to be so rare that of several rabbis consulted, even the rabbi who supplied the (anonymous) details of this real case claimed that he had never come across a similar occurrence. In other words, cases of women failing to accept a *get* are very rare. Unfortunately, the converse is not true: there are many instances of husbands refusing to issue a *get* for their wives.

This refusal results in the wife being classified as an *agunah*. An *agunah* is, literally, one who is chained or anchored. Originally the term was applied to women whose husbands had disappeared in such a way as to preclude certainty that the husband had died; death being the only way other than divorce to terminate a Jewish marriage.[7] The condition of the *agunah* was most likely to arise in instances when the husband went off to war and did not return, and no one was able to verify positively that he had died. Another important set of occurrences that can result in the wife being an *agunah* is when the husband is traveling and a calamity strikes on the journey—such as a ship sinking, a train derailing, or an airplane crashing—but there are no remains with which to verify the husband's death. While modern forensics and pathological sciences have reduced the possibility of remains going unidentified, the problem of the soldier missing in action is still a very real possibility. Just imagine the agony of the Jewish wife who lived through the Vietnam War—the most recent conflict that still accounts for a large number of soldiers missing in action—waiting for her husband to return only to find that he will not, not because of death but because he is missing. Not only has the wife lost her husband, but according to Jewish law she would be unable to remarry should the day come when she finds someone else. The Judaic code has attempted to provide a solution to the problem of the missing husband in time of war. The Talmud instructs that the soldiers who went out to fight in the Davidic wars all wrote a *get* before leaving;[8] this was done in order to free the wives in cases where the husbands did not return but were not declared dead. Moreover, the rabbis have erred on the side of leniency in the matter of determining if a husband is deceased. They have ruled that the normal rule for witnesses—two reliable males—can be waived in order to prevent a wife from becoming an *agunah*. In fact, they have ruled that the wife alone may provide the testimony.[9] Furthermore, Rabbi Goren, the former chief rabbi of Israel, ruled that in the case of Israeli naval personnel lost in a submarine accident it can be assumed that if modern scientific methods of search have failed to find any survivors, then there are none, and the wives may remarry. Other Israeli court rulings have come to similar decisions in regards to airplane crashes.[10]

What happens then to women whose husbands are alive but refuse to issue the *get*? The rabbinical courts and authorities attempt to compel the issuance of the divorce decree. Maimonides teaches that if one who may be legally compelled to divorce his wife refuses, then the courts may scourge him until he consents.[11] What happens where the Jewish courts have no jurisdiction? They may petition the secular/state authorities to compel the recalcitrant husband to issue the divorce.[12] There are several cases either pending or recently resolved in the United States—the most celebrated in New York—where the husband refuses to accept the compulsion. In Israel under a type of contempt charge, several men have been imprisoned because of their obstinacy—one for more than twenty years. In the New York case, a husband refused to grant a Jewish divorce because his wife's *ketubah* required the equal division of the assets acquired after their marriage, which meant the division of a considerable fortune would be required because the couple had become very wealthy after their marriage. Thus the husband has been penalized with fines and contempt rulings. In this instance the husband's greed and his animosity toward his wife has given him the strength to "dig in his heels" and endure a protracted fight. The unfortunate result is that the wife cannot remarry regardless of the dispensation of their marital assets.

The modern rabbinate have attempted to rectify this type of situation by suggesting writing stipulations into the *ketubah* to preclude the condition of the *agunah* from occurring. Unfortunately, however, none of the proposed conditions placed in the marriage contract have been found to be completely *halakhically* acceptable.[13] Moreover, attempts to conditionally modify the *ketubah* have been found to be unenforceable in the United States.[14] Recently, and in light of the New York case, a New York state senator has introduced legislation that would attempt to provide a secular legal remedy to this particularly religious problem. But despite all of this rabbinical and judicial concern, women who find themselves in the unfortunate condition of the *agunah* are still trapped. Eventually the Jewish authorities will have to provide a concrete and definitive resolution of this problem that afflicts only Jewish women. Such a resolution, unfortunately, is not likely to come any time in the near future, especially in Israel. In Israel there is a large movement of women who are attempting to pressure the rabbinate to resolve this issue once and for all; however, as the status of women is not very high in the eyes of some of the Orthodox rabbinate's members, very little of substance has been done.

Jewish Divorce and "A Tangle of Laws"

There are times when divorce does seem to be the only option; this would clearly seem to apply to the couple in the case at hand. Often the necessity for a divorce is the result of the fact that the couple should probably not have been married if, as with the husband and wife in "A Tangle of Laws," they had serious unresolved issues such as whether or not to reside in the United States or in Israel. In this case the wife's unwillingness to reside in Israel— one of the instances to compel a divorce for both husband and wife—seems to have caused a troubled marriage to break down completely. The wife requested and was granted a civil divorce in the United States after she fled there with her children. Moreover, in a vindictive move she has informed the INS that her husband only married her to receive United States citizenship. As a result, he has been barred from entering the United States, a move that effectively prevents him from coming to either see his children or to fight for their custody. Furthermore, his wife's refusal to accept the *get* prevents him from remarrying in Israel, the country wherein he resides, a country in which Jews are only married in religious ceremonies. While there are ways around the remarriage problem, the real tragedy here is that Yonaton Friedman is prevented from seeing his children.

Yonaton's wife's actions, essentially kidnapping their children and fleeing from jurisdiction, have stood with legal impunity through her lies to the INS, lies that prevent Yonaton from going to fight for custody of his children. It would seem obvious from her behavior that Ruth Friedman is not only a devious woman, but appears to hate her husband. If she did not, it would not be necessary for her to kidnap the children, flee the country, and then lie to authorities in another country about her husband. In fact many *ketubot* include stipulations that allow for the dissolution of the marriage in the case of hatred between spouses.[15] As things stand, Yonaton must certainly realize that his marriage is irretrievably broken and he must move on with his life.

Moving on, however, does not have to include giving up on ever seeing his children again or abandoning his responsibility towards them. Jewish law makes it quite clear that if the children reside with the mother after the divorce, then the father is responsible for paying for their support. As it stands, Yonaton does not have to fulfill this obligation because from a Judaic point of view the marriage is still intact until a *get* is issued and accepted. In the case of Yonaton and Ruth many issues remain unresolved. Among them are the final resolution of the marriage from the Jewish standpoint, child custody, child support, visitation, and education. In this case Yonaton, through the aid of the Israeli courts, needs to engage both a rabbinical legal advisor and secular legal counsel. By doing so he will be able to have the American rabbinical authorities request that the United States courts compel Ruth to accept the *get* or suffer the legal ramifications. Furthermore, the secular legal representation can begin to try to resolve the deception involving the INS as well as begin to deal with the matter of Ruth's kidnapping of the couple's children. This last matter should be a matter of great importance as its resolution will likely play a decisive role in the final custody decisions. It is unlikely that Ruth could be made to return to Israel to answer to questions about why she fled with the children, as the extradition relationship between the United States and Israel has recently been strained over another matter.[16] Nevertheless, Yonaton, acting through effective legal and religious counsel in the United States, can force Ruth into answering for her actions and resolve this matter in a much more equitable manner.

Conclusions

It is quite evident that the Jewish concepts of divorce are quite different from both secular and Christian concepts of divorce. Judaism, unlike Christianity, recognizes the unfortunate necessity that some marriages are either never meant to have been or have for various reasons broken down so completely that the husband and the wife need to be released from their commitments. In order to make this release as painless and effective as possible Judaism developed a system of divorce that is, in many ways, very close to the modern American concept of no-fault divorce. Another important aspect of Jewish divorce is that the wife has always had the right to request a divorce. This right is related to the wife's rights as outlined in the *ketubah*, or marriage contract. This formal document belongs to the wife and clearly details the husband's responsibilities to her. Moreover, the rabbis have created a list—one each for the husband and wife—that explicitly details what conditions can result in the request for a divorce.

One condition that appears in both lists, though in slightly different forms, is the condition that if, after ten years, the wife is barren or the husband is infertile, then they may divorce. This concept has evolved into the standard that if there are no children after ten years the marriage should be ended. It is important to note that this standard is not compulsory, merely suggestive.

Jewish concepts of divorce, and of the responsibilities of both parties to a divorce, do not end with the actual divorce itself but may extend for years afterward if there are children. *Halakha* also provides direction in regards to child support, and these suggestions are followed by the Israeli courts. Furthermore, many of the questions that go unresolved until the divorce is underway and relations have become acrimonious can be eliminated by adding provisions to the *ketubah*. For instance, provisions can be added that extensively detail the redistribution of property and assets in case of divorce. This would eliminate many of the contentious issues that can turn a divorce into a grueling ordeal where one or both sides intends to punish the other as much as possible.

In regards to the specific case in "A Tangle of Laws," Yonaton needs to avail himself of the ingenuity and creativity of both the Jewish and the American authorities in order to resolve his dilemma. Through a diligent religious and legal endeavor Yonaton should be able to resolve his problems with the INS and eventually secure a proper Jewish divorce as well as gain the right to see and interact with his children. This case clearly indicates the anger, bitterness, and emotional distress that can be caused when a marriage breaks down. It is unfortunate that the system of divorce that developed within Judaism, a system intended to minimize pain and suffering, has in the case of Yonaton Friedman been largely ineffective in resolving an absolutely horrific situation.

Notes

1. The Hebrew word *get* refers to the writ of divorce that must be delivered to the woman or her appointed agent.

2. Moses ben Maimon, *Mishneh Torah: The Book of Women*, trans. Isaac Klein (New Haven, CT: Yale University Press, 1972), 163–64.

3. Michael Kaufmann, *The Woman in Jewish Law and Tradition* (London: Jason Aronson, 1993), 190.

4. Kaufmann, *Woman*, 151.

5. The author's experience in regards to this matter of divorce is the result of clerking for an attorney during the summer of 1998. I personally attended a number of consultations with one potential party to a "no-fault" divorce. The process for determining what cause the client would cite in answer to the judge's question as to what caused the marriage to break down was that the attorney would produce two poster boards stapled together and tell the client to pick which of the generic item/items came closest to the problems with the marriage.

6. Mendell Lewittes, *Jewish Marriage: Rabbinic Law, Legend, and Custom* (London: Jason Aronson, 1994), 190.

7. There is, however, a way to annul a marriage, but it has not been used widely, if at all, since the medieval period.

8. *The Babylonian Talmud: Shabbat 56a and Ketubot 9b.*

9. Lewittes, *Jewish Marriage*, 182–83.

10. Lewittes, *Jewish Marriage*, 183.

11. Maimonides, *Mishneh Torah*, 177–78.

12. Lewittes, *Jewish Marriage*, 192–93.

13. Lewittes, *Jewish Marriage*, 192.

14. Kaufmann, *Woman*, 193.

15. Lewittes, *Jewish Marriage*, 172.

16. This matter involves an American-Jewish youth who fled to Israel and claimed citizenship under Israel's Law of Return in order to avoid prosecution for murder in the United States.

A ROMAN CATHOLIC RESPONSE by Diane M. Millis

It is incumbent on me to describe my location before responding to the case in question as where we stand determines what we see. Initially, I was invited to provide a Christian response to this case. I have elected to focus and frame my response as that of a Catholic Christian for at least two reasons. First, given that I am firmly committed to increasing ecumenical understanding, I am reluctant to speak for all Christians. Second, it seems to me that the issue of divorce and remarriage is much more problematic for Catholics than for Christians of other denominations, given our current church laws. Catholics are the only Christian denomination to require an ecclesial decree regarding the status of a previous marriage in order for a person to remarry and participate fully in the life of the church. Therefore, it seemed most appropriate, and in some cases situationally analogous, to consider this case from a Catholic perspective. In so doing, I do not claim to speak for all Catholics. However, the theologians to whom I refer are representative of the tradition.

As a college educator specializing in the study of family life and spirituality, the issues in this case examining the interface of families, cultures, and religion are of great professional interest for me. Moreover, as a child of divorced parents, I have seen my parents struggle with the way in which the Catholic Church responds to issues of remarriage. And for that reason, I feel a special sense of empathy with the family in this case.

After reading this case, I began thinking "we, as Catholics, also find ourselves amidst a tangle of laws" regarding questions of divorce and remarriage. Although the tangle does not result from ecclesial courts serving as state courts as it does in this case, a potential tangle nonetheless ensues.

In responding to this case, I will begin with a brief overview of the Christian theology of marriage and consider how the Catholic Church addresses issues of divorce and remarriage. I will then consider a basis for action given the current constraints on the Friedman family.

Theology of Christian Marriage

For Catholics, marriage is one of seven sacraments that comprise the practice of our faith. Since the fourth century and Augustine, the Catholic Church has insisted that there is a sacrament in marriage between Christians. Since the thirteenth century and Aquinas, it has insisted that a marriage between Christians is as much sacrament as the great sacraments of baptism and eucharist. Sacramental theologian Michael Lawler identifies the sacramental nature of marriage:

> A sacrament is a prophetic symbol in and through which the Church, the Body of Christ, proclaims, reveals and celebrates in representation that presence and action of God which is called grace. To say that a marriage between Christians is a sacrament is to say, then, that it is a prophetic symbol, a two-tiered reality. On one level, it proclaims, reveals and celebrates the intimate communion of life and love between a man and a woman, . . . On another, more profound level, it proclaims, makes explicit and celebrates the intimate communion of life and love and grace between God and God's people and between Christ and Christ's people, the Church.[1]

In modern sacramental theology, each individual marriage is considered a unique revelation of this covenant which is revealed differently in all stages of marriage and is expressed differently in various cultures.[2]

Divorce and Remarriage in the Catholic Church

The Catholic Church maintains that, in principle, every marriage is indissoluble. The church also maintains that, in principle, there are certain conditions under which a marriage believed to be valid can be dissolved: the marriage is not between two baptized Christian partners and/or was not consummated. To address all other types of conditions, a person is encouraged to petition for an annulment.

An annulment is an official declaration by the Catholic Church's external forum, the tribunal, that there never was at any time a *valid* marriage between two people. The tribunal is the church court through which a Catholic may be declared free of a first marriage and may lawfully marry a second time and continue to be a Catholic in good standing, i.e., she or he can remarry with the full public solemnity of Catholic rites and participate in the sacramental life of the church. For Catholics, a primary way of participating in the sacramental life of the church is through the sacrament of the eucharist and reception of communion. One of a Catholic's core beliefs is in the eucharist. It is a belief that the living body of Jesus Christ is actually and in fact present under the appearances of bread and wine. It is through the celebration of the eucharist that the Paschal mystery, i.e., the unique saving act of Jesus who we believe to be the Son of God who died for our sins and was resurrected, is represented, re-enacted, and remembered. Therefore, when a person receives communion, he or she is expressing faith in the Jesus both of past history and of the future promise of new life.

An annulment "is *not* the Catholic Church's form of divorce, as some mistakenly view the annulment process. Rather, it is a logical progression from our theological belief that the marital relationship is a permanent and faithful union and, therefore, not to be tampered with or interfered with or 'put asunder' by any authority, civil or ecclesiastical."[3] Ideally, the process of annulment is intended to be the Catholic Church's way of helping the divorced toward a healthy acceptance of life and spiritual growth.[4]

The annulment process consists of gathering, through the facts of a particular marital history and the substantiating testimony of witnesses, responses to one or more of the following questions:

1. Did both partners clearly understand the nature of marriage as a "community of life" and what such marriage would require of them?
2. Did both partners freely accept marriage as a lifelong commitment?
3. Did both partners have the personal capacity to carry out that to which they consented, i.e., to form a community of life with the chosen partner?[5]

Although the review process may differ in different dioceses, it always involves an objective, formal process of taking testimony regarding: the family background of both spouses, the courtship, the decision to marry, the marriage itself, and the problems in the marriage leading to the divorce.[6] While the tribunal is a judicial forum, court members look upon their work as ministry.[7]

A decree of annulment recognizes there are certain personal deficiencies that may make a person incapable of valid consent and sacramental commitment. Grounds for annulment are multiple: general immaturity at the time of the marriage; prior mental illness or alcoholism or psychosexual problems; prior intention to be unfaithful; lack of intention to have children; defective consent (marriage in the Catholic Church presupposes consent, freely given and with full knowledge); lack of the proper canonical form (i.e., wed in the presence of a designated priest and two witnesses).[8] Most annulments granted today in the United States are based on what is called a "psychological incapacity for marriage."

Alternatives to the External Forum

What does a person do, as in Yonaton Friedman's case, when legal or other types of obstacles impede the divorce process and preclude the rendering of an official decree of annulment? In the Catholic Church, there are currently two other options for those cases that cannot be brought before ecclesiastical tribunals. The first, referred to as a *brother/sister solution*, allows the parties to an invalid second marriage to receive the sacraments of the church if they refrain from sexual activity. The second is referred to as the *internal forum solution.*

The internal forum is based on a long Catholic tradition which insists that moral questions are not settled ultimately in the external forum, which is public, but in the internal forum of conscience and good faith, which is private. An internal forum requires an intensive personal and moral scrutiny. It is neither to be entered into lightly nor meant to bypass the external forum. Reasons for employing the internal forum include:

1. Lack of demonstrable evidence and witnesses;
2. Inability of parties to endure the annulment process or any other juridical procedure because it would cause excessive emotional strain and could seriously jeopardize the well-being of the parties;
3. Lack of access to a tribunal.[9]

An example of a case bearing some similarity to Yonaton Friedman's—in that the former spouse refuses to cooperate—is relayed here to illustrate more fully some of the conditions warranting an internal forum solution:

A young friend of mine, Bob I shall call him, had been married for seven years. To his sorrow, and with no apparent medical explanation, no children had been born in the marriage. One evening, out of the blue, Bob's wife told him that she was leaving him to marry another man. She also told him that the reason they had no children was that she had been aborting regularly during the marriage because she had never wanted children. It later transpired that, before their marriage, she had told two friends of her plan to do this. I explained to Bob that this was a solid case to submit to the local tribunal for an annulment of the marriage. When he tried to do so, he encountered a major legal obstacle: his wife and her friends refused to testify before the tribunal about her premarriage plan to abort any fetus. The tribunal was stymied, and the process ended without any resolution.[10]

The internal forum solution, also referred to as good conscience solution, is predicated on the belief in the primacy of conscience when making moral decisions. To employ the internal forum solution, a person begins by seeking the counsel of a priest. However, unlike the external forum, it is the individual's honest judgment of conscience that provides the solution.

How does a person arrive at a decision of conscience? Moral theologian Timothy O'Connell posits that a person's conscience operates on three levels: what he terms conscience/1, conscience/2, and conscience/3. Conscience/1 refers to the fact that human beings normally have an overall sense of values or "habit of conscience." O'Connell states that every discussion of moral values, every consideration of moral questions, has as its presupposition the existence of conscience/1. It implies a fundamental responsibility to do the good and avoid the bad.

When an individual seeks "to find and understand the concrete moral values" at stake in a given circumstance, conscience/2 comes into play. Conscience/2 must be open to every available source of wisdom: the Word of God, the witness or advice of others, consultation with theologians and ethicists, and the authoritative teaching of the church. Regarding the teaching of the church, O'Connell cautions: "The Church therefore has an important and responsible role in the process of moral education. But it is a limited role. It is limited by the possibility of error, the possibility of incompleteness, and the possibility of inadequacy. The prudent person acknowledges this, and yet seeks from the Church whatever wisdom it is able to give him or her."[11] O'Connell also cautions against equating feelings with the prompting of a moral conscience. He argues that because the origin of one's feelings on a given matter is often clouded in mystery, feeling or not feeling guilty is not a reliable measure for taking moral stock of ourselves.

If, after considerable prayer, study, reflection, and consultation, a person finds that the right thing to do in a given situation is action X (even though he or she recognizes that the action is possibly wrong), the decision or judgment upon which a person then acts is an exercise of conscience/3. At this level, conscience/3, a person is bound to follow what his or her conscience has discerned is the most appropriate action to take. Failure to do so is deemed to be sin because the individual has not given primacy to his or her considered judgment.[12]

Current Controversies

A current source of controversy within the Catholic Church is that some argue annulment has become too easy, while others argue it should be liberalized even further to respond to the needs of hurting people. As a result, one of the more pressing pastoral issues for the Catholic Church is how to minister to those who have divorced and remarried.[13]

Stephen Kelleher, a canon lawyer and former tribunal judge, argues that yet another alternative for divorced Catholics is needed. He refers to this alternative as the "Welcome Home" solution. If a person knows that the ending of his or her first marriage was due to willful wrong actions on his or her part, he or she should do penance for the fault. However, Kelleher believes that the church can and should allow for further exceptions so that Catholics who are remarried may participate actively and joyfully in the eucharistic celebration:

> All Catholics have a right and a need to receive Holy Communion. Aside from the area of sex and marriage, the Church very rarely denies this second right. In the areas of human behavior where millions are being killed, scarred, wounded and deprived by military, racial and economic injustices, the Church does not deny any sacrament or service to those Catholics who may be largely responsible for much of the

wounding and the suffering of multitudes. Why is the attempt to find in a second marriage a lasting love and the solace of the sacraments the great insufferable sin for Catholics?[14]

Responding to the Friedman Family

From my perspective, Yonaton Friedman's circumstances are quite exceptional. As the case states: he is a male *agunah*. For a man in his culture, this is a highly unusual situation within which to find himself. Given that his wife cannot be denied certain civil rights as a consequence of her actions, what recourse does he have? The case states that there would be a number of rabbis willing to sign off on a *get* given such extraordinary circumstances.[15] Yet, as stated, the divorce is not the main problem. If it were, I would encourage Yonaton to consider the internal forum solution. Rather, it is the implications of the divorce, namely citizenship and custody issues, that need to be addressed.

The criterion I propose we use to consider the implications of the case is: what actions lead to greater love? This question illustrates and employs the primary basis for moral decisions in the Christian tradition. Moral theologian Vincent Genovesi explains:

> We do best to say that as Christians we ultimately find our integrity both as human and as moral beings not in conformity to laws but in conformity to the person of Jesus Christ. . . Through his life and teaching, the Mosaic Law is turned inside out, and the hidden meaning and dynamism of the written Law are revealed. But more than this, we are invited and empowered by Christ and his Spirit to live a qualitatively new and different style of life, which consists in moving beyond the minimal commands of the Law's negative prohibitions so as to meet the maximal challenges of the positive demands of love.[16]

What are the positive demands of love for the Friedman family? Clearly, there is much more information that is needed. This case does not tell us much, if anything, about the relationship Yonaton and his wife, Ruth, shared. One can easily conjecture that she, or for that matter he, did not have the personal capacity to carry out that to which consent was given. Or perhaps both of them at the onset did not intend for their relationship to be a life-long commitment. Another possibility is that she and he *did* understand the nature of marriage as a "community of life" and what marriage would require, yet neither was able to live in a foreign country for an extended period of time. The case states that Yonaton and Ruth disputed over where they should live prior to her eventual leaving. There is too much room for speculation, therefore we must proceed with caution.

What we find in this case is a reductionistic appraisal of the marital relationship. The little that we do learn of the relationship is solely from the husband's perspective. The rabbis portray Ruth as intentionally malicious for not accepting the *get*. There seems to be no room for compassion for Ruth. In families, there is rarely a villain or a hero. To attempt to understand a marriage or family on the basis of one member's description is grossly inadequate because a family is more than the sum of its parts. Yonaton, in his discussion with the rabbis, needs to consider his role in the failure of the relationship and take responsibility for his part in it.

Therefore, what is needed is a systemic appraisal of the marital relationship. By utilizing a system's perspective, we can consider how family members influence and are influenced by one another along with how the surrounding systems of society, culture, extended family, and religion influence a family. Furthermore, just as we cannot reduce the cause of an ended marriage to any one person, we cannot reduce the increasing number of divorces to a single cause either. Many attribute the increasing number of single and divorced persons to the moral decay or loss of values by individual couples or parents. In so doing, they fail to consider the larger historical and economic forces that come into play.[17]

For whatever reasons, Ruth has maintained a position of complete cutoff from her former husband. This suggests the possibility that there was psychological cutoff between this couple while they were still living together. Moreover, she has prevented her children from establishing any contact with their father. Usually, one does not maintain such a position unless there is a reason for doing so—most often fear. A compassionate response would explore the source of Ruth's fear, rather than cast negative attributions on her behavior.

One thing does appear clear in this case. Yonaton wants to uphold his commitment to his children, and it is regrettable that Ruth has not at least allowed him to communicate with his children. Unfortunately, children's decreasing interactions with their father following divorce are all too common phenomena.[18] In this case, not only do Yonaton and the children suffer, but ultimately the entire family system does. Family therapists have found that cutoff between parents and children in a given generation increases the likelihood that cutoff will occur in a subsequent generation as cutoff becomes a learned pattern of managing stress.[19] The untold consequences are enormous. It is not only the children's Jewish identity and their sense of family identity that is at stake, but also their ability to interact in future intimate relationships.

Given the distance between the countries and differing legal systems, arranging for visitation presents an obstacle that may be insurmountable. Also, given the lack of communication between the couple, it appears even less likely that change will occur. However, the case does not make clear whether attempts have been made to communicate with Ruth's extended family. Has Yonaton attempted to communicate with his former in-laws? It appears incumbent on Yonaton or the rabbinic council to contact Ruth's extended family members. Presumably, Ruth's family may offer an untapped source of information regarding Ruth's current unwillingness to communicate with Yonaton or a potential source for mediation.

If all attempts at reestablishing communication have been exhausted, Yonaton may have to resign himself to accepting the situation as it is for the time being. When his children reach adulthood they may, of their own volition, reestablish contact with him. Until then, I can only imagine the tremendous agony he must feel in being separated from his children. As difficult as it is, such emotional agony is sometimes part and parcel of the vocation to family life. From a Christian perspective, it is often in our family relationships that we live out the Paschal mystery of Christ's suffering, death, and resurrection. However, on the basis of our faith, we believe that such suffering offers the potential for new life. What form that new life will take in this particular family remains to be seen. Ideally, on the basis of our faith, we would try to be mindful to pray for the grace to continue in faith, hope, and love until new life is recognized.

Conclusion

In considering this case from an American Catholic perspective, I have noted a similarity between current Catholic Church law and Jewish law concerning divorce and remarriage. Both laws require an official decree—for Catholics in the form of an annulment, for Jews, a *get*—designating the state of the previous marriage thus determining whether remarriage is possible. I would also note that both Catholics and Jews appear to share grave concerns about how both to minister to individuals and couples in a supportive pastoral fashion and to maintain the integrity of their respective religious traditions.

This case concludes by posing the question: Is separatism the only answer? Clearly, separatism is quite difficult to enact in our postmodern, information age. Perhaps equally difficult is engaging in dialogue, yet dialogue is undoubtedly the action that offers the potential for greater love. Dialogue, within communities and between communities, is our primary means for transmitting our faith to future generations:

> At their best, religious communities are communities of interpretation which also model love and care. The sacred texts and traditions of these religious communities should be constantly interpreted and reinterpreted in light of contemporary challenges. Parental authority is best established when it comes out of such communities of interpretation from which parents learn and which they use to model their convictions. . . Gradually the children themselves become involved in the interpretive task, becoming eventually equals in clarifying the narrative identities of the "communities of memory" to which they belong.[20]

Notes

1. Michael Lawler, *Marriage and Sacrament: A Theology of Christian Marriage* (Collegeville, MN: The Liturgical Press, 1993).

2. Michael Lawler and W. Roberts, eds., *Christian Marriage and Family: Contemporary Theological and Pastoral Perspectives* (Collegeville, MN: The Liturgical Press, 1996).

3. See C. Guarino, "Canonical and Theological Perspectives on Divorce and Remarriage," in *Perspectives on Marriage: A Reader*, ed. K. Scott and M. Warren (New York: Oxford University Press, 1993), 362.

4. Mary David Olheiser, "Media Concerns about Annulments," *Sisters of Saint Benedict* 8, no. 2 (1993):5.

5. Guarino, "Canonical," 362.

6. Olheiser, "Media," 5.

7. Mary David Olheiser, Ph.D., J.C.L., interview by author, 15 April 1998. Olheiser, a canon lawyer and member of Saint Benedict's Monastery in St. Joseph, MN, specializes in law for religious and marriage law.

8. Lawler, *Marriage and Sacrament*.

9. Guarino, "Canonical," 362.

10. Lawler, *Marriage and Sacrament*.

11. Timothy O'Connell, *Principles for a Catholic Morality*, 1st ed. (New York: Seabury, 1978), 96.

12. O'Connell, *Principles*, 96.

13. F. Foy and R. Avato, *1997 Catholic Almanac* (Huntington, IN: Our Sunday Visitor, 1996).

14. Stephen Kelleher, *Divorce and Remarriage for Catholics: A Proposal for Reform of the Church's Laws on Divorce and Remarriage* (New York: Doubleday, 1973), 189.

15. One finds an analogous occurrence among Catholic priests. It is a matter of finding a priest who is sympathetic to a couple's situation and allows them, even though they are remarried and have not sought an annulment, to receive communion.

16. Vincent Genovesi, *In Pursuit of Love: Catholic Morality and Human Sexuality*, 2nd ed. (Collegeville, MN: The Liturgical Press, 1996), 61.

17. Patrick McCormick, "For Better or for Worse: What's the State of the Marital Union," *US Catholic* 63, no. 5 (1998):47–49.

18. In the United States, only one child in six, on average, saw his or her father once a week in the first year after divorce. Ten years after divorce, more than two-thirds of children report not having seen their father for over a year. See K. Robinson, "The Divorce Debate: Which Side Are You On?" *The Family Therapy Networker* 18, no. 3 (1994):26.

19. Monica McGoldrick, *You Can Go Home Again: Reconnecting with Your Family* (New York: W. W. Norton, 1995).

20. Don S. Browning et al., *From Culture Wars to Common Ground: Religion and the American Family Debate* (Louisville, KY: Westminster John Knox Press), 298.

Bibliography and Suggested Reading

Browning, Don S., Bonnie J. Miller-McLemore, Pamela D. Couture, K. Brynolf Lyon, and R. Franklin. *From Culture Wars to Common Ground: Religion and the American Family*. Louisville, KY: Westminster John Knox Press, 1997.

Cunningham, Lawrence. *The Catholic Faith: An Introduction*. Mahwah, NJ: Paulist Press, 1987.

Genovesi, Vincent. *In Pursuit of Love: Catholic Morality and Human Sexuality*. 2nd ed. Collegeville, MN: The Liturgical Press, 1996.

Guarino, C. "Canonical and Theological Perspectives on Divorce and Remarriage."

In *Perspectives on Marriage: A Reader*, ed. Kieran Scott and Michael Warren. New York: Oxford University Press, 1993.

Hules, John M. *The Pastoral Companion: A Canon Law Handbook for Catholic Ministry*. Chicago: The Franciscan Herald Press, 1986.

Kaufmann, Michael. *The Woman in Jewish Law and Tradition*. London: Jason Aronson, 1993.

Kelleher, Stephen. *Divorce and Remarriage for Catholics: A Proposal for Reform of the Church's Laws on Divorce and Remarriage*. New York: Doubleday, 1973.

Lawler, Michael. *Marriage and Sacrament: A Theology of Christian Marriage*. Collegeville, MN: The Liturgical Press, 1993.

Lawler, Michael, and W. Roberts, eds. *Christian Marriage and Family: Contemporary Theological and Pastoral Perspectives*. Collegeville, MN: The Liturgical Press, 1996.

Lewittes, Mendell. *Jewish Marriage: Rabbinic Law, Legend, and Custom*. London: Jason Aronson, 1994.

Maimon, Moses ben. *Mishneh Torah: The Book of Women*. Trans. Isaac Klein. New Haven, CT: Yale University Press, 1972.

McCormick, Patrick "For Better or for Worse: What's the State of the Marital Union?" *US Catholic* 63, no. 5 (1998):47–49.

McGoldrick, Monica. *You Can Go Home Again: Reconnecting with Your Family*. New York: W. W. Norton, 1995.

O'Connell, Timothy. *Principles for a Catholic Morality*. 2nd ed. San Francisco: Harper and Row, 1990.

Oldheiser, Mary David. "Media Concerns about Annulments." *Sisters of Saint Benedict* 8, no. 2 (1993):5.

Scott, Kieran, and Michael Warren, eds. *Perspectives on Marriage: A Reader*. New York: Oxford University Press, 1993.

Zwack, Joseph P. *Annulment: Your Choice to Remarry within the Catholic Church*. Cambridge, MA: Harper and Row, 1983.

CHAPTER 4

Marriage Is for Life

A CASE STUDY by Regina Wentzel Wolfe

Sanjay was relieved when the markets finally closed. It had been a long week. The Bank of Japan had been in and out of the market, which resulted in wild currency fluctuations. As if that weren't enough, the Federal Reserve Board's announcement of a change in interest rates the previous day had caused the markets to explode. What a day it had been! At one point he had been exposed to a possible million-dollar loss in his positions.

"Not a good thing for a junior trader with sights on rising to the top," Sanjay thought to himself. Fortunately, so many central banks intervened that by early afternoon the markets returned to normal, he was able to hedge his position, and the day ended on a calmer note. Still, he was more than ready for the weekend. He needed the time to sort out his personal life.

His parents had called the previous Sunday night to inform him that they had found the right girl for him to marry. Sanjay wasn't sure why he had reacted so negatively to the news. Maybe it was the timing. His parents had agreed to wait until he had two or three years of work experience under his belt, so he wasn't expecting an announcement about a future wife. He was glad that he was meeting Anil for dinner. "Maybe he'll have some ideas about how I can get my parents to hold off for a bit," he said to himself.

It had been a couple of months since he'd seen Anil or any of the gang from school. Work had become all encompassing, and Sanjay had found himself drifting away from the close-knit group he had been part of at New York University where he did his M.B.A. After graduation he had taken a job as a currency trader with one of the big banks and settled into an apartment on West Fifty-Third. In the eighteen months since then, he had made new friends and been exposed to parts of New York he had not known existed. With the demands and pressures of his job, his life seemed to be on fast forward. He was constantly amazed that he had not only adjusted to the proverbial New York rat race but that he actually enjoyed it.

"What a difference a few years makes," he thought as he recalled his arrival in New York. He remembered the apprehension he felt when he first arrived at NYU. Greenwich Village had seemed so strange, and Washington Square Park with its share of street people and drug dealers had been frightening. Though he had spent his whole life in Chicago and thought of himself as a big-city type, he had not realized how protected his life had been. Fortunately he had met other Indian students through Shruti, the South Asian student organization which had been the center of his life outside the classroom.

"And I have so many good friends because of it," he thought to himself as he headed to the Indian Gardens Restaurant on Sixth Street. In the warm fall evening the smells and sounds of Little India wafted through the air. They reminded him of home and the sounds and smells that permeated the house as his mother prepared meals while listening to sitar music on the tape player. Ever since he had discovered it, he had considered this part of Greenwich Village his home away from home. In many ways, Sixth Street reminded him of Devon Avenue in Chicago, though it didn't have the quiet residential streets that he had grown up on branching off of it.

"I don't get down here nearly enough," Sanjay muttered to himself as he approached the restaurant where he was supposed to meet his friend. Walking through the door, he made his way through the fifteen or twenty people waiting to be seated.

"Hello, how's the big banker?" Mr. Patel, the owner, greeted him. "It's good to see you after so long. Anil is in the back at your usual place. I'll stop by to visit later on when the crowd thins out a bit."

Sanjay made his way through the restaurant trying to avoid the waiters as they scurried to serve people.

"Hello, stranger," Anil greeted him as he slid into the booth in the back corner. "How's the world of high finance treating you?"

"It was nip and tuck for a while this week, but things worked themselves out in the end. I'm glad the week is over though!" Sanjay replied emphatically. "Let's not dwell on that. Tell me what you've been up to and what you hear from the others, and then I've got a question for you," he continued, trying to keep from seeming overanxious.

Offering his friend the plate of pakoras and samosa, Anil began talking about his job. He worked for his father's cousin who had started a computer-consulting firm ten years earlier. Anil had recently been promoted to systems analyst and now had three programmers working under his supervision. Sanjay tried to focus on what his friend was saying, but he found it difficult. Finally, Anil stopped talking. "Sanjay," he said, "you haven't heard a word I've said. What is it? Why are you so preoccupied? What is it you wanted to ask me?"

"Well, it's not really a question; well, maybe it is. I don't know," Sanjay responded uncertainly. "My parents have arranged a marriage for me," he finally blurted out.

"That's wonderful," Anil replied. "Let's order some food and then you can tell me about your future bride," he said as he flagged the down waiter.

Once they had placed their order Anil bombarded Sanjay with questions. "Tell me all you know about your future wife. Where's she from? What's her family like? Is she fair or can't you tell from her picture?"

"She's from Bombay and she must come from a good family or my parents wouldn't have selected her," Sanjay replied in a dismissive way. "Look," he pleaded with his friend, "you don't seem to understand. The timing is all wrong, I don't want to get married right now."

"What do you mean you don't want to marry right now? What's the big deal? You knew your parents were going to arrange something, didn't you?"

"Yes, but not yet," Sanjay said. "They agreed to wait until I was settled in my job and had put some money aside. And now they're talking about going to India next month for the bride viewing. It's all too fast."

"What do you mean, 'all too fast'?" asked Anil. "There's never much warning once a suitable bride has been found. Look at Prakash. Once his parents found the appropriate girl he was married within two weeks. Besides, if the right girl has been found, why wait?"

"But I'm not ready. I'd like some time for myself before I settle down. Besides, I'm so busy at work I don't have time to get married," Sanjay said.

Anil stared incredulously at his friend. "You didn't say that to your parents, did you?" he asked.

"No, I'm not that disrespectful," Sanjay admitted. "I know they're only doing what they think is best. But I've got to figure out a way to get them to stop. You've got to help me."

"I don't know how I can do that," Anil replied. "I don't know why you'd want to stop them anyway," he continued. "It's a son's duty to marry and have children; how else will the family line be preserved? And your parents would be remiss if they didn't find the right girl to bear their grandsons. Besides, what do you know about choosing a bride?"

"Well, a lot actually," Sanjay retorted, "if choosing my cousin Ashok's bride is anything to go by. Though I must admit, the process seemed never-ending. First there was the matter of the bride's family. It had to be the same subcaste. Then there was the issue of class. My uncle insisted that the bride's family had to be people of means, just as he is. Of course, part of that had to do with the dowry. Given the size of my cousin's family any girl marrying into it needs a well-stocked bridal trunk if she's going to be able to meet the many gift-giving obligations. Needless to say, skin color also entered the equation, so the search for a light-skinned bride was on. As if that weren't enough, it was clear from the start that only a girl from India would do. My aunt and uncle have a poor opinion of most Indian-American girls. From their perspective only a 'real' Indian girl knows her place in the family."

"They have a point there," Anil interjected. "Look at many of the girls from Shruti; they're a pretty independent lot. I mean they're fun to be with, but I wouldn't want to marry one. They're just not trained properly. If they don't know their place in the household, how are they going to be able to show appropriate respect for and deference to the men in the family or the senior women? And they don't know all the customs. They're bound to be disruptive and inhibit the smooth functioning of the household. Also, its hard to check them out from the States, hard to be sure about their sub-caste, to determine if they can bear sons, to know something about their families and their ancestral villages. It's much safer to get help from relatives and long standing family friends in India. Then you'll be sure to get the right girl."

"I'm not so certain about that," Sanjay disagreed. "Mihir's wife, Sharmila, doesn't seem suited to him. She's so quiet it's hard to tell whether she even knows how to talk. And with her village ways, she seems more like his servant than his wife. I certainly don't want to marry a girl like that."

"You missed the point," his friend responded. "You don't have any older brothers whose wives have to be taken into consideration in choosing your bride the way Mihir does. Your wife will be the first daughter-in-law, not the fifth. Can you imagine the Singh household if the youngest daughter-in-law didn't know her place? Sharmila is perfect for that family."

"But I don't want a wife who's perfect for my family; I want one who's perfect for me," Sanjay insisted.

"So it's talk of marriage that has you two so deep in conversation," said Mr. Patel, whom neither young man had noticed approaching. "You both look so serious," he went on as he took plates of steaming food from the waiter's tray and placed them between the two young men. When the tray was empty, he waved the waiter away and pulled a chair up to the end of the booth. "Better take a time-out and enjoy your food before it gets cold," he admonished them.

His plate piled high with rice and fragrant mutton curry, Anil reached for the chutney. "Sanjay is to be married," he told Mr. Patel.

"Congratulations! I'm truly pleased for you. When is the big event?" Mr. Patel asked.

"Well, if my parents have their way, it will be next month," Sanjay replied in a dejected tone.

Mr. Patel leaned into the table and looked at Sanjay quizzically. "You don't seem too pleased about this turn of events. Is there something wrong?" he asked.

Sanjay was quiet for a moment. He didn't quite know how to respond. After all, Mr. Patel had been like an uncle to him and his friends for a number of years now, and Sanjay didn't want to be disrespectful. Picking his words carefully, he began to answer. "My parents and family have always given me guidance and support. If it weren't for them, I would not have been so successful in school or been able to come to NYU. And though I know they expected me to go back to Chicago right after I finished school, they've been more than understanding about the job at the bank," he said in a slow and deliberate voice. He paused for a moment and looked at the two men sitting with him. Neither said anything, so he continued, "I know my parents want the best for me, they always have. But for once I think they have it wrong. I don't think marrying now is the right thing, and I don't know how to tell them that without being disrespectful."

Nodding his head toward his friend, he turned to Mr. Patel and said, "I thought Anil could help me, but he just doesn't understand. Mr. Patel, you've seen and heard much. Tell me, what can I say to my parents?"

Mr. Patel was quiet for a long time. Finally he spoke. "You're right, I have seen much. I've seen children break their parents' hearts," he said in a pained voice. "I've seen parents disown their children. I've seen people insist on love marriages, only to be disappointed and brokenhearted in the end. I've seen people lose all sense of who they are and what their place in the family is. I'm not sure how to answer you, Sanjay. Surely, your parents wouldn't arrange a marriage if they thought it was not the right time for one. After all, at your age, you should be fathering sons. Maybe if you tell me why you think this is not the right time I can be of help."

"As I told Anil, when I took the job with the bank my parents and I agreed that I would settle in my job and put some money aside before I married. I've only been at the bank for eighteen months," Sanjay began to explain.

"But I thought you were doing so well," Mr. Patel replied. "By now you must have a considerable amount of money set aside. Besides, there will surely be gifts from the bride's family that are to be considered. This isn't really about money is it, Sanjay?" he continued gently.

"Yes. Well, no. Oh, I'm so confused," Sanjay said. As he stared at the food on the plate in front of him and pushed it around aimlessly, he spoke softly. "It's just that I'm not ready to be married. I'm so busy at work I don't have time to get married. What kind of husband would I make? There wouldn't be time for a long honeymoon, time to get to know my wife. And how would she settle into the family, into life in America? I would have to move back to Chicago so my mother could guide her and teach her the ways of our family. It would mean giving up my job here."

"You always said you didn't want to stay in New York, that you eventually wanted to go back to Chicago," Anil reminded him. "So what's wrong with getting married and doing that? Chicago's a big city; you're bound to find a job, especially with your family network there."

"Anil is right," Mr. Patel said. "There shouldn't be any trouble finding a new job."

Sanjay looked up at his two friends. "It's not finding a new job that's the problem," he said. "For the first time in my life I feel like I'm in charge. I've got a good job. I'm making good money. I'm meeting interesting people. It's just that, well, I'm my own master," Sanjay admitted to them.

"Sanjay, what are you saying?" Anil demanded.

"Anil, please be calm," Mr. Patel said in a firm voice. Then he turned to Sanjay, his tone gentle but serious. "Sanjay, it isn't the marriage you are questioning, is it? It's your whole way of life. I've seen it many times before. You are moving away from your roots, from your responsibilities to your family. And for what? To be your own master? Sanjay, you don't really mean that. I know you to be a loving and dutiful son. Perhaps you should go home for a bit? Visit with your family and talk to them. Whatever you do, don't act hastily. Don't bring rejection down on yourself."

The silence at the table drowned out the noise of the hustle and bustle around them. When Sanjay finally spoke, it was with great pain. "I'm not sure I want to go home. That's the problem. You're right, it is more than the marriage. The proposed marriage has forced me in a corner. I love my parents. I know they only want the best for me. But I live in a different world now. A bride from India isn't best for my world. I don't want to go back to the world I knew in Chicago. It will smother me. I want to be independent, to be self-sufficient. But I don't want to hurt my parents either. How can I find a way to balance what I want with what they expect? I'm meant to call them tomorrow with dates so they can book the flights to India. What am I going to say to them?" he pleaded.

A HINDU RESPONSE by Edeltraud Harzer Clear

There are five conceivable responses that Sanjay can consider as solutions to his dilemma.

1. Reasoned compromise. Sanjay could go home to his parents in Chicago and tell them that he is happy that they are taking such care of his future domestic life, but ask them if they could please find him an Indian girl who has studied in the United States, so that their backgrounds would be compatible.
2. Contrived resistance. After the bride viewing, Sanjay could refuse the bride. But he may find that he likes the girl that his parents have selected for him.
3. Go along. He could go along with his parent's wishes and not fight his situation so determinedly. After all, the prospective bride might be a city girl from Bombay. After he sees her, he might change his mind about not marrying. Thus, all ends well: the parents are happy with their choice of bride for their oldest son, and the son finds that he is happy too with a lovely and sophisticated bride.
4. Have his cake and eat it too. He could go along with his parents' arrangements for the marriage. After marriage he could return temporarily to his job in New York and leave his bride with his parents. As he says, he will not have time to introduce a new wife to life in America, but his parents could, in part, do that. He could then possibly choose to return to Chicago or break away and stay in New York. The latter would, again, involve a twofold choice: leave his bride with his parents indefinitely or, after a time, bring her with him to New York.
5. Disloyalty and disobedience. Conceivably, Sanjay could tell his parents that he does not want to go back to life as he knew it with them but wants time to see what the alternative might be like. Then he could reconsider whether or not to return to Chicago and have an arranged marriage.

Marriage in Hindu Society

According to the Hindu tradition, a man of the Brahman/Brahmin caste is born with three debts. The first is to the seers to study the Vedas (*sruti*). The second debt is to gods to perform sacrifice. The third debt is to his ancestors to ensure there are sons to perform rites for the deceased.[1] Marriage is the norm in Hindu society regardless of caste. As in any society, marriage is a rite of passage. These rites of passage (*samskara*) are rituals which allow members of the society to pass into the next stage of life. These *samskaras* enhance people's spiritual powers and facilitate personal achievement.[2] Of the many rites, three are of grave importance: birth, marriage, and death. Death is immediately expanded by the birth of one's own children who perform death rituals for family members, especially for their parents.

Marriage is viewed as part of the fourfold scheme of the stages of life—or Ways of Life (*asrama*)—of the classical Hindu system which society at large mimics, even in the present day. As Olivelle states, "The four *asramas* are regarded as paths (in the original system) or as a ladder (in the classical system) leading to the gods or to liberation. Especially in the classical system the *asramas* are presented as a gradual but sure way to advance spiritually and to attain the final goal of human beings."[3] These, along with the four castes, form the quintessential core of the Hindu religion.

As can be expected, there are regional differences surrounding marriage. For the Hindus in the north, the prospective groom and bride are strangers to each other. In the south of India, where marriage between cross-cousins occurs, the prospective couple may have been childhood friends and playmates.[4] According to the tradition there are some six to eight kinds of marriage,[5] ranging from kidnapping to marriage contests of royalty,[6] as in medieval Europe. Included among these marriage types is a "verbal contract" between two consenting adults to have sex (adulthood may be understood to be attained at the point of reaching puberty).[7]

The Importance of Compatibility

Just as the *asramas* constitute an essential part of the Hindu tradition, so also the traditional social order of the society is a distinctive aspect. It may be useful to think of the caste identity as a kind of ethnicity as Nayar puts it:

> Castes are communities, with their own histories, customs, and heroes. Moreover, their members tend to have similar ideas as to what Hinduism is, its good points and its bad ones. Even if a Brahmin utterly rejects Untouchability, for instance, he may find less reason to condemn traditional Hinduism than an Untouchable might. If such a Brahmin and such an Untouchable were to marry, their difference in attitude to Hinduism could create problems for their relationship. Such subtleties of attitude can explain a good deal about the persistence of caste, . . .[8]

Thus, caste and subcaste compatibility is very important. Yet, great care is taken that the marriage be outside one's own kin group.[9] The marriage of a daughter or daughters places a life-long strain on the family because of the dowry system. It might not be a monetary dowry, but rather an elaborate wedding and lavish gifts the costs of which are borne by the bride's family.

Often the marriage arrangements begin with the decision of the parents that their son or daughter has come of age and needs to be married. If education is involved, the plans for marriage are held off until the studies are completed. In the case of sons, the parents may wait for a while so that the young man can find a job and make himself secure in it. Today, such waiting for the completion of studies has more to do with practical issues than with the classical ideal of the *asramas*. The studies that are pursued by a member of the middle class of modern times have hardly any connection with the ancient traditional ways. First, traditional studies referred to the study of the sacred lore, studies that were intended for Brahmin males. Second, the four *asramas* were originally understood as four possible choices of vocation after completing education in the house of one's teacher and, as Olivelle has shown, not viewed as successive stages in an individual's life.[10]

Matrimonials or personal advertisements in newspapers are often, though not necessarily always, an initial lead for finding a suitable mate. Parents respond to advertisements, giving consideration to caste and subcaste and, of course, also to class. It is important that the bride be able to bring a sizable trousseau to meet the gift-giving demands. The parents may exchange photographs of the prospective bride and groom. They may make inquiries about each other's families. If the families find that they may be compatible, they will arrange for a social visit, often involving the bride viewing. The bride is usually shown in her own house. Of course, there are cases in which long distances will cause the interested parties to meet in a hotel of a big city that lies between their respective homes. Often the prospective bride will play the hostess to the visiting bridegroom and his family members, though at times she may simply be present so that she may be viewed. The viewing will definitely expose one of the important considerations, skin color. It is an enormous drawback for the bride to have dark-colored skin, which is considered an inauspicious sign. Popular as well as scholarly books that give advice about auspicious and inauspicious signs of a prospective marriage partner list skin color as one of the signs. Other inauspicious signs to watch for are low-caste origin, deformity, hereditary disease, and so on. Skin color is the most discussed sign and, also, the most subjective. Unfortunately, racism is not confined to the Western world.

For families settled abroad, either in Europe or the United States, the groom's party may insist on getting a bride from India, especially if it is a bride for a son who is not first born. The wives of the younger brothers have "to know their place in the family"—as Anil aptly reminded Sanjay. The wives are expected to show deference and respect to the men in the family and elders in general. Deference is part of social interaction in traditional societies. Just as the society is hierarchically arranged, so also the families have their hierarchies. The father is the most prominent figure and so will be his sons, from the eldest in descending order to the youngest. The order in which sons marry follows this hierarchy, with the eldest son marrying first.[11] The same ordering will apply to the brides, with the brides of younger sons expected not only to show deference to the men and family elders but also to the wives of the older brothers-in-law.

If, after the initial meeting, there appears to be a compatible match, the families may negotiate on a variety of items. Often the bride's family may not be able to meet the dowry demands at the time of marriage, despite having spent years accumulating a dowry. In such cases, future installments will be negotiated.[12]

The Marriage Ceremony

The Hindu marriage ceremony is very elaborate. Usually it lasts for three days. Food preparations and shopping for gifts and clothes for the various occasions during the wedding fill many days before the wedding. Large numbers of wedding guests are to be pampered. An ancient ceremony called *madhuparka* is observed, although in a much abbreviated form. *Madhuparka* means "offering honey by way of honour to a distinguished guest." Honey is to be poured into yogurt for the guests. The guest's feet are to be washed and so on. In ancient days the ceremony involved meat eating, in particular, beef, though the meat part has long been abolished.[13]

The law books divide the marriage ceremony into three parts: the preliminary, the essential, and the subsequent. There is some divergence of opinions on the preliminary and the subsequent parts. It seems that there is unison about the essential ones, for example, walking around the fire and the seven steps. The most important part of the wedding ceremony is the seven steps that the couple being wed take around the sacrificial fire .[14] The seven steps are somewhat analogous to the vows in Western marriage ceremonies. It is an ancient tradition that is well preserved into the present day and followed by even the most "modern" people. On the fourth day, the bride will leave her parent's house and will accompany her new husband into the home of his family. Often she may not know either the husband or the family into which she has married. It must be an extremely stressful situation for the bride. It is in the husband's home on the fourth night that the marriage is consummated.[15]

Honoring Filial Obligations

The son's obligation to his own family is to get married and to produce offspring, preferably sons, so that the family lineage may be preserved.[16] Marriage is not an event that affects only two people but it involves two families, and extended families at that. Therefore, it is important that the families should be compatible, not just the bride and groom. Compatibility is often assessed by means of an astrologer on the basis of birth certificates (*janma patra*) which describe in detail the position of heavenly constellations at the time of a person's birth. The astrologer's task then is to see if these two prospective marriage candidates have their birth certificates aligned.

Sanjay is fully aware of his obligation toward his own extended family and especially to his parents. His parents, probably with sacrifice, made it possible for him to go to school and to aim at the type of job that he now has. His ideals and dreams materialized with the help of his parents, not only in monetary terms but also in terms of a reliable support system that made his life a good one.

According to most traditional societies, younger persons are meant always to show a deference and proper respect for their elders, parents especially. Most often parents act selflessly in the interest of their children, even though it may not always be the case. Therefore, when parents decide that it is time for their son to marry, it is inconceivable that the son should try to change the course of planned events or disobey his parent's wishes. Sanjay's dilemma stems from having grown away from the traditional fold of his family and culture. He has acquired the ideas and lifestyle of his newly adopted country. His is not an isolated case. His position is not even as difficult as that of some of the young women who would like to study and qualify for a professional job but are unable to do so. There have been cases where a grandmother in India (who has never been to any Western country) will insist that the granddaughter has arrived at marriageable age and must marry. The parents of the young woman feel obligated to comply with the request. The young woman is left with no choice unless she rebels, and in such a case she may lose her family's support. Even today these daughters do not, for the most part, dare to break away because their families are tied together not only by customs, respect, and finances but also by strong emotions. Love among the family members is deep and very affectionate.

Sanjay has acquired a taste for independence. It is novel to him and, to a certain extent, intoxicating. He cannot imagine himself being stifled by the predictable and familiar ways of his tradition and his family within it. There is comfort and security in having a place in the family and in the society, but young people often tend to seek just the opposite. They like excitement, novelty, and challenge. Western society offers this abundantly.

Sanjay may be able to tear himself away from his tradition and make a life of his own. But just the fact that he hoped for advice and solace from his friend Anil and Mr. Patel, the restauranteur, shows him as someone who still relies on the security of his family and culture. Those who have severed themselves from the old traditions of their homes and have adopted the ways of their new country often experience terrible loneliness, sadness, inner exile, and a great sense of loss. This is recognized in the many excellent and eloquent writings and other artistic expressions of these people.

For an uninitiated Western public, the idea of an arranged marriage sounds like a horrific ordeal. In fact, to many it seems like trading cattle, nothing more or less. Yet, in many cases the whole affair can be sophisticated and cultured. Both involved partners will behave graciously, just as with strangers. Family members take it upon themselves to explain things material and immaterial to the newlyweds. And even if there is no love at first sight, it can develop. Salman Rushdie in *Midnight's Children* poignantly writes of the aunt married to a man whom she tries to love; she says to herself that every day she will try to love one part of this man, until she loves all of him.[17]

Western society is rather homogeneous. We westerners are unaware of the variety of life that exists in South Asia. That variety of life encompasses means for livelihood, lifestyles, and religious beliefs and attitudes. Means of livelihood are, for the most part, still hereditary, especially for the lower classes. The two highest castes—the Brahmins and Ksatriyas—are occupationally diverse. Lifestyles range from stereotypes found, perhaps, since antiquity, to varieties developed through the ages, to completely modern, which most of the time means Western. An example of the variety of lifestyles is found in Tehri Garhwal, a northern region in the hills, where there are communities with a fluid type of marriage. Here there are women who form polyandric unions, that is, one woman has more than one husband. At a different stage in their lives these same women will find themselves along with other co-wives married to one man. These hill country villagers are told that in the valley the people marry properly according to the norm. Apparently, the villagers are not greatly impressed with the ways of the valley people because the hill people have done little to change their own ways. Religion is the guide for an individual. Because life in India can hardly ever be without an expression of religious beliefs, the variety of beliefs is reflected in the simultaneous presence of different gods. It is not which god a person worships, but what he or she *does* that makes him or her a religious person, such as observing the daily rituals in one's home and honoring the traditions of one's society.

There have always been marriages out of love or choice. At times these have encountered resistance from the society, at times they have been endorsed. Still at other times one of the parties involved, usually the man, conveniently forgets a former alliance.[18] We may view another culture with our stereotypical preconceptions and find that the stereotype does exist. But we will also find the existence of numerous exceptions to the stereotype—those who opt for self-choice and self-determination.

Go Along

Of Sanjay's five options, outlined at the beginning of this response, the most suitable from the Hindu perspective is the third, "go along." The strength of this solution rests simply in the fact that one does not contradict one's parents, one's immediate elders, because hierarchy in the family, as well as in the society through the caste system, ensures order and a certain security in life. A person knows his or her place in the world and what it entails. From the facts of this case we can picture an Indian family with middle-class values who would like to operate according to the customs of their tradition.

Notes

1. Patrick Olivelle, *The Asrama System: The History and Hermeneutics of a Religious Institution* (New York: New York University Press, 1993), 2.1.3 The Theology of Debts, 46–53. Also see *Taittiriya Sanhita* 6.3.10.5.

2. Klaus Klostermaier, *A Survey of Hinduism*, 2ⁿᵈ ed. (Albany: State University of New York Press, 1994), 152.

3. Olivelle, *Asrama System*, 188.

4. Gavin Flood, *An Introduction to Hinduism* (Cambridge, England: Cambridge University Press, 1996), 205–6.

5. Krishna Nath Chatterjee, *Hindu Marriage: Past and Present* (Varanasi, India: Tara Publications, 1972), 35ff. Also see P. V. Kane, *History of Dharmasastra* (Poona, India: Bhandarkar Oriental Research Institute, 1974), 2, pt. 1, 516ff.

6. Kane, *History of Dharmasastra*, 502. Refers to *Manusmrti* 9.90–91 in which a girl who reached puberty had to wait three years before she had the full right to choose a husband and marry. This kind of marriage is known from the epics, the heraldic literature, and it applied primarily to princesses.

7. See Kalidasa, *Sakuntala*, Act 3. Recommended translation: Barbara Stoler Miler, *Theater of Memory: The Plays of Kalidasa* (New York: Columbia University Press, 1984).

8. Radhakrishnan Nayar, "Why Caste Persists," review of *Caste Today*, ed. C. J. Fuller, *Times Literary Supplement*, 8 May 1998, 12.

9. Chatterjee, *Hindu Marriage*, 151ff.

10. Olivelle, *Asrama System*, 74.

11. There are provisions in which the younger brother has the right to marry without his older brother having already married, if his older brother is unfit, e.g., ill, evil, impotent, and so forth. See Kane, *History of Dharmasastra*, 548.

12. Sometimes the bridegroom's family even insists. At times, the bridegroom's family gets very greedy and will try to extort more and more out of the bride and the bride's family. Such situations sometimes lead to the infamous incidents of bride burnings. The groom's family keeps pressuring the young wife to wrench more money and more goods out of her family, whether or not her family has already delivered the agreed amount. Out of desperation the young woman torches herself with the kerosene for the kitchen stoves used throughout the country for cooking. These bride burnings are reported daily in the newspapers.

13. Kane, *History of Dharmasastra*, 542ff.

14. Kane, *History of Dharmasastra*, 527ff, for a description of the marriage ceremony.

15. Kane, *History of Dharmasastra*, 541. It seems that the observation of the three days for the newlyweds to stay at the bride's home and leaving on the fourth day may have a connection with provisions established in antiquity for cases when the bride was menstruating during the wedding. Certainly, the marriage festivities do not always go on for three days.

16. Chatterjee, *Hindu Marriage*, 310.

17. Salman Rushdie, *Midnight's Children* (London: Jonathon Cape, 1981), 68.

18. See Kalidasa, *Sakuntala*, Act 5.

AN EASTERN ORTHODOX CHRISTIAN RESPONSE
by Stanley Samuel Harakas

Several dimensions of the case "Marriage Is for Life" compete for attention. Sanjay from the start is described as living in two vastly different worlds: the competitive modern world of a securities trader and the socially cohesive world of traditional Hindu society. The arrangement of his marriage by his parents is only one aspect of this larger situation. The case reveals a deeper incongruity. He isn't ready for marriage in the first place. He has absorbed enough of post-Enlightenment individualism in his new Western environment to be severely conflicted by the parental initiative.

Sanjay also sees a violation of his understanding of the agreement with his parents to wait several years for him to establish himself in his profession. In principle, he had not disagreed with an eventual arranged marriage. But his parents seemed to him to have violated the understanding they had about when it would take place. It might be that their understanding and his understanding were different from the start. It would not be surprising if deference and respect for his parents did not allow him to clarify what was meant, much less "get it in writing."

A critical aspect of this parental–son relationship is the powerful sense of conflicting values, duties, and rights that the telephone call has provoked in Sanjay. In classical moral terms the issue is how the duty to obey parents and the exercise of moral responsibility to and for one's self and others are to be reconciled.

In addition to these issues, there is the interesting and challenging issue of "arranged marriages" itself. At the end of the twentieth century in a nation founded on the principle of individual rights, in the context of 150 years of feminism and Freudian inspired sexual liberation, the question of arranged marriages would seem to be—if not a quaint social relic—a barbaric denial of individual liberty.

In the Greek ethnic tradition of Eastern Orthodox Christianity, which I know from personal experience, arranged marriages were at one time almost universal. Today they are not. For me, the most remarkable aspect of this change, one that I wish to reflect on for most of the balance of this commentary, is why there has been no theological or ethical negative reaction to the change from arranged marriages to free choice of marital partners in the Eastern Orthodox Christian tradition. I will conclude this commentary by briefly addressing the other issues raised above by Sanjay's dilemma.

The Tradition of Arranged Marriage

What contemporary people need to remember is that for eons, arranged marriages were essentially the only way young men and women entered into marriage. This is historically the case not only in far off India or Eastern Europe but also in the lands of Western Europe from which the majority of Americans trace their ancestry. It is also the case for those Americans who are descended from the tribal life of Africa, the ancient cultures of China, Japan, and Korea, and nearly every other place north, south, east, and west of the United States! No attitude, anthropologically speaking, could be more ethnocentric than for contemporary Americans to think that our present culturally approved system of spouse choice is "normal" and "universal."

I personally became aware of it when I was about eleven years old. On our block there were six Greek Orthodox families. The parents were about the same age and so were the children. We played together, spent much time in each other's houses, and—upon retrospect—were a tiny village in the larger society of a 1930s and 1940s Pittsburgh, Pennsylvania, suburb. The eldest of our playmates was Helen. When she was about eighteen years of age, seven years my senior, she appeared on a bright Sunday afternoon on our street, walking hand in hand with a young man from Ohio. I remember being shocked that such a public display of affection would take place on our street. I was calmed by the response. Their parents had agreed that they were to marry. It was also calming to my child's mind that they seemed to like the idea! The marriage took place and lasted for their lifetimes.

In 1995, the Long Island newspaper *Newsday* published in its "Remembering" column the story of another Greek Orthodox arranged marriage. Titled "Arranged Marriage Is Convenient—and Happy," it told the story of a Greek merchant marine sailor who jumped ship in Canada and made his way to the United States with the goal of marrying an American citizen in order to stay in the country. The lead paragraph of the column tells the story. "Steve needed a wife so he could stay in America. Mary's parents decided that their 17-year-old daughter should be married. Steve's uncle, the 'matchmaker,' arranged for an introduction—and the rest is history. The Johnsons of Hempstead have been married 54 years."

One of the most interesting aspects of the story is how the couple's moral and religious sentiments played out in the event. Steve presented himself to the family as an ethically responsible person. "When I met her with her parents, I told them I was honest, decent and hardworking and needed a wife." This was convenient, the story said, because Mary's parents "were looking to marry her off." Steve then described what happened:

"The next night, Mary's parents met with my aunt and uncle. The families decided that we were a good match and that we could be married. I bought Mary a ring on Monday, we had blood tests on Thursday, got a license and were married in a civil ceremony in Supreme Court in Brooklyn on Friday, April 5, 1940." Steve was then quoted as reporting, "I told Mary's parents that we would not live together as husband and wife until we could be married in a Greek church ceremony. After our (civil) wedding, Mary went to her house, I went to mine. I visited her two nights a week, sometimes taking her out to visit my uncle, but always having her home by 10 P.M., her curfew. We were finally married in the church on June 23, 1940."

The arranged marriage was one thing. The moral standards of sexual relationships taught by the church—no promiscuity, no premarital sex—were another. Further, though legally married for purposes of meeting United States residency requirements, both knew that they weren't "really married" until the Orthodox Church's Sacrament of Holy Matrimony had taken place.

Nothing about this story is unusual. During the first half of my forty-four years as a Greek Orthodox priest such arranged marriages were common, but not universal. They were an alternate pattern, rooted in old country village traditions. More often than not, they succeeded as marriages, though sometimes they did not. In September 1997 the British newspaper *The Independent* carried an obituary by Stathis Gauntlett about Sotiria Bellou, a famous Greek female singer of rebetiko songs, those melancholic Greek blues songs, with themes of dispossession, separation, and personal betrayal. Sotiria Bellou had been the granddaughter of a priest. At her death she had been given a state funeral. The obituary tells of the context: "She had left her native Chalkis for Athens . . . on the day after war was declared between Greece and Italy (1940), and, on her domestic front, between Sotiria and her parents, following the failure of her arranged marriage."

Another Social Reality

In short, for better or worse, in the cities, the countryside, and the islands of Orthodox Christian Greece and in the Greek immigrant communities of the United States until the end of World War II, arranged marriages were frequent enough occurrences to be considered normal and standard ways that marriages took place.

Now step across the World War II boundary. Greek Orthodox soldiers returning from war in Greece and in America; the promotion of education for both young men and women; social upheaval in Greece in the defeated post-World War II Communist revolution; the acculturation of ethnics into the values of Europe and of American pluralism: all lead to another social reality.

In my recent retirement, I was asked by some relatives and friends to conduct a weekly Bible study class. All the members of the group are retirees and all are married—five couples. The eldest member is in the mid-seventies. All but one couple are Greek-Americans. All are Orthodox Christians and actively involved in church life. I decided to ask them about their experiences and ideas about arranged marriages. The first surprising fact uncovered was that not one of the couples had an arranged marriage! All had been married after World War II. One couple, both Greek-Americans, had known each other from childhood and were attracted to each other. Another couple had eloped over objections to their marriage by their families. The third couple had met through the intervention of a cousin/classmate, with the woman finally proposing to the man! The fourth and fifth couples had especially interesting stories to tell.

A Cypriot-American had married a woman of German birth. They had met in the United States. She had, like a latter-day Ruth, adopted not only her husband's Greek Orthodox religion, but also his Greek-Cypriot popular culture, including Greek-Cypriot cooking and language. Clearly, their marriage, too, had not been arranged. However, the Cypriot-American described how until the Turkish invasion of Cyprus in July 1974, arranged marriages were the norm in Cyprus and how since then the institution has just collapsed. Arranged marriages today, according to his report, are rare, and they find little support in popular opinion.

Even more illuminating was the story told by the fifth couple. Actually, the story was told briefly by the husband to me after one of our Bible studies. Shortly thereafter, however, my wife and I were invited to a surprise fiftieth wedding anniversary celebration for this couple. The wife rose to thank those present but proceeded to tell how it came to be that she married her husband. Her parents had arranged a marriage with another man, then a close friend of the man she eventually married. There were several things about the parentally agreed on potential husband, however, that the nineteen-year-old potential bride did not like. Among these was his lack of religious belief and a cynical attitude. She dramatically and publicly described to her guests how she went to her parents and told them that she did not want to marry the man. When her parents urged her to proceed with the marriage because of the embarrassment it would cause, she responded, "Is it better to break it up now, or later?" The parents immediately drew back and agreed to accept her judgment. A few months later, at a church sponsored dance, the young woman saw the friend but did not approach him. It was her mother who admonished her to go over and greet him, which she did. Later, he began writing to her and several dates followed, after which he proposed marriage to her and she accepted. A fifty-year-long marriage was the result.

No Opposition to Change

My question is, why was there no observable comment or opposition to this radical change in the way people met and were brought together for marriage in the thought and official actions of the Orthodox Church? A potential case for supporting the cultural norm of arranged marriages could have been made. Without question, a church that is powerfully tradition-based, such as the Eastern Orthodox Church, could easily have sought to "maintain tradition" even though it was mostly cultural and ethnic rather than religious. But it didn't.

It could have put the social institution of arranged marriages on the same plane as other enduring conservative moral stances, such as the ethical rejection of premarital sex, fornication, adultery, and homosexuality, which it continues to teach and admonish as being opposed to the Orthodox Christian way of life. But it didn't.

It could have argued for a strict understanding of "honoring one's father and mother," one of the commandments of the Decalogue, that would require sons and daughters to be obedient to parental arrangements for their marriages—the kind of dilemma Sanjay was facing—thus giving the custom a religious ethical sanction. But it didn't.

It could have argued for arranged marriages and against the individual choice of a spouse by both men and women on the basis of an appeal to "order," an argument used in other cases regarding incest and the prohibition of marriages between close relatives in its canon law. But it didn't.

Arranged Marriage in the Orthodox Christian Tradition

There is no question that arranged marriages in antiquity were common and not at all unusual. The social systems of antiquity not only permitted but encouraged the practice. Arranged marriages were an accepted social convention. The Old Testament is filled with examples of arranged marriages in which a father exercises authority over his children regarding whom the child will marry even when there is personal attraction between the man and woman. For example, in Genesis 34 Hamor speaks on behalf of his son Shechem to the sons of Jacob to tell him that: "The soul of my son Shechem longs for your daughter; I pray you, give her to him in marriage" (Gen 34:8).

The law in Exodus gives power to a father to decide who his daughter will marry even in the case of rape (Ex 22:16–17). Later, the prophet Jeremiah instructs elders to "Build houses and live in them; plant gardens and eat their produce. Take wives and have sons and daughters; take wives for your sons, and give your daughters in marriage, that they may bear sons and daughters; multiply there, and do not decrease" (Jer 29:5–6). However, following the Babylonian captivity opposite instructions are given. These show again, however, the parental authority to arrange marriages. In the book of Ezra it is admonished after the captivity, "Therefore give not your daughters to their sons, neither take their daughters for your sons, and never seek their peace or prosperity, that you may be strong, and eat the good of the land, and leave it for an inheritance to your children for ever" (Ezra 9:12).

In the Deuterocanonical Septuagint book of the Wisdom of Solomon, also known as Sirach, the following indication of arranged marriages appears: "Give a daughter in marriage; you will have finished a great task. But give her to a man of understanding" (Sir 7:25). In another Deuterocanonical Septuagint book, 1 Maccabees, King Ptolemy proposes an alliance with another king, named Demetrius, by arranging a marriage with his daughter: "Come, let us make a covenant with each other, and I will give you in marriage my daughter" (1 Macc 11:90). Perhaps the most detailed account of an arranged marriage is to be found in chapters 3–7 of the Septuagint book of Tobit. Raguel and Edna, the parents of an only daughter Sarah, arrange her marriage with Tobias, the son of Tobit. At the center of this quite dramatic story we read the account of the marriage agreement where Raguel and Edna are persuaded to agree to the marriage. "Then he called his daughter Sarah, and taking her by the hand he gave her to Tobias to be his wife, saying, 'Here she is; take her according to the law of Moses, and take her with you to your father.' And he blessed them. Next he called his wife Edna, and took a scroll and wrote out the contract; and they set their seals to it" (Tob 7:13–14).

A similar assumption exists in the New Testament but with some apparent relaxation. We note that Jesus speaks of "marrying and giving in marriage" (Matt 24:38) in one place. Elsewhere he is presented as affirming that "The sons of this age marry and are given in marriage" (Lk 20:34). The formula appears again in an eschatological statement when Jesus is presented as saying "For in the resurrection they neither marry nor are given in marriage, but are like angels in heaven" (Matt 22:30). The difference between "marry" and "given in marriage" may be simply Hebrew poetic tautology, but it may imply that some married on their own initiative and some were involved in arranged marriages, that is, "given in marriage."

St. Paul seems to provide some evidence for individuals having control over their own marriage decisions. The argument that St. Paul gives in 1 Corinthians about engaged persons having the choice and the decision of going forward with the marriage or not in the light of the anticipated proximate Second Coming and end of the world, requires choice by the involved persons, not an arrangement at parental discretion. He concludes, "he who marries his betrothed does well; and he who refrains from marriage will do better" (1 Cor 7:38). Similarly, personal choice and volition are evident in this judgment: "Are you bound to a wife? Do not seek to be free. Are you free from a wife? Do not seek marriage. But if you marry, you do not sin, and if a girl marries she does not sin" (1 Cor 7:27–28).

A similar ambiguity appears in the subsequent early history of the Church. A brief search of Eastern Orthodox canon law provides evidence of different practices. Thus, the Epitome of canon 68 of Nicea I (325 CE) summarizes the ruling regarding "giving in marriage to an infidel a daughter or sister without her knowledge and contrary to her wish,"[1] which honors the will and desire of the woman, while at the same time sustaining the tradition of the arranged marriage. Another canon, Laodicea 31 (between 343 and 381 CE), holds that "it is not lawful to make marriages with all [sorts of] heretics, nor to give our sons and daughters to them; but rather to take of them, if they promise to become Christians,"[2] where the underlying social pattern seems to be exclusively that of arranged marriages.

Another canon, from the Fourth Ecumenical Council of Chalcedon (451 CE) seems to indicate both self-determined marriages and arranged marriages in the same paragraph. There follows the full text of canon 14 of Chalcedon; the two apparently conflicting passages have been italicized.

Since in certain provinces it is permitted to the readers and singers to marry, the holy Synod has decreed that *it shall not be lawful for any of them to take a wife that is heterodox.* But those who have already begotten children of such a marriage, if they have already had their children baptized among the heretics, must bring them into the communion of the Catholic Church; but if they have not had them baptized, they may not hereafter baptize them among heretics, *nor give them in marriage to a heretic, or a Jew, or a heathen,* unless the person marrying the orthodox child shall promise to come over to the orthodox faith. And if any one shall transgress this decree of the holy synod, let him be subjected to canonical censure.[3]

Chalcedon has another canon, canon 15, that indicates that women could contract their own marriages. It regards women deaconesses—who could only be unmarried—making the choice of marrying after they have served in the office. "A woman shall not receive the laying on of hands as a deaconess under forty years of age, and then only after searching examination. And if, after she has had hands laid on her and has continued for a time to minister, she shall despise the grace of God and give herself in marriage, she shall be anathematized and the man united to her."[4] This canon clearly speaks not of a young woman still under control of her family but of a mature forty-plus aged person. She can "give herself in marriage." The same rule holds true for a deacon or priest, who if celibate, may not marry after ordination, or if married, may not marry for a second time. So the Fifth/Sixth Ecumenical Council in Trullo (691 CE) decrees in the Epitome of its third canon: "Priests who shall have contracted second marriages and will not give them up are to be deposed."[5] Similarly, canon 16 of Chalcedon indicates that nuns and monks who leave their monasteries and marry are to be excommunicated, but at the discretion of the bishop they may be laicized.[6] Clearly, in these cases there is no arranged marriage, the principals decide for themselves.

Canon 22 in St. Basil's Second Canonical Epistle deals with men who have abducted young virgin women and sexually molested them. The men who had marital arrangements impending with these women had a choice whether to go forward with the marriage or not. The guardians of the women for whom there had not been any marital arrangement, could choose what should happen next: "it is at their discretion to give them in marriage to the raptors, or not."[7] This is obvious evidence of arranged marriage. Evidence, on the other hand, in St. Basil's canons that men and women were free to choose partners is clear in canon 23, whose Epitome says that "he who marries his brother's wife, be not admitted (to Holy Communion) till he dismiss her."[8] This could not have been an arranged marriage because it violated Church canons and civil law.

We see similar patterns in the writings of St. John Chrysostom. In section 81 of his *The Right Way for Parents to Bring Up Their Children,* Chrysostom speaks about the future wife of the young boy, emphasizing that he must be virtuous and of good character so as to be pleasing to this as yet unknown to him girl, who is eventually to be his wife. Characteristically, he urges the parents to say to the boy, "All that know thy bride—her father and mother, her servants and neighbors and friends—are deeply concerned for thee and thy way of life, and all will report to her."[9] Chrysostom adds, "Even if he cannot have a wife from his earliest manhood, let him have a betrothed from the first and let him strive to show himself a good man."[10] Chrysostom is speaking about an arrangement between two families for the engagement of children who are expected eventually to marry.

Nevertheless, there are other writings by Chrysostom that just as clearly assume that there is choice involved in the selection of a spouse. In his *How to Choose a Wife*,[11] Chrysostom argues that a man seeking to marry ought not to be primarily concerned about her wealth or even her looks, but rather, he should have as his highest priority her character. "Let us seek just one thing in a wife, virtue of soul and nobility of character."[12] But he also says, "Let us not investigate our bride's money, but the gentleness of her character and her piety and chastity."[13] All this, in spite of the existence of the institution of arranged marriages, indicates a measure of choice and selection by those persons seeking to marry.

Inviolability of Human Dignity

The biblical, canonical, and patristic examples provided above indicate that while the social institution of arranged marriages was considered a given in Greco-Roman society, it had far from an exclusive position. It would appear that it was possible that children and young people still under the care of parents could legally and socially become parties to arranged marriages, and that this could extend into adulthood. But it would also seem that many times adults, both men and women, could and did contract their own marriages.

In the context of the church, Christian teaching about personhood, freedom, virtue and vice, mutuality in marriage, and human dignity also played a role in the process of entering the marital state. Theologically, in the biblical and patristic mindset, the understanding of what it means to be a human being was rooted in the understanding of humanity's creation in the image and likeness of the Triune God, who is a community of persons in relationship, Father, Son, and Holy Spirit. The three persons of the Holy Trinity share one divine nature but are differentiated by their relationships of Fatherhood, Sonship, and Procession (the Holy Spirit). Human beings created in the image and likeness of the Triune God are consequently free and have a personal dignity that should not be violated.

When the social construct of arranged marriages lost its hold because of other disruptive social factors, such as World War II, the Greek Communist revolution, or the Turkish invasion of Cyprus, it was readily discarded. What remains is a sense of the dignity, self-respect, and freedom of the human person. It is this that the Orthodox Christian tradition will not back down on when it appeals to its faith tradition. It will not, however, feel itself obligated to support the socially constructed institution of arranged marriages.

In the story of the fifth of the bible class couples, the parents of the young woman who refused to accept the arranged marriage agreement gave "embarrassment" as their initial reason for opposing the breakup of the arrangement. It was not a trivial argument. They had given their word. As a value, this was a significant consideration. The values of trustworthiness, honesty, and consistency were operative in their initial response to their daughter. To some significant level, the integrity of their character was involved.

However, their daughter's objection that the marriage would not work and that sooner or later it would mean a break-up between her and the man, raised another, more significant set of values. Her brief statement was value-laden. It conveyed to her parents her personal assessment of the situation: that is, she was unwilling to compromise her faith, she judged the arrangement as inherently between two incompatible characters, and, as a consequence, she should not be forced to violate her personal integrity by entering into a marriage that she foresaw would fail.

By this, the parents were confronted with a conflict of values. There were the values associated with the maintenance of the arranged-marriage custom. Concurrently they were placed face to face with their daughter's personal integrity as embodied in her freedom to choose and in the value commitments she held precious, which caused her to oppose her parents' decision. The parents, confronted by such a choice, had no alternative as Orthodox Christians but to agree with their daughter's decision. The significance of the arranged marriage paled before their recognition of their daughter's personhood.

Alternatives Exist

How does this apply to Sanjay's situation? The dilemma of obedience to the parental decision for him to marry, in conflict with his desire not to marry at this time, need not be absolute. As Sanjay reflects on the situation, he still has alternatives between blindly submitting to his parents command and breaking with them as a result of his refusal to do as they wish. As an adult, he can respectfully make his case; agree but postpone; claim financial and personal hindrance at the present time; or even explain that he now feels— though he respects his parents, judgment—he needs to freely concur with it himself. Because this requires getting to know the bride-to-be, time is needed. Assuming that a break with his parents is not an option for him, he still can also make the claim to them that as an adult in a foreign land with alien customs, he cannot hastily enter a marriage which might easily end in misery for all involved.

Notes

1. *The Seven Ecumenical Councils: Nicene and Post-Nicene Fathers.* 2nd series, vol. 14 (Peabody, MA: Hendrickson Publishing), 50.

  2. *Seven Ecumenical Councils*, 149.

  3. *Seven Ecumenical Councils*, 278.

  4. *Seven Ecumenical Councils*, 279.

  5. *Seven Ecumenical Councils*, 363.

  6. *Seven Ecumenical Councils*, 280.

  7. *Seven Ecumenical Councils*, 600.

  8. *Seven Ecumenical Councils*, 606.

9. M. L. W. Laistner, *Christianity and Pagan Culture in the Later Roman Empire: Together with an English Translation of St. John Chrysostom's Address on Vainglory and the Right Way for Parents to Bring Up Their Children* (Ithaca, NY: Cornell University Press, 1951), sec. 82:120.

10. Laistner, *Christianity and Pagan Culture*, sec. 82: 120.

11. St. John Chrysostom, *On Marriage and Family Life*, trans. Catherine P. Roth and David Anderson (Crestwood, NY: St. Vladimir's Seminary Press, 1986), 89–114.

12. Chrysostom, *On Marriage*, 98.

13. Chrysostom, *On Marriage*, 99.

Bibliography and Suggested Reading

Chatterjee, Krishna Nath. *Hindu Marriage: Past and Present*. Varanasi, India: Tara Publications, 1972.

Constantelos, Demetrios J. *Understanding the Greek Orthodox Church*. 3rd rev. and enlarged ed. Brookline, MA: Holy Cross Orthodox Press, 1998.

Divakaruni, Chitra Banerjee. *Arranged Marriage*. New York: Anchor Books, 1995.

Dumont, Louis. *Affinity as a Value: Marriage Alliance in South India: With Comparative Essays on Australia*. Chicago: University of Chicago Press, 1983.

Flood, Gavin. *An Introduction to Hinduism*. Cambridge, England: Cambridge University Press, 1996.

Kane, P.V. *History of Dharmasastra*. Vol. 2, pt. 1. Poona, India: Bhandarkar Oriental Research Institute, 1974.

Klostermaier, Klaus. *A Survey of Hinduism*. 2nd ed. Albany: State University of New York Press, 1994.

Pelikan, Jaroslav. *The Christian Tradition: A History of the Development of Doctrine*. Vol. 1, *The Emergence of the Catholic Tradition (100–600)*. Chicago: University of Chicago Press, 1971.

———. *The Christian Tradition: A History of the Development of Doctrine*. Vol. 2, *The Spirit of Eastern Christendom (600–1700)*. Chicago: University of Chicago Press, 1974.

Rushdie, Salman. *Midnight's Children*. London: Jonathon Cape, 1981.

Ware, Timothy (Kallistos). *The Orthodox Church*. Baltimore, MD: Penguin Books, 1968.

CHAPTER 5

A Spectrum of Violence

A CASE STUDY by Christine E. Gudorf

Paul replaced the radio receiver on the console and turned to his partner, Diane, as she started the engine. "Here we go again," he said with a sigh. They had just received a domestic violence call from Scenic View, a public housing complex that had become notorious at the police station since 260 Afghani refugees had been placed there six months before.

The first calls had been from horrified neighbors who had seen animals butchered in the common yards, but almost immediately there had been other calls to report children, and in some cases adults, urinating and defecating in the yards. Every call meant long negotiations conducted through one of the two Afghani men who spoke English. They had explained that some of the refugees had lived in towns at least part of their lives and were familiar with outhouses, if not flush toilets. However, many of the refugees had always lived a nomadic life in the mountains and were finding it difficult to live "cooped up inside the belly of the concrete monster," as they had described the housing complex. Soon after the first calls, there had been a national news story about Afghanis in another city being arrested for selling young girls. It seemed the families in question had arranged what they regarded as good marriages within the Afghani community, complete with traditional bride prices, for their thirteen- and fourteen-year-old daughters. Local social services departments in the various resettlement locales remained stymied at how to deal with such a different culture within prevailing laws and policies.

Most of the officials of this small Midwestern city, and all of the police that Paul and Diane knew, were angry that the federal government had set this refugee group down in their town with no real preparation for either the refugees or the city. There had been no ongoing programs to help the refugees adjust to the new Midwestern American culture, no provision of translators who could assist the courts, the social service agencies, the police, or the schools. Just last week a woman had almost died at the local hospital emergency room because no one with her spoke enough English to tell the doctors her medical history. It had taken five hours to locate one of the two English-speaking Afghanis, then the doctors had to persuade both the family and the translator that it was necessary for this male translator to learn from the family this unrelated woman's gynecological problems and history and then tell them to another unrelated male doctor. In another year or two some of the kids would probably learn enough English in school to do translation of simple information for their parents and grandparents—if they could keep the kids in school. That was another bone of contention—many of the Afghanis did not understand compulsory education laws and assumed that children of eleven or twelve years of age, especially if they were girls, had had enough education.

As they approached the apartment complex, Diane, the senior of the two, suggested to Paul, "Why don't you go check out the scene and make sure everything is safe, while I try to locate Safed or Uri. We can't do much without one of them to translate. If everything is okay in 4G, you can go get a statement from Mrs. Johnson in 4E about what she saw or heard."

"Fine with me," responded Paul, climbing out of the car. He had adapted more easily to working with Diane, an African-American woman, than he had expected eight months ago, probably because she sometimes sounded like his older sisters.

"Be careful," Diane warned. "You think all these domestic violence calls here are just piddling misunderstandings of cultural differences. Some of them may be—but there's no reason to assume that domestic violence calls are only dangerous when it's Americans fighting. Remember Ralph." Ralph had been a fellow officer killed by a drunken husband from the tiny, usually quiet Korean community in town while investigating a domestic violence call two years earlier. Paul waved acquiescence as he slammed the car door and began walking up the sidewalk.

Half an hour later Diane had located Safed and brought him to 4G, and Paul had a statement from Mrs. Johnson, a portly African-American woman in her fifties who worked as a bailiff at the municipal court and cared for her paraplegic daughter and two grandsons. Mrs. Johnson, as they knew from her last call, was not happy that "these foreigners with their uncivilized ways" had been brought into the complex. She especially resented that the refugees had been granted special inclusion in welfare, Social Security, Medicare, Medicaid, and food stamps at the same time that federal and state policies were cutting the benefits to the working poor like herself. Her statement today said that when she looked out her kitchen window as she came into her apartment from court she had first seen the wife in 4G strike the son and then call to the husband, who immediately came over to the boy and began beating on him with a leather thong from around the father's waist. The boy, who told Safed that he was eleven, did have a swollen cheek and red, raised welts on his back.

Safed was engaged in an extended and animated conversation with the parents of the boy. Finally he turned to the police and said, "This has been a mistake. He is their son, and this is a private matter. There is no problem."

Diane replied, "There is a problem. It is against the law to beat children. We can see evidence of physical abuse."

Safed protested, "But even the boy agrees that he was disrespectful of his mother, and that it was right that he be punished!"

"His parents can certainly punish him, but they cannot beat him. To beat him is child abuse, and if the parents are guilty of child abuse they can be arrested and the child can be taken away from them and put into protective custody," Diane insisted.

Safed was clearly appalled by this and quickly translated Diane's statement to the parents. The father grabbed the son to him, as if daring anyone to try to take the boy away. Paul explained that they would make an initial report, and that Child Protective Services would investigate the home, and what happened would depend on their final report. The Afghanis were stunned. Safed tried to reassure the parents that nothing would happen soon. He then turned to leave with Diane and Paul.

In the lobby of the complex Safed demanded an extended explanation of the law and the social service procedures around domestic violence. There had been one incident of conjugal battery in the complex a month before, but that had, ironically enough, been dismissed. It turned out that while the husband had slapped his wife and split her lip—which, as physical evidence of abuse, would normally have required the police to press charges against the husband—both spouses had told the investigating officers from the beginning that the wife had hit the husband first, with a heavy wooden spoon in the back of the head, because he had insulted her family. Because nothing had come of this incident, neither of the translators had really understood how United States law treated domestic violence.

The idea that the law would jail a person for hitting his or her spouse or child—and take the child away from its parents—was beyond Safed's comprehension. In his society, these were family issues. If a man—or a woman—were abusive to spouse or child, the larger family would intervene to chastise the abuser or, in very severe circumstances, to separate the abuser from the victim. But even then the child or the spouse stayed within the extended family. But this happened only for what Safed called "real abuse." In his culture a slap, or even a light beating, for a wife or child requiring punishment for recognized infractions of social norms was considered the duty of the head of the household. How could it be that a man could go to jail or lose his children for doing his duty to his family? While they were talking, Diane took a call and interrupted Paul and Safed to say they were wanted at a four-car pile-up on the highway two miles away.

After dealing with the pile-up, Paul and Diane stopped for dinner before heading back to the station to write up their reports. They sat down with two other officers at the diner, and Paul brought up the subject of the Afghanis. "You know, guys, Diane and I have some differences of opinion about how to handle some of these calls with the Afghanis. Because she volunteers with Women Helping Women in their safe house, she sees broken bones, black eyes, and dead bodies every time we get a domestic violence call. My family came to this country from a little village in Honduras when I was a kid, and I remember how hard it was to learn American ways. I have two older sisters who really never did. They were fourteen and fifteen when we came, and my parents kept them at home to take care of the younger three kids—I don't know why nobody ever made them go to school. So they never learned good English, both married other Spanish-speaking immigrants, and neither of them got good jobs. But more than that, they, and my parents, stick to the old ways. Many a beating I got as a kid came from trying out the "freedoms" of American youth on my parents. I wanted to live like the American kids—who seemed to be able to go where they wanted, when they wanted, and to always have money. I always had responsibilities and no money, and sometimes I smarted off or just took off. I think there is a difference between beating a kid that needs it—what you call spanking— and abusing a kid. Abuse can be either too much force—broken skin or bones, internal damage, you know—or it can be hurting a kid for no reason or for reasons that have nothing to do with the kid."

Jack, the veteran cop in the group, asked, "Isn't this just a philosophical argument? We don't make the law, we just enforce it."

Diane responded, "No, it's a practical issue. Safed, one of the translators, wants to have a big meeting to negotiate some kind of agreement. They want to explain their culture and think that if use of domestic violence is okay within their culture, then officers of the law should respect that culture. I just don't think we can do that. How would we ever draw the line between 'light' beatings and criminal ones? Who gives us the authority to disregard the law for this one group?"

"But," Paul added, "these people are here for good. They'll need to be citizens if they're going to get Social Security when they retire, and Medicare, or Medicaid and SSI for their disabled. If they have criminal records, they can't be citizens. They don't know the culture, they are under all kinds of pressure in a strange land—do we really want to arrest them for what their whole community understands as acceptable, even commendable, behavior, knowing that a conviction on the arrest will prevent them from citizenship? If we give some of those men arrest records for hitting their wives, and they can't get citizenship, wives who don't work are going to be just as penalized as the men by the denial of Social Security."

Jack responded, "Tough luck. They'll have to learn quickly. These are the breaks. Life ain't fair. It didn't used to be fair to women and kids that neighbors and cops mostly ignored family violence. Now we have to investigate, and that's unfair to these foreigners."

"You know how much other residents like Mrs. Johnson would support going easy on the Afghanis and arresting everybody else for the same act," added Diane.

Steve, Jack's rookie partner who was working on a master's degree in sociology, spoke up, "Even if you could get away with not filing reports on some calls, the result would be that we'd have no paper trail for those calls. Lots of studies show that domestic violence often escalates and intensifies over time. If we don't keep a paper trail on a batterer, we can't see the escalation, and one day when we come his wife or kid may be dead. We all know that we only get called to a fraction of the incidents of domestic violence. With the Afghanis, because they see us as outsiders, the rate of reporting to police will probably be even lower. We can't disregard calls."

Diane spoke up. "But why even discuss it? You can't have all kinds of different groups in this city living under conflicting versions of the law. What makes respect for law is that everybody is held to it. I'm sympathetic to the culture shock these people must be going through, but they have to accept American law now that they are here, and the sooner the better. Ignoring their violations won't encourage them to adapt very quickly."

Steve looked up at Diane. "I just don't know. I hear Paul's argument. There is so much at stake for these people—losing citizenship, much less losing their kids—that it seems unfair not to give them any time, or any help in learning new ways. In my neighborhood when I was growing up, everybody hated the newcomers from the farm, because they didn't mow the lawn so often and kept noisy chickens and rusty old washing machines in their backyards. But the kids in those families grew up to become regular suburbanites. It just took a generation to learn the new rules, and the Afghanis have a lot more of them to learn."

As the waitress brought the checks and they all brought out wallets, Diane concluded, "Yeah, well, a lot of my people argue that blacks in northern cities are all transplanted poor rural Southerners, for whom corporal punishment of kids and slaps to keep wives in line have been part of the culture. But that has never kept black men from getting arrested for slapping wives or beating up on kids. I have seen, and even made, arrests of black parents for no more damage than that Afghani inflicted on his kid today, and those black parents lost their kids for months or years. We have foster parents who lose their foster care licenses for a single slap on the butt of a smart aleck kid. Why make exceptions for the Afghanis?" There was no answer to her question as they all filed out the door and entered the two cruisers.

Three weeks later another call from Mrs. Johnson brought Paul and Diane back to 4G. Safed was waiting for them anxiously. This time the father was not involved; he had not been home. Safed explained that the eleven-year-old boy had been told to watch his four-year-old sister and seven-year-old brother on the playground while his mother went to the grocery. After a while the boy had left the playground to join a group of his friends who were going to play soccer on a nearby lot. The mother had left the grocery to find the seven-year-old alone on the street outside and the four-year-old crying hysterically, also alone, on the playground. When the older son returned, his mother beat him for disobedience. Safed explained, "She remembered that her husband should not beat the child in this country, so she got the thong and did it herself. She thought that would be all right with the police. She does not consider herself capable of injuring the boy." By his expression, Safed understood that the mother's presumption would not be shared by the police.

Mrs. Johnson agreed that she had not seen the father all afternoon and confirmed that the four-year-old had been alone on the complex's playground. "I was thinking about sending my grandson down to get her when the mother returned," she added.

Diane went back to 4G and looked at the boy's back, and again saw a crisscross of red welts. The boy hung his head and appeared the picture of guilt. After he put his shirt back on he clung to his mother's side.

The mother demanded to know from Safed what would happen, and she became increasingly distraught when Safed was not able to reassure her that all was well. Diane promised to call Safed within the next few days.

As they walked out to the cruiser, Paul said to Diane, "I want to talk about this. If we just write this up like normal, that family is going to lose this kid within the week. You know that, and you know that would be wrong."

"But what else can we do?" asked Diane. "I don't see how to help this family without making things worse for others in the long run. Do you?"

A BAHA'I RESPONSE by Evaz Fanaian

From the perspective of the Baha'i faith, the problems in this case include the unquestioning use of violence to discipline children in the home, the United States government's move and subsequent abandonment of the Afghani war refugees, the pervasive attitudes of discrimination based on race and ethnicity, and the lack of clarity as to what justice for the Afghanis demands from the local community and its police officers. All of the problems are embedded in a network of particular circumstances and histories which make the application of religious teachings complicated and challenging.

Sources of Baha'i Revelation

The primary sources of Baha'i revelation which guide the life of the international Baha'i community are the more than 100 writings of Mirza Husayn-Ali (1817–1892), known as Baha'u'llah, the Glory of God. Baha'u'llah was the prophet-founder of the Baha'i faith, and his writings were interpreted by his son, 'Abdu'l-Baha, and Baha'u'llah's great-grandson, Shoghi Effendi. These writings are now translated into some 700 languages and dialects. The fundamental principles proclaimed by Baha'u'llah are that religious truth is a continuous and progressive process, that all the great religions of the world are divine in origin, and that their missions represent successive stages in the spiritual evolution of human society. Thus the revelation of other religions constitute secondary sources of revelation for the Baha'i community.

Within the writings of Baha'u'llah there are a number of teachings about both personal and communal behavior which are relevant to this case. Baha'is are nonpolitical in the sense that the Baha'i community is a voluntary, self-supporting community with no official relationship to any government. Its members are to refrain from any political office or partisan politics. All Baha'is are called to obey the civil laws of the nations and localities in which they live. One important influence on Baha'i abstention from partisan politics and fulfillment of the lawful duties of citizens is traceable to the life of Baha'u'llah and the lives of his followers: the intense persecution they have known, first in Iran and, later, in other nations as well.

Baha'i writings emphasize the need for peace in the world. Baha'u'llah recognized that one way in which this era is different from earlier eras addressed by other religious revelations is that the world is less and less ruled by the forces of violence and domination. The world civilization, which God is bringing about, has a balance which is shifting away from forceful and aggressive qualities both of body and of mind. The spiritual qualities of love and service are gaining ascendancy. Baha'i scripture emphatically states that women will be the greatest factor in establishing peace and universal arbitration and supports the entry of greater numbers of women into positions of prominence and authority as a necessary but not sufficient step in creating a just social order based in partnership, cooperation, and consultation.[1] There is, thus, some discrepancy between this emphasis on nonviolence and peaceable cooperation and this case's account of hitting children to train them to behave in acceptable ways. The use of corporal punishment to train children, though expedient and understandable in rare, emergency situations, is not a method conducive to children developing peaceable temperaments or learning cooperative techniques useful in building a peaceable world. There is, then, a general sympathy within Baha'i writings for the attempt of contemporary civil laws in the United States to move family discipline away from the use of force. 'Abdu'l-Baha specifically wrote:

> Let the mothers consider that whatever concerneth the education of children is of the first importance. Let them put forth every effort in this regard, for when the bough is green and tender it will grow in whatever way ye train it. Therefore it is incumbent upon the mothers to rear their little ones even as a gardener tendeth his young plants. Let them strive by day and by night to establish within their children faith and certitude, the fear of God, the love of the Beloved of the worlds, and all good qualities and traits. Whensoever a mother seeth that a child hath done well, let her praise and applaud him and cheer his heart; and if the slightest undesirable trait should manifest itself, let her counsel the child and punish him, and use means based on reason, even a slight verbal chastisement should this be necessary. It is not, however, permissible to strike a child, or vilify him, for the child's character will be totally perverted if he be subjected to blows or verbal abuse.[2]

At the same time, the writings of Baha'u'llah give a central place to justice, which is understood as basic to the peace and unity which should ultimately characterize the world. There is a question in this case as to whether the police will be furthering the cause of justice if they follow the local laws and regulations with respect to domestic violence among the Afghanis. Baha'is are taught to respect and obey the law in administrative matters but not to compromise in spiritual matters. Baha'is also doubt that the justice-based unity which should characterize the entire world community can be built on destruction of families by removing children from their parents and from their wider community. The failure of the federal government to provide the Afghanis immediate opportunities for basic acculturation was itself a denial of justice which sets the stage for further denials of justice. People who do not know the law, who do not understand the language in which the law is written and enforced, will not be equally or justly treated by strict enforcement of the law.

The Formation of Character in the Baha'i Community

The Baha'i faith contains not only social principles, but also strives to foster in individuals good character and spiritual qualities such as honesty, trustworthiness, compassion, and justice. Baha'u'llah wrote:

> The best thing in My sight is justice; turn not away therefrom if thou desirest Me, and neglect it not that I may confide in thee. By its aid thou shalt see with thine own eyes and not through the eyes of others, and shalt know of thine own knowledge and not through the knowledge of thy neighbor. Ponder this in thy heart; how it behooveth thee to be. Verily, justice is My gift to thee and the sign of My loving-kindness. Set it then, before thine eyes.[3]

Prayer, meditation, and work done in the spirit of service to others are methods of developing these spiritual qualities. The Baha'i faith recognizes that all persons have unique talents and abilities. It therefore strives to eliminate systematically, through the teaching and example of the Baha'i community, prejudices of race, creed, class, nationality, and sex. This focus on development of every person's God-given talents and abilities includes support for the pursuit of knowledge and the acquisition of skills for the practice of a skill or profession. Such education is to be available to all and not limited to either privileged minorities or to males; the call is to universal compulsory education. The use of such knowledge and skills is not only for the personal satisfaction and development of individuals, but also for the enrichment of society as a whole. Baha'u'llah taught: "It is made encumbent on every one of you to engage in some occupation, such as arts, trades and the life. We have made this—your occupation—identical with the worship of God, the True One. Reflect, O people, upon the Mercy of God and upon his favors, then thank him in mornings and evenings."[4] Support for a broad range of educational activities which prepare people for some occupation is one important aspect of Baha'i support for character development. The Baha'i community has earned a worldwide reputation for peaceful cooperation of peoples across various social, economic, political, and religious backgrounds within its international community. It is such skills and mindset that are required by the representatives of the American and the Afghani communities in the case in order to resolve the situation of the domestic violence calls among the Afghanis.

From the perspective of the Baha'i faith, both police and neighbors in this case need to ask themselves how well their service to the community has embodied justice, compassion, and lack of prejudice, just as the Afghanis need to develop the skills that will allow them to participate in, and share responsibility for, the larger community in which they now live. For Baha'is— and for many other religious persons—prayer and meditation hold a central position and are a positive help in developing these qualities of character. Baha'i services consist of the recitation of the scriptures of all religions and a cappella music. The readings remind individuals of the kind of persons God has repeatedly called humans to be, and the music serves to meld the collectivity gathered together into the unified community that will support individuals in becoming those kinds of persons in all the areas of their lives.

Toward Resolution

One way to decide what should be done in a specific situation is to imagine oneself or one's community in the various roles within the situation. If the civil community within which these refugees had been placed contained a Baha'i community, that Baha'i community would need to reach out to the Afghanis to the extent of their ability. This could take the form of Baha'is teaching English as a second language, or teaching more basic skills such as local customs around food preparation or garbage storage and disposal, appropriate use of health resources in the community, and, as would be so critical in this case, simple crash courses in basic legal rights and common police and social service interventions around family relations, domestic property, and employment. It is important that the Afghanis know that many of the functions that in their native situation belonged to the heads of families and clans here are assigned to impersonal police and social work officers.

Having come from a situation of war and now being confronted by the power of the American state in the form of the police, the Afghanis may need not only time to learn the new culture but also may need some help in shifting from changing behavior in response to superior power to changing behavior based on the needs and potential for development of the individuals and communities involved. That is, they should be helped to understand the reason for the law against beating children and should not be encouraged to acquiesce simply because the authorities demand it with dire threats. Different Baha'i communities will have different skills and advantages to offer to such refugee communities. What the Baha'i community in general could contribute is their experience in finding peaceable ways to bridge cross-cultural conflict and tension. They could mediate in the situation above, perhaps working with Mrs. Johnson as well as with the Afghanis, the police, and the domestic violence investigators who are not yet on the scene.

What if the police or the social workers or the eventual judge in this case were Baha'i? What would their faith direct? There is nothing specific in the

Baha'i tradition regarding work as police, though police work is not a common occupation for Baha'is, probably because of the Baha'i emphasis on peace and the historic use of police forces against Baha'is. Law and social work are more common occupations among Baha'is. All Baha'is are taught to be obedient to the government in power in the country in which they reside. Shoghi Effendi taught:

> For whereas the friends should obey the government under which they live, even at the risk of sacrificing all their administrative affairs and interests, they should under no circumstances suffer their inner religious beliefs and convictions to be violated and transgressed by any authority whatever. A distinction of fundamental importance must, therefore, be made between spiritual and administrative matters. Whereas the former are sacred and inviolable, and hence cannot be subject to compromise, the latter are secondary and can consequently be given up and even sacrificed for the sake of obedience to the laws and regulations of the government.[5]

There is little doubt that racism in the United States is the background into which the Afghani refugees have been inserted. The enforcement of laws—which are supposed to be for all—against some groups but not others in a society is unjust discrimination. Mrs. Johnson's attitude in this case—her seeming determination that child-beating by the Afghanis will be treated as abuse just as it is for African Americans—is supported to some extent by Diane, the police officer, and is almost certainly based in the centuries of differential treatment of whites and blacks under the laws of the United States. But there should be a difference between ignoring serious infractions of justice by one group while steeply punishing minor infractions by another group, on the one hand, and attempting to distinguish between applying the letter or the spirit of the law in shaping social justice. While Baha'is believe that law should be obeyed, they recognize that laws are means to justice and peace and not ends in themselves and, so, must be interpreted and followed in terms of how they will affect justice and peace.

Conclusion

This case is not insoluble. Most of the people seem to be people of general good will. They need to come together in the spirit of peace and cooperation to pursue justice. Attention to Baha'i teachings could be helpful, as could those of other religious traditions that emphasize the pursuit of peaceful civilization.

Notes

1. 'Abdu'l-Baha, *Baha'i: Teachings for the New World Order*, ed. Mouhebat Sobhani (New York: Waldorf Enterprises, 1992), 7.

2. 'Abdu'l-Baha, *Tablets of 'Abdu'l-Baha*, vol. 3 (Wilmette, IL: Baha'i Publishing Trust, 1988), 605.

3. Baha'u'llah, *The Hidden Words of Baha'u'llah* (Wilmette, IL: Baha'i Publishing Trust, 1982), 3–4.

4. Baha'u'llah, *Baha'i World Faith*, 2nd ed. (Wilmette, IL: Baha'i Publishing Trust, 1956), 195.

5. Shoghi Effendi in a letter written on behalf of Shoghi Effendi to an individual believer, 11 February 1934.

A CHRISTIAN RESPONSE by Christine E. Gudorf

From a Christian perspective this case has at least two major issues. One issue involves defining and evaluating domestic violence, and the other concerns the extent of and conditions for the authority of civil law. Does, or should, all use of corporal punishment—in this case of children—fall under the category of domestic violence? If a civil law reflects the cultural presuppositions of one group but not another, is it binding either on the group to which it is alien or to social agents pledged to equal treatment of members of both groups? Sources for investigating these issues include a number of specifically Christian ones, including the Bible and church teachings through the ages, as well as secular ethical traditions.

The Bible on Corporal Punishment

Any cursory reading of the Bible would reveal a position not unlike the one Safed described as Afghani. This is not surprising, given the common origins of the New Testament, the Jewish scriptures, and Islam among Semitic Middle Eastern peoples. The Afghanis are not only Middle Easterners, but also pastoralists like many of the peoples of the Jewish scriptures (the Christian Old Testament).

Until the twentieth century, Christian churches shared with both Western law and culture and the Bible the understanding that men were the heads of their families and had the duty of disciplining wives and children, which would sometimes take the form of physical chastisement. In fact, the use of the bride/groom analogy for the relationship of Yahweh and Israel in the Old Testament, and later by St. Paul in the New Testament for the relationship of Christ and the church, set up an analogy: men were to treat their wives—and, by extension, their children—as God treated Israel. While this analogy did permit physical punishment in response to disobedience because God was understood to have physically punished Israel with defeat and conquest, the analogy basically commanded that fathers' behavior be characterized by mercy and forgiving love. Prominent scriptural examples include the New Testament story of the prodigal son's forgiveness by his father (Lk 15:11–32) and the Old Testament story of Hosea's love for his unfaithful wife.

In the New Testament, the synoptic gospels, especially Matthew and Luke, relate a number of stories (Mt 18:1–4; Lk 10:14; Mt 18:10; Lk 12:32; Mt. 11:25) in which Jesus defends and reaches out to children, threatens those who endanger children, and demands that all those who desire to enter the Kingdom of God become as children—stripped of power and prestige. These narratives attempt to reverse the tendency to focus attention on those who have power, leaving the powerless outside the protective light of public scrutiny where they may be abused. Jesus' teaching on children in the New Testament did not lead Christians to treat children differently from the way the surrounding culture treated them. For the last 200 years, as Western society invented childhood—a period of protected innocence, idleness, and play for children—it tended to interpret Jesus' words as endorsing this social construction of childhood and, thus, shifted the meaning from a critique of the use of power in society to an endorsement of naivete.

In the New Testament books of Ephesians (5:25–6:9) and Colossians (3:18–4:1), the Roman household code was adapted to Christian usage. The code calls wives to be submissive to husbands, children to obey parents, and slaves to obey masters. Yet these passages also limit traditional patriarchy; husbands are also ordered to love their wives, fathers not to provoke their children, and masters not to abuse slaves. This love-patriarchalism was a Christian compromise between the prevailing patriarchal culture and the radical equality reflected in the early Christian baptismal formula—"There is no longer Jew nor Greek; there is no longer slave nor free; there is no longer male nor female; for all of you are one in Christ Jesus" (Gal 3:28). For almost 2,000 years, this love-patriarchalism was the model for the Christian family, and corporal punishment was taken for granted as the way of punishing transgressions.

During the first millenium when many Christian priests were married and had children, they were often admonished to beat their wives and children regularly in order to set a good example of well-ordered and disciplined households. This should not be surprising. Until two hundred years ago, physical torture was mandatory for certain kinds of civil offenses and was taken for granted as the method for extracting both confessions and true information for the state. Removal of fingers, hands, and feet were common punishments for relatively minor crimes; in some centuries, hanging was the most common punishment for thefts above the value of a loaf of bread. In periods where physical punishment was both so common and so severe, it is not surprising that the church did not see the use of corporal punishment for wives or children as problematic. Given the low status of women and children in society, and the understanding that their lower degree of rationality as compared to men excluded most noncorporal forms of punishment, it is perhaps not surprising that the Christian church contented itself with preaching that men should keep their wives and children in line, though punishment should normally stop short of death or disability. While the church may not have been the originator of the "rule of thumb," it did assist in the widespread teaching of the rule, which limited the size of a stick that a man could use on his wife or children to one with a diameter the size of his thumb.

Love-patriarchalism in the family endured in Christianity long after Christianity made peace with fewer and fewer patriarchal forms of social governance. As the Enlightenment produced new democratic political models of society, the church followed civil society in its separation of public and private realms which preserved inequality and hierarchy in the family—and church—by insulating them from the public world of equality and individual freedom. Until very recently, the recognition of abuse of power within the family was understood and treated by both civil society and church not as a result of the structure and ideology of the family but as the result of some accidental external circumstance, such as male alcoholism in nineteenth-century America. Attention was thus diverted to correcting the abuse of power in the family by discouraging alcoholism among men.

Civil law banning the use of any form of violence within the family is very recent and follows the success of the nineteenth- and twentieth-century women's movement in gaining recognition for the equality of women. Many argue that rates of domestic abuse against women and children rose in reaction to increasing social recognition of women's rights in the family and society. At any rate, one of the first specific issues within the mid-twentieth century women's movement focused on ending violence against women. As more public attention was paid to violence in the family, child abuse in the family quickly caught the attention of the public as well. The characteristic tendency of American society to solve social problems by recourse to law led to laws against physical or sexual abuse of spouses or children. Some states and even cities now legislate mandatory arrests when police find physical evidence of abuse, whether or not family members wish to press charges.

In an attempt to protect children from abuse or neglect within families, states have publicized child abuse hotlines where neighbors, teachers, health care workers, or others who have reason to suspect a child is being abused or neglected may report their suspicions and trigger an investigation. Evidence of abuse or neglect which threatens the life or health of the child usually brings criminal charges. Lesser degrees of abuse or neglect may result in temporary state oversight of parental care of the child, temporary removal of the child from parental care until the parents are either judged innocent or fulfill a required course of remedial action, or the permanent termination of parental rights. The case under consideration in this chapter accurately points out that the state systems for dealing with child abuse tend to be bureaucratically inflexible. No one involved in this case, including Diana who wants to stick by the rules, sees this child as seriously abused or as appropriate for removal from the home. Even so, both officers acknowledge that a second police call with evidence of a beating will have that result. Bureaucracies have no way to differentiate between a spanking and a beating because they adhere to law and regulations, which have little interest in motive or circumstances but tend to look to physical acts and a narrow range of consequences of those acts—in this case, marks on the body.

For these reasons, the question of what constitutes physical abuse of children is problematic in the United States, not only for immigrant groups from different cultures but also for fifth- and sixth-generation Americans, not only for Muslims but for Christians as well. Parents of difficult children, including mentally and emotionally handicapped children, delinquent children, and adolescent and teen drug users, are often caught in the middle. Society increasingly holds these parents responsible for the behavior of their difficult-to-control children—who may even be physically aggressive themselves—while at the same time penalizing those parents when they use physical coercion to control children. The church has been of little help. Church history provides little basis for banning all use of corporal punishment in the family, though church practice in this area has usually supported civil practice. Perhaps the two most helpful avenues to explore are: (1) the contemporary meanings of the restraints put on husbands, parents, and masters under Christian love-patriarchalism—to love wives as their own bodies, to not provoke children, and to not abuse slaves; and (2) the conclusions of scripture exegetes on violence. There is a general consensus outside the historic peace churches that Jesus was not an evangelical pacifist, though he was a pragmatic pacifist. Thus, for Christians, while recourse to violence is not forbidden, there must be a predisposition to nonviolence, and the burden of proof always rests with advocates of the use of violence. A parallel Christian teaching on corporal punishment, one that prefers noncorporal forms of punishment but recognizes that some use of corporal punishment could be justified, seems appropriate. In the same way, given contemporary understandings of the dignity and the embodied nature of the human person, it would be possible on the basis of the restraints on the patriarch in the New Testament household codes to argue that in our world we do not beat our own bodies and, therefore, should not beat wives we are to love as our own bodies. Similarly, it can be argued that consistent use of corporal punishment can easily be interpreted by a child as evidence of cruelty, even hatred and abuse, and can itself provoke the child to further inappropriate acts.

Equal Treatment under the Law?

As is often the case in difficult ethical situations, the predicament in the case study was caused by prior sin. The problem for the Afghanis began with Soviet control of their government and took its final shape when the United States government relocated them but failed to provide an orderly process of integration and temporary social supports for them in the strange land. Given the injustices of the past, what should be done now? There are a number of perspectives to be considered. Most of the discussion in the case focuses on how the law-enforcement establishment might itself mediate between the Afghanis and the law. But individual officers may well be caught in a dilemma. We do not know which, if any, of these officers are Christian, but Christians in this situation might well feel caught between their duties to their Afghani neighbors and their duties to fulfill their oath as law-enforcement officials.

The gospels describe Jesus as acting primarily on the basis of compassion for those who are needy, and as demanding of his followers obedience to the two greatest commandments: "You shall love the Lord thy God with all of your heart, with all of your soul, and with all of your mind, and with all of your strength... You shall love your neighbor as yourself" (Mk 12:30–31). Having compassion for the Afghanis to the extent of loving them as the officers love themselves would seem to conflict with removing Afghani children from their homes and denying the Afghanis citizenship for violating laws they either did not know about or could not yet understand.

But compassion is not the only characteristic appropriate for Christians. Christians are called to be good, as the heavenly Father is good. Goodness may begin with compassion, an openness to the needs of others, but it encompasses a great deal more. Justice, responsibility, and creativity are three other aspects of goodness necessary in this situation. Justice entails giving others their due, and what is due all others is not necessarily the same at any given time. Unless an act of corporal punishment either intends or results in serious damage to another, justice for the punisher will be different according to whether the law was broken knowingly or unknowingly. Responsibility is proportional to one's ability to impact a situation. Police officers in this case have a tremendous capacity to impact the lives of Afghani families and, therefore, a great responsibility to see that their impact is positive. It would be an abdication of responsibility for officers to take the position that their job is simply to enforce whatever the law says. Such a job is a job for robots, not for humans, who must always account for their actions. Creativity is a necessary aspect of goodness in that solutions to moral dilemmas such as this usually call for some degree of creativity, the ability to draw something new and better from the existing reality. In this situation and many others, the first step in creativity is to take the position of the other. This is what Paul does when he sees the Afghanis from the perspective of his Honduran immigrant experience. Diane cannot do this because child welfare authorities, including her fellow police, denied the existence or legitimacy of cultural change in her people's migration from rural South to urban North. To grant to the Afghanis what she cannot obtain for her own people would feel like disloyalty.

On the other hand, a righteous person fulfills promises, and the police officers have taken an oath to protect the community by enforcing the law equally and impartially. Jesus understood himself as a part of the Jewish covenant with Yahweh, in which obedience to the law was the means of Jewish fulfillment of the covenant. Fulfillment of contracted obligations is especially important when the obligation has entailed acceptance of certain powers and privileges necessary to protect the community, as is the case with the police in this situation. They have more than the ordinary obligation to protect the common good. The actions of the police, in whatever direction is decided, will have not only serious consequences for individual Afghanis but also for the community as a whole in terms of its understanding of respect for law, equality under the law, and the integrity and trustworthiness of police.

A quick reading of the New Testament might lead one to believe that, for the time being, Jesus would clearly be on the side of failing to file abuse reports on the Afghanis unless there were serious injuries. Jesus not only urged obedience to the spirit rather than the letter of the law, he also repeatedly condemned the Pharisees for blindly demanding the strict enforcement of the law—especially Sabbath law—regardless of the cost to human persons: "The Sabbath was made for man (sic), not man for the Sabbath; so the Son of man is lord even of the Sabbath" (Mk 2:27–28). Just as Jesus, in his compassion for the sick, possessed, and otherwise afflicted people of his time, did the work of healing on the Sabbath and, thereby, broke the letter of the law, so perhaps the police should, out of compassion for the Afghanis, give them a temporary reprieve from the full application of the law.

But it is important to note that Jesus also said, "I have come not to destroy but to fulfill the Law." Jesus might have been making a distinction between working on the Sabbath to heal the afflicted and other types of Sabbath work that he did not mean to justify. He was not setting aside the Sabbath law altogether, just as we should not disregard the secular law. Justice was also a concern of Jesus, and for Jesus justice consisted not only of the vindication of the innocent but also of the punishment of the guilty, especially of the guilty who prey on the innocent and weak. No one among the Afghanis or any other group can be allowed to abuse the weaker among them, even if that had been allowed in their old country. Some way must be found to move the Afghanis in the general direction of compliance with the law by first informing them of the law and policies of social agencies regarding physical abuse and then by providing training in other forms of disciplining children.

It is not enough simply to convey the law. Parents invariably pattern themselves on the way their own parents parented them and only make minor changes in those patterns with great difficulty. Even when individuals have voluntarily renounced corporal punishment as inappropriate, even barbaric, they often find themselves, as parents, unthinkingly smacking the bottom of the child who has just deliberately waked the baby or skipped her chores. How much more difficult it is to change one's parenting style if one cannot understand why this new community would condemn the well-deserved smack.

In the meantime, police teams or, preferably, a mix of personnel from the police, the district attorney's office, the local community, and the local department of children and families should work out some temporary policy. This might be an informal list of families with multiple but nonsevere domestic abuse calls, who might be targeted for special training efforts and/or more intensive investigation.

Bibliography and Suggested Reading

'Abdu'l-Baha. *Promulgation of Universal Peace*. Wilmette, IL: Baha'i Publishing Trust, 1982.

'Abdu'l-Baha. *The Secret of Divine Civilization*. National Spiritual Assembly of The Baha'is of the USA, 1957.

Adeney, Bernard T. *Strange Virtues*. Downers Grove, IL: Intervarsity Press, 1995.

Baha'u'llah. *Baha'i World Faith*. 2nd ed. Wilmette, IL: Baha'i Publishing Trust, 1956.

Baha'u'llah. *Gleanings from the Writings of Baha'u'llah*. Wilmette, IL: Baha'i Publishing Trust, 1983.

Baha'u'llah. *The Hidden Words of Baha'u'llah*. Wilmette, IL: Baha'i Publishing Trust, 1982.

Baha'u'llah. *Tablets of Baha'u'llah*. Wilmette, IL: Baha'i Publishing Trust, 1988.

Benhabib, Seyla. *Situating the Self: Gender, Community and Postmodernism in Contemporary Ethics*. New York: Routledge, 1992.

Brown, Joanne Carlson, and Carole R. Bohn, eds. *Christianity, Patriarchy, and Abuse: A Feminist Critique*. Cleveland, OH: Pilgrim, 1989. (The specific abuses treated are child sexual abuse and a variety of abuses against women, but the theology and analysis would apply equally well to physical abuse of children.)

Capps, Donald. *The Child's Song: The Religious Abuse of Children*. Louisville, KY: Westminster John Knox, 1995.

National Spiritual Assembly of the Baha'is of the United States. *Two Wings of a Bird: The Equality of Women and Men*. Wilmette, IL: Baha'i Publishing Trust, 1997.

Poling, James Newton. *The Abuse of Power: A Theological Problem*. Nashville, TN: Abingdon, 1991.

Sobhani, Mouhebat, ed. *Baha'i: Teachings for the New World Order*. New York: Waldorf Enterprises, 1992.

PART II

RELIGION AND THE STATE

CHAPTER 6

To Live among Dangerous Memories

A CASE STUDY by Christine E. Gudorf

Ben smiled at his son, Nathan, sitting in the seat next to him, and then turned back toward the small window of the airplane at which he had been gazing, unseeing, for the last hour. He and Nathan had flown from Dresden to Frankfurt this morning and were now en route from Frankfurt to Buenos Aires, back to their families. It had been a momentous trip for both of them, but the burden of decision was now Ben's. Nathan had repeated only yesterday what he and his wife, his mother, his sister and her husband had all told Ben when he returned to Argentina from Germany six months ago: "It is your decision. We will go where you lead." That was a tremendous responsibility.

The entire affair had actually begun in early 1991, when Ben's mother, Raquel, had been on her deathbed. When she realized that she might not recover from the heart attack that had hospitalized her, she demanded that her room be cleared except for Ben. She had then confessed that she was not his birth mother, that he had been smuggled out of Nazi Germany and into Spain as a one year old only weeks before the war began by parents who wanted to ensure his safety and who expected to escape themselves soon after. The Jewish group organizing the escape route had entrusted care of Ben to Raquel, a Jewish volunteer in Madrid, who became so attached to Ben that when she emigrated to Argentina in 1942 she registered him there as her son, assuming that his parents were dead. The following year she married another German Jew, and her new husband, Solomon, adopted the five-year-old Ben as his own. They had treated him as the elder brother of the four children later born to them.

While Ben had always known that Solomon was his adopted father, he had thought Raquel his biological mother and his father dead in the camps. This new information rocked the foundations of his life and his identity. Raquel produced the long-hidden documents sent with him as an infant which identified him as Benjamin Weismann, son of Samuel and Frieda Weismann of Dresden, Germany. Raquel died four days later.

During the following months, Ben struggled to mourn for Raquel, but found that her disclosures made it difficult to sort out his feelings for her. On the advice of his rabbi, he contacted a Jewish organization in Israel which specialized in tracing Jewish families separated by the Holocaust. Within weeks the organization came back with the information that Ben's father, Samuel Weismann, had died in the camps but that his mother, Frieda Weismann, had survived and was, in fact, still living in Dresden, though she was almost eighty years old and in poor health. Ben contacted Frieda Weismann, first through a Dresden rabbi and then by mail. They exchanged a few letters and pictures and finally spoke on the telephone, during which she begged him to come and see her before she died.

In May 1992, Ben flew to Dresden and saw his mother for the first time in fifty-three years. She introduced him to five or six elderly Jews who had known him as a baby, from his cousin Theodore to former neighbors who told him stories of his father, his aunt, and his grandparents, who had all died in the Holocaust.

Dresden had been a part of East Germany, but since the 1990 unification of the two Germanies, it was undergoing rapid change. One of the changes that preoccupied Frieda was the recent announcement that the unified German government would now make restitution to the estates of Jews who had had property in East Germany confiscated by the Nazi government between 1933 and 1945. West Germany had gone through this restitution process after the end of the war, but communist East Germany had never made reparations of any sort. Frieda wanted Ben to make a claim in her name for the restoration of both the piano factory owned by her father and the plumbing fixtures factory owned by her husband and father-in-law, as well as for the three houses that she and Samuel, her parents, and her in-laws had owned in Dresden.

All of those buildings had been destroyed in the Allied fire bombing, which had taken over 135,000 lives and obliterated central Dresden. When the city had been rebuilt after the war, the piano factory became part of a large bus station, new homes were built on the former sites of Ben's parents' and grandparents' houses, and the plumbing fixtures factory had been partly utilized for a dairy processing plant and partly for a new park. What would be restored would depend on when the claim was made. Under a May 1992 agreement, Jews had until December 31, 1992, to make claims for the restoration of property; after that date, claims were limited to cash awards based on the value at the time of confiscation, plus 3 percent interest per year. The destruction of all the buildings in the bombing of Dresden in 1944 made restoration of property in Dresden unlikely, though Frieda preferred that so that the properties, if not the businesses, would remain in the family. Her father had been the third generation of Hauptmanns to operate the piano factory. Frieda's goal in persuading Ben to make the claim in her name was to convince him to resettle his family in Dresden and continue those traditions.

Return to the Scene of the Holocaust?

The idea that Ben resettle his family in Germany struck him as absurd when his mother initially suggested it. It seemed masochistic to return to the place of so much hatred, so much suffering. "It hurts," he told Frieda, "to see that the Jewish community here is so old, that the families, spouses, and children of these survivors were either killed or driven off to Israel or the Americas by the hatred of the Nazis. How could I bring my children and my grandchildren here?"

But Frieda's response was that the centuries of Jewish communities in Germany and in other European nations devastated by the Nazis could not be abandoned. "Look at the Jewish cemeteries of Prague, of Berlin, of Warsaw, of Budapest! Look at the synagogues! Look at the artistic and cultural contributions of Jews to music, to philosophy, to medicine, to business and finance, to the history of Europe. For over a thousand years the history and the culture of Europe has been more than a little Jewish, and for that thousand years Europe has been the home of most of the Jews in the world."

"If you had taken your family to Israel, I would not ask this of you. But you have not taken the position that Israel is the only home of Jews; you live in exile in Argentina. My neighbor Emmanuel tells me that Argentina has its own share of fascist anti-Semitism and that it arrested and tortured prominent Jews during the unrest of the 1970s. What about the bombing of the Jewish Cultural Center in Buenos Aires last year—didn't ninety-five people die? If I, who have lived through Auschwitz, can believe that Germany can be a home for Jews, why is it so hard for you? The handful of crazies who knock over tombstones and spray paint slogans in places like Rostock are not the norm. And they are not people with power, either. I, too, hate to look around at the small numbers at the synagogue for Shabbat, and most, but not all, of them old. But people like you must come back so that the German Jewish community does not die completely, so that the madmen do not have the last word. How can you, who have lived your life unaware of how much you had lost in the madness, be willing to risk less than I?"

Frieda urged him to spend a week exploring Jewish history in Germany and speaking with Jewish communities and organizations throughout the nation. And he had promised—as a favor to the sick old woman who had given him life—to do that, but he had little expectation that exploration could make resettlement a real option.

After he went back to Buenos Aires and spoke with his wife, Sarah, his son, Nathan, Nathan's wife, Elena, his daughter, Raquel, her husband, Abraham, and their rabbi, it was decided that it was impractical for the whole family, including Nathan's and Raquel's three young children, to make the return trip to Germany but that Nathan, at least, should accompany Ben. They went first to see Frieda in Dresden and found her a little frailer but much encouraged by their trip. She gave them a list of names and organizations to talk to, addresses of Jewish synagogues, cemeteries, and museums to visit, and a stack of books on the history of the Jews in Europe to read. Many members of her synagogue, including its new rabbi, had contributed to her lists.

Nathan and Ben started touring in the former East Berlin at a small five-acre cemetery desecrated at the time of Kristallnacht and never restored. It included tombstones so old that the Hebrew carving was now faint. But some of the decipherable tombstones were four centuries old; the others probably much older. The Kristallnacht desecration was still apparent in the broken and fallen tombstones, and it appeared no one had cared for the cemetery because there were large trees growing out of the graves, vines had grown between the trees, and weeds abounded. From there they went to a much larger Jewish cemetery further out in the suburbs of East Berlin. It stretched on for over a mile on all sides, and the walls which surrounded it were composed of huge marble family monuments the size of small houses, most two and three stories tall, set side by side. The fronts of the green, white, black, or brown marble edifices, with names like Goldbaum, Baumburger, Hauptmann, Asher, and Rosenbaum etched over the portals, were still magnificent despite the fifty-year lack of care which had left some caved-in roofs and the inevitable vines and piles of detritus.

Inside this cordon, a few workers had obviously just recently begun to attack the neglect. Some of the larger paths had been opened, and one section which looked to be the most contemporary had been almost completely cleared of trees, vines, and weeds and had had the grass mown. As they approached it they realized that this section held monuments to Holocaust victims. As they wandered through they noted numbers of children, infants through teenagers, who died at various death camps, and periodically, the monuments of couples, some of which displayed death dates between 1939 and 1945 at Treblinka, Dachau, Auschwitz, Mauthausen, or Maidenek for one of the spouses and open death dates for the surviving spouse. As they left the cemetery, they passed a monument to a Nazi resistance group whose members had been captured and hung, their names and ages—mostly in their teens and twenties—listed on the sides of the monument.

"It is all so very depressing," commented Nathan as they walked to the nearby train stop. "It really makes you feel that the Jewish community is dead—there wasn't even anyone left to care for the graves of their dead." Ben said nothing, thinking that the combination of the Holocaust graves, the desecration from Kristallnacht, the human neglect, and the encroachment of nature combined to give the impression that nature and history had conspired to eliminate the Jews from the face of Berlin.

But in the following days they met with the living Jewish community in Germany and were impressed by the enthusiasm of many who pointed to the opening of the first postwar Hebrew day school for secondary students, to the growing numbers of Hebrew elementary schools, and to the beginning of the reconstruction of the central Berlin synagogue burned on Kristallnacht and left an abandoned shell for over half a century. They were also plunged into the ongoing debate among the 40,000 members of the German Jewish community. That debate seemed to have many aspects. Sometimes it seemed as if the question was the relationship of Jews to German nationality—were they Germans who happened to be Jewish in religion, or were they Jews who happened to be living in Germany? Many of the elders insisted they were German Jews; citizenship and not just residency were important. Many younger Jews thought this an inappropriate accommodation to the Holocaust. Another aspect of this same debate concerned how public the Jewish community should be. Many, especially the elderly, feared that for Jewish groups to publicize themselves in any way would invite increased anti-Semitism. This concern seemed especially strong in the former East, which, under communism, had not undergone the frequent public attention and debate concerning the Holocaust such as the Nuremberg trials or the reparations to individual Jews and to Israel, which had occurred in West Germany in the decades after the war. And yet, Ben observed that, even among the elderly in the East, there were persons like Frieda, his mother, who were not afraid for the Jewish community to assert itself, especially against any form of anti-Semitism.

One issue concerning their relations with the rest of Germany which divided Jews was the dispute over the Hamburg cemetery. The cemetery, which dated from 1663, had seen its tombstones bulldozed by the Nazis, who had dug through the human remains to build two deep bunkers. After the war, the land had been deeded to the surviving Jewish community in Hamburg, which sold it in 1950, perhaps without realizing that the cemetery's graves had not been entirely removed. In 1988, a contractor bought the land and planned a domed shopping center. Local leftists opposed to a shopping center in their neighborhood learned of the land's history as a cemetery and contacted Athra Kadisha, a Jerusalem-based Orthodox group dedicated to preserving holy places. Though the city and the contractor planned to exhume whatever remains could be located and rebury them at a nearby site that was dedicated as a permanent memorial to the lost Jewish community, the protestors were not satisfied, and groups of Orthodox Jews from France, Belgium, the United States, Austria, Switzerland, and Israel were blocking traffic every day, praying and singing. Most German Jews found the whole situation painful, and even many rabbis, including Hamburg's chief rabbi, disagreed with Athra Kadisha's insistence that Jewish law absolutely forbids the moving of human remains. Athra Kadisha members demanded that the city spend $30 million to purchase the land and restore it as a cemetery, a demand resented by many Hamburg taxpayers, who pointed out that the city had already given the land to the Jewish community who then sold it.

Despite such tensions, Ben and Nathan read surveys conducted in the Jewish communities of Germany that showed that only 10 percent of Jews believed that Gentiles who learned of their Jewishness might discriminate against them; over 70 percent had never experienced any prejudice from their neighbors, and only 1.6 percent indicated they were frequently confronted with prejudice. The survey reported that 62.9 percent of Jews in Germany have a circle of friends including both Jews and Gentiles, 11.7 percent have

a circle of friends that is predominantly Jewish, and 25.3 percent have a predominantly Gentile circle of friends. Furthermore, when asked about the
future of anti-Semitism in Germany, 8.8 percent thought it would disappear,
66.3 percent thought it would stay at the same low level, and 23.9 percent
thought it would intensify, based on recent anti-Semitic incidents.

The Central Council of the Jews in Germany, which speaks for the local
Jewish communities, denounced each new incident of anti-Semitism, but
pointed out that these are only a minor part of the larger picture of rising
xenophobia in Germany and Western Europe in general, a xenophobia aimed
principally against Turks, Romanian Gypsies, and sub-Saharan Africans,
groups with which Jews are sometimes lumped as foreigners. Leaders of the
Central Council viewed the incidents as sporadic and unconnected, and not
as an organized threat. Nathan and Ben reacted to their conversations with
Jewish leaders regarding recent anti-Semitic graffiti and cemetery desecra-
tions by observing that despite the deadly past, for almost fifty years the Jews
in Germany had been safer from bombings, arrests, torture, and imprison-
ment than some Jews in Argentina—and certainly safer from bombings than
Jews in Israel.

On the last day of their trip, Ben was touched, and even awed, when
Nathan informed him that the decision was Ben's to make, that he and Elena
would follow Ben and Sarah in whatever they decided. So now, Ben medi-
tated on the long flight back to Buenos Aires, he had to come to some decision. It seemed strange to him that Sarah, Raquel's family, and Nathan's
family had been open—more open than he, it seemed to him—to such a radical move. He had not been aware of anything missing in their lives in Buenos
Aires. They belonged to a close-knit synagogue community in which most,
but not all, members were of German descent. Ben and his partner, David,
owned and operated an office-supply service in downtown Buenos Aires,
which kept them all comfortable, if not rich. Why were they open to leaving
everyone and everything familiar? And to go to the land of the executioners,
the modern home of genocide? Did this make sense? Shouldn't Jews who
emigrate be heading for Israel? Ben hoped his family's attitudes were not sacrifices offered on his behalf.

He wondered if inherited Jewish cultural attitudes toward exodus and flight,
learned amid long persecution, had influenced them. How many times had he
heard his adoptive mother, Raquel, quote her grandmother on the necessity of
keeping their suitcases packed and near the door? Or was there, in his entire
family, a kinship with Germany based on the fact that German had been the
language of his homes both with his adoptive mother and with Sarah (though
it was a second language, after Spanish, for his grandchildren)? "Are we really
Germans as well as Jews, as Frieda says?" he wondered.

As he and Nathan gathered their things and prepared to meet the family's
questions in the airport Ben realized he did not yet have an answer to their
central question. He decided that he and Sarah needed to make an appointment to see the rabbi within the next few days.

A RECONSTRUCTIONIST JEWISH RESPONSE
by Mitchell Chefitz

Ben, Sarah, and Havurah of South Florida

Ben called me from Buenos Aires. When I heard his first words describing his situation, that he had been rescued out of the Holocaust as an infant, I jumped to an erroneous conclusion. I suspected that he had been born of a Jewish mother but raised as a gentile, or born of a gentile mother and raised as a Jew, and that he was suddenly bogged down in the quagmire of Jewish identity.

According to Orthodox tradition, one who is not born of a Jewish mother is not Jewish even though raised as a Jew, but from a Reform perspective, one who is raised as a Jew is considered Jewish even if not born of a Jewish mother. As a Reconstructionist rabbi, I keep one foot in the rabbinic tradition and one in the Jewish civilization. That is, I consult the tradition for its wisdom, but recognize the validity of the direction of the people. The tradition has a vote, but not a veto. When the people say that something is so, it is so, whether rabbinic tradition agrees or not. When I learned that Ben had been raised as a Jew, I was prepared to reassure him that even if his birth mother was not Jewish, if the community about him accepted him as a Jew, he was a Jew.

Before I could utter my response, he told me his birth mother was Jewish, so that wasn't his concern at all.

"My concern is this," he told me. "Should I follow my birth mother's request and move with my family to Dresden?" He wanted to know what rabbinic tradition might have to say.

I had a question for Ben. Why would he consult a Jewish renewal rabbi in Miami when he had his own rabbi in Buenos Aires? His answer did not surprise me. Ben and Sarah were secular Jews with an investment in the tradition. Although they were members of an Orthodox synagogue, they attended services only on the Holy days or when there was a family celebration. Their primary Jewish affiliation was with the community center where they could swim and play tennis, soccer, and basketball in the company of Jews. They felt very much part of the Jewish people, but their involvement with the religion, while existent, was distant. They chose not to seek the advice of the rabbi of their synagogue because they did not live fully within the Orthodox community. Their desire was to consult the tradition rather than to submit to it.

There are several Jewish organizations that wrestle seriously with the way we relate to God and Jewish texts and the means we use for involving the larger Jewish community in that struggle. The Havurah movement is one such agency. *Havurah* is Hebrew for fellowship and reaches out to Jews in their homes, bringing Jewish tradition to their lifestyle, whatever it might be.

The conventional synagogue draws Jews away from their homes to a central institution that does not as a rule enjoy the flexibility that allows for such risk and change. Havurah of South Florida in Miami is the closest fellowship to Buenos Aires. Ben and Sarah travel to Miami regularly on business. They made an appointment to spend time with me on their next visit to learn how Jewish tradition pertained to their situation.

What Is Jewish Tradition?

Jewish tradition is based on the Torah, the first five books of the Bible, Genesis through Deuteronomy. This is referred to as the written law. Appended to the Torah are the books of the Prophets and the Writings. These three together are referred to as the *TeNaCh*, an acronym for Torah, *Neviim* (Prophets), and *Chituvim* (Writings); Christians refer to this collection as the Old Testament.

Along with the written law there is an oral law. According to tradition, Moses received two bodies of law at Mount Sinai, the Torah and the Mishneh. The Torah contains in total 613 commandments, included among them the ten inscribed on the two tablets. The Mishneh consists of six volumes that outline the practical application of these commandments. The Torah contains not only the commandments, but also the narrative of the covenant between God and the Jewish people, stories of Abraham, Isaac, Jacob, and Moses. There is no such narrative in the Mishneh, only law.

This oral law was committed to writing at the beginning of the third century of this era for fear it would be scattered and lost as Jews spread throughout the world. No sooner was it set down in ink than it became the subject of argument in academies in Babylon and Jerusalem. These arguments continued for nearly three centuries. The shorthand Aramaic notes of the deliberations of the various academies, along with the Mishneh itself, are known as Talmud. The Talmud is encyclopedic in size and scope.

Some thousand years after the Talmud was redacted, a summary of its laws was published: the *Shulhan Aruch*. While other more eloquent codes had been written before, most notably the *Mishneh Torah* of Maimonides, the *Shulhan Aruch* was more politically correct and became the binding code of law for all of Jewry. It continued so until the development of a liberal expression of Judaism in the nineteenth century.

When Ben and Sarah arrived in my study, they did not expect from me any definitive instruction as to what they should do. What they hoped for was that I might make available to them some of the wisdom of the tradition and that this might serve as a marlin spike to insert into and loosen the knot of choices and decisions that was perplexing them.

Why didn't they expect from me a single definitive answer? They were familiar enough with the nature of Jewish thinking to know that there were two sides to most every issue. Consider the matter of the Hamburg cemetery. It had been desecrated by the Nazis, purchased by a developer in 1988, and then put into limbo as the Jewish community found itself immobilized by two conflicting rabbinic traditions. The Athra Kadisha in Jerusalem ruled that the graves could not be moved, but the chief rabbi of Hamburg ruled that they could. Which authority was correct? The astonishing answer is that they are both correct. *Aylu vi-aylu divrai eloheem hayeem*—both these and those are the words of the living God!

Ultimately the Jewish community in Germany will make a decision regarding the cemetery. There may be two correct opinions, but there can be only one course of action, and it is the majority that decides.

The *Shulhan Aruch*, the code of law, is at its essence the majority opinion of the rabbis. Sometimes, because only one course of action is indicated, one forgets that there were multiple expressions of the truth from which the majority opinion was derived.

There is a time-honored procedure for arguing complex issues. The first step is to isolate the variables. Often, when this is done, the whole matter falls apart into elements that are easy to cope with, but jumbled together they seem to defy analysis. Consider our difficulty. Does Ben have an obligation to honor his birth mother by moving to Germany, a nation which, in its recent history, perpetrated the most heinous atrocity upon the Jewish people? Let's isolate the issues:

Does Ben have an obligation to honor his birth mother?

Does one honor a parent by acceding to the parent's wishes in all instances?

If we choose not to keep a Jewish presence in Germany, has Hitler won? (This last question is not asked directly in our text, but it is implied. It was Hitler's intent to eliminate all Jews from Germany. He failed, but do we give him a posthumous victory by refusing to keep a presence there?)

Surely there are other elements, but even isolating the major issues in such a fashion renders the knot pliable.

Does Ben Have an Obligation to Honor His Birth Mother?

"Honor your father and your mother, so as to lengthen your days upon the land which the Lord your God is giving you" (Ex 20:12). This is the fifth commandment of the decalogue. It appears on the first of the two tablets, and we learn the depth of the commandment from its placement.

The second tablet consists of commandments that govern actions between human beings. It might be considered a table of civil rights. Our primary right is to life: "You shall not murder." Next is our right to family: "You shall not commit adultery." Then our right to material things: "You shall not steal." Not only are we enjoined not to violate these commandments directly, we may not do so even indirectly. Therefore, "No false testimony," for by false testimony we can deprive a person of his life, family, or material goods. And beyond that, "Do not covet," do not even obsess over what belongs to another, that it consumes your thoughts and leads you toward violation of any of the above commandments.

The first tablet consists of laws that govern the relationship between human beings and God. First, to acknowledge that there is an active relationship between us and God. It is written, "I am the Lord your God who brought you out of the land of Egypt, the house of bondage." The operative word is *your*, emphasizing a relationship. The essence of the commandment is that you are to have a relationship with *Me*. There shall be no idolatry to intervene in this relationship, nor shall you misuse (take in vain) the name of God. These are the second and third commandments. The fourth is to separate and sanctify a day of the week, a Sabbath, to intensify the relationship.

And then comes the commandment to honor one's father and mother.

Why is this commandment, which appears to speak to relationships between human beings, chiseled into the tablet of relationship between humans and God? There are various responses. We are taught that there are three partners in the formation of a human being: a father, a mother, and God. When one honors a parent, it is as if one were honoring the Holy One.

Also, we learn of relationship to God from relationship to our parents. As our relationship with our parents develops through stages, so does our relationship with the Holy One. Ideally, we learn ultimately to accept God for what God is, rather than what it is that we want God to be.

We learn then that Ben has an obligation to honor his birth mother. He has surely begun to do so. No sooner had he heard of her existence than he sought her out and acknowledged his relationship to her. We can only imagine how she responded when she learned that her son not only had survived the war but had flourished and grown into a family. Ben was not challenging his responsibility to honor his birth mother. He wanted to know the extent of that responsibility.

Does One Honor a Parent by Acceding to the Parent's Wishes in All Instances?

In wrestling with such a question the rabbinic technique is to argue from the extremes. Let's choose something trivial on the one hand and something major on the other. If a parent asked a child to get a glass of water, does the child have an obligation to do so? If a parent asked a child to violate one of the commandments, to murder, for example, or to be sexually licentious or to commit idolatry—all capital offenses, does the child have an obligation to do so? Does our obligation to honor parents have no limits?

The operative word is to *honor*. In Hebrew, *kibud av vi-em*. The Hebrew *kibud* is derived from the word to *weigh*, the implication being to give appropriate weight to the status and wishes of a parent. Tradition teaches that we do not call a parent by his or her first name, but rather always defer to the title which carries the weight of the relationship: Mother, Father. There is honor in these titles. We honor our parents when we receive them graciously in our homes, treat them with respect, attend to their wishes—but this with certain limits.

As individuals we have a primary purpose in this world, and that is the refinement and perfection of our own souls, which is done through study, prayer, and repair of the world around us. This is the intent of the commandments which govern Jewish life. The weight we give to the wishes of a parent is measured over against the weight of our obligation to our own responsibilities in the world.

The rabbis discuss at length in tractate *Kiddushin* of the Talmud how one establishes a balance between these two obligations. Ultimately the understanding is as follows: it is for the child to determine how best to fulfill the commandment to honor parents. The wishes of the parent are attended to, but not at the sacrifice of the child's other responsibilities.

A variety of anecdotal information is provided. We have an instance of a famous rabbi who himself fetched a glass of water at his aged father's request and returned only to find his father sleeping. He stood, holding the water, until his father should wake, lest his father not find him there and think that his son had not acceded to his wishes. What did that rabbi do while he was standing, holding the water? We are told that he considered a difficult problem in the Mishneh and found its solution. This was an instance in which the child was able to fulfill the parent's wish and his own obligation at the same time.

There is a story of a rabbi who honored his mother by making a stepping stone of his body to allow her to climb into bed. Yet another son served his father a banquet of pheasant, but did so with such a foul attitude that it was considered a dishonor. The intent behind the action is as important as the action itself.

We have another instance in which the son found it necessary to remove himself from the excessive and imbalanced demands of a mother. The only way he could fulfill his primary responsibility of refinement of his own soul was to put distance between himself and the demands of his parent.

We learn from these examples that the action alone does not describe honor or dishonor. One could accede to a wish and have it credited as dishonor or decline and have it credited as honor.

All of this I shared with Ben and Sarah. "Only you can determine how best to achieve that balance between your mother's wishes and your own responsibilities. Your mother can express her wishes, but only you can determine the balance."

Did this help him? It put him in the driver's seat. He learned that he was empowered to determine his own course.

In many ways he was fortunate. All too often the question of honoring parents arises when there is friction between a spouse and an in-law. There, by the way, the rabbis tend to side with the spouse. If necessary, separation is made between the couple and the in-law. In this situation Ben and Sarah were wrestling together and likely to be of a single mind.

Another difficulty arises when an aging parent is no longer able to care for himself or herself. There, the rabbis say, the child arranges care according to the best of his ability, but the funds of the parent are used to pay for it. Only when those funds have been exhausted is the child responsible to use his or her own resources.

"So it's for me to decide," Ben said. "I can make the decision to stay in Argentina or move to Germany, and either way I can be honoring my mother."

"If you do so with the proper intent," I agreed. "If you chose to stay in Buenos Aires and told your mother that this is where your work is and the very best place for you to develop your life, that you are sorry that you cannot be physically close to her but will still stay in touch, that would surely be honoring a parent."

"But I don't know if Buenos Aires is the best place for me and my family. What is the rabbinic view of moving back to Germany after the Holocaust?"

If We Choose Not to Keep a Jewish Presence in Germany, Has Hitler Won?

Here we have two paths of argument: one if it is dangerous for a Jew to live in Germany, and the other if the danger is no greater in Germany than in Buenos Aires. Ben's mother seems to anticipate this discussion and raises much evidence to indicate that Jews are as safe in Germany as they might be elsewhere, but let's look first at the ethics of putting oneself into a dangerous situation.

A fundamental rule of Torah is: "You should keep My laws and My statutes so that, when one does them, one might live by them . . ." (Lev 18:5). "Live by them, and not die by them," Maimonides reminds us in his *Mishneh Torah*, the twelfth-century fourteen-volume code of law that summarizes the principles of the *Talmud*. The essence of his teaching on this subject is that we have an obligation to stay out of dangerous situations. Faced with a choice between violating a commandment or saving one's life, we are to save our lives and violate the commandment in virtually all instances. Therefore, if we should determine that it is imperative for Jews to maintain a presence in Germany to assure that "Hitler doesn't win," then, according to Maimonides, even though we have established an imperative, if it is in the face of danger, we should not do it. We are not permitted to put our lives in danger to satisfy a religious obligation.

But we haven't yet determined any such an imperative. What does it mean that Hitler should win? Hitler lost. Germany lost. Germany suffered terribly. What other people other than the Jews might even suggest that Hitler could yet win? Is there any German living in Dresden after the fire bombing inflicted by the Allies who might suggest that Hitler has won?

It is the residue of Hitler that we remember: his desires, his legacy, his intent. We confuse that residue with the anti-Semites who might seek to destroy us today, but they are not Hitler. They are today's anti-Semites, not yesterday's. We confront them in this world, not Hitler's world. Hitler lost. God willing, the current wave of anti-Semites will lose too, long before they can inflict serious damage.

Still the memory of Hitler carries with it some serious baggage. Should this memory still have the power to influence and direct Jewish lives? Is there any wisdom in rabbinic tradition to teach us how to weigh this memory, how to keep it in proper perspective?

We learn by way of analogy, by comparison to a model that resembles it from which we derive some commandments. What applies there can be applied here as well.

The model is of Amalek, a nation that harassed the children of Israel during their march in the desert.

> Remember what Amalek did to you on the road when you came out of Egypt, what happened to you on that road, how he harassed those who were weak at the end of your march, the tired and weary. He had no respect for God. Now when the Lord your God gives you some rest from all of the enemies around you, in the land which the Lord your God is giving you as an inheritance to possess, you are to blot out the memory of Amalek from under heaven; do not forget. (Deut 25:17–19)

We are to blot out the memory of Amalek on the one hand and not to forget on the other! The instruction seems to be contradictory. Maimonides teaches in his code that there are certain wars that are commanded, among them the war against Amalek. We fought that war in Biblical times (1 Sam 15) and won it. Amalek was utterly defeated. That war cannot be fought again. From time to time a tyrant that resembled Amalek arose against the Jewish people, but this was not Amalek. It was a different tyrant that needed to be defeated in a different war.

We learn from this that Amalek was Amalek, and Hitler was Hitler, and each was defeated in his own time. God forbid there may rise up yet another tyrant, but he will be neither Amalek nor Hitler. He will be whoever he is, and be defeated on his own account. The commandment concerning Amalek demands that we first blot out his memory—that he should have no hand that reaches beyond his grave. His grave is sealed. But on the other hand, we are not to forget what we went through, so, should another tyrant arise, we might be quick to defeat him.

We learn from this that Hitler lost. We should blot out his effect, yet remember what he did, so that we should be quick to resist the efforts of any future tyrant.

How does all of this help Ben and Sarah? Ben knew already that he has an obligation to honor his birth mother. He has learned that honor does not mean always acceding to a parent's wishes. His obligation is to find a balance between honor due to a parent and responsibility to oneself, one's family, one's community. He has learned that there is neither obligation to return to Germany, nor any prohibition to keep him away. The decision is in his hands.

I hope the tugging and pulling with rabbinic tradition has loosened the knot. He and Sarah will be able to see the issues more clearly and make an educated and responsible decision.

A PROTESTANT CHRISTIAN RESPONSE
by Ludger Gaillard, trans. David Cotter, O.S.B.

A Home for Ahasver

Will Ahasver return?[1] Will he be able to find peace in Germany, the land where the worst anti-Semitism, the most horrible persecution and the most perfect genocide that the Jewish people ever experienced, took place? Will Ahasver, the ever wandering Jew, unable to find peace, finally settle there where Paul Celan, trying to find words to express the sheer horror, wrote: "Death is a Master from Germany."[2]

What a change! What a turnabout! Jews coming once again to *us*, immigrating *to* Germany. It is no longer just Israel or the United States, but *Germany* which has become a goal of Jewish immigration. Who would have thought it possible, or even hoped, that Ahasver would intentionally settle in the land of the Holocaust, a mere forty years after the monstrous and unprecedented crimes of the Nazis and their numerous "willing executioners."[3] Yet that is the astonishing reality. Jews from the former republics of what was once the Soviet Union are moving in great numbers to Germany, and it seems that in other parts of the world as well, people are seriously considering such a step. Among them is Ben, in Argentina. But he still hesitates, and the decision stills hangs in the balance. Will he come to Germany, the "modern homeland of genocide"? Would he and his family be welcomed by us? Would we, even if not the "Promised Land," be a hospitable and open home for Jewish people desirous of returning, people like Ben and Sarah whose connection to their German heritage was never entirely broken, despite the passage of time and great distance?

I would like to consider the situation from two perspectives: (1) the religious and (2) the societal.

The Religious Perspective

As a Protestant Christian of the postwar generation in Germany, I stand in a tradition which, because of the horror of the Shoa, has made a radical change of course in relation to "God's First Love,"[4] the Jewish people. This radical change is reflected in numerous official statements of the Evangelical Church in Germany issued between 1950 and 1995, in which it is asserted with ever increasing clarity and decisiveness that:

- Morally: Christians and their churches have long been complicit in the fatal tradition of anti-Semitism and in the inconceivable crime of the Holocaust.
- Theologically: God's Election of Israel is for all time.

- Ecclesially: All thought of Christian superiority over against Judaism and any behavior flowing from that, including the mission for the conversion of the Jews, must be ended.
- Practically: There must be further steps toward reparation, dialogue, and reconciliation.

This process of thought and clarification, which has lasted more than forty years among German Protestants, has reached the following conclusions:

- The question of guilt: "We declare that we, because of inaction and silence, stand before the God of Mercy, sharing the guilt of the crime that was committed against the Jews by our people." (Berlin-Weissensee Synod, 1950)
- The question of election: "God has not canceled his Covenant with Israel, nor rejected his People. His election continues." (Hanover Synod, 1995)
- The question of the mission: "Any mission to the Jews, in the sense of proselytism, is rejected. Christian witness can only be the respectful witness of one's entire life to the convictions of another." (Hanover Synod, 1995)
- The question of dialogue: "We have discovered that Israel is not simply a great relic of the past, but that Judaism has remained until our own day a living faith in our common God." (Hanover Synod, 1995)

As far as the official position of the Protestant Church (although generally speaking the Catholic side has been a bit more reserved, there is no practical difference between the two today), Ben and his family would come to a country where Christians are putting aside the horrible and inconceivable Shoa and are trying to open up ways of reconciliation for the future. It goes without saying, therefore, that those returning from Argentina would be welcome! However, we must admit that the realities of daily life may lag far behind the statements of good will found in these synodal documents. Forgiveness, reconciliation, understanding, and dialogue still need to be perfected and concretized in lived experience. However, because of the small size of the Jewish community this is not possible for most Germans and the result is a widespread ignorance—leading to what might seem to be the wholly paradoxical *anti-Semitism without Jews*. But if more Jewish people were to come to Germany, we would be able sooner—we hope!—to discover and to put into practice the conviction that there are many ways to God. On 14 January 1933, just a few days before Hitler's seizure of power, Martin Buber spoke these memorable words: "The gateway to God stands open for all. The Christian need not come through Judaism, nor the Jew through Christianity, in order to come to God."[5]

My hope is that if more Jewish people were to come to Germany to live, there would be a better chance—however late and after indescribable horror—to make Buber's vision a reality. This country might then, reconciled in their difference and mutually respectful, be able to experience that there is a real complementarity among religions, that they offer differing, but complementary, ways to God. In his own day, Buber could only dream that: "Then there would be no more sharp conflict between us and the Church, but something entirely different, which is today still beyond our capacity to express."[6]

More than sixty years later, I see both the necessity and the opportunity to give some shape to this other, which to Buber seemed still inexpressible: going together on the path to God, by separate paths indeed, but with tolerance, respect, and dignity with the same goal before our eyes. Jewish immigration to Germany would change, as indeed Islamic immigration already has, the religious geography of our nation and lessen the traditional monopoly of the Protestant and Catholic churches. But monopolies are never good things! In Germany, we need a genuine concert of religions and world views, and the Jewish voice should have a clear part therein.

In the summer of 1990, a few months after the fall of the Berlin Wall the well-known Catholic theologian J. B. Metz gave an impressive lecture in the Berlin Kongresshalle with the title: "The Church after Auschwitz." It is not possible to express more forcefully why we Christians in Germany need the Jewish people among us than Metz did: "We Christians can never more go back to the time before Auschwitz. However, we can come through Auschwitz if we come, no longer alone, but with the victims of Auschwitz."[7]

Metz makes clear that there can only be a final victory over the barbarism of Nazism in our country if we Christians in Germany can bravely look at ourselves in the mirror, seeing there the nearly unrecognizably sin-besmirched face of our nation, a nation which had seemed at one time so Christian and humanitarian. This is a necessary part of our inheritance, a task which we absolutely cannot refuse, even those of us born after the event. If it is only this look backwards, stripped of all pretense, that will help us to move forward, if it is in remembering what has been secret that salvation may be found (Elie Wiesel)—then what could be better than that ever greater numbers of Jewish people would come to live with us as neighbors and that we try to begin a new chapter of our common, now reconciled, history together. If Jewish people, such as these from Argentina, settled among us, it would be my wish that their presence would contribute to a change in the centuries old, deeply ingrained, patterns of religious life in Germany. Such a presence would provide an alternate theological model to that of the stone monuments in the medieval cathedrals which did, and perhaps for many, still do, influence the hearts of Christians. Again, J. B. Metz: "In the cathedral in Bamberg in which I was ordained, there is a pair of symbolic female figures 'The Church and the Synagogue' . . . and in Bamberg the figure of the synagogue is presented as being blindfolded."[8]

The synagogue, once depicted as blind by Christian power and ignorance, stands witness for all time to a profound recognition, one shared with her by the church, of the God who says: "You are my people." This means that the church, which by its adoption of the Hebrew Bible for its own use applies this declaration of love to itself, must reject both any hint of triumphalism of the past or faddishness in the contemporary religious scene. One who relies on the Hebrew Bible relies on a religion that presents itself in its deepest essence as defenseless and vulnerable, but which has never given in to the temptation to abandon what has all too often been a bitter reality by resorting to myths and ideologies. This is how a strong Jewish voice could contribute to the ongoing interreligious and social conversation in Germany: to act in opposition to the ideological obfuscation which is such a part of the oppositions that arise in society and its inhuman practices, and to work against the way in which modern plutocracy utilizes the trendy and faddish in religion. I desire a self-conscious Judaism in my country that—with Auschwitz behind us—may serve as an incorruptible and sober advocate of a religious and socially aware humanity, precisely because it has never forgotten its own special Election by God. For "Israel's Election, its capacity for God shows itself especially in its inability to take comfort in Myths or Ideas. It remains, as Nelly Sachs once put it, 'a landscape of screams.'"[9]

Jewish immigration to Germany would contribute to a strengthening of a Judaism that connects here with its great liberal and humanistic traditions, a flourishing of the Judaism that was nearly utterly destroyed in the cruelty of the Shoa and has gradually and quietly arisen again, a Judaism that knows itself, is sure of itself, and so is ready to enter into dialogue and conversation. In this way, it could be an anti-fundamentalist, not rigidly orthodox partner in a discussion in the midst of a German society undergoing a radical change, a human presence in the name of Adonai. Ben and his family will be welcome. Martin Buber gives them the reason for confidence in undertaking this difficult step towards Germany: "Nothing can dissuade me from believing that this is the time of the God of Israel."[10]

The Social Perspective

Jewish immigration to Germany touches on something that is a particularly critical part of contemporary Germany society. Both the official policy of the conservative government as well as unenlightened segments of the populace still hold to the mistaken opinion that this is not a land of immigrants. But nothing is less true! Nothing is more ignorant than the denial of the ever renewed waves of immigration through the centuries in Central Europe, especially during the period of Germany's industrialization 100 years ago, but continuing right up to the present day. But Jewish returnees would be differentiated from nearly all other immigrants because the great majority of those others—Poles, Italians, Spaniards, Serbs, Croatians, and Turks—came here, and still come, in search of work. Jews, however, come here as former victims of persecution—as is the case with Ben from Argentina—or quite recent discrimination—as is the case with the astonishing number from the former Soviet Union. Welcoming these people and integrating them into German society is a real act of reparation for the crimes of the Third Reich and is, at the same time, a burden and socially explosive.

After German reunification and the collapse of communism throughout the world Germany found itself in the midst of real upheaval as well as in the midst of worldwide economic turbulence stemming from a deregulated and globalized economy. This endangers in a special way the classical connection between the state and industry which has been so highly developed in Germany. What position would Jewish immigrants take on this current realignment of powers in eastern Germany, specifically Dresden? Most apparent is the possibility that Ben will apply for the restitution of real estate and property based on the problematic principle known as "Restitution as Compensation," set out in the 1990 Treaty of Unification between the two German states. In this way Ben would once again possess his family's factories and apartment houses, insofar as they were identifiable after the bombing campaign of 1944. If he were to succeed in this, there would immediately arise the question: What would become of those who are currently proprietors of these concerns (at least those that were not "People's Property" under the German Democratic Republic (GDR)? What would become of those living in the houses? Would this transfer into new, in this case Jewish, hands not simply increase the appearance that one's rights are not secure, of injustice? Could it be that property and homes which were, under the laws of the GDR, legally acquired and used would suddenly become, because of the political upheaval of 1989, illegal possessions, legally available for acquisition? What protection could Ben offer? What would become of the jobs in the factories, the tenants of the buildings? Would it result in increased unemployment and homelessness, or could Ben offer investments, make jobs more secure, and modernize the buildings?

One of the most difficult adaptations that people in the former GDR have to make in their transition to a Western lifestyle centers on their precarious situation with regard to property rights, the cause of which is, among other things, the principle of Restitution as Compensation. This says that little or none of the property in East Germany actually belongs to the people who are living there but that almost all of it belongs to those who, after the changes in East Germany, have moved there from West Germany or even from foreign countries. This is just as true for the ordinary citizen as it is for businesses.

Would it be helpful, although virtually inevitable because he would be both a foreigner and a Jew, for Ben to worsen this current German conflict? This would probably lead to a further increase both of the resentment directed at foreigners and of anti-Semitism. While no one is attempting to excuse this reaction, it must be understood against the background of an eastern German society which from the Nazi period to the present has been, for more than forty years, isolated, infantilized, and terrorized. Now, after the reunification of Germany, the great majority of these people still find themselves to be second-class citizens and still deprived. Would anyone want Ben and his family to live in this atmosphere? Would anyone want them to remain in the dark about these possible animosities? Might one expect that they would be generous to their potential employees and tenants?

The questions become even more intense when one considers the potential spectrum of Jewish immigration to Germany. There is in fact no single Judaism. So, *which sort* of Jews would come to us, with *which sort* of traditions?

What we desperately need just now in our country is to strengthen those parts of the society that feel a certain duty to building an emancipated society. There are certainly such people among the Jewish people of today, but would they be the ones to come to Germany? I wish there were a Jewish community here, with its commitment to progressive, socialist traditions, that would place those "Zionist virtues" in the service of our contemporary German society, though by no means hastening and furthering a runaway capitalist renaissance in the process. It would be tragic, if Jewish immigration reinforced, or somehow stabilized and perpetuated, the undesirable, ever-widening gap in income and property that has developed and that already endangers the increasingly unstable social consensus in Germany.

Economic creativity and social conscience must be joined anew in Germany. Can Ben help us to do that?

And can he encourage the "other" Germany, those people who even during the time of the Nazi regime acted against anti-Semitism and inhumanity, those many simple, "silent heroes"[11] who often without any recognition helped those who were being defamed or persecuted, even endangering their own lives for the others' sake? *This* tradition, fortunately, still exists in Germany and it would be good to have a visible Jewish counterpart. Ruth Kluger, with her mother and another Jewish girl, were helped by a Protestant pastor who, after their escape from a concentration camp in the winter of 1945, provided them with the papers and identification documents which were necessary in order for them to survive. She writes of him:

> It seemed like a crazy idea but, as it turned out, it was the only right one. The minister, to whom Mother and L.G. made themselves known, was a real Christian, as Christians would say. Jews would say that he was a Tzaddik, a righteous man. That he could have been punished for what he did simply meant nothing to him at all. He wanted only to make up for what had been done. . . . I think very often of this man I do not know, who remains faceless for me, into whose home my mother came covered with snow, and who gave her what we needed to carry on.[12]

Could a Judaism, established and growing in this country, be part of this beautiful German tradition and, precisely as Judaism, help to develop a human culture that understood itself to be bound by the principle of responsibility?

Germany faces many powerful social and ecological challenges at the end of this millennium. A German-Jewish culture, or a Jewish-German culture, could help us, at least according to Christian reckoning, to make a peaceful and life-serving transition to the next millennium. Since April 1, 1998, Greenpeace Germany has had a new leader, Walter Homolka, both a well-known economist and a brilliant rabbi. This bodes well for a future development.

At the end, let me ask again: Do Ben and his family really want to come to us, to Germany, one of the most difficult nations in the world? If so, they are welcome. Could it be, however paradoxical it may seem, that Ahasver will finally find peace here? That is what we desire. Let us give the final word to one of those who survived the Holocaust, the well-known author Ralph Giordano from Cologne, so that he might better define the task that awaits the Jews in this country, so that Ben and his family might better know what awaits them in Germany: "Let us make use of the opportunity which was frittered away after the First World War. We have paid such an awful price to become a democratic republic. Let us make it so that we could never turn back. Let us treasure it, for we have no other!"[13]

Notes

1. A brief review of the symbolic nature of the figure known as Ahasver [the ever wandering Jew] may be found in Hubertus Halbfas, *Religionen der Welt: Judentum* (Düsseldorf: Patmos, 1994) 5–6.

2. Paul Celan, "Todesfuge," *Gesammelte Werke* (collected works) pt. 1, (Frankfurt/M: Suhrkamp, 1983).

3. Daniel Goldhagen, *Hitlers willige Vollstrecker, Der ganz gewöhnliche deutsche und der Holocaust* (Hitler's Willing Executioners: Ordinary Germans and the Holocaust) (Berlin: Siedler, 1996).

4. Friedrich Heer, *Gottes erste Liebe, 2000 Jahre Judentum und Christentum, Genesis des österreichischen Katoliken Adolf Hitler* (München: Esslingen, 1967).

5. Martin Buber, "Zweite Antwort," in ed. Helmut Gollwitzer, Rolf Rendtorff, and N. P. Levinson, *Thema Juden, Christen, Israel: eine Gespräch*, (Stuttgart: Radius-Verlag, 1978), 9.

6. Buber, "Zweite Antwort," 8.

7. Johann Baptist Metz, "Kirche nach Auschwitz" (manuscript) 3 (Berlin, 1990).

8. Metz, "Kirche," 4.

9. Metz, "Kirche," 6.

10. Buber, "Zweite Antwort," 8

11. Eric Silver, *The Book of the Just: The Unsung Heroes Who Rescued Jews from Hitler* (London: George Weidenfeld and Nicolson, 1992).

12. Ruth Kluger, *Weiter Leben: eine Jugend* (Göttingen: Wallstein, 1992), 178.

13. Ralph Giordano, "Wohin, Deutschland, gehst Du?, Gedanken zur Vergangenheit und Gegenwart," in *Der Anfang nach dem Ende, Jüdisches Leben in Deutschland 1945 bis heute*, ed. Günther B. Ginzel (Düsseldorf: Droste, 1996), 300.

Bibliography and Suggested Reading

Arendt, Hannah. *Eichmann in Jerusalem: A Report on the Banality of Evil*. New York: Viking, 1964.

Bölts, R. "Der Rabbi kommt, Ein polyglotter Aufsteiger wird Greenpeace-Chef." *Die Zeit*, no. 14 (26 March 1998).

Buber, Martin. "Zweite Antwort." In Helmut Gollwitzer, Rolf Rendtorff, and N. P. Levinson. *Thema Juden, Christen, Israel: eine Gespräch*. Stuttgart: Radius-Verlag, 1978.

Celan, Paul. "Todesfuge." *Gesammelte Werke* (collected works) Pt. 3. Frankfurt/M: Suhrkamp, 1983.

Christen und Juden II: Zur teologischen Neuorientierung im Verhältnis zum Judentum. Eine Studie der Evangelischen Kirche in Deutschland. Gütersloh: Gütershoher, 1991.

Eisen, Arnold M. *Galut: Modern Jewish Reflections on Homelessness and Homecoming.* Bloomington, IN: Indiana University Press, 1986.

Gay, Ruth. *The Jews of Germany: A Historical Portrait.* New Haven, CT: Yale University Press, 1992.

Giordano, Ralph. "Wohin, Deutschland, gehst Du?, Gedanken zur Vergangenheit und Gegenwart." In *Der Anfang nach dem Ende, Jüdisches Leben in Deutschland 1945 bis heute*, ed. Günther B. Ginzel. Düsseldorf: Droste, 1996.

Goldhagen, Daniel. *Hitlers willige Vollstrecker, Der ganz gewöhnliche deutsche und der Holocaust* (Hitler's Willing Executioners: Ordinary Germans and the Holocaust). Berlin: Siedler, 1996.

Halbfas, Hubertus. *Religionen der Welt: Judentum.* Düsseldorf: Patmos, 1994.

Heer, Friedrich. *Gottes erste Liebe, 2000 Jahre Judentum und Christentum, Genesis des österreichischen Katoliken Adolf Hitler.* München: Esslingen, 1967.

Hertzberg, Arthur. *The French Enlightenment and the Jews.* New York: Columbia University Press, 1968.

Hilberg, Raul. *The Destruction of the European Jews.* Chicago: Quadrangle, 1967.

Holtz, Barry W. *Back to the Sources: Reading the Classic Jewish Texts.* New York: Summit Books, 1984.

Kaplan, Mordecai. *Judaism as a Civilization.* Philadelphia: Jewish Publication Society, 1981.

Kinzer, Stephen. "Cemetery Plans Divide Jews on Religious Law." *The New York Times* (International), 2 May 1992, 4L.

Kirche und Judentum. Beschluß der Landessynode der ev.-luth. Hannover: Landeskirche Hannovers, 1995.

Kurlansky, Mark. *A Chosen Few: The Resurrection of European Jewry.* Reading, MA: Addison-Wesley, 1995.

Lerner, Michael. *Jewish Renewal: A Path to Healing and Transformation.* New York: G. P. Putnam's Sons, 1994.

Metz, Johann Baptist. "Kirche nach Auschwitz." (manuscript) 3. Berlin, 1990.

Neusner, Jacob. *Self-Fulfilling Prophecy: Exile and Return in the History of Judaism.* Boston: Beacon, 1987.

Silbermann, Alfons, and Herbert Sallen. "Jews in Germany Today." *Society* (May–June 1995):53–64.

Silver, Eric. *The Book of the Just: The Unsung Heroes Who Rescued Jews from Hitler.* London: George Weidenfeld and Nicolson, 1992.

Twersky, Isadore. *A Maimonides Reader.* New York: Behrman House, 1972.

CHAPTER 7

A Matter of Veils

A CASE STUDY by Christine E. Gudorf

"It's so good to be back in Normandy," Patricia sighed, as she relaxed in the lawn chair and surveyed the surrounding flower gardens in the last gentle rays of the late June sunset. She sipped on the coffee flavored with Calvados, the local apple liqueur, that her cousin Jacques had handed her. "Visits to my French cousins have been the highlights of our vacations for over a decade now. Your seaside home in Montmartin must be the model for paradise."

Jacques sipped his coffee pensively and remarked, "Well, it is relaxing, and I can assuredly use that after these last few months."

Rochelle, his wife, added, "Thank *le bon Dieu* that the school year has ended, so the protests have, too."

"What protests?" asked Patricia. She knew that Jacques was an economics teacher for the highest level of students in a secondary school in Caen, the capital of lower Normandy. Both before and after he married Rochelle in his late thirties, he had taught in universities in Africa, first in French colonies, and then in independent Morocco. When their sons were to begin school, they had returned to France. Jacques had just yesterday finished grading exams for the students heading off to university in October.

"We are becoming diverse like your country, *cousine*," teased Jacques. "We now have a small Arab population in Caen, and fundamentalism is sweeping through all the Arab communities in Europe, just as it is in the Arab world. The result is that some Arab parents have sent their daughters to school with veiled heads. The school policy does not allow the veils, so the parents keep the girls home. But most are not old enough to quit school legally, so the parents are notified to send the girls to school or go to court and maybe jail. So, of course, the radicals seize the issue and make the schools out to be prejudiced against Arabs."

Patricia, who taught art history at a state university in Indiana, knew from past visits that cultural diversity was as touchy an issue in Europe as race was in the States. She had seen, both in France with her own relatives and in Germany with her husband's relatives, that most Europeans were less racist about skin color than Americans, despite the resurgence of occasional neo-Nazi and skinhead violence, but that the issue of cultural diversity was a minefield.

148

"Why are the veils against school policy?" she asked.

"Because they set off those Arab girls as different and apart, as people who don't accept being French," responded Rochelle, obviously surprised at the question.

"But isn't the wearing of the veil a religious practice, not a nationalistic one?" Patricia queried.

"For these people, their religion is their politics. That is one of the biggest problems. They want to use their religion as a way of controlling people. The government did not care if they wore the veils for religious ceremonies; they just couldn't wear them to school. What would be next? They would want to marry their daughters off at eight or nine. And look at that horrible case in Marseilles, where the woman had her two little girls mutilated in a religious practice and had to be sent to prison!" exclaimed Rochelle with disapproval.

"You mean the female circumcision case? But I thought that that was a non-Muslim African woman, Rochelle," said Patricia.

"But isn't it all the same? Religion should help bring people together in cooperation. When it hurts them, separates them, or makes them hate each other, it should be opposed, no?" reasoned Jacques.

Just then Patricia's husband, Marty, an attorney in Chicago, came outside. "What a nap! I was really exhausted after not being able to sleep on that flight. What have I missed?" he asked as he accepted a coffee laced with Calvados from Rochelle.

"Just a long walk to the shore and back. Now we have been talking about the Arab protests over the refusal of the schools to allow the veiling of girls," offered Jacques. "Our school has been in turmoil for months. Thank goodness the only Arab girls who take economics don't try to wear the veils, so I have never had to expel a student from class."

Patricia sent Marty a look that said "tread carefully." He hesitated a moment and said, "Good. I've wanted to talk with you two about this case ever since I read about it in the *International Herald Tribune* [the American English-language newspaper in Europe] a few weeks ago. It is really strange from an American perspective. In the States, the schools would be forced to allow the veils as a free exercise of religion. Private schools might be able to exclude them, but never a public school. Even if the veils weren't religious custom and protected by the free-exercise clause of the Constitution, the courts would almost certainly decide that public schools could not exclude any type of dress without a compelling reason—such as that it was unsafe, unsanitary, or otherwise hazardous to the welfare of the individual or the group of students. A ban on veils in the States would be interpreted like banning the Indian sari, or the yarmulkes of Jewish men, or the habits of Catholic nuns—as outright prejudice and discrimination. How is it so different here?"

"You Americans are never able to differentiate basic freedoms and radical individualism!" Jacques exclaimed. "Where else in the world is it understood that national schools cannot require uniforms because that would be a violation of student freedom?"

Patricia thoughtfully replied, "You know, that was one of the things that first surprised me when we began travelling in Latin America. Remember, Marty, how we assumed that the kids in uniform were all in private schools and thought there must be a huge network of private schools for the poor because so many of those uniformed kids poured out of the *pueblos jovenes* (young shantytowns ringing the cities)? Were we ever quickly disillusioned by visits to the public schools! And as we travel in Europe, both Eastern and Western Europe, it is true that we see lots of uniforms in public schools, from Spain to Poland."

"You make a very relevant point, Jacques," remarked Marty. " Perhaps it is peculiarly American to believe that kids should have freedom to wear whatever they want. As a parent, I sometimes overruled my sons regarding clothing. And if I were a teacher in the States, I would probably want to demand uniforms, perhaps even in university. Patricia has occasionally come home and told me of young women who come to class in bikini tops, short-shorts, and sandals. I don't know how coherent I would be before a jury dressed like that; I've often told her she's lucky she's a female and not so visually aroused. But isn't there a difference between demanding a basic uniform and denying students the right to add something required by their religion? What about Orthodox Jewish males—are they forbidden to wear yarmulkes in school?"

"I don't know. I don't think there are any Orthodox Jews in Caen, perhaps not in Normandy. Certainly not in the national schools. But I suspect that they would be allowed, and are allowed in other places because yarmulkes are perceived as different from veils," offered Jacques, looking to Rochelle. Rochelle was Jewish by birth, the daughter of a French rabbi who had moved his family from Morocco to Israel in 1965, about the time she married. She was not a practicing Jew, but still kept in touch with her family, though relations were somewhat strained after her marriage to a Catholic.

"But it is very different," insisted Rochelle. "The Jew in France is a Frenchman. We have been here for a thousand years, have been major contributors to the culture of France—to its music, its art, its philosophy, its architecture, its history and economy, as have Jews in other European nations. There is no lack of loyalty to France in the history of French Jews—rather, the issue is one of France's treatment of its Jewish citizens. It is only in the years since the war that it has become clear in France that to be true to its own history and culture, France must embrace its Jewish citizens—and that includes allowing for small distinctions such as the yarmulke, among the most traditional."

There was a silence in the little group for a minute or two, as they realized how quickly the conversation had gotten very heavy. Jacques was the first to stand, slapping his forearm at a mosquito and suggesting that it was time to go inside: "The night and the mosquitoes have arrived together." As they gathered up the cups and saucers, Marty remarked that if they thought these were mosquitoes, he couldn't wait to see what they would think of the mosquitoes in the Minnesota woods surrounding his and Patricia's summer cabin. As they walked into the house the conversation turned to the following year when Jacques and Rochelle were to make their long-anticipated trip to visit the American relatives.

The following day, the two couples drove to the lovely coastal town of Honfleur. After two hours of touring they paused for lunch at a little table under an umbrella on the harbor. As they sat, a family group with all the women dressed in Middle-Eastern robes walked past, and the conversation of the previous day resumed.

"You know, Patricia, we were surprised that you and Marty find it so hard to understand our national attitude toward the issue of veils in school. We spoke of it together last night and wonder if it is not a difference of historical culture. What defines me as a Frenchman is not a matter of believing in French law or a set of rules of behavior. What defines me as a Frenchman is a total history. In that history, it is as important that I live next to the castle of William of Normandy, across from the abbey his wife built to celebrate his victory at Hastings, as it is important that fifteen kilometers from here is the town of St. Lo where my father and my brother were killed in the Allied bombing in the invasion of Normandy in World War II. When Rochelle and I go to concerts we must wrap up in the winter, for our concerts are most often held in abbeys and cathedrals which were built almost a millenium ago. We live surrounded by France's past, its glories and its failures; they are a part of the air we breathe. I am not saying that we should be slaves to the past. Change and development are necessary and inevitable. But we are bound together in the nation by our common past. We do not have this sense that seems to characterize Americans, that they are starting afresh, that they can remake themselves, cut themselves off from the culture, the community, even the family that produced them, and be whatever they want to be or think they ought to be."

Rochelle added, "There are differences among us which we honor. You have seen how proud the Normans are of the Norman heritage—how we love our Calvados, our apple orchards, the thick hedgerows that line our roads, our buckwheat *galettes*, the traditional costumes, the local lace patterns. In Brittany, in Alsace, in Burgundy, in Paris, there are similar distinctions to be proudly preserved. And we Jews have our own specialties that we contribute to the cultural mix that is French. Last year we spoke with you about all the local squabbles occurring within the process of creating the European Union. Remember?"

"Yes, I remember," said Marty. "We were telling you how upset my German cousins were that the German laws on sausage making—especially the exclusion of male hog meat—would no longer be required of sausage marketed anywhere in the European Union [EU], including Germany, and that this would mean the end of real German sausage. And you responded with tales of how many special French cheeses would no longer be distinct because they could be made anywhere, with any milk, in any caves, so long as the basic process was followed. I also remember that Danes were unhappy that their national apple was no longer an apple because it was a centimeter or something short of the diameter specified in the EU's definition of an apple. I think I see the application here."

Rochelle nodded. "Yes, we are members both of France and of local provinces and towns which share in distinct ways in the general culture of France. And all these parts of our identity are important. There is a great deal of pressure on us to abandon local cultural identity—pressure from the European Union, for example, as well as from the contemporary "mass culture" exported from your own country to the rest of the world. We know that holding on to much of local culture will be increasingly difficult because culture in our age is increasingly sustained by the media, especially the electronic media, and that media is national and international, not local."

Jacques added, "But the fact that we are losing much of our local culture only makes it more important that we preserve national culture and identity; this, for us, takes precedence over what you call freedom of religion. We could not justify restrictions on how persons pray or when and where they gather to pray. But religion that divides cannot be protected. In the case of the veiling of Arab, or if you prefer, Muslim, girls, what is offensive is the rejection of French culture. This is the difference between the yarmulke of the Jew and the Muslim veil. The defenders of the veil also defend arranged marriage for young girls; some of them defend female circumcision, even polygamy, not to mention the complete subordination of women to men. They want to use their own language, their own neighborhoods, their own food and culture, as well as their own religion. They do not want to be French—they only want a piece of the French economy."

"This is what I cannot understand," Rochelle explained. "You are so much more the feminist than I, Patricia. How can you defend the veiling of girls that maintains such sex roles? Isn't it clear that this fundamentalism, this Islamicization movement, has as its center preserving the domination of women through polygamy, male-only divorce, harems, and veilings? I hear and read many Muslim women making this criticism."

"I agree, mostly. But I don't think the veil has to be a primary symbol of female subordination," responded Patricia. "Benazir Bhutto, the Prime Minister of Pakistan, wears a veil, as does the woman who is the Prime Minister of Bangladesh. Both of these are powerful, independent women who are trying to carve out new roles for Muslim women, to incorporate as much as possible of Muslim tradition while granting women equal rights and dignity with men both as citizens and in the family. Doesn't banning the veils make it seem to Muslims that France is an all-or-nothing option: give up their religion, language, customs, culture, everything, and accept those of the French, or hold out for preserving everything they brought with them?"

Jacques poured them all another glass of wine and remarked, as if incidentally, "When Erik came back from his first summer with you in the States ten years ago he was different. We liked that he seemed more spontaneous and gayer—he had, unlike our other children, always been a serious one. But we did not like the irreverent sense of freedom he brought back—he stopped greeting us in the morning and kissing us goodnight. He argued with us about everything and rejected our decisions. It seemed to us that he had lost the ability to think about what was best for the family as a whole. And that seemed to us characteristic of American culture; it worries about the rights of the minorities, of individuals, but no one ever thinks about the good of the whole community. I am sorry to sound so critical to guests, especially to relatives, and to such good friends."

Marty interrupted to assure Jacques, "Don't worry. Neither of us is particularly enthralled with the process of communal and cultural breakdown in our country, though we have not seen how to avoid that in defending the rights of minority communities."

Jacques finished, "It is as if you had all long ago concluded that it is not possible to have a unified community, regardless of what issue is under consideration. But to us the question is: How can the minority group or the individual flourish in the long run, if the community in which it is embedded disintegrates? I look at your country and I see an Anglo culture that has fractured just like your Humpty Dumpty. And no one knows how to make him whole again. We may have no choice; that may be our future, too. But we will resist."

AN ISLAMIC RESPONSE by Bahar Davary

The controversy that erupted in France in 1989 over the veiling[1] of female students in school led to the suspension of a number of Muslim girls. The justification of the action taken was that the wearing of the veil is a type of proselytism and thus unacceptable in public schools in France which have been secular since 1905. The *Conseil d'Etat* resolved the problem temporarily by allowing the veil as long as it was not disruptive to other students. The responsibility of judgment was put on each school. In 1994, once again the altercation was sharpened by the Minister of National Education, who instructed French school officials to ban any distinctive religious clothing. Nonetheless, the *Conseil d'Etat* exonerated a number of girls who had been put to trial for wearing the veil in school. Yet, the dilemma remains to be rectified.

In addressing this predicament in the framework of the case study, a number of questions come to mind. They are as follows: What is the significance of the veil? What are its premises and what purpose does it serve? Is the veil a religious matter or an affair of politics? Is it tantamount to fundamentalism or simply in keeping with tradition? Does the veil promote women's oppression and deny their rights within the family and the larger society? If so, is it legitimate to conclude that prohibiting the veiling of Muslim girls in schools is a step taken in the path of women's liberation, or is it denying their individual rights resulting from intolerance and prejudice?

Subsequently, these questions lead to the discussion regarding the value and significance of local, national, and international culture and spark a debate on the controversial issue of tradition versus pluralism. Is the presence of cultural, religious, or racial minorities a threat to endurance of a unified community? Is the communal and cultural breakdown of a country the indispensable result of defending the rights of minorities? Should, therefore, the rights of minorities be denied to ensure the vitality of a unified tradition or can a middle ground be reached? The following essay will address only the first part of this inquiry, namely, the issues that directly relate to the question of the veil in France. The principal element of this investigation is to be found in the meaning and significance of the veil within the Muslim tradition and culture.

The Veil according to the Qur'an and Tradition

According to traditional Islamic belief, the Qur'an, the sacred book of Islam and the primary source of the *shari'a* (Islamic law), commands women to veil. Making reference to particular verses of the Qur'an, the *'ulama* (religious scholars) have constituted an injunction for women to cover their body and their hair in their associations with men to whom they are not related. The two terms *sitr* and *hijab*, translated as "cover," "curtain," or "veil," are often used interchangeably by Muslim jurisprudents to connote the Islamic notion of modest dress. However, the Qur'an uses the word *hijab* only when it speaks of the wives of the Prophet and their distinctive position.

In addressing the case of Muslim women in general, other terms are used. In the Qur'an, Muslim men and women are instructed to "lower their gaze and (to) be modest." Women are further advised not to "display their adornments except for that which is apparent and to draw their *khumur* over their bosoms" (24:30–31). The word *khumur*, which is rarely used in the common language of Muslims, is translated as "the veil." Moreover, chapter thirty-three speaks of an outer garment or a loose flowing dress, a *jilbab*, that women are recommended to "draw close to them" for their safety and protection (33:59–60). According to proponents of the veil, this social function, namely, assuring women's safety, is only one among many benefits of the sanction of the veil.

There are some who suggest an economic factor is a dynamic element in returning to the veil in certain Muslim countries such as Egypt and Algeria. By adopting Islamic modest dress, lower-middle-class women, unable to afford expensive "Western" attire, recover an affordable means to gaining respect and status in society. True as this may be, there is much more to what the veil conveys than the economic factor.

In examining the purpose of the veil as presented by Islamic tradition, the crux of the matter seems to be the perpetuation of sexual attractions within the framework of the family. Thus, the expectation is that the veil should serve as a mode of limiting and safeguarding the association of women with unrelated married or unmarried men and thereby prevent extramarital relationships. It is in this context that the above-mentioned verses, and a few others regarding this issue, have been interpreted throughout centuries, as barriers that render sexual modesty rather than a restraint on active participation of women in society.

Indeed, much of the female Muslim population of the world has embraced the notion and practice of veiling as an essential element of virtue and religiosity. However, there are those who have a considerably different interpretation of the matter. A brief account of this Muslim-feminist perspective will be rendered later in the essay.

The Veil: A Religious Affair or a Matter of Politics?

"For these people their religion is their politics." This statement, often declared in describing Muslims, can hardly be repudiated. That is because, from the point of view of the Qur'an, religion is submission to the will of God, which is the literal meaning of Islam. This submission, if attained, entails all dimensions of human life, including economics, political, social, and spiritual dimensions. Therefore, a person who has submitted herself or himself to the will of God does so in her or his political, economic, social, and personal actions and not only in doctrinal issues. The example of the Prophet of Islam, who was at once the spiritual leader and the political head of the early Muslim community, supports this principle.[2]

Western scholarship emphasizes the inseparability of religion and politics in Islam, making comparisons with the Christian separation of the realm of God and that of Caesar. While this comparison may be theoretically true, it has not always been so in practice. There are instances in which fusion and propinquity of religion and politics is found among both Jews and Christians, as in the case of Zionism in Israel and of liberation theology in Latin America and Asia. Notwithstanding the fact that both of these political ideologies have encountered criticism, it is not often that one hears an objection regarding the merging of religion and politics in those circumstances. However, charges of amalgamation of religion and politics prevail when it comes to Islam. The veil, like all matters in the Muslim world, is politically interpreted.

In order to give a social and political analysis of the case study, we must recapitulate the history of the relationship between Islam and the West. That is because the effects of those events continue to mar the image of Islam in the West and vice versa. Historical evidence indicates that except in some isolated instances, authentic information regarding Islam was not available in the West until the nineteenth century when Muslims were no longer felt to threaten Western Europe. The memory of the Crusades lives on for Muslims as "an early harbinger of the aggression and imperialism of the Christian West,"[3] while Islam continues to be known not as the religion of the sword but of fanaticism and terrorism. The Muslims' notions regarding the hegemonic ambitions of the West were reinforced by the experience of European colonialism, by an era of neocolonialism with the creation of Israel and its subsequent exile of Palestinians, and by the politics of the cold war. For the purposes of this case, the focus will be on interactions between France and its Muslim colonies of North Africa, namely, Algeria, Morocco, and Tunisia.

In the years following 1882 and 1912 France spread its colonial power over Tunisia and Morocco, respectively. Algeria was a different case. In 1830 France not only took over the country but also attempted to demolish Islam and its cultural autonomy. During the 100 years that followed, the French felt free to establish economic, political, and social domination over Algeria and its people. The intense economic conquest and cultural disrespect on the part of the French administration resulted in considerable unemployment and migration, leading to one of the most strained political issues in the past few decades in Europe, namely, the problem of immigration. After World War II, a number of movements emerged whose aims were to resist and to restrict direct French domination. The 1954 movement *Front de Libération Nationale* (FLN) was organized with the goal of restoring an Algerian state while advocating social democracy within an Islamic framework. In the years that followed and before Algeria's formal independence in 1962, 250,000 Muslims lost their lives and many villages were destroyed in their struggle.

These events explain the underlying reason for the observation that "cultural diversity was as touchy an issue in Europe as race was in the States." The resentment and antagonism that existed among those who had been brought to slavery and their slave-masters is similar to that of the colonized and its colonizers. In order to regain their independence and identity, many Algerians turned to their religion. It was in this context that they "regarded Islam and the Muslim family law as sanctuaries from French cultural imperialism."[4] The return to tradition was one way of resisting foreign encroachment. In this circumstance, "the unveiled woman represented a capitulation to the European and his culture"[5]; she was one who had turned her back on her own identity. From this perspective wearing the veil, which is not intrinsically a political act, can become one by its transformation into a public symbol. In other words, the veil was reinforced not only as a religious criterion but also as a symbol of cultural, national, and political identity of Algerian women and men. It was not "a way of controlling people" but a retaliation and resistance towards oppression and restraint. This symbolism of the veil also prevailed among Iranian women at the height of the Iranian revolution of 1978–1979. The immense number of women who participated, despite their different motivations and ideologies, adopted the veil as a means of unity in their protest against the Shah's regime. Thus, the veil is "transformed into a symbol of contention" and "a means for women to assert some control over the ambiguous moral situation created by new economic and social pressures."[6] While for some Islamic dress had "little to do with Islamization . . . it conveyed the social message that a woman could hold a job" and participate in community affairs "without abandoning her roles of wife and mother. Wearing *hijab* showed respect for the boundaries of a well-ordered, moral society."[7] Thus, to repudiate the veil is tantamount to the loss of family values and social mores.

The Veil: Symbol of Fundamentalism or a Voice of Feminism

According to some, fundamentalism is at the root of the sanction and practice of the veil, and therefore, it must be opposed and demolished. While political oppositions have, at times, been conveniently labeled and defeated as being "fundamentalist," those who believe in the wearing of the veil cannot be easily identified with the radicalism or terrorism with which fundamentalism has been equated. The veil is not a symbol of fundamentalism in the political sense of the word or even in the literal sense of the word: adherence to orthodox religious belief. Many Muslim women, especially those of the young generation, are conscientious in their wearing of the veil, though they do not adhere blindly to tradition or to orthodoxy.

In contrast to the idea of abolishing the veil as a means of liberating women, these women perceive the veil as a token and symbol of their freedom and liberation. In this context the modest dress is the dress of one's thoughts, an intellectual dress reflecting a belief system that relates to one's own national identity. Women who wear this dress are not simply following the traditional mores and customs, but rather are saying no to all that negates their social, historical, and cultural values.[8] They have become self-actualized, by refusing to give themselves over to the culture of consumerism. They declare that the attempts of the West to dominate and impose its culture, civilization, and style have been in vain, for they still maintain their own identity and being in both their outer as well as inner selves.[9] In doing so they become liberated from the confinement of the foreign culture. In this context, the family and especially women and their self-definition constitute a cornerstone of cultural identity for the entire community. Women are transformed into a "symbolic embodiment of tradition . . . the ground on which tradition (is) debated and reformulated."[10]

Having realized this fact, the rhetoric of colonialism focused on women's oppression in the colonized societies, thus attaining moral justification for eradicating the culture of colonized people.[11] Consequently, the liberation of women proposed by the West is looked on with suspicion and mistrust on the part of some Muslims. From one Muslim perspective, that liberation movement, which started in the eighteenth century and has been strengthened in the twentieth century, suggests deliverance from family values and virtues. It gives way to exploitation of women in the name of freedom and modernity. Therefore, it is in opposition to the culture of Islam which acclaims motherhood above all other characteristics and capabilities of the feminine state.

Throughout history, the question of women's rights and their role has always been contemplated within the context of various religious, philosophical, and cultural systems. In this regard Islam has not been an exception. Until the eighteenth century, Muslim women were believed to have enjoyed more rights than their European counterparts. Today, many Muslim women are calling for the revising and revisiting of the rights of women in

Islam. Among these women, some have chosen to take up the veil as an option and a way to attaining the honor that Islam has promised them. They do not perceive the veil as part of a system of male dominance and female subordination.

From a different perspective, Muslim feminists argue that veiling and seclusion are ancient Near Eastern customs that have been adopted in the Middle East. Thus, they claim that the veil is an Islamic precept as much as it is a Christian or a Jewish one. According to some, the *shari'a* has established a clear regulation regarding the veil, however, they consider the *shari'a* as a historically conditioned human understanding of Islam. Based on this principle, they propose alternative interpretations with which to address the problem of maintaining the human rights of women in the modern context.

Similarly, some Muslim feminists consider the proclamation of the veil not as a necessary requirement of the Islamic faith but as a later adaptation of the prevalent custom. They argue that as early as first-century Islam, there were traditional Muslim women who did not exercise the veil. According to these feminists, the veil is the symbol of spatial boundaries, boundaries that were not established by God and his Prophet but by the male authority. In this context, the veil refers to a particular spatial dimension and indicates an assigned private space for women, a space that should not be trespassed.[12] Thus, the veil conveys a restriction and confinement and, therefore, should be repudiated.

The existence of these opposing views among Muslim women notwithstanding, they seem to agree that the rights of Muslim girls in France to veil does not deprive the rights of others in the community. The effort to unveil forcefully Muslim girls who have chosen Islamic attire would be akin to the intolerance of those who attempt to mask them by imposing the veil.

Notes

1. Here the word "veil" corresponds to the headscarf and not the *niqab* or the covering of the face.
2. It should be indicated that not all Muslims recognize this inseparability of religion and politics. There are some political leaders throughout the Muslim world who severely oppose the mixing of the two. At the doctrinal level there is the example of the Egyptian 'Ali 'Abd al-Raziq and his controversial book *al-Islam wa usul-al-hukm* (Islam and the roots of government), in which he excludes the Prophet's statesmanship from his prophetic mission.
3. John Esposito, "Islam and Christianity Face to Face," *Commonweal* 24, no. 2 (31 January 1997):12.
4. Valentine M. Moghadam, *Modernizing Women: Gender and Social Change in the Middle East* (Boulder, CO: Lynne Reinner Publishers, 1993), 83.
5. Moghadam, *Modernizing Women*, 83.
6. Dale F. Eickelman and James Piscatori, *Muslim Politics* (Princeton: Princeton University Press, 1996), 90–91.
7. Eickelman, *Muslim Politics*, 91.
8. Laleh Bakhtiar, trans. *Shari'ati on Shari'ati and the Muslim Woman* (Chicago, IL: Abjad Publications, 1996), 45–47.

9. Bakhtiar, *Shari'ati*, 48–49.

10. Farida Shaheed, "Networking for Change: The Role of Women's Groups in Initiating Dialogue on Women's Issues," in *Faith and Freedom: Women's Human Rights in the Middle East*, Mahnaz Afkhami, ed. (New York: Syracuse University Press, 1995), 82.

11. Leila Ahmed, *Women and Gender in Islam* (New Haven, CT: Yale University Press, 1992), 151.

12. Fatima Mernissi, "The Hijab" and "The Prophet and Space" in *The Veil and the Male Elite: A Feminist Interpretation of Women's Rights in Islam*, trans. Mary Jo Lakeland (New York: Addison Wesley, 1991).

A CHRISTIAN RESPONSE by Frances S. Adeney

This case is not a matter of veils but a clash of cultures. In 1989, Muslim girls wearing veils to public schools in France became a catalyst for a confrontation between customs of the French and those of Muslim immigrants.[1] All over the globe, societies are facing the same dilemma: groups of immigrants want to be included in programs of their host society while retaining customs from their particular cultural group. The societies to which they come want to retain traditional customs undisturbed. The ensuing conflicts have been dubbed "culture wars."

Contextual Factors

About three decades ago the French government granted asylum to hundreds of thousands of Algerians who had fought on the French side in Algeria's war of independence. An economic boom at the same time brought an influx of Muslim immigrants from former French colonies in Northern Africa to French provinces.[2] Many settled and became citizens. Along with their labor they brought their religion, customs, and patterns of dress. Although the economic boom has waned, three to five million Muslims now live in France.[3] Efforts have been made on both sides to implement the official policy of integration of these immigrants into French society. However, tensions remain.[4]

The conflict over veils in public schools in France addresses issues and fears that surround the increasingly close contact different racial and religious groups encounter in the world today. Globalization is creating economic structures that cross national lines with multinational corporations, free trade agreements, and a worldwide monetary system regulating money and the flow of goods. In this process, national affairs become subject to international economic forces.

Accompanying these economic factors are communication technologies and travel patterns that carry information and create consumer needs regardless of national or cultural boundaries. Mass culture begins to obliterate local values, styles of dress, attitudes, and patterns of consumption. Local languages are replaced by trade languages or English. Religious traditions find strange new religious groups springing up in their neighborhoods, sometimes proselytizing or demanding local change to accommodate their convictions.

These phenomena have resulted in battles over what language to use in certain settings, in dissension about religious rites, and in debates about multiculturalism. Discussions center around how much cultural unity is required to foster a healthy society and which customs are well-entrenched enough to be considered dominant. Fears of losing cultural identity and loss of ethnic distinctiveness intensify in many nations as numbers of "minorities" grow.[5]

Religious practices have been absent from French public schools since 1905 when the principle of secularity of public schools was established, removing Catholic influence.[6] Even though 71 percent of the Muslims in France support the secular education system,[7] many French people worry about the growth of an avowedly religious group in their midst.[8] Support of an active neutrality towards religion in the schools did not stop Muslims from wearing religious garb, seen by many as a form of proselytizing.[9]

While France has responded to the crisis of multiculturalism with a governmental policy of integration, repeated cultural conflicts show a re-entrenchment of social customs along traditional lines. The tensions around Muslim girls wearing veils to public schools have taken that direction. National authorities passed on jurisdiction to local leaders, many of whom supported the ban.[10] Sometimes minority groups that have shared the national history are included in the circle of tolerance. Other groups may be forced to accept traditional French ways or face ostracization and legal consequences.[11]

Dialogue Participants

The first step in understanding what is going on in the conflict of this case study is listening to the voices in the dialogue. These voices are those of a secondary school teacher from Normandy and his wife, and their American cousins, a university professor and a Chicago lawyer. Muslim voices, those of the students themselves or their religious leaders, are not included. Rather their positions are seen through the eyes of the French and American participants.

How do the French and American voices assess the conflict over veils in the public schools? What are the ethical issues in their estimation? How do they understand the opinions of the third and silent party, the Muslims themselves? What are the implications of the noninclusion of those voices in the dialogue?

Because the conversation partners are French and American non-Muslims, the core of the discussion shifts from the religious meaning of veils and their acceptability in French public schools to questions of nationalism and religious freedom, multiculturalism and minority rights. French and American viewpoints differ on these issues—it is here that the dialogue takes place.

Listening to the Dialogue

Rochelle and Jacques, the French couple, are both well-educated and have lived not only in France but also in French colonies in Africa and in Morocco. Their international experience has not dampened their loyalty to their home culture. They describe a limited and regulated diversity in French provinces—a diversity that does not threaten the stability of French society.

Foreigners staging protests in public schools is another matter. Jacques is relieved that the few Muslim women in his classes do not wear veils, allowing him to teach in peace. He wants to avoid conflict over difference while preserving all that he considers French.

Jacques sees the veil issue as a cover beneath which lie Arab demands for political power. The religious issue is used by fundamentalists to "make the schools out to be prejudiced against Arabs," he claims. Jacques feels that as long as religion fosters peace, it is good. But it must not be allowed to cause dissension or threaten French nationalism.

Rochelle, Jewish by birth, takes the religious agenda of the Muslim protests more seriously. She resists the veil because she links that issue with other Islamic values. She argues that if veils are allowed, soon Muslims will be demanding child marriages and female circumcisions. Unlike the Jews, who have been in France for a thousand years and have contributed to French culture, Arab girls, she claims, don't accept being French. The changes Muslims would institute, in her view, go against French values and must be resisted.

Rochelle draws the circle of who is included in French culture along historical lines. Whoever has been in France long enough to participate in the struggles and events of French life is included. On this basis she argues that the Jewish yarmulke would be tolerated in public schools, as a minor distinction. Muslim veils, by contrast, should not be tolerated. In a sense she is saying that newcomers have no claim to be French and notes that they do not *want* to become French.

Jacques agrees. He believes that the Arabs want to benefit from economic advantages they can receive by living in France while retaining their distinctive cultural ethnic identity. Such ethnic diversity, according to Jacques, results in culture wars that weaken society. In fact, he interprets the conflicts over cultures in the United States as a negative influence that is leading to a disintegration of American society. The French, he declares, will not allow that but will dig in their heels and attempt to preserve their culture.

Major issues for Jacques and Rochelle are the undisturbed continuity of their own cultural values as well as their economic and political advantage. Although Jacques states that he is not afraid of change, both he and Rochelle seem fearful of Arab religious influences upsetting French society, introducing values that run counter to their tradition while gaining economic and political advantage. How do the Americans respond to Jacques and Rochelle's assessment of the dilemma over veils in public schools? At first the conversation is lighthearted. Soon, however, differences emerge. Patricia, a professor at a state university in Indiana, cannot imagine state schools pro-hibiting dress that was required by religious convictions. Any school uni-forms at all seem antithetical to the freedom of expression these Americans espouse. Marty, Patricia's husband, a Chicago attorney, agrees that the free exercise of religion in the United States would protect religious practices of individuals in public institutions. Banning the veil in that context would be considered outright prejudice and discrimination. "How is it so different here?" he queries.

To Patricia and Marty, an emphasis on religious tolerance and equal rights of minority groups are important considerations. In their view religious con-victions cannot be subsumed under national interests. Jacques, on the other hand, sees preserving cultural and national identity as more important than the issue of religious freedom.

A bit further on in the dialogue with their American friends Jacques comes to another point of dissension: Americans, in valuing free speech, foster open conflict and a kind of brashness that are not helpful to society. As a French person, he does not emulate them. Underneath Jacques' emphasis on peace-ful coexistence and conflict avoidance is a different cultural style of com-munication and values that accompany that style. Valuing a more indirect and refined way of interacting may, however, be a stronger way of preserv-ing the status quo because protest and open debate are kept out of public discourse.

Ethical Analysis

A few salient issues are identifiable in this dialogue:

1. Is multiculturalism fracturing the unity of societies? Should it be toler-ated and to what degree? What are the essential elements that make up national identity?
2. Is nationalism more important than religious freedom? How should conflicts between common values and individual rights be ordered? What rights do minorities have to freedom of expression?
3. Underneath these obvious issues lies a deeper issue of inclusion or exclusion. Religions and nations both draw boundaries around their membership. Who should be included in French society? What groups should be able to act as participants, influencing customs and affecting values and practices in society?

Let us look at each of these issues in turn.

Multiculturalism

Some see the increasing cultural diversity of modern Western societal life as a disintegrating trend. Jacques remarks, "I look at your country and I see an Anglo culture that has fractured just like your Humpty Dumpty."

One need not be so pessimistic. While well aware of cultural diversity in the West, Charles Taylor outlines a list of common values that stabilize and unify Western society.[12] Those values of respect, equality, freedom, and benevolence are rooted in Western theistic traditions. New Testament accounts of the early church suggest that ethnic, economic, and cultural diversity was the norm. Respect for all and acceptance of all without partiality was required in the church.

Throughout Christian history, this standard of equal respect has been recalled again and again. Luther decried the practice of paying for pews, which marginalized the poor in the church. Catholic social teaching in this century posited a preferential option for the poor as a standard of Christian practice. Dorothy Day espoused manual labor and intellectual discourse as partners in Christian work among the disadvantaged. Martin Luther King called the United States to accountability to this Christian standard of equal rights for all, which American society had declared as national policy. National identity need not be linked to ethnic or cultural homogeneity. The Christian church, although failing at times to uphold its ideal, celebrates diversity within a larger unity of faith.[13]

Robert N. Bellah, in a recent address at the American Academy of Religion, made the argument that the United States has a cultural core that welcomes diversity.[14] Many of our foremothers and forefathers immigrated to the new world because they were being persecuted for their cultural distinctiveness. Freedom to worship as they saw fit required that sectarian groups allowed those of different convictions to do the same. Consequently, religious freedom and the right to believe and practice the dictates of one's conscience are highly valued in the United States. That central value not only allows for but also creates a society of diversity in which tolerance becomes a virtue.

During the 1950s John Courtney Murray argued that Catholics, while believing that their practices were closest to the truth, could tolerate those of other religious convictions in a situation of religious diversity in the United States. His ideas became incorporated into Vatican II documents under the rubric of "articles of peace."

Tolerance for diversity has grown into celebration of diversity among Christian feminists. Allowing others the freedom to be themselves, to hold the convictions dear to them without attempts to persuade or coerce has become a tenet of feminist theology among thinkers as diverse as Chung Hyun Kyung and M. Shawn Copeland. Because women's theologies arise from their experience, and experience is situated in various societies and histories, diversity becomes part of the discourse about God and human liberation.[15]

Jacques and Rochelle, however, see the public show of religious diversity in the wearing of Muslim veils in schools as an attack on French identity.[16] Charles Taylor notes that subaltern groups demand recognition based on a supposed link between recognition and identity.[17] Feminists and minority groups claim to be oppressed because they are not recognized as equal.[18]

Equality of respect and freedom to practice religious beliefs in visible ways announces the identity of a particular group within society. While Muslims demand this sign of recognition of their identity, French traditionalists are threatened by it.

But Taylor claims that both recognition and identity have changed their focus and meaning in the modern era. Whereas in the past, recognition was based on social status, he claims that today recognition is no longer related to social hierarchy. Instead, dignity and equality are universal values and must be respected. As a result, a universal politics of recognition calls for equal rights and expressions of identity for all groups.

This argument is supported by Christian moral sources that claim equal dignity and respect for all. In his epistles to the Ephesians and Colossians, Paul makes Christ the great equalizer, breaking down walls of partition between Jews and Greeks, and reconciling all in peace through his sacrifice. The "Declaration on Religious Freedom" in the Catholic Church's documents of Vatican II is a contemporary example of this theology.

Using this argument Jacques's definition of French identity related to historical participation in national life becomes obsolete. His demand that Arab customs be modified to fit into French life as it stands harks back to an ideal of social hierarchy in which groups with lower status are barred from participating in certain aspects of social life. Even though the stand of acceptance for Jacques and Rochelle is based on length of time a subculture has participated in French social life, an ethic of equality points out the limitations of this stance.

Here we see a classic battle between local customs and the traditions of subaltern groups. But Jacques doesn't stop at rejecting Taylor's modern idea of who should be recognized. He goes one step farther by turning the argument around. He sees the Arab insistence on veils as a rejection of French culture and a veiled (no pun intended) attack on French identity. While others may feel that France has a responsibility to care for Algerians who supported them in military conflicts in Algeria,[19] Jacques sees the assertive actions of Muslims in France as an act of subversion.

Jacques's American friends take a more modern, less traditional view, espousing the equal recognition that both Taylor and Vatican II claim is the modern alternative to old notions of honor and social hierarchy. To resolve the issue, one must take a stand on the debate about traditional and modern notions of honor, identity, and recognition. A Christian view cannot support a national identity based on ethnic or cultural hierarchies. Insofar as Christians support and influence societies on convictions about equality, respect, and tolerance, cultural diversity could become the norm rather than the exception in contemporary life.

Nationalism vs. Religious Freedom

France allows for diversity through practicing an active neutrality in its secular public institutions. An educational system that minimizes difference and keeps sectarianism out of the schools promotes equal education for all. It follows from this view that religion, while important to individuals and communities, should be kept out of the secular educational system. While ostensibly wanting to include Muslims in French society, a recent poll showed that in the French mind, Islam is linked with religious fanaticism. Bringing religious attire into the secular public schools is seen by many as an untenable compromise with France's secular tradition.[20]

Jacques views religion as something that should support national ideals and foster peace. If it does not, religion should be curtailed by law. He remarks, "We cannot support religion that fosters dissension." For Jacques, girls wearing veils to public schools present a direct attack on the active neutrality of the schools which has for so long fostered the common good.

Patricia and Marty, as Americans, understand the free expression of religious convictions to be a basic right that secular institutions should uphold. Free expression of religion, rather than conflicting with national identity for Americans, actually becomes a part of it. As Robert Bellah remarked, "We have a monolithic culture that is defined in part by respect of religious diversity. And that we owe to the Baptists."[21]

As a result of those differences, Americans are more concerned with protecting the rights of religious groups and individuals, while the French are concerned that the active neutrality of their secular institutions, which has served them well, may be eroded by sectarian groups insisting on bringing religious practices into those institutions. Religious freedom was a hallmark of the creation of national identity in the United States. France, by contrast, struggled against a dominant religion, founding its national identity on a freedom from religious oppression.

This part of the debate may need to be resolved differently in different contexts. What is good for France may not be what is good for the United States. Honoring difference may be what is needed here. Christian warrants can support either stance, depending on the context itself. The American concept of separation between church and state preserves individual liberty, allows for minority expression, and avoids imposition of religion on those of other faiths.

To support this view, some Christians turn to the saying of Jesus, "Render unto Caesar that which is Caesar's and unto God that which is God's" (Mk 12:17). Others reach a similar conclusion for the United States context by arguing from natural law. *Pacem in Terris* states that the Church has a duty to intervene if community leaders stray from those principles.[22]

The Apostle Paul's injunction in Romans 13 to honor the civil powers also supports a division of duties to the political and religious arenas which can be used to support secular public institutions.[23] John Calvin claimed that God ordains and places governments in power. The office itself demands respect and obedience as part of God's overall plan. While respecting secular powers, this view argues for more Christian influence in secular institutions because they are part of God's domain as is every area of human life.[24]

Inclusion or Exclusion

A deeper issue that surfaces again and again in this French-American dialogue concerns the boundaries of inclusion.

H. R. Niebuhr, as a German immigrant and Reformed Protestant, struggled with this issue in the 1920s. While lamenting divisions in the church along ethnic and theological lines,[25] his solution to the dilemma was to draw a larger circle of inclusion. Rather then center human notions of belonging in social or theological attributes, Niebuhr defined faith in God, who is beyond every human or historical representation, as the source for unity.

For Niebuhr, unity in God ultimately overcomes all relative moralities and boundaries of distinction among groups.[26] The community of faith transcends relativistic values and theologies and, ultimately, transcends time itself. "In that community of faith which we trust as loyal to God, loyal to men, loyal to us, there are no distinctions. There is here no Jew nor Greek. There are no B.C. and A.D. companies. . . It is a very catholic church, this community of faith to which we are related in memory and trust."[27] The question of inclusion disappears as the circle widens to include all those linked in faith in the God that transcends even religious boundaries.[28]

While unwilling to follow Niebuhr in that inclusive circle of faith, Miroslav Volf, as an evangelical Christian, proposes the idea of embrace as a theological response to the problem of exclusion. While not all people are within the circle of faith, justice must be sought by releasing all from oppression and embracing the other.[29]

Feminists go farther, celebrating diversity as contemporary women develop postpatriarchal values. Chung Hyun Kyung describes the diverse manifestations of emerging Asian women's theologies.[30] Those views culminate in a call to a life-centrism which eschews violence and values all creatures. Third-world feminist Christian theologians point to Jesus' identification with the suffering of the oppressed as a moral source for inclusion of minorities in the circle of acceptance.[31] Rita Gross, a Buddhist theologian, speaks of the importance of dialogue across cultures in revitalizing Buddhism today, another path to breaking down barriers of exclusion.[32] These women are discovering common values in their struggles and identity as women. In the process, divisions based on ethnicity, religion, or social hierarchy begin to be overcome.

Discussions about *the other* indicate that embracing the strangeness of the other can lead to a more complete sense of unity in oneself or one's group. Hans Georg Gadamer suggests that openness to the other is imperative in expanding one's own horizon of meaning.[33] Zaly D. Gurevitch claims that recognizing one's own inability to understand the other can become a beginning point for dialogue that leads to conflict resolution between opposing groups.[34] Carl Jung insists that unless one embraces the more sinister side of the self, projection of that shadow side onto others results in scapegoating and conflict among groups. To avoid that situation, "the conscious ego takes the trouble to detect the delusive projections and deals with these inside himself instead of outside."[35] These nontheological perspectives contribute to and augment Christian warrants for breaking down walls of division and including the other in the circles of acceptance that we draw.

Jacques and Rochelle see the Arabs as intruders in their tranquil cultural space. The otherness of that group leads them to make moral judgments based not on factual data, but on unstudied interpretation of their beliefs and actions, overgeneralizations, and fear of cultural change. That fear is exhibited in Rochelle's remark that, "For these people, their religion is their politics. . . They want to use their religion as a way of controlling people." Jacques makes a similar judgment: "They do not want to become French—they only want a piece of the economic pie."[36]

The resolution for this part of the conflict lies first in gaining knowledge of the other. Only by listening to Muslim voices can these prejudices and projections be assessed and diffused. The Christian ideal of hearing the voices of all parties concerned in an issue is crucial here. Jesus took time to listen to marginalized voices of children and women and ethnic outcasts. The dialogue between a French couple and an American couple must be augmented by information and opinions from that "other" cultural group, the silenced girls themselves.[37]

Having done that, Christians can use the Apostle Paul's vision for inclusion of those silenced by society. In Ephesians he outlines a vision of unity in Christ that welcomes the stranger, breaks down walls of division, and includes Jews and Gentiles, the two hostile groups of the day, in a peaceful dwelling place for God (Eph 2:11–22). This vision, expressed in various ways, can guide Christians in their assessment of issues of inclusion such as the veiling of Muslim girls in French schools.

Resolution

Actual resolution of the three issues discussed above in the real-life situation of French schools cannot come about merely by exploring Christian perspectives. Resolution can only come about through dialogue that includes Christians, secularists, and Muslims. Perhaps a compromise on the issue of multiculturalism can be reached. Certainly it is a phenomenon that will continue to occur. Jacques and Rochelle as French citizens need to face the reality of the changes taking place in their society and begin to listen to the voices of the Arab minority in their midst. However the issue of veils is resolved, French and Arabs need to learn to make compromises that will allow them to live together in harmony.

The question of religious freedom may come up more frequently as French society includes those with strong religious convictions. Although Jacques and Rochelle may not see religion as a crucial dimension of life, many people living in France today hold religion in very high regard. They will continue to press for religious freedoms and rights of expression.

The inclusion/exclusion debate will continue to rage. Thorough study of the traditions of "foreign" groups can lead to a clearer understanding that could reduce the anxiety of French citizens vis-à-vis Arab participation in public affairs. Arab interaction with French society could include reassurance that Arab minorities are not attempting to take over the French political system.[38] Fear and prejudice could be reduced by bringing Muslim voices into the dialogue about the meaning of veils and their place in the public settings.

As a global economy continues to develop and nations become more pluralistic, issues of this type will continue to demand resolution. Only through openness and education can understanding among diverse peoples build unity in diversity across the globe.

Notes

1. See Howard LaFranchi, "School Girls in Veils Spark Debate," *The Christian Science Monitor* (30 October 1989):6–7. See also "Compromise Eases French Dispute on Muslim Veils in Schools," *The New York Times International*, 3 December 1989 (Associated Press report from Creil, France, 2 December 1989).

2. Milton Viorst, "The Muslims of France," *Foreign Affairs* 75, no. 5 (September/October 1996):78.

3. Statistics vary: The most often quoted figure is three million (*Economist*, 9 February 1991), but numbers run up to four to five million Muslims, about two million of whom are citizens (*Foreign Affairs*, September/October 1996). France does not allow questions about religion to appear on their census data, so figures remain rough.

4. Viorst, "Muslims of France," 79.

5. Allan Bloom's book *The Closing of the American Mind* (New York: Simon and Schuster, 1987) sparked debate on this issue in the United States. Bloom argued that American culture was based in classical Greek roots, grown in European soil, and matured in the challenges of the new frontier. Classical Western education, he argued, was essential to preserving this cultural core and maintaining a unified society.

6. LaFranchi, "School Girls," 6.

7. Janice Valls-Russell, "A Restless Presence: Islam in England and France," *The New Leader* (7–21 August 1989):6.

8. "The 'Affair of the Veil,' as it was immediately dubbed, crystallized the debate on immigration around questions of national identity and revealed a deep French malaise about the Muslim presence in France, represented as a threat to French values" (Rachel A. D. Bloul, "Veiled Objects of (Post)-Colonial Desire: Forbidden Women Disrupt the Republican Fraternal Space," *Australian Journal of Anthropology* 5, no. 1–2 [1994]:113).

9. At the time of the crisis, Interior Minister Charles Pasqua rejected the veil on the basis that is was a mark of difference unacceptable in the secular school setting (LaFranchi, "School Girls"). "It is not enough simply to have Islam in France," he said. "There must now be a French Islam" (Viorst, *Muslims of France*, 81).

10. *The New York Times International*, 3 December 1989.

11. An example might be Muslim leader Larbi Kechat. After arrest and detainment along with twenty-six other Algerians in 1994, Kechat, who has lived in France for twenty-five years, said the arrests were symbolically directed at all the Muslims in France. He called them a "humiliation for our entire community" but insisted that Muslims would not be bullied by it (Viorst, "Muslims of France," 84). There is some debate about whether this and similar instances are motivated by political caution or racist motivations. See "The Islam Within," *The Economist* 318 (9 February 1991):50.

12. Those values include universal human rights, the demand to reduce suffering, and the ideals of freedom, equality, and self-determination. Frances S. Adeney, review of *Sources of the Self: The Making of the Modern Identity*, by Charles Taylor, *Theology Today* 48, no. 2 (July 1991):205.

13. See Romans 3:21–30, 1 Corinthians 12:12f, and Galatians 3:27–29 for the views of the Apostle Paul. Jesus himself was swayed to include those outside Judaism in his acts of mercy. See Mark 7:24–30.

14. Robert N. Bellah, "Is There a Common American Culture?" Plenary Address, American Academy of Religion, San Francisco, 22 November 1997.

15. See Elisabeth Schüssler Fiorenza and M. Shawn Copeland, eds., *Feminist Theology in Different Contexts*, Concilium, 1996/1 (Maryknoll, NY: Orbis Books, 1996). See also Ursula King, ed., *Feminist Theologies from the Third World* (Maryknoll, NY: Orbis Books, 1994).

16. For an interesting feminist appraisal of what the disruption over veils symbolized in terms of French identity, see Rachel A. D. Bloul, "Veiled Objects," 113–23.

17. Amy Gutmann, "Introduction," in Amy Gutmann, ed., *Multiculturalism and "The Politics of Recognition"* (Princeton: Princeton University Press, 1992), 25.

18. George Herbert Mead's notion of the social self, developed by H. Richard Niebuhr and others, would support this notion. How another responds to one's communication is integral to defining the meaning of that communication. Without recognition by others of one's status, that status itself becomes dubious. George Herbert Mead, *Mind, Self and Society* (Chicago: University of Chicago Press, 1934), and H. Richard Niebuhr, *The Responsible Self: An Essay in Christian Moral Philosophy* (San Francisco, Harper and Row, 1963).

19. Both England and Holland have allowed citizens from former colonies to immigrate to their countries. The basis for this is a notion of justice that focuses on fairness. Because Molukkans supported Dutch rule in Indonesia, for example, they were given asylum in Holland when the revolution of 1945 ousted the Dutch.

20. Viorst, "Muslims of France," 80f.

21. Bellah, "Is There a Common American Culture?"

22. Pope John XXIII, *Pacem in Terris*, 160.

23. "Let every person be subject to the governing authorities; for there is no authority except from God, and those authorities that exist have been instituted by God. Therefore whoever resists authority resists what God has appointed, and those who resist will incur judgment" (Rom 13:1f).

24. See *Calvin: Institutes of the Christian Religion*, ed. J. T. McNeill, IV. xx. 22, 23, 32; vol 2:1509–20 (Philadelphia: Westminster Press, 1960).

25. See H. Richard Niebuhr, *The Social Sources of Denominationalism* (New York: Henry Holt, 1929).

26. H. Richard Niebuhr, *Radical Monotheism and Western Culture* (New York: Harper, 1960).

27. H. Richard Niebuhr, *Faith on Earth* (New Haven, CT: Yale University Press, 1989), 113f.

28. Niebuhr argues that idolatry is attributing ultimacy to any notion of nation or of God that is historically bounded. While faith of necessity is linked to history, God is beyond any conception of God. Therefore the circle of inclusion must be drawn very widely. See Niebuhr, *Radical Monotheism*.

29. See Miroslav Volf, *Exclusion and Embrace: A Theological Exploration of Identity, Otherness, and Reconciliation* (Nashville, TN: Abingdon Press, 1996).

30. Chung Hyun Kyung, *Struggle to Be the Sun Again: Introducing Asian Women's Theology* (Maryknoll, NY: Orbis Books, 1990), 96f.

31. For various theologies along this line see King, *Feminist Theology.*

32. Rita Gross, *Feminism and Religion: An Introduction* (New York: Beacon Press, 1995).

33. Hans Georg Gadamer, *Truth and Method* (New York: Seabury Press, 1975).

34. Zaly D. Gurevitch, "The Power of Not Understanding," an unpublished paper based on a study of Jewish/Palestinian dialogue sessions (The University of Jerusalem, 1988).

35. Carl Jung, *Man and His Symbols* (Garden City, NY: Doubleday, 1964), 221.

36. This is an example of what Bloul dubs the "unconscious stakes: the insupportable presence of forbidden 'other' women on the collective French male territory of the republican institutions" (Bloul, "Veiled Objects," 120).

37. A political cartoon in *Le Monde* depicted a gagged Muslim girl held by the shoulders by an older man, presumably her father. An interviewer asks her, "*Êtes-vous pour ou contre le voile à l'école?*" (Are you for or against the veil in school?), 30 November 1989.

38. John Courtney Murray's book, *We Hold These Truths: Catholic Reflections on the American Proposition* (New York: Sheed and Ward, 1960), did that for the Catholic minority in the United States. By taking a nontriumphalist stance in American society, Murray led the way for Catholics to transform their public image from a feared minority to a fully included group in American societal life.

Bibliography and Suggested Reading

Afkhami, Mahnaz, ed. *Faith and Freedom: Women's Human Rights in the Muslim World.* New York: Syracuse University Press, 1995.

Ahmed, Leila. *Women and Gender in Islam.* New Haven, CT: Yale University Press, 1992.

Bakhtiar, Laleh, trans. *Shari'ati on Shari'ati and the Muslim Woman.* Chicago: Abjad Publications, 1996.

Bloom, Allan. *The Closing of the American Mind.* New York: Simon and Schuster, 1987.

Bloul, Rachel A. D. "Veiled Objects of (Post)-Colonial Desire: Forbidden Women Disrupt the Republican Fraternal Space." *Australian Journal of Anthropology* 5, no. 1–2 (1994).

Chung Hyun Kyung. *Struggle to Be the Sun Again: Introducing Asian Women's Theology.* Maryknoll, NY: Orbis Books, 1990.

Eickelman, Dale F., and James Piscatori. *Muslim Politics.* Princeton: Princeton University Press, 1996.

Esposito, John. "Islam and Christianity Face to Face." *Commonweal* 24, no. 2 (31 January 1997).

Gadamer, Hans Georg. *Truth and Method.* New York: Seabury Press, 1975.

Gross, Rita. *Feminism and Religion: An Introduction.* New York: Beacon Press, 1995.

Gutmann, Amy, ed. *Multiculturalism and "The Politics of Recognition."* Princeton: Princeton University Press, 1992.

Jung, Carl. *Man and His Symbols.* Garden City, NY: Doubleday, 1964.

King, Ursula, ed. *Feminist Theologies from the Third World.* Maryknoll, NY: Orbis Books, 1994.

Mead, George Herbert. *Mind, Self and Society.* Chicago: University of Chicago Press, 1934.

Mernissi, Fatima. "The Hijab" and "The Prophet and Space." In *The Veil and the Male Elite: A Feminist Interpretation of Women's Rights in Islam*, trans. Mary Jo Lakeland. New York: Addison Wesley, 1991.

Moghadam, Valentine M. *Modernizing Women: Gender and Social Change in the Middle East*. Boulder, CO: Lynne Reinner Publishers, 1993.

Murray, John Courtney. *We Hold These Truths: Catholic Reflections on the American Proposition*. New York: Sheed and Ward, 1960.

Mutahhari, Murteza. *The Islamic Modest Dress*, trans. Laleh Bakhtiar. Chicago: Abjad Publications, 1989.

Niebuhr, H. Richard. *Faith on Earth*. New Haven, CT: Yale University Press, 1989.

———. *Radical Monotheism and Western Culture*. New York: Harper, 1960.

———. *The Responsible Self: An Essay in Christian Moral Philosophy*. San Francisco, Harper and Row, 1963.

———. *The Social Sources of Denominationalism*. New York: Henry Holt, 1929.

Schüssler Fiorenza, Elisabeth, and M. Shawn Copeland, eds. *Feminist Theology in Different Contexts*. Concilium, 1996/1. Maryknoll, NY: Orbis Books, 1996.

Shaheed, Farida. "Networking for Change: The Role of Women's Groups in Initiating Dialogue on Women's Issues." In *Faith and Freedom: Women's Human Rights in the Middle East*, ed. Mahnaz Afkhami. New York: Syracuse University Press, 1995.

Valls-Russell, Janice. "A Restless Presence: Islam in England and France." *The New Leader* (7–21 August 1989).

Viorst, Milton. "The Muslims of France." *Foreign Affairs* 75, no. 5 (September/ October 1996).

Volf, Miroslav. *Exclusion and Embrace: A Theological Exploration of Identity, Otherness, and Reconciliation*. Nashville, TN: Abingdon Press, 1996.

Walther, Wiebke. *Women in Islam: From Medieval to Modern Times*. Princeton: Markus Wiener Publishers, 1995.

CHAPTER 8

A Bundle of Joy

A CASE STUDY by Regina Wentzel Wolfe

Chen Li-li felt weighed down as she turned off the quiet country road and walked along the path to the house where she and her husband, Liu Shun, lived with his parents and his brother's family. As she approached she heard Mei-Mei, her four-year-old daughter, laugh in childish delight. She stopped for a moment, taking in the scene before her. Mei-Mei was playing with her cousin Liu Fang, who was just learning to walk. The two children were under the large sycamore tree in the small courtyard in front of the house. Mei-Mei would hold out her hands to Liu Fang, who would hold on and be pulled to his feet. A few wobbly steps and the little boy would plop down to the amusement of both children. For a brief moment watching the two at play, Chen Li-li forgot about her awful condition. But as her mother-in-law came around the corner of the house calling out to Liu Fang, her mind exploded with the seriousness of the decision that now faced her.

For a few weeks now, Chen Li-li had suspected that she was again pregnant. The visit that afternoon to the village clinic had confirmed her suspicions. She hoped she would find some way to tell Liu Shun before the others found out. She hoped he would be pleased, even though they had wanted to wait another year or two before having their second child.

As she helped to prepare dinner she remembered how excited she and Liu Shun had been five years ago when she had found out she was pregnant. They shared the news with the family immediately. Her in-laws, Liu Bin and Wang Ping-ping, were excited with the prospect of their first grandchild. Despite the great anticipation, when Mei-Mei was born there was an unspoken sense of disappointment. Everyone had been so certain that Chen Li-li would give birth to a son.

"No matter," Liu Shun had said. "This is not the city, we can have a second child; we can have a son. He will be fortunate to have an older sister to care for him."

Things were fine for a number of years. Mei-Mei was idolized by everyone. Her grandparents spoiled her, as did her auntie and uncle. Despite all the doting on her, or perhaps because of it, she was an undemanding little girl, happy and carefree, with an angelic smile that seemed to bring out the best in people.

"Things changed," thought Chen Li-li to herself, "when Liu Fang was born."

He was the first child of her brother-in-law Liu Guang and his wife Zhang Hong. There was much celebration when Liu Fang was born. Chen Li-li was as delighted as anyone. She was pleased for the new parents and understood the delight that Liu Bin and Wang Ping-ping took in their only grandson.

The attention given to Liu Fang didn't really bother Chen Li-li. After all, she was used to the attention that a number-one son received. In her own family her brother had commanded most of the attention, but she had never felt left out or unwanted. However, she was afraid that things would not be the same for Mei-Mei.

During the last year Chen Li-li had sensed a change in her husband. He seemed to be less involved with Mei-Mei. At first Chen Li-li had attributed it to the stress and strain of working the land. Last year's heavy spring rains followed by an extremely dry summer had been difficult. But as Liu Fang began to grow and she watched Liu Shun spend more and more time playing with his nephew she began to have her doubts. Again and again she found herself thinking, "He is disappointed that he does not have a son like his brother." Now she wondered how he would respond to her news.

As they did most summer evenings Chen Li-li and Liu Shun went to walk by the stream that wove its way through the fields. When they stopped to sit on their favorite log Chen Li-li picked up a small tree branch blown down from a recent summer storm. She began to play with it, putting the end in the stream and letting the water flow through the leaves. She hated to break the peacefulness of the evening, but knew she had to speak.

"Liu Shun," she said softly, "We are going to have another child. I went to the clinic today and the doctor confirmed what I already knew."

He said nothing; he just continued to sit there looking across the stream at the late evening sun beginning to set. Finally, he turned toward her and with his hand gently turned her face toward his.

"I am not unhappy to have another child, Chen Li-li. But I so want to have a son," he said wistfully. "I have always wanted one but never knew how much until Liu Fang was born. Watching him grow these past few months, seeing my brother with him has only strengthened my desire for a son."

"But what if we have another girl?" asked Chen Li-li, not quite sure she wanted to hear the answer.

"I'm not sure," her husband responded. "The government is starting to enforce the law on family size. If it's not a boy, it might be difficult to try again and have another child. If we didn't have to be concerned about the number of children it might not be so important. But even if there were no restrictions, we still have to consider how we will be able to provide for our children."

Chen Li-li had heard this all before. She saw the sense in the policy. There were too many people in China. If the population continued to grow it would be impossible to feed all the people, to educate all of them, and to find jobs

for all of them. Even so, some in the village had chosen to have large families. Others had not. There was often talk about who could afford to pay the
fine for having illegal children, who could afford the money to send them to
school.

Everyone realized it was easier in the country than in the big cities. In the
cities people lost their jobs if it became known that they had more than one
child. In the country, when a couple who had two children had another child
they were fined 500 or 600 yuan, though Chen Li-li knew some people who
were very lucky and were never fined. But the government seemed to be
cracking down again. Recently a family in the village had to pay the fine;
they could afford to pay it. But for her and Liu Shun such a fine would be
almost impossible to pay. And she had heard that Wang Ying, the Women's
Committee member who enforced the birth control policy in the village, was
pressuring people, especially women, to be sterilized in order to prevent any
illegal births.

As they walked back toward the house, Chen Li-li's mind was racing. She
felt as if she were watching some other person in a play. It seemed unreal that
she was facing this problem. When Zhang Hong first found out she was pregnant she had decided to go to Nanjing where the doctors could run tests and
tell her the sex of the child. How happy she and Liu Guang had been when
they found out that their first child would be a boy! There were no problems
to consider, no discussions to have, no decisions to be made. There was only
a name to be found, and that was easy. The boy would be called Liu Fang—
an auspicious name that was the same as that of his great-great-grandfather
who had lived a long life.

Now here she was, pregnant for the second time. Should she follow her
sister-in-law's example? Should she ask for an appointment in Nanjing? But
what would she do if the answer were not the one her husband desired? She
was too confused to think about those questions.

The next morning, after Chen Li-li had dropped Mei-Mei off at the village nursery, she went to visit Chen Maio-maio, her best friend since childhood. The two women sat at a small table that had been moved into a shady
spot under the eaves of the house. Having told her story, Chen Li-li peered
over her teacup at her friend.

"You must talk further with your husband," Chen Maio-maio insisted.
"He has not said he would not accept a second daughter. He has not said
he will not have a third child. Many prefer sons but are quite content with
daughters. You should not trouble yourself so much without knowing his
mind."

By the time Chen Li-li returned home she had calmed herself. "Chen
Maio-maio is right," she thought as she made her way into the garden to
help with the weeding. "I am upset for no reason. I will talk once more with
Liu Shun."

As she approached, her mother-in-law stood and turned toward her.
"Daughter," she said, "I am happy for you and wish you the good fortune
of a son to care for you in your old age."

Chen Li-li was surprised that the older woman knew about the pregnancy, but thanked Wang Ping-ping for her good wishes.

"Liu Shun must be pleased after all," she thought to herself. "Otherwise, he wouldn't have told his mother."

The two women had been working side-by-side for more than an hour pulling weeds, staking the young bean plants, and generally tending to the family garden when they stopped for a rest. They sat together on an old stone bench set along the hedgerow that acted as a windbreak. There was not much relief from the sun, but a slight breeze in the air cooled them.

"Daughter," Wang Ping-ping began, "you know how much Liu Shun desires a son, someone to care for you both in your old age. I hope you will think about his wishes and what they mean for the family? Please talk to him again and let him know you understand. It is very important to him to have a son."

"Mother-in-law, I know how much Liu Shun wants a son. I am his wife; I can tell these things. But here I am, already pregnant. The die has already been cast," Chen Li-li responded.

"Talk with Zhang Hong," Wang Ping-ping encouraged. "Remember, she went for the test. You could do the same. You could be lucky like her and find there is no need to worry."

Chen Li-li did not reply. She slowly stood and returned to the rows of young plants in the garden. She began to understand that Liu Shun had told the family so that he would have others to support him. She got along well with her in-laws. She had known them from childhood. The two families often visited with one another, and she knew early on that she would some-day marry Liu Shun. When that happened she was fully accepted as a daughter in Liu Bin's household. There had never been any serious disagreements. But now she felt abandoned; she felt as if she were an outsider. She did not know what to do. Perhaps in the morning, after she brought Mei-Mei to the nursery, she would be able to visit with her mother.

By the time that Chen Li-li reached her parent's house, which was a mile or so distant from the village, she was very upset. Yao Ling, her mother, had seen her coming and came out to greet her. The smile evaporated from her face when she saw how upset Chen Li-li was.

"What is wrong? Why are you so upset?" Yao Ling asked as she put her arm around Chen Li-li and led her into the front room of the old house.

Sitting beside her mother, the young woman began to speak haltingly.

"I am pregnant. I am going to have another child. But my husband is not happy; no one in the family is happy," she began, her eyes beginning to fill with tears.

"Surely, Wang Ping-ping is pleased," Yao Ling replied, trying to calm her daughter. "She loves children. Why I remember when we were young girls how she used to always stop and play with all the nieces and nephews. All the children called her 'Auntie.' She was much loved by them."

"But it is Liu Shun. He wants to have a son. He says it is good to have a son who can care for us in our old age. They all agree with him. They want me to go to Nanjing and have the test," she said, her voice hardly audible.

Yao Ling felt the shudder go through her daughter's body as the young woman continued to speak.

"It is all because of Zhang Hong and her big city ways. I didn't even know of the test before she married Liu Guang," Chen Li-li said, "but now everyone thinks it is a good idea. They say I can know in only a few weeks whether I will have a son or not."

"And if it is not a son?" Yao Ling asked, hardly believing that she had been able to speak the words.

"No one really says. They are all certain it will be a boy. But I know that if it isn't then they will want me to kill my child," Chen Li-li said and began to sob uncontrollably. When she finally regained control of herself, she continued, "It is all so terrible. I think we should just wait. If it is a son, we will all rejoice. We will have our two children, I can have the operation, and we will not have to be concerned with Wang Ying and the Women's Committee. If it is a girl, then we could try once more for a son. I know Wang Ying will come each month to talk. But I am strong; I am not afraid to listen to her, she will not convince me!"

Chen Li-li paused for a moment before continuing. "Liu Shun says waiting is pointless. He wants me to have the test, but he won't say much more. He is certain it is a son, and says there will be nothing more to be concerned about."

"He must be very upset and confused, too," Yao Ling said taking her daughter's hands and gently holding them in her own. "He is not thinking clearly. You must help him to see that."

"I have tried," Chen Li-li said mournfully. "I told him that if the tests show the baby is not a boy and I kill the child, there is no guarantee that the next time it will be a boy. I cannot keep killing children like that. It may never be a boy. Look at Peng Dan who works at the nursery. She has five daughters!"

"He says that he would not keep insisting on a son, just this once. He says that we cannot afford more than two children. We do not have the money to pay the fine or to educate a third child. So he does not want to take a chance on waiting. Besides, he is afraid that if I have another daughter, I will let Wang Ying convince me to have the operation, and then it will be impossible to have a son. He does not believe that I am strong enough to reject her."

Yao Ling felt helpless. It was not her place to interfere; she could only console Chen Li-li. Later that evening, she related the afternoon's conversation to her husband.

"Chen Li-li understands her situation well. Liu Shun is really asking her to kill the child if it is not a boy. And it appears that his family supports him in that request. If she does not honor his request, she will have to live with the consequences. She will certainly no longer be the honored daughter-in-law, and who knows what effect such a decision will have on the marriage. I would never have believed this could happen to a member of the Liu household.

"On the other hand," Yao Ling continued in her soft yet pained voice, "if she does as Liu Shun requests, she will always have to carry the burden of having destroyed her own child. I don't know what to do, what to tell her. I simply want to hold her and make all the pain and anguish go away."

"There is not much for us to do," Chen Xin replied. "We cannot interfere; it would be inappropriate. But we can make certain that Chen Li-li knows that she is our daughter and that she and her children will always be loved and welcomed in this house."

A CONFUCIAN RESPONSE by Charles B. Jones

On the third day after the birth of a girl the ancients observed three customs: to place the baby below the bed; to give her a potsherd with which to play; and to announce her birth to her ancestors by an offering. Now to lay the baby below the bed plainly indicated that she is lowly and weak, and should regard it as her primary duty to humble herself before others. To give her potsherds with which to play indubitably signified that she should practice labor and consider it her primary duty to be industrious. To announce her birth before her ancestors clearly meant that she ought to esteem as her primary duty the continuation of the observance of worship in the home.[1]

The case study entitled "A Bundle of Joy" is ironically named; it seems that no one in the entire story exhibits happiness at the news of Chen Li-li's pregnancy. The reason for the general unease surrounding the diagnosis of her pregnancy stems from a conflict between state policy and traditional values, and the near-impossibility of adjudicating the conflict to everyone's satisfaction. In this evaluation, we will consider Chen Li-li's case from a Confucian perspective, noting along the way the fundamental differences between the worldview and value system that inform the Confucian ethical critique of the case and the corresponding Western (particularly Christian) worldview and values.

First, we must understand the ethical bind in which Chen Li-li finds herself. She is pregnant and must decide whether or not to accede to family pressure to go to Nanjing and undergo an ultrasound test to determine the sex of the child. Although no one in her husband's family will say so outright, the purpose of the test would be to allow her the opportunity to have an abortion should the fetus turn out to be female. Thus, a decision to have the test done would constitute an implicit agreement to abort, and Chen Li-li feels uneasy about having an abortion for purposes of sex-selection.

While the problem may thus be simply stated, the reasons why the sex of the fetus constitutes a problem at all are complex and require some elucidation. Traditional Chinese family values, which the reader must not facilely confuse with specifically Confucian values, placed a premium on sons. When a woman married in traditional China, she cut off all connections with her natal family and joined her husband's family. Her children became part of her husband's patriline and carried on his family name exclusively, even though, contrary to the Western custom, she did not adopt his family name herself. This meant that daughters did not count as part of her husband's family, as they would eventually marry and join their own husbands' families. We can see this situation reflected in the rules for compiling the family genealogy that the Liu family of Anhui province published in 1870. The decorum of language in this genealogy is as follows:

> those who had daughters only are said to have "no heir," because, although the line has stopped, the family's essence remains. . . Female members who died before they were betrothed are not mentioned in this genealogy, for they did not become wives. For the same reason, women who were betrothed to members of our lineage yet died before the marriage ceremony could take place are not listed in our family genealogy.[2]

In addition, sons, and their wives, bore the responsibility for caring for parents in their old age and maintaining the offerings to them as ancestors after their passing.

Under this system, daughters were unprofitable investments. When a family had daughters, they bore the financial responsibility for feeding and educating them, and frequently, they had to pay for ruinously expensive weddings to marry them off, after which they got no further return from them as mature adults in terms of financial contribution, emotional support, domestic labor, or worship and offerings. This gave rise to the maxims, "Daughters are goods on which one loses" and "Many sons, much happiness."

This did *not* mean, however, that families uniformly despised daughters. Throughout most of Chinese history, when traditional social arrangements encouraged the ideal of many children, parents could be content with a good mix. A didactic poem of the Tang dynasty (618–907), entitled "A Woman's Hundred Years," which delineates an idealized course of life, depicts the woman at forty as "mistress of a prosperous house" with "three sons and five daughters."[3] A satirical play entitled "The Shrew," which dates either from the Southern Song (1127–1278) or Yuan (1206–1341) dynasty, contains a blessing pronounced over a marriage that wishes for the bride and groom:

> May they be merry as fish in water
> and their union prove sweeter than honey
> Blessed with five sons and two daughters
> A complete family of seven children.[4]

Thus, while the exact numbers may vary, the ideal family always comprised both sons and daughters.

However, in 1979, under the shadow of a population explosion that threatened to overwhelm the social structure, the central government of mainland China instituted a strict one-child-per-family statute, with severe penalties for violation. As the case study notes, the authorities in rural areas often look the other way when a family has two children, but can become very harsh when they have three. In addition, the financial burden of raising children has increased to levels no longer affordable, motivating families to limit themselves to no more than two children, another factor that appears in the case study. Thus, the family of seven or eight children idealized in previous eras is no longer a possibility. This means that, while rural Chinese still strive for a mix, noting in interviews that their desire is to have one son and one daughter,[5] the desire for at least one son is still intense, only now the number of chances a family has for producing a son has decreased to two.

This has led to a number of social phenomena as families plan their reproductive strategies. Susan Greenhalgh and Li Jiali report that in many areas the traditional belief that holds the mother responsible for the sex of the child persists, and women have been subjected to verbal and even physical abuse by angry husbands and in-laws after the birth of a daughter.[6] A repentant husband, in a letter to the editor published in the journal *Zhongguo Fun (Chinese Woman)* in 1982, said, "Because I . . . did not understand basic biological facts, I believed it was my wife's fault that she gave birth to a daughter. I cursed her and beat her, and I even proposed divorce."[7] In our case study, although Chen Li-li does not fear actual abuse of this sort, she does anticipate a sharp decline in her status within the family or some other form of reprisal if she fails to produce a son.

Thus motivated, many women, especially those who already have a daughter and thus only one more chance to bear a son, have submitted to ultrasound tests to determine the fetus's gender in spite of a 1993 law forbidding the administration of the test for this purpose. As a result of the information gained from these tests, many female fetuses have been aborted, neglected, or even abandoned after birth, with the result that the ratio of male-to-female births reported in some rural areas is as high as 125 males to 100 females, a staggering imbalance.[8] The outlines of the problem should now be clear: Chen Li-li is pregnant, and she and her husband already have a daughter, so have only one last chance to produce a son under current legal and economic conditions. Consequently, her husband and his family are applying pressure on her to have an ultrasound test so that if the fetus is a girl, she can abort and they can try again. The only other option any of them can see is to accept the baby even if it is a girl, and risk running afoul of the authorities later by having a third child. One other possibility that, according to the case study, they appear not to consider is that of hiding the pregnancy and birth from the authorities and putting the baby up for adoption.[9]

Before we begin a specifically Confucian critique of this situation, we must note that the classic texts of Confucianism, like the Bible, say nothing explicit

about the issue of abortion. In addition, Confucianism lacks any unified cler-
ical tradition or teaching lineage with the authority to pronounce on the
issue. Because of this, our remarks on this case must be extrapolations from
what the tradition *does* say. With that understanding, let us first look at
aspects of the Western debate on abortion that do *not* have a place in Chen
Li-li's decision-making process.

A recent survey of the issues and the terms around which the American
debate revolves includes two major considerations: the nature of personhood, which bears on deciding whether abortion means killing a person and
on whether the fetus has "rights," and the rights and interests of women and
the state. In adjudicating the first, Ted Peters, the author of the survey, strives
to find a point in fetal development before which a person is not present, but
after which a person exists. With regard to the second, in considering the
question of rights, the author considers only three agents: the mother, the
fetus (after it attains personhood), and the state.[10]

From a Confucian perspective, neither of these considerations has any relevance to the process of moral decision making. Confucianism defines personhood in a vastly different way than does the West, and it allows other
people with whom the mother shares a relationship a stake in the decision
that the West seems not to recognize. Because of these differences, the question that Chen Li-li must settle—whether or not to have the ultrasound test
done and possibly expose herself to pressure to have an abortion—will be
resolved using a different process of moral reasoning under a different conception of what is at stake.

Let us turn first to the issue of personhood. As we read the case study, we
see that Chen Li-li is in no doubt that the unborn child is a person. Both she
and her mother refer to abortion as "killing the child." However, from the
Confucian perspective, this does not imply that the fetus is a full person. In
fact, even Chen Li-li herself would not be considered a full person, although
if she successfully negotiates this difficult situation, she will advance closer
to this goal.

Within Confucian thought, personhood is not a static category that one
either fits or does not fit. Whereas Peters's book seeks to find the point, be it
conception, the "primitive streak," or birth, at which the child becomes a
full person, in Confucian thought, one works over a lifetime to become more
and more fully human. Confucius himself first expressed this idea in an autobiographical poem that appears in his *Analects* (2:4).

> At fifteen I set my heart upon learning.
> At thirty, I had planted my feet firm upon the ground.
> At forty, I no longer suffered from perplexities.
> At fifty, I knew what were the biddings of Heaven.
> At sixty, I heard them with docile ear.
> At seventy, I could follow the dictates of my own heart;
>   for what I desired no longer overstepped the boundaries of right.[11]

Although neither this nor any other passage in Confucius explicitly raises the issue of personhood, it did set the overall vision of Confucianism as one of continuous effort that always approximates more closely, but never reaches, the goal of full moral development.

Mencius, who lived about two centuries after Confucius, did talk quite directly about human nature and what it means to be human. He saw moral development as grounded in human nature, which included the "four beginnings" or "four sprouts": (1) our natural tendencies to feel compassion, (2) our sense of shame, (3) our natural deference to our parents, and (4) our preferences for one thing over another. If properly cultivated and neither neglected nor forced, these four seedlings would grow into the fully mature moral virtues of benevolence, righteousness, propriety, and wisdom. Not only that, but failure to cultivate these virtues destroys that which makes one human at all. The person who has eradicated these tendencies has lost all claim to be human; he or she is little more than an animal.[12]

The subsequent Confucian tradition has maintained the view that personhood involves a lifelong transformation, and is never simply assumed or given. Following Mencius, it also affirms that the mechanism for cultivating one's full humanity lies in repeated application of moral reasoning and repeated right-doing. The virtues that make one a true person, in other words, come about when one consistently follows the right. In this light, one may not ask whether either Chen Li-li or her unborn child enjoy the status of "personhood." Rather, one can only say that both are on the way towards personhood and are either nearer to or farther from the goal.

In addition to demonstrating that the issue of determining the humanity or personhood of the fetus lacks coherence within a Confucian worldview, we can also see what is at stake for Chen Li-li herself in the very process of making the decision. Her own advance towards full humanity depends on how she walks the road set before her. If she negotiates the situation reflectively, with constant self-scrutiny, and finds an appropriate solution, she will have strengthened her own moral character and thus have come closer to achieving the goal. The right decision, in short, will make her more fully human; the wrong decision will cause her to backslide.

The other main factor in Chen Li-li's situation is the network of relationships within which she must make her decision, and to what extent others should or should not influence her final decision. As noted above, in America the issue concerns only the fetus (once it attains personhood), the mother, and the state. The "pro-choice" position in American abortion politics seeks to make the decision of whether or not to abort a pregnancy the woman's alone, to the extent that, in many localities, pregnant minors may seek an abortion without the knowledge or permission of their own parents or the father of the fetus. Tyrene White, a Western scholar, has criticized the Chinese government's imposition of the one-child policy from this pro-choice perspective: "Women's sovereignty over their own bodies is muted, while elite struggle over the direction of socialist transformation and development looms large."[13] The United States Supreme Court, in the *Roe v. Wade* decision of

1973, cast the whole issue as one of privacy rather than human rights, and on this basis declared that the state had no compelling interest in interfering with the woman's decision.

The Confucian tradition would find such a moral procedure appalling. Confucianism has never concerned itself in the slightest with the rights of the individual or permitted a person to make moral decisions without reference to the feelings or opinions of those to whom he or she stands in relationship. As the eminent Confucian scholar Tu Wei-ming has pointed out, privatization of the self is selfishness and is the antithesis and enemy of Confucian self-cultivation. The moral growth of the self manifests itself precisely in a growing concern for familial, social, and national well being.[14]

All Confucian values are social values and are based on five fundamental human relationships, each of which is marked by a particular kind of virtue, as outlined in *Mencius* (3A:3):

> The Sage Emperor (Shun) worried about it and he appointed Hsieh to be minister of education and teach people human relations, that between father and son, there should be affection; between ruler and minister, there should be righteousness; between husband and wife, there should be attention to their separate functions; between old and young, there should be a proper order; and between friends there should be faithfulness.[15]

The reader should notice that all but one of these relationships are hierarchical, implying that one has authority over the other. In the case of husbands and wives, the husband has clear authority over the wife, who should follow his directives.

In fact, if she does not, then the Confucian tradition would hesitate to call her a wife at all. One of the first proposals Confucius put forward for the governing of the state was the "rectification of names," a program of reforming language so that words would correspond to the realities to which they pointed. In the *Analects* 6:23, Confucius scoffs at the idea of using the Chinese word that means "cornered vessel" to refer to a vessel without corners. Although this may seem a frivolous point, it becomes quite serious when applied to people who occupy a role that carries a certain name but who do not discharge the obligations connected with that role. A wife who does not act like a wife, then, is not a "bad wife" or a "disobedient wife"; she is not a wife at all. From the Confucian perspective, then, Chen Li-li is right to worry about the loss of her place in the family if she fails to produce a son.

Nevertheless, she does have a personal conscience; if she were in complete agreement with her husband's family, there would be no problem. She does not want to have the ultrasound test because, if the fetus turns out to be female, she does not want to "kill her child." What does the Confucian tradition have to say when someone subordinate to another has an honest difference of conscience and finds that he or she cannot simply obey? Here are some relevant passages, the first from another Confucian text, the *Classic of Filial Piety*. Although it refers to fathers and sons, we may substitute "husband" and "wife" in the relevant places and not be far off the mark:

> Tseng Tzu spoke: ". . . Dare I ask if a son, by obeying all of his father's commands, can be called filial?" The Master answered: "What kind of talk is this? . . . If a father had one son to reason with him, he would not be engulfed in moral wrong. Thus, in case of contemplated moral wrong, a son must never fail to warn his father against it."[16]

This passage makes clear that, even in a subordinate position, one must not fail to remonstrate with one's superior when one's conscience dictates, and so Confucianism would clearly see Chen Li-li as well within the bounds of propriety in making her objections known to her husband.

But what would happen should the husband stand his ground and demand that she go through with the test and possibly have an abortion? Confucius makes clear the course to take in the *Analects*: "The Master said, in serving his father and mother a man may gently remonstrate with them. But if he sees that he has failed to change their opinion, he should resume an attitude of deference and not thwart them; [he] may feel discouraged, but not resentful" (4:18).[17]

Again:

> The Duke of She addressed [Confucius] saying, In my country there was a man called "Upright Kung." His father appropriated a sheep, and Kung bore witness against him. [Confucius] said, In my country the upright men are of quite another sort. A father will screen his son, and a son his father—which incidentally does involve a sort of uprightness. (13:18)[18]

Extrapolating from the prescriptions of these texts, we may assume that the proper course for Chen Li-li is to assume the correct attitude of a wife, which means to be willing to discuss her own convictions with her husband, but then be willing to abide by his decision. For her to assert a "sovereignty over her own body" or to maintain that the fetus is a "person" with a "right" to life—in other words, to assert either a pro-choice or a pro-life position—would be meaningless.

To summarize, the Confucian would say that Chen Li-li is, first of all, in a difficult position because an unrighteous central government has put her there by imposing a limit on childbearing that makes having a son in the first two pregnancies imperative. Given this situation, she must then make a moral decision that takes into account her relationships with her husband and his family. She is perfectly free to make her own views clear to them, and to let them know what her own conscience dictates, but under no circumstance is she to assert a right to make the decision on her own or follow any other "selfish" course of action. If she follows the proper moral course in both the process of decision making and in the outcome, she will nourish her own inherent virtues and thus take another step towards full humanity. If she does not, then she will fall back from the goal and become less human herself. Thus, the Confucian sees every aspect of the problem as a "dangerous opportunity" for further growth in social virtue and full humanity or for degradation to the less-than-human.

Notes

1. Pan Chiao (48–112 CE), "Lessons for Women," in *Chinese Religion: An Anthology of Sources*, ed. Deborah Sommer (New York: Oxford University Press, 1995), 108.

2. Patricia Buckley Ebrey, ed., *Chinese Civilization and Society: A Sourcebook* (New York: Free Press, 1981), 239.

3. Ebrey, *Chinese*, 56.

4. Ebrey, *Chinese*, 87.

5. Susan Greenhalgh and Li Jiali, "Engendering Reproductive Policy and Practice in Peasant China: For a Feminist Demography of Reproduction," *Signs: Journal of Women in Culture and Society* 20, no. 3 (1995):514.

6. Greenhalgh and Li, "Engendering," 609–10.

7. Quoted in Emily Honig and Gail Hershatter, *Personal Voices: Chinese Women in the 1980s* (Stanford, CA: Stanford University Press, 1988), 204.

8. Greenhalgh and Li, "Engendering," 601. On page 627 they mention that the rate has been known to climb as high as 153:100 during periods when the government cracked down hardest on violations of the policy.

9. For this option, see Greenhalgh and Li, "Engendering," 630–32.

10. Ted Peters, *For the Love of Children: Genetic Technology and the Future of the Family* (Louisville, KY: Westminster John Knox Press, 1996), 90–118.

11. *The Analects of Confucius*, trans. Arthur Waley (New York: Vintage Books, 1938), 88.

12. See, for example, Mencius's parable of Ox Mountain in the *Mencius* 6A:8. The man here who has uprooted all of his sprouts of virtue through repeated wrongdoing "becomes not much different from the beast."

13. Tyrene White, "The Origins of China's Birth Planning Policy," in *Engendering China: Women, Culture, and the State*, ed. Christina K. Gilmartin et al., Harvard Contemporary China Series, 10 (Cambridge, MA: Harvard University Press, 1994), 251.

14. Tu Wei-ming, *Confucian Thought: Selfhood as Creative Transformation* (New York: State University of New York Press, 1985), 75.

15. *Mencius* 3A:3, translated in *A Source Book in Chinese Philosophy*, trans. Chan Wing-tsit (Princeton: Princeton University Press, 1963), 70.

16. *The Hsiao Ching*, trans. Mary Lelia Makra (New York: St. John's University Press, 1961), 33. In the original Chinese, the word translated here as "reason with him" is actually closer in meaning to "strive" or "struggle" with him.

17. *Analects*, 105.

18. *Analects*, 175–76.

A CHRISTIAN RESPONSE by Frances S. Adeney

"A Bundle of Joy" describes one woman's dilemma in a common situation in China today. Along with India, Pakistan, and South Korea, nations that together make up 40 percent of the world's population, China grapples with population control in a context of a cultural preference for boys.[1]

Contextual Factors

In China, the dilemma presented for families is influenced by four major factors:

1. Economic factors: Sons are needed to support aging parents. Because there is a large social and economic gap between the sexes, daughters are not as able to do this.[2] In rural areas, sons are also needed to work on the farms. Throughout the 1970s the Chinese government made sustained efforts to bring China's burgeoning population under control. In 1979 when China's baby boomers began to reach adulthood, a strict one child policy was instituted by the government.[3] By the early 1980s, that policy severely affected the rural family economy and policies in rural areas were relaxed in the mid 1980s.[4] However, birth quotas are still in effect, and both individual taxes and group sanctions are imposed with the birth of a second child.[5]

2. Social factors: When young women marry, they leave their family and attach themselves to the family of their spouse. The relationship with one's in-laws and husband's siblings becomes very important because the young woman lives the rest of her life in the household of her husband's family. A commonly expressed attitude is that one raises boys for one's own family, but girls for someone else's family. As in many Asian societies, one's sense of identity is strongly influenced by family relations. If a daughter-in-law does not produce a son, criticism and ostracization often result.

3. Political factors: The authority of the state to control lives of individuals is much greater in China than it is in the United States. Decades of self-examination in neighborhood groups during Mao's rule regulated personal lives through peer pressure. Strictly enforced laws prohibiting religious gatherings, controlling travel, and regulating career choices and farming practices fostered a submissive attitude toward the state among Chinese citizens.

   People in China today have grown accustomed to state regulation of birth control and birth quotas.[6] Since the early 1970s sustained government attempts to limit family size to one child in urban areas and two, or at the most three, in rural areas effectively reduced China's population growth.[7] Enforcement is carried out locally, centered in the workplace. Groups of workers are subject to punishment for individual behavior. If a woman goes over her birth quota, others suffer. Community censure, abortion or infanticide, and enforced sterilization may be imposed on those who do not conform.[8]

4. Cultural factors: Traditional religion requires Chinese families to bear sons to offer worship to the ancestors in household shrines, an important part of everyday life in China. Confucianism, a life philosophy prevalent in China, applauds large families. "Among the three vices that violate the principle of filial piety, the biggest is to be without offspring," Confucius said. "The Chinese turned this negative warning into a positive maxim, 'More children, more virtues.'"[9] Many children are seen as a blessing and a source of happiness and wealth. Sons, however, are valued more highly. In discussing an almost universal preference for male offspring, Alison Dundes Renteln reports that "In China there is a saying, 'Even a deformed son is better than the brightest, most skilled girl.'"[10]

These factors in recent years have led to a high birth rate of males due to selected abortion of females and a high rate of female infant mortality.[11]

Conflicting Values

Because of these factors, the one-child policy presents burdens and value conflicts to women and their families. Patriotic duty to control population conflicts with traditional values of large family size. The older generation's expectation that a daughter-in-law produce a son conflicts with a mother's desire to bring to birth the life that is growing within her. A husband's duty to bear a son for parents and posterity conflicts with a wife's responsibility to care for a daughter. Peer pressure and sanctions imposed on the community conflict with parental longings to have more children.

Chen Li-li's case must be considered in this context of conflicting values. Without population control, China could not sustain its population and many would die of famine. Without state regulation and peer pressure, women would have more than one child. Without selective abortion, traditional cultural forms of ancestor worship would disappear and the economic situation of aging parents would worsen. There are no automatic solutions or easy answers in this situation. Chen Li-li's struggle is real.

Cross-Cultural Assessment of Values

The easiest and most common response to this issue is to make an assessment on the basis of one's own cultural values. As a westerner, human rights issues come immediately to mind. Protection of human dignity and freedom to pursue a good life are basic human rights. State controls of private affairs such as birth control and family size seem invasive to one brought up with democratic freedoms. Our society has known little of the ravages of mass famine, making it difficult to appreciate government intervention for population control. Christian understandings of the value and dignity of each life predisposes many to reject abortion as a solution. Selective abortion of female fetuses seems unjust. An emphasis on human rights, free choice, and minimal state involvement in private affairs characterizes the views of middle-class United States citizens. These values are dearly held and are understood to be universally applicable.

The first task in assessing Chen Li-li's situation is to lay aside those values briefly and attempt to listen to her speak in her own voice—to appreciate her situation as she sees it. Beginning the interpretive task of understanding that which is strange requires one to become open to the voice of the other.[12] By accepting that one's own view is limited by context and perspective, one opens oneself to the task of cross-cultural understanding.[13] Only after careful and respectful listening can an ethical assessment that has credibility to cross cultural lines be attempted.

However, believing that there *can be* an evaluation that has validity across cultural lines is crucial for Christian ethics. There are various ways of arguing for that possibility, such as a creation theology of moral anthropology used in the Catholic tradition or an "inner light" view of the Holy Spirit as understood by Quakers.

Another way to understand the possibility of values that transcend the particularities of history and culture is by conceiving values themselves to be oriented around a Center of Value that transcends culture. H. Richard Niebuhr describes values as relational. That is, they arise not from individuals or from principles but in the interactions between and among people. Values cohere in the way persons or groups *respond toward* one another. Moreover, Niebuhr argues that all human values orient themselves around God, the Center of Value.[14]

Along with listening with openness, a faith in the possibility of congruence among differing cultural values because they are somehow oriented around a common Center of Value provides one with resources for discerning goods in common and standards around which different cultural groups can organize those goods. Various perspectives on values differ among Christians. But those differences are part of a dialogue within a shared faith. That dialogue results in finding universal elements within relative moralities and the particularities of different historical and cultural situations.

The same thing can be said for dialogue across cultures. As we listen to Chen Li-li, our various religious traditions inform both our listening and our assessment of her dilemma. Niebuhr sees all values as relational and penultimate. Through dialogue, we can augment and correct our own values by relating to those in other situations with both parties orienting their longings for the good around a Center of Value. Christians define that center as God. But dialogue between people and oriented toward understanding values in the broadest possible way results in a triadic relationship about values among two parties and the third Center of Value. Niebuhr's stance affirms the faith-based or confessional nature of ethics. Ethical reflection is a way of believing both that the good can occur and that it is somehow organized around a larger Center that goes beyond any human or cultural apprehension of the good. For this reason, Niebuhr's ethics of response was never complete. It was constantly revised and revisable, an exercise in living dialogue about value.

Listening to Chen Li-li

It becomes immediately apparent that Chen Li-li is troubled. She is worried about her pregnancy and her husband's obvious desire for a son. She is concerned that he has begun to favor his nephew over their own four-year-old daughter. She worries that the suggestion of doing a laboratory test to determine the sex of the fetus may result in pressure for her to abort if she has conceived a girl.[15]

Her distress leads Chen Li-li to seek communication with her husband and counsel from her parents and a friend. She understands herself and her life in a web of family and community relationships.[16] She considers not only her own anguish about the possibility that she may be pressured to "kill my child" but the impact of her actions on others in her family and work situation. She thinks about social pressures that will be brought to bear on her if she goes through with testing for sex determination of the baby. She reflects on the implications for her family and coworkers of having a second girl. She thinks about the economic hardships of a possible third pregnancy to attempt to bear a son. She considers her relationships with her husband, her mother-in-law, and the extended family that she has become part of through marriage. Chen Li-li desperately wants a resolution to family tension surrounding her pregnancy. Yet she longs to bring her pregnancy to term and bear a healthy child.

As she reflects on her dilemma, Chen Li-li gains an appreciation for the views of others in her relational world. She empathizes with her husband Liu Shun's desire for a son. She remembers his disappointment when their daughter Mei Mei was born: a firstborn son is most to be desired. She muses on his change in attitude toward their daughter and wonders if he still feels disappointed that he did not have a son while his brother did. Her conversation with Liu Shun confirms these suspicions. He speaks as well of government enforcement of family size and the difficulties of providing economically for more than two children.

After speaking with her mother-in-law, Chen Li-li sees that Liu Shun is rallying the family in support of testing so that they can be sure that Chen Li-li's second child is a boy. She knows that there will also be pressure from Wang Ying, the Women's Committee member who enforces birth control policy in the village. There would be fines to pay and pressure to be sterilized after her second child was born. Chen Li-li had said to her mother-in-law, "The die has been cast." This strong statement indicates her determination to go through with the pregnancy no matter what. Yet, as Chen Li-li sees the forces arrayed against her, she feels abandoned.

She confides in a friend who counsels further discussion with Liu Shun, counting on his good will to accept another daughter. But Chen Li-li goes next to her mother where her feelings of anguish about the situation burst out. She now becomes clearer about the seriousness of the situation and begins to formulate a plan of action. At first she thought that she was over-reacting. Now she realizes that the implications of getting the test are no less than facing family and social pressure to have an abortion if the fetus is not male.[17] She decides to attempt to delay having the test. She reasons that if it is a boy, all will be well. She can be sterilized and still have her two children. If it is a girl she is willing to face the disapproval of the Women's Committee and try once more for a son. She seeks and receives the support of her own parents in the event that ostracization from her husband's family results from her convictions and actions.

It seems that Chen Li-li has already decided to attempt to bring her baby to term, honoring the life within her. At the same time, she attends to her relationships with husband and family and works out a plan for having a son if it is possible within three pregnancies. She is willing to face financial hardship and loss of respect in her husband's family in order to have her baby.

The dilemma is not resolved, but Chen Li-li's course of action is set. Given the factors of the situation, there is no way to satisfy the conflicting claims placed on Chen Li-li and Liu Shun. They cannot satisfy the one-child policy without giving up their dream of having a son. They cannot assure themselves of a comfortable old age if they do not have a son. They cannot change the traditional value that a son holds or his place in performing rituals of ancestor worship and carrying on the family name. Furthermore, Chen Li-li cannot independently fulfill the course of action she has determined for herself. If she avoids the testing she may still lose her baby at birth through infanticide.[18] She may still be forced to be sterilized if a live baby girl is born and is not killed.

Chen Li-li realizes that she is not an independent agent. Her web of relationships supports her but at the same time exerts control over her behavior. She does all in her power to support those relationships. Nonetheless, she makes a choice, prioritizing the goods she must choose among. She is aware that damaged relationships and personal hardship may result from her choice. She realizes that personal moral strength is required to carry out her course of action to attempt to bring this baby to birth. She is convinced that she has that strength. One can only hope for Chen Li-li that she will succeed.

Ethical Analysis

Having listened to Chen Li-li's own voice in the situation, we see that she faces two major ethical issues. The first is the issue of *life*. Both she and her parents see abortion as morally equal to infanticide, as "killing a baby."[19] Given the strength of that conviction, one must applaud her willingness to accept dire economic and social consequences in attempting to preserve that life. Although others in China may not see abortion as a moral issue in the same way, it is clear that in this case, abortion is anathema to the one most responsible for bringing that life into the world—the mother.[20]

In the Christian tradition, there are three major theological warrants for valuing and preserving the life of the unborn. First, each person is *created in God's image*, designed and destined to be a unique human being. Questions about early versus late abortion, the viability of the fetus, and similar issues are hotly debated because the value of each individual life is assumed because it is the handiwork of God. A second reason for valuing the unborn is that each individual is valued by virtue of *being in relation to God*. God not only creates but also loves and remembers every individual, thereby bestowing on each value and inherent worth. Theological arguments for the *eternal nature* of the soul and the possibility or assurance of salvation and eternal life with God present a third set of warrants for caring for the unborn.

A Christian feminist perspective builds on these warrants, affirming Chen Li-li's deep sense of reverence for life. Theological assertions that each person is loved by God and created in God's image bring me to the same conclusion that Chen Li-li reached: each life, male or female, is precious and should be preserved if at all possible. The deep feelings of people in many societies concerning the tragedy of abortion and infanticide point to a universal value of preserving life and protecting the innocent and weak.

A Christian feminist analysis, however, brings the mother into the circle of value as a unique person deserving honor and care. Not only the unborn but also the embodied self of the mother is valuable as created, eternal, and loved by God. This widened circle of value presents immediate conflicts as the well-being of the mother may conflict with bringing a new life into the world. In this case, Chen Li-li's life and needs must also be taken into consideration in deciding whether or not to agree to allowing a pregnancy to be terminated. The possible consequences facing Chen Li-li are extremely serious—to be ostracized by the family of in-laws with whom she must live would be difficult; to be sent away, disastrous. Chen Li-li considered these potential effects, ensuring that her own parents would receive her back and care for her and her child in the event that her husband's family rejected her. If her own parents were unable to do that, Chen Li-li's refusal to cooperate with her in-laws' demands might have placed her own life in jeopardy.

How best to insure human flourishing, a goal of Christian ethics, may not be so clear in this case. The situation becomes ambiguous; trade offs may be necessary. A Christian feminist analysis addresses the ambivalence of the situation, realizing that the good of the mother is as important as the good of the unborn child. Chen Li-li's awareness of her situation and the strategic moves she makes to insure both her welfare and the welfare of her unborn child are exemplary. She considers carefully what consequences she may incur if she has this baby. She considers relations at her workplace, the impact of her decision on others, how she would deal with rejection, poverty, and the burden of more children. None of these factors are determinative, but all are important in deciding the least damaging way to proceed.

Christian feminist ethics considers this conflict of goods because of its strong emphasis on the worth and freedom of women. In this view, it is right for women to love themselves and choose paths that lead to their own flourishing. Traditional Christian theologies of self-sacrifice have dominated women's lives, leading them to choose against their own welfare in order to support the welfare of others. This imbalance may be redressed by calling on Christian women to love themselves and honor their own needs. Creating this new balance enhances women's ability to choose wisely, sacrificing when appropriate while retaining their own sense of value. This approach does give leeway for women to choose to end a pregnancy, although it is never demanded by feminist Christian ethics. How to balance self-love and love for others becomes an appropriate part of deliberations in dilemmas fraught with ambivalence and conflicting goods.

That leads us to the second and related issue of *coercion*. The Chinese government, in enforcing its one-family, one-child policy has used extreme measures to insure lowered birth rates. These include punishments for factory workers if they do not meet their birth quota as a group.[21] One person having an extra baby influences the welfare of all. In Chen Li-li's case, a Women's Committee enforces the one-child policy, taking measures as extreme as forced abortions and sterilization. Chen Li-li's responsibility to her community and their welfare is not absent from her mind. Yet, the more dominant concern, the higher value in her view, is the preservation of life.

Under what circumstances, if any, is it ethically responsible to force a woman to abort a fetus? Is it right for the state to impose such action on families and individual women? International questioning of governmental policies that lead to forced abortions and sterilizations are the responsibility of a world community that attempts to develop humanitarian practices and foster the common good. In assessing China's policies, ethicists and demographers alike have indicated that current policies may not be the best path to population control due to problems in rural areas and sex-ratio imbalances.[22]

General Issues

How should the international community respond? While Chen Li-li grapples mainly with her responsibilities to her community, her family, and her own deep convictions about life, a number of other issues are important in the general assessment of abortion policies in China. Should education redirect traditional value for male children to egalitarian notions of gender equality? Should sex-selection techniques be used to identify female fetuses when the known result is so often abortion? Is the one-child policy leading to a potentially harmful imbalance in the population as fewer girls are born and survive infancy? Can more education and effective birth control lessen the number of women that face the abortion or death of their infants?

The question of sex-ratio imbalances as well as the injustice of selective abortion of female fetuses need to be addressed. The world population is being adversely affected by sex-selective abortion. Yet population control is

an absolute necessity in China and other countries to insure that food short-
ages and widespread famine are averted. Women with Chen Li-li's deep convictions about the potential lives they are responsible for should not have to
stand alone. Yet, imposing a Western standard of free individual choice for
women ignores the complexity of an issue that has personal, communal, and
societal impact.

While Christian feminists deplore patriarchal conditions that so severely
limit a woman's freedom, we must take cognizance of the population issue
and the question of the value of traditional ways of life in Chinese society.
We need to be aware that work for change that would give women more control over their own lives subverts traditional Chinese cultural traditions. With
that awareness, a shift in values that honors women's choices and values the
lives of female children may be advocated for the sake of a higher goal of
gender equality and an end to oppression of women. In fostering those
changes, extreme care must be taken to honor the modes of transformation
arising from Chinese women and men in their own context. The path to
achieving gender equality and ending oppression of females, born and
unborn in China, can only arise from the Chinese community in dialogue
with international human rights and religious voices.

In the broad scheme of things, one can see the wisdom of population control in countries such as China. However, there may be more humanized
ways to achieve that goal.[23] Effective, nonhealth-threatening birth control
techniques such as use of condoms could be increased. Differences in family
size according to occupation, economic status, and moral convictions could
be instituted. Education about gender equality and the wisdom of delayed
childbearing could be effective in reducing both abortions of female fetuses
and lack of self-determination on the part of parents in designing their family life. In the year 2000 China is scheduled to lift its population control policy.[24] These alternatives could be part of a new millennium that values
responsible and healthy family planning, gender equality, and freedom of
choice in Chinese society.

Practical Reason in a Postmodern Context

Implementing changes on an international scale requires ethical approaches
that go beyond convictions of a particular religious tradition. Understanding
similarities among Christian and philosophical approaches to ethics can foster a meaningful dialogue about common values in the world today.

Chen Li-li makes her choices using a relational mode of ethical reasoning.[25]
She sees her decisions and choices in the context of caring for relationships.
She considers her husband's views, the needs of his extended family, and the
quality of life for her daughter and other children she may bear. As she practices an ethic of care, she communicates with those she loves, constantly seeking mutual understanding. She faces up to the possible consequences of going
along with the family's wish to test or abort and then having a girl. Realizing
that her husband could send her back to her own family, she speaks to her

mother and secures her parents' support. An ethic that cares for relationships may not succeed in preserving those relationships. As much as she tries, Chen Li-li must be prepared for retribution if she persists in what may be perceived as an independent and foolish course of action. Chen Li-li's approach is consistent with the ethic of care purported by Carol Gilligan.[26] Rather than focus on principles of justice or human rights, Chen Li-li makes her decisions in connection with others.

This approach is consistent with a Christian approach to working out ethics in the community of the church. The Apostle Paul's letters to the early church show a similar care for understanding and cooperation in the community. In 1 Corinthians 12–14 he likens the community to a body in which each part fits together in harmony with the others. He goes on to enumerate various gifts, comprising roles that must of necessity be carried out in the community. The working of the whole body proceeds most harmoniously, however, if persons have love toward one another.

At the same time, Chen Li-li demonstrates the communicative action that Jürgen Habermas puts forward as a type of reason that can balance the procedural reason that governs so much of modern life.[27] She seeks mutual understanding, she counts on the truthfulness and right intentions of others, she acts by speaking truth as she understands it. Chen Li-li's approach is relevant, productive, and modest. Rather than claim the higher ground of a moral universal stance, she works within her context, seeking understanding without letting go of her own deep convictions.

This emphasis too is consistent with the narrative approach to ethics put forward in many biblical texts. For example, personal integrity vindicates Job in his struggle against evil. Truth, rightness, and sincerity are the linchpins in his dialogue with God and others. He seeks knowledge from God and mutual understanding with his friends. He puts reason to work in seeking understanding. Ultimately, Job confesses his inability to understand his oppression but never lets go of his deep conviction that he belongs to God. It is here that he differs from Habermas for whom reason alone is the ultimate court of appeal.

With a postmodern realization of the limited situatedness of all ethical convictions, Zygmunt Bauman suggests another approach to ethics that seems to be operating here. He claims that the security of universal values upheld by reason or extrinsic authority disappears in the postmodern context. Without the ability of reason to legislate morality and without a socially underwritten moral code, individual conscience comes to the fore. Ethics can now be reconstructed in a productive way, on the basis of situatedness and personal convictions.[28] Christian ethics makes a similar appeal to conscience, that inner sense of right and wrong that calls us to action.

Chen Li-li, living in a society that has undergone a kind of postmodern deconstruction with the demise of Maoism, presents an example of just such a reconstructed postmodern ethic. Although utilizing communicative rationality in her relational approach to her dilemma, she seems to make her moral assessments precognitively, appealing to no extrinsic authority or moral code, but speaking from the inner convictions of conscience.[29]

We see that Christian warrants and theologies of the good, as well as how ethical decisions are processed, are reflected in both Chen Li-li's deliberations and other approaches to ethics. Limiting oneself to one simple rubric, be it human rights, reason, feminism, or a particular religious tradition, hampers dialogue and prevents us from understanding the complexities of ethical dilemmas and the rich resources available to understand them. In reaching across cultural barriers, diverse points of view can enable us to find common values and approaches that make greater understanding possible.

Notes

1. Anna Maria Gillis quoting statistics of Marcus Feldman in "Sex Selection and Demographics," *BioScience* 45, no. 6 (June 1995):384.

2. Susan Greenhalgh and John Bongaarts, "Fertility Policy in China: Future Options," *Science* 235, no. 4793 (6 March 1987):1169–70.

3. Virginia C. Li et al., "Characteristics of Women Having Abortion in China," *Social Science and Medicine* 31, no. 4 (1990):445–46.

4. "Under the present policy one child is advocated for all couples, but rural couples with 'real difficulties' *(a euphemism for one child families without a son)* are allowed to have two children, as long as they do so in a planned way" (emphasis mine) (Greenhalgh and Bongaarts, "Fertility," 1168).

5. "If you give birth to a second child, you will be fined *and* the rewards of all of your colleagues will be deducted" (Qui Ren-Zong, Wang Chun-Zhi, and Gu Yuan, "Can Late Abortion be Ethically Justified?" *The Journal of Medicine and Philosophy* 14, no. 3 [June 1989]:346).

6. "The product of both the *'wan, xi, shao'* and one-child family campaigns is a family planning effort that touches upon virtually all aspects of a couple's social, economic and personal lives. . . The strictness with which these policies were enforced reached a zenith in late 1982 and early 1983, during which circulars called for mandatory IUD insertions for women with one child; sterilization for couples with two or more children; and abortions for unauthorized pregnancies" (Susan Greenhalgh, "Shifts in China's Population Policy 1984–1986: Views from the Central, Provincial, and Local Levels," *Popular Development Review* 12 (1986):492–515, quoted in Li et al., "Characteristics," 446).

7. "As a result fertility fell from 5.4 to 2.7 in the years between 1971 and 1979." (D. L. Poston, "Patterns of Contraceptive Use in China," *Studies in Family Planning* 17 [1986]:217–27, quoted in Li et al., "Characteristics," 446).

8. "Couples had an increased incentive to avoid a higher-order female birth after 1980 because of the one-child policy introduced in 1979: this policy was administered at the local level to induce couples to avoid having a second (and especially a third or higher-order) birth. Apparently the tradition of infanticide was restored somewhat" (Ansley J. Coale and Judith Banister, "Five Decades of Missing Females in China," *Demography* 31, no. 3 [August 1994]:475). See also Steven Mosher, *A Mother's Ordeal: One Woman's Fight Against China's One-Child Policy* (New York: Harcourt Brace, 1994).

9. Qui, Wang, and Gu, "Late Abortion," 345.

10. Alison Dundes Renteln, "Sex Selection and Reproductive Freedom," *Women's Studies International Forum* 15, no. 3 (1992):407.

11. "'In rural areas ratios can be 130 or 140 to 100,' says Tuljapurkar. 'There's no biological reason for it.' In *Science*, the researchers say, 'This imbalance of the sexes implies many millions of "missing" females. Some of these are unreported births, but a substantial number are missing because of high early female mortality or selective abortion'" (Gillis, "Sex Selection and Demographics," 384).

12. Hans Georg Gadamer describes an interpretive path to knowledge that he considers ontological. The process begins with approaching the foreign "text" with openness, then learning from it, and finally integrating it with one's own views in a "fusion of horizons" (Hans Georg Gadamer, *Truth and Method* [New York: Seabury Press, 1975]).

13. Charles Taylor asserts that meaning is always "for a subject, of something, and in a field" (Charles Taylor, *Philosophical Papers II* [Cambridge, England: Cambridge University Press, 1985], 32–33).

14. This assessment contains my own appraisal and application of Niebuhr's ethics. See H. Richard Niebuhr, *The Responsible Self: An Essay in Christian Moral Philosophy* (San Francisco: Harper and Row, 1963), and J. S. Bixier, R. L. Calhoun, and H. R. Niebuhr, eds., "Value Theory and Theology," *The Nature of Religious Experience: Essays in Honor of Clyde Macintosh* (New York: Harper and Brothers Publishers, 1937), 106.

15. "In the literature on sex selection it appears that most of the preconception techniques that are being developed are designed to guarantee male offspring. The same pattern can be discerned in the use of post conception measures, namely selective abortion" (Renteln, "Sex Selection and Reproductive Freedom," 409). Renteln also reports that "It is undeniable that the determination of fetal sex has led to the abortion of essentially only females" (Renteln, "Sex Selection and Reproductive Freedom," 410). This statement is followed by a list of eleven studies documenting that finding.

16. Shripad Tuljapurkar notes: "In China, like other traditional societies, identity comes from being part of a family." Quoted in Gillis, "Sex Selection and Demographics," 384.

17. Although she does not mention it, Chen Li-li may fear that even if she avoids abortion her child will be killed if she delivers a female baby. "In China, according to Stephen Mosher, director of the Asian Studies Center at California's Claremont Institute, as late as 1980, village midwives were often instructed to 'draw a bucket of water when a woman went into labor. If the newborn had the misfortune to be a girl, she was plunged into the bucket before she had a chance to draw her first breath'" (Jo McGowan, "Little Girls Dying: An Ancient and Thriving Practice," *Commonweal* 118, no. 14 (9 August 1991):481). Renteln also notes, "The one child per family policy resulted in a resurgence of female infanticide, as thousands of parents killed their female children because they wanted the one child to be a boy" (Renteln, "Sex Selection and Reproductive Freedom," 411).

18. Hospital techniques used by doctors in late abortions, infanticide, and sterilization are described in Trish Saywell, "Abortions for the Masses," a review of *A Mother's Ordeal* by Steven Mosher, *Far Eastern Economic Review* 157, no. 23 (9 June 1994):54.

19. Contradictory evaluations of Chinese attitudes toward abortion are found in the literature. Lee Yueh-Ting et al. report that ". . . it appears that a majority of people in the PRC consider it morally right or at least acceptable to have an abortion" (Lee Yueh-Ting et al., "Cross-Cultural Research on Euthanasia and Abortion," *Journal of Social Issues* 52, no. 2 [1996]:143). To support this claim Lee quotes H.

T. Engelhardt, "Bioethics in the People's Republic of China," R. M. Veatch, ed., *Cross-cultural Perspectives in Medical Ethics: Readings* (Boston: Jones and Bartlett Publishers, 1989), 112–119. "Abortion appears to be accepted without problem as the second procedure of choice for the control of unwanted pregnancies. Fetuses are not considered to be persons, either before the law, or as objects of revolutionary humanitarian concern" (Engelhardt, quoted in Veatch, "Cross-Cultural Perspectives," 117). This represents a governmental perspective rather than views of pregnant women or physicians. In contrast, Li reports ". . . growing domestic opposition to what is probably one of the most unpopular policies promulgated by the state to date" (Li et al., "Characteristics," 446). She is referring here to rigorous enforcement of sterilization and abortion policies in the early 1980s. Qiu, Wang, and Gu say that, "There is a schism between physicians, ethicists, and the public over late abortions." They report perplexity on the part of most physicians as they attempt to decide between social responsibility and preservation of life (Qiu, Wang, and Gu, "Late Abortion," 347). The study reported that 77 percent of physicians questioned believed late abortion should not be performed (Qui, Wang, and Gu, "Late Abortion," 348). Lee's research, while indicating that Chinese students favor abortion more than American students, looked only at evaluations of abortions of a deformed fetus (Lee et al., "Cross-Cultural Research," 143). From these reports, it is not at all clear that abortion is accepted unreservedly. Despite the tradition of infanticide and the great numbers of abortions in China, a case like Chen Li-li's is probably not exceptional.

20. There is even more pressure in her situation than we as westerners may imagine because Chen Li-li is acting out of a personal moral conviction in a society where the conflict around abortion is "structured almost wholly in terms of corporate groups, like the state and the family, and centers on the needs of and the duties owed to such groups" (Laurence H. Tribe, *Abortion: The Clash of Absolutes* [New York: W. W. Norton and Company, 1992], 63).

21. One example is the case of a woman worker for a state-owned factory who would not consent to abortion. "The cadres of her factory complained that if she gave birth to a fourth child, the rewards of all of the workers would be diminished, because they had broken the birth quota assigned to the factory." Although in this case the physician at first refused to perform a late abortion, he was finally convinced and gave the fetus an injection of Huangyan Flower. The next day the woman gave birth to a live baby who was later adopted by an infertile couple (Qui, Wang, and Gu, "Late Abortion," 344).

22. See studies cited: Greenhalgh and Bongaarts, Coale and Banister, and Renteln.

23. Qui, Wang, and Gu suggest ". . . a more human way. We should make every effort to avoid late abortions, i.e., to use effectively the contraceptives and to perform the abortions earlier. In the case of a late abortion, voluntary consent of the mother is indispensable. The physician should determine whether the late abortion would cause any harm to the mother's health or endanger her life, and he should refuse to perform it if there is a high risk" (Qui, Wang, and Gu, "Late Abortion," 349).

24. Greenhalgh and Bongaarts, "Fertility," 1167.

25. Carol Gilligan treats the same issue among women in the United States and shows how women make ethical decisions about abortion in the context of relationships and care (Carol Gilligan, *In a Different Voice: Psychological Theory and Women's Development* [Cambridge, MA: Harvard University Press, 1982]).

26. Carol Gilligan, Janie Victoria Ward, and Jill McLean Taylor, eds. *Mapping the Moral Domain: A Contribution of Women's Thinking to Psychological Theory and Education* (Cambridge, MA: Center for the Study of Gender, Education and Human Development, Harvard University, 1988), 8.

27. Jürgen Habermas, *A Theory of Communicative Action, Vol. 1: Reason and the Rationalization of Society* (Boston: Beacon Press, 1984), 398. Habermas outlines a kind of reason geared toward mutual understanding. Persons engaging in dialogue each have the expectation that the other party will speak with truth, rightness, and sincerity. It is this type of communication that Chen Li-li engages in as she grapples with her dilemma in the relationships of her social and cultural world.

28. Zygmunt Bauman, *Postmodern Ethics* (Cambridge, MA: Blackwell Publishers, 1993), 248–49).

29. In the postmodern milieu, "We learn again to respect ambiguity, to feel regard for human emotions, to appreciate actions without purpose and calculable rewards. We accept that not all actions, and particularly *not all among the most important of actions*, need to justify and explain themselves to be worthy of our esteem" (emphasis mine) (Bauman, *Postmodern Ethics*, 33).

Bibliography and Suggested Reading

Bauman, Zygmunt. *Postmodern Ethics*. Cambridge, MA: Blackwell Publishers, 1993.

Bixier, J. S., R. L. Calhoun, and H. R. Niebuhr, eds. "Value Theory and Theology." *The Nature of Religious Experience: Essays in Honor of Clyde Macintosh*. New York: Harper and Brothers Publishers, 1937.

Chan Wing-tsit, trans. *A Source Book in Chinese Philosophy*. Princeton: Princeton University Press, 1963.

Coale, Ansley J., and Judith Banister. "Five Decades of Missing Females in China." *Demography* 31, no. 3 (August 1994).

Ebrey, Patricia Buckley, ed. *Chinese Civilization and Society: A Sourcebook*. New York: The Free Press, 1981.

Fingarette, Herbert. *Confucius: The Secular as Sacred*. New York: Harper and Row, 1972.

Gadamer, Hans Georg. *Truth and Method*. New York: Seabury Press, 1975.

Gilligan, Carol. *In a Different Voice: Psychological Theory and Women's Development*. Cambridge, MA: Harvard University Press, 1982.

Gilligan, Carol, Janie Victoria Ward, and Jill McLean Taylor, eds. *Mapping the Moral Domain: A Contribution of Women's Thinking to Psychological Theory and Education*. Cambridge, MA: Center for the Study of Gender, Education and Human Development, Harvard University Press, 1988.

Gillis, Anna Maria. "Sex Selection and Demographics." *BioScience* 45, no. 6 (June 1995).

Gilmartin, Christina K., et al., eds. *Engendering China: Women, Culture, and the State*, Harvard Contemporary China Series, 10. Cambridge, MA: Harvard University Press, 1994.

Greenhalgh, Susan. "Shifts in China's Population Policy 1984–1986: Views from the Central, Provincial, and Local Levels." *Popular Development Review* 12 (1986).

Greenhalgh, Susan, and John Bongaarts. "Fertility Policy in China: Future Options." *Science* 235, no. 4793 (6 March 1987).

Greenhalgh, Susan, and Li Jianli. "Engendering Reproductive Policy and Practice in Peasant China: For a Feminist Demography of Reproduction." *Signs: Journal of Women in Culture and Society* 20/3 (1995):601–41.

Habermas, Jürgen. *A Theory of Communicative Action, Vol. 1: Reason and the Rationalization of Society*. Boston: Beacon Press, 1984.

Honig, Emily, and Gail Hershatter. *Personal Voices: Chinese Women in the 1980s*. Stanford, CA: Stanford University Press, 1988.

The Hsiao Ching. Trans. Mary Lelia Makra. New York: St. John's University Press, 1961.

Hsieh Kuang-hua, and Robert L. Burgess. "Marital Role Attitudes and Expected Role Behaviors of College Youth in Mainland China and Taiwan." *Journal of Family Issues* 15/3 (September 1994):403–23.

Judd, Ellen R. *Gender and Power in Rural North China.* Stanford, CA: Stanford University Press, 1994.

Lee Yueh-Ting, et al. "Cross-Cultural Research on Euthanasia and Abortion." *Journal of Social Issues* 52, no. 2 (1996).

Li, Virginia C., et al. "Characteristics of Women Having Abortion in China." *Social Science and Medicine* 31, no. 4 (1990).

McGowan, Jo. "Little Girls Dying: An Ancient and Thriving Practice." *Commonweal* 118, no. 14 (9 August 1991).

Mosher, Steven. *A Mother's Ordeal: One Woman's Fight against China's One-Child Policy.* New York: Harcourt Brace, 1994.

Niebuhr, H. Richard. *The Responsible Self: An Essay in Christian Moral Philosophy.* San Francisco: Harper and Row, 1963.

Peters, Ted. *For the Love of Children: Genetic Technology and the Future of the Family.* Louisville, KY: Westminster John Knox Press, 1996.

Poston, D. L. "Patterns of Contraceptive Use in China." *Studies in Family Planning* 17 (1986).

Qui Ren-Zong, Wang Chun-Zhi, and Gu Yuan. "Can Late Abortion be Ethically Justified?" *The Journal of Medicine and Philosophy* 14, no. 3 (June 1989).

Renteln, Alison Dundes. "Sex Selection and Reproductive Freedom." *Women's Studies International Forum* 15, no. 3 (1992).

Sommer, Deborah, ed. *Chinese Religion: An Anthology of Sources.* New York: Oxford University Press, 1995.

Taylor, Charles. *Philosophical Papers II.* Cambridge, England: Cambridge University Press, 1985.

Tribe, Laurence H. *Abortion: The Clash of Absolutes.* New York: W. W. Norton and Company, 1992.

Tu Wei-ming. *Confucian Thought: Selfhood as Creative Transformation.* New York: State University of New York Press, 1985.

Veatch, R. M., ed. *Cross-cultural Perspectives in Medical Ethics: Readings.* Boston: Jones and Bartlett Publishers, 1989.

Waley, Arthur, trans. *The Analects of Confucius.* New York: Vintage Books, 1938.

White, Tyrene. "The Origins of China's Birth Planning Policy." In *Engendering China: Women, Culture, and the State,* ed. Christina K. Gilmartin et al., Harvard Contemporary China Series, 10. Cambridge, MA: Harvard University Press, 1994.

Wolf, Margery. *Women and the Family in Rural Taiwan.* Stanford, CA: Stanford University Press, 1972.

CHAPTER 9

What Model of Development?

A CASE STUDY by Christine E. Gudorf

Keke Omuji waved his arm to dispel the flies that hovered over his glass of juice and continued to ponder the meeting he had attended the previous day. Keke was a district official in a small state in southwestern Nigeria, the most populous nation in Africa. Keke's district consisted of eleven Yoruba villages and one town of 20,000 that housed the regional market. Yesterday's meeting had been an economic planning meeting for all the agricultural, health, and commerce administrators of all the local districts in this state. Economic planning meetings had been grim since the late seventies when Nigeria's oil-based economy began to go sour. Since then all statistical indices of development had either stagnated or gotten worse. After more than a decade of military rule the government, even at the district level, tended to focus only on conserving "political stability" by opposing calls for civilian rule and free elections and by keeping the national economy afloat.

This morning's meeting had been both refreshing, in that a truly ambitious plan covering agriculture, health, and population had been proposed, and a cause for anxiety, in that Keke had some reservations about some of the plan's aspects, and he expected strong opposition in his district. Though the colonel who had presented the plan was one of the more enlightened army officers Keke had known, he had nevertheless emerged not only from military culture in which orders were determinative and eliminated any need to consult with subordinates, but he was also from the North, where Muslim Hausa culture dictated less independence and fewer economic roles for women. Keke feared that army authoritarianism and Hausa attitudes towards women could be real problems in dealing with health and work issues that affected individuals, families, and tribal groups among the Yoruba.

Eight days later, Keke stood in front of the crowd assembling in the shade of the trees at the edge of the market. He had called together the village chiefs and elders, the president of the market association, the officers of the women's Trader Clubs, and the doctor and the nurses who ran the six health clinics in the district to explain the proposed plan to them.

He first described the agricultural component: "The plan's target is as we anticipated: next year our district should harvest 10 percent more, with about half in food for our local market and half cocoa for export."

There were nods and thoughtful murmurs from many of the elders, indicating that they were considering his ideas, and the president of the local market association beamed at the idea of having more food products to send to the large markets in Ibadan and more cocoa to sell to the Marketing Board for export. But the women from the Trader Clubs were waving their arms and speaking rapidly to the female health workers.

Christine Ciroma, one of the health workers and a member of a prominent local family who had trained as a nurse practitioner in the United States, spoke up. "The women are upset. Your plan sounds simple, but you ignore issues of ownership and income. Women own little land; women earn their money in petty trading, and get nothing of the profit from their husbands' fields. But when extra help is needed in the fields, it is the women who do it, especially weeding. Now you speak of 10 percent more crops, which means 10 percent more work. Who is to do the extra work? The women think it will be them, and this will take time from their trading, which they need to be able to buy necessities for themselves and their children that husbands do not buy. More crops may help the men and the government, but they can be bad for women and children."

Keke insisted this was not a problem. The women could either be paid for their labor, or the income from the extra crops could be used for family expenses by agreement of the spouses. Both the men and the women objected, raising numerous problems, some based in the complexities of polygamous family structures. For example, the men objected that paying women wages for their fieldwork would take all their profit from the extra production. But some cowives objected that if they weren't paid, the income generated by one wife's work in the husband's fields could either be spent by the husbands on their own pleasure or be used for other children of the household, those of other wives. Some women responded to this concern by reminding others that the children of a sick, very pregnant, or newly delivered wife, who often watched the children of other wives while they farmed or traded, should not be discriminated against. The majority of women argued that women would not do more work unless they knew that they and their children would be better off.

Keke interrupted, "But you have not yet heard the whole plan. The health workers were invited for a reason. In 1989, the national government adopted a population policy which aimed at four or fewer children per mother throughout at least half the population by 2000. Nigeria has one of the highest crude birth rates in the world—seven children per woman." Many of the faces in the audience beamed at this last statistic, because large household size carried status and signified power in Yoruba society. "We need not only to revive agriculture to the production yields of twenty years ago in Nigeria, before so many workers left for the cities, but we also need to lower the birth rate so we do not eat up the increased production. Each subdistrict in Nigeria is to come up with a plan under which we decrease the birth rate by 15 percent over the next three years."

Edward Oyeluso, an elder from a distant village, was the first to respond. "But what of men who want more than four children? Or what if a man's wife has four children and they are all girls? Must he marry another wife if he doesn't want to? Look at me. My two wives have birthed nine children, but only three were sons, and two of them have died. The other one is still young. Must I marry a third wife to have sons?"

Chief Simi said, "Most men can only afford one or, at best, two wives, so that one can act like a wife after the other has a child or becomes a grandmother. Now to limit each woman to four children—it makes families too little! How will we have enough young people to work in the fields with so few babies born? What if a woman has four children and then most of them die?"

Christine spoke up, "What contraceptive technology do you plan to use to limit women to four children? And how will the plan be enforced?"

Keke answered, "Women will be required to attend the clinic once a year. Each woman would have proof of her last visit to the clinic, and women found without such proof would be fined the first time and arrested after that. The method of contraception would depend on what was available and what the woman chose. But women with four living children would be required to choose and use a method."

"And if a woman with four children chose oral contraceptives and then next year showed up pregnant?" Christine asked.

Keke smiled at her and asked, "Do you normally recommend oral contraceptives for the village women? I suspect not. But in any case, we would have to assume oral contraceptives don't work for village women and find a different method."

Betty Olusanye moved to the front of the group and said, "So the army is going to decide about women having children, hum? That may work in the North, but it is not the Yoruba way. Where is the benefit to women in this plan? It sounds like all we do is more work, with less money and more hunger for us and for our children, while the army makes us have fewer children."

"There are some benefits for women and children in this plan," Keke explained. "You know that fewer of the older children die now since the clinics began the vaccination programs. But fourteen of every hundred babies still die in the first year, and six more of every hundred children die between one and four. Now the national government will have some funding, pledged by rich countries at the United Nations' meeting in Cairo in 1994, for improving the health of women and children, and it will be distributed to the clinics. We will have clinic hours in each village, each pregnant woman will get vitamins and check-ups so that babies will be bigger and stronger, and children will get medicines if they get sick. Fewer children will die, and more will be strong and healthy."

As the meeting ended and people gathered in groups to drive, catch buses, or walk to their homes in town or in the outlying villages, Christine stopped for coffee at a market stall with Siti and Alice, two other nurses.

"I have a problem with this plan of Keke's," Christine said to the other two after they were served. "We are going to be expected to police the women because we run the clinics. We will be the ones who are supposed to record how many children each woman has, and make the women with four children use contraception, and record when each woman last came to the clinic, and then report the results to some authority. Should we be doing this? What about confidentiality? And families here do not want fewer children. Whether they are Catholic or Muslim or simply Yoruban, almost all of them believe that God sends as many children as God wants and that big families are healthy and prosperous. And if Keke is serious about increasing production by 10 percent or more, families are going to be wanting more children as laborers. This concern for smaller families is not Yoruban, not Nigerian, not African. It comes from the developed nations. This whole plan was put together by people who think that we should all have small nuclear families like they do. That is why the plan didn't see the women's problem with working in the men's fields—they think all real families have single budgets."

"You know," Siti added, "many men now observe the traditional three-year sexual abstinence after childbirth for fear of the public censure a pregnancy would bring. But if women go to contraception, how could a woman say no to a husband who wants sex before the three years? Contraception would interfere with the mother–child bonding that sexual abstinence protects."

But Alice, whose brother was Keke's assistant, said, "I don't deny that these are all problems. But what's this I'm hearing? I don't understand. Christine, you have always said you married Akoye partly because he was Catholic, so you knew he could never marry a second wife. And Siti, as a Muslim woman you had it written into your marriage contract that your husband can only take a second wife with your permission, which you claim you will never give. Is polygamy a good thing just because it is Yoruban or Muslim? How many times have we talked about the fanatics who promote anti-Western Islamicization movements in the North and how the Qur'an allows women more freedom than do these fanatics who claim to represent Islam? Now you want to defend the traditional Yoruban family? Does that mean returning to the days when Yoruba women could not inherit land and sons had to work for their fathers and could not own land or businesses of their own? The decline of the extended family is linked to these new rights. If we go back to traditional Yoruban culture, we can junk contraceptives and all the modern medical treatments we were taught and heal only with roots and incantations. Is that what you want?"

A YORUBAN RESPONSE by Leke Adeofe

The concerns of an African (Yoruban) traditionalist with this case focus on the notion of human rights that informs the events and the misunderstanding of the traditional African culture exhibited by the actors. The traditionalist does not understand rights in terms of a lone individual crying out for protection against the community. She does not merely think there is an alternative to individual-based rights, she thinks the latter approach is misconceived. Individual-based rights presuppose that the best interests of the individual do not necessarily constitute the best interests of the community. Indeed, there is the further presupposition that the interests of the individual and those of the community might actually be in conflict with each other. Moreover, where such alleged conflicts exist, they are to be resolved in favor of the individual, otherwise the community risks being coercive and tyrannical. This is the underlying assumption in the conversation between Christine Adeniyi (Ciroma) and Kole (Keke) Omuji.

A traditionalist finds this kind of thinking strange. She opposes coercion and tyranny as much as anybody else does. What troubles her is the thinking about rights and associated notions, for example, personhood, which undergirds such resolutions of conflicts. Rights, she thinks, are essentially communal, and talk about the rights of individuals only makes sense from this vantage point. As John Mbiti notes, "I am because we are, and since we are, therefore I am."[1] The alleged conflict between the rights of the community and those of the individual is an illusion. The illusion is due to a misconception about the robust ontological status of communal rights. It is not accidental that in a traditional African society, a person is characteristically defined in reference to his environing community. This can be contrasted with the Western approach that typically aims at abstracting some feature of a person by which to define him. The Western approach to defining a person relies on two main criteria, the physical continuity criterion and the psychological continuity criterion. The physical continuity criterion aims at defining a person by virtue of the person being a human organism. In this view, it is the physicality underlying the traditional life history of a human being that makes that human being a person. This can be contrasted with the view that it is the psychology underlying such a life history that makes a human being a person. In this view, it is the continuity of a person's psychology, that is, her beliefs, intentions, memories, and other forms of mentation, that makes the person. Some psychological continuity theorists have gone so far as to claim that the preservation of a person's psychology in a human organism is true but unnecessarily so.

Continuity theories are not very useful from an African view point. To be sure, the Africans, say, the Yoruba, conceptually distinguish between the body *(ara)* and the soul *(emi)*. Some traditional Yoruban thought systems even distinguish between the seven phases of the soul and make metaphysical assumptions about the various parts of the body. The complexity of the system notwithstanding, it is the third constitutive element of a person—the metaphysical head *(ori)*—which essentially defines a person. But the notion of a metaphysical head and the psychic unity it fosters can be understood only in relation to the community. Thus, even within the metaphysical realm, the reality of the community seems to take precedence.[2]

The notion of communal rights is more than an emergent phenomenon of a communal view of personhood. Also to be considered in this communal web are such factors as ownership, family structure, children, inheritance, religious worship, and architecture. Land, which remains the principal mode of production in African communities, is communally owned. Land is viewed as that which ought to be communally owned, and this is understood in the religious attitude that surrounds its ownership. Land is the link between the ancestors, those now living, and the future generations. Individuals are neither invested with property rights in the land nor given the right of possession of it. The elders of a community act as custodians and give others the right to use the land, but it is clearly understood that a piece of land is held in trust for the community.[3] The religious rituals associated with the use of land—say, before cultivating the land or building a house—help to reinforce the sacred but communal nature of land transactions.

A community that owns together lives and worships together. The family is the smallest unit of a community. But because the family is defined through a common ancestor, a whole clan may conveniently constitute a family. Land cultivation is the principal economic activity, and the whole family constitutes the force of production. The available wealth is thus communally produced and understood to be communally owned. Normally, marriages function to link and expand families and, hence, increase economic strength. Children are viewed as blessings, and these are not to be counted or tabulated. But this attitude is not a manifestation of the desire to have as many children as possible. It is an attempt to protect the ancestral integrity and well-being of the children. The children of a family are not traditionally viewed in possessive terms: my children, theirs, or hers—at least not within the same family. The eldest male in a family ordinarily serves as the father, or "greater father" as it is traditionally labeled, to all the children in a family. The children's various uncles, who are themselves biological fathers, take their instructions from the head of the family and assume their roles accordingly. Similar considerations with appropriate changes apply to the eldest female and the other mothers in the family. Subject to availability of resources, this family structure is reflected in the architecture of the dwelling places. Perhaps more important for our purpose here, issues of inheritance are to be understood against the background of the architectonic family structure prevalent here.

We might wonder if and how traditionalists would respond to tyranny. Attempts to justify tyranny are usually based on the view that communal interests, however defined, do override personal interests. Of course, there are various degrees of tyranny. Those who argue against tyranny argue that certain personal interests can never be overridden by communal interests. Common to both positions is the assumption that personal interests and communal interests are, metaphorically, two trains scheduled for two opposite destinations. But because in the traditional African view, communal interests always override personal interests, how does a traditionalist respond to tyranny against the individual members? The question becomes more pertinent when one understands that with the traditionalist, the notion of personal interests independent of communal interests is not meaningful. But the way the question has been posed is misleading.

Communal interests are not deemed communal just by the wishes of the leaders. There is a complex societal structure, in addition to tradition, that helps to define communal interests. Contrary to the customary practice of military governments, communal interests are not defined to be so by fiat or decrees. This is important to note because of the current attitude among military administrators—and politicians—to assume that the interests of the government as defined by them are communal interests. The problem here is not just that the interests of the government are narrowly defined or the fact that such governmental interests are dictated by neocolonial considerations. The problem is that the commonality of interests in the traditional Yoruban society has been misunderstood. Apart from the traditional head of a Yoruban community, there is a council of chiefs. There is also a wider council of lesser chiefs. In the domain of each chief, there is a council of elders. Parallel to these divisions are various group associations based on the traditional divisions of labor and religious practices. For example, hunters, healers, market women, warriors, and worshippers of Sango and Egungun would have their different group associations. What makes an interest communal is that it emerges from a decision process that includes this plethora of groups. It is reasonable to expect such an interest to be beneficial to all, but that is not what makes it communal. Of course, in actual practice, customary services properly grounded in tradition help to speed the process along.[4]

Underlying the various events in this case is the breakdown of the traditional African society. All the various issues about land ownership, income, children, gender, and spousal wealth sharing are due to this breakdown—or so a traditionalist would surmise. In what follows, I offer traditionalist perspectives on the issues.

Population Concerns

The concern with population is perplexing. Nigeria's population, for example, is supposed to be too high. But what ought to be the ideal population figure, and why? There is no empirical evidence that countries with the highest populations are necessarily the poorest. On the contrary, there are many countries with low populations that are also among the poorest. The common denominator apart from their poverty is that these are countries characterized by dependent capitalism. "Dependent capitalism" refers to the system operative in countries that are integrative participants in the global (Western) capitalist market but without an indigenous capitalist class. It would seem then that the status and, hence, level of participation of the poor countries in the global capitalist market ought to be the real concern. Unnecessary confusions are sometimes added to this debate with references to corruption in the mismanagement of funds and resources. Sometimes, references are made to the perpetual political instability in these countries. But is corruption, endemic as it is in many poor countries, the cause of poverty or its effect? And how are we to understand political instability except as a struggle for resources deemed to be scarce and exhaustible?

The truth is that the naked interests of the Western countries are not served by population growths in capitalist dependent countries, at least not at the present stage of global capitalist development. There was a time when millions of African hands, including those of children, were forced to cultivate rubber for Firestone in Liberia or mine gold for De Beers in South Africa. Taxes were introduced to force the populations into a monetary economy that was designed to benefit Western countries. Africans who refused were beaten and tortured, and they had their lands confiscated. All this barbarism served to make them participants in the Western capitalist market. The current African elites are the latest group of beneficiaries of this inhumane structure. Because the elites are not ready to commit economic suicide, the exploitative colonial arrangement remains essentially intact. But the economic activities that gave rise to them can now be done with very little manpower. What a large population does is to create social and economic pressure on a country's elites to restructure fundamentally the country's economy.

The argument is not that population growth ought not to be a concern but that it should be properly motivated. The underlying assumption seems to be that poor countries are operating at their best possible level in terms of available resources which are poor and which they are incapable of changing for the better. The only factor within their control is their population. There is even no advocacy for restructuring the economy *and* controlling the population. The International Monetary Fund and the World Bank do not qualify as advocates for restructuring poor economies for the better, at least not from the available evidence. Western countries cannot continue to consume most of the world's resources while advocating higher population growths for themselves.

The perplexing question remains: who declared population a concern, and why? An African (Yoruban) traditionalist sees plenty of uncultivated farming land all around him. It reminds him of the "housing shortage" in the country when many Yoruban towns have unoccupied houses and many occupied ones are rented out for a pittance. The population issue seems like another mirage. The situation is not helped by people like Kole (Keke) Omuji who speak for the government. He represents a long tradition in deception that dates back to colonial times. It is difficult to know when these officials are speaking the truth; their job is to enhance government revenue and make general administration easier. Anyone who genuinely wants the people's input knows where to initiate the traditional process—the council of chiefs through the king (*oba*). It is a long process to consensus, but the decision will be greatly respected by all. Government functionaries, whether representing military or politicians, like their colonial predecessors, have never had the patience needed for the traditional process to work. Forums like the one Kole (Keke) Omuji called are meant to ratify, not deliberate on, government policies.

Health

Everybody, at least within traditional communities, knows that malaria is best cured by herbs. The same consideration applies to many other diseases, especially mental diseases that have defied Western cures. The problem with these Western doctors and nurses is that they hardly believe claims that are not Western. This is the legacy of colonial chauvinism. But the country continues in its unenviable colonial status as the dumping ground for deficient and rejected drugs of the Western pharmaceutical companies. Even under the best of circumstances, the efficacy of imported drugs has always been in doubt. This is not surprising given that the trial tests were done on other people. It is noteworthy that these days many wonder whether drugs tested on Western men are equally efficacious for Western women. Nigeria and other African countries must produce their own drugs tapping into their own herbal traditions. And they must hurry if it is not to cost them much more than it already has. Japanese pharmaceutical companies have been scrounging African forests asking about the various plants and their medicinal powers. There is already a "controversy" about medicines that might come out of a similar sojourn into the Amazon forest. The upshot is that when Alice rhetorically asks Christine whether she is prepared to "heal only with roots and incantations," it is the virus of colonial chauvinism at work. Given the devastating effects of AIDS, it is easy to lose focus of long-term planning. It is AIDS today, but it will be something else tomorrow.

Recuperative and therapeutic aspects of health delivery are important, and the African social structure is particularly useful in this regard. Those who suffer from AIDS perhaps need these more than anyone else does. The African family has traditionally demonstrated ethics of care and affection to their afflicted members. The shock that village dwellers feel on seeing the mentally insane wandering on city streets is due to this. Even in the cities, there is a reservoir of such sentiments of communal goodwill that can be tapped into when helping the afflicted.

The actors in this case think and behave as if the traditional Yoruban society is just facing its first health crisis. Barely forty years ago, it faced influenza. Between that time and now, it has survived a couple of epidemics. The only difference between all these other crises and the current crisis is that, unlike before, there is, among the elites, a lack of confidence in the traditional process. Decisions concerning oral contraceptives, possible sexual promiscuity, and male attitudes are all within the purview of the traditional culture. Twenty-year-old nurses are hardly positioned culturally to dictate to anyone what ought to be done. The issues should have been presented to the traditional women's associations. They would have come up with solutions they could live with and ways to enforce those solutions, and there would be no doubt about enforcement. The problem for the elites, however well intentioned they are, is the nature of the final decisions from such a traditional socio-political process. The elites want to be sure that the final outcome matches what they believe it ought to be. On the one hand, they fear losing the power to control the people, and, on the other hand, they fear losing the neocolonial privileges associated with such a control. The colonial interlude is an offensive interruption in an otherwise wonderful history. The African elites think and behave as if the history of the people started to unfold with colonialization. All their indices, paradigms, and adopted categories of development are biased from this perspective.

Land and Agriculture

For the traditionalist, current state policies on land embody the confusion with which the postcolonial period is identified. As Léopold Senghor and Julius Nyerere make clear, land is traditionally viewed as a communal property, though there are instances where anomalous holdings are allowed. Communal ownership of land is consistent with the extended family system that characterizes Yoruban society. Communal ownership allows for a certain level of well-being among the individual members of the various clans. Individual members of the community enjoy temporary ownership rights over land lasting for the duration of use. But, on the whole, the community traditionally relies on the clan to provide the required labor to cultivate the land and harvest the crops.

Christine Adeniyi's (Ciroma's) reflective instincts are on the right track about this case. Any plan that requires higher productivity will fall more heavily on the women than on the men. This is partly because with a wage economy, more women than men are left at home in the clans. Men are encouraged to seek paid jobs outside the clan or township. Land cultivation is now perceived somewhat as an extension of household chores. It is relevant to understand that the traditional Yoruban family maintains two farms, one near the homestead, the other far away. The homestead farm is devoted to crops like vegetables and fruits. The far away farm is reserved for crops such as yams or cassava or cash crops such as cocoa or rubber. The latter farm, unlike the former, is usually maintained by men. Planting for cash crops was a distortion brought about by colonialism, but the greater distortion was in the social roles that were fostered. Gradually, men have come either to plant and cultivate cash crops or to engage in wage labor, while women tend to cultivate food crops and take care of day-to-day necessities.

For a traditionalist, Christine's rhetorical question, "Who is to do the extra work?" reveals the current malaise that affects the traditional social structure and blurs its network of obligations. Kole's (Keke's) proposal to pay the women is a false solution for the reasons stated in the story. The network of interdependencies is still very strong and singling out a particular segment of the community and paying them for their work will lead to chaos. If the women are paid, what about those women who principally care for the children in the family or clan? Are those who have carried out obligations in the past on behalf of those women now to be paid?'

Conclusion

For the traditionalist, the social trauma evidenced in this story is rooted in the colonial and postcolonial epochs in Africa. The seeming futility in fashioning out solutions by the actors and the various groups they represent or exemplify is due to their neglect of traditional social structures and institutions. A traditionalist is not committed to an idealized view of traditional institutions in Africa. Traditional institutions have serious deficiencies. Everyone, including the traditionalist, knows that much. However, the traditionalist wants to claim that any serious solution to these social problems must start with ideas and precepts grounded in the traditional institutions.

Notes

1. John Mbiti, *African Religions and Philosophies* (New York: Doubleday, 1970), 141.
2. Ifeanyi A. Menkiti, "Person and Community in African Traditional Thought," in *African Philosophy: An Introduction*, ed. Richard A. Wright (Washington, DC: University Press of America, 1979), 157–67.
3. Leopold Senghor, "On African Homelands and Nation-States, Negritude, Assimilation, and African Socialism," in *African Philosophy: A Classical Approach*, ed. Parker English and Kibujo M. Kalumba (Englewood Cliffs, NJ: Prentice-Hall, 1996), 44.
4. Segun Gbadegesin, *African Philosophy: Traditional Yoruba Philosophy and Contemporary African Realities* (New York: Peter Lang, 1991), 61–82.
5. Gbadegesin, *African Philosophy*, 215–53.

A CHRISTIAN RESPONSE by Christine E. Gudorf

In this case there are a number of different religious traditions present within a generally Yoruban cultural tradition. While Christian, including Catholic, missionary work in Africa until the mid-twentieth century did not differentiate European culture and Christian faith, there has been since Vatican II (1962–1965) a conscious attempt in most Catholic quarters of Africa to enculturate Catholic Christianity in indigenous forms, though within limits which tend to reflect European rather than African traditions. Polygamy and widow remarriage/levirate marriage have tended to be more problematic than the introduction of African cultural expressions—drums, dancing, reconciliation rituals—into the liturgy.

Because of the emphasis on enculturating Catholic faith within the indigenous culture, which in this case is distinctively Yoruban, though with Muslim as well as Christian influences, a Catholic Christian perspective will also need to respect and consult these other religious traditions.

There are two central Christian values threatened by the unfolding events in this case. The first is justice, which is involved in the question of how to distribute appropriately the extra work and wages resulting from expanding production. The second is human freedom, which is denied/abridged in the proposals to force both contraception and AIDS testing on women. Understandings of both these values have evolved gradually throughout the history of Christianity and the world. For most of human history, justice has been regarded as a virtue of the public realm, seldom sought in the domestic realm in the relationships between spouses. Similarly, for most of history, basic freedom to control one's body and its activity has been the privilege of a rather small portion of the human population, usually rather elite groups of ruling-class males. Coercion of the bodies of male slaves, male servants, women, and children—in terms of work, sexuality, reproduction, and other activities—was often taken for granted. So while the issues raised by these women are very old issues, the applications here are relatively new ones in the history of Christian ethics.

On the other hand, in Yoruban tradition individual freedom takes a second place to concern for the family community. Notice that Alice's rebuke at the end, in which she claims that none of the group really wants to return to traditional Yoruban values as a whole, cites changes that empowered individuals at the expense of family solidarity and traditions such as those that required sons to work for their fathers and not have their own fields or businesses and prevented women from owning land. The values of Western modernity have changed Yoruban culture in the name of justice and rights for individuals but in ways that introduce divided loyalties and interests into the extended family. In this regard, Muslim influences more closely resemble the Yoruban emphasis on family solidarity.

Scripture on Workplace Justice

Christian teaching on justice in the workplace has a number of sources, beginning with the Mosaic law, which forbids the mistreatment of slaves and servants, and extending through the prophets' denunciation of injustices against the poor, but is most explicitly grounded in Jesus' parable about the workers in the vineyard (Mt 20:1–16). In that parable, Jesus defends the right of the owner of the vineyard (God) to distribute the same day's wage both to the workers who worked the entire day and to those who only worked the last hour. The point of the parable is that God is just and that a basic level of justice requires meeting human need. Therefore, whether workers managed to obtain work in the morning or were unemployed until the late afternoon, they all received the same amount of income necessary to feed themselves and their family for the day.

Christian churches have addressed the issue of just wages in many different ways. Catholic social teaching from *Rerum novarum* in 1891 initiated a great deal of Christian deliberation on just wages when it defined a just wage as the level of wages that would allow a worker to support himself and his family and, with thrift, to save some capital. Some Christian thinkers in the twentieth century have advocated a "family" wage, which would increase with the size of a family, but this concept has never been endorsed because of the great risk within capitalism of increasing unemployment among heads of large families, who would be more expensive to hire. In general, the Christian churches have insisted that wages be sufficient to supply basic needs of a family, and the Catholic Church and many others have condemned unequal wages or hiring discrimination based on race, sex, or other ascribed factors. In this case condemnation of sex discrimination is very much to the point, because cocoa workers are both paid-itinerant workers and family members, especially wives. Of course, sex discrimination is not only at stake in the issue of payment for work but also in the issue of how procreation and AIDS transmission are to be regulated.

Christianity on Freedom

Freedom is understood somewhat differently in the modern world than it was in biblical times. It is easy to go back to scripture and find treatment of freedom, but it is usually not unfettered human choice that is being promoted or defended. What is being promoted is human responsibility, that is, writers such as St. Paul insist that in Christ Jesus we are free, and thus we must take responsibility for our salvation, for following the Way of him who saved us. While there is a general recognition within the community of followers of Jesus that membership was nonexclusive, it was also understood that all were sisters and brothers, that as the baptismal formula in Galatians 3: 28 says: "There is no longer Jew nor Greek, slave nor free, male nor female, for you are all one in Christ Jesus." This was why Paul, while sending the slave Onesimus back to Philemon the legal master whom the slave had fled, challenged Philemon, a Christian, to recognize Onesimus as more than a slave. Paul called him to recognize the slave as a brother Christian, at the same time noting that while he could command Philemon to follow this call, he preferred to allow him to respond freely with love to Paul's appeal for Onesimus (Philem 1:8–18). While respecting the legal conventions of his society, Paul clearly recognized that the gospel of Jesus Christ is incompatible with ownership of one person by another. Thus, even in the earliest church it was understood that there is some relationship between this interior attitude of freedom that forces us to take responsibility for our lives and our salvation and the conditions which limit or enlarge the choices open to us.

While the Christian gospel does not produce an understanding of freedom in terms of rights, the practice of Christian love of neighbor involves respect for the dignity of the human person, which, in turn, forbids denying to individuals or groups any responsibility for basic areas of their lives. Specifically, Christianity has always insisted that men and women cannot be denied the right to marry or to have children and has, for centuries now, denounced torture and other nonconsensual invasion of the body. But Christian tradition has allowed society to regulate human freedom to marry and have children by such methods as setting minimum ages or health conditions (freedom from sexually transmitted diseases, for example), or, in ages past, by removing children from the care of unmarried mothers. One issue for today is whether the proposed regulations fall within these historic limits or constitute a more basic denial of human dignity.

Population Concerns

Within the dialogue of the case a number of other issues arise. Christine views the concern for population stabilization as imposed through the economic and cultural imperialism of the developed nations of the world and seeks to defend traditional values. Many women and men from the developing world who took the floor at sessions of the Nongovernmental Organizations (NGO) Forum at the Cairo ICPD in 1994 echoed her perspective. Noting that both the donor nations and the recipient nations were clear that the population rate should be lowered indirectly by targeting improvements in maternal and infant health, female education and status, and access to clean water—all conditions that influence the poor to have fewer children—doctors and nurses from developing nations demanded to know why the closets of their clinics were devoid of aspirin, antibiotics, rehydration salts, and vaccinations but were full of condoms, intrauterine devices (IUDs), and oral, injectable, and implantable contraceptives? It is a good question, and it reflects a long colonial and neocolonial history of unequal power relations between what are now rich and poor nations. Many in the poor nations understand that unequal power relation as having not only generated prevailing patterns of wealth and poverty today, but also as seeking to preserve it through population controls on the poor nations. Consequently, they are suspicious of Western population or ecological concerns, whether or not Western churches are involved.

Nigeria is the most populous nation in Africa and is a part of the sub-Saharan area of Africa which has, by far, the highest total fertility rate in the world—6.4 children per woman, compared to the next highest region, North Africa, at 4.7 children per woman.[1] The total population of sub-Saharan Africa was about 502 million in 1990. By 2030, depending on which of four scenarios of the Population Reference Bureau one uses, the estimated population of this region will be somewhere between a low of 1,199,000,000 and a high of 1,825,000,000. Extending the central scenario to the year 2100, the population of the region is likely to be 2,700,000,000[2]—and that assumes significant lowering of the total fertility rate of the region. In other words, the population of sub-Saharan Africa is now so young, and so large, and reproducing at such a high rate that even with significant reductions in the fertility rate the population will increase four to six times its present size. And Nigeria has resisted lowering fertility rates. Although total fertility rates in Latin America, for example, fell from over 5.5 to 3.6 children per woman between 1970 and 1990, Nigeria's fertility rate declined only from 7.1 to 7.0 in that same twenty-year span.[3] Christianity has not seriously addressed the issue of population levels apart from defending the right of persons to marry and have children. The Genesis command to "Multiply and fill the earth" has generally been cited in the past to support a right and, especially in some varieties of Protestantism, a duty to procreate. Today in light of the population crisis, the churches are having to evaluate that command more seriously. Once the earth is filled, how binding is the command to multiply? What does love of neighbor dictate in an overpopulated world in which so many of those already living have inadequate food, shelter, and basic services such as safe water and electricity?

Ecological Concerns

One absent perspective or issue in this case concerns the health of the earth. In many parts of the world talk of population immediately leads to issues of environmental degradation/regeneration. While there are certainly environmental issues raised in regard to urban growth in Nigeria, as well as issues such as international dumping of toxic waste in Nigeria and pollution of land and water in the oil-producing regions of Nigeria, for the most part the depopulation of the countryside by urban migration has prevented much concern that there might be too many people for the land to accommodate. Furthermore, the level of poverty is so high relative to the rest of the world that, aside from food, individual resource use levels are a tiny fraction of the average levels in developed nations. But projected population growth alone, even without amelioration of consumption rates from poverty, will further increase Nigeria's present dependency on food importation. If economic development increases per capita income for an expanded population—and increases in per capita income virtually always increase resource use—the drain on natural resources, such as clean air, water, and cleared land for housing as well as oil, minerals, and ores, will also be significant.

In Christianity, humans are understood to have been given the task of being stewards of God's creation. Increasingly, churches are recognizing that this means that humans are not only obliged to conserve those resources necessary for human survival, but to value and conserve all elements of creation as important for their own sake. African tribal religions have always understood humans as a part of the earth and dependent on it. Lack of ecological concern among tribal peoples is not rooted so much in alienated attitudes toward nature, as in much of modern Christianity, but rather in a failure to understand the implications of present population structure and the development process. The present ravages of HIV/AIDS in sub-Saharan Africa where twenty-one of the world's thirty million living cases are located, presents people with such constant images of population devastation that overpopulation is difficult to take seriously, even though the deaths only serve to reduce one small part of the population increase.

Women's Concerns

Siti seeks to defend women and the traditional culture that has supported them. Yoruban women have been internationally renowned for their economic independence, demonstrated in their traditional roles as traders. Women traders have complete control over their income, though women with working-class husbands are expected to cover children's school fees, clothes, and health care—the extras.[4] Siti understands that AIDS in Africa is spread almost exclusively by heterosexual sex, and that for biological reasons it is many times easier for men to transmit the virus to women than vice versa. Unlike nations such as Rwanda, Zaire, Tanzania, Uganda, Zambia, and Zimbabwe, which have been devastated by AIDS, Nigeria is just beginning to see signs of massive coming troubles.[5] Arguing that wives are only sexual recipients of the virus, not transmitters of it, Siti suggests that, instead of testing women in general, transient workers, who are mostly male, and prostitutes be tested for HIV.[6] According to prevailing research, she is largely correct, except, of course, that wives are the principle transmitters of HIV to children. This would not seem to justify mandatory testing of all women because it is extremely unlikely that this district has available the expensive AZT treatments which can drastically reduce the rate of HIV-positive children born to HIV-positive mothers. Theoretically, it might be possible to justify mandatory testing if by so doing one could see that pregnant HIV-positive women got AZT, but the frequency of the testing and, therefore, the degree of invasiveness would probably need to be unacceptably high if AZT intervention were to be timely and effective.

Siti also opposes the use of contraceptives—not merely their imposition—on the ground that they leave women no ability to persuade their husbands to wait out the traditional Yoruban three-year sexual abstinence for mothers after the birth of a child. This ban on sex after childbirth is paralleled by a permanent ban on sex for women after becoming grandmothers;[7] both bans facilitate devotion to the care of children and/or grandchildren. Siti's concern here is for maternal–infant bonding which, from her perspective, suffers if women are preoccupied with catering to the sexual demands of husbands.

The analysis of the traditional sex-ban practice is important. Was the original purpose of the ban contraception, maternal-infant bonding, discipline for husbands, or rest and regeneration for new mothers? Often cultures give no specific reasons for such rules of conduct; reasons must be inferred. Sometimes the original reasons are shrouded in mystery and defenses of the rules that are provided are, often, later inventions designed to answer attacks on traditional practice. If the original purposes can be inferred, does religio-cultural loyalty require obedience to the ban or protection of whatever purposes the ban was designed to serve? In terms of medical or health reasons alone, one could guess that the ban kept the birth rate from maximizing, allowed women's bodies to heal fully from childbirth, and gave mothers more time to spend with the new baby and other children. Siti worries about maternal–infant bonding, but if this is the concern, a mother who has three children instead of seven or eight already has had a great deal more time to bond with her children, even if she has resumed sexual relations with her husband. The only remaining concern would then be to ban resumption of sexual relations until the woman is fully healed from childbirth, but this is a matter of weeks or, at most, a few months, not years. Furthermore, it is assumed by most public health authorities that the three-year ban on post-partum sex contributes to male adultery, which, in turn, contributes to the spread of sexually transmitted diseases (STDs) and AIDS between adults and to children.

Structural Analysis

The economic aspect of the proposed plan is dictated by structural adjust-ment policies imposed on debt-ridden developing nations—including virtu-ally all African nations—during the 1980s. Based on its oil exports, Nigeria's economy had boomed in the 1960s and especially the 1970s. This allowed the rapid expansion of national government services and employment,[8] to the detriment both of agriculture in general and of cocoa, the country's prin-cipal nonpetroleum export. So many Nigerians left rural agricultural work for urban jobs that agricultural production decreased, food importation increased, and the shift toward waged cocoa workers more than consumed the rise in cocoa revenues, undermining the stability of cocoa production.[9] So the concern of the husbands—that giving wages to wives will eat up all the profits—has some support. It might be better to raise more food instead of cocoa, because Nigeria imports food, but the government needs to export cocoa in order to earn foreign exchange necessary for buying imported goods such as machinery for water treatment plants, technology for communica-tions and transportation systems, or military weaponry.

Possible Resolutions

Keke, as the district official, must work out two sets of resolutions. One set of resolutions will be between the farmers and their wives and will involve agreement over the amount of additional work the women will contribute to agriculture as well as how compensation will be arranged for that work. The second set of resolutions actually has three parties: Keke representing the state, the women's clinic staff representing the health care profession, and the local population—especially of women, because they are primarily con-cerned here. Initially, however, the negotiations could proceed between Keke and the women's clinic workers, since their code of professional ethics forces them to defend the individual rights of their patients.

Health care ethics in the West, where at least Christine was trained, require practitioners to refuse to participate in procedures such as forced abortion, forced sterilization, and forced implantation of contraceptives, to insist on gaining informed consent of the patient for all procedures, and to protect the privacy of patient records. If regulation of fertility is a legitimate interest of the state, then procedures that flow from that state interest, such as state access to individual health care records or legal limits on the num-bers of children couples may have, will conflict with the professional ethics inculcated in health care workers. It would be in the interest of the clinic workers to persuade Keke to institute incentives and disincentives rather than to criminalize uncontrolled fertility beyond four children. It is unlikely, though, that this conflict between the public interest in lowering fertility and professional ethics based on liberal theory of individual rights can or should be completely avoided over the next century.

Notes

1. Wolfgang Lutz, "The Future of World Population," *Population Bulletin* 49, no. 1 (June 1994):17.
2. Lutz, "Future," 27.
3. *The World's Women: Trends and Statistics, 1970–1990* (New York: United Nations, 1991), 60–69.
4. Simi Afonja, "Changing Modes of Production and the Sexual Division of Labor among the Yoruba," in *Women's Work*, ed. Eleanor Leacock and Helen Safa (South Hadley, MA: Bergin and Garvey, 1986), 122–35.
5. Jonathon Mann, Daniel J. M. Tarantola, and Thomas A. Netter, eds., *AIDS in the World* (Cambridge, MA: Harvard University Press, 1992), 908.
6. Her argument is supported by research: O. Orrubuloye, "Sexual Behavior of High Risk Groups and the Implications for STDs and HIV/AIDS Transmission in Nigeria" (delivered to the AIDS and Reproductive Health Network Working Group on Sexual Behavior Research Conference: International Perspectives in Sex Research, Rio de Janeiro, 22–25 April 1993).
7. Agnes Reidman, *Science That Colonizes: A Critique of Fertility Studies in Africa* (Philadelphia: Temple University Press, 1993), 1–32.
8. Patience Elabor-Idemudia, "The Impact of Structural Adjustment Programs on Women and Their Households in Bendel and Ogun States, Nigeria," in *Structural Adjustment and African Women Farmers*, ed. Cristina H. Gladwin (Gainesville, FL: University of Florida Press, 1991), 128–50.
9. Sara Berry, *Fathers Work for Their Sons: Accumulation, Mobility and Class Formation in an Extended Yoruban Community* (Berkeley, CA: University of California Press, 1985), 64–70.

Bibliography and Suggested Readings

Berry, Sara. *Fathers Work for Their Sons: Accumulation, Mobility and Class Formation in an Extended Yoruba Community*. Berkeley, CA: University of California Press, 1985.

Bratton, Susan Power. *Six Billion and More: Human Population Regulation and Christian Ethics*. Louisville, KY: Westminster, 1992.

English, Parker, and Kibujo M. Kalumba, eds. *African Philosophy: A Classical Approach*. Englewood Cliffs, NJ: Prentice-Hall, 1996.

Gbadegesin, Segun. *African Philosophy: Traditional Yoruba Philosophy and Contemporary African Realities*. New York: Peter Lang, 1991.

Gladwin, Christina H., ed. *Structural Adjustment and African Women Farmers*. Gainesville, FL: University of Florida Press, 1991.

Hartmann, Betsy. *Reproductive Rights and Wrongs: The Global Politics of Population Control and Contraceptive Choice*. New York: Harper and Row, 1987.

Lutz, Wolfgang. "The Future of World Population." *Population Bulletin* 49, no. 1 (June 1994).

Mbiti, John. *African Religions and Philosophies*. New York: Doubleday and Company, 1970.

Reidman, Agnes. *Science That Colonizes: A Critique of Fertility Studies in Africa.* Philadelphia: Temple University Press, 1993.

Wright, Richard A., ed. *African Philosophy: An Introduction*. Washington, DC: University Press of America, 1979.

CHAPTER 10

Fighting for a Homeland

A CASE STUDY by Regina Wentzel Wolfe

Dan had recently been named to succeed Jake Miller as export administrator for AGEX, an import-export firm located in Chicago's western suburbs. This meant he was responsible for ensuring that the company complied with the Export Administration Regulations governing the export of military or dual-use goods. Dealing with military goods was fairly routine; any export of them always required an export license. But, as Jake had noted before he left the company, the export of dual-use goods wasn't always as clear because items in that category had civilian as well as military applications. Companies only had to apply for validated export licenses for dual-use goods when they had knowledge that the items were for end-uses listed in the regulations provided by the Department of Commerce or if there were suspected irregularities, such as questions about the end-use of the item or about the end-user. Looking at the paperwork in front of him, it was clear to Dan that some of the export items listed there fell in the dual-use category.

"This looks pretty straightforward," Dan thought remembering what he had learned at the training course. He turned to his computer and called up the account information on the Aishagu Import-Export Trading Company. Dan didn't know much about the company, though he was familiar with the name because AGEX had been doing business with the Turkish company for a number of years.

"It can't possibly be the same person," Dan said to himself as he stared at the computer screen. It listed Mustafa Bahdiri as the managing director of the company. His mind flew back to his college days, more than twenty years earlier. He remembered the first time he had seen the tall and ruggedly handsome young man with his dark hair and thick mustache. He was just coming out of the room across the hall as Dan and his parents were carrying in clothes, books, and all the other paraphernalia that goes with moving into a freshman dorm. They hadn't officially met until the first hall meeting. Mustafa Bahdiri, a student from Turkey, was the first of his family to attend university in the United States. Turkey seemed a strange and far-off country to Dan that night. But by the time the two were seniors, Dan had come to know something about the country and the place of Mustafa's people, the

Kurds, in it. Actually, thanks to Mustafa, Dan knew more than most Americans about the Kurds and their struggle for a homeland.

"It has to be him," thought Dan. "There can't be two Mustafa Bahdiris in Diyarbekir. Funny, after losing touch for all these years, here he is—name, address, phone number—on my computer screen. What a small world! I wonder if he ever gets to the States. I'll have to call Aishagu's East Coast rep and ask. Meanwhile, I'd better get on with the paperwork."

The files indicated that Aishagu imported a few small household appliances, but that their main line of business with AGEX was in photographic equipment and supplies. It was a well-established relationship, and it looked like his predecessor, Jake, had always approved the paperwork. There was no indication that export licenses had ever been required.

Dan began dealing with the forms but had a difficult time concentrating on them. His mind kept shifting from the training session he had just completed to the numerous late-night conversations he and Mustafa had had years ago as college students.

"I'm not really Turkish," Mustafa had said one night, "I'm a Kurd." He went on to explain to Dan, "We are an ancient people with our own language and culture and have been struggling for more than a century to establish our own land. No one seems to understand us or wants to assist us."

Dan had found the history of the Kurds very confusing, and as he tried to recall what he once knew, it seemed even more muddled. He knew that repeated but unsuccessful efforts to establish an independent Kurdistan had been made for the better part of the past two centuries. External or internal forces of one sort or another always seemed to thwart independence.

"Mustafa really used to get agitated about it all," Dan thought to himself, "particularly when he'd talk about the mistreatment his people had suffered after World War I."

Sometimes it would be discussing the infighting among the tribal chieftains that would get Mustafa riled up. At other times it would be the British, the French, the Russians, or even the Persians. It had seemed to Dan that from Mustafa's point of view there wasn't anyone who had treated the Kurds fairly. The worst offenders seemed to be the Turks, particularly Kemal Ataturk who led the Turkish war for independence.

"Ataturk used the Kurds for his own nationalistic purposes," Mustafa had said in a pained voice. "He got some of the Kurds to fight with him by appealing to their common religious heritage and declaring that there would be a land where Kurds and Turks would live side by side as Muslim brothers. But when it was all over, Ataturk betrayed the Kurds."

"Was it some kind of religious war?" Dan had asked.

"No, not really. Yet, there were clearly religious overtones," Mustafa had replied. "The Turks had appealed to the Muslim sense of community and claimed to be fighting a *jihad*, or holy war, against the Christian infidels who occupied the western part of the country. The mullahs and other religious leaders encouraged my people to fight. But Ataturk wasn't really fighting a holy war, and he had no real interest in the independent future of his Kurdish brothers. He really wanted to establish a nationalist state controlled by the Turks and in which the Kurds would be assimilated.

"Just look at the treaty Ataturk signed with the Allied powers!" Mustafa had exclaimed. "The Kurdish province of Mosul, which just happened to have extensive oil deposits, went to Iraq which was under British mandate. The French got their share, too, when some of our lands were given to Syria, then under French mandate. Were my people asked about all this? No, their land was simply divided among Turkey, Iraq, Iran, and Syria, with the majority of the territory going to Turkey. In Turkey the Kurds were given no rights at all because the treaty only protected non-Muslim minorities there. The Western powers could have made a difference. But they bought into the Muslim 'brother' rhetoric and let Ataturk have his way. We were a people without rights, without a homeland, much as the Palestinians are today. In the end, it was as if the Kurds didn't even exist."

Dan pulled himself back to the present. "Maybe a cup of coffee will help," he said and headed for the work area.

"The damnedest thing just happened to me," Dan said, as Jim, AGEX's accountant, handed him the coffeepot. "I started on that stack of papers I inherited from Jake, and the first one is a deal with Aishagu, that Turkish company we work with. Well, it turns out the managing director is a guy I went to school with. At least I'm pretty sure it's the same fellow. There can't be two people named Mustafa Bahdiri from Diyarbekir."

"What the hell are you talking about? What's Diyarbekir?" asked Jim with a quizzical look on his face.

"Oh, sorry," said Dan. "I guess I'm not making much sense. Diyarbekir is a city in southeastern Turkey. That's where Aishagu Import-Export Company is headquartered, and that's also where this fellow I went to college with was from. I haven't heard from him in years, and then a couple of minutes ago his name pops up on my computer screen big as life. Apparently he's head of Aishagu."

"It's a good company," Jim replied. "Solid credit, timely payments, never any problems. Wish all of the people we dealt with were like them."

"Oh, that's good to hear," Dan said. "I was sort of wondering about the company, especially since they import some dual-use items. Being new at this stuff, I wasn't sure if we need to apply for an export license."

"Don't ever remember that happening before," Jim said. "Isn't all that history in the files? Jake was always so meticulous about details, I would have thought that if licenses were needed that information would be in the files."

"Yeah, you're right," Dan agreed. "All the data is there. I don't think we ever got export licenses for Aishagu's orders before, but I wonder if we ought to."

"What do you mean?" Jim asked.

"Well," Dan responded, "when we were in school he was always talking about the Kurds. You see, Mustafa's not Turkish, he's a Kurd. He was always going on about how the Kurdish people in Turkey were facing a classic case of oppression. I remember one night he went on and on about the way the government was destroying all references to the Kurdish people, their history, their culture, their language. He said that the names of their towns and villages were changed. Books were burned. Calling yourself a Kurd or speaking Kurdish was a criminal act. Very few Kurds could speak Turkish, so they couldn't go to school. Without an education they were effectively cut out of politics and business.

"What really would send him off was the constant threat to their existence. Mustafa used to tell unbelievable stories about commando raids in Kurdish territory. Groups of government commandos would go into the villages and round up all the inhabitants, under the pretext of searching for contraband weapons. But their real purpose seemed to be to intimidate the villagers and peasants of the Kurdish countryside. He said that sometimes they would beat or torture people. Sometimes they would rape the women. Often, a person would be executed as an example to other villagers. I never really believed all of what he said, but with everything that's gone on in Bosnia, I wonder now if maybe he wasn't exaggerating. Regardless, I always wondered why he wanted to go back," Dan said, his voice trailing off.

"You've been out of school for quite a while. Things have changed a lot, I'm sure," Jim said.

"I'm not so sure about that," Dan countered. "That's really what concerns me. I remember him telling me about the number of people who were jailed or executed for speaking out in support of the Kurds. In fact, he had an uncle who had been imprisoned in the early sixties for writing about Kurdish language and culture. And there was also the family friend who had been imprisoned for being involved in a bilingual publication.

"Look, Jim," Dan said in response to the skepticism evident on his colleague's face, "I know this must sound melodramatic. But you have to understand my position. You see Mustafa always said he was going back because he wanted to help his people. I never did understand how working in the family business was going to help, but I do remember his answer when I asked him that question. Mustafa was clear in his reply. He told me, 'I don't want the lives of those who struggled for freedom to have been given in vain. Someone has to do something. I have the advantage of an education. I will be able to educate my people. With the resources from the business I can help them gain a better economic footing. They need to become involved in the economic expansion that is to come. I can help them become involved in the political process. Already, there have been a few Kurds elected to the national assembly. If my people are ever going to have autonomy, we must be active in government.'

"Now, here I sit, trying to figure out if I need to get in touch with someone down at Export Administration, if Mustafa's involved with the Kurds? He could be supplying them with all sorts of stuff, including some of the photographic material we're shipping."

"Dan, don't you think you're overreacting?" Jim asked. "Look, I've got to get back to work, but I think you ought to call Aishagu's man out East. First of all, it may not be the same guy. But if it is tell him who you are and ask what he's up to. I can't imagine that Jake would have been approving things if there were any doubt at all. Jake was very careful and a real stickler for following the rules. How else do you think he made it for thirty-five years in this business?"

Dan watched Jim disappear down the long hall. "Jim doesn't know Mustafa," thought Dan. "I do, and I know that if it's the same person there's a possibility, however remote, that the items might go to an inappropriate destination or end-user. It was made clear in the training session that I'm bound to report any suspicion to the Office of Export Enforcement. I'd better call the fellow in New Jersey right now."

Dan hung up the phone, stood up, went over to the window, and began staring at the planes making their final approach to O'Hare International Airport. He was even less sure of himself now than before. When he had contacted Aishagu's East Coast office he'd found that Mustafa's nephew, Abdul, was in charge. Bits and pieces of their almost hour-long conversation popped in and out of Dan's head.

"Oh, my uncle is very well. He is the elder of the family now. He has built the company into one of the most successful in the region," Abdul had said proudly.

After a while, Dan had been able to steer the conversation to politics. Abdul seemed to respond naturally, though he didn't say much more than what Dan already knew from following news reports. After the fall of the Shah and the almost decade-long war between Iran and Iraq, the Kurds were still without a homeland. The Iran-Iraq war was particularly gruesome for the Kurds, though they had once again become a military force to be reckoned with. Unfortunately the Kurds didn't limit their attacks to the Iraqis, but, as in the past, they often attacked one another. It wasn't until 1987 that the Kurdish Front was established and they joined forces. That was also the year that Iraq began to use chemical weapons against the Kurds.

"The stakes were raised for our people during the Iraq-Iran war," Abdul had said matter-of-factly. "It had become a war of genocide. Thousands of Kurds were killed. No one would respond to calls for help, not the United Nations, not foreign governments. The international community seemed more interested in courting Saddam Hussein whose power was solidifying. Only human-rights groups and a few reporters seemed to care. But they were ineffective in their pleas. So we Kurds remain a people with no political or economic influence and no support from our Muslim neighbors. But this time there was no retreating to the mountains for safety. Chemical-weapon attacks prevented it. Tens of thousands became refugees in Turkey. But they are treated more like prisoners in concentration camps, much like the way the Vietnamese boat people have been treated in Hong Kong."

Dan had asked if things had improved when the international community turned against Iraq.

"Well," Abdul replied, "things started to look up for us after Hussein's invasion of Kuwait. The rapid response of the United States and its Arab allies gave Kurdish patriots new hope. In the first place, the Kurdish Front was recognized, and international support was given, and promises were made to secure the rights of the Kurdish people. But now, things seem to be in a holding pattern with nothing much happening."

Dan remembered that after the Gulf War the papers were full of news about "Operation Provide Comfort," Washington's response to securing the Kurds against future attacks and persecution from Baghdad. Dan had read somewhere that the real intent of creating the no-fly safe zone for Kurds in northern Iraq was to protect Turkey from an influx of Kurdish refugees similar to that at the end of the Iran-Iraq war. The papers were full of praise for the American, British, and French efforts and concern for the Kurds.

"I think my uncle has been successful because he is one of the few people able to bring goods into the area. He is a very good businessman and a fair one, too. He doesn't try to inflate prices, so people trust him. That's always good for business," Abdul noted proudly. "Though it has not been easy. You know, Diyarbekir had been under emergency rule since the beginning of the influx of refugees in 1987. In addition, the embargo against Iraq after the Gulf War has closed down the major overland route for trade between Europe and the Middle East. It is a problem because that trade route has always been the source of the little economic stability that we had in southeastern Turkey."

Abdul hadn't said anything Dan didn't already know. Because of his friendship with Mustafa, Dan had always read with interest any reports on Turkey or the Kurds. He was convinced that the embargo had to be catastrophic for the local economy and those living there—Kurd or Turk.

"But," he often asked himself, "wouldn't you think that being in the same boat and suffering the same hardships would bring them together and give them a common cause? Apparently not. Territorial disputes somehow seem to be built into human history both past and present. Look at Bosnia or Tibet or Sudan. Is there really a right to a homeland? Are we bound to give every group its own territory? Can't we learn to coexist so we can live in peace together?"

Suddenly, the telephone rang, its sharp ring jolting Dan back to the present. Joe was on the other end. "Do you have the paperwork on the Aishagu Import-Export Trading Company deal?" he asked.

"I'm almost finished with it. You'll have it by the end of the day," Dan replied, stalling for a little extra time. "If I'm finished sooner, I'll call you right away."

The conversation with Abdul left Dan believing that Mustafa's analysis of his people's situation would still be the same as it had been when they were in college.

"What is the international community's concern for my people? Does it really want to help us establish a homeland?" Mustafa had always asked. "Members of the international community seem to be interested in helping my people only as long as we can help them further their own interests in the international arena. And when we are no longer useful, that will be the end of any aid or assistance. We Kurds have to rely on ourselves."

"Well, from what Abdul says, it's obvious that Mustafa hasn't changed a lot," Dan concluded as he finally turned away from the window and sat down at his desk, "I'm not surprised that he's been involved helping his people, he was so determined to preserve their culture and heritage. Abdul talked about how his uncle helped poor kids go to school and worked with people who provide food and medical treatment for the refugees. Certainly that isn't a problem. That's simply good old philanthropy. But I wonder if that's all he's doing? If I could answer that, then I would know how to proceed. How much more do I need to pursue this? Maybe I should just let this go; otherwise, there's a chance that shipments will be canceled and the charity work he's doing will come to a halt. After all, this order is for photographic paper and other film processing supplies, and Jake has been okaying transactions just like this for at least five years. If he hadn't retired, this would have been on Joe's desk by now."

As Dan picked up his pen, ready to sign off on the paperwork, he wondered if he was acting irresponsibly and putting himself and his company in a position that might result in government sanctions. He'd heard of people and companies being fined or, in extreme cases, being prosecuted for not following the regulations. On the other hand, he had the required declaration from Aishagu Import-Export Trading Company stating that the goods were for commercial nonmilitary use only, plus a long history of exporting to Aishagu without any problems. That history should be sufficient if any inquiries were made. Still, pen poised on paper, his mind continued to reel with questions: "Should I sign this? Is this really the right way to help the Kurds? Will I make trouble for Mustafa if I don't sign it? Somebody needs to take responsibility for the situation the Kurds are in, but is it me and is this how to do it?"

AN ISLAMIC RESPONSE by Ismail H. Abdalla

Ethically, Islam as a religion recognizes the rights of all individuals to life, property, and, within limits, freedom. The *shari'a*, or Islamic law, specifies individuals' responsibilities to God (prayer and fasting), to one another (alms giving), and to the Islamic state (defense). Ideally, in an Islamic state governed by the *shari'a*, all Muslim individuals are equal before God. This unity of believers was central to the community that the Prophet founded. Non-Muslim minorities (Christians, Jews, and the Sabaians or followers of the old religion of Persia) enjoyed the protection of the state and were free to continue practicing their faith against the payment of a special tax called *gizya*. They, however, were not allowed to hold sensitive state posts such as the head of the state or the commander of the Muslim armies or to be judges except in their own communities adjudicating among their own people. Because the Islamic state recognized religion as the only valid criterion for citizenship, all those who professed Islam as their faith were, therefore, full citizens. Those heathens who professed none of the accepted monotheistic religions of Islam, Christianity, Judaism, or Sabaian, were not considered citizens, though often they, too, were tolerated.

From a theological point of view, Islam does not recognize "nationalism" as a defining characteristic of humans. It is faith rather than ethnicity or geography that counts. A Muslim fighter dies in the name of God, not in defense of a particular territory or special ethnicity. This is why there is now tension between Islam and the ideology of nationalism. This tension has been there from the beginning of Islam. Upon the death of the Prophet Muhammad, the founder of Islam, unity among believers was seriously threatened when Muslims from Medina made strong objections to the selection of Abu Bakr as successor or Caliph because he was from Mecca, the rival city. Ever since that time to the present Muslims have tried with various degrees of success to reconcile loyalty to their faith with loyalty to their tribal, ethnic, or regional group. The reason is that Islam itself, while uncompromising about unity and equality among all believers regardless of color, race, or origin, made significant concessions to relations based on blood, such that these relationships acquired legitimacy, even sanctity, in the eyes of the believers. This is clearly the case in the rules covering inheritance and the individual's obligations toward close relatives up and down the descent line. Muslims are obligated, for example, to help other Muslims, starting with close relatives first.

The ideal egalitarian *umma*, or community of believers, that the Prophet Muhammad was able to establish in Medina did not survive his death. And while faith remained an important unifying factor after that, it was not uncommon to see this or that region of the vast Islamic empire controlled by dynasties whose claims to legitimacy were based solely on the manipulation of sanguinity, what Ibn Khaldun, the famous fourteenth-century Muslim philosopher-historian, called *asabiyya*. Such were the Umayyads, the Abbasids, the different Seljuk sultanates, and, most importantly, the Ottoman Turks. Islam, as interpreted by the *ulama*, or clergy, quickly learned to tolerate power in the hands of powerful tribal or ethnic chiefs, giving them in due course the legitimacy they needed to govern. Some *ulama* went even further and declared that Muslims must always live under some system of government and that any ruler, no matter how unjust he might be, was preferable to the alternative, which was anarchy.

This was the prevalent political culture in the Muslim community that imperial Europe encountered when it came to dominate the area we now know as the Middle East. It was a community of Muslims "united" by faith against non-Muslims but divided according to ethnicity or region. The Kurds were one among many other ethnic groups. They were Sunni Muslims which set them apart from the Shi'i of Iran to the east, while their language and the secluded mountainous terrain where they lived for millennia separated them from neighboring Muslims, from the Arabs to the south and west, and from the Turks to the north. Colonial rule brought with it significant changes, however. One important change was the complete separation between church and state, or Islam and politics. Islamic law, which once informed every aspect of the life of the believer, was systematically being confined to the realm of personal matters: marriage, divorce, or inheritance. Politics remained the domain of the new European masters and of their protégées from among loyal subjects. Europeans brought yet another change which was to have grave consequences for the peoples of this region. In their attempt to divide and rule, the colonial masters strengthened whatever tendencies for autonomy and independence existed among the different groups. Kurds, Arabs, and other minorities in the former Ottoman Empire were led to believe that they were cultural and national units unto themselves, distinct from and opposed to the Turks, and that their different languages, histories, and traditions, even their sectarian religious beliefs, were worthy of preservation, cultivation, and development. They were also encouraged, through education and practice, to believe that such desirable goals were achievable only within the newly introduced political framework of the nation-state.

Unfortunately, only the Arabs, the Turks, and the Jews were able to push the demand for autonomy and/or independence to its logical conclusion, the creation of an independent state. The Kurds and the Armenians were left out. Neither the Turks nor the Arabs were willing or prepared to grant them freedom, and the European powers were not, until recently, agreeable to fight regional powers on behalf of the Kurds.

All in all, there are about ten and one-half million Kurds living in their ancient homeland, Kurdistan. This rugged mountainous terrain in the Anti-Taurus and the Zagros range is divided among four countries: Turkey, Syria, Iraq, and Iran. Although Iraqi official records are suspect, there are about three million Kurds in Iraq alone, thereby constituting the largest minority in that country. While Kurds have had a strong sense of nationality from very early in their history, intertribal rivalry and foreign domination led to frequent alliances with intruding Arabs, Turks, or Iranians against local rivals. Such political expediency, more than anything else, impeded the Kurds' progress toward self-determination and independence. But this is changing. Urbanization, education, and social and economic mobility all combined to arouse, among urbanite Kurds in Turkey as well as in Iraq, intense nationalism, a nationalism that is growing rapidly at the expense of the traditional tribal loyalty and particularism. This is especially the case in urban centers such as Kirkuk, Mosul, and Sulaymaniya.

Religion plays a strong role in the lives of the Kurds, even among those with a considerable degree of Western education. Most of the Kurds are Sunni, though in Iraq many are Shi'i. Compared to those who are Iranian or Turkish citizens, the Kurds in Iraq have long actively participated in the political development in that country. This is because, unlike Iran where Shi'ism has been politicized to an extreme since the Iranian revolution of 1979 or Turkey where Turkic nationalism has practically suffocated to death all other forms of loyalty, the Ba'ath Party in Iraq has always accommodated minorities and incorporated then into its ranks. This was so because the founding father of this secularist and revivalist party, Michael Aflaq, was himself a minority, belonging, as he did, to the Greek Orthodox Church in Syria. Thus it is misleading indeed to try and read the intractable conflict between the Kurds and Baghdad in terms other than what it is, a rivalry between two nationalities, one "Cowardice," the other Arab, or more precisely Iraqi Arab. The intense hatred that the leaders of Baghdad reserve for the Kurds stems largely from the feeling that the Kurds on more than one occasion betrayed them to the enemy. This was the case when Iraq fought Iran in the 1980s and again during the recent Gulf War. In both cases, the Iraqi leadership could not count on the loyalty of the Kurds, some of whom took advantage of Iraqi troubles and opened a war front in the north. Thus is explained the ruthlessness with which Baghdad treated the Kurds whom it regarded as traitors deserving the same bloody punishment that is meted out to all opposition groups regardless of their ethnic or religious affiliation. If Saddam Hussein can be as ruthless as he was with members of his own family, it is not at all reasonable to expect him to be more merciful to others. To him, political power comes first, not Islam, or, even Arabism. Otherwise, he would not have invaded the country of his "brothers," the Kuwaitis.

Islam, as noted above, is against nationalism understood to mean identity based on ethnic, geographic, or linguistic affiliation. It is precisely because of this that neither the leaders of Baghdad nor their Kurdish opponents can manipulate Islam effectively in the pursuit of their secular goals. However, because Islam stresses justice and equity and implores all believers to strive hard to achieve them and live lives according to their dictates, injustice can be and often was a sufficient justification for disobedience, even rebellion, against an unjust ruler. But such a rebellion is to redress a bad situation or to replace an unjust ruler, not to divide the Muslim community into entities based on ethnicity, language, or geography. From an Islamic point of view Kurds as Kurds do not exist. Only as Muslims do they have rights to life, security, property, and freedom, and as Muslims they individually or collectively can take redemptive actions to injustice inflicted upon them. Indeed, it is their duty and the duty of all believers to see to it that injustice is removed, by force if necessary. Seen in this context, the plight of Kurds and indeed of any other "minority" in the Middle East is against Islam and contrary to its teachings, not so much because these peoples are separate communities, for they are not, but because they are individual Muslims who are denied their rights.

A ROMAN CATHOLIC RESPONSE by William P. George

In this "case of conscience," the primary actor, Dan, is faced with a dilemma: should he sign off on a business transaction when not only livelihoods but also the life of an entire people appear to be at stake? A primary aim of Roman Catholic moral theology has been to help individuals like Dan to resolve such questions. This is serious business because matters of morals—how we ought to live in the world—are not merely ancillary to the "Godly" life. Catholics believe that, in the person of Jesus Christ, God has entered our world with a redeeming and healing love, a love that continues to dwell in human hearts and communities through the Holy Spirit. Business transactions, government regulations, and many other "worldly" affairs are not beside the point of a "faith-full" life.

In addition, from a Catholic point of view, one will necessarily inquire immediately about Dan's religious faith commitments. Grounded in the doctrine of creation is a Catholic conviction that all people share the call of conscience to live fully human lives. Such a conviction is expressed, for example, when papal documents on such varied issues as war or euthanasia or economic justice are addressed not only to Catholics but also to all people of good will.

There is a particular feature of Catholic theology that bears on this case and others like it, namely, the tendency towards balance and inclusiveness, a "both-and" as opposed to an "either-or" stance. So, Catholic theology, including moral theology, stresses grace and nature, faith and reason, scripture and tradition. While concern for "subjective" morality (being a good person) may be primary in Catholic theology, morality's "objective" side (doing the right thing) is crucial, too. In other words, from a Catholic point of view, good intentions are necessary but not morally sufficient; as Dan seems to recognize, *what* he does and *how* he does it are as important as his good will. The dangers of legalism and objectivism notwithstanding, the Catholic tradition has consistently stressed the importance of an objective moral order.[1] Similarly, while this tradition affirms the primacy of individual conscience (such that Dan is obliged to follow his conscience, even if in error), so also does it stress the arduous duty to inform one's conscience through careful attention to the wider and longer moral wisdom of the tradition and its moral sources among which are scripture, official church teaching, theological opinion, and the example of good and holy people.

Catholicism's reluctance to place exclusive emphasis on one or another aspect of morality is shown again in the degree of pluralism it recognizes on certain substantive issues. This is due in part to the opaqueness of many situations that call for prudential judgments, those wise and subtle judgments that, in the midst of very particular circumstances, exceed the straightforward application of moral principles.[2] But a degree of pluralism may also be rooted in the various roles and vocations that individuals assume or have chosen. What is required of a corporate CEO may not be required of a college student, and what is required of a diplomat may not be required of a middle-level manager of a multinational corporation. As one of Catholicism's most important moral guides, Thomas Aquinas (1225–1274), puts it, while all are called to imitate God, each is called to do so according to his or her own "mode."[3] Thus, in a particular situation, what is morally required will depend in various and sometimes complex ways on which moral actor(s) we are considering. This consideration, we shall see, is critical to the case at hand.

It is not as though the Catholic tradition does not draw moral lines in the sand. Certainly it has and does—although sometimes these lines relax or harden,[4] and sometimes they are contested even from within the tradition. Still, much of the Catholic approach to morality is a balancing act, seeking a moral mean between unacceptable extremes.[5] If one thinks this is easy or an exercise in fence sitting, then one might recall a famous Catholic apologist's comparison of "orthodoxy" to the equilibrium displayed by one who expertly holds the reins behind a brace of madly rushing horses.[6] How might this search for the moral middle ground—the "both-and" or the "neither-nor"—be relevant here? The Catholic social activist Dorothy Day used to say that hers was a two-fold mission: to comfort the afflicted and to afflict the comfortable. Surely there is much in this case to suggest that many "comfortable" people need their consciences afflicted or shaken up with regard to the reprehensible treatment of the Kurds. I do not want to minimize this "prophetic" dimension of Catholic moral thought and action.[7] "Cheap grace," "moral laxism," and rationalization are, of course, real dangers, as Blaise Pascal (1623-1662) demonstrated with biting wit.[8] Still, Catholic moralists (and, it may surprise some, canon lawyers, too) have often also been intent on relieving individuals' consciences of burdens they ought not be asked to bear—for such unburdening is surely grounded in the Gospel, too (Mt 23:4). For instance, Catholic pastoral practice has regularly included care for persons who suffer from "scruples," a fear that even the slightest transgression cannot be forgiven. While scrupulosity in this technical sense may be rare in American corporate life and elsewhere, an obsessive worry about "doing something wrong" *can* lead to moral paralysis or unintended harm. So, the question is, what is required in this case—comfort or affliction?

Dan is arguably placing on himself an excessive moral burden. Thus Jim's remark that he is "overreacting" may unwittingly be on the mark. How is Dan overburdened? Let me suggest three ways. First, assuming that he takes seriously the directives he learned in his training session, the case presents no solid evidence to sustain suspicions that his old acquaintance, and now his transaction partner, is in fact engaged in the sort of military procurement that would require a license for "dual-use goods." On the contrary, Mustafa Bahdiri's strong convictions about the treatment of his people and their heroic stand notwithstanding, Dan knows from his conversations with Mustafa only that Mustafa is intent on the economic advancement of his people, helping them to work within the economic and political system. There is, in other words, no justification for Dan to override the presumption of truth that ought to be given the declaration from the Aishagu company as to the nonmilitary use of the goods.

Second, Dan is faced with a prudential judgment, and, as Thomas Aquinas explains in his treatise on the virtues, prudence often requires that individuals seek the counsel of experts.[9] In the case at hand, this certainly includes legal counsel. For we should not forget that AGEX is a legal as well as a moral entity. If Dan has genuine concerns (or even unfounded scruples), the prudent thing to do would be to place a call to AGEX's corporate counsel. After all, this is precisely the sort of expert advice that competent attorneys retained by corporations in Chicago's western suburbs can and ought to provide. In fact, if Dan is seriously worried that he might be in violation of export regulations such that his signing of documents jeopardizes AGEX and the welfare of its employees, one could argue that he is acting irresponsibly if he does not consult his company's attorney(s) before moving forward. If Dan has time for a one-hour call to Aishagu's New Jersey office, he surely has time for a ten-minute call to AGEX's lawyer, and if the lawyer truly believes that the transaction poses problems, then the paperwork can wait another day.

Now, introducing a corporate lawyer into the case raises any number of broader questions that might be pursued. These include the complex relationship between law and morality, the possibility that business ethics might degenerate to "what we can legally get away with," the possible overemphasis in the United States on law and lawyers, and so on. The Catholic tradition has something to say on these issues and a longer commentary on the case at hand might move the discussion in these directions. The basic point, however, is that Dan's moral responsibility is a shared responsibility, and in this case it is shared with, among others, the corporation's legal counsel. This is not just "passing the buck." It is an implicit acknowledgment of some very Catholic themes: human beings are by nature social; individual moral agents do not operate in moral or legal vacuums (again, AGEX is a legal and thus a social entity); the virtue of prudence is oriented to the common good; and the call of conscience, though profoundly personal, is never wholly private. Conscience is a "knowing with"—a moral knowing and striving that reaches out to other moral agents, traditions, and spheres, with their distinctive competencies and moral perspectives. As noted above, the duty to "inform" one's conscience by reaching beyond oneself is critical to the moral life.

This leads to a third way in which Dan may be unduly burdened. A component of prudence, Aquinas tells us, is "circumspection"—awareness of facts and features morally relevant to this case.[10] Now, it may seem that morally relevant circumstances are endless. Dan has a breadth of knowledge about the particulars of this case that, for instance, his coworker Jim does not enjoy, and surely the complexity of the Kurdish situation overflows the case as it is written.[11] When Dan muses that perhaps he needs more information, it is easy to surmise that the complexity of the issue will only increase as the moral sphere of the case is allowed to grow to include the complex history and factionalism of the Kurds, the behavior of Turkey and other states, and so on—and he has only given himself until the end of the day to reach a decision!

Indeed, the problem of circumscribing a particular case often seems so daunting that, in his treatise on prudence, Aquinas considers an objection: circumstances are infinite and therefore unknowable; thus circumspection cannot be a part of prudence. But to this objection Aquinas replies: "Though the number of possible circumstances be infinite, the number of actual circumstances is not; and the judgment of reason in matters of action is influenced by things which are few in number."[12] Prudence is oriented towards decision, and deciding necessarily involves "cutting" (from the Latin:

decidere: to cut down, cut off). Circumspection, as a part of prudence, involves cutting away that which impedes a good moral choice. In the case at hand, such cutting or circumscribing arguably requires Dan's humble admission that, on the spot, he cannot—and need not—resolve the enormously complex case of the Kurds in search of a homeland, or the more general case of self-determination of peoples as this has been debated for decades now in international law.[13]

The point is that, while an expansion of moral horizons and thus an ever wider awareness of circumstances is crucial to the moral life (hence the need for education on several fronts), so too is it critical to remain focused on the moral task at hand. In this regard, the title of the case, "Fighting for a Homeland," may be a somewhat imprudent title. It seems to suggest that resolution of Dan's dilemma rests on his ability morally to resolve a case that is far more complex and burdensome than whether or not he should apply for an export license. Catholic moralists have often engaged in casuistry— the sophisticated use of cases to help clarify how stringently moral principles ought to apply in particular circumstances. If this case method has a legitimate purpose, it is, in part, to help people to resolve difficult moral issues precisely by starting with that which is more solid and certain and then moving to the intellectually and morally more challenging case. Putting the major emphasis on the "Kurdish question" or the "self-determination of peoples," as the case title might suggest, is to invert that order, moving instead from the difficult or even intractable case to the simpler and more manageable case at hand.

More to the point, perhaps, because case studies are meant to lead the user to a deeper level of moral reflection, the reader may be led astray as well, burdened by the assumption that he or she must resolve the Kurdish question if he or she is to resolve Dan's dilemma—and thus similar moral issues in his or her own life that seemed tied to some moral issue of near global proportions. In short, the case of Dan and his paperwork is distinct from the enormously complex case of the Kurds and similarly oppressed peoples fighting for a homeland. If this distinction is kept in view the resolution of the case appears relatively easy: Dan should either complete the transaction without applying for the export license, or, if he has doubts, phone AGEX's legal office and go from there.

But this is not to say that Dan's case is entirely separate from broader questions that have immense moral weight. It is not to say that Dan's knowledge of the Kurdish situation imposes on him no obligations whatsoever to work, within the various moral spheres he occupies as parent, citizen, voter, business leader, etc., towards a resolution of that profoundly important and difficult moral case. And it is not to say that the Catholic tradition has nothing to offer in terms of reflection on the question of the Kurds or the larger question of the rights of peoples that emerges in Bosnia, the Americas, the Middle East, Africa, and elsewhere—though it is doubtful whether, in Catholic moral reflection and social teaching, that larger question has been fully worked through.

The case ends with an apt question: "Somebody needs to take responsibility for the situation the Kurds are in, but is it me and is this how to do it?" Convinced that human beings are bound by their common humanity and thus by principles of solidarity, which in turn are grounded in the two-fold Gospel commandment to love God and neighbor, the Catholic tradition would readily agree that, yes, somebody does have to take responsibility for the situation in which the Kurds find themselves. But it is a responsibility shared by many: those who sit on the United Nations Security Council or in the General Assembly, individual state leaders and diplomats, religious leaders and organizations, contributors to international law journals, corporate executives doing business in Turkey, voters, human-rights activists, journalists, and many others—not least of whom are the Kurdish people themselves. Were the reader asked to consider a second case, inquiring for example about the moral responsibility of a legal adviser to the United States Secretary of State faced with a question of United States policy bound to affect Kurds in Turkey or Iraq, or of a Kurdish leader locked in a bitter struggle with other Kurdish factions, then this shared responsibility would quickly become apparent.

Granting this division of duties, the Catholic tradition does affirm certain principles that can and ought to guide moral reflection on the Kurdish and similar situations. For instance, the principle of "subsidiarity," so central to Catholic social thought, holds that "it is an injustice and at the same time a grave evil and a disturbance of right order, to transfer to the larger collectivity functions which can be performed and provided for by lesser and subordinate bodies."[14] And in keeping with its longstanding suspicion of statism, whether of the Right or of the Left, the Catholic tradition also holds that culture ought to maintain its relative autonomy vis-à-vis political authority. Furthermore, Catholic social teaching has affirmed a theologically backed "preferential option for the poor" and marginalized peoples.

These and similar principles provide a basis for the moral and legal claims of identifiable cultural entities such as the Kurds, although the extent of those claims may well be limited (recall Catholicism's "middle way").[15] "Catholic" moral principles will not necessarily yield immediate policy prescriptions regarding particular situations, that is, prescriptions that bypass very difficult prudential judgments of how best to operate in an imperfect world. To give but one example, clearly one of the most problematic aspects of the Kurdish question is the manner in which self-determination of peoples, an accepted principle of international law, quickly butts up against an even more deeply entrenched principle, namely, state sovereignty—whether of Turkey, Iraq, or the United States—such that the Kurdish "people" lose out to the Turkish "state" and its allies.

Fifty years ago, a famous Catholic thinker, Jacques Maritain, delivered a scathing philosophical critique of the concept of sovereignty, which, in the extreme, places individual states above the good of both individuals and the global community. Still, Maritain was realistic enough to know that an alternative vision of world order could not be realized easily or soon.[16] He was surely right about that, recent challenges to the principle of state sovereignty notwithstanding. What is required, then, is creative moral activity in a less than perfect international legal situation. Despite the measure of sham and posturing that arguably passes for diplomacy and international affairs—for example, the questionable altruism of "Operation Provide Comfort," mentioned in the case—it is worth noting that international lawyers and state leaders are not insensitive to the dilemmas posed by sometimes conflicting principles. So, while the international community has until now staunchly resisted claims for self-determination that seek to define peoples apart from existing territorial boundaries—which in turn are tied to the colonial system—it is sometimes acknowledged that in particular situations the claims of peoples without a legally recognized territory may yet gain a degree of acceptance.[17]

Such considerations go beyond the scope of this commentary, for as I have emphasized, Dan need not resolve all these problems in order to make a good decision. But in closing, it should be noted that just as the challenges posed by the Kurdish question should not paralyze individual decision makers such as Dan, so too it must not be supposed that even the larger issues that Dan mulls over (but need not resolve) are intractable in every respect. As noted above, despite its reticence to bypass the role of prudence in specific cases, the Catholic tradition does draw some clear moral lines. Much of what is reprehensible about past and present treatment of the Kurds, whether self-inflicted or at the hands of others, falls under the heading of attacks on the person, thereby violating what is perhaps the fundamental principle of Catholic social thought, and a principle that implicitly grounds human-rights law: respect for human dignity.

So, one should not allow the contested nature of the self-determination of peoples issue to obscure the fact that much of what is wrong in the Kurdish situation—for example, the gassing of Kurds in Iraq—is already contemptible under widely accepted human rights principles and law. The case of the Kurds and other marginalized peoples is, to be sure, on the growing end of international law and, I would suggest, Catholic social thought. As Dan and other moral agents acting in other spheres seek to resolve this larger case with its several unknowns, they should root themselves in that which is already solid and clear and then with courage and wisdom forge ahead into this moral frontier.

Notes

1. While it goes beyond the scope of this commentary, it should be noted that this "objective moral order" may be understood in dynamic and heuristic rather than fixed and static terms. See, e.g., Richard M. Gula, *Reason Informed by Faith: Foundations of Catholic Morality* (Mahwah, NJ: Paulist Press, 1989), esp. Chapter 2, "The Context of Contemporary Moral Theology."

2. For instance, as the United States Catholic bishops emphasized in their 1983 pastoral letter on war and peace, while certain moral principles governing the use of force may be binding on all, in concrete circumstances good and reasonable people

will not always agree on how these fundamental principles might best apply. See National Conference of Catholic Bishops, *The Challenge of Peace: God's Promise and Our Response* (Washington, DC: United States Catholic Conference, 1983), par. 9.

3. Thomas Aquinas, *Summa Theologica* II–II 64, 4, reply obj. 1.

4. One could argue, for instance, that the "official teaching" on the death penalty has moved from acceptance of this practice to a virtually absolute prohibition.

5. For example, in the economic sphere, official Catholic teaching has repeatedly rejected both communism, on the one hand, and unbridled liberalism, on the other.

6. Gilbert K. Chesterton, *Orthodoxy* (New York: John Lane Company, 1906), 185.

7. For example, it seems that such a concern has motivated Pope John Paul II's frequent condemnations of Western consumerism and what he perceives as its "culture of death." Catholic versions of liberation theology also display a powerful prophetic dimension.

8. See Blaise Pascal, *The Provincial Letters*, trans. A.J. Krailsheimer (New York: Penguin Books, 1967).

9. Aquinas, *Summa Theologica* II–II 49, 3.

10. Aquinas, *Summa Theologica* II–II 49, 7.

11. See Gerard Chaliand, ed., *A People without a Country: The Kurds and Kurdistan* (New York: Olive Branch Press, 1993).

12. Aquinas, *Summa Theologica* II–II 49, 6, Reply Obj. 1.

13. See Louis Henkin, *International Law: Politics and Values* (Boston: Martinus Nijhoff Publishers, 1995), 197–98.

14. The statement is from the encyclical of Pius XII, *Quadragesimo anno*; quoted in John XXIII, *Mater et Magistra*, par. 53. Not only does this principle have something to say about the rights and duties of groups, but it also serves as a reminder that, sometimes at least, individuals such as Dan, or individual groups such as the Kurds, *do* require the aid of a "larger collectivity" such as the United Nations if a particular moral challenge is to be met.

15. For instance, with its emphasis on the common good, the Catholic tradition will be sympathetic to the warning of former United Nations Secretary General Boutros Boutros-Ghali who acknowledged that the United Nations "has not closed its doors" to such claims, but then warned: "Yet if every ethnic, religious or linguistic group claimed statehood, there would be no limit to fragmentation and peace, security and economic well-being for all would become even more difficult to achieve" ("Agenda for Peace," UN Doc. S/24111, para. 11 [1992]).

16. Jacques Maritain, *Man and the State* (Chicago: The University of Chicago Press, 1951), 28–53; 201.

17. Henkin, *International Law*, 197–98.

Bibliography and Suggested Reading

Arfa, Hassan. *The Kurds: An Historical and Political Survey*. London: Oxford University Press, 1966.

Bates, Daniel and Bassam. *Peoples and Cultures of the Middle East*. Englewood Cliffs, NJ: Prentice-Hall, 1983.

Chaliand, Gerard, ed. *A People without a Country: The Kurds and Kurdistan*. New York: Olive Branch Press, 1993.

Edmonds, C. "Kurdish Nationalism." *Journal of Contemporary History* 6, no. 1 (1971):87–107.

Gula, Richard M. *Moral Discernment*. Mahwah, NJ: Paulist Press, 1997.

———. *Reason Informed by Faith: Foundations of Catholic Morality*. Mahwah, NJ: Paulist Press, 1989.

Hannum, Hurst. *Autonomy, Sovereignty, and Self-Determination: The Accomodation of Conflicting Rights*. Philadelphia: University of Pennsylvania Press, 1996.

Henkin, Louis. *International Law: Politics and Values*. Boston: Martinus Nijhoff Publishers, 1995.

Jonsen, Albert R., and Stephen Toulmin. *The Abuse of Casuistry: A History of Moral Reasoning*. Berkeley: University of California Press, 1988.

Kinsman, J. "The Changing Face of Kurdish Nationalism." *New Middle East* 20 (1970):19–20.

Maritain, Jacques. *Man and the State*. Chicago: The University of Chicago Press, 1951.

National Conference of Catholic Bishops. *The Challenge of Peace: God's Promise and Our Response*. Washington, DC: United States Catholic Conference, 1983.

The New Dictionary of Catholic Social Thought. Ed. Judith A. Dwyer. Collegeville, MN: 1994. Entries especially pertinent to the issue of the rights of peoples include: "Culture" (Allan Figueroa Deck, SJ); "Genocide" (John T. Pawlikowski, OSM); "Human Rights" (Thomas Hoppe); "Poor, Preferential Option for" (Donal Dorr); and "Solidarity" (Matthew L. Lamb). Each includes references to relevant papal encyclicals as well as a bibliography.

O'Ballance, Edgar. *The Kurdish Revolt: 1960–1970*. London: Faber and Faber, 1973.

PART III

RELIGION, ECONOMICS, AND ECOLOGY

CHAPTER 11

A Conflict of Interest

A CASE STUDY by Christine E. Gudorf

Margaret responded respectfully, "Yes, Jim, I have the last set of legal memos, and I'll review the entire project and give you an initial impression on Monday. No, it's no trouble; I know you're anxious for some feedback. Talk to you Monday." As she hung up the phone she groaned out loud and thought to herself, "Big trouble ahead, and none of the paths look promising." She carefully selected those memos she wanted to reread at home that night, placed them in her briefcase, and began straightening her desk, thinking to herself, "I always suspected it might come to something like this."

Margaret Grey Bull was an associate vice president with the Project Development Division of Crayrock Mining Company. She was also a non-reservation Lakota Sioux. Even before her mother had died when Margaret was eleven, they had not lived on the reservation. Her mother had told stories about the government's policy to depopulate the reservations both by failing to deliver food and supply shipments due the Natives under treaty and by promising young Natives jobs and health programs if they moved off the reservations to the cities—thereby forfeiting their reservation rights. Both of Margaret's parents had been urban Lakotas. After her mother's death, her father, unable to find steady employment—and increasingly under the influence of the alcoholism that killed him when she was sixteen—surrendered the eleven-year-old Margaret and her seven-year-old sister, Rose, to state foster care. After some months in a shelter, they were eventually placed in a neighboring state with a non-Native family, a minister and a schoolteacher with two young sons. The minister had pastored a largely Native congregation, so Margaret and Rose Grey Bull had not been entirely immersed in non-Native culture, though the congregation was not Sioux.

Margaret's foster parents had encouraged her to finish high school and go to college, where she completed a B.S. in environmental studies and, later, an M.B.A. About halfway through her environmental studies program it occurred to her that her Native American background might well have influenced her interest in the environment. She was even clearer that one part of her interest in business was her abhorrence of the poverty that mired so many Native Americans and the areas around their reservations. When Margaret began interviewing for jobs she had quickly learned that her Native American background, indicated by both her appearance and her surname, Grey Bull, made her especially attractive to the corporations recruiting environmental staff.

Though she had initially been put off by the idea that employers might see her as a token Native American and use her hiring to deflect charges of environmental despoliation or racial discrimination against other minorities, Margaret had decided that her suspicions of the motives of Crayrock's personnel director in hiring her did not extend to Peter, a vice president and the director of Project Development, and, in any event, need not affect the integrity of her own work. "Besides," she had laughed at the time to her cousin Dan, "it's about time that being Indian gave somebody an advantage somewhere!"

Margaret had begun as Peter's technical assistant and had quickly learned how central the environmental impact office at Crayrock was. It had an important role in new project development as well as in Crayrock's interaction with the media, the courts, state and federal regulatory offices, and the public in general. The longer Margaret had remained at Crayrock, the more often it had occurred to her that environmental engineering was even more critical for the company's external relations than it was for planning new projects. For the first six years she had obtained options on land, visited proposed sites, reviewed the analysis of ore samples, investigated development costs, written reports on this data, and sent them to Peter, the vice president who headed her office. Peter had commented more than once that her B.S. in environmental studies had saved Crayrock hundreds of thousands of dollars by allowing her to recognize immediately sites that would never make it past the stage of filing environmental impact statements.

Two years ago Peter's heart attack had forced him into early retirement, and she had been stunned when he recommended her to replace him as an associate vice president in Project Development. For the two years in which she had headed Project Development, there had been no major new projects. Until now most of the work in Project Development had been in refining plans for projects already on the board.

The stack of memos she was taking home laid out the problems in getting the company's newest mining project approved. The proposed project was a huge new mine which would cover over 600 acres and produce daily over 10,000 tons of ore containing copper, zinc, and lesser amounts of gold. The mine was to be situated on privately owned land, most of which was surrounded by several Indian reservations as well as some state and federal wilderness lands. A big piece of the land had already been acquired through a three-way trade with another company and the state. Margaret anticipated some problems because she knew the entire region around the proposed mine was wet—full of lakes, rivers, and a high underground water table. Wet areas were the bane of Margaret's work, for the sulfide wastes produced by mining metals combine with water or air to make sulfuric acid, which remains toxic for many centuries. The sulfide wastes of so large a mine would not be easily contained, and so posed a danger to both the surface and the underground water and to any life forms dependent on them.

As she left the office and began the three-hour drive to her sister's home, where she would spend the weekend, she worried that the land trade made the proposed project seem already near the implementation stage when it arrived at her desk. She was upset that she had not been consulted before Crayrock agreed to the trade, but she understood that the first negotiations had taken place during the period immediately after Peter's heart attack and before she had been named to succeed him. During that period Alex, the lawyer and vice president who directed land acquisition, had made sure to have the ore samples carefully analyzed, but the whole issue of environmental impact had been ignored, all the more easily because the state had been a party to the trade. Now she was afraid that Jim, the president, and the Board itself would understand her role as getting the project through any environmental scrutiny. But it was clear to her after the first read-through that it would be impossible to plan a mine that both utilized the entire site and passed environmental muster even if she were willing temporarily to set aside her conscience and values. Pulling into the driveway of Rose's house, Margaret was relieved at the chance to unburden herself to Rose and her husband, Ray.

Ten minutes later, sipping on a glass of tart lemonade in Rose's backyard, Margaret recounted the story of the new project. Ray, who was turning hamburgers on the grill while Rose set the picnic table for dinner, remarked to Margaret, "You haven't told us where this proposed mine is, Margie. But if this is the land trade written up in the paper a few weeks ago, then I think I know where it is. If so, the problem is bigger than you think. This is not just a matter of your conscience and your job, or your company fouling the land they think of as theirs. If what they do will kill the fish in the reservation rivers and lakes, if it will poison the game and kill the groundcover that prevents erosion, if it can make the people sick, then this is an issue for the tribes—and if I'm right, there are at least four different tribes at stake here. As a Native, you have an obligation to tell the tribes of the dangers."

"I can't do that and work for Crayrock," Margaret responded firmly. "It would be a conflict of interest. I can only work with the tribes if I quit first, if I determined that nothing could be done to make this project safe where it is planned and that nothing I do can persuade the company to give it up. It may come to that, Ray, but for now I have to work within the company."

Rose, a school cafeteria cook who had married Ray right out of high school, had always treated Margaret's education and job with great deference. Now she responded, "Margie, do you think the company deserves this respect when they traded for this land without even asking what the effect of a mine would be? Do you really owe them anything?"

But Ray interrupted before Margaret could reply. "I understand what she means, Rose. Maybe they don't deserve to be treated honorably, but she wants to keep her own self-respect. We shouldn't push her to go behind their backs just because they're no good," Ray said and turned to call their three sons from the baseball game next door.

Chuckling wryly, Margaret remarked, "I take it you do intend to push me to go to the tribal councils, only for different reasons?" Ray only smiled. Margaret asked, "What do you think the tribes would say if the company offered to give the tribes first crack at the jobs at this site? Would that alter their willingness to take risks? We're talking about a few hundred jobs, most relatively well paying."

"I think that would make it tougher, because unemployment and under-employment are so high, but I have no doubt that the tribes will act to pre-serve the reservation. In the last analysis, the reservation is all they have. It is the tribe's past and future," answered Ray.

Having sent the boys to wash their hands, Rose added very seriously, "Margaret, this is a life-or-death issue. That mining project might very well be the direct cause of Indian deaths, but if it ruins the reservations, it will be the end of these communities. I know you have never been very interested in reservation affairs because the poverty and alcoholism make you uneasy, though Ray's boss mentioned to me last year that you were one of the clinic's biggest private benefactors. We were surprised, but proud. But Margaret, the environment is not only important in its own right, but also to the tribes—and to people like you. How many times have you come back from your soli-tary hiking and camping trips in the wild and told me how they are the only thing that renew and energize you to return to work? How many times have you heard Ray telling stories of the elders who come into the clinic under pressure, because they insist that the reason for their illness is not in their body, but that the people suffer because the land is afflicted, because the spirits of the animals are disturbed?"

"Remember," Ray added, "the sobriety conference I went to in Gallup last year that focused on Native spirituality? I've been keeping tabs on three of the local groups that started working with teenagers following that con-ference, and so far I'm very impressed with them. They treat sobriety, both directly and indirectly, by involving the kids in tribal lore and rituals with elders who give them a healthy identity and sense of community with the tribe and with the land. As the kids learn the old ways, they have a better sense of themselves as Natives and are more committed to the tribal com-munity and its structures and traditions. I sent a young delinquent from one of my families in counseling to one of these groups, and four months later he was a new kid, alcohol-free, whose life revolved around sweat lodge, learning ritual prayers, and preparations for his vision quest."

"I'm happy the programs are working, though I don't understand why. But what does this have to do with the mining project?" asked Margaret.

"Everything," Ray answered. "The health of the land and the communal life of the people are inseparable. If the waters, animals, and plants die, then the link with the territory that sustains the people's identity is destroyed and even prayer is impossible. The soul of the people will be at risk. So this is not just the business of the tribal council. This is also the business of the people's spiritual guides, the elders who retain the sacred rituals." Margaret did not respond. She loved her brother-in-law and knew that his tribal folklore expressed much of the same reverence toward nature that she expressed in more scientific language, but she had always felt unable to follow him when he talked this spirit language. As the boys filed out from washing their hands and sat at the table, the talk turned to Little League competition and the prospects of their team which Ray coached.

Two weeks later Margaret had completed her inspection of the proposed mine site and, setting aside the geological reports she had just reviewed again, she addressed her assistant, Stan Bilkowski. "Well, Stan, let's review the problems and the options."

Stan, accustomed to his role of organizing the options and being the sounding board Margaret used in deciding her initial steps, began. "Well, the one positive note is that northwest corner of the site, where the water table is significantly lower and the surface less permeable, and there are no surface waters near. On the other hand, in the southeast area there is just no way to safely mine. Even transporting all the slag, which would be prohibitively expensive, would still leave a virtual certainty of significant contamination of the river. The area is simply too marshy—though even the EPA [Environmental Protection Agency] concedes it is not (legally protected) wetland. I don't think we need to worry about this area—there is no way the EPA can possibly approve mining there. And it's state Forest Service land that is nearest to that piece, so they will have some say, too."

Margaret responded, "Don't be too sure. I made a remark about that likelihood in the elevator the other day when one of the VPs asked me about how our evaluation was going, and he replied that the state had assured the company that it promised to approve the project and argue for its safety with the EPA. He even said they had obtained data to back up the argument. He said that the promise of jobs in a project this big was a powerful motivator with the state. Maybe so. And maybe some official will have a luxury retirement from this. We are a subsidiary of one of the most powerful corporations in the world—who knows what kind of power it exercises?"

Two hours later they were finished. Margaret wearily summarized, "So we propose a medium-to-small mine that uses less than half the property; ban open-pit mining; treat, and then triple the proposed depth of, the clay linings of the tailings ponds. Reducing the size of the mine and going from full open-pit to partial underground drilling will greatly reduce the amount of sulfide waste. Tripling the linings on the tailings pond should take care of leaks. But according to environmental engineering, there are only two choices for where to divert the rest of the runoff. What a choice! A trout-filled river designated as scenic or the headwaters of a major national river network! But there really isn't a question—the company would rather see the wastes get "lost" in the multi-state river network than ruin the local scenic river where the damage could be blamed on us alone. Politically, there is simply no choice, as PR would say."

Dan queried gently, "Can you really propose that the company not use more than half the land and mine only a small piece at a time for years longer? The earnings rate from this project will be very low, and the longer the company mines the land, the longer it must take responsibility for the environmental effects of its mining—and the more likely effects are to show."

"I know, Dan. That's the problem. And I can already hear the responses if I propose this: 'The project will produce necessary metals and provide jobs. Why are you being so conservative if the state and the EPA will approve more?' They will tell me that I can't hold back progress, that this size mine is not economically feasible, and that Crayrock can do what it pleases with its own land."

Dan commiserated, "It's going to be awful for you. I'm glad I don't have to be there. But you only have another week before the report is due. What are you going to do?"

"I don't know," Margaret admitted.

Two days later she called in sick, then flew to Chicago to keep a last minute appointment she had wangled with an old university classmate who had done a law degree after his environmental studies B.S. and now worked in environmental law. Rich greeted her warmly and walked her into his office. "It's so good to see you, Margie. It's been too long. Beth wanted to drop downtown and see you, but our youngest son woke up with a fever and she felt she ought to stay home."

"I hope he's okay," Margaret began, but Rich broke in to say, "He's fine, he's just teething, and nobody but Beth will put up with him when he's uncomfortable. He's a real holy terror. But Beth asked you to call her before your plane leaves."

When Margaret had called for the appointment, she had told Rich she wanted to consult him about the law regarding Indian rights over reservation land, especially migratory resources near or on reservation land. Now Dan asked for a quick rundown on the proposed project, so that he could better understand how to answer her questions. After she was finished with her explanation, Dan asked: "I take it that you feel it's not advisable to ask these questions of Crayrock's fleet of attorneys?"

"No," Margaret admitted, "I need to know all the implications of the situation before I decide whether there is any use in putting my career on the line. What does the law say?"

"Well," Rich began, "the basic case decision governing this type of situation was the 1908 *Winters* decision that says that water rights in treaty land were reserved to the tribes, so that persons upstream could not dispossess the tribes by excessive use. *Winters* began a system of water appropriation that says the first people to acquire legal right to land get first use of the rivers or lakes, and that what water use is left passes to the next people to get legal right to land, etc. But rights to water can be sold separately from the land, too, in the west. In most cases Natives were the first—or near the first—to have legal land rights and, therefore, water rights. But your question is about quality of water, and the courts have been largely silent about what quality of water can be provided to the tribes in order to fulfill their treaty rights. Furthermore, since the fifties there have been a series of encroachments on *Winters*; the effect of much federal legislation and policy has been to force the tribes into negotiating the limitation of their water-rights treaty.

"The EPA has been the best friend of the Indians in these cases, arguing the tribal side against the states' efforts to implement lower standards in environmental policy for reservation lands. The ruling that comes closest to your situation was a New Mexico one. In 1993, the Isleta Pueblo required that the water in the Rio Grande be sufficiently clean for ceremonial and recreational purposes and set specific standards of water cleanliness. The EPA approved the tribal standards, which then required the city of Albuquerque, five miles upstream, to treat and clean the sewage it now discharges into the river. The estimated cost of meeting the new standard is over $200 million, and the city is in court to reverse the ruling. One important question for you is the nature of the land that Crayrock plans to mine. You said it was privately owned. Is it within the boundaries of the reservation?"

"Some of it may be, but at least two-thirds has never been part of the reservation. Why? Does it make a difference whether it is or was part of the reservation?" asked Margaret.

"It may make a significant difference," replied Rich. "In *Montana v. the United States* (1981), the Supreme Court ruled that while tribal authorities do not have general authority over non-Indians owning private land within the reservations—so-called fee lands—the tribe may retain sufficient sovereignty to control non-Indian conduct that has some direct effect on the political integrity, economic security, or the health and welfare of the tribe. In 1989, this exception allowing some tribal regulation of non-Indian land and conduct was narrowed. The court, in *Brendale v. Confederated Tribes and Bands of Yakima*, ruled that tribal authorities could regulate non-Indian land and conduct when those non-Indian lands were small and the majority of land was tribal-owned, but could not regulate where ownership was checkerboarded between non-Indians and the tribe. However, the EPA has tended to ignore *Brendale*, because effective regulation of any kind of migratory resource is impossible where sovereignty is divided into tiny geographical bites. Because *Brendale* came from a divided court and is not considered clear, many authorities argue for ignoring it."

"How checkerboarded must land ownership be for the courts to deny regulation by tribal authorities?" asked Margaret.

"That is the million-dollar question. No one knows for sure what the limits are. In these two parcels the court allowed tribal regulation where the tribes owned 97 percent of the land and denied it where ownership was nearly equally divided between tribal lands and fee lands. Where the court would draw the line between those limits is not yet clear," Rich responded.

Twenty minutes later, after making a brief call to Beth and thanking Rich for his time, Margaret headed for the elevator, thinking to herself, "I can call Stan from the airport and get him to locate a map of the entire area which lays out tribal land, fee lands, and which fee lands are Crayrock's. I have a vague recollection that there is very little fee land involved, but whatever fee land is part of the project would be in that northwest corner. But then what do I do? How far will the state go in supporting advocacy for a large project covering the entire parcel? Is there any way to convince the Board to adopt a medium to small site without presenting them with massive opposition from the tribes and the EPA? Can I go to the tribes and the EPA while I still work for Crayrock? Can I work against the company that employs me?" Margaret sighed as she slid into the taxi for the ride to O'Hare. By the time she sank down in her window seat on the plane she had concluded: "The basic question for me is: Which of my responsibilities are primary? Am I first a Native American, as Ray and Rose insist? Or am I first associate vice president at Crayrock? Or am I first an ecologically committed citizen? In growing up and being educated I was taught environmental ethics and business ethics and Christian ethics, and I guess there is at least as much Native in me. But all the ethical principles and systems I have been taught push me in different directions all of which stem from only one of my roles. How do I decide among my roles?"

A NATIVE AMERICAN RESPONSE
by Carol J. Gallagher

Introduction

Margaret's struggles are rooted in a common contemporary native situation. They are neither only a dilemma of cultural responses, nor are they solely spiritual (theological). Margaret's struggle is a struggle at the core of her being for a fundamental understanding of who she is. The issues of land use, her own personal and professional integrity, and her tribal identity are enmeshed with her past as well as her future. To understand Margaret and the importance of her decision-making process, we need to understand both the historical context of her place in history and the unique nature of her spiritual grounding. To say this grounding is complex is to oversimplify the situation. And to say that the dilemma she faces is solely personal is to misstate the critical and primary issues at hand.

Margaret lives biculturally or transculturally, across cultures. She lives between two worlds—at least—and struggles with what she needs to do to survive in her corporate job while she attempts to define who she is in relation to her tribe, her family, and her heritage. It is important to begin this commentary with a brief explanation of the differences in worldviews between the various realms in which she is operating. Although not brought up on a reservation, Margaret is a Native woman who is—through family members—in contact with and invested in tradition and tribal values. She believes with some certainty that being Indian makes her different. She may not be able to articulate why she understands herself to be different, but it is clearly essential to her frame of reference. For much of the world, identifying and labeling difference is the only work that needs to be done. But to understand Margaret and the depth of her dilemma, we must identify some critical differences in the way Native peoples in general understand relationship, spirituality, and identity.

Overview

What follows are some general statements about the unique perspective with which Native people view the world. When I speak of Native, Native Americans, or American Indians, I am referring to those peoples whose heritage is *indigenous* to the North American continent, including mixed race, full blood, urban, and reservation persons. There is incredible diversity among these 530 distinct tribes, more than 450 of which are recognized by the federal government and have official status with the Bureau of Indian Affairs (BIA). The differences in tribal governments, worldviews, and religious practices make generalizations and universalization impossible. The predominance of my particular and personal experience has been in an urban setting, where Native people come together in multitribal gatherings. I am a Cherokee, an Episcopal priest, and mother of mixed ancestry. Throughout this commentary I hope that it is understood that I do not speak for all Indian people but only from the experience of my particular nation and family. For clarity I will make some general statements, but to understand best what it means to be an urban Lakota woman one must find a Lakota woman source. I will try, from my own perspective, to shed light into a very complex circumstance. There is—and should be—a great difference between the local tribal perceptions and the understanding of Native urban dwellers. Home, whether recognized reservation lands or not, is the blessed place of the people. This sacred homeland is always brought forth, remembered, and recreated in strange and alien environments. All that said, there are common themes and threads that create comparability among tribes and peoples of this hemisphere that might offer a framework for understanding the nature of Margaret's dilemma.

Relatedness

Common to most Native worldviews is a unique understanding of relationship. We as individuals are not only related to those with whom we share common blood lines but to all beings and all aspects of the form and function of the world. This understanding of our relatedness demands, from the individual, a responsibility to all of creation and to all generations, living and dead and as yet unborn. University of Colorado professor Vine Deloria, Jr., a Yankton Sioux, explains that "the personal nature of the universe demands that each and every entity in it seek and sustain personal relationships. The broader idea of relationship, in a universe very personal and particular, suggests that all relationships have a moral content. The spiritual aspect of knowledge about the world taught the people that relationships must not be left incomplete."[1] As Native people, part of who we are is embedded in this complex understanding of relationship and responsibility. David and Derald Sue, prominent human psychology researchers, have noted that "Indians see themselves as an extension of a tribe. This identity provides them with a sense of belonging and security, with which they form an interdependent system."[2] In understanding Margaret and the choices before her, we must engage this both personal and profound sense of relationship.

Power

For Indian people, understanding power means understanding place. Vine Deloria writes: "Power and place are dominant concepts—power being the living energy that inhabits and/or composes the universe, and place being the relationship of things to each other . . . power and place together produce personality."[3] For Native people each place has significance and power and each person is affected by and a participant in each place's power. Each individual's self-identity is defined by the interaction of the force of power and place. Wisdom, garnered by years of engagement with the totality of local place, is one way Native people identify authentic power in a person's life. The presence of wisdom signals the presence of power. For this reason, elders are revered for they provide wisdom and knowledge about the power of the place and demonstrate the person's integrity with their surroundings and the created order. Young people are not excluded from having wisdom as Native people believe that each individual is born with the potential of having vision and insight into the heart of the Creator. For Margaret, this means that her struggle with the issues at hand is not only an obvious corporate power struggle but also a conflict both personal and communal in scope. It calls her not only to seek advice but also to seek wisdom, the evidence of power, in her family and community.

Traditional Religions, Native Christians, and Spiritual Formation

For many American Indian people, cultural identity is linked to one's religious or spiritual upbringing. People often ask, "Can one be Christian and Indian, too?" Since the time of Columbus' arrival the debate over whether one can be Native and Christian has been waged. In fact, many tribes—for example, the Cherokees—were introduced to Christianity very early in the formation of the United States, and many embraced the religions of their missionaries and conquerors. James Treat, in his book *Native and Christian*, writes: "The blatant opportunism and oppressive dogmatism of the missionization process, the open complicity of white religious leaders in the widespread land dispossession, and the growing strength of the traditionalist revival work together to challenge the legitimacy of the personal religious choices many Native Christians have made."[4] To evaluate the complexity of the situation before Margaret, a Lakota woman brought up in a Native Christian environment, we must understand the staggering stratified levels of problems faced when trying to integrate Christianity in a culturally authentic tribal context. The complicity of missionaries in the past, their willingness to degrade and destroy people's culture and identity for the sake of religion, must be called into question. One must examine the dark history of the tribes and the United States government in federally funded, denominationally sponsored boarding schools. This commentary cannot encompass nearly all of the concerns provoked by the centuries of interaction between Native people and the church. Suffice it to say that the legacy is filled with pain which will not be resolved easily or soon. As a Native Christian, I choose to live in the "unresolved" ambiguity, striving to live faithfully and responsibly, informed by both traditions. For many, this is an impossible task. Margaret stands at the center of this ambiguity, and she is not alone.

Tribal religions are embedded in the power of place, relatedness, and interdependence with the whole created order. Ritual and story help bring the people to a place of hearing, respect, and wholeness. The ritualistic practices of traditional Native religions are varied and broad. Native people were and are people of prayer who daily seek the blessing of the creator and the cooperation of all their relations. Native people, unlike their European neighbors, do not distinguish between secular and religious, between holy and ordinary, between body and soul, between human and nonhuman. The integration that was referred to earlier when speaking of place and relatedness is in operation here. There is no concept of personal religion in our tradition, although private expressions are integrated as part of the whole. Paula Gunn Allen, professor of literature at the University of California, explains:

"The private soul is the public wall" is a concept alien to American Indian thought. The tribes do not celebrate the individual's ability to feel emotion, for they assume that people are able to do so. . . . The tribes seek—through song, ceremony, legend, sacred stories (myths), and tales—to embody, articulate, and share reality, to bring the isolated, private self into harmony and balance with this reality, to verbalize the sense of majesty, and reverent mystery of all things, and to actualize, in language, those truths that give to humanity its greatest significance and dignity.[5]

Rather than a private piety most common in Christian traditions, traditional practices among the tribes focused on integration of the larger whole as the primary religious expression. For Margaret truly to grapple with the issues at hand she must also be honest about the dissonance found in these clashing worldviews and wrestle with her place within the ambiguity of the circumstances. There are no simple answers to the decisions before her, but we also know she is not alone.

Commentary

Margaret asks, "Can I go to the tribes and the EPA while I still work for Crayrock? And can I work against a company that employs me?" Margaret wants to know how to prioritize her world, how to order her cosmos and find her place within it. She is faced with a decision to make, a task that is mired in the various roles within which she finds herself. The problem for Margaret is really developmental. I don't mean to say that she has some unresolved conflict left over from her early teen years. Margaret's crisis is developmental because of the nature of the circumstances. When we progress through the stages of our lives, we are faced with conflicts that push us beyond what we were in the past. Scholars like Eric Erickson spend their entire careers examining those moments of push—when we simultaneously grow into a new sense of self-knowledge, while some part of our personality or past self-knowledge is put aside. These are times of choosing one road over another, and they are times when our latent or dormant tendencies, if not addressed earlier in life, might need acknowledgment and employment in our personality.

Margaret is struggling to know how to resolve these issues from the norms of the ethics that she has been taught in church and school, both products of a culture and socialization method vastly different than that of her first years. But she also is aware that the part of her that was lying dormant is speaking to her on these issues, and she is less and less able to silence this voice or intuition. She knows that this is a struggle for herself. And although her sister and brother-in-law are the active voices of the "Indian" way, she is inherently struggling with who she is in light of what she has become.

Once we have identified this as a developmental conflict, and a conflict that is about identity, we can reflect back to some of the observations that were made earlier. Remember that a sense of relatedness, the power of place and wisdom, the notion of the importance of entire gathered community, and the unique and different worldview are all associated with Margaret's early developmental culture. Margaret faced a series of losses early in her life that she has overcome but not integrated. At least a part of her is pushing to the integration, that wholeness and sense of place in the created order that so dominates the consciousness of Native peoples. Simply put, for Margaret to find answers to resolve her conflict, she will have to find out who she is in the midst of the people who formed her culturally and who inform her sense of self.

Donald Fixico writes:

Among Indian people, role and responsibility are essential to the survival and prosperity of the community. . . . In this effort to fulfill roles and responsibilities, the final value will be achieved—harmony and balance. Harmony in each of us occurs as an internal struggle every day. . . . Balance in life is the key for harmony as intended by the Creator, but it has also been intended that we must struggle. We must understand the need for struggle as a daily endeavor to expend energy and work for the conservation of nature. Thus we build for the future.[6]

Fixico helps us to understand that Margaret's struggle is defined by her Native worldview.

Margaret is at a transitional place in her life. She has worked through the strata and structure of the educational system. She has worked her way to a place of responsibility and confidence in her world of employment. But she needs to know who she is. She needs a sense of her relatedness; she needs to see the place from where she came. She needs to go home and listen to the very core of her being. She needs to seek the advice of elders, the healing power of ritual, and her voice in the midst of her people. She needs to go home. And for someone who has been estranged from her home, who has lost so much of her family, and who has been separated from so much that defines her, this will be the most difficult task. Margaret will have to open herself to the spiritual power and grounding in her life in order to find answers. And the answers might be very hard to take.

Margaret wonders if she can keep her job and still go to the tribe. But there is a much larger and deeper question that looms on the horizon for her. With all that she knows and the evidence of history behind her, can she believe that the profit of Crayrock and other mining operations will not compromise the integrity, health, and future of the people of this region, both Native and non-Native alike? Does she truly believe that she can choose for the good of the tribes on one day and the next do what is necessary to keep her job? Margaret knows that her honesty will compromise her job and that all her hard work will be called into question. She has been defining herself as the non-Native world does—by the job she does. She has been judging the world from this perspective, but she is now at a place of no return. She wants and needs to know who she is and whose she is. She needs to be integrated into the larger community. Margaret needs to go home, back to the place she was forced to leave by circumstances over which she had no control. She needs to hear her name in the midst of her people. And for Margaret to resolve the great dilemmas that face her, she will have to find a way to bring that home, that sacred place with her wherever she goes. The time has come in her life that she has been avoiding. The answers will be found in hearing the voices of her ancestors, in touching all her relations, and in finding herself at home.

Notes

1. Vine Deloria, Jr., *Indian Education in America* (Boulder, CO: American Indian Science and Engineering Society, 1991), 10.

2. Derald Wing Sue and David Sue, *Counseling the Culturally Different: Theory and Practice*, 2nd ed. (New York: John Wiley and Sons, 1990), 176.

3. Deloria, *Indian Education*, 14.

4. James Treat, ed., *Native and Christian: Indigenous Voices on Religious Identity in the United States and Canada* (New York: Routledge, 1996), 9.

5. Paula Gunn Allen, *The Sacred Hoop: Recovering the Feminine in American Indian Traditions* (Boston: Beacon Press, 1986), 55.

6. Donald L. Fixico, "The Struggle for Our Homes," in *Defending Mother Earth: Native American Perspectives on Environmental Justice*, ed. Jace Weaver (Maryknoll, NY: Orbis Books, 1996).

A HINDU RESPONSE by Christopher Key Chapple

I write this as a guest representative of the Hindu tradition, having studied the yogic disciplines of India for several years, both as a scholar and as a practitioner. The Yoga tradition, which dates to the early phases of the Indus River Valley civilization (ca. 3500 BCE), has served as an underpinning for India's religious and cultural consciousness, with its ninety-one disciplines spanning Hinduism, Buddhism, Jainism, and Sikhism. In its devotional forms (*bhakti*) it speaks a language recognizable to Islam and hence might be termed a technology of religiosity rather than a distinct religious tradition.

In my studies of Yoga, I have explored Hinduism's advocacy of human will in the pursuit of psycho-spiritual freedom, known as *moksa* among the Hindus, *nirvana* among the Buddhists, and *kaivalyam* among the Jainas. I have also probed the complex strands of Indian thought that reflect themes of pre-Socratic Western philosophy. Each of these traditions itemize essential components of reality that include the gross elements, sense perception, modalities of conditioning, and varying descriptions of human consciousness. This itemization of the building blocks of reality emphasizes the interrelatedness between the world we perceive and the intention and desires of the perceiver. In short, Indian thought places the human person at the critical juncture of world construal. Through the disciplines of Yoga, one comes to understand how the thinking process governs, forms, and shapes our perceptions and reminds us that the world utterly depends on our perception of it.

From within this complex philosophical context, specific traditions arose that have put into place social norms and conventions that govern all aspects of daily life in India. The Brahmanical tradition gradually established a rigid system of caste that, in general terms, placed religious, legal, and instructional authority in the hands of the Brahman priests; assigned landholding, defense, and political concerns in the hands of the Ksatriya warriors; and delegated mercantilism to the Vaisyas. These three upper castes, comprising less than a quarter of the overall population, became the educated elite. They dominated the much larger peasant caste (Sudras) who tilled the soil, took up arms when needed, and filled occupations such as latrine cleaning deemed unworthy for the higher castes. A process of gradual "Hinduization" or "Brahmanization" or "Sanskritization" recruited workers from indigenous populations that spoke non-Aryan, non-Dravidian languages; today these people are known as tribals or members of "scheduled castes."

The Buddhists resisted the caste system, preferring to require all its members to renounce family life and caste status and enter monastic orders. Although the Buddha himself came from the landed class (Ksatriya) and many of his disciples were drawn from the merchant caste, all such distinctions disappeared once one joined the Buddhist community, or sangha. After 1,500 years, the Buddhist religion largely faded from India as Buddhist ideas and stories became subsumed within Hinduism, but Buddhism survives as the primary tradition throughout Southeast Asia and as an important component of cultural life in East Asia.

The Jainas, generally known for their success as merchants, developed both communities of renouncers (monks and nuns) and a significant lay community. In tandem, the Jain renouncers and laypersons have maintained a vital presence in India since at least 800 BCE.

Each of these traditions has developed a unique attitude toward the natural world. In addition to their formal, classical ontological assessments of the natural world, each tradition has accrued a history of interactions with the land and has adapted certain behaviors and attitudes toward the land that can be readily seen in daily life. By drawing from both the theories of these traditions and the observance of daily living in India, I will attempt to respond to the crisis of conscience faced by Margaret as she contemplates land use issues.

Let us proceed by contemplating the landscape and climate of India. India stretches several hundred miles from the Arabian Sea to the Bay of Bengal, tapering to a point that faces the Indian Ocean. To the north lie the Himalaya Mountains; to the west, the deserts that distinguish South Asia from the Middle East; and to the east, dense jungles and mountains that separate the subcontinent from Southeast Asia. Great river valleys gave birth to the civilizations of India: the Indus River, flowing through modern Pakistan; the Ganges River, flowing from the mountains and creating a great fertile flood plain in north India that supports a huge population; and smaller rivers such as the Godavari and the Cauvery. The tropical climate of India allows a year-round growing season, with monsoon rainfall augmented by irrigation from the rivers and wells. Great productivity in food has enabled India to support a huge population, which has been governed at various times by local kings or Rajas, the Buddhist empire of Asoka, the Hindu Gupta empire, the Delhi Sultanate and Mughal empire in the north, and European colonists, most notably the British. Since 1947, India has operated as a united, sovereign nation, which dominates the South Asian region and, occasionally, is in tension with its neighbors, particularly Pakistan and China.

The literature of India extols the beauty of the subcontinent. Banabhatta, author of the *Kadambari*, describes the vast stretches of forest in north India, writing, "There is a forest named Vindhya which touches the tide line of woods of both the Eastern and Western Oceans and which, like a girdle, adorns the middle region of the Earth. Its trees . . . bear masses of blown white flowers which, because of the great height of the trees, look like clinging star-clusters."[1] The luxuriant language of this expansive poetry reflects the natural splendor of the subcontinent.

The *Ramayana*, a great epic tale of love, banishment, and revenge, includes detailed descriptions of India's geography, flora, and fauna. Looking into the wild Dandaka forest into which he was banished, Rama called out:

Look, the *kimsuka* trees are in full blossom now that winter is past. Garlanded with their red flowers they almost seem to be on fire. Look at the marking-nut trees in bloom, untended by man, how they are bent over with fruit and leaves. I know I shall be able to live. Look at the honeycombs, Laksmana, amassed by honeybees on one tree after another. They hang down large as buckets. Here a moorhen is crying, and in answer to it a peacock calls through delightful stretches of forest richly carpeted with flowers.[2]

The natural beauty of India has long inspired its poets and storytellers. It also inspired words of protection by philosophers and writers of the law books. The *Atharva Veda*, which serves as the foundation for the traditional system of Indian medicine (Ayurveda), described the earth as the mother and states, "What I dig out of thee, O earth, shall quickly grow again: may I not, O pure one, pierce thy vital spot, (and) not thy heart!"[3] This verse states a need to protect the earth.

An example of the practice of protecting the earth can be found in the tradition of the sacred grove. The life of India even today takes place primarily in village communities. Many of these communities have included common space for grazing of animals and, in some instances, forest preserves attached to temples. Frederique Apffel Marglin writes:

The network of sacred groves . . . in India has since time immemorial been the locus and symbol of a way of life in which humans are embedded in nature and in which the highest levels of biological diversity are found where humans interact with nature. . . .

The sacred grove is the keystone in a way of life that has maintained such astounding sustainability. Far from being a mini nature preserve, the sacred grove is both locus and sign of the regeneration of body, land, and community. It stands for the integration of the human community in nature. . . The sacred grove, with its shrine to the local embodiment of the Great Goddess, is the permanent material sign of periodical processes of regeneration. It is because of the existence of the Great Goddess in her sacred grove that the body, the land and the community can be integrated into a single process.[4]

An annual festival at the sacred grove of the Goddess Haranchandi in Orissa takes place every year, drawing people from approximately sixty villages in a twelve-mile radius. Those celebrating set aside their normal work and, regardless of caste or status, join in the festivities; as Apffel Marglin notes, "all hierarchy is set aside for the duration of the festival."[5] One participant in the festival, Banambar Barala, observes:

no one owns the sacred grove; it belongs to every one; it is common land, the land of the Goddess. Just as the Goddess, and women too, must be undisturbed and pleased during their menses, the sacred grove as the material of this state is the locus where all the male villagers live in common. In this communal state, this unified household, they treat each other as brothers, undisturbed by quarrels or dissension. And it is in that very harmony that marriage exchanges, the first step towards village regeneration, are first discussed.[6]

The fertility of the forest facilitates the process of matchmaking for the villagers.

During a visit to India in 1997, I visited the Mannarassala Temple in Harippad, Kerala, to which a fourteen-acre sacred grove is attached. During the time of our visit, several parents had brought their babies to the temple for the feeding of their first solid food. These parents had first sought blessings from the temple priestess when they wished to become pregnant. They returned to the temple with offerings equal in weight to each baby. After receiving a new name and their first taste of rice, these five- to six-month-old babies were taken to the priestess for another blessing before returning home. The ceremonial songs and music pierced the quiet of the canopy of dense forest that surrounded the temple. A woman chanted praise verses in honor of various gods and goddesses. Retired people lingered at the temple even when the blessings concluded, and various temple attendants carried on their work of crafting offerings from palm thatch.

Village life in India, as well as urban life, follows the rhythms of the natural world. Electricity, though increasingly common in the cities, does not provide a reliable source for light, so the pace of life slows quickly after dark and begins with the first glow of sunrise. Animals, including monkeys, goats, cows, and dogs, roam the streets and road freely. The boundaries between the human and natural orders are much more fluid and permeable than in northern climates where sheer survival requires sequestering oneself from nature.

In the Hindu tradition of India, the earth is revered as a goddess, the Bhu Devi. She finds multiple manifestations, such as the Orissan goddess Haranchandi mentioned above. The Devi also empowers various priestesses, such as the Great Mother of the Serpent Temple at Mannarassala, to perform the rituals that ensure the smooth continuation of life. In philosophical Hinduism, the earth mother or Prithivi of the Vedas supports all life; Prakrti, the creative principle of the Samkhya tradition, permeates and includes all manifestations of reality.

In the Buddhist tradition, one meditates on a mound of earth for an extended period of time, reciting to oneself various epithets for her power: Prithivi, the earth goddess; Mahi, the great one; Medini, the friendly one; Bhumi, the ground; Vasudha, the provider of wealth; and Vasudhara, the bearer of wealth. In time, one internalizes the vision of the earth mound, taking its firm foundation throughout daily life. According to the *Visuddhimagga*, this concentration exercise helps still the mind: "The hindrances eventually become suppressed, the defilements subside, and the mind becomes concentrated."[7] This focus on the earth allows one to draw back from attachment to particularities and embrace the broader context from which all manifestations arise.

In the Jain tradition, the earth, in addition to being a constituent ingredient of weighty materials, also holds living spirit. According to Jain cosmology, earth bodies, found in clumps of dirt, in minerals, and in things made of metal, plastic, and other earthy materials, possess a living consciousness characterized by their sense of touch. In other words, when I walk upon the earth, the earth feels the weight of my footsteps. In Jain spirituality, harm to any being, including the earth, results in the accrual of negative *karma* that impedes the spark of one's own soul, or *jiva*. By taking care to not harm life, one enters into states of increasing spiritual purity. Acknowledging that the all-pervasiveness of life makes harmlessness an endlessly complicated task, the Jains allow for some differentiations among life forms. Animals, including fish, humans and other mammals, and birds carry all five senses and the mind. Worms possess only the senses of touch and taste. Jain ethics mandates that only one-sensed beings such as plants may be used for food sources and in one's livelihood. Hence, Jains are vegetarian and tend to take up occupations within such fields as commerce and publishing that minimize direct violence to life forms.

So far, we have investigated three distinct worldviews on the earth that can help Margaret look at her circumstances from different perspectives as she attempts to arrive at a decision. From the perspective of Hinduism, the *Atharva Veda* advocates protection of the earth. In the daily life of Hindus, examples of this approach can be found in the setting aside of sacred groves for ritual celebration and in temple observances that integrate the cycles of human productivity and reproductivity with the cycles of nature. Will the development of this mine violate the basic premises of this relationship? If contained to a small area, the benefits to human flourishing might outweigh the disadvantages. But if, as Margaret suggests, the mine will introduce toxins into the river systems, it will be risky. In the example of contemporary India, industrialization has overpowered vast tracts of land surrounding the major cities. Bombay, Delhi, and Bangalore are now ringed with districts of heavy industry. The waters and air have suffered immensely. In New Delhi, the particle particulant level regularly reaches 400 to 500 parts per million; in Los Angeles, the most polluted city in the United States, children and the elderly are advised to stay indoors on those rare days when the count reaches 200 parts per million. The waters of India have been severely polluted as well. The Ganges, the largest river of India, has been declared unfit for human use in many areas due to its high level of heavy metals and human waste products. Environmental regulation has lagged in India and elsewhere, with the argument that the luxuries afforded by increased industrialization and modernization counterbalance the inconvenience of foul air and water. Yet, despite the large task of meeting basic survival needs for nearly a billion people, India, nonetheless, has initiated some steps toward environmental responsibility, enacting vehicle emissions standards for the first time in 1997. The leading party of the 1998 coalition government included as one of its slogans, "Clean air, clean water."

With the proposed massive damming of the Narmada River for purposes of irrigation and generation of electricity, contemporary India struggles with land use issues similar to those found in the American West. The Narmada River Valley basin, a vast area of 98,796 square kilometers and home to twenty-two million people, will displace at least 100,000 people from 245 villages and disrupt the property of 140,000 farmers.[8] Proponents argue that the project, when completed, will provide drinking water for forty million people and irrigate desert areas in the state of Gujarat. Opponents claim these numbers are inaccurate and do not fully take into account the devastation to the largely tribal peoples slated for displacement. Of the thirty dams planned, one has been built; the sad story of the people displaced by this phase of the project has been recoreded in the documentary film *Kaise Jeebe Re! How Do I Survive, My Friend!*, produced in India by Jharna Jhavaeri.[9]

If contemporary Hindus were presented with the array of issues faced by Margaret, they would recognize several themes: disruption of rural land, weighing the benefits against the costs, and concern for the broad reach of industrial effluent. They would also recognize the profit motive driving the Crayrock Mining Company and the arguments put forth by the company that industry benefits people. They would also be impressed with the care and consideration on Margaret's part in consulting the legal precedents and with the fact that the company staff includes an environmental specialist.

From the perspective of Indian Buddhism, the response would be somewhat simpler. To what extent would the development of this mine project enhance one's advancement toward the liberating experience of *nirvana*? Buddhism in India, recall, was a religion of monks and nuns. To be a Buddhist meant that one renounced involvement with worldly concerns. The benefits derived from the mining operation would simply not benefit a monastic lifestyle and hence the Buddhist would reject the project. However, as noted earlier, Buddhism long ago disappeared from India. If we observe parallel conflicts in contemporary Buddhist countries such as Thailand and Sri Lanka, the answer would not be as simple.

The Jain tradition would provide a slightly more complicated response to Margaret's dilemma. On the one hand, mining requires harm ostensibly to one-sensed beings: plants and the earth. The animal life could be moved; humans would not be directly displaced. In India, granite and marble quarries are owned by Jains, who also control much of the jewelry business. Jains discovered mining to be lucrative and an acceptable source of livelihood for the lay community. And with the wealth generated by their many enterprises, Jains have long supported large communities of monks and nuns, as well as temples and libraries. However, from a contemporary perspective, the scientific data has revealed that the slag from the mine will pollute the water and might enter the food chain (for those non-Jains who fish and eat trout) or the source of someone's water. Including these considerations would cause a Jain to move slowly in making a decision. From a monastic perspective, similar to that held by the Buddhists, the mine is useless. From a lay or worldly perspective, the mine might serve some economic benefit, though, in this instance, it would appear likely that a Jain would support the small-scale project if any support at all were to be given.

The religions of India offer many resources for arriving at ethical decisions regarding the environment. I have summarized only a few. What I find most interesting is that issues such as the one faced by Margaret are now confronting people throughout the world. Just as Margaret has struggled with her conscience to reach an appropriate compromise drawing from her training as an environmentalist and her upbringing within Native American culture, so peoples throughout the world are grappling with finding a balance between an industrialization that enhances human comfort and well-being and an industrialization that attacks the very premises for a life of being well.

Notes

1. Gwendolyn Layne, trans., *Kadambari: A Classic Sanskrit Story of Magical Transformations* (New York: Garland, 1991), 136.

2. Sheldon Pollock, *Ramayana of Valmiki* (Princeton: Princeton University Press, 1986), 2:190–91.

3. Maurice Bloomfield, trans., *Hymns of the Atharva Veda*, (Oxford: Oxford University Press, 1897), 12:35.

4. Frederique Apffel Marglin with Purna Chandra Mishra, "Sacred Groves Regenerating the Body, and Land, the Community," in *Global Ecology: A New Arena of Political Conflict*, ed. Wolfgang Sachs (London: Zed Books, 1993), 198.

5. Apffel Marglin, "Sacred Groves," 205.

6. Apffel Marglin, "Sacred Groves," 206.

7. Buddhaghosa, *The Path of Purification* [*Visuddhimagga*], translated from the Pali by Bhikkhu Nyanamoli (Boulder, CO: Shambala, 1976), 130.

8. William Fisher, ed., *Toward Sustainable Development: Struggling Over India's Narmada River* (Armonk, NY: M. E. Sharpe, 1995),130.

9. Jharna Jhavaeri, producer, *Kaise Jeebe Re! How Do I Survive, My Friend!* (Bombay, India: film, 1997).

Bibliography and Suggested Reading

Allen, Paula Gunn. *The Sacred Hoop: Recovering the Feminine in American Indian Traditions.* Boston: Beacon Press, 1986.

Apffel Marglin, Frederique, with Purna Chandra Mishra. "Sacred Groves Regenerating the Body, and Land, the Community." In *Global Ecology: A New Arena of Political Conflict*, ed. Wolfgang Sachs. London: Zed Books, 1993.

Buddhaghosa. *The Path of Purification* [*Visuddhimagga*]. Translated from the Pali by Bhikkhu Nyanamoli. Boulder, CO: Shambala, 1976.

Deloria, Vine, Jr. *Indian Education in America.* Boulder, CO: American Indian Science and Engineering Society, 1991.

Fisher, William, ed. *Toward Sustainable Development: Struggling Over India's Narmada River.* Armonk, NY: M. E. Sharpe, 1995.

Hessel, Dieter, ed. *After Nature's Revolt: Eco-Justice and Theology.* Minneapolis, MN: Fortress, 1992.

Hymns of the Atharva Veda. Trans. Maurice Bloomfield. Oxford: Oxford University Press, 1897.

Jaimes, M. Annette, ed. *The State of Native America.* Boston: South End Press, 1992.

Jharna Jhavaeri. Producer. *Kaise Jeebe Re! How Do I Survive, My Friend!* Bombay, India: 1997. Film.

Layne, Gwendolyn, trans. *Kadambari: A Classic Sanskrit Story of Magical Transformations.* New York: Garland, 1991.

Monet, Don, and Skanu'u. *Colonialism on Trial: Indigenous Land Rights and the Gitksan and Wet'suwet'en Sovereignty Case.* New Haven, CT: New Society, 1992.

Pollock, Sheldon. *Ramayana of Valmiki.* Vol. 2. Princeton: Princeton University Press, 1986.

The Red Road to Sobriety. San Francisco: Kiaru Productions, 1995. Film.

Sue, Derald Wing, and David Sue. *Counseling the Culturally Different: Theory and Practice.* 2nd ed. New York: John Wiley and Sons, 1990.

Treat, James, ed. *Native and Christian: Indigenous Voices on Religious Identity in the United States and Canada.* New York: Routledge, 1996.

Weaver, Jace, ed. *Defending Mother Earth: Native American Perspectives on Environmental Justice.* Maryknoll, NY: Orbis Books, 1996.

CHAPTER 12

A Long Awaited Call

A CASE STUDY by Christine E. Gudorf

"What will you do when he is dead, Raoul?" asked Marta as they sat in the garden outside their father's bedroom. Raoul did not immediately answer his sister. The doctor had just explained that his father, Dom Pedro, had lapsed into a coma and was expected to die without recovering. Dona Elena was prostrate at the side of the bed, clutching her rosary and flanked by her two elder, married daughters. Her sons-in-law, Jorge and Luis, had just gone downstairs. They had not been particular admirers of Dom Pedro and were likely discussing the probable size of a daughter's share of Dom Pedro's estate, though both came from comfortable families and had never been dependent on Dom Pedro.

As Marta sat silent beside him, Raoul thought, "Ah, Father, but you have left me with a terrible mess!" In three days' time, there was to be a meeting of the local Rural Democratic Union (UDR), a group that opposed land reform in Brazil. His father had been well known both as one of the larger landowners in the region and as a founding member of the UDR in 1985. The UDR had been inactive since 1994, following critical national and international press on the UDR's hiring of a mercenary army which had assassinated campesinos in the landless movement. Now it was meeting again, as landowners became disturbed at the increasing level of national support for both land reform and for the landless movement. While Raoul's sentiments on land reform had always conflicted with his father's, he needed to know what the meeting decided. Perhaps he could moderate their plans; this was more likely if he could present himself as spokesperson for his ailing father, assuming, of course, that his father was still alive.

"Raoul, you will be careful, won't you?" Marta begged. Younger than their older sisters by over ten years, Marta and Raoul had always been close. She alone in the family had supported Raoul when he left the seminary to work for a social service agency in the slums of the state capital six years ago.

"You know I don't disagree with your goals," Marta went on, "but you have responsibilities for the welfare of many of us, both our safety and our support. You can only fill that responsibility if you are alive. We both know the possibility of violence has been increasing." Unspoken between them was

260

the accusation of a neighboring widow in 1990 that Dom Pedro and his friends in the UDR had threatened, harassed, and finally killed her husband, a small estate owner who had refused to join UDR and had publicly criticized its tactics.

Solemnly, Raoul replied, "Of course I remember my responsibilities to my family, Marta. I'm Dom Pedro's son, aren't I?" They both grimaced, remembering the many times Dom Pedro had denied them permission to do something they wanted by citing their responsibilities toward the family, its name, and its honor.

"Why don't you go see Bishop Silva? You and he have been close since you were in the seminary, and he certainly is well informed about the land reform issue," suggested Marta.

Turning quickly, Raoul kissed her on the forehead and replied, "I have an appointment tomorrow morning. Don't worry. Now let's go to Mama."

The next day Raoul met with the bishop who offered his sympathy for Dom Pedro's illness and, upon hearing the dire prognosis, remarked, "Such a relatively young man—Dom Pedro is hardly retirement age! And such a burden for your shoulders, Raoul. I am very sorry."

"I need some advice, Monsignor, and to talk the situation through with someone I trust," Raoul explained. "I fear the present circumstances here in Para [a northern state in Brazil]. The threat of violence looms over all of us. Within days I will have legal responsibility for my family estate. The estate manager tells me there are about 120,000 hectares of land in the estate, in three major parcels. Only 30,000 are worked, and 5,000 of that is leased out. Another 30,000 were acquired for speculation, and we are still making payments on that parcel. About 20,000 hectares will belong to my sisters and cannot be touched. I can afford to distribute up to 20,000 hectares to the landless. Two thousand families could get 10 hectares each. But I am afraid of inciting violence from both sides.

"There is a possibility that when the UDR learns of the proposed distribution, they will have me killed in the hopes of preventing my family from carrying through with the plan. I fear not just for myself, but also for my family. Maybe they would burn the hacienda in the night or cause a car wreck when I am not alone—or even machine-gun the family as we go to church," Raoul said earnestly.

"I know the possibilities, too, Raoul. I have had threats myself from the UDR for my condemnations of the UDR violence against the landless. I am still alive—but who knows for how long. On the other hand, I am an old man," replied Bishop Silva.

"But that is not all, Monsignor. I am also afraid of the landless movement. There are over five million landless campesino families. Some of them are desperate. I understand that if my family were hungry, I would be desperate, too. If word gets out that there is a land giveaway, how many thousands will make their way to our estate? Once the 2,000 families have the land, what will the others do? They will squat on the rest of the estate, and they will be angry. Like many of the local landowners, we are land-rich and cash-poor.

If they prevent us from farming the 30,000 hectares or cause large expenses in guards to keep the access roads open, I could quickly be in deep trouble. I need to talk to my sisters and their husbands, too. Their land is a major piece of the land that is worked, and if they intend to claim it now, or sell it, I will need cash to clear and prepare other sections to be worked if I mean to maintain the present level of income. Massive invasions of squatters could paralyze and bankrupt the estate."

Bishop Silva broke in, "But you must understand their desperation, Raoul. They have nothing. They watch their children die of hunger, of diseases that would never kill healthy children. They see access to land as their only hope."

"I understand, Monsignor. I am not blaming them. I might do the same if I were them. In fact, I know I would, and that's what scares me. I don't want to put myself in a position where, in order to save my family estate, I have to hire thugs to clear the squatters from my land. How likely is that to happen?" asked Raoul. "I don't see how to do what I know needs to be done."

"The risks are real enough from the UDR," responded the bishop. "When one of the UDR leaders is quoted as bragging to reporters about not only buying police officers and justice department officials, but also about poisoning Bishop Hanrahan of Conseicao de Araguaia in 1993 for supporting the rights of the landless, we must consider them likely to do violence to you. They have no conscience, no shame, or they would not have massacred the thirty-two landless men, women, and children here in Para in April '96. I am not sure how to advise you about the threat from the UDR. Everything depends on their mood and the leadership of the moment. You could deed the land to the church for distribution, and we could keep it quiet until the property has transferred, so that killing you would not prevent the distribution. But some of them might still want vengeance against you for betraying your class. Just last year they killed Natan Periera just for being a journalist who covered the massacre."

"I appreciate your offer, especially with the National Union of Rural Producers [another landowner association] already threatening to sue the bishops for supporting the landless movement. Deeding the land to the church would certainly be better than deeding it to the Institute," said Raoul flatly. They both knew that the government's National Institute of Colonization and Agrarian Reform had only given land to a third of the 43,000 families pledged by President Cardoso in 1995 and to fewer than a third of the 60,000 pledged for 1996. At the same time, the news media, alert to the solid majority of Brazilians who now supported land reform, had made clear that the Institute's inefficiency was politically selective. In almost ten years, the Institute had made no move to assist in expelling the mining and lumber companies illegally occupying Quilombo lands in Para, though the 1988 Constitution had given the Quilombos title to the interior Amazonian lands first settled by communities of their escaped slave ancestors. Neither had the Institute acted to evict or arrest large ranchers who had illegally seized public land in the Pontal de Paranapanema region of São Paulo. But the Institute had acted quickly and efficiently to coordinate evictions of poor landless squatter families and of organized mass occupations by the Movement of the Landless (MST). The Institute had even tried and imprisoned MST leaders and advisors, including priests, for planning illegal occupations of unused land.

"Raoul, I am impressed that you want to do the right thing. I know how ashamed you have been of the UDR and your father's role in it. I think you need to meet some of the leaders in the MST. Only they can answer your questions about the risk of squatters and violence from the landless. Let me set up a meeting here," proposed Bishop Silva. Raoul agreed to the meeting and promised to await the bishop's call.

Two evenings later, Raoul returned from the UDR meeting to find Marta waiting. "Well, what happened?" she asked, as she poured herself a cup of coffee. "Mama told me where you had gone, though she doesn't know why."

"Not much happened. I wanted to feel out the leaders, see how they reacted to my presence, see if there were divisions among them. No one challenged me—Father's pride must have kept him quiet about our arguments over the UDR and its thugs. Some of the more militant owners expected me to echo father, and some of the more moderate questioned me to find out where I stood. I let them know I deplored violence, which made me pretty conservative. Most of the discussion was about the new tax law. I agreed that, like most of them, I am land-rich and cash-poor, so paying 20 percent tax on unused land in estates of more than 20,000 hectares is impossible. If the government tries to collect the new taxes, we cannot pay without selling land. If all the landowners are forced to sell land to raise tax money, the price of land will fall drastically, and that will be a problem for people who borrowed against their land at higher prices, even if we can get the assessors to tax at the new lower value. And of course, we can't afford to have squatters disrupting our farming by either blocking the access roads or squatting on piecemeal parcels that prevent efficient use—or, God forbid, using their occupation as the basis for piecemeal land claims."

"And what of the MST? What did they say about them?" demanded Marta.

"They are angry at the MST and beginning to fear them, because of the change in public opinion. They reported on the March 1997 poll of the National Federation of Industry which showed 85 percent of Brazilians supported nonviolent land occupations. Ninety-four percent said the MST's fight for land reform was just, and 88 percent said the government should confiscate unused land and distribute it to landless campesinos. The UDR see this as a very dangerous shift in public opinion. They may not be able to buy off the politicians much longer. They blame the MST, and now the bishops supporting it, for encouraging millions of campesinos in what the UDR sees as illegal theft that campesinos would never have thought of without encouragement. The UDR see themselves as an oppressed and vilified minority. It's scary."

After a moment of silence, Marta informed him, "Bishop Silva called while you were out. The MST meeting is in the chancery at 3:00 tomorrow afternoon. May I go with you?"

"Of course, if you like. Mama will not object to your visiting the chancery, I suppose," replied Raoul. They turned out the lights and walked arm in arm up the stairs to their rooms.

The following afternoon, Raoul and Marta were escorted by a young priest into a conference room where they met Bishop Silva and the archbishop. They were introduced to four MST leaders, three from the Para region and one from the capital. The archbishop began the meeting by suggesting, "Raoul, I think you should describe what you are considering doing and the problems you see in doing it. Then they can respond."

So Raoul described his willingness to distribute 20,000 hectares to 2,000 families as well as his fears of UDR retribution on the one hand and the operation of his estate being paralyzed by thousands of disappointed squatters on the other.

"There is nothing that can be done about landowner violence unless landowners themselves are willing to bring those responsible to justice," said Eduardo, the MST lobbyist from the capital. "We have had forty to fifty of our people killed every year since the late eighties. Welcome to the club."

Diego, one of the local officials, immediately jumped in. "Perhaps there are ways to appear to your neighbors as if you were forced to surrender the land, so that they will not blame you."

Bishop Silva nodded. "I had suggested something like that to Raoul. A deathbed gift to the church from Dom Pedro, perhaps."

Diego went on, "About squatters, we can take care of that. If you allow us to select the 2,000 families, we will make sure that you do not have a squatter problem on the rest of the estate. We will, in effect, police it for you, and remove squatters. We can usually do it peacefully enough with a show of force and by registering the squatter families in our program so that they have hope of getting legal land from which they cannot be evicted. They trust us, because we are campesinos like them, and they know we will not sell them out. We have planned the majority of land occupations since 1988. We had forty-three occupations involving 11,000 families in 1990, but by 1996 that had increased to 176 occupations involving 45,000 families."

The archbishop remarked, "Before we move to specific strategies, I would first like to know from Raoul why it is that he pursues this path and what path he sees himself pursuing."

Raoul hesitated and then volunteered, "I have often argued with my father that violence is not the way for our society and that the distribution of land is too unequal. If I am to take responsibility for the estate, my conscience demands that I do something that moves us toward greater social justice."

Diego inquired, "How did you come to decide on 20,000 hectares?"

Raoul explained that it was the largest figure that he and the manager thought the estate could spare without any significant risk to operations or cash flow. Gazing probingly at Diego, he demanded, "Are you suggesting that I should offer more? Isn't that being somewhat ungrateful?"

Marta reached over and placed a calming hand on his forearm. "He just asked how you arrived at that figure," she reminded him.

The archbishop intervened: "Raoul, the MST has an interest in your intentions and motivation if they are to work with you. That is a very practical level for this inquiry. At another level which concerns me even more, your motivations seem religious and moral, and from what I know of you and have heard from Monsignor Silva, you are a good man. As your pastor, I want to make sure you have thought through the different options for discipleship here. Giving the land is a good thing, an action toward greater justice. But to whom much is given, much will be demanded. The MST needs people like you who will publicly support them. Your help—even aside from the land itself—could make a tremendous difference for millions of campesinos. But it would be a great risk for you, a changing of sides, and a risk of being a target of violence."

Before Raoul could respond, Rosario, a young MST official from a local village, explained, "There are many things that you could help us with. You could help the campesinos who get your land to organize a cooperative or two and have your marketing agent also handle the marketing of the cooperative's crops. Many times the local estate owners shut out from the markets the small campesinos who have received land. You, your estate manager, and workers who know this land and how to farm it successfully, could also instruct campesinos just beginning."

"But even more necessary," explained Eduardo, the lobbyist from the capital, "is a landowner who is willing to talk to other landowners about ceding land, about the justice of our cause."

Marta recoiled from these suggestions. "You are asking him to be a martyr," she accused.

Archbishop Muneres gently replied, "Sometimes the cost of discipleship is martyrdom, Marta, but we cannot know that in advance. There is a risk, I would be the first to admit. But Raoul would not be alone in that risk. Most of the people in this room have lived with that very risk for years now, and will go on living with it. The landless families these men represent often live not just with the risk of death, but with death itself. They bury their prematurely dead children in the dark of night because they could not afford medicines or burial fees. The plight of the landless is a blight on the nation, and it has to be addressed. We are asking Raoul to consider giving more than an anonymous gift of land that he does not need. It is up to him to decide what more he can or cannot do."

"I am not a leader. I am not a brave man," insisted Raoul. "I cannot be the man you need."

Eduardo replied, "Do you think that any of us was born to be brave leaders? We take one step at a time, just like you. And we know fear, too. But we understand our faith in terms of following Jesus' preferential option for the poor. And in Brazil today, the poor of Jesus are the landless campesinos. Once you make the commitment, it is a matter of living one day at a time."

Rosario, the youngest man present, said in a tone of finality, "I do not have the education to speak well, but I know that you have much to offer us. You bring your land, your education, and your family background and respectability. We can show you the campesinos from whom you can learn bravery and leadership."

"Think about it, Raoul," insisted the archbishop quietly. "If you decide to appear to surrender the land involuntarily, you will need to decide before Dom Pedro's will is announced. The gift of the land itself will be a great act of justice. We know that we ask for more than simple justice."

At this last, Eduardo added teasingly, "But know that if you join us there will come a time when we will start to make demands on some of the rest of the 100,000 hectares."

At this last, Marta was incensed, and as she and Raoul walked to their car, she fumed, "Who do they think that they are, Raoul, to be so ungrateful as to want more than 20,000 hectares? They will not be satisfied until we, too, are reduced to 10 hectares and living in a shack!"

But Raoul absentmindedly replied, "No, Marta, I don't disagree with him. If I hadn't had to worry about the mortgages on the northwest section, I would have offered them another 30,000 hectares. That's not the real issue. I just never expected to be in a position where I have to decide once and for all what kind of Christian I will be. It's almost as if Jesus, while collecting apostles, had walked up to me and said, 'Come, follow me.' Do I drop my life as it is and go? That's my choice. All my life I have waited for such a call. I left the seminary because I couldn't hear it. Now that I finally hear it, I don't know if I want to answer it. I never thought it would be like this. I don't know what to think of myself, much less what to do."

A ROMAN CATHOLIC RESPONSE by Christine E. Gudorf

Land reform in Brazil, as in much of Latin America, has been one of, and often, the most pressing demand(s) of the popular majority, due to long-standing monopolization of land ownership in Brazil by a small minority. While the roots of the present conflict extend back into the colonization process itself, the latest stage can be said to have begun forty years ago. In the 1950s came the establishment of leftist-organized grassroots peasants' leagues and then parallel local church-sponsored organizations of peasants.

In 1964 the military coup forced both peasant and Indian organizations pressing for land reform into defensive positions through strong persecution. The Catholic Church responded to the deaths, arrests, torture, and disappearances of those opposed to military policies by taking up the role of defender of human rights in Brazil. As was often noted by churchmen and international observers during the period of the military government, there was no other social institution capable of such defense.

With the return of civilian rule in the 1980s, the organization of peasants and Indians struggling to gain or retain land accelerated. Now, for the first time in Brazil, there is clear national sentiment for land reform, demonstrated in a variety of polls, though the shape and size of the majority favoring land reform shifts with the particulars of any plan.

In this case the central issue for Raoul is not so much whether land reform is just but rather how to distinguish between the demands of simple moral justice and those of Christian discipleship within the extended social process of obtaining land reform. Are the demands of simple moral justice, the justice owed to one's fellow citizens, satisfied by transferring one's excess property to those without land to work? Is the Christian call to "Follow Me" that Jesus made to his disciples supererogatory—not for all those who would be saved, but only for the special saints and martyrs pursuing perfection, whose excess virtue enriches the community as a whole?

Reflection on Christian Sources on Justice

The church in Brazil has led much of the Latin American church in reflection on the suffering and persecution, including martyrdom, experienced in the church and by others working for justice during the years of military rule. That reflection was based in scripture, in the record of God's presence in human communities extending from Abraham through the early Christian church. Scripture pointed to an understanding of God as a liberating God who covenanted with humans to care for them, intervened to free them from the slavery and oppression of Egypt, formed them into a people, delivered them to a promised land, and continued to care for them through messengers called prophets. All this was done despite the constant failures of fidelity on the part of the people during the Exodus and throughout the period of kingdom. The New Testament presents Jesus as God's ultimate intervention in human history, sent to both announce and reveal the inbreaking of God's reign as well as to embody the perfect response to God's love.

In the examples of God in the Old Testament and Jesus and his followers in the New Testament, the Brazilian church detected a clear preference for the poor, including the powerless, the marginalized, the despised, and the sick, as well as the economically poor. As the result of reflection on scripture within the church communities of Brazil, the call for Christian discipleship came to be understood as including a preferential option for the poor. Raoul reflects this basic understanding of a connection between a preferential option for the landless and his own Christian discipleship. His question is a practical one; he wants to know if there are any limits to the preferential option for the poor, because he does not feel equal to the task facing the landless movement.

Concern for the poor, as a Christian duty, is not a new or recent idea in Christianity. In the earliest church in Jerusalem a communal purse supported widows, orphans, and the sick (Acts 4:32–36). The epistles of St. Paul refer to the collections regularly taken up in the mission lands for the suffering poor of Jerusalem (Gal 2:10, 1 Cor 16:1–3, Rom 15:31). Caring for the poor distinguished many, many of the saints long recognized by the church. In the centuries after Christianity became the religion of the Roman Empire, especially during the medieval period, the church developed many of the institutions devoted to care of the poor, including hospitals, orphanages, and poorhouses for the homeless destitute, not to mention the food and/or lodging that monasteries and convents frequently furnished to beggars and weary travelers.

This tradition of care for the poor in Christian history had at least two distinctive characteristics not apparent to the contemporary person. First, it was structured as charity to alleviate the situation of the poor momentarily. The inevitability of poverty, and thus the dependency of the poor, were taken for granted so that a just sharing of resources which would allow the poor to care for themselves was not in question. Second, saints, monks, and nuns who cared for the poor were often understood to answer to higher standards of virtue than ordinary Christians. Personal involvement in the care for the needy fell to the religious orders, whose efforts were financially supported by the laity.

Ordinary lay Christians were not absolved from the duty to care for the needy, but that duty was interpreted within a hierarchical framework which dictated what was due to persons of different social rank. Thus while all Christians had a duty to contribute to the welfare of the poor from their excess, the calculation of excess was based on what level of consumption was thought necessary and/or appropriate to persons of various social ranks. The maintenance of different social ranks—one of which was the dependent poor—was thus understood as foundational for the implementation of the command to love one's needy neighbor.

Contemporary Church Teaching on Poverty

Christian reflection on poverty has undergone a revolution in the last two centuries. There have been two major causes of that revolution, one economic and the other political/philosophical. The industrial revolution, in both its agricultural and manufacturing applications, created the possibility of such great improvements in productivity as to make abject poverty no longer inevitable for many workers, even without a tremendous leveling of consumption. At the same time, Enlightenment political thought led to democratic revolutions which redistributed political power more broadly. One effect in the West has been to charge governments with responsibility for a stable, healthy economy and for economic safety nets for citizens in times of need. Catholic social teaching, begun in 1891, reflects this expectation of governments at the same time that it draws on democratic thought to support the formation of workers' unions with the right to strike for just wages and working conditions.

It was this Catholic social teaching, developed by the popes in a series of documents, which was the foundation for the Catholic Action movement in Brazil in the 1940s and 1950s, led by Bishop Helder Camara of Recife/Olinda. This Catholic Action movement became the nucleus for the Pastoral Plan that the Bishop's Conference developed to deal with the civil crisis in the wake of the military coup of 1964. That plan both divided up large parishes into smaller communities for purposes of evangelization and support and outlined a program of the defense of human rights. At base, Catholic Action and the Pastoral Plan drew on Catholic social teaching to assert that the ordinary person has a certain inherent dignity and consequent rights, not merely as a citizen but as a child of God, and that denial of that dignity and those rights is a violation of the entire Christian community and must be opposed by the church. The analysis and initial organizing of Catholic Action later supported the formation of Catholic peasant organizations, forerunners of the MST which Eduardo and his colleagues represent, as well as of the defense of indigenous peoples' habitats.

Social Analysis

As the case makes clear, both the justice of land reform and its political necessity are clear to most Brazilians, though there is no clear consensus about any particular plan. The majority—most of whom are city dwellers—are so clear that land reform justice has been unconscionably delayed that they even support land invasions by the landless peasants.

Land reform is actually bigger than the distribution of either government or private land to landless families; it has come to include the allied issue of indigenous land rights. The land rights of the indigenous—who include some communities of former African slaves who escaped into the interior where their communities continued for hundreds of years—have been an issue for the church since the military coup, when indigenous land was seized and cleared, community leaders killed, and communities dissolved in the name of national development, often with terrible ecological as well as human consequences.

The situation in this case is not usual. Few large landowners decide to give away 20,000 hectares of land to landless families. While Raoul's sister seems to support his decision, seeing it as motivated by his faith and consistent with his vocational commitment as a social worker with the urban poor, it is not at all clear how his mother or his two other sisters and their husbands will respond. Raoul seems to know that the conditions of the will leave him the bulk of the land, but he indicates that his older sisters could decide to use their inheritance in ways that would complicate the estate's ability to bear the donation to the landless, at least initially.

The questions in this case are not about the rightness or wrongness of the land transfer. Instead, they focus on more personal questions concerning the level of commitment Raoul is willing and able to make. For this reason social analysis is less critical. Though, because Christian principles—such as the command to love one's neighbor or the more specific preferential option for the poor—link degree of obligation to the degree of need present in the other as well as to the degree of risk to oneself, some social analysis is necessary. Such analysis assists in determining the level of need among the landless and identifying how the satisfaction of that need might be affected by Raoul's options. He could give the land either covertly, as if from Dom Pedro's will to the church, or openly in alliance with the MST. The level of need is clear—five million landless Brazilian farm-worker families. It is more difficult to predict the degree of risk to Raoul or to estimate how closely increasing his collaboration with the MST would increase his risk.

The consequences for the landless families of Raoul's deciding for active or passive assistance can only be roughly estimated. Many landless farm workers would almost certainly be encouraged to see a landowner openly acknowledge the justice of their cause; perhaps a few other landowners would be encouraged to make similar decisions if Raoul survived the announcement of his support for the MST. On the other hand, the reactions of the landless and of the landowner organizations to Raoul's becoming a public supporter of MST and then being killed for doing so might well increase the potential for an escalation of social violence.

Personal Spiritual Journey

The crux of this case lies in Raoul's own intentions and aspirations. There are a number of possible interpretations of the action up to this point. Raoul may have been motivated as much by a desire to spite his seemingly authoritarian father as by his concern for the poor when he decided on this gift. Humans often have complicated, even sometimes conflicting, reasons for a single action, and a less than charitable motivation does not make evil an otherwise good action—though it certainly reduces or removes any merit for that good act! The danger comes when the uncharitable motivation becomes controlling and influences how, when, or in what circumstances we act. For example, if Raoul were to decide to spite his father by allowing his father's pride and joy, the family estate, to go to ruin, and in the process his family and the estate workers were all impoverished, this would be an evil act.

Raoul may be acting out of guilt at having been gifted with so much wealth and privilege in a society where so many have so little. Again, we would not want those who have abundance when others have nothing to be free of guilt—their very guilt is a sign of their Christian conscience at work. But guilt alone as a motivation is inadequate for producing good. Guilt might lead Raoul to dispose of that excess, which is the source of the guilt, without being responsible for what was done with the excess. For there is never any real excess; the earth was made for the use of all. Resources are meant to supply the needs of all, and unused resources belong to the needy. Thus it would be wrong to simply give the land, unencumbered, to the Institute, or even to the church, unless one were sure, as Raoul seems to be, that the archbishop would convey the land to the landless.

What seems most likely is that Raoul is motivated by both guilt and spite, in addition to a real concern for the welfare of the poor understood as brothers and sisters in the Lord. The deeper question is where Raoul is in his own faith journey. There are, for all of us, stages in our journey toward communion with God. While we can and do experience moments when the path momentarily disappears and we fall, feeling lost and alone, only to recover our feet and continue more competently than before, progress through such traps is not completely random. There are preconditions for our progressing through them.

Raoul is not a beginner at the business of spiritual journey. He has been trying to find his way for some years. The journey led him first to the seminary and then, having decided he did not hear the call to that life, to his work with the urban poor. Now he recognizes the call to discipleship he had sought, but he is tempted to imitate Peter on Holy Thursday and deny the Lord. Raoul says: "I am not a leader. I am not a brave man. I cannot be the man you need." But the answer from the MST—interestingly enough, not from the bishops—is that brave men aren't born, they are just ordinary people who live one day at a time with fidelity, in the midst of danger. Rosario says, "We can show you the peasants from whom you can learn bravery and leadership."

The question of bravery is a response to the real danger of martyrdom. The Brazilian church has been no stranger to martyrdom over the last thirty years. Most of their martyrs have been people who took stands for justice that were unpopular with the military government or with organizations of the rich, such as the UDR. The martyred have included priests, sisters, and many thousands of anonymous poor people. Marta describes Raoul as having been close since seminary to a bishop who, with his archbishop, openly supports the MST. This probably indicates that Raoul's vocation to seminary was linked to an understanding of Christian vocation as a call to serve those in need and as a willingness to risk martyrdom.

Raoul's confusion and temptation at the end of the case—his recognition that this is the call he has sought and now he is not sure he wants to hear it—is neither unusual nor a negative sign. Faith that is not tempted by doubt or fear does not grow stronger. Hesitation from doubt and fear might be a healthier initial response than to embrace the dangerous option offered by the archbishop and the MST immediately. For martyrdom should never be sought. It is, rather, an honor to be evaded for as long as possible. Christians are not called to die because Jesus did but to live as Jesus did serving others and, like Jesus, to accept death only when there are no honorable alternatives, no other ways to serve. If Raoul decides to support the MST openly, he must seek action that promises the greatest benefit to the landless and the greatest safety to himself. Heightening risks to oneself is not courageous but reckless; it squanders the crucial resource God gave us to ensure our own and our community's well-being: our lives.

Raoul feels the dilemma of the rich young man in the gospel, who asked Jesus, "Good Teacher, what must I do to inherit eternal life?" Jesus recited the commandments to him, to which he replied that he had observed them from his youth. To this Jesus replied, "You lack one thing; go, sell what you have and give to the poor, and you will have treasure in heaven; and come follow me" (Lk 18:18–22). Raoul's problem does not seem to be so much the giving up of possessions, for he is not upset at Eduardo's teasing him about the MST demanding more of the estate in the future. But like the rich young man, Raoul fears giving up control over his life. He fears committing himself completely to the struggle for rural justice. To side publicly with the MST, even if it does not result in great physical danger, will brand him in his society for all time. It will determine his relations with his neighbors, with his extended family circle, with his social class.

And yet, as Raoul already feels, it is not easy to ignore that voice when it says, "Come, follow me." For in the voice is the implicit message, "Truly I say to you, there is no one who has left house or wife or brothers or parents or children for the sake of the Kingdom of God who will not receive manifold more in this time, and in the age to come eternal life" (Lk 18:29–30). Many of the pastoral agents who work with the poor in Brazil as elsewhere continue to report that this promise is repeatedly fulfilled—they do receive manifold more than they sacrifice—in their own lives. Even though they work among families where children and adults alike die before their time, they understand themselves as involved in communities committed to the God of life and to the fullness of life for all. In many different ways they maintain that it is these communities struggling against the death-dealing structures of injustice who give life to those from outside who join them, and not the reverse.

Raoul's reluctance may be rooted more in his apprehension of leadership responsibilities than in his fear of martyrdom. Even when he speaks of his fear of the UDR, he seems to fear that his family, and not he alone, might be targets of violence. His feelings of responsibility for them and his need to protect them from harm might well make a leadership role with the local MST difficult. Others in his situation have felt it necessary to make public breaks with their families in order to protect the families from misplaced vengeance. Another possibility is that if Raoul worked with the MST he would develop the same feelings of responsibility for all the landless families with whom he worked. It is not easy for elites raised in hierarchical systems to shift from feeling responsible for others to feeling responsible to others. The difference is critical. We do not know much about Raoul's urban social work in the state capital, but we can expect that he is exposed to the sufferings inflicted on the poor by poverty and cannot totally distance himself from the sufferings of the clients with whom he works. How much worse to care about and feel responsible for poor families who are the victims not only of the violence of poverty but also of physical violence by those committed to continuation of that poverty, especially when those committing the violence are persons from one's own social class, one's neighbors, childhood friends, and even relatives.

Conclusion

It seems likely that Raoul will decide to work with the MST, though he may or may not decide to announce his land gift publicly, depending on the position of his mother, sisters, and their husbands. Once committed to the gift of land to the landless, Raoul's working with the MST offers, as the bishop suggested, his best chance of avoiding the danger of large-scale land squatters that could provoke not only violence but economic disruption of production on his family estate. For this reason, working with the MST is both practical as well as a service to the needy. The shape of Raoul's support is, however, open. He could decide to let the MST choose the families to receive the land, help the new landowners organize into cooperatives, and offer those cooperatives technical and marketing support. All of this would inevitably be known to the local UDR and would expose him to some danger. But it would be more covert than advocacy for the MST with other estate owners, with politicians, or with human rights groups investigating the beatings and deaths of MST members.

This case offers drama, but not much suspense. It is not difficult to predict that Raoul will decide to work with the MST, though he may well choose to keep that collaboration as quiet as possible. But one may fairly comfortably predict also that as Raoul gains personal exposure to the level of need among the landless, to the depth of commitment within the MST, and to the courage and discipleship among its leaders, that Raoul will gradually increase his involvement. This is not a lesser path to discipleship. It is merely human.

Peter is the paradigm of the Christian disciple. When he is called to come follow Jesus, he goes without a qualm. But later, when confronted with the suffering and dangers awaiting Jesus in Jerusalem, he not only protests Jesus' insistence on leadership as service at the Last Supper, but he falls asleep at watch in the garden and then denies Jesus three times in the courtyard of the Temple. It is only after the catastrophe of Jesus' death, and the second chance offered him by Jesus' resurrection, that Peter begins to rise to the demands of discipleship. Faith is a *process* involving successive victories over doubt and fear. That process needs to be supported by exposure to the faith of others. Hundreds of thousands of church personnel in Latin America in the last decades would suggest that Raoul might be changed by working with the peasants who, the MST leaders promise, will teach him bravery and leadership.

A BUDDHIST RESPONSE by David McMahan

If Raoul counted himself among the small number of Brazilian Buddhists and wanted to make his decision based on Indian or Tibetan Buddhist principles, he would have a variety of resources from which to draw. In fact, the giving away of property, including land, was an important issue in the early Buddhist community. Buddhist monks and nuns in India were originally homeless wanderers who had renounced their families, professional affiliations, and social status. They did not handle money or generate income and were reliant on gifts of food from lay supporters for their sustenance. The climate in India allowed for homeless wandering most of the year, but during the intense annual rainy season, these mendicants would stay together in makeshift shelters. These shelters eventually became more permanent residences of the community, or *sangha*, developing sometimes into large monasteries. Often, land was provided by wealthy, land-owning supporters of Buddhism who would donate considerable resources to the *sangha*.

The reliance of the monastic community on the laity for material well-being was one historical/cultural factor contributing to the development of a strong emphasis in Buddhism on giving *(dana)*. The ethic of giving involves a relationship of mutual exchange between the monastic community and the laity that still persists in Buddhist countries. The latter provide food and donate land and other forms of wealth to the monasteries, and the monastic community in turn provides spiritual and moral guidance to the wider society. The practice of giving illustrates two more principles basic to Buddhism that Raoul would be considering in his decision, those of nonattachment and *karma*.

One of the most fundamental doctrines of Buddhism is that suffering, frustration, and dissatisfaction (all possible translations of the Sanskrit term, *duhkha*) are caused by craving and greed, and among the most pernicious forms of greed is the unbridled lust for material acquisition. Placing one's hopes for true happiness and meaning in life on the acquisition of wealth is, in the Buddhist view, simply inviting more frustration and discontent. The observation that everything is impermanent highlights the transience of wealth, possessions, and their associated power and implies that making such acquisition one's primary focus is doomed to failure. Thus, the Buddhist teachings advocate nonattachment to wealth and possessions. This does not mean that material prosperity in itself is seen as evil; in fact, many people highly esteemed in Buddhist traditions are laypersons who have been quite wealthy. Rather, it indicates that one should neither have an attitude of possessiveness or greediness regarding money, nor hesitate to use it for the good of society. One source says of wealth:

> Take note of this, my people, and make your wealth bear fruit by giving it away and spending it. This is the way to fame and happiness, in this world and the next. Money is in itself a meaningless trifle; only when someone bent on being of use to the world gives it away does it come into its own. Giving money away is like laying up treasure— hoarding it spells ruin.[1]

That "giving money away is like laying up treasure" implies the universally held belief among Buddhists in action *(karma)* and its effects. The notion that all morally significant actions bring forth results is common to virtually all Buddhist schools. The performer of virtuous deeds can be assured that future benefits will result, as the performer of evil can expect misfortune as a consequence of his or her unethical actions. The most common metaphor for the operation of the principle of *karma* is that each morally significant action plants seeds which, in this lifetime or a future one, come to fruition and produce plants of a kind determined by those seeds. Donating to the *sangha* is considered to be highly meritorious and will insure a later harvest of positive karmic results.

But the ethic of giving is not just confined to gifts to the *sangha*; giving to the poor and unfortunate is also considered highly meritorious. When given with the right attitude, such charity exemplifies nonattachment to material things as well as compassion, another cardinal virtue in Buddhism. Although greed and attachment to money and property are discouraged, poverty is in no way glorified in Buddhist literature; in fact, it is seen as detrimental to societal well-being, producing greed and social instability. Descriptions of an ideal society in Buddhist literature nearly always indicate that such a society will have abundant food and material goods.[2] Such abundance, whether of a society or an individual, is often taken to be the result of meritorious *karma*, and the unselfish acquisition of wealth is often considered to be the karmic result of previous generosity. Of course, the attitude with which something is given is of utmost importance—giving away wealth not out of compassion and charity, but in hopes of acquiring more wealth as one's karmic reward, will backfire. A small gift given unselfishly will generate more meritorious *karma* than a large gift given with ulterior motives.

From the Buddhist perspective, *karma* will always have its results, so if Raoul takes this principle seriously, he can expect great rewards in this life or another for unselfishly giving away his land to the landless. This is where the function of the doctrine of rebirth comes into play. Buddhists do not, of course, fail to notice that good people suffer and evil appears to go unpunished. The explanation for this is that *karma* takes a while to come to fruition, and if good and evil actions do not reap corresponding results in the present life, they will in a future one. Nothing in Buddhist doctrine, therefore, would assure Raoul that performing ethical or meritorious actions will guarantee his and his family members' immediate good fortune. While he could be confident that he will eventually reap the rewards of his deed, as would those who would harm him reap theirs, his immediate danger is in no way mitigated by the notion of *karma*. He may indeed be hurt or killed by the UDR.

Yet, another aspect of *karma* is that if he or his family were to be hurt or killed, that would ultimately be the result of their own past actions as well, which would inevitably come to fruition no matter what his decision regarding the land. If there are no negative karmic consequences ready to emerge among Raoul and his family, they will be safe; if there are, they will experience those consequences either way. The degree to which any individual could be at peace with this depends on his or her confidence in the ultimate efficacy of *karma*. We should not confuse such a peace with resignation or fatalism, however. Granted, the effects of past *karma* will inevitably come to fruition (although some practices have emerged in Buddhist traditions whereby one can supposedly nullify the negative *karma*), but each moment offers a person opportunities to shape future destiny, so that each decision has great consequences. Even if one cannot change the momentum of past *karma*, one is always in the process of shaping one's future.

Given that karmic reward is often presented in material terms with virtuous acts begetting material prosperity, one might be tempted to interpret this as a kind of determinism regarding material inequality and social injustice. If one's lot in life is determined by past *karma*, then perhaps Raoul might reason that the landless are in such a desperate situation because of their own past deeds and, therefore, it is not incumbent on him to help them. While it would be true on a Buddhist account that the landless have arrived at their condition by means of their own past misdeeds, this would not release Raoul from the Buddhist ethic of universal compassion for all living beings. No matter how a person has gotten to a position of wealth or poverty, social elevation or degradation, the appropriate response to all suffering, according to Buddhist ethics, is compassion. If one enjoys wealth and high standing in society, simply to be self-satisfied that one's own virtuous actions brought about this good fortune and that, conversely, those in less fortunate circumstances are reaping their just rewards and thereby not deserving of compassion, might have the effect of reversing one's own good fortune.

That unselfish giving is one of the highest virtues in Buddhism is attested to by the many "birth stories" (*jataka*) of the Buddha's previous lives chronicling the kinds of actions that he performed in his long career as a *bodhisattva*—a being on his or her way to full enlightenment. These are mostly simple tales rife with hyperbole and designed to illustrate some of the core values and attitudes deemed essential for awakening to full human potential. In one, the *bodhisattva* gives his own flesh to a starving tiger so she can feed her cubs. In another, he gives away his eyes to a blind man. In the story of his penultimate lifetime before being born as Gautama in India, he is a prince named Vessantara who has a nearly compulsive habit of giving away anything that is asked of him. Upon giving away his white elephant, a state symbol of great auspiciousness, he is driven from his kingdom, along with his wife and children. Rather than taking his possessions with him, he gives them all away and goes to a remote mountain hermitage, where he even gives his children and wife away to wandering Brahmins who ask for them.[3]

The ethical problems of such extreme generosity were not lost on the Buddhist tradition. In the *Questions of King Milinda*, a well-known text in which a Greek king questions a monk named Nagasena about Buddhist doctrine and practice, Milinda notes that Vessantara's generosity, though admirable, caused suffering for his wife and children. Nagasena concedes this point but suggests that such extreme generosity was a necessary part of Vessantara's attaining Buddhahood, an end which justified the means. Nagasena likens the suffering caused by Vessantara to the suffering inflicted on bullocks by rushing a sick man to the doctor on a bullock cart.[4] Here we see the subordination of all goals, even those of dedication to family, to the quest for enlightenment. Gautama the Buddha, in relating this story of his past life as Vessantara, assures his listeners that it is not that he "loved [his wife and children] less, but Buddhahood more," for by becoming a Buddha, he could be of service to all beings.[5]

This story suggests that the ideal is to delight in giving without a thought for oneself and that such an attitude is prerequisite for becoming a Buddha. Whether the examples in such stories help in a concrete way with Raoul's dilemma is open to question. The fact that the being who would become the Buddha is the actor in all of these dramas perhaps does not speak to the poignant exchange between Raoul and Eduardo, the lobbyist for the campesinos, in which Raoul protests that he is not a courageous or exceptional man, to which Eduardo replies that none of them are either—that they make their ways day-by-day trying to do what is right. The hero in the *jataka* tales is always the exceptional, courageous, virtually ideal person. Raoul may be tempted to think that only future Buddhas are capable of performing— and therefore required to perform—great selfless acts. And even though in most of these tales everything often works out in the end—good is rewarded, evil nullified, wisdom achieved—a real-life Buddhist in Raoul's situation would not be so naive as to think that his situation did not pose a real threat and true danger, belief in the ultimate balancing of *karma* notwithstanding. The significance of such stories, though, is that they present idealized images of certain fundamental Buddhist values that are meant to be put into practice in the very nonideal situations of the real world. Recalling such stories, Raoul might reason that if the *bodhisattva* could without hesitation make such immense sacrifices, then he after all might be able to make this comparatively smaller sacrifice. Drawing from the doctrines of *karma*, compassion, giving, and nonattachment, as well as the *jataka* stories, Raoul would likely be compelled to conclude that following the *dharma* meant giving away as much land as he could possibly give in the spirit of compassion.

The decision about whether to take the public political stand in favor of land reform brings more nuanced complications into the picture. Here, Raoul is being asked to put himself and his family in danger. For guidance on this aspect of the problem, Raoul might do best to look to examples of contemporary Buddhists' struggles against oppression and violence. Buddhism is often thought to be a religion of passive nonaction and withdrawal from the world, a purely introspective orientation that eschews political and social action. The most prominent Buddhist leaders of today, however, belie this assumption, at least regarding Buddhism in the modern world. Indeed, the most prominent contemporary Buddhist leaders are quite outspoken on social and political issues, attempting to combine traditional contemplative attitudes with vibrant social commitment. Various Buddhist "liberation movements" have arisen in Asia resembling in many respects the Christian liberation theology prominent in Central and South America. Buddhist liberation movements explore ways of addressing social injustice, poverty, war, and oppression according to Buddhist principles and through nonviolent means.[6]

Some of the most notable Buddhist leaders involved in issues of peace and justice are those who have themselves been directly affected by war and political oppression and have responded by resolutely espousing nonviolence. Thich Nhat Hanh, a Vietnamese monk nominated by Martin Luther King for a Nobel Peace Prize, was active in opposing the war between capitalism and communism that ravaged his country. He and many other Vietnamese monks faced peril for opposing the violence, often putting their bodies literally in the line of fire. Aung San Suu Kyi, a leader of the opposition to the repressive Burmese government, was elected as national leader in 1989 but held under house arrest and never allowed to take power. In the face of constant threat, she has continued to speak out against the military regime. She won a Nobel Peace Prize in 1991 for her efforts at social reform in her country.

The most famous Buddhist leader in the world, Tenzin Gyatso, the fourteenth Dalai Lama of Tibet and also a Nobel laureate, has been a leader in the struggle against violence and political oppression, not only in Tibet but also around the world. Having been forced into exile from Tibet by the invading Chinese, he continues to be one of the world's leading figures in the search for peace and justice through nonviolence.

What any individual Buddhist does in a given situation may, of course, vary considerably according to individual and historical circumstances. A great deal of diversity exists among Buddhists and one tradition may give answers different from others. No one unambiguous answer exists for Raoul, far away in time and place from where the earliest Buddhists formulated the principles that the great diversity of Buddhists have interpreted for two and a half millennia. But if Raoul wanted to make his difficult decision drawing from the earlier doctrines and narratives of Buddhism in India as well as some of the exemplars of Buddhism in the modern world, he would find it difficult to avoid the conclusion that he must not only distribute the land but also use his position to cast his lot publicly with the displaced and destitute, despite the possibility of danger.

Notes

1. *Once the Buddha Was a Monkey: Arya Suras' Jatakamala*, trans. Peter Khoroche (Chicago: University of Chicago Press, 1989), 10–17.

2. See *Cakkavatti-Sihanada Sutta* in Maurice Walshe, trans., *Thus Have I Heard: The Long Discourses of the Buddha* (London: Wisdom Publications, 1988), 395–406.

3. John S. Strong, *The Experience of Buddhism: Sources and Interpretations* (Belmont, CA: Wadsworth, 1995), 23–25.

4. T. W. Rhys Davids, trans. *The Questions of King Milinda*, Sacred Books of the East Series, ed. Max Müller (Dehli: Motilal Banarsidas, 1988), 114–32.

5. John S. Strong, "Rich Man, Poor Man, *Bhikkhu*, King: Quinquennial Festival and the Nature of Dana," in *Ethics, Wealth, and Salvation: A Study in Buddhist Social Ethics*, ed. Russell F. Sizemore and Donald K. Swearer (Columbia, SC: University of South Carolina Press, 1990), 107–23.

6. See Christopher S. Queen, "Introduction: The Shapes and Sources of Engaged Buddhism," in *Engaged Buddhism: Buddhist Liberation Movements in Asia*, ed. Christopher S. Queen and Sallie B. King (Albany: State University of New York Press, 1966), 1–44.

Bibliography and Suggested Reading

Dalai Lama. *A Flash of Lightning in the Dark of Night: A Guide to the Bodhisattva's Way of Life*. Boston: Shambhala, 1994.

Gombrich, Richard F. *Precept and Practice*. London: Oxford University Press, 1971.

Gutiérrez, Gustavo. *We Drink from Our Own Wells: The Spiritual Journey of a People*. Trans. by M. J. O'Connell. Maryknoll, NY: Orbis Books, 1983/84.

The Journal of Buddhist Ethics (Online journal at http//jbe.1a.psu.edu).

Kalupahana, David J. *Ethics in Early Buddhism*. Honolulu: University of Hawaii Press, 1995.

Lernoux, Penny. *Cry of the People: The Struggle for Human Rights in Latin America*. New York: Doubleday, 1980.

Newton, Lisa H., and Catherine K. Dillingham, eds. "The Diversity of Life: Chico Mendes and the Amazonian Rainforest" *Watersheds: Classic Cases in Environmental Ethics*. Belmont, CA: Wadsworth, 1994.

Nhat Hanh, Thich. *Vietnam: Lotus in a Sea of Fire*. Foreword by Thomas Merton. Afterword by Alfred Hassler. New York: Hill and Wang, 1967.

Nolan, Albert. *Jesus before Christianity*. Maryknoll, NY: Orbis Books, 1992.

Once the Buddha Was a Monkey: Arya Suras' Jatakamala. Trans. by Peter Khoroche. Chicago: University of Chicago Press, 1989.

Queen, Christopher S., and Sallie B. King, eds. *Engaged Buddhism: Buddhist Liberation Movements in Asia*. Albany: State University of New York Press, 1996.

Rhys Davids, T. W., trans. *The Questions of King Milinda*. Sacred Books of the East Series. Ed. Max Müller. Dehli: Motilal Banarsidas, 1988.

Sizemore, Russell F., and Donald K. Swearer, eds. *Ethics, Wealth, and Salvation: A Study in Buddhist Social Ethics*. Columbia, SC: University of South Carolina Press, 1990.

Sobrino, Jon. *Christology at the Crossroads*. Trans. John Drury. Maryknoll, NY: Orbis Books, 1978.

Spiro, Melford. *Buddhism and Society*. New York: Harper and Row, 1970.

Strong, John S. *The Experience of Buddhism: Sources and Interpretations*. Belmont, CA: Wadsworth, 1995.

Walshe, Maurice, trans. *Thus Have I Heard: The Long Discourses of the Buddha*. London: Wisdom Publications, 1988.

CHAPTER 13

The Successful *Sarariiman*

A CASE STUDY by Regina Wentzel Wolfe

Twenty-some years ago, when he was a recent graduate of Tokyo University, the thought of being named a general manager at one of the large banks was beyond Takeo Mashimoto's wildest dreams. When he had thought of the future, which was not often, he had aspired to be a loyal and dependable *sarariiman* (white-collar worker) who, by contributing to his company's success, would be contributing to the country's success. Yet, here he was, about to become one of the bank's most senior executives.

"The bank has depended greatly on Mr. Ito," Mr. Yamaguchi began, once Takeo had been seated. "He has served well and been a valued contributor to the bank's success. Unfortunately," the bank's president continued, "he will retire soon, and we will need someone dependable to replace him as the general manager of the global securities group. The Board has decided that you are the person to do so."

Takeo sat silently for a moment, absorbing the full meaning of what had just been said.

"I am not worthy of this great honor," he insisted softly.

"It has been decided," replied Mr. Yamaguchi in a no-nonsense manner. "In two months' time, the announcement will be made that Mr. Hadeo Ito is retiring and that Mr. Takeo Mashimoto will assume the vacant position. You should continue for a week or two with your current duties while a suitable replacement is found. Once that has been accomplished, you can begin working with Mr. Ito and his staff to familiarize yourself with the day-to-day requirements of the position. All the staff members will continue in their positions so that there will be a smooth transition as you take up your new duties. Obviously, people in the company will be aware of the changes, but there will be no formal announcement until the next full board meeting. The board members place much confidence in you, and I am sure that you will not disappoint them," Yamaguchi said as he rose to signal the conclusion of the meeting.

Takeo noted his unworthiness once again, then, promising he would do his best for the company, thanked Mr. Yamaguchi, proffered the customary bow, and returned to his office. He was grateful that it was the end of the day, and he could sit at his desk for a minute and consider the news. He wasn't stunned by the news; he knew that his superiors saw him as a valued employee and contributor to the bank's long-term strategic goals. However, he had not expected to be named to such a prestigious position, particularly since his life seemed to be in such a flux following his return to Tokyo from the London branch.

"Aren't you ready?" Tsuda Nakamura asked, poking his head into Takeo's office. "Half the group is already at the bar."

"Just give me a minute," replied Takeo. "I'll meet you at the elevators, and we can walk over together."

When they arrived at the bar, they found the group sitting at the big table along the rear wall. Takeo sat down with Hosoi Sato, Shigeo Fujita, and some of the other fellows from commercial banking who had started out as management trainees with him. Sato nodded acknowledgement of Takeo's presence and continued with what he was saying.

"I tell you, I am very impressed with NJ Heavy Industries (NJHI). The company is becoming a bigger and bigger player in the international scene," Sato told his colleagues. "Only last week they substantially increased their borrowing ability and added another bank to the list of those willing to lend them funds. They are looking for a new lead bank for their international business. And they have big expansion plans. The new manufacturing process which they developed last year has really taken hold, driven their costs down, and given NJHI a significant competitive advantage. Now they are going to expand their market share by buying out the competition, especially in Europe. Takeo, you must know much of this. Didn't NJHI's managing director meet with Ito to arrange a Eurobond issue? In fact, I think they may be going after a U.K. company," Sato concluded.

"Yes, but just preliminarily. The frequent swings in the global bond and equity markets during the past year have made everyone cautious. We'll have to see where that meeting leads us," Takeo answered, waving at the waiter to bring another round of drinks.

In fact, Takeo knew full well that it was his relationship with NJHI's General Manager of Finance, whom he had met in London, that had brought this opportunity to the bank. To be the lead underwriter for NJHI's first Eurobond would be a real coup both for him and for the bank. The decision was to be made at NJHI's next board meeting.

"Is it a coincidence that NJHI's board meeting is the week before our next board meeting?" Takeo wondered, thinking back to his conversation with Yamaguchi.

Realizing that it was getting late, Takeo stood up to make his good-byes, as did his friend, Katayama. The two men lived in the same suburb of Tokyo and often took the train home together after these weekly Wednesday-night drinking parties. They had known each other since university days and had grown to be close friends.

"You seem rather distracted tonight, I think," Katayama commented breaking the companionable silence as the two walked toward Tokyo Station to catch the 10:55 train. Takeo did not respond until they were on the train and then did so only indirectly.

"It has been a long day, hasn't it?" he said, looking at his friend seated opposite him.

"Yes, I think so," Katayama replied and paused for a moment. "Perhaps it has been particularly long for you?" he asked tentatively, not wanting to appear rude or intrusive.

"It's difficult to say; perhaps, similar to many others," Takeo said non-committally. He wanted to share the news with his friend but did not want to appear self-serving. "Besides," he thought to himself, "Katayama will soon hear the news from someone else. There isn't any hurry for me to tell him. The only people to know will be my parents and Fumiko. I hope this will please her and bring her back to her senses."

Having arrived at their stop, the two men said their good-byes, and Takeo turned to walk the few blocks to his home wondering how Fumiko, his wife, would react to the news of his promotion. Even though it had been almost a year since their return from the London assignment, his wife had still not adjusted to being back in Japan. From her perspective everything was wrong: the housing was inadequate; transportation was overcrowded; the people were too provincial; the structure of Japanese society was too confining— she just wanted to return to London. He couldn't understand it. She was unreasonable, almost to the point of irrational, about everything. Ignoring her old friends, she had joined one of Tokyo's international women's groups. She had even refused to support his decision to place the children in the public school system, insisting that they go to one of the modern private schools. She and the children argued that to go back into a traditional Japanese public school after five years in London would be nearly impossible.

"I can't go back to being a robot," his son Hiroshi had said. "The teachers only want you to memorize and recite facts. It is dull and boring. And I'd have to spend hours going to *juku* (cram school) to prepare for the national exams. Besides, what's the point of sitting the exams when I want to go back to England to university—Oxford or Cambridge, with luck."

"It would be more difficult for me," his daughter Yoko had added. "Nobody would care what *I* think, just because I'm a girl. And we'd have to wear uniforms and be like everyone else. It would simply be too dreadful. It's all so regimented that I'd feel like I was in the military or something."

"How could things get so out of control?" Takeo asked himself, turning into the narrow lane leading to his home.

Life had been relatively uncomplicated before he took the overseas assignment. Like every other Japanese *sarariiman*, he had known what was expected of him. There was a clear path to be followed with no surprises as he moved up the ranks at the bank, and he had followed it conscientiously.

For as long as he could remember, Takeo had been dutiful and responsible, always doing what was expected of him. His childhood was remarkable only in its conventionalism. His father worked the long hours of a junior civil servant in loyal service to Japan. Though he was often physically absent from home, his presence was always felt by his wife and son. He was particularly insistent that Takeo should do well in school, and it had been his mother's duty to ensure that that happened. To her credit, she had been a successful *kyoiku mama* (education mother). Her life had been devoted to the task of seeing Takeo through the various levels of entrance exams. When he was young, she doggedly accompanied him to the *juku* that was so much a part of educational success in Japan. And when he finally matriculated at Tokyo University his father showed his pleasure with her and acknowledged her efforts by taking her out for dinner at one of Shinjuku's finest restaurants.

It had to be one of the few times that his mother had ever been in a restaurant. He remembered the girlish giggle she had given as his parents passed through the gate and headed down the lane to the main road. It was the first time he had ever seen his mother dressed in so fine a kimono. And he had known that, though they weren't visibly watching, it would not be lost on the neighbors that she was being honored for a job well done.

"Imagine if I suggested to Fumiko that I would honor her with a fine restaurant dinner for the service she provided to the country by seeing to it that Hiroshi passed the exams for Tokyo University!" he exclaimed to himself and almost cringed as he imagined her response.

"What has happened to my wife? She is not the same girl I married. And my children, why can't they see that they have no future if they are not part of the system? Where did I go wrong? I've always done what was expected of me," he muttered under his breath as he stepped into the *genkan* (entryway) and bent down to remove his shoes.

He walked quietly down the hallway and sliding back the *karakami* (paper-paneled sliding door) saw that Fumiko was sound asleep. "I'll tell her the news in the morning," Takeo thought to himself, turning over on his futon and drifting off to sleep.

"It is quite an honor to be appointed general manager," Fumiko said as she served her husband his breakfast the next morning. "It will mean a great deal of traveling, I suppose. I'm already looking forward to returning to Europe for visits."

"Fumiko, you know that it would not be appropriate for you to accompany me on business trips," replied Takeo curtly. "When are you going to come to your senses and behave as a proper wife?" he asked rhetorically as he stood up and headed toward the *genkan* to put his shoes on and leave for the long commute to work.

"If only things could be like they were before," he thought ruefully, recalling the simpler days of his early adult years. As was the case for most graduates of Tokyo University, life had progressed well. Takeo had been hired by the bank right after graduation. He began as a management trainee, spending the first few years moving through the various departments and mastering the finer points of the behind-the-scenes technical aspects of banking and finance. He worked hard in those early years. With the two-hour commute from his parents' home to Tokyo's financial district, his days were long.

Often, he didn't return home until close to midnight. But the hard work was rewarded both by the pride his parents had for his success and by his steady progression up the ranks at the bank.

Eventually, he found himself in the foreign exchange and money market department. He had a real gift for trading that was not lost on his superiors. It soon became clear that he was viewed as a rising star and was being groomed for rapid advancement. "Everything seemed so uncomplicated and straightforward in those days," Takeo thought to himself as he stared out the train's window. "It was easy. The rules were simple: apply all that has been taught, follow directions, work hard, and be a success."

Things were simple on the home front, too. With his parents' help, he found a bride and was married. Takeo and Fumiko lived with his parents at first while they set aside money to get their own place. In just a few years, their savings, coupled with the salary increases that went along with Takeo's promotions, enabled them to move into their own home. The births of their children completed the picture perfectly.

At the end of 1989, in recognition of his ability to understand financial markets, Takeo was sent to London to head the new securities operation there. "I wonder if I'd have been so elated at that appointment if I knew then what I do now?" Takeo asked himself. The overseas assignment had been a clear signal that Takeo continued to be a rising star. Because the posting to London was to be for three to five years, the company would pay to have his family accompany him if he wanted.

"Deciding to bring them to London was the start of it all," Takeo muttered to himself as he stepped off the train and made his way along the platform and into the crowded station hall. "If Fumiko and the children had remained in Japan things wouldn't be so bad," he thought to himself. "I should have listened to Murata and the others." He recalled the advice he had received from colleagues who had had overseas assignments.

"It is very bad to bring your family," Murata had insisted. "Your children will suffer because their education will be interrupted. It will be especially hard for your son, Hiroshi. His chances of following you to Tokyo University will be lessened and that could cost him a good career. Your daughter will have a difficult time, too. I've met girls who spent time overseas. They are too independent and don't know their place in society; they become too Western. Your wife will change, too. She'll start taking English lessons. 'Just enough to do the shopping and manage the household,' she'll say. But learning English only leads to trouble. She'll start making friends with the neighbor women, and then she'll be taking classes in cooking or art history. It doesn't matter the subject. The result is the same: she'll begin to neglect her duties. Pretty soon your home life will be completely unsettled!" Murata had concluded emphatically.

"It's almost as if he were a fortune teller," Takeo thought wryly as he moved through Tokyo Station with the mass of morning commuters.

Takeo's parents had been concerned, also. They had suggested that Fumiko and the children move in with them. That would have made it possible for her to oversee the children's education and to help Takeo's parents who were getting on in years. In the end, Takeo had decided it would be difficult for him to be so far from home without his family for such a long assignment. "Besides," he had convinced himself, "we're not going to the United States but to England which is a very traditional country."

Walking through Chiyoda-ku, the heart of Tokyo's financial district, toward the bank's headquarters where his office was located, Takeo had to admit to himself that the years in London had been good ones, both personally and professionally. He had found working in the City of London exhilarating. And, though it took a while to adapt to local customs and the more open manner of the Europeans, he had come to enjoy the people and the less-rigid lifestyle. "And I wouldn't have been named Ito's successor without the London experience," he acknowledged. "This promotion will certainly put a capstone on my career. And things are bound to improve on the home front, too," he thought to himself optimistically as he entered the building and headed toward the elevator lobby.

Dropping his attaché case on his desk, he went to the third floor to make his courtesy call on Mr. Ito.

"Ah, Mashimoto, so you have received the good news. Congratulations!" Mr. Ito greeted him and waved a hand toward the sofa indicating that Takeo should be seated.

"Thank you very much. It is a great honor to be named your successor, though I do not deserve it," Takeo politely responded before sitting down.

Over tea, the two men discussed the general state of the financial services industry from both a domestic and an international perspective. They had been chatting for some time when the final cup of tea was offered and declined. Just as Takeo was preparing to take his leave, his soon-to-be predecessor spoke.

"Before you go, there is a matter that needs to be considered," Ito said. "The board has decided to add to the bank's investment portfolio. With our increased international activity, it wants some exposure to other markets but in industries about which we have some knowledge. It has been decided that the bank should, over the next two months, acquire five million shares of Midland Specialty Steel, Plc. Because you are going to take over the global securities group, it will be your responsibility to acquire the shares and build this position."

Before Takeo could respond, Ito's phone rang.

"The delegation visiting from the Chamber of Commerce must be here. We'll have to continue later," Ito remarked. He stood up, gave a nod indicating that the meeting had ended, bowed slightly, went to his desk, and lifted the receiver.

Takeo returned to his desk. Swinging his chair around, he stared blankly out the window. It was a quiet day for the Japanese markets. The U.K. markets were closed for a holiday and the United States markets wouldn't open until after the close of business in Tokyo.

"Midland Specialty Steel, Plc.," he thought to himself. "We were part of a bond syndicate for them a few years ago—good company; good market share but lacks the capital and foresight to develop their technology. A good target for a takeover," he thought—and suddenly sat upright.

"Didn't Sato say last night that NJHI was on the acquisition trail? Midland might be a great match. With NJHI's technology and Midland's clients, the combination could be extraordinarily profitable, and it could establish NJHI in the U.K., giving it an opening in the European Union. NJHI could afford to pay a very high price right out of the box. There would be some resistance to the acquisition for cultural reasons, but the price could lead to a quick closing.

"The bank could make a huge profit on holdings of Midland. That would significantly help our sagging domestic portfolio, which has been hurt by the fall of the Nikkei from its highs of several years ago. Plus, all the problems we've had with our loans to real-estate developers and local finance companies have hurt profits. We could certainly use a boost. NJHI could turn out to be a 'white knight,' in a way. The profit on the holdings, fees on the Eurobond issue, and the bank's enhanced position with Japan's new rising star could certainly put us back on track again," Takeo mused as he stood and began pacing in front of his desk.

"Is this all too much of a coincidence?" he asked himself. Questions he would rather not consider began to form in his mind. "Is there something more behind this? Is Ito trading on inside information? Is the bank? Could we be accumulating this position in Midland stock to help NJHI with their acquisition? Does Ito expect to sell these shares to NJHI? Is there some kind of agreement that Ito has struck with them in order to protect the bank against losses or unforeseen problems? Oh, it can't be that; surely the bank isn't involved in parking securities! But if we are quietly buying all these shares for NJHI at their request in order to facilitate their acquisition without the market or Midland's shareholders being aware of their intention, parking securities is just what it would be! And Ito would be sure to see that the bank would be nicely compensated and would not be exposed to any losses."

Takeo was uncertain of how to respond to the situation, and he did not have the time to consider it thoroughly. After all, he did need to get some work done. The rest of the day was a long one for Takeo. His conversation with Ito kept replaying itself, despite his best efforts to keep it at the back of his mind. It was after seven o'clock before most of his colleagues had left for the evening, and he could take time to consider the situation.

"What is really going on, here?" he wondered, as it registered with him that NJHI's next board meeting would take place a week before the bank's own board met. "Ito wants the stock accumulated over the next two months; just in time for the board meetings. Is this a test to see how clever and loyal I am?" Takeo could hardly believe he had formulated the question.

All of a sudden the office felt claustrophobic. Takeo had to get out of the building. He quickly got his things together and left. He was thankful for the extended daylight of late summer as he headed toward Hibiya Park. He had always enjoyed walking among the *hinoki* (Japanese cypress) and often found he did his best thinking in the peaceful environment they provided.

It was obvious that the bank could benefit from the purchase that Ito instructed Takeo to make.

"But is it truly in the bank's best interest?" Takeo asked himself as he tried to weigh his options. "What if it is discovered? The press would certainly report it, and while it might die down soon enough here at home, the international press would not ignore it. That could really hurt the bank's credibility in overseas markets. And what about Midland's shareholders? They would certainly be disadvantaged by such an acquisition."

Coming upon a stone bench in a quiet section of the garden, Takeo sat for a moment. The irony of the situation was not lost on him. Had he not spent so long in London, he might not be as familiar with the legal and ethical implications of such a transaction, and he wouldn't question the request. But then, without the London assignment, he wouldn't be in line to succeed Ito.

"If only I were still in London. The people working in the compliance group there were really on top of things and were a great help in sorting out the legal and ethical dimensions of complex situations. And, most of all, they could be counted on to respect the confidential nature of requests for assistance in compliance matters," Takeo thought wistfully. "We don't have a truly dependable compliance group here. Besides, before being named the chief compliance officer, Watanabe used to be Ito's boss, and everyone knows that Watanabe was given the job because the Board wanted a team player in that position. If I go to him, I'll be shipped off to some small country branch in Hokkaido. I can't imagine how my family will accept such an assignment," he thought dejectedly as he rose and headed out of the park toward the station.

"I don't have much time to decide on a course of action," he said quietly to himself, knowing that to accumulate such a large holding without attracting attention, he would have to begin acquiring Midland stock almost immediately.

A BUDDHIST RESPONSE by Richard K. Payne

Prefatory Disclaimer

It is not my intent to write the following reflections on the case of the unfortunately successful *sarariiman* from a position of abstract authority, claiming to speak for "Buddhism." Rather, I speak from my own particular locatedness as a late twentieth-century Anglo-American Buddhist convert. It seems to me wholly in keeping with my understanding of the Buddhist tradition to reject the idea that any claims could be made for the entirety of the tradition. Indeed, the vast majority of those who, over the course of time, identified themselves as Buddhists would have been very hard pressed to even comprehend the case at hand. Further, it would be absurdly presumptuous of me to claim to know what the Buddha Shakyamuni would have made of it. My own experience with Buddhism has been largely with the Mahayana traditions, though I have had some exposure to various Theravada practices.

Within the Mahayana I was, like so many of my generation, first exposed to Zen. Following this I spent several years practicing under the guidance of a Tibetan master and eventually wound up in Japan practicing Shingon, an esoteric form of Buddhism related to the Tibetan Vajrayana forms but with its own lineage back to India. I was eventually ordained as a Shingon priest, though since then I have been largely involved professionally with the Pure Land tradition here in the United States. Now that I have established that I am only speaking for myself, and the reader has some inkling of who that is, let me abandon further qualifications of the form "It is my understanding of Buddhism that. . . ."

On Differentiating Buddhism and Christianity

American culture is so deeply imbued with preconceptions concerning the nature of religion and ethics that are based on Protestant Christianity that it is often difficult for people to understand just how fundamentally different Buddhism is. The difference goes far beyond giving different answers to the questions of life, but rather it has to do with asking different questions. Where for Christianity ethical action is central to the logic of salvation, for Buddhism the central concern is practice conducive to realizing how the world works. In other words, for Buddhism ethics is subservient to epistemology. For this reason it is necessary to distinguish between the worldview of Buddhism and the application of Buddhist thought to ethical evaluation.

In order to explicate the difference between Christianity and Buddhism, let us examine how the two describe the human condition (ground), the goal of the religious life, and the path from the ground to the goal. For Christianity, that is, for the popular religious conceptions of American culture based in Protestant Christianity rather than sophisticated theology, the ground of human existence is marked by sin. Sin in its turn is understood as disobedience to God's will. In this way ethical action is action congruent with God's will and is required for salvation from sin. Salvation from sin leads to eternal life in the presence of God, that is, to heaven. The ground is sin, the goal is eternal life in heaven, and the path is redemption from sin. (Because belief in a single God who is creator and therefore legislator of the universe is foundational to all three of the major Western monotheistic traditions—Judaism, Christianity, and Islam—I would suggest that this logic of salvation through ethical action is also shared by all three of them.)

Some Protestant formulations of Christianity questioned whether human action could ever be ethical enough and, if it could not, replaced action with faith as central to the issue of salvation. Salvation is achieved through faith in the redemptive power of Jesus' sacrifice. However, even without the rhetorical question of whether faith is an action or not, this still did not displace ethics as a central concern of Christian culture.

In contrast to sin, Buddhism describes the starting ground of the religious life as one of ignorance (*avidya*). Because we do not understand how the world works, we repeatedly get caught up (*samsara*) in activities that are inevitably the source of suffering (*dukkha*).[1] Holding to the mistaken notion that we are separate, independently existing selves, we have the mistaken expectation that we are capable of achieving eternal happiness. The goal of the religious life is awakening (*bodhi*, same root as in the title Buddha, meaning "one who has awakened") from both the intellectual and emotional mistakes (*klesas*)) that prevent us from seeing the world as it actually is.

The path (*marga*) leading from ignorance to awakening is the main topic of Buddhist thought. Indeed, one could argue that the history of Buddhism is the history of the development of the variety of methods by which one moves along the path to awakening.

While the ground from which we start is characterized by ignorance, much of East Asian Mahayana Buddhism shares the idea that the mind is fundamentally pure. The two kinds of mistakes that we make—intellectual and emotional—are not the foundation of our consciousness but rather accidental acquisitions which obscure the clarity of pure consciousness.[2] One of the most common metaphors for this idea is that of a mirror which has been covered over with dust. Although the dust interferes with the mirror's ability to reflect the world, the dust is only an accidental acquisition which can be cleared off from the mirror, returning it to its original clarity.

The various means by which one may realize the original purity of consciousness are usually referred to as types of meditation. The Shingon tradition shares the idea that consciousness is fundamentally pure and therefore already awakened. What distinguishes the Shingon tradition is its use of ritual practice as the meditative means of realizing original awakening.

As mentioned above, ethical action is valued because it is conducive to practice. For example, it is very common for Buddhist laypersons to take the five lay precepts: to abstain from killing, stealing, sexual misconduct, lying, and intoxicants. The point of these is not that these actions are in themselves morally wrong or sinful, that is, counter to God's will. Rather, it is that such actions arise from the delusion that one is a separate, independently existing self. Such actions therefore only further enmesh one in the round of delusional thinking, including justifying the actions, which supports the fundamental delusion of independent existence. Taking the precepts means being willing to confront the delusion of independent existence. It is for this reason that a breach of the precepts is best seen as an opportunity for learning, rather than as a moral failing endangering one's possibility of salvation.

In addition to the five lay precepts, many Buddhist practitioners within the Mahayana tradition also take the bodhisattva precepts. Although there are various forms of the bodhisattva precepts, one of them is:

> Living beings are infinite, I vow to free them.
> Delusions are inexhaustible, I vow to cut through them.
> Dharma gates are boundless, I vow to enter them.
> The Buddha Way is unsurpassable, I vow to realize it.

In general, the main intent of the bodhisattva path is to perfect wisdom (insight into the delusional character of the idea of separate, independent existence) and compassion (assisting other living beings also to awaken from the delusion of separate, independent existence).

The interdependence of all existence is the positive expression of the denial of separate independent existence, that there is nothing that is absolute. This applies to ethical standards as well. However, if ethical standards are not absolute, are we then left only with ethics as social convention—a total relativity of values: whatever a society says is right is right in that society?[3] The Buddhist response is no, not because of the existence of any absolutes but rather because of the way that the world works. All of our actions (*karma*) have consequences. Self-reflection upon the interdependent character of our own existence leads to awareness of how our actions affect other living beings. In his classic description of the bodhisattva path, the medieval Indian Buddhist monk Shantideva expresses this line of thinking as follows:

> One should first earnestly meditate on the equality of oneself and others in this way: "All equally experience suffering and happiness, and I must protect them as I do myself."
>
> Just as the body, which has many parts owing to its division into arms and so forth, should be protected as a whole, so should this entire world, which is differentiated and yet has the nature of the same suffering and happiness.
>
> Although my suffering does not cause pain in other bodies, nevertheless that suffering is mine and is difficult to bear because of my attachment to myself.
>
> Likewise, although I myself do not feel the suffering of another person, that suffering belongs to that person and is difficult [for him] to bear because of his attachment to himself.
>
> I should eliminate the suffering of others because it is suffering, just like my own suffering. I should take care of others because they are sentient beings, just as I am a sentient being.
>
> When happiness is equally dear to others and myself, then what is so special about me that I strive after happiness for myself alone?[4]

Mashimoto's Quandary

The vignette does not tell us about Mashimoto's religious status. Let us assume, therefore, that like probably the majority of contemporary Japanese he has taken neither the five lay precepts nor the bodhisattva precepts. He is, rather, an ordinary person, caught up in the round of repetitive actions motivated by the mistaken notion that as a separate, independently existing person he can achieve a permanent state of happiness. Now let us imagine that for whatever reason Mr. Mashimoto comes to me for advice. What is my responsibility as someone who has taken the precepts—lay, bodhisattva, and others—to him? I cannot tell him what to do, but I can attempt to help him to see that this situation arises from his own mistaken view of himself as separate from others.

Most importantly I would want him to consider the motivation of his actions in this situation. Is he—still—trying to achieve permanent happiness? His nostalgia for a simpler time in the past when he was not plagued by the competing demands of the present indicates that he is still motivated by such a hope. The fine irony of being in a situation where the very expertise that has led to his promotion also makes him more bound by complex social expectations and ethical standards is an opportunity to realize the frustrating character of human existence. Having gotten what he wanted, he now doesn't want it.

Further, I would ask him to identify just what the problem he faces is. Is he primarily concerned with the conflicting expectations that are being placed on him by his employer, family, and society? Or with the fear of being caught breaking the law? Or with the possible embarrassment to his company? Part of Mashimoto's problems result from the contemporary breakdown of the value system widely propagated by the Japanese government from the middle of the nineteenth century to the middle of the twentieth century. Under neo-Confucian standards as understood in China, Mashimoto's top priority would have been to his family. These standards were themselves modified in premodern Japan so that one's primary duty was to the line of social authority that culminated in the emperor. This was based on the analogy between the duty of obeying one's father and a higher duty of obeying the emperor as the (metaphoric) father of the nation as a whole. In postwar Japan such service to the country was again transformed into serving one's company— its economic success meant the economic progress of the country. Having attained economic success, Japan has now entered a world in which at least some of its citizens are now exposed to the different standards of other countries. His wife and children, having adopted some of the values to which they were exposed in England, now find Japanese values constricting in contrast to the openness and individual freedom they experienced while abroad. On the other hand, his employers still expect him to adhere to the standards of devotion to the company according to which as long as he did what was best for the company he would be taken care of. Thus, for Mr. Mashimoto there is no shared social consensus that he can depend on to justify his actions.

In the absence of any social consensus, is he attempting to resolve the conflict by clinging to some abstract absolute? In an important way making an ethical decision is only complicated, rather than simplified, by the existence of formalized ethical and legal strictures, such as those associated with banking. First, although such strictures attempt clarity for the sake of a standard understandable by all and, therefore, applicable to all, they necessarily are always going to be applied to situations requiring personal judgment. Second, there is the problem identified by Kierkegaard: no matter what standards one chooses to act on, one is responsible for choosing those standards.

Are the possible courses of action he is considering motivated by greed, hatred, or delusion? If they are based on the illusion of separate, independent existence, then no matter what action he takes, it will only further contribute to his own enmeshment in a frustrating situation. Acting defensively—attempting to protect his sense of self-identity from the perceived threats to it: loss of love, position, respect, and life itself—is the automatic response of a mind constrained by intellectual and emotional mistakes. When we identify with those things that are necessarily subject to change, we are necessarily creating fear because when change occurs—which it will—we will experience a loss of self-identity. It is the task of Buddhist meditative practices to bring about a shift of the center of self-identity from our possessions, accomplishments, and relationships, which create the fear-driven mind, to the pure, enlightened consciousness which is the foundation of our existence.

If Mashimoto pays attention (the basis of meditation) and takes responsibility for his actions (becomes aware of *karma*), including his choice of standards of behavior, then he can move a step closer to awakening from the delusion of separate, independent existence. Because of the interdependence of all living beings, his movement toward awakening benefits all others.

Notes

1. "Suffering" as a translation of the Sanskrit *dukkha* is used in English language discussions of Buddhism as a cover term for a wide range of experiences. *Dukkha* apparently originally was used in reference to situations in which "things don't work right," such as when a wheel is off its axle. The broad meaning then is that human existence is such that our expectations of how things ought to be are not met. Thus, although there is a significant difference between the physical suffering of a broken bone and the emotional suffering of disappointed love, both are considered forms of suffering. In this analysis of human existence even happiness is a source of suffering because the conditions that create happiness (or which we respond to as producing happiness in us) will necessarily change, leading to frustration and disappointment, that is, to suffering.

2. The use of the term "pure consciousness" here refers to consciousness that is unobscured by the twin obscurations of intellectual and emotional mistakes, not to the idea of "pure consciousness" as existence of subjective consciousness independent of an object of consciousness. Indeed the latter idea would be rejected by Buddhism which considers all existence as relational.

3. This approach to ethics appears to be very fashionable today. It seems to be given validation by the methodological concept of cultural relativity found in anthropology. But appropriating this methodological value as a standard for ethical judgments is a misappropriation.

4. Shantideva, *A Guide to the Bodhisattva Way of Life* (Bodhicaryavatara), trans. Vesna A. Wallace and B. Alan Wallace (Ithaca, NY: Snow Lion Publications, 1997), 100–01.

A JEWISH RESPONSE
by Ehud Ben-or and Ronald M. Green

Talmudic Advice for the Sarariiman

Takeo Mashimoto is facing one of the greatest trials of his life. Ahead of him lies a course that seems to represent the path of least resistance: obedience to the requests of his superiors, promotion, and, very likely, continued prosperity, esteem, and career advancement. Japanese culture rewards loyalty to one's firm and many Japanese values make that loyalty appear to be the center of one's moral universe, even eclipsing obligations to oneself and one's family. But the price of these rewards is involvement in dealings that Takeo knows to be morally and legally wrong. Having lived abroad, he can have had no illusions. Stock parking and insider trading may be relatively commonplace practices in Japan, but they are nevertheless against the law. Overseas, among Japan's trading partners, involvement in them is grounds for severe legal punishments. Making matters even worse is the turmoil in Takeo's home life. With his wife and children struggling with the clash of Japanese and Western values, he feels that he cannot look to them for clear support or guidance.

What Judaism has to say about ethics and business conduct at first seems infinitely remote from the quandary that Takeo faces. What relevance can biblical norms developed first for a small agrarian nation in the Middle East and later applied by generations of Talmudic sages to the life of a Diaspora community of small traders and artisans have to the affairs of an international banker in a modern Asian industrial nation? As a Buddhist or follower of Shinto, Takeo probably does not even share Judaism's monotheistic presuppositions.

Nevertheless, over the centuries Jews developed a significant body of teachings about ethics in commercial life. Behind these teachings was the Jewish impulse to shape a community whose members sought in all their dealings to imitate the lofty justice and righteousness of God: a holy community. Because of the deeply ethical and spiritual nature of this quest, the heritage of Jewish thinking on business ethics is not as remote from Takeo's dilemma as it might seem. Takeo himself faces a spiritual crisis: a choice about the very meaning and direction of his life. The deepest principles of Jewish teaching in this area point to a standard of personal—and communal—integrity which Takeo would do well to consider as he struggles to preserve his self-respect amidst the seemingly irresistible pressures exerted by his own cultural environment.

The repository of Jewish ethical teachings is the Talmud, the many volumes-long collection of rabbinic discourses, debates, homilies, and commentaries on biblical texts. The most prescriptive of these teachings compose *halakhah*, the body of Jewish law whose norms govern every feature of the Jew's life, from ritual matters to the conduct of business dealings. Less authoritative, but often instructive, are the *haggadic* portions of the Talmud, comprising depictions of saintly lives, moral parables, stories, and, sometimes, even jokes. In these *halakhic* and *haggadic* materials, the requirement of honesty in business dealings and the avoidance of all forms of fraud and deception emerge as the leading themes relating to Takeo's dilemma.

These themes are expressed in two basic norms. One is the prohibition of *genevat da'at* (literally "stealing the mind") of a Jew or non-Jew. In sales transactions, this rules out any conduct by the seller that creates a false impression and that misleads the purchaser about the nature or value of the product being sold. For example, it is forbidden to dress up or doctor meat so as to convey the impression that it is fresh when it is old, or fat when it is lean. It is forbidden to sell a barrel of wine with a small amount of oil floating at its top, thereby giving the misleading impression that the whole barrel contains the more valuable oil. The Talmud (Tractate Hullin 94a) illustrates the meaning of forbidden deception with a tale about Samuel who, crossing a body of water on a ferryboat, asked his attendant to reward the ferryman. The servant did so by giving the ferryman a ritually unclean (*trefah*) hen. Samuel grew angry on learning of this because the servant's deed misrepresented the reward as being of greater value than it was. Lest we mistakenly conclude that the wrong here was merely a ritual one (the attendant's possession or bestowal of a ritually unclean animal), the text goes on to offer a parallel tale of Samuel's anger when he learned that an attendant had given someone watered wine while representing it as undiluted.

A second relevant norm prohibits "overreaching" or "overcharging" *(ona'ah)* in sales transactions by exploiting for one's own advantage the neighbor's naivete or trust. The biblical basis for this prohibition was found in the verse, "When you sell to your neighbor or buy from your neighbor's hand you shall not oppress one another" (Lev 25:14). One oppresses the neighbor in this sense when one extracts an unduly high price for something one is selling. A buyer, too, engages in oppression by asking the price of an article he or she has no intention of purchasing, thereby encouraging false hopes in the seller. Conduct that violated the *ona'ah* requirement typically involved less overt acts of deception and more subtle forms of misrepresentation than that of *genevat da'at*. Unlike the *genevat da'at* prohibition, the requirement to avoid *ona'ah* did not extend to gentiles but applied only in commercial relations between Jews. This in-group/out-group distinction— which over the years unfortunately contributed to anti-Semitism—had its basis in the assumption that the highest standards of commercial dealing can take place only in a context of reciprocal relationships and mutually assured obligations.

Takeo and his bank clearly violate the letter and spirit of both these traditional Jewish norms. This scheme is actually a conspiracy to deceive many other individuals and firms in the securities marketplace. Those who sell

Midland Specialty Steel stock to the bank unaware that it is "parking" these securities for NJ Heavy Industries (NJHI) are deprived of the added value that NJHI's intended acquisition will give to the stock. It is one thing for a seller to conceal his or her plans to acquire large blocks of property or stock if making one's intentions public will have the effect of greatly increasing the cost of these items. Jewish law permits this.[1] Unless the seller is explicitly asked for information, he or she is not required actively to reveal every detail of his or her commercial plans in ways that reduce the prospect of profit. But the bank is not acting for itself here. It is serving as a "front" for NJHI in a way that is meant deliberately to obscure buyers' understanding of the economic signals being sent. Furthermore, because it cannot possibly make its intentions known without rendering itself susceptible to prosecution for securities fraud, the bank cannot comply with any purchaser's requests for disclosure.

This transaction also involves trading on insider information. Knowing that NJHI will ultimately buy its Midland shares at an attractive price, Takeo's bank is both protected from risk in its investment and guaranteed a large profit. Insider trading is against the law in Japan, where, as in the United States from where it drew these laws, it is conceived as a form of marketplace fraud. It represents a breach of the informational expectations of all actors in the market. They assume either that valuable commercial information about publicly traded firms will be made available to all willing to exert themselves to find it through adequate research or that such information will otherwise be securely retained inside the firm generating it. Insider trading is especially profitable when it exploits these expectations and takes advantage of others' unwarranted confidence in the openness of information and markets.

It might be objected that in the past, at least, insider trading statutes in Japan have been widely ignored and unenforced. On an ethical level, this calls into question the pattern of expectations that makes insider trading wrong. If others fail to respect an ethical standard, how can one be expected to be the sole holdout? This logic, we saw, to some extent underlay the Jewish teaching that the highest forms of commercial honesty and avoidance of misrepresentation applied only among coreligionists and within a community of mutual responsibility. If Japan's standards were very high on this matter compared with those of its trading partner nations, this logic might authorize some relaxation of standards in situations abroad where insider trading was rife. But the facts of this case are just the opposite. Takeo's bank is willing to impose its lax commercial standards on other international commercial partners and stockholders whose laws are far better enforced. The reasoning that sometimes authorizes an in-group/out-group distinction in Jewish ethical teaching thus works here to accentuate the wrongfulness of the bank's conduct.

One other feature of Jewish law rounds out this condemnation. This is the particular disdain Jewish teachers held for covert deeds of theft or misappropriation. Classical Jewish teaching makes a distinction between the thief and the robber. The former is one who takes movable property from another clandestinely; the latter steals openly, perhaps using force to do so. Of these two, the Jewish sages ruled, the thief is the more reprehensible: he must repay twice the value of the goods he takes while the robber must only restore what was taken. Why is this so? Because the thief combines misappropriation with the effort to conceal his deed from both God and man. In this sense, there is a sort of practical atheism at the heart of the thief's deed: the conviction that no one will see what he is doing. In addition, the rabbis reasoned, because of its covertness people can be victimized by theft without ever realizing it. This reduces both the chance of punishment and the victims' recovery of what they have lost.

Clearly these conceptions are relevant to the scheme in which Takeo is becoming embroiled. Many people will have their faith in the market exploited and will be financially damaged without ever realizing it. Even if this scheme is eventually exposed and the perpetrators are punished, how will all those other people be repaid? In the rabbinic sense, there can be no doubt that Takeo is being asked to be a thief, with all the opprobrium attaching to this term in Jewish teaching.

What then should Takeo do? Jewish teachings indicate that on a purely personal level the stakes for him are considerable. His self-respect is on the line. He is also alert enough to international standards to realize that this scheme imperils his bank. Already buffeted by poor economic decision making, it could fail if this scheme became widely known. Unemployment and a prison sentence are far greater evils than his current fears of demotion and assignment to frigid northerly Hokkaido.

Takeo has two resources. One is his wife Fumiko. What he regards as her aberrant wish to free herself from the suffocating embrace of local culture could be a maturing point of view that would allow him to see his dilemma in a larger perspective.

Takeo could also turn for confidential assistance to his company's London-based compliance group. We know that Takeo believes that these people can be of great help in sorting out difficult situations and can be relied on to preserve confidentiality. By contacting or even visiting them, Takeo can at least get a second opinion based on a solid knowledge of the law and international market conditions. Having stepped into the international milieu, Takeo cannot go back. He is now responsible, both for his own sake and for the bank's, to global standards. Jewish ethical thinking on business conduct is one contributing source to those standards from which Takeo might learn.

Notes

1. For a discussion of this permitted exception to the requirement of disclosure, see Aaron Levine, *Economics and Jewish Law* (New York: KTAV, 1987), 17–18.

Bibliography and Suggested Reading

Jones, Donald E. *Business, Religion, and Ethics: Inquiry and Encounter.* Cambridge, MA: Oelgeschloger, Gunn & Hain, 1982.

Levine, Aaron. *Economics and Jewish Law.* New York: KTAV, 1987.

Shantideva. *A Guide to the Bodhisattva Way of Life* (Bodhicaryavatara). Trans. Vesna A. Wallace and B. Alan Wallace. Ithaca, NY: Snow Lion Publications, 1997.

Smith, Patrick. *Japan: A Reinterpretation.* New York: Pantheon Books, 1997.

Taka, Iwao. "Business Ethics: A Japanese View," *Business Ethics Quarterly* 4, no. 1 (1994):53–78.

Takada, Noriko, and Rita L. Lampkin. *The Japanese Way: Aspects of Behavior, Attitudes, and Customs of the Japanese.* Lincolnwood, IL: Passport Books, 1997.

Werhone, Patricia G. "The Ethics of Insider Trading." In *The ACT Guide to Ethical Conflicts in Finance,* ed. Andreas R. Prindl and Bimal Prodham. Oxford: Blackwell, 1994.

CHAPTER 14

For the Good of the Children

A CASE STUDY by Regina Wentzel Wolfe

It was hot and humid with the morning sun beating down, but the women seemed not to notice. "I still say she has no business coming here and telling us what our daughters should do," Berna insisted as she fanned herself in the shade of one of the market stalls. "She thinks it is so simple. 'The girls belong in school,' she says. What does she know about it? She's from Manila. Things here are different."

"Yes," agreed Rosa. "All our girls can read and write. What would they do with more schooling?"

"If they go back to school they will be too old to get jobs in the factory when they finish. What will they do then?" added Lourdes. "I don't know why she keeps coming back here. We should tell her to go bother the people in some other barrio."

"We can't do that," said Fele. "She's a good friend of Father Ramos and the sisters from the clinic."

"I know, but every time it's the same," replied Lourdes. "She thinks that with more education the girls will have a better life with more opportunities than we had. But that would mean they might go to the city for jobs, and I don't want my Rosita there."

"I agree," said Leah. "The city is a dangerous place for girls from the countryside. They could get sold into slavery or end up as show girls in Taipei or Tokyo."

"That's right," said Marcelina joining the conversation. "Remember what happened to the Zaragosa girl? She went to Hong Kong as an amah, and her employer took her passport away from her and locked her in the house. She didn't get her Sundays off and worked for months without a break or a paycheck. It's only because her cousin was persistent and kept going to the consulate complaining that something had to be wrong that she was rescued," she recounted.

The women, familiar with the horror stories of overseas employment, nodded knowingly. "Gloria didn't have any trouble," Fele reminded them. "Look at what she was able to do for her family. They have a bigger bungalow and some land of their own to grow food on. And they don't just have chickens like the rest of us. They have two carabao. You know the wages over-seas are often five times what they are in Manila. That's why Leena stopped teaching school and took a job as an amah for a family in Hong Kong."

"They were lucky. I still say the factory is better," insisted Berna. "I want my daughter to stay home. Besides, we need the money she makes now. We can't wait three more years for her to finish school and then find work."

"Berna's right, we know what's best for our own children," Lourdes said. "This evening we just have to tell Father Ramos that we are decided. Our daughters are not going back to school. He shouldn't keep asking that woman to come here. You can see that, can't you, Fele?"

"I'm not sure. Father Ramos says Maria is right about the girls staying in school. You should go with me this evening and listen to her. We can talk more about this then. Now, I've got to get the laundry out to dry and the bedding needs airing," Fele answered as she gathered up her shopping bas-ket and balanced it on her head in preparation for the walk home.

That evening Father Ramos greeted people as they began gathering in the small courtyard of the church. He hoped the meeting wouldn't be too con-tentious. Recently Maria had become involved with an international advo-cacy group and had been collecting data on illegal child employment. Tonight she was going to try to convince people to take their daughters out of the local factories. And she wanted his help. He had told her he thought it was a nearly impossible task. But more disconcerting was her intention to file a report with the regional office of the Department of Labor and Employment.

"That will cause an uproar," thought Father Ramos to himself, ponder-ing his own feelings toward such a move.

The long shadows of the setting sun were fading into dusk as he invited people to come in and find a seat. They sat on the long narrow benches wait-ing for the discussion to begin and conversing quietly, the smell of melted candle wax permeating the warm, humid air. Fele looked around for the oth-ers. Berna and Marcelina were in front, but she didn't see Lourdes. Maybe she wasn't coming after all.

Father Ramos moved to the front of the church and began, "You all know Maria Peña from the bishops' office in Manila. She's visited us many times in the past few months to speak about our young people's education. Tonight she wants to talk about a different issue. Tonight she will talk about the prob-lem of children working in factories." Over the murmurs he continued, "She has some important things to say, so we should all listen carefully."

"You know that I help the bishops in their work to further the opportu-nities for children and youth," Maria began. "The bishops are very con-cerned for our country's children and want the best for them as they grow. I am concerned for our children, too. I've spoken to you before about the importance of education for *all* our children, not just the boys, but the girls also. Tonight I'd like to tell you about the way some of our children—your children—are being exploited.

"Since I began my visits to you, I have become increasingly aware of the number of underage children working in some of the factories in the area. I am very concerned about this. We all know it is illegal for children below 15 years of age to be employed, but that is not my main concern. My main concern is for the children. Most of them work under conditions that threaten their health and safety, and all are underpaid. They are being exploited," Maria said passionately. "I'm here this evening to ask you to help change this situation. I'm here to ask you to take your children out of the factories," she pleaded.

Before she could continue, one of the men stood up. "That's not possible," he protested. "How are we to survive? Those are the only jobs available, and the family would not be able to eat without that income. What do you know about it?"

Maria had heard that and other protests before.

"There are ways," she replied. "There are alternatives. I am here to help you find them. That is part of the work I do with the bishops. Please, let me tell you about one of the girls I've been working with; let me describe a typical day in her life. It might help in understanding why she and others shouldn't be in the factories."

As people shifted uncomfortably, Father Ramos intervened, "Please, let's at least hear what Maria has to say."

"The young girl I've been working with is eleven years old, and she lives with her parents and five brothers and sisters. I'll call her Luisa. Luisa's day starts around nine in the morning. She wakes, washes, dresses, and has something to eat. Then she cares for her two younger sisters and brother while her mother goes to the market. When her mother returns, Luisa helps her prepare the midday meal. After eating, she has a little time to play, to go outdoors for a walk, to be a child. By two in the afternoon she has to get ready to go to work.

"Luisa lives a fair distance from the factory where she works the three-to-eleven shift. She has a bicycle that she rides to and from work, but it takes over half an hour to get there. Some of the roads she rides on are very busy with trucks, buses, and jeepneys roaring by her. It is dangerous, especially when she comes home late at night, in the dark. Louisa and many of her friends have been knocked down by passing vehicles. In fact, one of her friends was killed when she was hit by a jeepney as she rode home one particularly dark and stormy night!" Maria paused a moment to let her point sink in.

"It is also unhealthy to be breathing all the smoke and fumes that the vehicles spew out," she said as she continued her story.

"Luisa tries to arrive at work a few minutes early so she can visit with the other girls on the shift. The factory is in a compound enclosed by ten-foot-high walls. Near the gate there is a small shed where the watchman lives with his family. Not far from that is a small building where the manager has his office. The workshop itself is a bit farther along in a building made of corrugated metal with windows along both sides just under the eaves. The space in which Luisa and her friends work is about thirty feet wide and eighty feet long. It takes up most of the building. When you walk into the workshop, you look down a center aisle, with row after row of sewing machines on either side. The windows are so high that they provide little ventilation and even less light. Luisa's work station is at the end of one of the rows pushed up against the outer wall of the building. A light bulb dangles about four feet above her head. The company is a subcontractor for a company that makes doll clothes for a doll manufacturer. Her job is to sew the left shoulder seam on the doll dresses that the company produces.

"At three o'clock sharp Luisa and the other girls are at their places. Sitting on a wooden chair in front of her machine, Luisa reaches into the large basket on her left and takes out the back of a dress. The basket on her right contains the front of the dress. She sews the pieces together and lets the partially completed garment fall into the basket on the floor behind her machine. Small particles of dust from the fabric fill the air. She's at it for almost eight hours straight. This is wrong!" Maria proclaimed.

"It is wrong not just for Louisa, it is wrong for all our children," Maria continued. "Many of you have daughters working in similar conditions. I'm here tonight to plead with you to take them out of those places. Children should not be working under those conditions. They should be in school."

The group had become silent, many were staring stonily at Maria. "He always has something to say," Fele thought to herself as Pablito stood up to speak.

"Why do you think you can tell us what to do with our daughters?" he asked angrily. "First you come to talk about school. They all know how to read and write. They don't need any more schooling; it will only give them big ideas and they won't be able to find husbands. Now, you tell us they shouldn't work. That it is not healthy for them. Look around you. Most of the women in this room worked in the factories when they were that age. They did it to help support their families just as our daughters do. This is not Manila! Things are different here. You should return to the city."

Most in the church were nodding in support of Pablito's comments as Maria began to reply. "It's not simply a matter of schooling. Your daughters face real hazards in the factories. Things that might be all right for an adult are not safe for growing bodies. I'll give you just one example. The benches and other equipment in factories are designed for adults. Children are forced to stretch or otherwise accommodate themselves to equipment that is oversized for them. This can hamper their muscle and bone development leaving them more susceptible to neurological complications when they get older. If they are really unlucky, it can leave them severely deformed."

"Another thing," Maria continued, "children get tired more easily than adults and aren't able to concentrate on what they're supposed to be doing, so they're more prone to accidents. These jobs are hazardous for them. Can't you see that?" she pleaded.

Father Ramos looked around. There seemed to be a few people who were sympathetic to what Maria was saying. "Why don't you tell us about the project, Maria," he prompted.

Maria gave him a quick glance, acknowledging his comment, and turned back to the people assembled in front of her. "What Father Ramos is talking about is a series of meetings where we could come together and talk about our children and the type of work they are doing. Some people from the bishops' Commission on Social Action, Justice and Peace will come to help us and be able to answer questions for us. We would be able to talk about the children's needs and ways to protect them. The commission also has people who can work with you to see if there aren't other ways to help with family income, ways that might enable you to move into better paying jobs so that there wouldn't be a reason for your children to work."

Jose Ocampos stood up to respond, "We are too busy for senseless meetings. There is nothing wrong with our daughters working at the factories as their mothers did. Pablito is right. You should go back to the city." With that, he motioned to his wife, and she got up and followed him out of the church.

A few began to leave as Fele stood up to speak. Looking around at her neighbors she said, "I think we should listen to Maria. She is right about the dangers. Have you all forgotten that my sister, Joanna, lost the tips of her fingers when her hand got caught in the machine she was operating? She was only thirteen at the time, and she was not the only one of us girls who got hurt! Pablito, you and Jose and the others should ask your wives and sisters to tell you what it was really like. It's not just the few girls who were involved in road accidents or those who lost hands or arms or were maimed in some way. Ask them to remember the girls who used to pass out and those who seemed always to be coughing and wheezing. How easy it is to forget, especially when some of them are no longer with us. I think we should listen to Maria. She is only concerned for the good of our children. I think she's right that our girls should stay in school. I'd like my Josefina to go back to school, but we need the money she makes. Maybe Maria can help find a way to solve the problem. I'll come to your meeting," she said, turning to Maria.

"Thank you," Maria replied and then asked the rest, "are there any others who want to join? If so, why don't we gather at the side over here, and we can decide on a good time to meet."

Only a few people came forward. Fele watched to see if any of her friends would join her, but was not surprised to see Berna and Marcelina leaving the church. "They will probably tell me I'm stupid," she thought to herself as she went up to join Maria and the five or six people she was speaking to.

When she was finished, Maria headed toward the rectory to see Father Ramos. Sister Joseph from the clinic was with him. "Well, I gather you stirred things up a bit. I only came in at the end. People were so upset they didn't even notice me as they walked out," she said.

"I get so frustrated," Maria told them. "I tried to get them to see that they should keep their daughters in school, but that never seems to work. And it's just as difficult to get them to see that working in the factories can really hurt their daughters. I don't know why they are unable to see that their daughters are being exploited!"

Maria plopped into a chair and tried to keep from becoming too agitated. It was at times like this that her friends accused her of getting on her soapbox. She would list all of the ways in which working children were exploited: they received inadequate pay; they were specifically targeted because they were disadvantaged; their physical, mental, and social development was thwarted; they were trapped in a cycle of poverty because as adults they could only do unskilled low wage work. "And for girls it's worse," Maria said out loud. "The boys often get to continue in school, the girls are not only sent to work, they have to do household chores, too."

"Look, don't get so emotional about it," said Father Ramos. "Why don't you wait and see how the meetings go. Maybe in time more people will come around."

"But there isn't any time, at least not for the children," Maria retorted. "Someone has to look out for their interests. If their parents won't, or can't, then I guess I'll have to."

"That sounds like some sort of threat," Sister Joseph remarked.

"I think it is," Father Ramos said. "Maria wants to report the factories to the Department of Labor and Employment. That will get the girls out of the factories, but it will also cause trouble for a lot of people."

"If you mean the employers," Maria responded sharply, "what they are doing is illegal, and they should be stopped."

"But don't you see," Father Ramos said with a soft but deliberate tone in his voice, "they're trapped, too. I spoke to some of them about your project a few days ago, and they made it clear that they can't afford to pay higher wages for adult workers and stay competitive. Believe me, these are not wealthy men. Like everyone in the barrio, they are struggling to support their families and provide a future for their children."

Father Ramos stood up, moved to the window, and looked out into the night. "Have you been out to the 'factories' and seen the condition they're in?" he asked Maria as he slowly turned to look at the two women. "One look at the overgrown grounds and the rusting corrugated buildings should be enough to realize they can't pay higher wages and stay in business. Maria, these are little guys," Father Ramos insisted. "They're as much at the mercy of the system as the girls and their families are. The contractors they work with aren't going to pay more for the work. And if you close them down by reporting them to the authorities, the contractors they work with will only go to some other barrio and find someone else to subcontract the work to.

"I'm not just concerned for the girls' employers. I'm concerned for their families, too. As it is they can barely make ends meet; losing the girls' wages will put some of them over the brink and could force families to be split, especially if one of the parents has to go to Manila or somewhere else to get work. Maria, you've got to reconsider, at least for the time being," insisted Father Ramos.

"I can't," replied Maria as she got up to leave. "My mind is made up. I'll send in my report tomorrow."

Father Ramos paced for a long time after the two women left. He agreed that something had to be done in the long run, but he wasn't sure that Maria had looked at the problem from all sides or thought things through. Not only was he concerned for the economic havoc that her decision would wreak on so many of his parishioners, he was also concerned for the girls themselves. It wasn't simply a matter of getting them out of the factories. It would take time to make plans for them so they wouldn't end up in circumstances that were even worse. He had listened to stories of girls who ended up in domestic work which could be much worse than the factories or, even more horrendous, the stories of those forced into prostitution.

Father Ramos had a difficult time falling asleep. He felt caught. He was pretty certain Maria would follow through on her threat to file a report; if he was going to do anything about it he had to act first thing in the morning. "I could warn the factory owners," he thought to himself. "They would most likely dismiss the girls until the inspectors came. It would be hard on everyone for a few weeks, but eventually the girls could go back to work. Then there would be time to think things through and come up with a solution that might work for all concerned. If anyone found out, though, there would be big trouble—from the labor people and from the bishop. I'm not sure I could cope with that," he admitted to himself as he finally drifted off to sleep.

A ROMAN CATHOLIC RESPONSE
by Michael J. Naughton

Within Catholic moral theology, in order to penetrate the ethical dimension of human actions one must understand three aspects of the human act: the end (what are we doing it for?), the means (what will we actually do to achieve our end?), and circumstances (what are the extenuating circumstances of the particular act or situation?). I will use these three aspects of the human act to understand the ethical dimensions of this case as we examine the many stakeholders: Father Ramos and the local church, Maria and the archdiocese, the girls who work in the plant, the parents of the young girls, government officials, employers (contractors, retailers, customers), children in other plants, trade organizations, international advocacy groups, and so forth. While the girls at the plant are the most important stakeholders, they seem the least empowered in the case. Their immediate fate lies in the actions of Father Ramos, Maria, their parents, their employers, and the government.

The End

What do Father Ramos, Maria, and the parents want? They all seem very concerned with the development of the children, although they seem to have different notions of human development. Two seemingly conflicting notions of the girls' development are found to exist between Maria and the children's parents. Maria wants the girls to develop their talents, skills, and knowledge through education. She sees the current employment situation for the young girls as detrimental to their development. The parents are concerned about economic survival and family unity. While their concerns sound somewhat parochial and their arguments against Maria somewhat self-serving, they see Maria's plan as a threat to the economic and familial goods they wish to preserve.

Father Ramos has a difficult situation in front of him, but he has within his Catholic tradition a social philosophy and theology that can frame the problem for him. A critical cornerstone principle to the Catholic social tradition is Integral Human Development. This development has multiple dimensions to it. We survive. Economic goods serve as a floor to the rest of

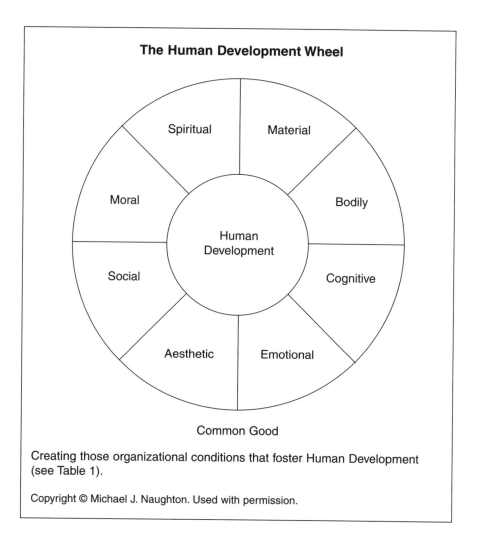

The Human Development Wheel

Spiritual · Material · Moral · Bodily · Human Development · Social · Cognitive · Aesthetic · Emotional

Common Good

Creating those organizational conditions that foster Human Development (see Table 1).

Copyright © Michael J. Naughton. Used with permission.

Table 1: Human Development

The purpose of any organization must be the development of the human person. While revenue, efficiency, and quality are all necessary means to human development, they are only means. Pressures of organizational life all too often lead us to invert ends and means.

a. *Material development:* Create and distribute the world's resources so as to meet people's needs (common use). Dominion of the earth is a gift to all humanity. When people have little or no access to this gift while others have plenty, the created order of the earth is distorted.

b. *Bodily development:* Negatively speaking, one's work should progress in mitigating physical disabilities. The science of ergonomics has been very helpful here.

c. *Cognitive development:* Train and develop the talents and skills of employees to have them engage in challenging work that exercises their intellectual abilities.

d. *Emotional development:* Freedom to act without fear or reprisal. Allowing people to exercise responsibility and take accountability for their work (subsidiarity).

e. *Aesthetic development:* Through work, people can gain a sense of craftmanship in making their work beautiful, elegant, and harmonious with nature.

f. *Social development:* The ability to participate in other social institutions to contribute to society's welfare, particularly one's family, but also religious, educational, community, and political institutions.

g. *Moral development:* Through work, people participate in the edification rather than the degradation of society (stewardship). Character development.

h. *Spiritual development:* Collaborate with God for the human race. "We are not here to transform the world. We are here, instead, to be transformed singly and collectively, by the powerful presence of God in our midst" (Haughey). "We become persons, we develop personality, precisely in engagement with the incarnate Christ who disclosed to us the unexpected possibility of fullness of life" (Briel).

The reason why human development is the primary goal is that if one fails in this task, all other goals are corrupted and worthless. An organization must always be evaluated on the basis of "what it is doing to people."

human development. Yet, our goal in life is not merely to survive. We have families to nurture, an intellect to develop, friendships to mature, a soul to nourish. Father Ramos seems to recognize a fuller notion of the children's development, which is why he is bringing Maria and the parents together.

Unfortunately, he is not having much luck communicating a fuller vision of development to Maria and the parents.

The Means

Pope John XXIII defined the common good as "the sum total of those conditions of social living, whereby men are enabled more fully and more readily to achieve their own perfection."[1] Within the Catholic social tradition there are two critical dimensions to the common good. The first is achieving human development, and the second is creating conditions that lead to human development. Concerning the case we ask, "What are the necessary conditions for development to take place in the barrio outside of Manila?" While both the parents and Maria want the girls to develop, they disagree on what their development means and on the conditions necessary for that development.

As the unofficial mediator, Father Ramos has a special responsibility to work toward the common good, that is, to create conditions that foster human development and in particular for these young girls. His faith does not allow him to escape this situation by capitulating to the implied parochialism of the parents: "Who is to tell us what to do with our daughters!" Likewise, faith, and in particular the common good, does not allow him to join Maria in imposing rigid solutions without consideration of the economic and familial consequences.

If there is no change, certainly the young girls will not be developing their full potential within the present conditions. If Maria calls the authorities, the animosities between employer and community, and the parents and Maria, will grow more severe. What is necessary here is what John Paul calls the virtue of solidarity, that "firm and persevering determination to commit oneself to the common good; that is to say, to the good of all and each individual, because we are all really responsible for all."[2] For John Paul II, the fact that people are interdependent in their work demands solidarity. People do not work only for themselves. They also work for their family, their community, their nation, and for all of humanity. Hence, in *Laborem Exercens*, he explains that solidarity does not represent a struggle against a particular class or power. Rather, solidarity reflects unity in struggle "for" justice, not "against" a particular group.

In part, it is the lack of solidarity that is preventing a possible resolution and that is leading to an impasse on the proper means necessary for the girls and their families to develop. Parents are refusing to collaborate with Maria, and Maria is refusing to collaborate with the employers. While Maria's plan to remove the girls from the plant and move them into school is critical to their development, it is irresponsible without some alternative to the loss of income the families will endure after the girls leave employment. Joseph Ratzinger points out that "a morality that believes itself able to dispense with the technical knowledge of economic laws is not morality but moralism. As such, it is the antithesis of morality."[3] While Maria has a good end, her failure to supply sufficient means to carry it through indicates a lack of prudence on her part. She needs first to present to the parents some economic alternatives, then begin to address removing the children from the factories. While comments from Pablito seem from a Western perspective to smack of sexism, he and the other parents see Maria's comments as anti-family and anti-economic. There are survival and familial needs that Maria has to address first before the parents can begin to consider removing their children from the factories. She also needs to contextualize her comments so that they are focused more in terms of strengthening the family and less in terms of individualizing the young girls' development.

So, what means are available to address the issue at hand? This problem will not be solved by one or two stakeholders but by several working in collaboration. This is precisely why the problem is so difficult to solve. Father Ramos seems to be the only one on the right track here. He realizes two things: this problem of child labor is part of a systemic or structural construct, and the only way to deal with this structural problem is through collaboration, particularly collaboration with employers.

His first task is to set up a meeting with people from the diocese, with the employers, and possibly with some parents. If Maria refuses to attend the meeting, then he needs to go to her superiors. If this meeting fails then it will be simply each party attempting to outdo the other through legal and manipulative means.

If they succeed in a meeting together, they need the good will of all parties in order to collaborate toward a solution. This moral commitment of solidarity is never easy. Father Ramos and the local church play a critical role here. Father Ramos as pastor serves as part of the moral formation that his parishioners receive. He can help his parishioners—both parents and employers—to become sensitive to the development of the young girls and their inherent dignity through preaching, confession, counseling, pastoral visits, faith formation, and so forth. The church's role is primarily a cultural one, although the diocese with its international contacts can offer models. For example, Levi Strauss, in collaboration with their subcontractors, sent its underage employees to school while continuing to pay them wages and agreeing to hire the girls back after they finished school.[4] Unfortunately, most multinationals do not seem to be so creative.[5]

Members of any group Father Ramos calls together will also need to evaluate the economic situation. There seems to be a deterministic attitude on the part of both Father Ramos and the employers that wages cannot be higher. Such determinism tends to be bad management. The variables involved in making a profit are too complex to say "wages can't be raised," or, conversely, to say that wages can be raised. Without proper investigation we simply do not know. A couple of issues need to be addressed: the efficiency and productivity of a child worker as compared to an adult worker; the quality of goods produced by a child compared to those produced by an adult; the ownership of the company; and so forth. Children are more concerned about socializing with other children than they are about the company for which they are working (as they should be). They do not feel any sense of ownership of their productive efforts. Economic conditions must be established to serve the development of the families in this barrio outside of Manila. Essential to those conditions are efficient, productive, and, above all, humane work processes where human development can take place and an ownership structure that avoids what Jeff Gates calls "disconnected capital" can be created.[6] It is far from clear that these goals cannot be achieved with adults at this plant rather than children.

The Circumstances

A much larger problem looms for Father Ramos, Maria, and this small community outside Manila. It has been estimated that between 100 and 145 million children in Asia, some as young as four years of age, work, most in appalling conditions.[7] The problem is exacerbated by the international flight of capital, an ineffective enforcement of labor legislation within the Philippines, and very few effective labor laws within international trade agreements. What we are dealing with in this case is what John Paul calls structures of sin—those particular conditions that prevent people from flourishing. Within this labor market, subcontractors as well as multinationals will, depending on how well managed they are, be pressured in economic ways to continue child labor practices. Along with many others, the Catholic social tradition has maintained that while the market is an effective tool in creating and allocating resources, it is only one tool and, by itself, is insufficient in promoting human development.

While Father Ramos, Maria, parents, local employers, and government can do much to achieve the common good, they cannot do it by themselves. The common good is the task of both the public and the private sectors, as well as local, national, and international bodies. Some matters belong to one or the other, but many matters—such as the distribution of goods—belong to both. However, as articulated in the principle of subsidiarity, social and economic control should be kept at the lowest possible level, thus giving primacy to individual initiative. Intermediate associations—families, local communities, employers, unions, and so forth—should be free to perform operations proper to them without interference from the state. The state, as well as international bodies such as the World Trade Organization and the International Labor Organization, in their vigilance over the common good are to encourage, assist, and, when necessary, supplement this private initiative. It is naive to think the market can solve all our problems. Child labor problems in the United States were solved through legislation and enforcement. While some labor markets, left to themselves, will provide living and equitable wages, other markets will not and will need creative solutions from what John Paul calls indirect employers—such as states, unions, international agencies, and financial institutions—to create "structures of the common good."[8]

There is, of course, no easy resolution here, but that does mean the solution is merely relativistic. There is a possibility that Maria's solution of calling in the Department of Labor and Employment may be the best solution; but at this point in time it should be seen as the last alternative, not as a club with which to threaten people. Maria's desire for justice does not have an equal consideration to the means of accomplishing justice. In other words, her justice is, at least initially, without prudence, resulting in a sort of "justicism" that has a good end, but defective means. At this present time, Maria has failed to consider all the means available. It should be pointed out that without Maria this issue of child labor most likely would not have gotten this far. Her role is critical to a solution. Somewhere along the line some form of creative government help will be necessary such as tax breaks, favorable credit policies (microenterprises), training and development programs, and so forth.[9] What is needed is social justice, which mandates not merely one person but the institutions in society acting in concert for the common good, that is, acting to create conditions in society that enable people to develop.

Notes

1. Pope John XXIII, *Mater et magistra*, 15 May 1961, para. 65.
2. Pope John Paul II, *Sollicitudo rei socialis*, 30 December 1987, para 38.
3. Joseph Ratzinger, "Market Economy and Ethics," in *Ordo Socialis: Making Christianity Work in Business and Economy*, ed. Association for the Advancement of Christian Social Sciences (Philippines: Divine Word Publications, 1992):62–67.
4. See Russell Mitchell and Michael Oneal, "Managing by Values at Levi's," *Business Week* (1 August 1994):44–51.
5. See the National Labor Committee's Web page for critiques of practices by Disney as well as other American corporations (http://www.nlcnet.org).
6. Jeff Gates, *The Ownership Solution* (Reading, MA: Addison Wesley Publishing, 1998).
7. See *(http://www.nando.net/newsroom/ntn/world/0918995/world179_9.html)*.
8. See the document by the Pontifical Council *Cor Unum* "World Hunger," in *Origins* 26 (7 November 1996):342.
9. For more information on microenterprises, see the Woodstock Theological Center Web page (http//www.guweb.georgetown.edu/woodstock/gl-micro.htm).

AN ISLAMIC RESPONSE by Mohamed Adam El-Sheikh

As we move into the twenty-first century, we are going to face a number of moral and ethical issues that deserve immediate attention from policy makers and religious leaders. There are three important developments in world affairs that warrant new thinking and new action.

The first factor is the globalization process that is affecting all parts of the world. This is evident in the telecommunications revolution, which is best exemplified by the CNN factor, the BBC outreach, and the Sky TV invasion of the airwaves. This globalization has created and opened new markets for the products of multinational and transnational corporations. Globalization has also affected the world system in another sense. This is to say, globalization has created an international labor market which allows multinational corporations to find the cheapest labor markets for the mass production of their goods. A widely celebrated example is the Indonesian workers producing Nike shoes, footwear that is now a status symbol for young people all over the planet. In the special case of the United States, the Nike phenomenon has become a bone of contention following media reports that Nike not only employs child labor in its factories in Indonesia, but it also sells its shoes briskly at exorbitant prices in the inner cities of the United States where the underclass of American minorities resides.

The second factor that deserves our attention is the evidence of migration all around the world. Not only do we witness internal migration which creates the conditions for child labor within nations, but across the globe we also have seen international migration which engenders human exploitation and worsens the problem of child labor. Because of this globalization, a chaotic mobility of the masses has become a distinctive phenomenon of our time. People now flood the borders of more developed countries in search of livelihoods. Such persons, who most often are illegal immigrants, are targets of labor recruiters who take advantage of the immigrants' poverty and vulnerability. Child labor is very much a product of this new process of internal and global migration. The children are not only recruited to work on agricultural farmlands, but they are also secretly and illegally drafted to work in sweatshops. This phenomenon is well known in the developing areas of the world. Examples from Thailand, Bangladesh, and India have attracted the attention of the media, and efforts have been made to bring this state of affairs to an end.

The third factor centers on the role and place of moral and religious leadership in the protection of workers, regardless of their ages. This is an important area of life which religious leadership must address. A combination of the three factors identified above has made it categorically clear that political and religious leaders all over the world must focus their attention on this new trend in the world economy. The increased attention paid to this matter by religious and moral leaders has made it clear that families struggling to make ends meet and multinational corporations trying to make their bottom lines look good for investors' meetings must face the moral dilemma of these times.

Islam and the Question of Labor in Human Society

In order for us to understand the Islamic perspective on child labor, we must first address the Islamic view of labor and work in human society. The point of departure for any discussion on the Islamic view of work and labor is found in the second chapter of the Qur'an. In this section of the Muslim holy text is the story of creation. We learn from this narrative that humans were created to be the *khalifa* (vicegerents or deputies) of Allah on the earth. This responsibility gives humans both spiritual and secular responsibilities. The

Qur'an states categorically that humans were created purposely to serve Allah. It is their responsibility to serve the Creator in a world of phenomenon. Humans have to labor in the sublunary world so that they can succeed in this life and in the next.

In fact, one of the most widely recited prayers of Muslims is that which calls on their Creator to grant them success in this life and in the next life. To be successful in this life, therefore, humans have to accept the responsibility of being *homo laborans* (working humans). They cannot be *homo faber* (tool-making humans) without being *homo laborans*. The Qur'an makes it clear to believers that to work is an obligation placed on the individual in the community in which he or she lives. Allah says, "work, soon will Allah observe your work and His Apostle and the believers" (9:105). It is also the obligation of the community and society to help provide suitable job opportunities to each and every capable member of that community and society. Along these lines, Muslim workers have the right to demand just and fair wages and humane working conditions.

Muslims believe that when Allah created the earth, He bestowed His blessing upon it, provided humankind with all the means of sustenance, and made all creatures subject to the will of humans. The following Qur'anic verse captures this meaning well: "And the earth We have spread out (like a carpet); set mountains firm and immovable; and produced therein all kinds of things in due balance. And We have provided therein means of subsistence,—for you and for those for whose sustenance ye are not responsible" (15:19–20).

This same message is restated in Chapter 41:9–10. Indeed the divine provision of livelihood to humans and their brief authority over the rest of creation are linked together in Chapter 7, where Allah states: "It is We who have placed you with authority on earth, and provided you therein with means for the fulfillment of your life. Small are the thanks that ye give" (7:10). This linkage between the divine creation and the human uses of the resources of this earth is stressed over and over again in various verses in the Qur'an. The matter is decreed this way: "We have honored the sons of Adam; provided them with transport on land and sea; given them for sustenance things good and pure" (7:70). As Dr. Hussein Hamid Hassan wrote in his book *Right to Work*:

> In this holy verse, the honor and distinction conferred on mankind by the Almighty have been connected to the facilitation of means of living for him on the earth and the way Allah has provided him with easy means of transportation to acquire his sustenance and seek bountiful provisions of Allah. And when he obtains his daily bread with his efforts and endeavor he will lead an honorable life and bow down to none other than his Creator and his Provider.[1]

What is evident from these verses is that humans are privileged creatures in the universe and have the responsibility to earn a living on this earth and to serve Allah throughout their lives. This call to service is both spiritual and secular as we have said earlier. On the spiritual plane, humans are expected to use their physical, mental, and emotional energy to worship Allah. They are also expected to carve niches for themselves within the social universe through the job market and through networks of relationships with other human beings. Ideal Muslims are those who internalize the Qur'an while living harmoniously with their fellow human beings. This can only come about when they are in full control of their bodies and are not at the mercy of an employer or a state.

On the secular plane, individuals are called on to remember that they are, in Adam, brothers and sisters to other human beings. This common humanity should not be violated through injustice. This moral teaching of Islam is closely connected to the khalifahood, or the act of being a vicegerent or deputy. This sense of being the *khalifa* is not only confined to the spiritual role humans play in this world. It is also evident in the social universe where humans have secular responsibilities.

In light of the above discussion of creation and the role humans are expected to play in this world, we can say that work is essential in all human societies, especially in Muslim societies where Muslims strongly believe that working is part of our role as vicegerents or deputies of Allah. Why is work essential? It is essential because it is a prerequisite for the construction of the earth. Without human labor and human creativity, many things that we now enjoy in human societies would vanish. The Qur'an makes it clear that Allah's mercy is showered on humanity so that humans can accomplish both their spiritual and their mundane needs on earth before their lives come to an end. The Qur'an states the matter in the following verse: "It is He Who has made the earth manageable for you, so traverse ye through its tracts and enjoy of the sustenance which He furnishes: but unto Him is the resurrection" (15:67). "And when the Prayer is finished, then may ye disperse through the land, and seek of the Bounty of God" (62:10). In reviewing these verses of the Qur'an, one is led to the conclusion that Islam considers work to be the basic factor for distribution of wealth and the main source of its private ownership. Almighty Allah says: "Whoever works righteousness benefits his own soul; whoever works evil, it is against his own soul" (41:46).

Islam and Child Labor Process

Having examined the Islamic view of work and labor in general, let us now analyze the Islamic perspective on child labor in particular. First, we must ask, what is the Islamic position on child labor? The answer is that children aged seven and above may do some work for their families in order to receive training. They can work on their family farmlands or care for the herd or work in the family workplaces where their dignity is not violated and abused by parents or older family members. Children under thirteen years of age, ethically and customarily, are not subject to outside labor. In light of the prerequisite respect for the dignity of children, one can argue here that Muslims can allow their children to work so long as the employers operate within the bounds laid down by the Qur'an and *Sunna*.[2] This is to say that the Muslim tradition tolerates child labor under three major conditions: (1) the child must be seven years of age or older; (2) the workplace should be owned and run by the child's family; (3) the objective of the child's work must be oriented towards training the child and not for making money. Islamic *shari'a* takes into consideration that children are the potential providers for their families and member of the society. Because of this potentiality, they should be trained in preparation for their future responsibilities.

Child Labor and Islamic Shari'a

Muslim scholars unanimously agree that after birth human life is divided into three consecutive stages. The first stage is from birth to the age of seven; during this stage the Islamic *shari'a* identifies the child as *sabie ghair mumaiz* (one who lacks the capacity to distinguish good from bad). In this stage children are totally dependent on others; they have no independent will, therefore, they are neither accountable religiously nor liable criminally. Their good deeds are added to their parents' good deeds while their bad deeds are nil because legally they are not answerable for their deeds. The *shari'a* determines that, during this stage, children should not be subject to penalty for wrongdoing because they lack the two essential factors on which liability and accountability are based: comprehension and will.

Because they lack the capacity to perceive the ultimate result of their actions, children younger than seven years of age cannot conceptualize and comprehend the consequence of their deeds, such as entering into an agreement with a factory or signing a contract with an enterprise. Therefore, they should not be allowed to buy, sell, employ, or be employed by other parties. According to the Islamic *shari'a*, any interactions of the above nature entered into by a child younger than seven years of age are null and void, regardless of the outcome of the deal or the approval of parents or guardians.[3]

However, the *shari'a* determines, in principle, that the property of others must be protected. Therefore, if an action of a child younger than seven years of age results in the destruction of someone else's property, that child shall be held liable monetarily. That is, the liability is held against the child's property and the compensation for the loss is to be paid from the child's wealth, if the child has any wealth. Otherwise, compensation should be made by the child's parent.

The second stage of human life is from age seven to age fifteen according to the majority of Muslim *Fuqaha*. Though according to Imam Abu Hanifah[4] and some *Fuqaha* in the Imam Malik[5] School of thought, the age of the second stage of human life is considered to be from age seven to age eighteen.[6] In this second stage of life, the child is classified as *sabie mumaiz* (one who can easily distinguish between what is legal and what is illegal and between what is benevolent and what is detrimental). In this stage, the child's good deeds are still recorded on behalf of his or her parents as long as the child has not attained actual puberty. Due to the child's vulnerability, in this stage he or she shall not be held accountable for any crimes committed.[7] And as a minor, the child is not morally responsible for bad deeds.

According to the *shari'a*, a child under the age of fifteen is not competent to buy, sell, employ, or be employed by others. However, if such a child does engage in any of the above mentioned interactions, the *shari'a* determines that any commitment, agreement, or contract signed by him or her is null and void unless it is thoroughly reviewed and approved by his or her parents. Additionally, the *shari'a* vigorously instructs parents and guardians not to approve any deal entered into or made by their children who are under fifteen years of age unless that deal or contract is geared, without any shadow of doubt, to the interest of the minor. For instance, if a contract or deal could jeopardize the child's life, affect his or her physical or mental health, lead to risking his or her wealth, or risk his or her potential welfare, then such a contract or deal must be rendered void and the parents must terminate such a transaction.[8]

The third stage of human life begins at age fifteen. According to the *shari'a*, upon reaching his or her fifteenth birthday the child is no longer a minor but is an adult even if he or she has not yet attained puberty. The parents or guardians should examine the child's maturity, if he or she is found mature and competent, then the child is eligible to receive his or her wealth and deal with his or her own businesses independently. Allah says in the holy Qur'an: "Make trial of orphans until they reach the age of marriage, if then you find sound judgment in them, release their property to them" (4:6). This verse and verse 24:59 quoted above both indicate that the factor that distinguishes between childhood and adulthood is puberty. According to the *shari'a* the signs of puberty are characterized either by the physical changes in the child's body associated with menstruation, impregnation, or pregnancy or by reaching the fifteenth birthday even if the child has not experienced any physiological changes.

Therefore, the age of fifteen is the boundary between childhood and adulthood. It has been reported that while Abdullah bin Umar was fourteen the Prophet Muhammad (Peace be upon him) did not allow the boy to join the armed warriors at the battle of Uhud, though following his fifteenth birthday he was allowed to join the army in the battle of Trench.[9] This Prophetic approval provides the religious evidence that the age of fifteen is the age that differentiates between adulthood and childhood.

This is the public opinion of the Muslim scholars except for Imam Abu Hanifah and the majority of the adherents of Imam Malik School of *Fiqh* who have determined eighteen to nineteen years of age to be the age of majority for males and seventeen years of age to be the age of majority for females.[10] It is worth knowing that these two schools of *Fiqh*, that is, the Hanafi and Maliki schools, are the largest and most popular in the Muslim world today, yet their findings in this particular issue are not widely supported.

Conclusion

The Islamic view is that labor is a form of worship; this is in contrast to other views of labor. For example, the Marxist view upholds labor for the economic good of the state, while decrying private ownership by the individual. In comparison to the Marxist view, the Islamic view towards private ownership is very favorable, especially in regards to the ownership of small businesses. The capitalist view upholds work primarily for the good of the individual and/or family rather than for the state, and it encourages private ownership. However, the encouragement of private ownership, with its high value on the bottom line sought by enterprising capitalists, has often led to a less than fair distribution of income and wealth in society, a result that Islam does not accept.

One fundamental reason for these differences of opinion between the Islamic perspective and the perspective of other systems of thought lies in the fact that Islam considers both physical and metaphysical dimensions of work and labor in this life. Work in this life cannot be separated from worship. These two modes of operation—work and worship—which are expected of humans are indeed two sides of the coin of existence. It is also noteworthy that the Islamic view of child labor is in accord with that of the International Labor Organization in that both emphasize that children below the mandated age limit of fifteen must be exempted from sweatshops and other harmful forms of labor.

Children should not expend their time working to the detriment of their schooling. Lack of education will negatively affect their future careers because it will leave them without training. This will adversely affect their productivity in their future lives, leaving them dependent on others and unable to support themselves. Thus, it is extremely vital to maintain equilibrium, and that is what Islam is calling for in this particular matter.

Islam encourages children to learn and practice housework and allows children, if old enough, to work for their family-owned business. Children who help their parents in the household by shoveling snow from the driveway, emptying garbage in the dumpster, helping their mother in the kitchen, or undertaking other such tasks are viewed by their parents as a blessing, and the parents are proud of their children's concern for the family.

To combat inappropriate child labor, various sectors of the human community must assume their responsibilities. A joint effort between policy makers and religious leaders should be established. The formal and informal business sectors must be in accord with the religious and ethical rules as well as the International Labor Organization's regulations.

To insure effective regulation and oversight of child labor, governmental agencies must play an active role in preventing all products made by children from entering the country. The role of the consumer in combating the problem of child labor is vital. Consumers, as well as community activists and conscientious government leaders, must educate people about the detrimental consequences of child labor. This can be done by boycotting all products made by children, writing warning letters to factories that produce items made by children, and supporting human rights organizations which protest child exploitation. Through these efforts on the part of each of us, the problem of child labor can finally be addressed and brought to an end.

Notes

1. Hussein Hamid Hasan, *Right to Work* (Islamabad, Pakistan: Da'wah Academy, University of Islamabad, 1995), 4–5.

2. *Sunna* means actions, sayings, or approvals of the Prophet Muhammed (Peace be upon him).

3. Sahih Bukhari, "A Man's Work and Earning by His Hands," *Book of Sales Transactions*, vol. 1, sec. 431 (Beirut, Lebanon: Dar Ihyaa al Turath al-'Arabi, 1979).

4. Al-No'man Abu Hanifah Thabit: 80–150 AH (*Anno Higerae* [year of the *Hijra*; Islamic calendar]), 699–767 CE. He is the founder of the Hanifi school of *Fiqh*.

5. Malik bin Anas, 93–179 AH, 712–795 CE. He is the founder of the Maliki school of *Fiqh*.

6. Muhammed Abu Zahrah, *al-Jariema wal- aquobah*, sec. 478 (Cairo, Egypt: Dar ul-Fikr al 'Arabi, 1976).

7. Abdul Kadir Audah, *Al-Tashriri'e Al-Janaie fi al-Islam*, vol. 1, sec. 432, 4th ed. (Beirut, Lebanon: Dar Ihyaa al Turath al-'Arabi, 1985).

8. Sayid Sabiq, *Fiqh al-Sunnah*, vol. 3, 1st ed. (Beirut, Lebanon: Dar ul Kitab al 'Arabi, 1971), 181. Also see Al-Juzairi, *Kitab al-Fiqh 'ala al-Mathahib al-Arba'ah*, vol. 2 (Beirut, Lebanon: Dar-al-Kotob al-'Elmeiyah, 1990), 145.

9. Abu Dawood, *Sulaiman bin al Ash'ath: Sunan Abu Dawood* (Beirut, Lebanon: Dar al Jeil Press, 1988), vol. 4, 139.

10. Muhammad bin Ahmed Ibn Rush, died 595 AH, 1211 CE. *Bidayat al-Mujtahid wa nihayaat al-Muqtasid*, vol. 2 (Beirut, Lebanon: Dar ul Fikr, 1995), 226–29.

Bibliography and Suggested Reading

al Ahdath, Qanun. *Regulations on Minors*. Cairo, Egypt: Egyptian Government General Corporation for Publishing Affairs, 1981.

Alwaan, Abdullah. *Tarbiyatul awlaad fi al Islam* (Raising Children in Islam). Vol. 2. Beirut, Lebanon: Dar al Salaam Press, 1981.

Audah, Abdul Kadir. *Al-Tashriri'e Al-Janaie fi al-Islam*. Vol. 1, sec. 432, 4th ed. Beirut, Lebanon: Dar Ihyaa al Turath al-'Arabi, 1985.

Bukhari, Sahih. "A Man's Work and Earning by His Hands." *Book of Sales Transactions*. Vol. 1, sec. 431. Beirut, Lebanon: Dar Ihyaa al Turath al-'Arabi, 1979.

Gates, Jeff. *The Ownership Solution*. Reading, MA: Addison Wesley, 1998.

Gini, A. R., and T. Sullivan. "Work: The Process and the Person," *Journal of Business Ethics* 6 (1987):649–55.

Lutfiyya, Abdulla M., and Charles W. Churchill. *Reading in Arab Middle Eastern Societies and Cultures*. New York: Humanities Press, 1970.

Naughton, Michael J. *The Good Stewards: Practical Applications of the Papal Social Vision of Work*. Lanham, MD: University Press of America, 1992.

Ratzinger, Joseph. "Market Economy and Ethics." In *Ordo Socialis: Making Christianity Work in Business and Economy*, ed. Association for the Advancement of Christian Social Sciences. Philippines: Divine Word Publications, 1992:62–67.

Sabiq, Sayid. *Fiqh al-Sunnah*. Vol. 3, 1ˢᵗ ed. Beirut, Lebanon: Dar ul Kitab al 'Arabi, 1971.

Walsh, Michael, and Brian Davies, eds. *Proclaiming Justice and Peace*. Mystic, CT: Twenty-Third Publications, 1984.

Zahrah, Muhammed Abu. *al-Jariema wal- aquobah*. Sec. 478. Cairo, Egypt: Dar ul-Fikr al 'Arabi, 1976.

PART IV

RELIGION, MEDICINE, AND PUBLIC HEALTH

CHAPTER 15

Children: Parental Right or Gift of God?

A CASE STUDY by Christine E. Gudorf

Shirley concluded, "Yes, we have to talk. I'll see you at home in an hour, Ted," and hung up the phone. She gathered her briefcase and purse, locked her door, and headed for the parking lot, shoulders drooping. Ted had called to tell her that he had received the final results of his fertility tests that afternoon: normal. He was openly pleased and relieved, and she felt glad for him. Her feelings of discouragement now were not due to the knowledge that her scarred fallopian tubes were the probable cause of their infertility, but emanated rather from qualms about the choices open to them if they wanted children: adoption or in vitro fertilization (IVF).

Shirley and Ted had married in their early thirties. Having known that her fertility was doubtful after a serious bout with PID (pelvic inflammatory disease) in high school, Shirley had worried that her possible infertility would prevent her marrying until she met Ted. He had reassured her that infertility was a risk in all marriages and that they would deal with whatever happened. Only when she learned that he was an adopted child did she relax. Though they never talked about what they would do in case of infertility, she had always assumed adoption would be their choice. Shirley was now thirty-six; she and Ted both felt that they had to make some decision soon. They did not want to be raising children in their retirement years. Remembering Ted's impassioned speech the previous week, she was fairly certain that Ted was going to push for recourse to technology. Ted had declared, "I was an adopted kid, and I always promised myself that my children would never have to wonder if they really belonged to me or were only substitutes for the real thing. It feels like, until I met you, I was always second best. Even though Mom and Dad never did anything to make me feel that way, being adopted has always been an interior wound I carried around with me. I really don't want to have to deal with it again, from the other end, feeling frustrated because there is nothing I can do to make my child feel completely loved."

For Shirley, the emergence of Ted's feelings about adoption pushed them in the direction of in vitro fertilization, about which she had had very ambivalent feelings even before she began working for the Population Information Bureau four years before. In her job she did research and advised officials of foundations, donor governments, and governments of developing nations about demographic behaviors and connections between population and other elements of development. Now she thought bitterly, "How ironic! Last month I published an article on the disparity between the millions of working poor without insurance for the most basic medical care and those whose insurance pays many thousands of dollars for experimental fertility treatments. Now I have to choose whether to make use of the inequitable privilege I criticized."

Over dinner that evening, Shirley and Ted discussed their feelings in the face of the latest test results. Ted admitted that he leaned much more strongly toward in vitro fertilization than adoption, but realized that his feelings about adoption were not fully rational. "I know that adoption works, because it worked for me. I had a good home, good parents whom I still love dearly and who, I know, love me. But I remember so vividly how I never could purge the fact of my adoption from my mind—whenever I misbehaved and they punished me I wondered if they would have punished a natural son the same way, and if they didn't punish me I wondered if they would have punished a natural son. When I turned out to be half a foot taller than anyone in their families, I cursed my height even though it was the envy of all my family and friends. Maybe if I could put all the pain behind me, I could be a good adoptive father. But right now adoption strikes me as a way of extending, even doubling, my pain from wanting a relational fit that isn't possible."

Shirley shared her reservations about in vitro technology. "In my work I have seen lots of abuses of reproductive technology. Manual Vacuum Aspiration [MVA, or suction abortion], for example, is often misused as a substitute for much safer and more preventative methods of birth control, but in many parts of the developing world MVA is a godsend in dealing with incomplete, botched, illegal abortions in that it frees up hospital beds and surgeons, with fewer risks than surgical D&C. We can't make judgments about these technologies in themselves, but must look at why they were developed, who owns and controls them, and what their consequences are in specific situations."

"What problems do you have with in vitro itself?" inquired Ted.

"In vitro fertilization can offer a real benefit to some infertile couples. But there are problems, too. Isn't it crazy to invest in techniques to help infertile people have children at a time when we are attempting to limit immigration to the United States and when the basic survival of life on the planet requires that humans produce fewer children?"

"But doesn't distribution count? Because some people have more children than they should, other people should have none? Is that fair? Don't we have a right to be parents just like other people?" asked Ted.

"Is there a right to be parents, regardless of the cost?" responded Shirley. "In vitro is a very expensive technique, with a very low success rate. We could undergo three, four, even ten or more cycles of in vitro fertilization without a pregnancy. IVF technology in the United States has only a 12 percent rate of success in achieving a live birth. And that doesn't even count all the women who have to drop out because even the powerful fertility drugs like Clomid and Pergonal are unable to produce multiple mature ova. If our insurance pays $6,500 for the first cycle, and we pay $6,500 each for the following attempts, it would cost $26,000 for four cycles, in addition to the funds the government has invested in the education and training of the doctors involved, and the thousands more that foundations, hospitals, research institutes, and pharmaceutical companies have invested in the research and equipment used. How many more failed attempts would our right to be parents require? Do we only have a right to be parents if we can afford to pay? Should public monies be supporting such rights?

"And I have a lot of unanswered questions about IVF. How large is the increased risk of ovarian cancer from fertility drugs? And what about risks of fetal abnormalities? I remember reading that Australian studies show IVF babies with higher rates of abnormalities. And I am not sure how I feel about the need for selective abortion if I should get pregnant with more fetuses than I could carry to term. IVF seems to present more risks and problems than solutions," said Shirley.

"Then there is a whole other realm of global questions. The biggest dilemma for me," Shirley declared earnestly, "is that my work concerns whole populations in which three out of ten children die of measles because they are malnourished, where diarrhea is the number-one killer of children, and where hope for improving living conditions depends on both economic initiatives and drastic reduction of the birthrate. How could I explain to Acholla Ndeti, the director of the Women's Clinic in Lagos, Nigeria, who is also infertile, that I had bought a technique that would give me a child when the cost of that technique not only makes it out of the question for her, but also is sufficient to provide prenatal care, childhood inoculations, and basic medical care for more than 5,000 children in her city who otherwise would have none?"

"This is going to sound crazy, but I think it is true, Shirley," said Ted as he reached for her hand. "I can agree, given both the ecological crisis and the terrible poverty in our world, that no society should provide a minority of its people with access to such expensive and uncertain techniques as in vitro fertilization. But the world is not just; existing structures and institutions favor people with money. I would vote to have the world arranged more justly, but while it isn't, I feel I have a right to make use of those things within my reach which offer me real improvements in my life if they don't directly harm others. Poor handicapped people in India can't get expensive artificial limbs or motorized wheelchairs, either, but you don't object to handicapped persons here having these. Poor people don't get good dental care, either, but you didn't tell your mother to switch to soft foods instead of spending thousands for new bridgework and implants in her mouth last year. I don't see a consistent principle here. How much of your preference for adoption is pride and fear that your coworkers will disapprove?"

"I don't know, Ted. I need time to think. A child seems different from wheelchairs and false teeth. Children are not possessions; parenting is a relationship. Can anyone have a right to any particular relationship? And besides that, if people who recognize the inequity and inhumanity in resource distribution around the world rationalize taking their disproportionate share, then how can we expect to change patterns of access toward greater justice? You met Acholla last year in Lagos—what would you tell her?"

"I don't know, Shirley. Maybe we both have some thinking to do about this. I haven't thought this through; I just have this need to feel genetically related to at least one person on the face of the earth. I didn't know there were any possible risks to you or a child from in vitro. We need to look further into both adoption and in vitro. Can we agree that in the next few weeks you will look into in vitro and I will look into adoption? Maybe we can talk to somebody with expertise about each option. Okay?"

Shirley nodded and smiled. "Thanks. I'm too tired to continue tonight."

Three days later, on the way back from their shared aerobics class, Shirley confided in her friend Harriet about the dilemma she and Ted faced. Harriet, a social worker who lived a block away, looked at Shirley for a long moment and said, "I'm really surprised at Ted. Part of me understands his hurt and hesitation, but another part wants to shake him and shout, 'Don't you know how lucky you were? How many African-American children—especially males—were never adopted but shuffled from orphanage to foster home and back while you were raised in a two-parent family with sufficient resources to send you to college and law school!' Between poverty, drugs, crime, and AIDS there are hundreds of thousands of unwanted, abandoned, abused, and neglected African-American kids in this country, Shirley. You are arguing about having moral obligations to medical and health equity with people in other societies. What about obligations to these kids here? It seems to me that obligations to the wider society—to both your race and your global community—point to solving your infertility problem through adoption, especially because you can get an African-American child of any age or condition relatively quickly. It's not like waiting years for a white baby."

"That may sound logical, Harriet, but it ignores Ted's feelings," said Shirley. "I don't think that is a very good way to begin parenting, by ignoring a parent's feelings. Those feelings could bring on a lot of problems down the line. To parent well, Ted would have to cleave to the child without reservation—and he has reservations. How could we gamble that they would go away when presented with a child?"

By the following week, Ted had arranged a meeting for the two of them with the local Health and Human Services Child Welfare Division which supervised adoptions, and Shirley had arranged a meeting with the local hospital's Reproductive Services Director. On the day before the first appointment, Shirley's supervisor, Ojiwa Kerula, knocked and walked into her office. He congratulated her for having been chosen to collaborate with two researchers from Egypt and Bangladesh on a project that would examine global uses of reproductive technology, both technology aimed at expanding options for reproduction (such as in vitro) and technology aimed at controlling fertility (such as RU486, the French abortifacient drug). The aim of the study would be to suggest appropriate roles for new reproductive technologies in global public policy initiatives. The cost/benefit analysis involved would include not only material factors, such as the probable effects on the health and welfare of women and children, but also more ineffable factors such as justice between and within societies and groups.

"I'm really in for it now," Shirley thought to herself as Ojiwa walked out and closed her door behind him, "there will be no compartmentalizing my work from my personal life. What is the right thing to do?"

A BUDDHIST RESPONSE by Ronald Y. Nakasone

Increased knowledge of human biology and technological advances have improved health and medical options in ways that were never before thought possible. Couples can control fertility through RU486, an abortifacient drug, while reproductive technologies (such as in vitro fertilization) expand options for couples unable to conceive a child. Shirley would not have faced the dilemma of choosing between adoption and in vitro fertilization twenty-five years ago. The dilemma faced by Shirley and her husband emerges from technological miracles. The Buddha, who lived 2,500 years ago, was not confronted with questions of begetting life through in vitro fertilization or other such reproductive technologies. Recently developed biotechnological therapies raise such issues as distribution and allocation of scarce resources, exploitation of the poor, conflict between personal and global community needs, and the imposition of values by the powerful on the weak. While these dilemmas often involve agonizing choices, they also offer an unprecedented opportunity for Buddhists to examine the relevance of the insights of their faith tradition and expand their moral imaginations.

Buddhist ethical deliberations are tempered by realism, humility, and optimism. These attitudes emerge from a legacy of "benevolent skepticism,"[1] a belief in the truth that we live in an interdependent world and an aspiration of spiritual ease for all beings giving Buddhists powerful tools for considering medical and societal dilemmas. We will reflect on these ideas within the context of the dilemma that in vitro fertilization poses for Shirley. I begin with a brief overview of the Buddha's skepticism and the doctrine of *pratityasamutpada*, or interdependence.

The Buddhist Posture

The Buddha underscored that his *dharma*, or teaching, is only a guide and that he was not an authority. The Buddha urged his followers not to accept any of his teachings without first critically examining them. Only if any of his teachings leads to spiritual ease should they be observed and accepted.[2]

For those who either could not accept his teaching or did not wish to follow his method for spiritual liberation, the Buddha recommended other paths. More recently, Thich Nhat Hanh, the Vietnamese Zen monk, reflected on the Buddha's attitude toward overreliance on doctrines. The experience of the Vietnam War forced Thich Nhat Hanh to reinterpret the traditional Buddhist precepts and condense them into Fourteen Guidelines for Engaged Buddhism. The first Guideline reads: Do not be idolatrous about or bound to any doctrine, theory, or ideology, even Buddhist ones. Buddhist systems of thought are guiding means; they are not absolute truth.[3] "Even meritorious teachings become a burden if one does not know when to discard them."[4] The *dharma* is simply a guide from which we should make decisions and conduct our lives. It is the finger pointing to the moon, not the moon.

Buddhists' attitudes toward their own doctrine and other meritorious teachings are supported by the doctrine of *pratityasamutpada*. The doctrine articulates the Buddhist belief that we live in an interdependent world and that all beings and all things are mutually dependent. As the basis for Buddhist ethics, interdependence provides Buddhists with a vision of identity and responsibility to all beings. Interdependence also quickens a sense of gratitude for all things and beings. Mahayana Buddhist documents that appeared during the first century of the Common Era interpret *pratityasamutpada* to be compassionate and morally purposeful. The *Larger Sukhavativyuha sutra* casts the doctrine of *pratityasamutpada* in the myth of the Bodhisattva Dharmakara, a spiritual hero who vows to forgo supreme enlightenment until all beings enter the Pure Land, the realm of spiritual ease. The myth tacitly assumes that the universe is warm and caring and that interdependence is the truth of the universe. Dharmakara's vow crystallizes the responsibilities we all have to each other and to the world. The myth expresses an optimism of the eventual destiny of all beings. Further, a vision of an interdependent world asks that we see everything from every point of view. The doctrine of *pratityasamutpada* asks that we recognize relative values. No one person or community commands absolute truth or value. Predicaments arise from conflicting values and loyalties as well as from competing interests. Further, there is good and bad in every situation and being. We learn from our mistakes, and even good deeds may have unintended evil results. Appreciating relative values is grounded in the reality of competing viewpoints. It also nurtures humility.

Ethical deliberation and exercise that posit an interdependent world consider a microscopic view alongside a macroscopic one. The symphony offers an analogy. To grasp the beauty in a Beethoven symphony, for example, it is not enough to listen to the individual instruments sequentially. One must hear the instruments together, as each musician modulates his or her instrument and timing in response to the other instruments. Each instrument participates in creating a greater whole. The whole, in turn, gives value to the sounds from each instrument. The microscopic and the macroscopic resonate together. This symphonic analogy is useful in formulating a Buddhist approach to ethics and deliberation. Like a symphonic composition, we must see ourselves as parts of a larger whole. The whole, in turn, gives us value and worth. The idea of interdependence links our individual lives to each thing and each being in the universe. To act, according to this vision, is to work to nurture the lives and relationships that enrich and sustain the life of individuals and this whole universe. The ideal is difficult and almost always impossible to realize. I am reminded of Thich Nhat Hanh who commented on the conflict between our good intentions and the reality of our lives.

> The problem is whether we are determined to go in the direction of compassion or not. If we are, then can we reduce the suffering to a minimum? If I lose my direction, I have to look for the North Star, and I go to the north. That does not mean that I expect to arrive at the North Star. I just want to go in that direction.[5]

A decision to move in the direction of compassion is a personal one. Moreover, even if we commit ourselves to compassion, we are often thwarted by circumstances and events beyond our control. Thich Nhat Hanh recognizes the fragility of the human condition. Even if we are determined to move toward compassion, "can we reduce suffering to a minimum?" The best we can do is to try. Our relationships to others and events constantly shift. Good intentions and ideas, like nations, rise and fall. "The strong are like dust before the winds of change."[6] Suffering is endemic to a transient and interdependent world. The best we can do is to minimize suffering.

Eight centuries earlier, Shinran (1173–1262), a Japanese cleric, poignantly illustrated the difficulties of living in a world of conflicting karmic forces. In the thirteenth chapter of the *Tan'nisho*, Shinran underscores the reality that we are often swept up in events that thwart our best intentions. Our lives are intimately linked with the karmic tide of others to society and even to the whims of nature.[7] We know from experience that we can never realize our every intention. Some forces work to nurture our lives. Others frustrate our wishes. No decision or act is ever generated in isolation. Innumerable causes and conditions affect all things.[8]

Buddhist ethical deliberation and opportunity lie in the understanding that we live in an interdependent world and that we are irrevocably intertwined with the destinies of the world and all beings. Such an interpretation of life dictates the various virtues and ends that we should consider when reflecting on ethical questions. A sense of fair play, compassion, gratitude, humility, and patience are some virtues to nurture and bring with us in reflecting on such questions as euthanasia, allocation of resources, organ donations and transplants, and relating to the most vulnerable in our society.

A Right to Parent

Shirley struggles to reconcile her desire to have her own children through in vitro fertilization with the issues of global overpopulation and the equitable distribution of resources. Shirley's scarred fallopian tubes, the probable cause of her infertility, have pushed her to find alternatives: adoption or in vitro fertilization. Her husband Ted, who experienced the uncertainties and the stigma of growing up as an adopted child, does not want to deal with those issues from the other end, as the parent of an adopted child. Ted's feelings toward adoption pushed the couple in the direction of in vitro fertilization. Her job as a researcher at the Population Information Bureau introduced Shirley to the disparity between availability of medical resources such as in vitro for the rich and lack of basic medical care for the poor. In vitro is not an alternative for her Nigerian colleague, Acholla Ndeti, who is also infertile. Shirley struggles to justify the costs of in vitro therapy that could provide prenatal care, inoculations, and basic medical care for 5,000 children in Lagos, Nigeria. Shirley is troubled by ineffable issues of "justice between and within societies and groups." In addition to the cost, Shirley is concerned about the risks of ovarian cancer and fetal abnormality. Finally, she is concerned with population growth and survival of life on the planet. The narrative concludes with Shirley contemplating her options. Further, she is ambivalent about the need for selective abortion, should she become pregnant with more fetuses than she could carry to term.

How will Shirley resolve her conflicts? Ethical deliberation grounded in a vision of an interdependent world considers all elements of Shirley's suffering. In a symphonic performance the composer subsumes the musical score of each instrument within the larger rhythm of the entire composition. While the composer may feature some instruments at different times, each instrument must fulfill the integrity of the finished composition. The vision of symphonic harmony is an aspiration: only rarely do personal commitments resonate with global reality. Realistically, personal deliberation weighs the most relevant elements first. Shirley's wishes for justice within and between society and groups do not mesh with Ted's desire for them to have their own child. What issues should Shirley consider to be of primary importance? What might be of secondary importance? She does not want, it appears, to compartmentalize her personal and professional life.

Fa-tsang (643–712), the Hua yen master, may offer a partial explanation. Fa-tsang reasons that in an interdependent world no *dharma* is independently established. All *dharmas* are mutually supportive and mutually dependent within the *dharmadhatu*, the realm of *dharmas*: each *dharma* is thus of equal importance. However, when a *dharma* is arbitrarily singled out for consideration, that *dharma* becomes the principal *dharma* and the remaining *dharmas* take on a secondary role. Each *dharma* has the potential of alternately assuming the principal role or a secondary role. The role a *dharma* assumes is determined by what is weighed to be important at any given moment.

When we apply Fa-tsang's reasoning to Shirley's dilemma, it simply means that whatever issue is important at the moment becomes the principal concern. When she considers her desire to have children and Ted's feelings, those concerns take precedent. On the other hand, when she bears in mind the suffering of children in Nigeria, her sympathies for their well-being and her idea of justice become primary. Fa-tsang's explication of *pratityasamutpada* can explain the overlapping spheres of interest and why one sphere would take precedence over another. How does Shirley decide which sphere is to take precedence over others? Why should personal desires supersede moral and ethical considerations? Why should Shirley ignore Ted's feelings and needs? Is her responsibility to the cause of saving the planet from overpopulation more important than her relationship with Ted?

In a world of conflicting demands, what are the parameters of ethical responsibility?

Where does the ethically responsible, moral decision making lie in an interdependent world? If we accept the Buddhist position that we live in an interdependent world, each and every one of us bears direct responsibility for the survival of the planet. We rise and fall together as one living body. The idea of interdependence links our individual lives to each thing and each being in the universe. To act according to this vision is to work to nurture the lives and relationships that sustain life. In a world where lives are inexorably intertwined, like ice and water, our concern should be extended to all beings. Essentially, we should focus our energies where we can make a difference rather than trying to embrace all lives and relationships. Shinran endorses this attitude in Mattosho: "Whether one is left behind or goes before, it is surely a sorrowful thing to be parted by death. But the one who first attains nirvana vows without fail to save those who were close to him first and leads those with whom he is karmically bound, his relatives, and his friends."[9]

Yet, we have a responsibility to restrain and prevent individuals and events from demeaning our humanity. We work to prevent child and elder abuse. We intervene to end war and fight famine. Shirley works to save the planet.

Thus far, our attention has focused on ethical deliberations in a world of conflicting karmic forces. Perhaps the question is not how we are to resolve the legal, ethical, or medical concerns in deciding life or death. We could conceivably rephrase Shirley's dilemma by asking how we are to understand her suffering. Shirley's anguish is not hers alone; it is also ours. "Your suffering is my suffering," said the Buddha. When we prevent and are prevented from the exercise of compassion, we must turn the question towards ourselves. By redirecting the question inward and struggling to resolve suffering, we are asking what it means to be human. We read in the *Vimalakirtinirdesa sutra*:

> Buddha-qualities do not grow in living beings destined for the uncreated but do grow in living beings who are like swamps and mud banks of passions . . . Buddha-qualities do not grow in those determined for the absolute but do grow in those who conceive the spirit of enlightenment . . . Without going into the ocean of passions it is impossible to obtain the mind of omniscience.[10]

The decision to move to the direction of compassion is the moment our lives are transformed, perhaps irrevocably. The rest of the world may not have changed or may be affected only incrementally. By moving in the direction of compassion we can reduce suffering to a minimum.

The vision of an interdependent world can serve as a context for conducting ethical deliberations. We see ourselves as parts of a larger whole, which, in turn, gives us value and worth. We can rationalize and subsume our predicaments with a macro, all-encompassing vision. Fa-tsang's vision of a symphonic and interdependent world may fail to reconcile individual karmic choices that conflict with others. Shinran, on the other hand, understood the difficulties faced by individuals living in a world of conflicting karmic forces. Appreciating the complexity of ethical and moral dilemmas and ethical decision making and working within that limitation to minimize suffering are, undoubtedly, the most powerful exercises in deepening our understanding of the human condition. With an awareness of why our good intentions may often be thwarted, we should continue to exercise our compassionate aspirations in the belief that, no matter how insignificant, an act of kindness resonates throughout the farthest reaches of the universe. Still, as we have learned from Shinran, we are often unable to fulfill our good intentions. Under those circumstances we yield—mournfully and, perhaps, even justifiably—to the dictates of more powerful karmic forces.

Ultimately, Shirley's decision is her own to make. She must take into consideration her personal desires and suffering and weigh them in the context of her desire for justice and the countless children who seek loving parents and a home. Whatever Shirley decides will result in unforeseen consequences, good and bad. There is no one right answer. Whatever decision she makes will bring her joy and conflicts. I am optimistic that whatever step she takes, she will move in the direction of compassion. She will do her part to minimize suffering.

Notes

1. Edward Conze, *A Short History of Buddhism* (London: Unwin Paperbacks, 1982), 2.

2. Sanghabhadra, *Shan-Chien-P'i P'o-Sha*, a Chinese version by Sanghabhadra of the *Samantapasadika*, trans. P. V. Bapat and Akiva Hirakawa (Poong, India: Bhandavkar Oriental Research Insitute, 1970) 171–73.

3. Thich Nhat Hanh, *Old Path White Clouds: Walking in the Footsteps of the Buddha* (Berkeley, CA: Parallax Press, 1991), 213. In his retelling of the life and teachings of Gautama Buddha, Thich Nhat Hanh interweaves several incidents of the Buddha's life. He interweaves the Parable of the Raft with the Parable of the Finger Pointing to the Moon with the Buddha's instruction to Dighanakha. The Parable of the Raft (*Alagaddupama sutta* 22:13) and the Buddha's instruction to Dighanakha (*Dighanakha sutta* 74) appears in the *Majyhima Nikaya*.

4. Thich Nhat Hanh, *Interbeing* (Berkeley, CA: Parallax Press, 1987), 27.

5. Nhat Hanh, *Interbeing*, 98.

6. *Heike monogatari [The Tale of Heike]*, in *Heike monogatari zenchushaku*, annotated by Tokujiro Tomikura (Tokyo: Kadokawa, 1969), 33.

7. Shinran, *Letters of Shinran: A Translation of Mattosho*, ed. Ueda Yoshifumi (Kyoto: Hongwanji International Center, 1978), 32–35.

8. Ronald Y. Nakasone, *The Ethics of Enlightenment: Sermons and Essays in Search of a Buddhist Ethic* (Fremont, CA: Dharma Cloud Publishers, 1990), 36–40.

9. Shinran, *Letters*, 49.

10. *The Holy Teaching of Vimalakirti: A Mahayana Scripture*, trans. Robert Thurman (University Park, PA: The Pennsylvania State University Press, 1986), 67.

A CHRISTIAN RESPONSE by Christine E. Gudorf

Technology has been developed to alter both fertility and infertility in humans, for the most part in females. New reproductive technologies which increase or create fertility include improvements in artificial insemination, in which male semen is collected and then manually introduced into the vagina rather than introduced by a male penis within intercourse, as well as various technologies that use fertility drugs and/or build upon in vitro fertilization (IVF).[1] Fertility drugs such as Clomid and Pergonal can be given to women in whom ovulation is irregular or absent to produce the release of a mature ovum or, more frequently, multiple mature ova. In vitro fertilization involves obtaining semen from a male (usually through normal ejaculation) and multiple ova from a female (through use of strong fertility drugs which produce the maturation of multiple ova in the female which are then surgically removed). The ova are then fertilized through laboratory contact with the sperm in the semen. Multiple fertilized ova are separated, with one or more implanted into either the uterus or the fallopian tube of the female, and the rest are frozen for future implantation(s). In a slightly more effective modification of this technique called GIFT (gamete intrafallopian transfer), the ovum and the sperm are collected, combined, and immediately placed in the fallopian tube, so that fertilization occurs within the female body. In embryo transfer, the fertilized egg is flushed from the uterus five days after fertilization and implanted in a different uterus which has normally been chemically adjusted to accept implantation.[2]

Other new assisted reproductive techniques include collecting multiple ejaculations of semen, concentrating the sperm in the semen to improve the fertility of men with low sperm count, and confining that concentrated semen with an ovum for extended periods. Sperm with limited motility have been exposed to a variety of substances that improve sperm function, such as TEST-yolk buffer, which increases the ability of sperm to penetrate the ovum by 45 to 55 percent.[3] In the near future it is expected that microinjection techniques for injecting sperm into an ovum will be perfected, thus rendering more infertile men fertile. And it is likely that the cloning of humans will be technically possible within the next decade or so—whether or not human society is prepared, or can be prepared, to confront the social and moral implications of such practice.

There are yet other types of medical technology which are not directly reproductive but which can assist either in creating or limiting fertility. One such technology is ultrasound. Ultrasound is a diagnostic technique for imaging the fetus within the uterus. It can be used to diagnose both treatable dangers to the life or health of the fetus, and sometimes to the mother, as well as untreatable conditions which, when known, sometimes become cause for terminating the pregnancy. One very common abuse of ultrasound technology is its use in sex selective abortion, especially in parts of Asia. In some nations the use of ultrasound for sex selective abortion is a major commercial enterprise which has become so popular that India, for example, blames the practice for a severe imbalance in the number of males and females under ten years old and has acted to ban commercial use of ultrasound for sex selection.

While all research in reproductive technologies is expensive, those technologies treating infertility are much more expensive than those treating fertility and have much lower rates of success. One reason for the higher costs of fertility treatments is that the number of persons pursuing greater fertility is miniscule compared to the billions seeking fertility control. As for effectiveness, chemical contraceptives have typical effectiveness rates of over 98 percent; barrier methods have effectiveness rates of 94 to 98 percent. By contrast, in the much more complicated task of creating human fertility the effectiveness rates are much lower. Many clinics claim effectiveness rates of around 20 percent for IVF techniques in achieving live births, but the overall effectiveness rate per implantation of fertilized ovum in the United States is only 9 to 12 percent.

Issues in the Case

At first glance, the central issue in this case seems to be whether or not it can be responsible to derive personal advantage from using technological privileges from which other equally desirous persons are barred without just cause. Upon further reflection, however, what is at stake is not just privileged access. If the technology were, for example, a new long-term contraceptive, it would be much easier to justify use, however privileged, on the grounds that in a situation of global overpopulation the use of more effective contraception benefits the common good. But in this case, where the technology is IVF, it is difficult to argue that the benefits accrue to society beyond the small circle of intimates around Ted and Shirley. Not only are the benefits much more narrowly distributed, but the possible hazards in enhancing fertility are far greater than in fertility control due to the greater fragility of the developing embryo/fetus compared to adults.

Low birth weights, inadequately developed lungs, and elevated cystic fibrosis and spina bifida rates in IVF babies have all been alleged;[4] all are extremely serious, immediately handicapping, and life-threatening medical conditions. On the other hand, our society has only a few thousand IVF babies each year; though individual risks of cancer and heart disease from chemical contraceptives may be less severe, there are millions of persons running those risks.

Other issues in the case involve how couples should negotiate differences around reproductive options: should, for example, Ted and Shirley forgo a child because of their reciprocal reservations about the other's preferred method? Another way of asking this question is whether it is responsible to have children when one parent has severe reservations about the reproductive method, reservations which could affect interaction with the child.

Christian Religious Resources

Biblical treatment of reproduction includes a number of clear, prominent, and oft-repeated themes but suffers from inconsistency nonetheless. On the one hand, children—posterity—are commanded by God of humans in the creation process: "Be fruitful and multiply, and fill the earth and subdue it" (Gen 1:28). Children are also presented many times as gifts of God, as in the birth stories about Isaac, Jacob, Samuel, John the Baptist, and Jesus. On the other hand, because men were assumed in the Mosaic law to have a right to children (sons), they were allowed to divorce women in search of sons and were required to beget and raise posterity for their male relatives whose widows were childless (Gen 38). Throughout the Hebrew scriptures women are depicted as needing sons to ensure secure marriages, economic security, and social status. In the New Testament, Jesus rebukes the woman who says his mother is blessed for her motherhood (Lk 11:27–28) and insists that, "Those who do the will of God are my brother, and sister and mother!" (Lk 8:21), but the author of 1 Timothy says that women will be saved through childbearing (1 Tim 2:15).

While the biblical treatment does not indicate any human right to have children, favoring instead the concept of children as God's gift, neither does it place any special limit on human actions to secure children. This becomes important as Ted argues that while IVF is a scarce resource to be allocated with justice, children are also a resource to be allocated with justice. A comparison of Jewish tradition or common Greco-Roman practice with the early church reveals that the early Christian church relativized the reproductive family. This was both because the teachings of Jesus emphasized a universal solidarity—"Love your enemies"—over the traditional family, group, or religious solidarity[5] and because conversion to the early church often resulted in estrangements from family with the faith community itself becoming the new family. However, beginning with the gradual triumph of patriarchal sex roles and hierarchical social distinctions in the second-century church, the Christian community gradually came to see the procreative family as basic to church life, originally in that it produced the vowed, celibate men and women who exemplified the Christian ideal and, later, as the domestic church and the essential unit of society.

It was not, however, until the twentieth century that technology for augmenting human fertility was developed, beginning with artificial insemination. Most of the ethical questions raised concerning those technologies have centered on the relationship between the technology and traditionally Christian sexual rules. That is, any technology that involved sexual or reproductive activity between unmarried persons or involved any traditionally forbidden sexual act, such as masturbation or artificial contraception, was prohibited. Other religious criticisms were made, but few were widely accepted. In the nineteenth century, some Protestant clergy in the United States objected to the use of anesthesia in childbirth—but not dentistry—because they felt it violated God's biblically stated intention that women deliver children in pain (Gen 3:16), but eventually they were overridden. Today the Catholic Church finds morally objectionable a variety of types of reproductive technology. The overarching teaching is the Christian insistence that genital sexual activity is restricted to marriage, an exclusive and permanent union between a man and a woman. The specifically Catholic principle at stake in reproductive technology is that the reproductive and unitive aspects of sexuality may not be separated. This is interpreted to refer to individual acts, so that a couple may not pursue reproduction outside the act of sexual intercourse, thus in vitro fertilization is rejected as an acceptable method of conception. This interpretation also precludes the use of donor ova or sperm, surrogate wombs, or masturbation in order to obtain semen.

It is only in the last two or three decades that Christians have come to see a case such as this as involving justice as well as violations of the traditional Christian sexual code. Sexuality has often been understood as the central aspect of private morality governing personal relations, as opposed to the social demands of the gospel such as justice, solidarity, and participation. But with increased attention to third-world poverty and first-world medical ethics in the 1960s, Christian ethics began to deal with issues in the allocation of scarce social resources in general.

Christian theologians of the last few decades have reflected in new ways on the implications of creation, incarnation, and redemption for human embodiment. Most applications of the resulting concept of human embodiment have related embodiment of sex, gender, and sexual orientation issues. Application in the area of human reproduction has been largely limited to treatment of abortion, contraception, and sexually transmitted diseases, not parenthood. Christian feminists have perhaps come closest to connecting embodiment and reproduction, but even for feminists, for whom the focus has been on parenting (mothering) as an activity impacting both adult and child, there is little evaluation of the importance of genetic connection between mother and child, only discussion of whether mothering is learned or inherent behavior.

One aspect of theological treatment of marriage and family with implications for the evaluation of adoption is the treatment of reproduction as a way in which humans participate with God in the process of creation. To the extent that reproduction has been understood as the exclusive or primary way in which humans share in the act of creation, adoption could be seen as a poor second as a method of becoming a parent. Many theologians, for this and many other reasons, have begun to stress in the last half-century the many different ways in which humans are cocreators with God. Ongoing human responsibility for the maintenance of creation—of the environment and all the species and social relationships that it contains—is one important aspect of human cocreation.

When Christian norms such as justice, solidarity, and participation are brought to bear on the use of specific technologies in specific cases as illuminated by social analysis, they produce evaluations of the moral adequacy of technological use in those situations and practices. But when a specific situation is found to be morally lacking, the principles do not necessarily indicate how an individual or a group should respond to the existing situation in order to ameliorate it. In order to determine which specific action most adequately shifts the situation in the direction of Christian moral norms, one must morally evaluate the probable consequences of possible options in light of social analytic trends.

Social Analysis

Shirley explains her reservations regarding IVF in terms of the differential access to IVF technology in developed and developing worlds. But differential access to reproductive technology—indeed even to basic health care—characterizes not only the global situation but also national and local situations in the United States. Catholic social teaching, beginning in 1967 with Paul VI's *Populorum progressio* and including John Paul II's *Sollicitudo rei socialis*, has focused on the Christian imperative to solidarity with the poor and marginalized in every society. Such solidarity forms the foundation from which social analysis should be done.

The United States is in the midst of an ongoing controversy around how health care should be organized. By the mid 1990s the health care system was a synthetic mixture of market-driven and government-funded provider programs, with forty million persons—many employed, many with chronic health problems—excluded from the system for all but emergency care. Government-funded programs include Medicare (chiefly for the elderly) and Medicaid (chiefly for the poor who qualify for assistance); market-driven programs include both HMO (health maintenance organization) and PPO (preferred provider organization) group plans, some of which are fully employer-funded, some of which are individual plans, but most of which divide costs between employer and employee. Among plans there is great disparity in the treatment of fertility. Some plans will cover the costs of contraceptive methods and/or abortion, while others will not. Most plans will cover some types of infertility treatment, though not necessarily in vitro methods. There are, however, eight states that require commercial insurance companies to include in vitro within normal medical coverage.

The situation in most of the world, and certainly in the developing world, is very different. Most infertility treatments are unavailable in most areas of the world, and the vast majority of the world's population could not afford even the least expensive of the infertility treatments, such as artificial insemination, much less fertility drugs or the very expensive in vitro-based methods. Where there exists provision of health care to the population in the developing world, the care provided is basic, and only in recent years has it begun to aim at relatively inexpensive goals, such as universal childhood immunizations (less than $2/child) and universal access to rehydration techniques (about $.10/treatment) and, following the 1994 United Nations conference in Cairo, universal access to a variety of contraceptive methods.

Ted's resistance to adoption as a response to infertility, rooted in his own experience as an adopted child, is apparently strong. In the United States, the context for adoption has changed drastically in the last few decades due to increases in contraceptive use, abortion, and unmarried mothers[6] keeping their babies. The rate at which children born to unmarried women are placed for adoption has dropped from 9 percent prior to 1973, to 4 percent between 1973 and 1981, to 2 percent between 1982 and 1988.[7] At the same time that the rate of adoptive placement of out-of-wedlock newborns has declined, the birthrates among unmarried women have soared; between 1970 and 1988 the birthrate for unmarried women rose from 26.4 to 38.6 per 1,000 births.[8]

At the present time there are both private, commercial adoptive networks and public, usually local, governmental agencies arranging adoptions. Public adoptions range from a low of 4 percent of all adoptions in Arkansas to a high of 48 percent in Wisconsin, with a national average of 16 percent.[9] Independent adoptions (nonpublic) cost from $6,000 to $20,000 and tend to be of white infants or very young children, though increasingly foreign children, especially Asian, Latin American, and Eastern European children, are included.[10] Within public agencies, waits for young white children are usually long unless the children have health problems and/or disabilities. Preference in adoption is usually given to placing children within the racial, religious, and ethnic group of origin and to keeping siblings together, but agencies differ on the point at which these preferences are abandoned in favor of placing the child in a permanent home. The numbers of hard-to-place children are increasing rapidly under the impact of AIDS and the drug epidemic. About 60 percent of the 36,000 children languishing in foster care in the United States are seriously ill (AIDS or HIV positive, for example), seriously handicapped (Down's syndrome, fetal alcohol syndrome, or other forms of mental retardation and/or physical disability), or are dark skinned, or older children, or children in sibling groups.

Adoptive children fare differently depending on a number of factors, of which the most important seems to be the quality of the child's fetal environment and relationships during the first five years of life. In many cases adoption dramatically improves both the health and the measured IQ of children. While some studies have shown that adults who were adopted as children make up 2 percent of the population and yet make up one quarter of the patients at psychological treatment facilities in the United States,[11] many of these children were only adopted after they were abused, neglected, or shuffled for years through institutions and foster homes. On the other hand, while adoption often cannot eradicate the damage done by abuse and neglect, it does in many cases dramatically and permanently improve the health and the measured IQ of children.

In postmodern life, human relationships, especially intimate relationships, are increasingly voluntary rather than ascribed. The shift to urban living, the demise of the extended family household, the increasing interpersonal expectations of marriage, and, underlying all these, the mobility of individuals, both geographically and occupationally, all pressure humans into directly or indirectly chosen communities. This differs from most individuals who lived a century ago, for whom the majority of family, neighbors, and coworkers were all ascribed and relatively constant throughout their lives. While this shift has undermined the strength of most adults' ties with their parents, this lessening of genetic ties has not necessarily created more social openness to adoption compared to biological parenting. In fact, many therapists maintain the contrary: that loosened connections with our own parents have made us crave closer, less voluntary relations with our children. We are needier, both with our spouses and with our children, as our ability to rely on others for meeting interpersonal needs declines.

Possible Resolutions

Shirley and Ted face the systemic problem of unjust global access to human resources, which they themselves cannot solve. But there are a number of avenues that could be pursued to resolve their infertility problem while ameliorating or at least not aggravating the present injustice. One obvious avenue is for Ted to explore adoption and his reaction to it further. This could involve airing to his parents his questions and suspicions of them and their parenting of him or, alternatively, exploring his feelings with a trained therapist. Ted could also explore adoptable children available in his area through local agencies. The protective feelings of biological parents faced with their newborn children are not completely rooted in their shared genes but in a more generalized human impulse to protect vulnerable innocents. Such feelings often bond prospective adoptive parents to available children until more specific feelings of love for the unique child develop. In short, while Ted's preference to be genetically linked to another person is an understandable and legitimate expression of human desire for solidarity and acceptance, as an absolute condition for parenting it raises new and serious questions about his ability to be a good parent. For if the Bible is right that children are a gift and if they are, like the rest of creation, only entrusted to our care and not given to our undisputed ownership, then the role of good parents is to assist the child in discerning and preparing to cooperate with God's plan for that child and eventually to let that child go. The desire to produce a child in the parents' image and likeness—or in the image and likeness of the person the parent would like to be—is an idolatrous desire. That parent has set himself or herself up in the role of God. The goal of the parent is the responsible exercise of freedom by the child; it is ultimately to accept the child as one's peer—and perhaps, in one's fading years, even to become dependent on the child without fear.

It may be that resolution of these issues for Ted is a long-term project, in which case adoption might be as risky as Shirley fears. If their exploration of IVF turns up little risk to them or to a potential child so that the just allocation of resources is the basic problem, they might consider some kind of compromise. For example, they might agree that for every cycle of IVF they undergo, they will fund a cycle of IVF for an indigent infertile couple in the United States or abroad. Or they might agree to donate the cost of each cycle of IVF to provide basic health care to a community without it. Such schemes do not address the systemic inequalities of power that determine unequal access to resources. But Shirley is committed to undermining that system in her work. This action distributes more new resources to the deprived than would Ted and Shirley accepting childlessness or adopting a child, who, if young and healthy, would be adopted regardless. It would also be important to thoroughly research any prospective IVF program. If the cost of IVF will inoculate thousands of children, then that cost should not be risked on programs that have nonexistent or low rates of IVF success, but only on proven, responsible programs.

At the same time, how Shirley and Ted understand their decision may be at least as important as what action they decide on. Realism and humility force us to acknowledge that our context exerts tremendous influence on our actions. All the options in a sinful situation are tinged with the sin of injustice. Only solidarity to redress the unjust distribution of power and resources could truly resolve this dilemma. Choosing IVF on Ted's fatalistic argument— that individuals can't change the system, so the privileged should accept the advantages they are offered—violates a well-formed Christian conscience. But Ted is right that to forgo IVF because of Shirley's reservations would not in itself improve the access to medical care for any needy people anywhere. From a Christian point of view, what is at least as important as what specific option they choose is that the option they choose fits within a general orientation to compassion for and solidarity with the needy. The prayer of the Pharisee in Jesus' parable of the Pharisee and the publican (Lk 18:9–14) was neither disrespectful nor insincere. The Pharisee failed to please God because he refused to understand the publican and himself as both children of God and, therefore, as related to and responsible to and for each other. From a Christian point of view, we are called to follow the teaching and example of Jesus, who is more than a system of ethical principles.

Notes

1. Marc Goldstein, Mark Fuerst, and Gary S. Berger, *The Couple's Guide to Fertility* (New York: Doubleday, 1989).

2. William H. Masters, Virginia E. Johnson, and Robert C. Kolodny, *Biological Foundations of Human Sexuality* (New York: HarperCollins, 1993), 130–36.

3. Interview with Dr. Richard Paleness of the University of Southern California, in Robert Crooks and Karla Baur, *Our Sexuality*, 5th ed. (Indianapolis, IN: Benjamin Cummings, 1993), 356–59.

4. Janice Raymond, *Women as Wombs: Reproductive Technologies and the Battle over Women's Freedom* (San Francisco: Harper San Francisco, 1993), 11–14.

5. See Luke 12:49–53 and Albert Nolan, *Jesus before Christianity* (Maryknoll, NY: Orbis Books, 1976), 59–64.

6. In the United States this is based on participation in a legal marriage ceremony; in some contexts it refers to single women who are not part of a couple or partnership relationship.

7. Christine A. Bachrach, Kathy Shepherd Stolley, and Kathryn A. London, "Relinquishment of Premarital Births: Evidence from National Survey Data," *Family Planning Perspectives* 24, no. 1 (1992):29.

8. Bachrach et al., "Relinquishment," 29.

9. Victor Eugene Flango and Carol R. Flango, "Adoption Statistics by State," *Child Welfare* 72, no. 3 (May–June 1993):316–19.

10. Nancy Gibbs, "The Baby Chase," *Time* (9 October 1989):87–88.

11. Gibbs, "Baby Chase," 87.

Bibliography and Suggested Reading

Bachrach, Christine A., Kathryn Shepherd Stolley, and Kathryn A. London. "Relinquishment of Premarital Births: Evidence from National Survey Data." *Family Planning Perspectives* 24, no. 1 (January–February 1992):27–32.

Conze, Edward. *A Short History of Buddhism.* London: Unwin Paperbacks, 1982.

Corea, Gena. *The Mother Machine: Reproductive Technologies from Artificial Insemination to Artificial Wombs.* New York: Harper and Row, 1985.

Fa-tsang. *Hua-yen-ching tan-hsuan-chi. Taisho* 35, no. 1733 (1912–1926).

Flango, Victor Eugene. "Adoption Statistics by State." *Child Welfare* 72, no. 3 (May–June 1993): 311–19.

Flack, Harley E., and Edmund D. Pellegrino, eds. *African-American Perspectives on Biomedical Ethics.* Washington, DC: Georgetown University Press, 1992.

Heike monogatari [The Tale of Heike]. In *Heike monogatari zenchushaku,* annotated by Tokujiro Tomikura. Tokyo: Kadokawa, 1969.

Hirakawa, Akira. *A History of Indian Buddhism from Sakyamuni to Early Mahayana.* Trans. Paul Groner. Honolulu: University of Hawaii Press, 1990.

The Holy Teaching of Vimalakirti: A Mahayana Scripture. Trans. Robert Thurman. University Park, PA: The Pennsylvania State University Press, 1986.

Nakasone, Ronald Y. *The Ethics of Enlightenment: Sermons and Essays in Search of a Buddhist Ethic.* Fremont, CA: Dharma Cloud Publishers, 1990.

Nhat Hanh, Thich. *Old Path White Clouds: Walking in the Footsteps of the Buddha.* Berkeley, CA: Parallax Press, 1991.

———. *Interbeing.* Berkeley, CA: Parallax Press, 1987.

Raymond, Janice. *Women as Wombs: Reproductive Technologies and the Battle over Women's Freedom.* San Francisco: Harper San Francisco, 1993.

Sanghabhadra, *Shan-Chien-P'i-P'o-Sha,* a Chinese version by Sanghabhadra of the *Samantapasadika.* Trans. P. V. Bapat and Akira Hirakawa (Poona, India: Bhandarkar Oriental Research Institute, 1970.

Shannon, Thomas A., ed. *Bioethics.* 4th ed. Mahwah, NJ: Paulist, 1993.

Shinran. *Letters of Shinran: A Translation of Mattosho.* Ed. Ueda Yoshifumi. Kyoto: Hongwanji International Center, 1978.

Tachibana, Shundo. *The Ethics of Buddhism.* London: Curzon Press, 1975.

United States Congress, Office of Technology Assessment. *Infertility: Medical and Social Choices.* Washington, DC: Government Printing Office, 1988.

CHAPTER 16

An Unlikely Donor

A CASE STUDY by Regina Wentzel Wolfe

It was finally quiet on the floor. The patients were settled for the night, and the lights had been dimmed. Carole Bennet sat at the nurses' station and sighed as she finished with the paperwork and began filing patients' charts. Only thirty minutes before the shift ended and she passed the watch over to Julia Swindon. She was anxious to get home. In two days' time she and Marshall would be off to Cornwall for a well-deserved holiday. "Imagine, a full fortnight away from the Northumberland Gate Hospital," thought Carole, a ward sister at one of London's many private hospitals.

It would be a well-earned rest. Except for the odd long weekend off, Carole had not had a real holiday in over two years. In part this was a result of choice, in part a result of circumstance. The nursing staff was below complement. Though not as bad as public sector hospitals where pay, benefits, and working conditions were deplorable, the Northumberland Hospital was understaffed as it tried to cope with the flight of British nurses to the Middle East and Australasia where working conditions were superior and more money was to be made.

It had been a hectic afternoon and evening—the three-to-eleven shift was always busy and for the past few weeks the ward had been full. Going over each chart, Carole began a mental review of the patients she had seen that day. Most were recovering well from their surgeries, though Mrs. St. John seemed to have lost the will to live. There were only four patients scheduled for surgery in the morning. Even so, she'd need to spend a little extra time on those charts to make sure Julia followed up on the special pre-op instructions. Then there was Mr. Simonies who had been admitted for pre-op testing.

"There's something peculiar about all this," Carole thought to herself when she saw the name. Mr. Simonies was the most recent of a string of middle-aged men, all of whom were kidney donors. "I wonder if Julia thinks so, too?" she asked herself as she set his chart aside and turned to the others.

She wrote out the more perfunctory notes first and then spent a bit of time on Mrs. St. John's record. Her care that evening had been a rather trying experience. The old woman had at first refused to take her medication. "Ninety-three years is long enough. I don't know why the Lord doesn't just take me," Mrs. St. John had said. "I'm just a good-for-nothing old woman who's tired of living."

"If only her children hadn't been there," Carole thought. "I could have handled the situation and gotten her to take her medication. The daughters' responses were quite inappropriate." The memory of the event came flooding back. Though visiting hours were almost over, three of the four children had still been at Mrs. St. John's bedside when she refused her medication. Inexplicably, the two daughters became very near hysterical. Crying and begging their mother to take her medication and trying to convince her that she still had many good years ahead, they had made things worse. The old woman had only become more adamant in her refusal. When James St. John began to remonstrate with both his sisters and his mother, fireworks really erupted. It had taken Carole and another ward sister quite a while to calm everyone. They finally succeeded in getting the siblings to leave hospital and in getting Mrs. St. John to take her medication. "Hopefully," Carole thought to herself, "Mrs. St. John will have been released by the time I come back from holiday." She glanced at her watch, which read 10:45, and quietly said to herself, "Back to business."

Only Mr. Simonies's chart was left when, out of the corner of her eye, Carole saw Julia come out of the lift and head toward the nurses' lounge. Mr. Simonies had been admitted that afternoon for intensive final testing in the morning before undergoing surgery the following day. He was providing the kidney needed for Mrs. Amin's transplant surgery. "I wonder what's really going on," Carole said to herself, her suspicions beginning to return. "Why would a healthy man choose to come to a foreign country in order to donate an organ to a complete stranger? They aren't even compatriots; Mrs. Amin is from Kuwait, and Mr. Simonies is Turkish. It just doesn't make sense," Carole muttered to herself.

This was the seventh time in three months that Mr. Mathers-Smith had performed a kidney transplant. "How," she thought to herself, her mind now racing, "does Mr. Mathers-Smith find these donors? He's the only transplant surgeon whose donors are all foreigners." At first Carole had not thought much about it. But now, as she perused the chart she began wondering more about the situation. Somehow, it seemed odd. She turned to Julia who was just signing in at the nurses' station. "You know there's another transplant scheduled this week," Carole said holding up Mr. Simonies's chart. "I've been wondering about it. There seem to be quite a number of them recently." When Julia didn't respond Carole continued, "Don't you think it's odd that there are so many of them recently and that all the donors are foreigners? The last two couldn't even speak a word of English. And then this afternoon this other foreign organ donor was admitted to hospital. When I checked on him a bit ago he was very distraught."

"What do you mean?" Julia inquired.

"I've been here five years, and there've been more kidney transplants the past three months than in that whole time." Turning to look directly at Julia, Carole continued, "It just seems odd. All the donors are healthy men with no relation to the recipients and no real sense of what is going on. I'm not sure that they truly understand what's happening to them. Undergoing any kind of surgery always has an element of risk, not to mention an increased health risk later on from having only one kidney. Removing a kidney is so much harder than inserting one. Mrs. Amin may be up and moving in six to twelve hours, feeling good, but Mr. Simonies is going to have a longer surgery with much more internal manipulation, which is going to cause much more pain and tenderness. He'll be convalescing for two to four weeks at least. Would you do that for a total stranger? Even if it didn't leave you at higher risk of kidney failure?"

"All of them signed the consent forms, didn't they?" Julia responded.

"Well, yes," Carole replied hesitatingly. "But the forms are supposed to elicit informed consent, and I don't think that they know what they are agreeing to. Take Mr. Simonies, the one who was just admitted. He was really agitated this evening. When I went to prep him he was almost hysterical. He kept grabbing my arm and was going on in some strange language. He really looked frightened. I could see it in his eyes. I tried to calm him but he kept thrashing about until the sedative finally took hold. It just wasn't normal."

"Well, what would you expect?" Julia exclaimed as she looked over Mr. Simonies's chart. "If you'd read the chart carefully, you'd see he's Turkish. It's only natural to feel strange and out-of-place."

"That's not the point," Carole persisted. "Who on the staff speaks Turkish? Does Mr. Mathers-Smith? I've never heard him speak Turkish to any of these other donors. If nobody speaks their language, what does this signature on an English form mean?"

"Look, there's nothing to be concerned about. Mr. Simonies is in great hands; Mr. Mathers-Smith is an excellent surgeon," Julia concluded as she turned to look over the other charts. "Besides, maybe both the donor and the recipient are Muslim; it may be a religious support program we're seeing. If it were your mother getting the kidney, would you want somebody suggesting things weren't cricket?"

"But that's another thing, too," continued Carole in a perplexed voice. "All the foreign donors have been from Turkey, and they've all been under Mr. Mathers-Smith's exclusive care. I think that's odd, too. What if this is a network for buying and selling organs from poor people? I really think it should be reported to the chief surgeon."

"You've been watching too much telly," replied Julia. "It's a good thing you're going on holiday. Much more talk like this and people will think you're mad. Besides you could get yourself in real trouble and lose your job if someone thought you were accusing Mr. Mathers-Smith of misconduct," warned Julia. "Then where would you be? This is not our responsibility, Carole. We don't do the kidney extraction or the transplant. We only supervise the donor testing in this unit. We don't even secure the signature on the consent form. It isn't our responsibility. The responsibility belongs in surgery and ICU where they do the transplants and aftercare. We are only a medical floor. How would you like them to start asking questions about our procedures?"

Trying to keep the pique out of her voice, Julia turned to Carole and continued, "Look, it's already five of eleven. Why don't you let me take over now?"

Ignoring Carole, Julia began reviewing the charts. Realizing there was nothing more to be said, Carole turned away and headed down the corridor to the nurses' lounge. Absentmindedly, she opened her locker and began placing things in her carryall. She really didn't think she was overreacting. Yet, there wasn't anything concrete to her suspicion, just her own conviction that things were not as they appeared to be.

"Maybe I'll be able to think more clearly about this after a good night's sleep," Carole told herself as she walked out to the car park where Marshall was waiting to give her a lift home.

"You're a few minutes early tonight," he noted as she got into the car. "Everything must be going smoothly, then."

"I don't know that I'd say that," replied Carole and repeated her conversation with Julia.

"Julia's right, it's not your responsibility," Marshall responded when she was finished. "You've got enough of those as it is with your mother, as you always seem to be reminding me." Marshall had an annoyed tone in his voice.

Carole was silent, hoping to avoid starting a row just as they were to leave on holiday. The topic of her mother was always a delicate one.

"If it weren't for my mother," thought Carole as she stared out the car window, "I'd go out to Bahrain or one of the Emirates for a few years. Marshall would be bound to follow and we could put enough aside so that we could marry." She sighed again at the thought of her recurring dilemma.

Though she felt fortunate to have the job at the Northumberland, Carole felt trapped by having to care for her mother who was housebound. Never an adventurous woman, Mrs. Bennet had begun to retreat from the world five years earlier when her husband died. A bad fall three years ago exacerbated the situation, and she had, for all practical purposes, become a recluse. Carole was frustrated. She loved her mother and didn't want to put her into a home, but caring for her was putting an ever-greater strain on her relationship with Marshall. Only the night before last Marshall had insisted, "You can't let your mother run your life. Besides, you're really not helping her. Can't you see that! She's not yet sixty and is physically fit. You must stop giving in to her every wish; that only makes her more dependent and less able to cope on her own. You really must get her help."

Carole hated these rows. Marshall wanted to get married but insisted that he would not move in with Carole and her mother. He just didn't seem to understand. How could Carole leave her mother on her own? As it was it had been a chore to find a place for her mother to stay for the coming fortnight. "Give it all a pass for now, or you'll ruin the fortnight's holiday," thought Carole, determined to put work and home out of her mind.

Carole was up early the next morning. She still had a few last-minute errands to run before bringing her mother to the convalescent home where she would be staying for the fortnight and settling her in there.

"I can't believe I'm not going to be late for work," she thought to herself as she waited for the tube at Clapham South Station. To Carole's surprise, her mother had not been at all difficult, and reassured that her mother was in good hands, Carole was already in a holiday mood. Unfortunately, as she entered the train her eye caught an advertisement for a ten-day Turkish odyssey. The tension seemed to rush back into Carole's body as she remembered Mr. Simonies's plight the day before.

"What am I to do?" she asked herself, trying to identify alternatives.

The conductor's voice crackled over the train's public address system, "Next stop Bank. Mind the gap."

"That's it," Carole thought. "I could get off here and go see Father Smythe."

Coming out of Bank Street Station she headed down Lombard Street to St. Edmund the King where Father Smythe was the canon. Carole had first come to the small Wren church for the occasional organ recital and had soon become involved in their work with one of the East End missions.

"Father Smythe is just the person to help me sort through this muddle," she thought to herself as she entered the parish office.

"I'm really in a hurry," Carole said declining the offer of a cup of tea. "I go on duty in half an hour's time, but when I heard the conductor say, 'Bank,' I knew I had to get off and seek your advice."

Carole told her story to Fr. Smythe.

"It seems to me that you need to communicate with your Mr. Simonies before you do anything else," Father Smythe responded after considering Carole's story for a few minutes. "There's a fellow down in Whitechapel at the mission who speaks Turkish. What if I ask him to come by and visit with Mr. Simonies? That should ease your concern."

Carole, relieved that some action was being taken, thanked Father Smythe, said her good-byes, and headed back to the tube.

Her shift at Northumberland was proving to be uneventful. Later that day, Carole was at the nurses' station enjoying the after-supper lull when a young man approached her.

"Excuse me, sister. I am Mahmut Kemal. I am looking for Sister Carole," he said softly, his eyes taking in the patient-monitoring board on the far wall.

"I am she," Carole replied, somewhat startled.

"Oh, good evening," the young man said. "Father Smythe asked if I would come and visit one of your patients. He told me of your concerns for him. I think he and I must be countrymen."

"Oh, yes," Carole replied wondering, now that someone who could communicate with Mr. Simonies was standing in front of her, if she had done the right thing. "Too late for second thoughts, now," she thought to herself as she led Mr. Kemal down the corridor.

Mr. Simonies was propped up in his bed resting when the two entered the room. Carole was about to speak, but Mr. Kemal did so first. Mr. Simonies's facial expression was all the indication Carole needed to know that the two men spoke the same language.

"No, no. Please remain," Mr. Kemal said to her as she turned to leave the room. "It is not a problem for you to be here."

Carole stood at the far corner of the bed as the two men conversed. At first Mr. Kemal was doing most of the talking. Then Mr. Simonies began to speak. As he went on he became more and more agitated. Finally, Carole stepped in.

"Please, Mr. Kemal. You are upsetting the patient. He is scheduled for surgery in the morning and mustn't be disturbed," Carole said authoritatively, the nurse in her coming to the fore.

Mr. Kemal stepped back a bit and said something to Mr. Simonies who became a bit more composed.

"What is the trouble?" Carole asked the young man.

"Mr. Simonies is afraid that you will stop the surgery. I tried to explain that I had come because you were unsure that he understood the seriousness of his proposed action. He is only concerned that the surgery be completed."

"I don't quite understand," Carole replied in a perplexed voice.

"Apparently, he has agreed to this surgery in exchange for 10,000 pounds sterling, but he will not get the money if there is no surgery and will not be able to get a ticket to fly home," Mr. Kemal told her.

"That can't be possible!" Carole cried. "Surely, you've misunderstood."

The two men spoke again, this time in calmer tones. Mr. Kemal kept nodding in a reassuring manner, while Mr. Simonies spoke earnestly. Carole could only be a silent bystander. Finally, Mr. Kemal turned to her.

"Yes, it is true," he said. "Mr. Simonies is from a small village in eastern Turkey, not far from Lake Van. A number of people from there have come for similar operations. They were all recruited by the same man who visits the village every so often."

"But I don't understand," Carole repeated to herself. "Why would he sell his kidney? Doesn't he realize the health risk involved? It's absolutely mad."

"Sister Carole, you don't understand. For him, it is *not* mad. He comes from a part of Turkey that is like—what do you British call it?—the Moors. It is rocky, forbidding land. In good years it is difficult to make a living, in bad—well, some are not so fortunate. With the money from this surgery, Mr. Simonies will no longer be concerned about rain or cold or wild animals or any of the things that go with living in such a harsh land. He will have sufficient money for him and his children to see old age. The others who have come to England from his area have no problems. He will be the same," Mr. Kemal insisted. "He says you don't worry. All will be well."

"I'll leave you two for a few minutes. I've been away from the station too long," Carole replied, not knowing what else to say.

By the time she returned to the nurses' station her mind was racing, "What am I to do with this new information? Julia won't listen. She thinks I'm a headcase, and what if she's right about me losing my job? Marshall will simply say I'm a silly cow and keep me from doing anything." Looking at her watch, she saw that it was almost 9:30. "Not much time to decide," Carole concluded. "If I'm to say something it must be soon. The transplant is scheduled for 6:30 tomorrow morning."

A HINDU RESPONSE by Rebecca J. Manring

The Vairagi Vaishnava tradition developed in north central India in the fifteenth century under the leadership of Ramanandin, who had previously been a follower of the Vishishtadvaita (qualified nondualism) school of the eleventh-century South Indian philosopher Ramanuja. Ramanuja taught an essentially monistic ideology but recognized that monism is much too abstract for most seekers and so advocated a preliminary stage of devotion to a personal god. His chosen deity was Rama, the seventh incarnation of the god Vishnu, usually worshiped along with his wife Sita as the example of the perfect married couple. Ramanuja felt that if one began one's spiritual quest with devotion to a perceptible form of the divine, one could train one's mind and senses to focus on that god and, through that focus, would gradually develop the understanding that Ultimate Reality is actually all-pervasive and beyond name and form. Like the other major Vaishnava sects of the medieval period, Ramanuja's school asserted its legitimacy with the production of a commentary on the *Brahmasutras*, and in this commentary this group propounded its qualified nondualism.

Ramanandin, known to have taken the socially radical step of welcoming followers from all social groups and to have ordained women as well as men as renunciates, broke off from Ramanuja's school to form the Vairagi Vaishnava sect. Unlike many of the other Vaishnava orders, the Vairagi Vaishnavas are renunciates. As such they are as likely to be found living alone as in organized monasteries.

Since the late 1960s when many Westerners began traveling to India in search of spiritual refreshment, a number of religious adepts have come to the West to teach. Among these is a Vairagi Vaishnava *mauni sadhu* (a holy man who observes a vow of perpetual silence) from Almora District in the Kumaon region of the Himalayas. He received his initiation from a Vairagi *sadhu* named Raghubir Dass and, therefore, considers himself a member of that lineage. His teachings are based on Patanjali's *Yogasutras*, the *Bhagavadgita*, and his own experience and contain little specifically sectarian doctrinal material other than that outlined above. This would appear to be typical of Vairagi Vaishnavas. The group holds to the idea of Ultimate Reality as nondualistic, with qualifications, and sect members most often rely on their individual studies and life experiences to interpret the world around them and to teach.

The Vairagi Vaishnava tradition is a renunciate tradition and, as such, one that does not have large numbers of followers in diaspora. As renunciates, its adherents would have little interest in or use for the money they might earn by selling their own organs and would be unlikely to seek out an organ transplant for themselves.

These facts notwithstanding, I will attempt herein to respond to the case study given from the Vairagi Vaishnava perspective as propounded by Baba

Hari Dass. The case does present some interesting problems which can be discussed on ethical grounds. These are, first of all, the basic issue of organ transplantation itself; secondly, that of informed consent; and thirdly, the ethics of organ selling, especially in light of its significant impact on the lives of the sellers.

Most religions that arose in India accept the idea, in some form, of transmigration of souls, with one's actions in the current lifetime determining one's future circumstances. The goal of existence is to attain liberation, which is understood by Vairagi Vaishnavas to be specifically the realization that the individual soul is no different from Ultimate Reality. Although there is an implicit assurance that everyone will eventually "make it," no matter how many lifetimes it takes, a good devotee seeks liberation—for us all—sooner rather than later and so strives to make as much spiritual progress as possible in a given lifetime. At the same time aspirants are counseled not to be attached to the ever-changing objects and conditions of this world—which objects include our own bodies. But as the body is the vehicle through which we seek and attain liberation, we must take proper care of it: feed it nourishing food that will not agitate the mind and senses, exercise it to keep it fit for meditation, clothe and house it to keep it free of disease so that our meditation practices are not disturbed, and so forth. And in time of crisis, we must do whatever we can that might prolong its life, so that we can continue our efforts as long as possible.

The body is simply the temporary container of the soul. We leave one body at death and come to inhabit a new one at the time of rebirth. It has no permanent existence. So surgery, even the removal and/or replacement of body parts or organs, would not be viewed as defiling in any way, as it is understood that the body is perishable. Thus organ transplantation in and of itself is not problematic for an aspirant in the Vairagi Vaishnava tradition.

Let us now examine the issue of informed consent. In the last century or so medical doctors have managed to accrue tremendous power in the eyes of their patients. Their pronouncements are taken as the final word in any situation, and it is only very recently, and then only in the West where higher levels of education are more or less universally accessible, that patients have learned to question their physicians. In many parts of the world, and indeed in less privileged sections of Western society, if a medical doctor is consulted, that doctor's word is not likely to be questioned. So if a doctor instructs such a patient to donate a kidney, and mentions compensation, the patient will simply acquiesce.

The most troubling aspect of this particular case is simply that kidneys are being purchased from healthy men in hopelessly impoverished circumstances for implantation into the bodies of wealthy patients. The surgeon's trips to a remote Turkish village in search of organ donors indicate that he has carefully researched and orchestrated the entire procedure. The donors receive an amount of money so large that their families will be able to live the rest of their lives in comfort, without regard for the vagaries of nature that can wreak havoc on farming communities. The high price connected with the surgery will then be borne by the organ recipient—and that high cost renders the procedure inaccessible to many potentially needy recipients and available only to the very wealthy.

If the entire undertaking is viewed as a commercial transaction it at first glance appears perfectly acceptable. However, as mentioned above, Vairagi Vaishnavas are noted for their egalitarian attitudes in spiritual matters. It is only reasonable to assume that this egalitarianism would extend to other issues as well, particularly because the culture from which they spring does not compartmentalize the various elements of life. Thus, reserving a life-saving medical procedure to those who can pay a foreign donor and thereby bypassing the usual roster for organ transplants and the system whereby priorities for receiving organs are determined—in effect, "jumping the queue"—is indeed ethically problematic. Further, the large payments made to the donors will alter the standard of living in their village, creating tremendous economic disparity between organ donors and other villagers. The money the donors receive will certainly improve their lives, but can also only create friction and resentment among the villagers and, as such, will not, in the long run, really improve life for the community as a whole.

Among the monastic vows taken by Vairagi Vaishnavas is a pledge to adhere to the truth. Perhaps even more important than the principle of honesty is the commitment Vairagi Vaishnavas make to *ahimsa*. The word *ahimsa* is most often translated as "nonviolence," but encompasses the entire range of thoughts, words, and deeds capable of causing harm to others. Maintaining this ideal requires tremendous self-discipline. Many Vairagi Vaishnavas feel *ahimsa* to be the anchor of their practice, and so if there is ever a situation representing an apparent conflict between *ahimsa* and one of the other principles, the Vairagi Vaishnava will choose to act in accord with *ahimsa* over all else. The present case presents such a set of circumstances: the Turkish kidney donors appear to have been told what is involved in their organ donation. They have had the opportunity to discuss the surgery and recovery prospects with previous donors in their villages, and the entire undertaking appears to be quite an open business in the village.

What is not clear is whether prospective donors clearly understand who is to be the recipient of their kidneys. That is, are the villagers told that they will be saving the life of a deathly ill patient—which is probably true—or are they also told any of the economic circumstances of the whole transaction which allow the recipients, by virtue of their wealth, simply to purchase anything they require? Are these indigent people led to believe that they are helping someone whose circumstances are as difficult as their own? I suspect, although this is not entirely clear from the case study, that for the villagers, this is purely a business transaction too good to pass up. They are paid an amount which is not extravagant by Western standards, but which looks to them like an enormous fortune. And so it appears to be a very magnanimous, win-win situation.

Yet one cannot help returning to two very troubling aspects of the problem. First, the sale of organs seriously upsets the economic balance of the

Turkish village. This upset will change the economic base of life there, taking agricultural workers out of the work force and giving them instead a new and foreign lifestyle, largely reliant on Western consumer goods, while their neighbors continue to try to eke out a very humble living from their land. Second, the recipients are able to bypass the usual transplant waiting list system. They, thus, have an unfair advantage over other kidney patients who do not have the financial resources to simply purchase their own kidneys.

When presented with the facts of this case study, Baba Hari Dass wrote, "Donating organs to give life to others is a good *karma* but selling organs is not a right thing." For him, the leading exponent of Vairagi Vaishnavism in the West, the issue is quite clear.

A BUDDHIST RESPONSE by Ronald Y. Nakasone

Developments in medical science and technology have brought us to a state where organ transplant surgery is commonly accepted as standard medical treatment. Organ transplant technologies enable physicians routinely to harvest organs from donors and implant them to improve the quality of life and extend the life of another. In the absence of modern surgical techniques and the development of antirejection therapies, Carole Bennet would not be agonizing over her discovery that an impoverished Turkish peasant had agreed to give up one of his kidneys in exchange for 10,000 pounds sterling. As with Shirley's dilemma with in vitro fertilization discussed in the previous chapter, the Buddha who lived 2,500 years ago would not have to weigh the questions Carole confronts. The ramifications from the sale of human organs call for similar opportunities for Buddhists to consider the significance of the insights of their faith tradition and broaden their moral imaginations.

Consideration of the moral quandary that faces Carole with new information concerning a scheduled kidney transplant operation will be done in light of the doctrine of *pratityasamutpada* discussed in the previous chapter and the Buddhist notion of health and care giving. The question of human suffering, the impetus for Siddhartha Gautama's quest for and eventual realization of the truth of *pratityasamutpada*, defines the Buddhist attitude toward medicine and biotechnology and the changes they have brought or will bring. The Buddha's insight of *pratityasamutpada* and his notion of health and spiritual well-being that emerged from this vision temper decision making.

The Buddhist Posture

Health and healthcare are metaphors common to Buddhist thought and practice. Buddha, the great physician, dispenses the *dharma*, or teaching, the medicine that leads humanity away from suffering to spiritual ease. Though spiritual suffering was of paramount concern, the Buddha understood that spiritual well-being necessarily involved physical health,[1] which is in turn dependent on a wholesome community and sound management of natural and human resources.[2] The Buddha and his devotees attended to their spiritual ills through self-cultivation and served as sick nurses with compassionate deeds.[3]

Buddhist medical theory reflects the Buddhist belief in an interdependent world. In such a world, balance, mutuality, and reciprocity are prime virtues. Health involves a balance of the physical components of the body, of a wholesome environment, and of equitable distribution of goods and services. Physical health requires a balance among all the four elements that constitute the human body. The four elements are: (1) earth or the solid element, (2) water or the wet element, (3) fire or the hot element, and (4) wind or the mobile element. Illness arises when the body experiences an abnormal augmentation or diminution of any of the four elements. Diet, daily regimen, change of the seasons, stress from unusual physical activities, and past actions were understood to affect physical well-being.[4] Medicine and medical therapies prescribe the means to restore and maintain the healthy physical balance needed to cultivate the spiritual life. The Buddha placed a high value on physical fitness and freedom from disease as a basis for mental and spiritual development. In addition to the disequilibrium among the four elements, Buddhist medical theorists took into account external and societal conditions in considering the cause of a disease.[5] In keeping with the belief that prevention is the best guarantee against illness and disease the Buddha urged moderation against harsh spiritual austerities and overindulgence of food. His monastic rules emphasized personal hygiene and public health.

Medicine and care giving were integral parts of the early Buddhist community. The model for care giving is the Buddha himself. On an occasion, the Buddha chanced on a sick, unattended monk wallowing in his own excrement. "O monks, if you do not nurse one another, whoever will nurse you?" Thereupon the Buddha bathed the monk, changed his garments, and laid a bed for his ailing comrade. This experience led the Buddha to declare, "Anyone who wishes to make offerings to me, let him make offerings to the sick."[6] Initially, the early community focused medical treatment and nursing activity on the care of monks and nuns by fellow cenobites or by pious lay devotees. Caring for their compatriots became part of the monastic code. From around the mid-third century BCE medical care was extended to the population at large. Later, the medical arts became part of the curriculum at Nalanda and other monastic universities.

An Unlikely Donor

Carole Bennet, a nurse at Northumberland Gate Hospital, faces a host of dilemmas when her suspicions are confirmed that something is amiss with Mr. Simonies, a potential kidney donor. She learns through Mahmut Kemal that Mr. Simonies is a poor Turkish peasant who speaks no English and has agreed to give up one of his kidneys for 10,000 pounds sterling. Mr. Simonies's kidney is intended for Mrs. Amin from Kuwait. Because a market in organs would foster inequities and promote injustice and exploitation of the poor,[7] many countries only permit the donation of organs. Regardless of the legality surrounding the sale of organs, Carole is bound by her professional nursing ethics and the ethics of the health care delivery system. She raises the question of the appropriateness of the informed consent that Mr. Simonies and Mrs. Amin signed. If they do understand English, "do they know what they are agreeing to?" In addition to her professional responsibilities, Carole confronts more fundamental issues of justice. Clearly this case is a question of fairness and access to medical services. The rich can purchase health. Biotechnology has enabled the rich to exploit the poor of their birthright, their organs. Mrs. Amin appears to have the financial means. Besides purchasing Mr. Simonies's kidney, she must pay for hospitalization and physical services. In a case such as this, which involves foreign nationals, British national health insurance does not pay for renal therapy, such as dialysis and kidney transplants. Carole has also learned that in exchange for his kidney, Mr. Simonies will have enough "money for himself and for his children to see old age." The cash for a kidney exchange is an exchange for health and financial security for two generations of Simonies who will not suffer privations.

The narrative closes with Carole contemplating what to do. It is 9:30 P.M. and the transplant is scheduled for 6:30 the next morning. "Not much time to decide."

Reflections

Buddhist documents abound with medical injunctions and prohibitions. The *Anguttara Nikaya* lists the five qualities of those who attend to the sick. The competent caregiver possesses (1) knowledge of medicaments and their application, (2) tends to the sick with amity of mind and without thought of personal nourishment and profit, (3) is not lazy, (4) or prone to annoyances and does not loathe removing excrement, urine, sweat, or vomit. Because the early Buddhists linked illness with mental states gone awry, (5) the competent caregiver should delight in sharing the Buddha's *dharma* and conversing with the sick.[8] Sakyamuni Buddha, the great healer, appropriately dispensed the teaching of impermanence to the terminally ill and meditative exercise to those who could be cured.

Carole as caregiver satisfies the fifth requirement of a Buddhist nurse who converses with the patient. She hears the pleas of Mr. Simonies and discovers his poverty and his generosity toward his family.[9] Should Carole report her newfound knowledge of cash for an organ? She could be without a job. Julia, the other nurse on duty, cautions her to mind her own business. "Besides you could get yourself in real trouble and lose your job if someone thought you were accusing Mr. Mathers-Smith of misconduct." Julia implies that Carole would be challenging the judgment of the surgeon and possibly hospital policy. Julia seems to suggest also that there is a conspiracy within the hospital. Further, if Carole chooses to report her newfound information, she may not be able to leave on her planned vacation to Cornwall with Marshall, and she may jeopardize their plans for marriage. Beyond her own personal dilemmas, she must consider the motivation of the donor, and wishes of the recipient, the attending surgeon, hospital policies, professional responsibilities, medical ethics, and international and British law.

The appropriateness of Mr. Simonies's exchange of his kidney for 10,000 pounds sterling is a question of some importance. How do we reconcile the ideal with an individual's immediate survival? Laws prohibiting the sale of organs attempt to insure that the poor are not exploited. Yet, Mr. Simonies's sacrifice will insure financial security for himself and his family. He appears willing to undergo postoperative complications. His devotion to his family is admirable and not unlike the sacrifices parents endure to see that their children have a better life. If Dr. Mathers-Smith were to remove one of Mr. Simonies's kidneys and transplant it into one of his children, I doubt if Carole would have a problem. Aside from the efficacy of Mr. Simonies's sacrifice, is there a significant moral difference between Mr. Simonies donating a kidney to his child and selling his kidney? Giving a kidney would help only one child. With the money he will be able to provide better for his entire family. Further, should he not be appreciative of Mrs. Amin for having a dysfunctional kidney, for having the right genetic match, and the means for having a transplant? What right does Carole have to deny Mr. Simonies and his family their only recourse for a secure livelihood? Interestingly, we know next to nothing about Mrs. Amin. Why is she a recipient? Are her needs greater than Mr. Simonies's needs? We can think of other hypothetical scenarios.

The cash for a kidney transaction calls for the consideration of a multiplicity of factors. The Buddha's original insight, the truth of *pratityasamutpada* or interdependence, affirms the reality that we live in a complex, ever-changing web of interrelationships. No single cause can explain how an event transpires. A multiplicity of causes and conditions converged at Northumberland Gate Hospital on that fateful night, including Carole being on duty, that gave rise to her dilemma. As noted in the previous article, "A Right to Parent: A Buddhist Response," Fa-tsang (643–712 CE) described the complexity of a single event. Moreover, each cause and condition offers a different perspective of how a thing or event arises. No thing or event is ever the locus of attention for everyone. Further, in a world of conflicting demands and responsibilities, we need to clarify all of the relevant facts before passing judgment. This daunting task may prove impossible. Too often we act or make decisions before we have explored all causes and investigated all alternatives. Though this may be cumbersome, believing that we are right and that we have all the answers is to fail to appreciate other points of view. Knowing that we live in an interdependent world means that we may never fully discover the truth that is embedded in complex issues. Issues may be unresolvable and may remain forever ambiguous. Living and working in ambiguity is often the most productive way of ethical deliberation and action. Such an attitude forces us to deliberate, make decisions, and act knowing that others are not going to approve or follow our example. This humble attitude permits us to see many points of view, just as a Cubist painter renders an object from different perspectives. In contrast, perspective, a visual rendering technique perfected during the European Renaissance, sees a view from a single-fixed point. To be objective is to consider all points of views.

The question of the appropriateness of the pending transplant involves a host of questions that Carole cannot resolve alone. To begin, does she have enough information? The first question is: What is her professional responsibility as a nurse? In California, a nurse acts as an advocate for the patient "by initiating action to improve health care or to change decisions or activities which are against the interests or wishes of the client."[10] A nurse has a responsibility to challenge a physician's judgment, if there is sufficient cause. If Carole were licensed in the State of California, she would need to communicate and document her concerns to the head nurse or the chief surgeon. Does the hospital have an ombudsman? Are the nurses unionized? If so, the shop steward should be approached. If she suspects some criminality, she should contact the police. In the United States, the state and county have agencies that investigate abuses and irregularities. If Dr. Mathers-Smith performs an illegal transplant, he may lose his medical license, and the hospital may lose its accreditation. She has an obligation to report her newfound information, to clarify the situation, and to abort a possible illegal operation. Carole has not exhausted her avenues of appeal. Her dilemma can be mitigated with more information. She must report her concerns.

The cash for a kidney transaction calls into question other issues of health care ethics. The Buddha traced much of human illnesses to poverty. The poor have limited access to material and nonmaterial resources that ensure basic necessities: food, clothing, shelter, medicine, and education (i.e., spiritual development). Political leaders, either through ignorance or greed, institute public policies that result in the unequal distribution of goods and services. A Buddhist state would provide a pleasant living environment by safeguarding the natural environment and protecting the poor and dispossessed against exploitation of human and other resources to ensure everyone has life's necessities. Proper education enables the poor to have access to information and helps them procure goods and services for a comfortable life. These measures would maximize the psychological and physiological well-being that provide the basis for spiritual development.[11] We must consider all aspects of suffering. In an era of real-time communications and globalization, we can no longer think simply of nation-states. An individual must be seen globally. International laws must be enacted to insure that the poor and dispossessed in one country are not exploited by the rich of another. In an interdependent world, we rise and fall together as one living body.[12]

Pratityasamutpada, or interdependence, provides Buddhists with a vision of identity and responsibility to all beings. Interdependence also quickens a sense of gratitude toward all things and all beings. Ethical deliberation and opportunity lie in our understanding that we are irrevocably intertwined with destinies of all beings. The world evolves through our individual efforts and at the same time we are molded by events in which we are caught up. Echoing this idea, James Gustafson writes, "Man (individual persons, communities, and species) is a participant in the patterns and processes of interdependence of life in the world."[13] By voicing her concerns, Carole Bennet acts out the vision that we live in an interdependent world.

Notes

1. *Gandavyuha sutra*, Taisho 11:710–712, quoted in Paul Demiéville, *Buddhism and Healing: Demiéville's article "Byo" from Hobogirin*, trans. Mark Tatz (Lanham, MD: University Press of America), 44.

2. Nanadasena Ratnapala, *Buddhist Sociology* (Delhi: Sri Satguru Publications, 1993), 99–100.

3. While illness testifies to the frailness and transiency of the human condition, caring for the sick is also an opportunity for spiritual quickening. The sick, in turn, have an opportunity for abundant giving. Spiritual health means to realize and to live with gratitude for and responsibility to all things and beings. (Ronald Y. Nakasone, "Abundant Giving: A Buddhist Reflection on Caregiving," working paper for the Stanford University Geriatric Education Center, 1998.)

4. Ratnapala, *Buddhist Sociology*, 180–81.

5. Kenneth G. Zysk, *Asceticism and Healing in India: Medicine in the Buddhist Monastery* (Delhi: Oxford University Press, 1991), 29.

6. *Dharmagupta-vinaya*, Taisho Shinshu Daizokyo 1428:41:86lb–c, ed. Junjiro Takakusu et al. (Tokyo: 1929), quoted in Demiéville, *Buddhism and Healing*, 32.

7. Nanette Newel, "Biotechnology," *Encyclopedia of Bioethics*, ed. Warren Reich (New York: Macmillan Publishing, 1995), 285.

8. *Anguttara Nikaya*, quoted in Demiéville, *Buddhism and Healing*, 34.

9. Conversing requires the art of listening which is personified in Avalokitesvara, the Bodhisattva of Compassion. "Avalokitesvara" or "Kanzeon," the Japanese rendering, clearly captures the Bodhisattva's special talent. "Kan" means "to hear," "ze" means "world," and "on" means "sound." Avalokitesvara, who hears the pleas of the world, is the ideal caregiver. Listening to the outbursts of anger, despair, and hurt, the Bodhisattva attends to the journeying spirit, not the momentary stammer. Likewise a good listener hears not what is said, but what underlies that which is spoken.

10. State of California Department of Consumer Affairs, *Nursing Practice Act with Rules and Regulations* (Sacramento: Board of Registered Nursing, 1997), 63–64.

11. Ratnapala, *Buddhist Sociology*, 97–115.

12. Francis H. Cook, *Hua-yen Buddhism: The Jewel Net of Indra* (University Park, PA: The Pennsylvania State University Press, 1977), 118.

13. James Gustafson, *Ethics from a Theocentric Perspective: Ethics and Theology* (Chicago: University of Chicago Press, 1984), 145.

Bibliography and Suggested Reading

Cook, Francis H. *Hua-yen Buddhism: The Jewel Net of Indra*. University Park, PA: The Pennsylvania State University Press, 1977.

Demiéville, Paul. *Buddhism and Healing: Demiéville's article "Byo" from Hobogirin*. Trans. Mark Tatz. Lanham, MD: University Press of America, 1985.

Nakasone, Ronald Y. "Buddhism." In *Encyclopedia of Bioethics*, ed. Warren Reich. New York: Macmillan Publishing, 1995.

————. "Probing the Limits of Buddhist Thought." *Essays in Honor of Professor Watanabe Takao*. Kyoto: Nagata, 1998.

Newel, Nanette. "Biotechnology." In *Encyclopedia of Bioethics*, ed. Warren Reich. New York: Macmillan Publishing, 1995.

Ratnapala, Nanadasena. *Buddhist Sociology*. Delhi: Sri Satguru Publications, 1993.

State of California Department of Consumer Affairs. *Nursing Practice Act with Rules and Regulations*. Sacramento, CA: Board of Registered Nursing, 1997.

Tachibana, Shundo. *The Ethics of Buddhism*. London: Curzon Press, 1975.

Ubel, Peter A., and Mary B. Mahowld. "Ethical and Legal Issues Regarding Living Donors." In *Encyclopedia of Bioethics*, ed. Warren Reich. New York: Macmillan Publishing, 1995.

Ueda, Yoshifumi. "The Status of the Individual in Mahayana Buddhist Philosophy." In *The Status of the Individual in East and West*, ed. Charles A. Moore, 77–90. Honolulu: University of Hawaii Press, 1968.

Zysk, Kenneth G. *Asceticism and Healing in India: Medicine in the Buddhist Monastery*. Delhi: Oxford University Press, 1991.

CHAPTER 17

An Issue of Murder?

A CASE STUDY by Christine E. Gudorf

The Swiss doctor panted as he tried to keep up with Sister Dolores's pace on the mountain path. "How can you not think it is a scandal, Sister? Incidence of mental retardation in the developed world is 3 percent, with 1 percent severely affected. We have only found a quarter of that rate anywhere in the altiplano, either in Bolivia or Peru. Do you really think that significantly fewer children are born mentally retarded here?" asked the slender man in his early forties as he gingerly touched his balding pate, which had baked to a bright scarlet in the thin Andean air and strong mountain sun.

Sister Dolores smiled and paused. She was a short compact woman in her early sixties whose face suggested her Irish roots. "No, Dr. Renseur, I suspect the incidence at birth may even be higher here. But I still do not think that programs for the mentally retarded should take priority here in the altiplano."

Dr. Renseur was a Swiss physician who was a part of a World Health Organization study team on special populations of the mentally retarded in the developing nations. He sputtered. "But you are a nun. How can you countenance the killing, active or passive, of innocent children? Virtually none of them live to adulthood here!"

Sister Dolores began walking again, her walking stick making a regular but slow tapping on the rocky path. "Let me tell you of a couple you will meet in the next village, Maria Amparo and Francisco. They have a one-room house on a small farm outside the village. Maria Amparo began taking contraceptives after the birth of her third child. When that child was two, measles came to the village, and he and his sister both died, leaving one son. She stopped taking the contraceptives and got pregnant with twins, Rosalia and Diego. Diego was never "right," as they say. He was just always weaker, slower, duller than Rosalia. They are six now. Diego goes out with Rosalia or with their older brother, Juan, to feed the chickens and herd the goats, but he could never do it alone. He is only Rosalia's shadow. He is not coordinated and is only slightly trainable. He can't be trusted to remember to close gates or stake the animals.

"Diego will die this year. He is not ill now, only weak, but he will die. No one will kill him. He will just be too weak and ill-fed to fend off the first viruses that come with the winter, and sooner or later, as the food supply dwindles over the winter, he will succumb. I have seen it too many times to doubt. It could have happened the last two winters, but it will happen this winter."

Dr. Renseur queried as he again struggled to match Sister Dolores's pace, "Don't his parents feed him? How can you be sure?"

"Yes, he gets fed with the rest. Perhaps a little less, but not so much that anyone would notice. He makes fewer demands for food—he talks very little, and that not clearly. When he and Rosalia are passing the fields on the way to the pastures, Rosalia will dig up a potato or a carrot and munch on it. If Diego sees her, he will ask for some, but it would never occur to him to dig his own. It is the same on market day. Rosalia and her brother run errands in return for food snacks, but Diego merely stares at the vendors' food," explained Sister Rosalia.

"Don't their parents see that he needs more food?"

"They all need more food, especially in winter. But Diego needs more, because he cannot pursue it so well. And when he gets ill and dies, his family will weep and mourn and then agree with the neighbors that the death of this little angel was God's will," commented Sister Dolores ruefully.

"But surely you don't let that happen! It's not God's will that retarded children die!" protested Dr. Renseur.

"No? Are you sure? On one level, I'm sure that's true. God would undoubtedly prefer that we humans shared the resources of the earth so that everyone was fed. But I am not so sure that God would act any differently in the place of Maria Amparo and Francisco. From whom in the family would you take the food that you would give to Diego?" asked Sister Dolores.

"What a question!" snapped Dr. Renseur. "Surely the little bit of extra food to keep this small child alive could be managed without significantly depriving anyone else."

"No," responded Sister Dolores gently. "Here we are at Santa Catalina, and I see the crowd at the church pastoral room. Looks like you will have a full afternoon of children's clinic. We can finish this discussion on the way back. *Hola, Juanito, como estas? Y su familia?*" called Sister Dolores to the young boy running out to greet her.

Almost five hours later the two returned to the mountainous path that would lead them from Santa Catalina back to San Angelo. Dr. Renseur was trying to clarify some of the procedures in the clinic that had puzzled him. "The overall health of the children was better than I expected," he commented, "considering the difficulties of living without piped water and sewage. And most of the mothers seemed to know the basics of rehydration for children with diarrhea."

"Yes, the *promotores* for this inner ring of villages have done a good job on the basics. The infant mortality level was halved within less than five years after they began, though it is still high compared to your world. Their *charlas* (presentations) have become popular among new mothers, who sometimes walk many miles from surrounding villages to learn these techniques, and sometimes to get inoculations," added Sister Dolores.

"What I can't understand is why, if these people are open to modern med-icine and hygiene, they remain so backward about mental retardation? Or other disabilities, either. Did I understand that little old woman correctly, that she had found a baby who had died from exposure because it was born with what sounded like spina bifida?" inquired Dr. Renseur.

"Yes, it did sound like spina bifida, and the child was exposed and died. And I suppose that exposing infants does sound backward to you. It doesn't happen often—it's really rather rare. But do you really think that that child could have lived here? I do not condone exposure, but I am hard-pressed to condemn these parents. Think how much harder it is to give birth to such a child, and to hold it, and feed it, and love it, knowing that it can never, never survive," said Dolores, her voice choking as she remembered one such child in her first year in the altiplano. "In your world a baby like that is born and stays in the hospital or specialized-care center until it dies; only if it has a very mild case does the child go home to be cared for by family. We have no hospitals or nursing homes here; the parents must provide all the care. Family survival requires the work of the entire family; to try and save the doomed is to endanger the whole family."

"Look, I understand that, somewhat," admitted Dr. Renseur. "I heard the woman who measured the children's growth conferring with the mothers, and I understand that many of them are simply shifting a familial caloric deficit around from one member of the family to another so that no one is permanently affected. The first few times, I looked for some other answer, but there just isn't any. When the baby gets extra food or fat because he did not grow this quarter, one of the other children, often the one who had a growth problem last quarter or the one before, will get shorted. I caught myself about to suggest that the parents forfeit the food, and then asked myself what would happen to a family if the working father or the caretaker mother got ill. Clearly, the suffering to be shared would be exacerbated. But Sister, surely there are organizations that could distribute subsidized food here and enable more children to live. Why isn't that being done?"

"Cahatalca has a Vaso de Leche program which makes a daily glass of milk made from powder available to all children and pregnant and nursing mothers, and Caritas distributes oil to some *comedores*, but that is the limit of food distribution," said Sister Dolores stepping back to avoid rock rolling down the steep side of the mountain.

"What is a *comedor*, and why oil?" asked Dr. Renseur.

"You remember the *comedores*, I know you saw some in Lima. They are the women's group kitchens that collectively buy, prepare, and serve meals to all the families that contribute. Pooling resources allows people to eat better, and, periodically, while the women are gathered to prepare the meals, local NGOs [nongovernmental organizations] send in nutritionists to teach the women how to use their limited resources to prepare the most nutritious meals possible. Oil is the cheapest source of fat, and in the diets of poor children, fat is often the missing element that prevents growth," reminded Sister Dolores.

"Yes, I remember hearing that now. You know, for years now, I have heard the criticisms that medical training neglects nutrition, but until I came to the altiplano, I didn't really understand how important the connection is. The case for the importance of nutrition is much more compelling among the poor."

"I'm not so sure about that. In my aging religious congregation we have had to deal with lots of nutrition issues in medical care—low-fat diets for clogged arteries, low-salt diets for hypertension, sugar restrictions for borderline diabetics. It seems to me that the problem is that medical training is too focused on the medical problems of rich people who eat too much fat and sugar and salt, and it ignores the plight of the majority of people who lack calories, protein, and fat. If you go down to the jungle around Iquitos, you will find that tropical diseases and parasites are other areas of medicine you haven't been trained in. The local healers are often much more successful than the trained doctors, and the doctors can't even figure out—oh, look!" Sister Dolores began vigorously waving at a battered old truck coming toward them on the one-lane dirt road they were approaching. As the truck slowed down, she begged a ride back to San Angelo.

* * *

The members of the study team greeted each other in the conference room of the university in Bogota. The six of them had covered different areas of Latin America over the previous two weeks. Dr. Lars Olafson, the head of the team, called the meeting to order, suggesting that each person take five to ten minutes to detail the highlights of their findings and impressions before they got down to outlining a common report. Five heads nodded, and the team members, one by one, sketched their experiences in the field, with Dr. Olafson last.

Almost an hour later, the reports completed, Dr. Olafson remarked, "What we just heard is somewhat different from the expectations I understood the group to have as we began this study. As we began, I heard complaints of a lack of documentation concerning the incidence of, and care of those with, mental retardation. I also heard strong suspicions that changes in law, social policy, and religious attitudes, as well as strong international leadership and support, are necessary here. But most of your reports seem much more tentative. Do we still begin with a statement to the effect that treatment of the disabled is the best test of the humanity of a nation?"

"Yes," declared Dr. Maria Tesoro, a pediatrician from Barcelona. "The mentally retarded should have the same rights to life as others, and that is clearly not the case on most of this continent."

Dr. Renseur, who had decided to listen to the others in hopes of clearing up the confusion he felt, found himself speaking. "I am not so sure that treatment of the mentally retarded is the best test of the humanity of a nation. Perhaps it is a good test of the development of a nation, but not its humanity." Thinking of Sister Dolores and some of the medical personnel he had met in Bolivia and Peru, he continued, "Some of the most dedicated people I met who care for the mentally retarded reject the assumption that the mentally retarded should be a priority in Latin America. Many of them would oppose enacting a policy that supported equal life expectancies for the mentally retarded and the normal population. And many of these people work within the churches."

Dr. Tesoro was indignant. "Surely we cannot take seriously such an attitude. Why shouldn't the mentally retarded live as long as persons of normal intelligence? This is unjustified discrimination. The present laissez-faire policy supports widespread murder!" Two other members of the team nodded their heads. Another, Dr. Richard Sommers of the United States, objected, "I am uncomfortable with calling it 'murder.' There probably are some murders, but what most of us reported was neglect, a kind of systematic discrimination in feeding and medical care. Stories of exposure in rural areas, which tended to involve severe deformity in infants—many of whom would not have survived regardless of their care—are the only intentional killings I came across. On the other hand, I agree that it is totally intolerable. I understand that many of these people are poor, but if their process of development does not recognize the rights of the retarded or otherwise disabled, what kind of a society can they hope to build? I agree with Dr. Tesoro that we should insist on equality."

Dr. Chung Kim Sung from Korea interjected, "But that is the crux of the problem. What do we mean by equality? Equal length of life is a very different social policy goal than ensuring that mentally retarded children get fed as much as their siblings. Ensuring equal length of life to the mentally retarded would require a tremendous social intervention by the government that would cost billions on the continent as a whole. Nations that cannot provide all their normal, healthy children with schools, or all their schools with teachers or supplies, or all their towns with hospitals or clinics, cannot provide the institutions that would be required to house and feed and clothe the mentally retarded as adults—even if all their families raised them to adulthood despite the risks of depriving other members of the family."

Dr. Kefe Olanje of Zaire asked, "Are we speaking of recommending legislation or of implementing broader social policy? If we speak of legislation, it must be somewhat minimalist, so that it will be accepted by a broad enough majority so as to be enforceable. Social policy, on the other hand, can be more ambitious. It can work in incremental stages."

Dr. Chung responded, "Kefe, I agree that we need to decide. I think that law cannot make the same demands here that it can in the developed world where families have more support in dealing with mentally retarded kids—even in South Korea we have institutions to which families can surrender mentally retarded children and know that they will be fed and cared for. Most of the profoundly retarded persons in the developed world are in some kind of supported program, whether it is a residential institution, a publicly-supported job training program, an educational program for the mentally retarded, or a group home in the community. Families here have nothing like this—nor do they have any government income or free medical care for their adult retarded children, as families in the developed nations have for their retarded children."

Dr. Tesoro interjected, "But why did these programs arise? Because these societies valued the mentally retarded. We cannot let poverty justify barbarism—that is not doing these poor people a favor. I wonder if the mentally retarded—the disabled as a whole—are the only casualties of this social attitude of human dispensability. What about the sick and the old? What is their incidence? The only way to value life is to place an equal value on all life. I understand the distinction between law and broader social policy, and I am willing to focus on social-policy formation rather than law. But I believe that international pressure must be brought to bear on these nations in order to raise the survival rates of mentally-handicapped children and adults, and that this must be done immediately." Dr. Olafson asked if Dr. Tesoro wanted to make this a motion, and after a few moments to frame the wording, a formal motion was introduced to this effect.

"You would want to make various kinds of international-development assistance to these nations depend on their transferring scarce resources from the social-welfare sector of the budget—from medical care, education, clean water, sewage, and electricity services—to programs for the mentally retarded?" asked Dr. Renseur. "Isn't that likely to bring the general life-expectancy rate down? Is that really the way to produce equality of life expectancy? Most of these nations have already cut their social services budgets by 30 to 50 percent over the last ten to fifteen years under neoliberal austerity programs."

No one responded. Dr. Olafson called for an initial straw vote on Dr. Tesoro's proposal. The result was two yeas, two nays, and two abstentions, and the meeting was adjourned for lunch. Wondering who the other abstainer had been, Dr. Renseur left the room asking himself, "What is the best way to move toward justice for the mentally retarded in poverty-stricken areas?" He had two hours to decide.

AN AYMARAN CHRISTIAN RESPONSE
by Diego Irarrázaval

Care of persons who are "unsuccessful" in the eyes of the modern myth points to an alternative meaning of life and also demonstrates faithfulness to the gospel and its ethical demands.

This essay examines one case of violence against a mentally retarded indigenous boy in the Andean highlands. We can see how this case is misinterpreted by people who have a Western mentality. More importantly, the case illustrates how first-world persons can learn from the indigenous ethics of Latin America. During the last seventeen years, as a theologian and a missionary in the midst of the Aymara people in the Peruvian altiplano, I have been introduced to the other side of reality, to the wounds, the joys, and the wisdom of the poor of the earth. This has been more enriching than my twenty-one years of formal education among the elite. I hope that readers of this essay may engage in dialogue with an indigenous worldview; such views invite us to reconsider Christian ethics.

My commentary has four sections: first, the socio-cultural scenario; second, our biblical and theological principles; third, interpretation of this indigenous case; and fourth, intercultural ethical concerns and opportunities, particularly in developed nations.

Socio-Cultural Scenario

Andean peoples have their own worldview, which includes an appropriation of dominant global categories.[1] Briefly I will underline four dimensions in this Latin American reality.

Life and Death: All is alive in this autochthonous *pacha* (cosmic and historic space and time); all is mutually connected, sacred, and has both good and evil dimensions. Life begins with birth, with marriage, with physical death (one who dies is born). Dead persons are alive, in a special manner. Fullness of life is a gift of God. Creation and humanity cooperatively nurture life. Material products and physical existence are important, but not absolutes.

Sickness and Healing: Indigenous peoples are aware of both supernatural and natural causes of illness, and they have a holistic therapeutic system. Though fatalistic as a result of facing harsh situations, people do everything in human and spiritual terms to heal and be healed. The mentally retarded are usually seen as victims of evil superior forces, such as a bad place or spirit, an accident, or a bad experience, and are treated with compassion. They are often considered close to God, so they lead some rituals.

Conflict and Harmony: Every society has its own ways of resolving contradictions and building peace. Indigenous peoples seek, among themselves, reconciliation, and, at times, vengeance and destruction. When they interact with more powerful racial/economic groups, they either build alliances or tolerate subordination. In the case of sick persons—whose condition is often interpreted as due to evil forces—rituals re-establish physical, social, and spiritual harmony.

Violence in the Social Order: Thorough analysis shows the structural nature of violence. Structures, both of the world and internal to the society, are the roots of impoverishment, the lack of public services, and the cause of sickness among the majority of people. From our perspective, this is the central ethical problem, and not what Dr. Tesoro unjustifiably calls "widespread murder" among Indians. Our Christian discourse confronts structural violence. For centuries in Latin America, the poor have been "socially murdered" through hunger, discrimination, capitalism, and co-optation. It is in this context that one must consider a case of neglect towards handicapped persons. It is evident in this case study that first-world professionals cannot assess our reality and are therefore incapable of proposing world policy.

What does this scenario say to persons concerned about Christian ethics? First, it invites us to cross-cultural sensibility and understanding. One may not handle concrete issues without thorough historical and religious study. Only with these resources is it possible to do an ethical critique of, for example, how another culture handles its sick members.

Second, our Indo-American scenario contains its forms of Christianity, which some call syncretic; these Christian forms have their own symbols, codes, and wisdom. A foreign theologian must be in dialogue with local, inculturated Christianity, as well as with other religions and with indifferent and nonreligious groups. Experience shows that dialogue is difficult between indigenous Christianity and contemporary first-world Christianity, characterized by Western rationality with postmodern perspectives.

Third, in our scenario there is a need for both holistic insight—clearly absent in the medical doctors quoted in the case study—and a theological understanding of this reality. We acknowledge, within the human condition, varied forms of revelation and salvation in Christ. An external observer cannot decide what is authentically Christian or moral in any specific situation. Rather, with eyes of faith one gradually discovers in the situation the presence of God and the ways Christian love is or is not put into practice.

Biblical and Theological Principles

So far we have seen the locus, the concrete place and spiritual reality, of Christian ethics. Now we examine people's, preferentially the poor's, right to life, in the struggle for which God is encountered (see Mt 25:31–46; Jn 1:27, 2:14–25, 5:1–6). This is the source of our theological ethics. St. Augustine called the world a first book and the Bible a second book. Revelation comes to us through the Spirit of truth (Jn 14:17). So, Creation/Word/Spirit are the sources of Christian ethics; they sustain church guidelines and discourses. We will consider these elements in terms of care of our neighbor, especially the sick and marginalized.

Imagery of God: Indigenous spirituality admires all as sacred, as signs of God's saving presence. From this starting point, the good news says that women and men are created as images of God (Gen 1:27) and recreated in Christ who is image of God (Col 1:15, 3:10–11, Rom 8:29). Due to this theology of creation-salvation, we relate among human beings without discrimination, because each is a divine image. Positively, we acknowledge the crucified and risen Jesus in handicapped persons, who both carry the cross and are glorified.

Unconditional Love: The old law and new law are summarized in love, which implies solidarity with the downtrodden (Mk 12:28–31, Lk 10:27–37). With this ethic of love, Jesus and all his disciples remove evil forces and relieve the suffering multitude (Lk 6: 17–19, Mk 6, 7, 12). We also accept children and the poor as the most important concern (Lk 9:46–48, 22:24–27, Mk 9:33–37, Mt 18:1–4). This is a qualitative, unconditional love. God is who loves first, sending Jesus Christ to save all. Human beings are respected, not in retribution for something good they have done, but simply because the example of God's merciful, gratuitous love calls us to do so. Furthermore, in imitation of Christ, love is the gift of life (Jn 15: 9, 12, 13). Everyday Christian witness and the Latin American martyrs of today signal this mystery.

As Christians we are moved, and judged, by these unconditional relationships. These principles guide our care of the sick and the impoverished, including the mentally retarded. The ethical norm is unconditional care of such persons, following Christ's gift of life. The living Word forbids indifference toward and killing of handicapped persons. This saving law comes from God, whose Spirit leads all toward life.

Guidelines and Discourses: According to Catholic tradition, the people of God have sensibility and wisdom, a *sensus fidei*.[2] Thus, the body of the faithful recognizes what is true or false, good or evil. So, normative and doctrinal roles belong to both the laity and the hierarchy. In this case study, the Irish nun voices the sense of faith of the common people: "the death of this little angel was God's will," the God who prefers that "everyone was fed."

The Catholic hierarchy gives us guidelines—from within the local church, from the councils of bishops presided over by the pope, from the teachings of the pope and institutions of the Vatican. These permanently remind us that the sick are to be taken care of, that no one may be killed outside of situations of self-defense. All human beings, regardless of their particular features or religious affiliations, are neighbors—sisters and brothers in the universal Body of Christ.

A special issue is euthanasia, that is, helping the very sick to die when they wish to do so either by not providing extraordinary, disproportionate care which extends their physical existence, or by directly providing a therapy that leads the sick to death. The Vatican Congregation for the Faith clearly states that no one may authorize death or determine it for oneself or for others; however, it is licit to refrain from extraordinary treatment which extends a painful existence. These principles, originally developed for and usually applied to medical ethics, are also critically important in socio-economic terms. Most poor peoples of the world are undergoing unjust death while they barely survive, due to malnutrition, unemployment, a merciless global market, endemic sickness, and exploitation of women and children. This "world order" kills our people prematurely, even before their definitive death.[3]

Ethical discourse by Catholic scholars and ministers[4] offers both good insights and open questions. Most consider euthanasia an evil that is ethically unacceptable, because life is a fundamental, though nonabsolute, value. However, some of these scholars and authors defend euthanasia of newborns who are not normal. Some consider that, in subjective terms, euthanasia is not necessarily murder. All the authors claim the sacred character of life, giving preference to the most vulnerable and poor. Physical existence is defended together with quality of life. There are many questions and there is much debate over the loving responsibility to alleviate suffering while not destroying life.

Our Christian principles are not mere objects of truth; they require the community of faith, the church, who develops its discernment and who prays over its ethical responsibilities.

A Case of Omission

The case study focuses on indigenous mistreatment of a retarded child. He is given less food and care than other persons are; he is weak and will probably die during a harsh winter. This case and its context demand some clarifications.

The extended indigenous family normally takes excellent care of the sick, the elderly, and orphans. I have firsthand knowledge of these common situations. My work includes deep interaction with different social and ethnic groups in Latin America. I strongly affirm that native peoples take care of persons judged useless in the modern myth of economic utility. However, among indigenous persons there are some blatant injustices. The less poor and the men receive more food and social opportunities than do those who are poorer and women. I am told by health specialists that only in very rare cases are infants and children with physical and mental handicaps neglected and led to death.

Critique of Professionals: In impoverished regions we urgently need collaboration among all agents of humanization. Those of us with a professional status must interact deeply with the local population, as the medical doctors in this case study do not do. In a brief two weeks, they supposedly cover (!) our continent; they alone, without joint planning with the poor and local health personnel, decide on a policy of international pressure. Their judgments of the situation range from "barbarism" and "widespread murder" to "neglect" towards the mentally retarded. It is their behavior that seems immoral, not that of indigenous peoples.

Matters of life and death demand that professionals and common people work seriously and strategically together. Those excluded from modern well-being are neither heard nor consulted by those in power. We need an honest critique of the neocolonialism shown by these professionals.

Ethics of the Voiceless: In this case study, only a Catholic nun is in communion with the poor: She says it is not a case of murder, and she favors grassroots organizations to diminish poverty. Indigenous Christians have their ethic of care for mother earth, of symmetric relationships, of walking in community and with God. In this particular case, parents and "health promoters" are ethically responsible: they have lowered infant mortality by half in five years. So, ordinary people are bearers of an evangelical ethic of love.

This happens in the midst of institutionalized violence. The data is overwhelming, making us cry for justice.[5] In Peru, the infant mortality rate is forty-eight out of 1,000 live births; 40,000 Peruvian children under five years of age die every year because of diarrhea, pneumonia, etc.; 49 percent of children suffer physical abuse; 94 percent of the mentally retarded have no professional health attention. In this case study, the family has a one-room house, two sons died of measles, and two are alive. In the midst of this modern holocaust, one admires the ethical dignity and solidarity of the poor, the autochthonous norms in favor of well-being. In a special way I admire how they take care of the sick and retarded.

Urgent Strategizing: Ethical behavior by ordinary persons is admirable, especially under difficult circumstances. But there is also evidence of active abuse—physical, psychological, sexual, and socio-economic—and also of neglect and omission concerning children's fundamental rights. These facts are like a siren, calling us to intelligent and efficient strategy, so as to provide better private and public care of all children, and in a special way, of retarded children.

On the part of health personnel, prevention and education in human rights goes hand in hand with both assisting the sick and effecting structural social changes. The family and the local community may strengthen care networks and autochthonous wisdom so as to improve care for sick and mistreated persons. But all this strategizing has powerful cultural enemies: contemporary family disintegration; persons measured by monetary benefits so that the sick, elderly, and the retarded are discarded; and more indifference because the "I" has become absolute. As these modern factors infect previously healthy cultures such as the indigenous, they have devastating effects.

On the issue of death inflicted on the mentally retarded, health professionals of different areas tell me it is most exceptional. When there is a case, it is kept secret. There is no official data, because it is murder, punishable by law. What does happen more often is neglect of and discrimination against the mentally retarded. These evils can be resolved through local community agents of change, as a part of a larger strategy that confronts the social order which silently kills the poor's right to thrive.

Intercultural Ethical Concerns

Due to globalization, most people live in multicultural realities which have specific ethical and theological challenges. Indigenous peoples face these challenges; so do peoples in the First World.

Secular and Traditional Values: Modern, secular values—freedom from external norms, autonomous action, being a person, religious pluralism, and moral positivism—are reshaping the mentalities and behavior of so-called traditional peoples. The other side of the story is that secular sectors are confused and wish to reinforce family values, religious truths, and norms of natural law. So, many intercultural challenges are good.

There are also negative realities. Modern "success" has no mercy for handicapped persons. Massacres of handicapped persons, like the Nazi elimination of 80,000 retarded persons, do not happen anymore. Today's violence against the retarded is more subtle and widespread: hedonism destroys personal and cultural hopes, moral relativism allows domination over the weak, and the mentally retarded are rejected by a rationalist society and by a unilateral market economy.

Dialogue among cultural worlds is for the sake of ethical corrections, of transforming social evils. It is not a question of choosing either the secular or the traditional perspective. In both, one discovers some moral good and theological truth. With what criteria should we examine these perspectives?

The Christian criteria are life, created and saved, and love in an unconditional way, as lived and taught by Jesus of Nazareth.

Global Solidarity: Ecologists and feminists of today, and indigenous peoples of the last 20,000 years, remind us that earth is life's mystery and a common house, though exploited by humans. Real solidarity is global; it is joyous sharing among plants, animals, minerals, humans, spirits, artifacts, and arts.

Therefore, our moral responsibility is holistic. Any abuse against a flower, animal, handicapped child, and so on hurts the whole universe and hurts the living God. On the other side, kindness and collaboration with any being benefits all. We either destroy or build life together. Theologically speaking, on the one hand we share evil and sinfulness, and on the other hand we share grace and justification through faith.

Intercultural Challenges: Indigenous persons, as in this case study, learn from others, just as others grow because of them. There are also mutual confrontations and challenges. One may question the other, due not to ethnocentricity or to cultural manipulation, but rather in terms of the fundamental value of life, nurtured and loved by all.

In terms of health care, societies develop different types of knowledge and therapy; these enrich each other. This mutual exchange is an ethical duty; for example, for the sake of integral care of vulnerable individuals and groups. City people could well imitate the way the indigenous poor treat their elderly, and indigenous peasants may benefit from modern prevention of infant mortality.

Moreover, each person and each society must contribute to the holistic healing of creation and of globalized modernity. In this context, care of marginalized persons goes together with, or is part of, the struggle for holistic development. This, in an Indian or any other situation is not done from outside. Rather, "traditional values harbor within them a latent dynamism which can serve as the springboard for modes of development that are more humane than those derived from outside paradigms."[6] Authentic and deep development starts and finishes at the heart of each people's journey. This journey—rooted in each cultural and religious universe—inspires others to continue along their different paths toward a new earth and a new heaven.

Conclusions

A case study of neglect towards the mentally retarded is placed within the global norm of solidarity, of nurturing in this earth a renewed human condition. We examine a local form of world Christianity, enlightened by the principle of being images of God and the principle of Christ's and the disciples' unconditional love. We underline intercultural challenges, including a critique of medical personnel who unethically say that Indians murder the mentally handicapped. The ethical values of the poor contribute to other sectors of society. So, first-world persons—like myself and like you, patient reader of this essay!—are enriched by so-called primitive peoples, peoples who, rather than being primitive, are primordial communities inviting us all to rediscover our humanity within the earth and to redesign global development so it will be at the service of poor and hope-filled persons.

Notes

1. See Xavier Albo, *Raices de America, el mundo aymara* (Madrid: Alianza, 1988); M.S. Cipolletti, *La muerte y el mas alla en las cultural indigenas latinoamericanas* (Quito, Ecuador: Abya Yala, 1992).

2. Vatican II, *Lumen Gentium* (Dogmatic constitution on the church), n. 12, in Austin Flannery, OP, ed., *Vatican II: The Conciliar and Post Conciliar Documents* (Collegeville, MN: Liturgical Press, 1975).

3. Congregation for the Doctrine of the Faith, "Declaration on Euthanasia" (5 May 1980), in Austin Flannery, OP, ed., *Vatican Council II: More Postconciliar Documents*, vol. 2 (Northport, NY: Costello Publishing, 1982), 510–17.

4. See L. Rossi and A. Valsecchi, eds., *Diccionario enciclopedia de teología moral* (Madrid: Paulinas, 1980), 368; M. Vidal, *Moral de actitudes II* (Madrid: PS, 1978), 244; E. Lopez, *Etica y vida* (Madrid: Paulinas, 1990), 114, 220–24; F. Moreno, *Teología moral desde los pobres* (Madrid: PS, 1986), 91–119; A. Moser and B. Leers, *Teología moral: conflictos y alternativas* (Madrid: Paulinas, 1987).

5. See UNICEF/INEI, *Estado de la niñez: adolescencia y la mujer in el Peru* (Lima: 1996), 5 and 9; Conferencia Episcopal Peruana, *Campana Compartir 1997: enfermos mentales, Documento de base, 1997*.

6. Denis Goulet, "Development: Historical Task or Opening to Transcendence?" *Cross Currents* 46, no. 2 (1996):225.

AN INDO-TIBETAN BUDDHIST RESPONSE
by Vesna A. Wallace

The tragic situation of mentally handicapped children in the altiplano and other impoverished areas of Latin America and the difficult choices that their parents face would likely evoke different responses from different Buddhist traditions and communities. Such different Buddhist responses would not stem from some fundamental disparity in their doctrinal and ethical teachings but rather from the ways in which they interpret and practically apply their common principles of the ethical evaluation of action (*karma*). Another contributing factor to the possible diversity of responses would be the influences of the prevailing local cultures and social norms within Buddhist communities. One of the essential Buddhist principles of the ethical evaluation of action, which is common to all Buddhist traditions, is the principle of intentionality. The Buddhist principle of intentionality emphasizes the motivation behind the action, and not the action itself, as the determining factor of the ethical quality of the action. If one's motivation for action comes from a malevolent attitude toward others, the resultant action is considered nonvirtuous, even though it may outwardly appear virtuous. On the other hand, if one's underlying motivation is based on compassion and sincere interest for the welfare of others but circumstances require harsh action, the resultant action is considered virtuous. For example, in the broader context of Mahayana Buddhist ethics, one is allowed—although not encouraged—to perform harsh acts, including killing another human being, if doing so would save the lives of a larger group of people. This is permissible, however, only if one's underlying motivation is compassion for the individuals whose lives are in danger and for the perpetrator who is about to commit an evil act and suffer the negative karmic consequences. Unfortunately, the Buddhist canonical texts that assert intentionality as the factor determining whether a specific action is virtuous or nonvirtuous do not offer ample examples of situations to which this principle of action applies. Thus, they leave space for ambiguities and for different interpretations that depend on the degree to which a particular Buddhist community chooses to extend this principle.

Furthermore, within Buddhist canonical literature I have found no illustrations of mental retardation and of the ways in which the mentally handicapped are to be treated. The reason for that may be two-fold. First, Buddhist scriptures are primarily aimed at leading people to spiritual liberation, but the mentally handicapped are, on the whole, regarded as incapable of engaging in that discipline. Second, although Buddhist literature includes many references to medicine, mental retardation was thought to be incurable, and, therefore, it has received little attention even within the medical context. The closest references to mental retardation can be found in several Buddhist texts[1] that mention the inopportune times and unfavorable conditions for practicing Buddhist *dharma*, into which one can be easily born. One such unfavorable condition is the impairment of the sense-faculties, including the mental faculty. In the *Sangiti Sutta*, Buddha Sakyamuni states that even though one may be born in a Buddhist country where Buddhist teachings are easily available, one can be born mentally retarded, deaf, dumb, or unable to discern whether something has been correctly or incorrectly taught.[2] Due to their inability to evaluate teachings and to participate in rigorous monastic discipline, those with impaired mental faculties have not been allowed to join the Buddhist monastic order to this very day. To my knowledge, this is the only restriction that has been imposed on the mentally handicapped by the Buddhist tradition.

Somewhat different ethical evaluations of the treatment of mentally impaired Latin American children may also be made on the basis of the Buddhist awareness of the relativity of ethical judgements, which is based on Buddhist teachings that encourage one to use one's own intelligence and power of judgment, instead of relying on doctrinal principles alone. *The Sutta on the Advice to Rahula at Amballatthika* defines the ethical quality of an action on the basis of its result. If an action—whether bodily, verbal, or mental—ultimately leads to unpleasant results for oneself, for others, or for both, it is considered nonvirtuous; but if in the long run it brings about pleasant results for oneself, for others, or for both, it is considered virtuous.[3] In the same text, Buddha Sakyamuni insists that on repeated reflection, each individual has to decide for himself or herself whether a certain action is virtuous or nonvirtuous.

When taking into account the Buddhist perspective on the role of intention in determining the ethical status of action, the manner in which mentally handicapped children are treated in Latin America represents a challenge to any Buddhist tradition for ethical evaluation. The motivation behind parents' neglect of these children seems to be based on their genuine concern for the physical welfare of the remaining members of the family who are struggling to survive in difficult circumstances. On the other hand, their intentional negligence regarding the mentally handicapped child's physical needs, their awareness that such oversight will indirectly cause the child's premature death, and their deliberate disregard for the child's right to live are serious violations of the leading principles of Buddhist ethics—namely, nonviolence (*ahimsa*) and compassion (*karuna*).

The first precept of Buddhist ethical discipline is not taking the life of any sentient being and not encouraging others to do so. This initial precept does not merely apply to the avoidance of killing but to the abstention from all forms of injury to others. It is founded on the recognition of the inherent worth and equal right of all beings to life. In the Indo-Tibetan Buddhist tradition, the inherent value of all sentient beings is based on the Buddhist Mahayana view of the ultimate nature of sentient beings and their consciousness. According to some Indo-Tibetan Mahayana schools, all sentient beings are endowed with the potential for spiritual awakening, regardless of their present condition. According to others, all sentient beings are already buddhas, or spiritually-awakened beings, even though their enlightenment has not yet manifested itself. Hence, by bringing harm to someone, one inflicts harm either to a potential buddha or to an actual buddha. Even though a mentally retarded individual is unable to pursue the path to spiritual awakening in this life, he or she is still recognized as a potential buddha or essentially as a buddha. The rationale here is that he or she may have the opportunity to follow the Buddhist path in another life and eventually to actualize either his potential or inherent spiritual awakening. Also, it is said in the *Vasala Sutta*, an early Buddhist canonical text, that "whoever destroys life, whether bird or animal, insect or fish, has no compassion for life. . . ."[4]

When compassion is to be extended to all living beings, including the smallest of animals, it goes without saying that in the light of Buddhist ethics, one must regard all human beings, *without exception*, with compassion. According to Buddhist teachings, compassion is not merely sympathy for those who are in distress or a desire to remove the suffering of others; it is an active engagement in counteracting and annihilating others' suffering. It manifests as nonviolence, or absence of cruelty, and it is directly aroused by seeing the helplessness of those in distress.[5] Compassion is seen in Buddhism as one of the four most virtuous attitudes toward sentient beings. The other three are loving kindness (*maitri*), empathetic joy (*mudita*), and equanimity (*upeksa*). They are regarded as complementary to compassion and are closely interconnected with it. Loving kindness is a desire to bring well-being to all sentient beings, and it is seen as directly arising from perceiving all beings as lovable.[6] It is manifest as an altruistic sentiment, described in the *Metta Sutta* in the following way: "Whatever living beings there be: feeble or strong, tall, stout or medium, short, small or large, without exception; seen or unseen, those dwelling far or near, those who are born and those who are to be born, may all beings be happy."[7] Empathetic joy means rejoicing in others' happiness. Equanimity refers to the feeling of impartiality toward all beings and seeing all beings as equal in terms of their desire for happiness and their wish to escape suffering. If an Indo-Tibetan Buddhist were to evaluate the treatment of mentally handicapped children in Latin America from the standpoint of these four attitudes, he or she could not condone it, for it clearly defies these four Buddhist ethical ideals.

The Buddhist ethical ideals discussed here, together with the Buddhist Bodhisattva ideal of cultivating the spirit of awakening (*bodhicitta*) and sacrificing oneself for the sake of others, have constituted the foundation of Buddhist social activism and the Mahayana call for universal responsibility. Already, in its early stages in India, Buddhism expressed interest in the social, economic, and political welfare of every individual in society. As the *Cakkavattisihanda Sutta* attests, since its inception, Buddhism recognized poverty as one of the leading causes of numerous social problems, beginning with crime and violence and ending with the short life span of children.[8] Another early Buddhist canonical text, the *Kutadanta Sutta*, proposes the following solution to social problems induced by poverty: improve the economic conditions of farmers, ranchers, merchants, and government workers by a ruler or a government, and provide them with grain and fodder, investment capital, and proper wages.[9] Buddhism would offer to today's governments of Latin America the same advice it gave to ancient Indian society.

Later Indian Buddhist Mahayana texts continued to teach that the socioeconomic administration of society should be based on prudence and compassion. According to the Mahayana *sutra* called the *Dasacakrakṣitigarbha*, one of the ways to maintain social welfare is to create opportunities for incapable people to earn a livelihood.[10] This text advocates that those with little knowledge and education, and *unintelligent* individuals as well, should be provided with work suitable to their abilities and needs, thus enabling them to generate moderate wages. This recommendation implies that mentally handicapped individuals who can be trained to perform limited tasks should not be discriminated against or discarded as useless members of society. Rather, they should be allowed to lead active and meaningful lives. With regard to individuals who are either unable to work or cannot find work, Nagarjuna, a renowned Indian Buddhist adept of the second century CE, in *Precious Garland: An Epistle to a King*, advises the king to provide provisions for those who are unable to take care of themselves. He counsels: "Allow the blind, the sick, the downtrodden, homeless, destitute, and handicapped, all equally, to find food and drink, without omission."[11] Thus, from the Buddhist perspective, treatment of the disabled is, undoubtedly, one of the best tests of the humanity of a nation. At the same time, it may also indicate the inadequate economic and social development of a particular nation. As I pointed out earlier, the Indo-Tibetan Buddhist tradition recognizes that poverty may lead to inhumanity and cruelty. Therefore, we could say that in view of Buddhist social teachings, treatment of the disabled in Latin America is a test of both the humanity and socioeconomic development of Latin America. Even Buddhist medical texts assert that inadequate diet, whether during gestation or after birth, causes humoral imbalances in the body that may result in different types of mental disorders. However, Buddhist medical texts also teach that loving care is a crucial treatment for mental disorders. According to Indo-Tibetan Buddhist medicine, even though positive surroundings and nourishing food cannot eliminate mental retardation, they can build the individual's strength and resistance and thereby induce occasional moments of lucidity, during which a spiritual teacher may affect the individual's consciousness and secure a better rebirth for that person.[12] Thus, in terms of Indo-Tibetan Buddhism, poverty should not be used as an excuse for the ill-treatment of mentally disabled children, but it should be treated as an unfavorable condition that at times can bring out reprehensible qualities and actions of individuals and of a nation as a whole.

In solving this societal problem, the Indo-Tibetan Buddhist tradition would recommend the same methods it implements in solving the problem of individual suffering. That is, once the primary and immediate causes of one's suffering are identified, the antidotes that can eradicate these causes are sought out and applied. This approach is based on the common Buddhist principle of causality, or the principle of interdependence, according to which every event arises only from its own causes and conditions. If poverty and inadequate social welfare in Latin America are the primary social conditions for the existence of mental retardation and the bad treatment of mentally disabled children there, then that nation should seek ways in which its economic and social conditions can be improved. Just as the spiritual development of an individual in Indo-Tibetan Buddhism is a gradual process that requires the individual's sustained effort and determination in spiritual practice, so the social and economic development of a nation entails a gradual process that requires the sustained effort of the entire nation.

At the same time, whenever there is suffering and negative actions, Mahayana Buddhism sees an urgent need for eradicating such suffering and negative deeds. Thus, in the context of Indo-Tibetan Buddhism, the tragic situation of mentally disabled children in Latin America calls for the urgent intervention on the part of everyone—from each individual to each nation as a whole—even if there is only a little benefit at the beginning. The contemporary spiritual leader of Tibetan Buddhism and the Nobel Peace Laureate, the Fourteenth Dalai Lama, commented in his booklet entitled *The Global Community and the Need for Universal Responsibility* that "in our present circumstances, none of us can afford to assume that somebody else will solve our problem; each of us must take his or her own share of universal responsibility."[13]

In that respect, from the Indo-Tibetan Buddhist perspective, the treatment of disabled children in Latin America is also seen as one of the best tests of the humanity of the entire global community. Buddhist texts of different traditions and periods have equally advocated generosity and sharing of material resources with those in need. Mahayana Buddhism strongly emphasizes generosity (*dana*) not only as a soteriological virtue—that is, a virtue that one must practice in order to achieve liberation—but also as a social virtue arising from compassion and from the feeling of universal responsibility that manifests itself in social action. Therefore, when a poor community or a nation is unable to provide adequate conditions for its mentally disabled children and adults, then the task of helping the undeveloped nation to cope with such social problems becomes the responsibility of economically more developed communities and nations. According to Mahayana Buddhism, universal responsibility stems primarily from seeing the equality between oneself and others, disregarding race, nationality, and so on. The eighth-century Indian sage Santideva expressed it in these words:

> I should eliminate the suffering of others because it is suffering, just like my own suffering. I should take care of others because they are sentient beings, just as I am a sentient being.

> When happiness is equally dear to others and to myself, then what is so special about me that I strive after happiness for myself alone?[14]

Thus, Buddhist teachings on social ethics and universal responsibility of the individual and community urge all—Latin American nations and the communities and the nations of the world—to take on their responsibility to mentally handicapped individuals everywhere.

Notes

1. The *Digha-nikaya*, III, 265; *Dahmmasangani*; *Siksasamuccaya*, ch. 1 [2], which cites the *Jayosmayatanavimoksa* passage of the *Gandavyuha*; *Suhrllekh*, vs. 63–64.

2. The *Sangiti Sutta* of the *Digha Nikaya*, III, 265 (4), in *Thus Have I Heard: The Long Discourses of the Buddha*, trans. Maurice Walshe (London: Wisdom Publications, 1987), 507.

3. *The Ambballatthikarahulovaddasutta* of the *Majjhima Nikaya*, I. 414, in *The Middle Length Discourses of the Buddha: A New Translation of the Majjhima Nikaya*, trans. Bhikhu Nanamoli and Bhikhu Bodhi. (Boston: Wisdom Publications, 1995), 523–26.

4. The *Vasala Sutta* of the *Suttanipata.*, trans. H. Saddhatissa. (London: Curzon Press, 1985), vv. 117, 13.

5. See Bhadantacariya Buddhaghosa, *The Path of Purification* (*Visuddhimagga*), trans. Bhikhu Nanamoli (Kandy, Sri Lanka: Buddhist Publication Society, 1979), IX, 92, 94, 343–44.

6. See Bhadantacariya Buddhaghosa, *The Path of Purification*, IX, 93, 344.

7. The *Metta Sutta* of the *Suttanipata*, trans. H. Saddhatissa. (London: Curzon Press, 1985), vs. 146–47, 16.

8. The *Cakkavattisihanada Sutta* of the *Digha Nikaya*, III, 65–73, in Walshe, *Thus Have I Heard*, 398–402.

9. The *Kutadanta Sutta* of the *Digha Nikaya*, I, 36, in Walshe, *Thus Have I Heard*, 135.

10. *The Dasacakraksitigarbhanamamahayanasutra* (preserved in Tibetan transla-tion as *'Dus pa chen po las sa'i snying po'i 'khor lo bsu pa zhes bya ba theg pa chen po'i mdo*), in the Derge edition of the Kangyur, *mdo, zha*, 101.1.

11. *Ratnavali*, Ch. 4, v. 20. For a slightly different translation see Acarya Nagarjuna, *The Precious Garland: An Epistle to a King*, trans. John Dunne and Sara McClintock (Boston: Wisdom Publications, 1997), 60.

12. See Terry Clifford, *Tibetan Buddhist Medicine and Psychiatry: The Diamond Healing* (York Beach, ME: Samuel Weiser, 1992).

13. Tenzin Gyatso the Fourteenth Dalai Lama, *The Global Community and the Need for Universal Responsibility* (Boston: Wisdom Publications, 1990), 6.

14. Santideva, *A Guide to the Bodhisattva Way of Life*, trans. Vesna A. Wallace and B. Alan Wallace (Ithaca, NY: Snow Lion Publications, 1997), ch. 8, vv. 94–95, 101.

Bibliography and Suggested Reading

Albo, Xavier. *Raices de America, el mundo aymara*. Madrid: Alianza, 1988.

Cipolletti, M.S. *La muerte y el mas alla en las cultural indigenas latinoamericanas*. Quito, Ecuador: Abya Yala, 1992.

Clifford, Terry. *Tibetan Buddhist Medicine and Psychiatry: The Diamond Healing*. York Beach, ME: Samuel Weiser, 1992.

Goulet, Denis. "Development: Historical Task or Opening to Transcendence?" *Cross Currents* 46, no. 2 (1996):225.

Lopez, E. *Etica y vida*. Madrid: Paulinas, 1990.

The Middle Length Discourses of the Buddha: A New Translation of the Majjhima Nikaya. Trans. Bhikhu Nanamoli and Bhikhu Bodhi. Boston: Wisdom Publica-tions, 1995.

Moreno, F. *Teología moral desde los pobres*. Madrid: PS, 1986.

Moser, A., and B. Leers. *Teología moral: conflictos y alternativas*. Madrid: Paulinas, 1987.

Rossi, L., and A. Valsecchi, eds. *Diccionario enciclopedia de teología moral*. Madrid: Paulinas, 1980.

Santideva. *A Guide to the Bodhisattva Way of Life*. Trans. Vesna A. Wallace and B. Alan Wallace. Ithaca, NY: Snow Lion Publications, 1997.

Tenzin Gyatso the Fourteenth Dalai Lama. *The Global Community and the Need for Universal Responsibility*. Boston: Wisdom Publications, 1990.

Thus Have I Heard: The Long Discourses of the Buddha. Trans. Maurice Walshe. London: Wisdom Publications, 1987.

Vidal, M. *Moral de actitudes II*. Madrid: PS, 1978.

CHAPTER 18

Parental Rights in the Age of AIDS

A CASE STUDY by Christine E. Gudorf

Anna gave a sigh as she pulled into the parking lot at the juvenile justice complex. "Not a vacant spot in sight at 8:15," she thought out loud. "I bet our first few cases are double-booked again." Pulling out of the crowded lot, she drove down the street and found a spot several blocks away. She began to walk away from the car, then doubled back, unlocked the door and reached into the car. "Last month this ignition-kill switch probably saved me a stolen car," she thought, remembering her panic at returning to her car at the end of the day to find the trunk ajar and the driver's door lock punched in. As she locked the door and walked toward the court building she reflected on the irony of the fact that the juvenile justice complex should be the center of so much crime.

"We have a full schedule all day, and we're double-booked for the first three slots due to resets from last month," announced Paula, the review specialist, as Anna entered the hearing room and greeted the other members of her judicial panel. Anna was the chair of the panel of the Florida Foster Care Citizen Review Program which met on the fourth Wednesday of every month. Foster care in Florida had had such poor case management in the past that state law now mandated that the case of every child in foster care be reviewed twice a year by a panel of trained volunteers. The panel sent the judges both evaluations of the adequacy of the casework by county workers in Florida's Department of Children and Families (DCF) and specific recommendations regarding the care and placement of children in foster care. Each panel consisted of four trained volunteers, three of whom were required for a hearing, as well as a staff member of Florida Foster Care Citizen Review, called a review specialist, who prepared the case summaries in advance, set cases on judges' calendars, and sent the panels' recommendations on to the judges. In some cases, only the DCF caseworker appeared at the hearing before the panel, while in others the hearing room would be bursting with the children, the foster parents, the parents, the DCF worker, a guardian *ad litem* for the child or children, and attorneys for some or all of these.

"This is the first hearing of this first case," Paula explained as she distributed the case summaries. "You'll notice that all four children came into DCF care five years ago when the mother became too ill to care for them. She subsequently died. The children were placed with a couple who a few months later moved to Sarasota and were allowed to take the children with them. But there was a glitch in the system, and the case hasn't been followed or reviewed either there or here for five years. The file was lost until the foster parents recently contacted DCF about a problem with one child's Medicaid card."

"Wonderful," said Sissy, a long-term panel member. "Another DCF screw-up. Undoubtedly the excuse will be that the old DCF worker quit at the same time." The turnover in DCF workers, due to low pay, high case loads, and a terribly inefficient bureaucracy, was notorious. Few cases kept the same worker longer than six months because every resignation and hiring created a wave of reassigned cases in each unit. Fully half of all reviews involved caseworkers who had been on the case less than eight weeks.

"But wait a minute," said Earl, another panelist, peering at the case summary. "From their names, these kids seem to be Haitian, and it says the first and second graders are in ESL (English as a second language) programs. But the name of the church where the foster parents have the twins in kindergarten has a Spanish name. Tell me these Haitian kids weren't placed with foster parents who only speak Spanish!"

"It gets worse," said Patricia, the fourth panelist. "Look on page eleven; it says that the foster mother is fifty-six and in poor health but wants to keep the children as long as possible."

Paula suggested, "Let's start the hearing so we can get some answers from the DCF worker." At nods from the rest of the panel, Anna walked to the waiting room. The DCF worker was the only person waiting for this case. As she sat down at the table in the hearing room, she handed Anna the telephone number of the foster mother in Sarasota who wanted to be present by speaker phone. The worker confirmed that the foster mother spoke only Spanish and so needed a translator.

"Well, that answered that question," muttered Sissy as Anna called for a court interpreter and then dialed the foster mother's number. The translator arrived and the hearing formally began.

After questioning both the foster mother and the DCF worker, the panel learned that both parents were dead, that the four United States-born children of Haitian descent had come into DCF care at the ages of two-and-a-half, one-and-a-half, and the twins at six months. They had all been placed with a Hispanic couple of fifty-one and fifty-six who had one eight-year-old adopted child of their own in their home. The wife had severe diabetes, which was now causing circulatory problems and vision impairment; the husband had recently quit work due to unspecified health problems. The couple wanted to keep the children for now but did not expect their health would allow more than another few years of care.

As the DCF worker walked out and Anna hung up the phone, the panel gave a collective sigh. "What a terrible way to start a long day!" exclaimed Sissy. "There's not even anybody to yell at now. What do we do? Tear the kids away from the only home they remember? I'm not even sure that this couple can effectively parent now. How does a person with swollen purple legs like Mrs. Martinez describes—or a sixty-one year old on disability— keep up with five, six, and seven year olds?"

Earl responded, "For me, it doesn't matter whether or not they can effectively parent now. They say that there is no way their health will allow them to raise these children to 18. These kids are probably adoptable now, but by the time the Martinezes have to give them up, they almost certainly won't be, and certainly not as a group." They all knew that the younger the child, the more adoptable, and they frequently struggled to balance the need for due process in terminating parental rights with the need to get homeless children into adoptable status as soon as possible. Many of the "foster homes" into which they placed children, especially children over twelve, were more like small institutions than families and had anywhere from eight to fifteen teenagers, usually all of the same sex, living with a couple who simply could not provide the care and attention that so many of these children desperately needed, especially those who had suffered abuse or neglect before they came into foster care or in earlier foster placements.

"Do you really think they have a chance of being adopted as a group now?" asked Anna. "It would be very unusual. Maybe when they were babies. But four children is a lot to take on at one time, and black children are sometimes harder to place—and these are four black children who speak only Spanish, which pretty much rules out adoption by Haitian or Anglo families."

"I know it doesn't do any good to cry over spilled milk," added Patricia, "but why on earth were these children not put on the adoption exchange when they first came into care? The mother was dying, the father was dead— and they were all babies! Why any delay at all in pursuing adoption?"

"Which brings up the question of what the parents died of," said Earl. "I know it's stereotypes, but we have two dead young Haitians here—was it AIDS?"

Anna and Paula immediately responded, "We can't ask that question." Paula waved to Anna to continue. "It's a matter of confidentiality, and with AIDS the consequences of dissemination of health information can be so harmful. So the nature of an illness or the cause of death is not specified— that's policy. If they died of AIDS we just say "terminal illness.""

Sissy replied, "That's the dumbest thing I ever heard of. If we can't ask what the parents died of, then how can we know whether or not to inquire as to whether the children were ever tested for HIV, or whether they should be tested now? DCF has a duty to the foster parents, to the health care workers who care for HIV-positive children, maybe even to the teachers who might bandage a bloodied knee, to let them know so that they can protect themselves. Why should we assume that DCF did the proper thing five years ago with regard to testing, when they didn't with regard to adoption or appropriate foster placement? They didn't even obey the law that requires a review every six months!"

Anna responded, "Okay, I see the problem. How about we set the case before Judge Weinstein next month and order DCF to either have the children tested for HIV and bring the results or to provide the judge with evidence as to why HIV testing is unnecessary?"

"That seems okay," said Sissy. "Will the judge take the time to look at the file and figure out why the issue came up?"

"I'll send a memo to the judge's clerk that will explain our concern," said Paula, at which the panel members nodded. They decided to recommend that DCF should, at the same time, defend both the out-of-language placement and the case goal of long-term foster care; DCF should explain to the judge why adoption had not been and still was not the goal of the case.

Patricia noted that it was about ten, and they had not yet heard the second case set for nine o'clock, much less the two set for 9:45. "I guess I can forget running to the bank over lunch hour," muttered Sissy.

Two minutes into the second case, they were into controversy again.

Anna had asked the DCF worker, "What can you tell us about how Jorge is doing since the last review?"

The worker had replied, "There have been no changes."

Patricia followed up: "Do you mean that the results of the psychiatric tests still haven't come back after six months?"

"I don't know. I am just the DCF worker for judiciary hearings. This child has been assigned to an outside agency, the Children's Welfare Service, and is being followed by their caseworker. I only handle the court aspects," explained the worker. "I have never seen the child or any personal records."

"Then," said Anna, "you are not in a position to be able to give us any information about the health, education, or mental status of this child, or how he is relating to his foster placement?"

"No, ma'am," said the worker.

"In that case," said Patricia, "I think we need to set the case before the judge and send notice to the caseworker from Children's Welfare Service to be there." The rest of the panel nodded in agreement.

"But I'm the worker who handles the judiciary aspects," insisted the DCF social worker vehemently. "That is the arrangement that DCF made with the Children's Welfare Service—they don't have to come to any of the court proceedings."

Paula stood, and walking toward the worker, explained, "Our job is to investigate the adequacy of the care of this child. We can't do this by interviewing someone who has no contact with the child, his immediate caretakers, or his personal records. We are setting this one before Judge Crandall as soon as possible. Thank you for coming."

In the discussion immediately following, the panel surmised that DCF's contracting out supervision may have been aimed at saving money by hiring other companies to supervise cases. Those companies were not required to pay benefits to workers and could have even lower standards for hiring than DCF—and it was a perennial joke around the courts that the impossible would happen when any applicant flunked the DCF test for employment. But whatever the motives, the effect of the contracting out of supervision was to nullify judiciary supervision of cases unless the contracted company had to send their workers to the panels. Paula assured them that none of the judges, in her view, would uphold DCF.

By four o'clock, the panel was dragging. They had worked through lunch, gulping Cokes and candy bars delivered between hearings by Serafina, the clerk, and they were still running almost an hour behind. But most difficult had been a string of terribly depressing cases: a twelve-year-old boy who had been physically and sexually abused in a series of foster homes and was now in a psychiatric hospital where his doctors had pronounced him a sexual psychopath without much hope of cure; a sixteen-year-old girl with a two-year-old child in foster care with her had just miscarried after being beaten up by her boyfriend; a ten-year-old child whose mother had attempted to strangle him during postpartum depression continued to languish on a respirator with permanent severe mental impairment.

As the door closed behind the mother's attorney and the DCF worker in the next-to-last hearing of the day, Paula said, "I know this is a hard one, but we need to deal with it quickly because we still have one more. Let's lay out the chief issues. Anna?"

"You know, I have been a panel chair for five years, and I have never doubted the wisdom of the policy on AIDS. But after this case I have to agree with Sissy—it's silly to treat AIDS as if it were asthma or hypertension. Ms. Clark's attorney more or less admitted that this woman has AIDS—she is not just HIV-positive, she has advanced AIDS and has spent much of the last year in and out of the hospital, where she is today. The normal question of whether this woman has fulfilled all the tasks set for her in order to get her children back is just not the central one anymore. I don't care if she did find adequate housing and complete a parenting course and test drug free for 180 days. These kids need a permanent home. They were taken away from her because of her drug use and neglect, they have been in a shelter, then separated into different foster homes for four years, and now she wants them back for a few months—at most a year or two. But their being with her can only be temporary, because she has no family or friends to take care of her kids either when she is too sick or when she is dead. The kids will be back in the DCF system again. I can't agree that another cycle of temporary homes is best for them. As soon as it was clear that she had full-blown AIDS and that the new protease inhibitor drugs were not keeping her helper T-cell count up, the children should have been registered on the adoption exchange."

Earl nodded, then offered, "I hear you, and part of me agrees. But I just remembered a similar case in the panel I was on before I transferred to this one. The only difference was that that mother was white, and we recommended reunification with the kids. I wonder if we, and I include myself in that, are more punitive with black mothers."

"But Earl, I think there are other relevant issues. The older the kids are, the shorter their stay in foster care, the more willing I would be to reunite, even when the mother has a very limited life expectancy. Older kids who want to be reunited, who have good memories of their mother, who have kept in touch with their mother, and who because of their age would be less dependent on her when reunited might have a very hard time with a decision not to reunite. But for younger kids, like these eight and ten year olds, especially as here where there is no larger family network to oversee the situation or take over care when the mother dies—reunification just seems too chancy to me," insisted Sissy. "I would support her right to visitation until she dies, but I wouldn't give her custody. These kids have been jerked around enough. We are supposed to seek safe permanent homes for them."

"I don't want to make problems," inserted Patricia, "but I don't think we can just ignore the fact that the goal on this case has been reunification from the beginning. For four years this mother kept up visitation, though sometimes irregularly, and though it took three years to find a program that could help her kick her habit, she completed the list of tasks that DCF set for her and that we approved as conditions for getting her children back. Now that she has finally done it all we're going to tell her 'Sorry, we changed our minds. You did it all for nothing. Go and die alone?' Doesn't our legal charge by the state say that we are supposed to make recommendations based on the welfare of families, both children and parents? What right have we to put the possible welfare of the children over the clear welfare of the mother?"

At that moment, a loud ringing began. As all of them reached to muffle their ears, the clerk, Serafina, bustled in and shouted over the din, "It's the fire alarm! Probably nothing dangerous, but everybody down the outside stairs. We won't get back in today; take your things with you!"

As they filed down the stairs, Paula shouted that they had no choice but to reset this Clark case for next month, when everyone should come ready to make recommendations. As Anna trudged to her car in the heavy humidity of the Miami summer, she pondered the case and Patricia's question, wondering, "Whose rights and whose welfare take precedence here? And who are we to decide?"

A VODOU RESPONSE by Terry Rey

AIDS demonstrates how economics and politics cannot be separated from disease; indeed, these forces shape our response in powerful ways. In the years ahead we will, no doubt, learn a great deal more about AIDS and how to control it. We will also learn a great deal about the nature of our society from the manner in which we address the disease: AIDS will be a standard by which we may measure not only our medical and scientific skill but also our capacity for justice and compassion.

Allan Brandt[1]

One of religion's most appealing and thus most enduring faculties is its guidance in the negotiation of human suffering and bereavement. The attempt to fathom the issues of pain and death has forever been among the chief generators of religion, as seeking meaning, strength, and solace in the face of insurmountable, seemingly arbitrary, misery and loss is arguably the greatest of religious needs. AIDS has amplified this need for millions over the last quarter-century and in ways that perhaps no other tragedy has because of the stigma and shame that ignorance, homophobia, xenophobia, and racism have cast on the HIV/AIDS community. In light of religion's traditional role of support for the infirm and bereaved, it is as ironic as it is appalling that some religious leaders share the blame for this stigma and shame, as from Nashville to Kinshasa preachers have labeled the AIDS epidemic God's punishment for licentious sexuality, drug abuse, or some other unthinkable, irreligious transgression. Fortunately, the more mindful of Jewish, Muslim, and Christian clerics have not been so woefully oversightful of either the twentieth-century plague's blindly amoral pervasiveness or that staple Semitic doctrine of forgiveness.

Less mainstream traditions in the United States, such as Vodou, which has long been relied on for the negotiation of survival, displacement, and suffering, and independent African-American churches (quite possibly the religious backgrounds of the subjects of the two case studies, respectively), have likewise been forced to confront concretely the epidemic and to serve their practitioners accordingly in the age of AIDS. While certain dimensions of Vodou's reading and negotiation of AIDS are comparable with those of other religions, the Vodouisant[2] etiology of the virus is refreshingly free of the victim-blaming of which some religious communities have been guilty. Vodou's response to AIDS, as will be illustrated below, echoes concerns of the afflicted wherein resonate, through another form of blame, lessons not only about sickness and poverty but also about the unjust social structures that in large part cause them and make HIV/AIDS a "misery seeking missile"[3] on a projection "along the path of least resistance, rapidly becoming a disorder disproportionately striking the poor and the vulnerable,"[4] like the subjects of the two case studies at hand.

Religious Responses to AIDS

In a study of religious responses to AIDS in the United States, Mark Kowalewski concludes that "American society has constructed AIDS as a disease affecting 'sinners,' primarily 'promiscuous' gays and secondarily drug abusers."[5] While Fundamentalist Protestantism has been the most unabashed in equating AIDS with divine punishment,[6] even some churches with AIDS ministries have continued implicitly to link AIDS with sin. The Catholic Church, for example, in virtually every official proclamation that it has made on the AIDS epidemic, has framed its calls for compassion towards persons with AIDS (PWAs) with reiterations of its sexual morality, thereby reminding the majority of American PWAs—homosexual males and intavenous drug abusers—of the "sinfulness" that caused their infection in the first place. The sobering question for the Catholic Church is, does not such rhetoric compromise compassion and the holistic nature of healing or genuine care for the infirm, which is, after all, in many ways the most traditional of Christian ministries? The commentary of one American Catholic priest who ministers to PWAs suggests the harm that such an association in religious discourse causes: "A lot of times people with AIDS feel, 'My God, this is the end, and not only is it the end, but I'm going to hell too.' They have very much of that hell-fire-and-damnation thing."[7]

Kowalewski identifies three basic categories of religious "constructions" of the AIDS crisis in the United States. The first category, "blaming the victim," is that into which fit Jerry Falwell and his "moral majority" flock, who regard AIDS as "God's punishment for moral failing" or "the logical outcome of violating natural law."[8] Into the second category, "embracing the exile," are placed those progressive religious groups that insist that "AIDS is separated from sexual morality,"[9] a distinction that is reflected in the position of the United Church of Christ, whose 1986 pronunciation on AIDS criticized both the Fundamentalist and Catholic overemphasis of the AIDS/sexual morality connection.[10] The Catholic position, which preaches compassion while exploiting the AIDS epidemic to reiterate in dramatic fashion its objection to homosexuality and sexual freedom, best typifies the third category. While devoid of the AIDS equals divine punishment equation of the first category, proponents of this position, nonetheless, "give a medical validation for their moral teachings and attempt to enforce proscriptions against extramarital sexual behavior with fear of a life threatening disease."[11]

Having outlined Kowalewski's "exploratory typology of religious responses to AIDS," we will attempt below to determine into which of these categories, if any, fit the traditions of the subjects in the narrative. Because the religious affiliations of these individuals is nowhere explicitly stated, it will be assumed that in the first case the deceased Haitian parents of the children, if not the children themselves, were from a Vodouisant background—a distinct possibility—while in the second case, it is at least as possible that the subjects belong to an African-American Protestant church, perhaps Baptist. While admittedly we are operating on assumptions in designating religious backgrounds here, the traditions that we shall explore, Vodou and African-American Protestantism, certainly confront the issues of AIDS on a daily basis, especially in poor minority communities in urban America, amongst whom most new cases of HIV infection are now being reported.[12]

What Is Vodou?

Vodou is a religion that blends a variety of traditional African (mainly Fon, Yoruba, and Kongo) elements with Catholicism. While decidedly more akin in its forms of ritual and belief to African traditional religion than to Catholicism, it is important to recognize that Vodou is not an African religion, but is rather very much a product of the Haitian experience of and response to reality. That experience began in, and has forever been conditioned by, the injustices and brutality of plantation slavery in the French colony of Saint-Domingue (1697–1804), which was renamed Haiti after independence. Vodou, as it were, is a religion born of displacement, suffering, and the negotiation thereof.

Slaves brought to the colony from Africa were baptized Catholic on arrival and given minimal religious instruction by Dominicans, Capuchins, and Jesuits, who struggled to convey to their displaced, tormented flock the orthodox meaning of Catholic symbolism. In the absence of an effective catechism, syncretism immediately resulted, as the Catholic saints were identified as the African spirits, and crosses, holy water, and incense were freely adopted as powerful religious trinkets to be used in conjunction with the amulets and fetishes that the slaves reproduced from African religious memory. The Catholic "pantheon," with its single high creator God, who in popular devotion is often relegated to the background, its Virgin Mary, and its host of dead individuals, the saints, who can intervene to affect life in the material world, actually lent itself quite fluently to assimilation with the traditional African community of spiritual beings, which likewise has a single distant creator God and numerous spirits and ancestors who, much like the Catholic saints, are perceived of as readily accessible and as the vehicles through whom most human/divine commerce transpires.

Spirit possession and divination are the main forms of communication with the dead and the spirits in Vodou and are thus the focal ritualistic elements of the religion. While varying widely throughout Haiti and the Haitian diaspora, Vodou altogether posits that life in our world is intricately linked to the existence of the spirits and the dead. Put simply, when our relationship with them is in harmony, life will be full and pleasurable, whereas when there is discord in this relationship, suffering and loss usually result. When such misfortune occurs, ritual specialists are engaged, who, either through divination or the orchestration of ceremonies aiming to provoke spirit possession, effect communication with the spirits or the dead in order to determine the cause of the disorder and to learn how to reestablish harmony. Both the maintenance and the reconstitution of this harmony rely primarily on sacrifice in various forms.

As Karen McCarthy Brown has demonstrated, Vodou is first and foremost a religion of healing and survival: "Vodou is a religion of survival, and it counsels what it must to ensure survival."[13] The Haitian experience of the world has been one permeated by struggle and pain, and Vodou, as the religion of the majority of the Haitian people, has succeeded as a religion because of its deft negotiation of such existential realities. The main functions of its religious specialists are the diagnosis and remedy of individual, social, national, and even international disorders in the form of either sickness or discord. Like the traditional African religions out of which it emerged, along with the other African-derived religions of the Americas, such as Santeria, Umbanda, and Candomblé, healing is the principal service that Vodou performs. Writes Brown, "healing is the *primary* business of these religious traditions. In fact it is not an overstatement to say that spirituality and healing are synonymous in the Afro-Caribbean."[14]

In the ritual context of these traditions, healing takes two basic forms depending on the cause of the disorder. The first class of disorders are those "sent by God" (Haitian Creole: *maladi bondyè*—sickness from God), or those that have natural origins, much like natural catastrophes which insurance companies designate as "acts of God." These are further subdivided into treatable and nontreatable-because-serving-some-higher-purpose. Once diagnosed as the former, such illnesses are treated through herbalism, which in Haiti is a tradition so rich and effective that Western-trained physicians have sought insight into treatment through consultation and training with folkloric herbalist healers (*medsin fey*—leaf doctors). Disorders that are diagnosed as not being *maladi bondyè* are concluded to be caused either by discord in the ill person's rapport with the spirits or the ancestors, which might demand various sacrifices or ceremonies to placate the responsible spiritual agent, or by sorcery, where human agency would be to blame (*maladi nèg*—sickness from man). If sorcery is suspected, once the sorcerer responsible for "sending" (*voye*) the sickness is identified, that sorcerer and her or his client become the target of a ritualistic counter-attack. As with most illness, AIDS is usually diagnosed as such a "sent sickness" by Vodouisants.

It should be clear from the foregoing summary that because Vodou's AIDS etiology does not link the affliction to sexual morality, because it understands the syndrome as "sent" rather than "acquired," Haiti's popular religion clearly falls outside of either the first or third category of religious constructions of the virus, each of which makes, explicitly or implicitly, a causal link between AIDS and sin. While there certainly is a theodicy of blame operative in Vodou's response to AIDS, it is aimed at the agent responsible for "sending" the disease, whether human, spirit, or ancestor, and not at the afflicted. The infirm are very much *embraced* by their family and community, groupings which, incidentally, are intrinsically religious in the Vodou context. We may thus place Vodou into the second of Kowalewski's categories, "*embracing* the exile," for as Paul Farmer, reflecting on the care of PWAs in rural Haiti, explains, Vodou is characterized by "a humane discourse about suffering. The advent of *sida* (AIDS) did not change this. At no point did the family members of the ill refuse to care for their kin, as has been the case in the United States and elsewhere."[15]

Vodou, Death, and the Therapy of Ritual

Experts on the therapeutic treatment of the children of deceased PWAs argue that "the strengths that exist within the family's community, through religion, and from intrafamily dynamics need, in each case, to be marshaled to respond to each individual situation."[16] In other words, since the "struggle to create meaning is often intense when children are confronted with suffering, illness, and death, . . . (c)aregivers first need to understand the child's spiritual framework."[17] In the case of young Vodouisant survivors of

deceased PWAs, like the children in the first case considered by the panel, the
dimension of the survivors' "spiritual framework" that should most carefully be taken into consideration pertains to the care of the departed spirit.
In Vodou and other African-based traditions of the Americas, as is true of
African traditional religion in general, the dead remain integral members of
the family and are possessed of mysterious powers by which they can and
do intervene in the lives of their descendants in the world of the living. Vodou
thus stresses the importance of respectful burial, gravesite maintenance, and
reverent, often sacrificial, recollection or memorial of the dead. "The family
dead are buried on the family land (in rural Haiti) and the cemetery is the
major center for religious activity." It is considered of highest importance
"to honor, entertain, and feed the ancestors and the Vodou spirits which these
ancestors served."[18] To neglect such religious obligations is to invite wrath-
ful retribution from the world of the dead and the spirits. Uncertainty as to
the spirits' and ancestors' degree of satisfaction breeds great anxiety among
the living. It is possible, therefore, that the children of the deceased Haitian
PWAs suffer from such anxiety, which could obviously exacerbate their
trauma and inhibit effective grieving. Thus, the suggestion that they be
accorded access to a Vodou priest or priestess for consultation, divination,
and, if necessary, ceremony and that they be allowed to visit their parents'
gravesites regularly, would seem constructive and potentially therapeutic:

> One of the most powerful manifestations of spirituality lies in rituals.
> At best, rituals can be highly therapeutic. They can provide psycho-
> logical comfort, social support, and spiritual meaning.
> *For many children the power of therapeutic rituals is untapped.* The
> reasons for this are twofold. *In some cases, the child simply does not
> have the opportunity to attend or participate in rituals,* perhaps because
> the child is not living with the parent at this point or because caregivers
> wish to protect the child from what is perceived to be a troubling or
> problematic event.[19] (emphasis added)

In many religious contexts it is the funeral that is the most effectively therapeutic ritual for the bereaved. This is especially true for religions such as
Christianity, whose soteriology and funeral discourse usually offer the reassurance that the deceased now rests eternally in peace with God. In Vodou,
on the contrary, there is "no vision of heaven,"[20] although, as we have seen,
"there is a sense in which the dead continue to exist."[21] In spite of the absence
of an idea of heaven, nonetheless, a comparable catharsis to that engendered
by the Christian notion of salvation can be occasioned for the living through
Vodouisant rituals that ensure that the dead are satisfied or placated.
Paramount among such rituals is that of *manje mò* (food of the dead), which
is described by Gerald Murray:

> It . . . involves an elaborate and somewhat expensive banquet for the
> deceased, in which the food which the dead person liked during life

will be prepared, but in which special foods liked by the dead in general are also prepared. The preparation of this banquet in many instances involves a direct consultation with the dead person . . . it is a demonstration of the fulfillment of a serious duty on the part of the children. . . There is a sigh of relief when the meal is over, and people were heard to say happily: *kounyéa m pa dwé ankò*, I'm no longer in debt. This is a very serious duty which children owe to their parents. It is a loose end which most hope to tie up before their own death.[22]

The *manje mò* ritual is thus understood as essential for the well-being of the living, since hungry ancestors are perceived as capable of wreaking havoc in the lives of their negligent descendants. In Vodou, it is thus the domain of people in the world, rather than of a God "who art in heaven," to ensure the rest of the departed. Rituals such as *manje mò* afford the living the prime opportunity to do so, in turn performing therapeutic functions for the bereaved themselves.

AIDS and the African–American Church

Students of African-American culture since W.E.B. DuBois have recognized that the African-American church "began as a spiritual sanctuary and community against the violent and destructive character of the slave world," and has since "remained a wall of defense and comfort against racism and its accompanying attacks on Black dignity, relevance, and social worth."[23] Indeed, "Black faith (has) provided the entire breadth of human hope in the face of pain and suffering."[24] AIDS represents yet another form of suffering confronting African Americans, particularly in urban communities where the spread of the virus in the nineties has been especially alarming. It would be expected that the African-American church would thus take on a central role in the struggle against AIDS:

> The African-American church has long been perceived as an organizing and life-sustaining institution within the African-American community. Social, political, and public health mobilization has historically been rooted within these community establishments. The situation with acquired immune deficiency syndrome (AIDS) warrants similar conscription by the African American clergy.[25]

While African-American Protestantism in general does not equate AIDS affliction with divine punishment,[26] which would suggest placing it into Kowalewski's "embracing the exile" category, its clergy, according to a study in the *Journal of Community Psychology*, generally have been slow to regard AIDS as a serious problem facing their communities: "Results from a survey of African-American Baptist ministers toward acquired immune deficiency syndrome (AIDS) revealed that most of the clergy did not perceive human immunodeficiency virus as being a significant risk to their communities."[27] One troublesome result of such a perception is "that the number of prevention, education, and intervention services the African-American Baptist church is providing for its members are few."[28]

Although based on sound research, these observations cannot, however, be extended to characterize African-American Christianity at large. For one, the study is of ministers and says nothing of the African-American mothers, fathers, sisters, brothers, and *neighbors* whose religious belief daily inspires in them the courage and compassion to help PWAs confront their sickness with dignity and strength. Compassion, moreover, cannot be measured merely in terms of formal support programs, especially among communities with marginal financial resources. Finally, the study's narrow focus belies the essential fact that African-American religious life is primarily communal, and communal rituals that are characteristic of African-American spirituality, such as the revival, best generate strength and familial unity in the face of suffering:

> Along the continuum—from speaking in tongues to less overt forms of expression—the revival represents a time for coming together, a time of support, and a time for asking forgiveness and praying for self and others. These rituals help to reframe a negative experience, such as death, through religious teaching and reaffirmation of faith.[29]

In the second case discussed in the narrative, the negativity of the subjects' experience was exacerbated by the mother's drug use and abusive behavior, which ultimately drove the state to take her three children from her. The central question under consideration by the panel is whether the children should be reunited with their evidently socially rehabilitated mother, who is now critically ill with AIDS. At least one of the points made against reunification (that since "there is no larger family network to oversee the situation—reunification just seems too chancy") would be offset by a sound understanding of the nature and function of the African-American church. As has been demonstrated consistently over the course of its history, the African-American church, beyond its stabilizing function of "spiritual leadership and emotional and financial supports," has always itself represented first and foremost "a viable extended family."[30] The "larger family network" of support for an AIDS-afflicted mother longing for reunification with her children thus could very well lie within the African-American church, which, since its inception in the brutal realities of servitude and bondage, has always "sustained familial and communal networks of support."[31] African-American Christians might also advance another important consideration that is altogether ignored by the panel discussing the case—or at least one that the untimely fire alarm cuts off: That the union of family and the miraculous power of faith might generate a response in the mother's T-cell count to protease inhibitors. As the Negro spiritual so beautifully and forcefully proclaims:

Children, we shall be free,
For the good Lord
Give ease to the sick, give sight to the blind,
Make the cripple walk.

Vodou, "Blackwater," and the Geography of a Plague

Typical of the racism that has shaped so much American discourse about Haiti and Haitians, during its early stages the AIDS epidemic was widely perceived by Americans as coming from Haiti, and even medical researchers were suggesting in refereed journals that Vodou might be responsible for its spread. "In the October 1983 edition of *Annals of Internal Medicine*, for example, physicians affiliated with the Massachusetts Institute of Technology related the details of a brief visit to Haiti and wrote, 'It seems reasonable to consider voodoo practices a cause of the syndrome.'"[32] In reality, Vodou not only does not contribute to the spread of AIDS, but it has proven to be one of the most compassionate religions in the face of the plague. Furthermore, as Farmer forcefully demonstrates, the Haitian epidemic was triggered mainly by North American sex tourists in Haiti, and thus the geography of AIDS must be considered in the context of global economics, geopolitics, and the historical domination of one people at the hands of another:

> It may be argued, endlessly no doubt, that it was the political economy of the region which. . . sent sickness. . . [T]he overwhelming impact on Haiti of plantation slavery, a component of international economies centered in Europe, cannot be overemphasized. Haiti, the world's first underdeveloped nation, was born of this template. Similarly, Haiti's place in the West Atlantic system, an international economy centered in the United States, helped determine the current epidemiology of HIV.[33]

The "advent of HIV," Farmer goes on to argue, must therefore be understood "in the context of larger forces—the push of rural poverty and the pull of urban factories and tourism catering to North Americans."[34] Thus the blame that Vodou seeks to place on human agency for "sending" AIDS, along with the conspiracy theories that circulate both among Haitians and African Americans that AIDS was created by white Americans or their CIA to eliminate blacks, however fantastic, serve to remind "us to explore the notion of 'sent sickness' in all its symbolic register."[35]

To engage in such an exploration of the historical and geopolitical/economic forces at play in the ever-unfolding epidemiology of AIDS casts light upon the very structures of domination and oppression against which Vodou and the African-American church have always struggled. Manning Marable, among others, finds that this struggle for survival, cultural authenticity, and social, this-worldly liberation represents half of the essence of African-American spirituality:

The conservative tendencies within Black faith reach for a Spirit that liberates the soul, but not the body. On the other hand, the radical consciousness within Black faith was concerned with the immediate condition of Black people. This other half of Black faith, which I shall refer to as "Blackwater," provides a spiritual equilibrium with its conservative counterpart. Blackwater is the consciousness of oppression, a cultural search for self-affirmation and authenticity.[36]

Vodou and Blackwater thus combine to demonstrate what is, along with loving compassion, perhaps the most important response that religion can make to the AIDS crisis: To struggle against social injustice and the ignorance, poverty, and despair that it engenders; that is, against the "larger forces" that drive a single African-American mother to heroin addiction, North American sex tourists to frolic in the Caribbean, and Haitian parents to immigrate to the United States.

Notes

1. Allan Brandt, "AIDS: From Social History to Social Policy," in *AIDS: The Burdens of History*, ed. Elizabeth Fee and Daniel M. Fox (Berkeley, CA: University of California Press, 1988), 168.

2. Etymologically, the word "Vodou" derives from the Fon *vodu*, meaning sacred being or thing. From among a litany of variations of the term, with Leslie Desmangles and others I choose *Vodou* "because it is phonetically more correct, and because it corresponds to the nomenclature used by the Haitians themselves for their own religion." Also following Desmangles, I have opted when referring to Vodou practitioners, to employ the French word "*Vodouisant*" which is a derivative of the word Vodou and which strikes me as preferable over the English term "Voodooist," if for no other reason than a concern for eloquence. And just as the word Christian serves either to designate a follower of Jesus or as an adjective modifier, so too is the term "*Vodouisant*" usable as an adjective (e.g., Vodouisant belief). Leslie G. Desmangles, *The Faces of the Gods: Vodou and Roman Catholicism in Haiti* (Chapel Hill, NC: The University of North Carolina Press, 1992), xi–xii.

3. AIDS has been termed a "misery-seeking missile" by Renee Sabatier in *Blaming Others: Prejudice, Race, and Worldwide AIDS* (Philadelphia: New Society Publishers, 1988), cited in Paul Farmer, *AIDS and Accusation: Haiti and the Geography of Blame* (Berkeley, CA: University of California Press, 1992), 259.

4. Farmer, *AIDS and Accusation*, 259.

5. Mark R. Kowalewski, "Religious Constructions of the AIDS Crisis." *Sociological Analysis* 51 (1990):91.

6. This position is perhaps encapsulated most poignantly in the title of the Jerry Falwell article "AIDS: the Judgment of God." *The Liberty Report* (April 1987):2–5.

7. Mark R. Kowalewski, *All Things to All People: The Catholic Church Confronts the AIDS Crisis* (Albany: State University of New York Press, 1994), 89.

8. Kowalewski, "Religious Constructions," 93.

9. Kowalewski, "Religious Constructions," 92.

10. National Council of Churches of Christ in the United States, *Resolution on the Churches' Response to the AIDS Crisis*, 22 May 1986. The Council's document argues that such an overemphasis has "contributed to the disproportionate devastation of

AIDS among racial and ethnic minorities. . . . Much more attention has been given to education and care of the predominately white male homosexual population." Cited in Kowalewski, "Religious Constructions," 94.

11. Kowalewski, "Religious Constructions," 94.

12. "From 1995 to 1996 . . . the greatest proportionate increase in AIDS-OI (opportunistic illnesses) occurred among non-Hispanic black men (19%), Hispanic men (13%), and non-Hispanic black women (12%) who had heterosexual risk/exposures." Centers for Disease Control, *Morbidity and Mortality Weekly Report* 46:862.

13. Karen McCarthy Brown, *Mama Lola: A Vodou Priestess in Brooklyn* (Berkeley, CA: University of California Press, 1991), 254.

14. Karen McCarthy Brown, "Afro-Caribbean Spirituality: A Haitian Case Study," in *Healing and Restoring: Medicine and Health in the World's Religious Traditions*, ed. Lawrence Sullivan (New York: Macmillan, 1989), 257.

15. Farmer, *AIDS and Accusations*, 120.

16. Barbara Blum, forward to *AIDS and the New Orphans: Coping with Death*, ed. Barbara O. Dane and Carole Levine (Westport, CT: Auburn House, 1994), 2.

17. Kenneth J. Doka, "Suffer the Little Children: The Child and Spirituality in the AIDS Crisis," *AIDS and the New Orphans*, ed. Dane and Levine, 37.

18. Brown, "Afro-Caribbean Spirituality," 261.

19. Doka, "Suffer," 38 (emphasis mine).

20. Brown, "Afro-Caribbean Spirituality," 258.

21. Brown, "Afro-Caribbean Spirituality," 284, note 2.

22. Gerald Francis Murray, "The Evolution of Haitian Peasant Land Tenure: A Case Study in Agrarian Adaptation to Population Growth" (Ph.D. diss., Columbia University, 1977), 532.

23. Maulana Karenga, "Black Religion," in *African American Religious Studies: An Interdisciplinary Anthology*, ed. Gayraud S. Wilmore (Durham, NC: Duke University Press, 1989), 286.

24. Manning Marable, "Religion and Black Protest Thought in African American History," in *African American Religions Studies*, ed. Wilmore, 323–24.

25. Isiaah Crawford et al., "Attitudes of African-American Baptist Ministers Toward AIDS," *Journal of Community Psychology* 20 (October 1992):304.

26. "Many of the respondents (60 percent) very strongly disagree that AIDS was God's way of punishing homosexuals or drug abusers. Similarly, 70 percent of the ministers strongly to very strongly disagreed that people who contracted AIDS deserved their illness" (Crawford et al., "Attitudes," 306–7).

27. Crawford et al., "Attitudes," 306–7.

28. Crawford et al., "Attitudes," 306–7.

29. Penelope Johnson-Moore and Lucretia J. Phillips, "Black Communities: Coping with Death," *AIDS and the New Orphans*, ed. Dane and Levine, 111.

30. Barbara O. Dane and Samuel O. Miller, *AIDS: Intervening with Hidden Grievers* (Westport, CT: Auburn House, 1992), 148.

31. Cornell West, "Nihilism in Black America: A Danger that Corrodes from Within," *Dissent* 3 (1991):221–26, cited in Johnson-Moore and Phillips, "Black Communities," 110.

32. Farmer, *AIDS and Accusations*, 2.

33. Farmer, *AIDS and Accusations*, 258.

34. Farmer, *AIDS and Accusations*, 258.

35. Farmer, *AIDS and Accusations*, 259.

36. Marable, "Religion and Black Protest Thought," 327.

A CHRISTIAN RESPONSE by Christine E. Gudorf

This case assaults the sensibilities of any religious community that understands children as a sacred trust, as gifts of God to be cherished and nurtured and eventually entrusted with responsibility for the community and for its relationship with God. The cruel neglect of these children by the entire society cries to heaven. Where are the extended families, the church communities, the neighbors, and friends of these children? Why have these children been left to the less than tender mercies of an inefficient court bureaucracy? And why is the bureaucracy that deals with a resource so precious as children allowed to become so negligent and inefficient?

How could participation in the panels, however well-motivated, not produce callousness, even fatalism, toward the suffering of children—suffering that seems so pervasive within a system so resistant to improvement? One advantage of outside volunteers is that they are less susceptible to bureaucratic fatalism, but that advantage diminishes over time as the volunteer is immersed in the way things work within the institution. But the Christian imperative is not merely to feel love; we must love these neighbor children effectively. Christ's resurrection must mean there is hope for overcoming even the complacent fatalism of a foster care system that deals death to the spirits—and sometimes even the bodies—of its children. Without such hope, effective love will be difficult.

As Beverly Harrison wisely pointed out,[1] situations such as those presented in this case call for anger. Anger at the injustice done to these children and at the callous disregard for their lives and their spirits is appropriate and is, in fact, the source of the energy to get involved on behalf of the children. Anger signals that something is wrong, something that could and should be righted; it signals that someone we care about is being mistreated. Though misdirecting anger can be dangerous and lead to further injustice, anger itself should not be understood as sinful or dangerous but should be seen as a valuable indicator of something wrong.

There are a number of specific ethical issues in this case. How should the parent–child relationship and its inherent rights and duties be understood? Should the rights of parents and children be equal, or do the rights of one or the other predominate? Should medical diagnoses of HIV/AIDS in parents and children be open to the panels, or should they be treated as confidential? Should full-blown AIDS—as opposed to HIV infection—in a single parent requesting return of her children justify the panel in demanding a continuity of care plan from the parent? How does one effectively evaluate and predict how the welfare of children will be affected by adoption, foster care, or return to parental custody? These are questions of both value and fact. Christian revelation and teaching speak primarily to the value issues, though the voices of religious revelation and tradition are always culturally and historically conditioned. Christian answers to these questions vary depending not only on the Christian denomination involved but also on the cultural situation of the Christian respondent—his or her nationality, race, class, and, perhaps, even sex. Because the case is set in the United States, this commentary will present American Christian responses to the case.

A Structural Issue

The structure of the foster care system must be examined. Orphanages and foundling hospitals in Europe have been operated by Christian communities for well over a millennium, especially in Catholic Europe. In the last forty years in the United States, foster care has replaced both religious and public orphanages and foundling hospitals as the long-term method of caring for children whose parents are dead, unknown, or otherwise unable or unwilling to care for them. The few surviving orphanages tend to be used as short-term shelters for children in transition. Social science initiated the shift to foster care by demonstrating that the physical health and growth, the mental development and IQ, and the psychological health and well-being of children require personal, consistent one-to-one relationships with a primary adult caretaker. Especially among younger children, impersonal care frequently produced "failure to thrive" which was connected with an abnormally high death rate, delays in or lack of growth in basic physical and interpersonal skills, and low resistance to disease. Thus, a system of foster homes was developed. Many foster homes are excellent, offering exemplary care to children who must temporarily be separated from their families while parents shake addictions, are incarcerated, require extended medical or psychological hospitalization, or find adequate shelter or employment with which to support their children. But a shortage of such foster families leads to both overcrowding in existing foster homes and insufficiently high standards for foster homes, thereby undermining the superiority of foster care over orphanages.

In addition, foster care is often misused by the inclusion of children who cannot safely return to their original family and should be placed in permanent adoptive homes. Recent state and federal legislation is forcing states and counties to take no more than twelve to eighteen months, instead of the average three or four years, to move each foster child into either reunification with family or adoption following termination of parental rights. This move represents a shift in direction from a strong concept of parental rights to the primacy of children's rights to stable homes.

Many parents cannot get their lives together within the allotted time. The foster care population is disproportionately poor for two basic reasons. First, abuse and neglect of children in middle-class families are not nearly so likely to come to the attention of authorities, because those families have access to additional layers of resources such as private doctors, insurance funded addiction programs, and lawyers. Middle-class families, therefore, are not nearly as likely to lose their children to the state even when they suffer from the same problems as poor families do. Second, poverty itself is a major stress on families and can help create the problems that lead to neglect or abuse of children. Homelessness, for example, is, in many places, grounds for child removal. Unemployment is a prime stressor for domestic violence. Escape from the apparent hopelessness of multigenerational poverty through drugs and alcohol, which often results in child neglect, is a long-standing curse of the communities of the poor. Both domestic violence and addiction are common grounds for child removal. Addiction, whether to alcohol or illegal drugs, is not easily vanquished in the twelve to eighteen months the new foster care guidelines allow, because the waiting lists for government funded residential programs on which the poor who lack private medical insurance depend can be that long or longer and frequently exclude pregnant women altogether.

Patricia's last question, "Who are we to decide?" brings up the issue of representation. This was raised by another member of the panel specifically with regard to race. Earl asked if the panel could be treating black and white mothers attempting to regain custody differently, presumably because the panels are largely white. Obviously, the ideal situation would be to have the make-up of citizens review panels reflect either the population whose children are in the foster care system or the general composition of the city. But recruitment of representative panels is difficult because all panels are staffed with citizen volunteers who have completed twenty-five to thirty hours of initial training, six to ten hours of annual continuing training, and must serve nine to twelve workdays a year. Despite continuing special efforts to recruit a more diverse pool, panels are disproportionately made up of retired persons, unemployed housewives, the middle-class self-employed, and professionals with flexible work schedules. The poor and working class—disproportionately nonwhite—are under-represented on the panels, though over-represented among foster care clients. Because children have traditionally been considered the responsibility and interest of women, the panels turn out to be not only disproportionately white and middle class but also largely female.

At the same time, the panels came into existence and continue to spread across the nation in response to a terrible crisis of mismanagement in foster care. Children have been lost without supervision in the system, placed in or left in neglectful or abusive living situations, or returned to unsafe homes. Hundreds of thousands of children in the United States have been languishing in overcrowded foster care homes for years without either being placed for adoption or being aided in safe supervised return to parents or other relatives.

The basic problems can be traced to poor management and lack of money, both of which result from traditional relegation of families to the feminized private realm, rather than the higher status—and masculine—public realm. Lack of money was and is a major cause of the mismanagement, because the salaries of caseworkers and supervisors are so low and average caseloads so heavy that burnout is frequent and turnover rapid among both caseworkers and supervisors. In many units, the level of resignations and consequent case transfers ensures that the average foster-care child has a new caseworker every few months. By the time the case-worker knows the situation of the child, the options available within the system, and the procedures for implementing those options, she or he is gone, and another caseworker begins the learning curve. Even if they have not been abused or have not had their physical needs neglected, children who have been in fifteen to thirty different foster homes and had fifteen or more caseworkers would be extraordinary if they retained any sense of self-worth or any expectation of ongoing care and concern from others. In the-ory, the court system safeguards the interests of the children. However, there are not enough juvenile court judges to replace the panels or to con-duct regular reviews of more than a small fraction of the foster care place-ments. In the opinion of most analysts, outside supervision, even when unrepresentative, is better than no supervision. After all, recommendations of the panels are reviewed before being ordered by judges.

However much the foster care system may need to retain nonrepresenta-tive panels for the immediate present, individual panel members need to ask the question, "Who am I to be deciding the future of this parent or this child?" The purpose of such a question is not to paralyze the panel mem-bers, preventing them from making decisions, but to remind the panel mem-bers of the need for social analysis to inform their questions and decisions. One of the functions of training for panel members is to sensitize them to the need for social analysis, so that they recognize that not all social groups oper-ate from the same assumptions, are structured in the same way, or interact in the same manner to which they are accustomed. There are different ways to achieve equal treatment in the return of children to dying mothers, with-out compromising the concern of panel members that the children have sta-bility and security in their lives. For some families the solution is finding a relative of the mother or father who will agree to take the children upon the death or incapacitation of the mother. In another family the solution might be provided by an agency that finds an adoptive family willing to take in not only the children but also the dying mother. In yet another case it may be a fictive relative, a neighbor, or a church friend who will maintain the children in the same local community. European-American, African-American, Hispanic, Native-American, and other minority groups have different fam-ily and social patterns which must be understood in order to treat all chil-dren equitably.

Christianity on the Parent–Child Relationship

Christian understandings of the parent–child relationship have evolved con-tinuously since the beginning of Christian revelation in the Jewish scriptures. Old Testament stories, law, and genealogies together focus on two distinct aspects of the parent–child relationship: the importance of children to par-ents and the authority of parents over children. The patriarchs and their wives not only rejoiced in their children and understood them as gifts from

God, but they also understood childlessness as a terrible curse that deprived men and their lineages of immortality and deprived women of status, social function, and even the protection of marriage (Gen 16:1–4; 29:31–30:24). Abraham's and Sarah's yearning for a son and their joy in Isaac was paradigmatic: the son promised by God becomes the symbol of the posterity that Israel is promised in the covenant (Gen 17:1–21). No other sacrifice could have proved so strongly Abraham's loyalty to his God as his willingness to sacrifice this son. The value of children, especially sons, is echoed not only in the genealogies of the Old Testament (e.g., Gen 36:9–43) but also in the Mosaic law's requirement that the firstborn son, being a gift of God, must be ransomed back from God by his parents (Num 3:44–51).

At the same time, the Hebrew scriptures make clear that fathers have control over children. As in the story of Abraham's sacrifice of Isaac (Gen 22:1–14), there is no doubt that fathers exercised the power and the social authority to dispose of their children as they see fit. It was assumed that the value of those children to the father would prevent abuse of that power. But Old Testament understandings of abuse are not the same as contemporary understandings. Jepthah vows to sacrifice the first living thing to meet him upon his return if God will grant him victory in war (Judg 11:30–33); his sacrifice of his daughter is presented as praiseworthy both for him and for her (Judg 11:37–40).

Some Old Testament texts indicate an ongoing attempt to moderate the powers of parents over children. For example, the Deuteronomic text forbidding incest begins with the principle that men are forbidden sex with any blood relative, which would exclude one's children (Lev 18:6). But children are conspicuously absent from the following list of persons with whom sex is forbidden; instead the list appears based on respect for male owners of women in that it includes many women not related by blood, but forbidden because they "belong" to male relatives, either as wives or concubines (Lev 18:6–18). Interpreters have suggested that the text reflects an early attempt to moderate the power of patriarchs by demanding that they respect the female ownership rights of other men in the family and by introducing the idea that sex with blood relatives is abominable to God.

Interestingly enough, the teaching on the value of children is transformed in the New Testament, which reveals a continuing tradition of strong parental control over children as well as ongoing attempts to moderate that power. Along with the sick, the poor, women, and foreigners, Jesus included children among the powerless groups he championed. (Mt 18:1–6, 10–14; Mt 19:13–15. He promised woe to those who abuse children (Mt 18:5–6) and insisted that all who want to be saved must throw in their lot with children (Mk 9:33–37; 10:13–16; Lk 9:46–50). Jesus treated children as valuable, a treatment not in accordance with their low status in his society. In his relativizing of the family in his teaching and in his own example, Jesus supported neither the traditional Jewish emphasis on the importance of having children that was still strong in his time (Lk 1:7–25), nor the traditional emphasis on patriarchal authority. Not only do Jesus and his followers not teach that

Christians have an obligation to marry and have children, but in the Pauline epistles there is advice not to marry (1 Cor 7:8). This advice is later emphasized in the patristic tradition to the point that vowed celibacy becomes the path to the ideal Christian lifestyle. Furthermore, Mark tells us that Jesus was at least temporarily estranged from his own family over his mission (Mk 3:20–35), and his teaching frequently presented the gospel as disruptive of family (Mt 10:21–22, 34–39; Mk 13:12–13). His disciples, like he himself, must be willing to break with their families when loyalty to the gospel is at stake. To the one man who said he must go bury his father and then would return to discipleship, Jesus responded, "Let the dead bury the dead" (Lk 9:59–62). Such a teaching must have scandalized most of his own society, which understood duty to and reverence for one's father as surpassing all others. For Jesus, however, the priority of obligation depended on the degree of need of the other and not the degree of personal affinity one had to the other (Mt 12:46–50).

Jesus' example and teaching could thus support the direction of policy in foster care, which relativizes parental rights and authority over children in favor of providing children with more stability and support. However, in the case of the woman with AIDS who wants her children back, the application of scriptural insight actually raises a new question. If we understand Jesus' treatment of children as similar to that of the poor and marginalized, then we can assume that he was not merely advocating charity for them but was insisting on their full inclusion into society. That inclusion involves duties and obligations. This is why, though Jesus in a number of situations champions women, his response to the woman who called out, "Blessed is the womb that bore you and the breasts that nursed you!" was "Blessed rather are those who hear the word of God and keep it!" (Lk 11:27–28). Jesus' defense of women—and children—was not intended to put them on a pedestal as objects to be protected and admired but was to include them in the work of discipleship.

Women are not minors as are children; the obligations of discipleship must increase with the age of the child. But the questions "at what age or level of maturity do children begin to have responsibilities for others, and at what age might even children have a role in supporting their dying parent?" must at least be posed. That is to say that Jesus' remarks on children are misinterpreted when assumed to present children as innocents to be preserved from responsibility, work, and knowledge of suffering. Such an idea of childhood is a modern invention with no analogy in the first century. Jesus demands that children be protected from victimization to which they are very vulnerable, but he does not argue for any special privilege for children. All are called to be disciples. Discipleship requires training; one cannot adopt the mantle of discipleship out of the blue at eighteen or twenty-one years of age. To say that the children of a dying mother may have some responsibility for supporting her in her dying process does not override in any way the children's need for stability in their lives. The ideal situation would be for the mother and the caseworker to find a relative or friend who is willing to be present to some degree through the mother's final months and to raise the children after the mother's death. If the children knew such a plan had been agreed to by all parties from the beginning, there is less likelihood that their own needs would overshadow the possibility of responding to their dying mother's needs.

In this case the panel questions the placement of the four Haitian boys with a non-English-speaking Spanish family. They view such a placement as a problem for adoption, in that it is unlikely that English or Creole speakers will adopt boys who only speak Spanish, and most Spanish-speaking adoptive families in the United States seek light-skinned children. This is especially serious because sibling placements are difficult, and the placement of older sibling groups is especially difficult.

But a lessened likelihood of adoption is not the only problem. Most Christian denominations recognize that persons have a right to be raised in their native culture. Christian churches responded to the situation of Christian missions in colonial lands by gradually coming to repudiate the view that there was one Christian (European) culture and many pagan peoples without real culture. Instead, they came to see that other peoples had rich cultural traditions that generally fit the economic, geographical, and social situation of their lives. By early this century, Catholic popes began insisting that native peoples should have their own native priests who should be in control of the mission churches and not merely assistants to European priests. By mid-century increasing numbers of Catholic and Protestant bishops and other church officials in Asia, Africa, and Latin America were natives, and since the second Vatican Council (1962–1965) native culture has been increasingly important in local theologies and liturgies within Catholic as well as many Protestant and independent (often syncretic) churches. Gained originally in foreign missions, this understanding of the importance of culture for grounding identity forms the basis for Christian church insistence today that children have a right to be reared within their birth culture.

Similarly, most states have adoption laws that insist that whenever possible children be placed in adoptive families similar to their racial, ethnic, and religious backgrounds. Yet adoptions across these lines occur frequently because adoption is much more beneficial to children than foster care is. If there are two families approved for adoption and one of them better matches a child's background, other factors being equal, that family will be preferred for that child. But a child up for adoption is not generally retained in foster care when there is an approved family requesting him or her, regardless of whether or not the family's background matches the child's. The most basic need is a stable, loving family. Yet the child's adolescence, and indeed her or his longer process of identity formation, will be easier the fewer obstacles there are to the child's modeling of and identification with the adoptive parents. Many religious communities have taken seriously the importance of placing their children up for adoption in homes within the same religious community. Historically both American Jews and Catholics have established organizations that actively recruit religiously similar homes for Jewish and Catholic children up for adoption. In most parts of the nation today, Jewish children seldom remain within the public foster care system but are channeled through Jewish social services to Jewish placements.

With regard to the review panel's policy on AIDS, the issue is complicated. At the beginning of the AIDS crisis hysteria and discrimination against persons with AIDS (PWAs) were so widespread that confidentiality policies were widely adopted to prevent further victimization. Most Christian churches supported this move and condemned discrimination against PWAs, though there remain small fringe groups of Christians who insist that AIDS—but not hepatitis, or herpes, or lung cancer, or stroke—should be understood as God's judgment on those affected.

Many groups today insist the time has come to treat AIDS like other serious, potentially fatal diseases and not as a special case with its own rules. Confidentiality policies should withhold private information from those with no need to know it. Generally only one's doctor needs to know one's health status, but there are exceptions. A sexual partner needs to know if one has a sexually transmitted disease, and coworkers and family need to know if one has a readily contagious disease such as tuberculosis. Caseworkers, foster parents, and panel members need to know children's HIV status in order to care for them properly and prevent HIV spread to others. Unless AIDS testing becomes automatic for children in foster care, panels must be able to follow up clues such as the separate deaths of two young parents. Privacy has not been one of the most crucial values within Christianity. Though some instances of privacy, such as the seal of confession, have been defended absolutely, rights to life and health generally take precedence over a right to privacy. In this case the compromise of revealing information to the judge instead of the panel meets the situational need, but it may not be practical given the large volume of cases.

Conclusion

Christian perspectives on this case are not radically different from other secular perspectives concerned for justice and the welfare of children. Aside from the need to correct the sentimental pedestalization of children as innocents without responsibilities—a pedestalization often wrongly attributed to Jesus—Christian contribution to this case lies not so much in original analysis as in potential for involvement. Where are the churches in this social crisis? Many churches advertise themselves as children- and family-friendly, with many activities and organizations for all age groups. But how many churches actively encourage adoption, much less fostering? How many recruit foster children in the mentoring or Big Sister/Big Brother programs they operate? Many neglected, abused, or abandoned foster children are as needy as the traveler aided by the Good Samaritan; virtually all are both more needy and less prodigal than the Prodigal Son of Jesus' parable. Indeed, recent research in many cities has shown that young adults recently released from foster care constitute disproportionately large segments of the homeless population. Where are the Christians in this Christian nation?

Notes

1. Beverly Wildung Harrison, "The Power of Anger in the Work of Love: Christian Ethics for Women and Other Strangers," in *Beverly Harrison, Making the Connections*, ed. Carol Robb (Boston: Beacon, 1985).

Bibliography and Suggested Reading

Brandt, Allan. "AIDS: From Social History to Social Policy." In *AIDS: The Burdens of History*, ed. Elizabeth Fee and Daniel M. Fox, 149–171. Berkeley: University of California Press, 1988.

Brown, Karen McCarthy. *Mama Lola: A Vodou Priestess in Brooklyn*. Berkeley: University of California Press, 1991.

———. "Afro-Caribbean Spirituality: A Haitian Case Study." In *Healing and Restoring: Medicine and Health in the World's Religious Traditions*, ed. Lawrence Sullivan, 255–85. New York: Macmillan, 1989.

Crawford, Isiaah, Kevin W. Allison, W. LaVonne Robinson, Donna Hughes, and Maria Samaryk. "Attitudes of African-American Baptist Ministers Toward AIDS." *Journal of Community Psychology* 20 (October 1992):304–08.

Dane, Barbara O., and Carole Levine, eds. *AIDS and the New Orphans: Coping with Death*. Westport, CT: Auburn House, 1994.

Dane, Barbara O., and Samuel O. Miller. *AIDS: Intervening with Hidden Grievers*. Westport, CT: Auburn House, 1992.

Desmangles, Leslie G. *The Faces of the Gods: Vodou and Roman Catholicism in Haiti*. Chapel Hill, NC: The University of North Carolina Press, 1992.

Falwell, Jerry. "AIDS: The Judgment of God." *The Liberty Report* (April 1987):2–5.

Farmer, Paul. *AIDS and Accusation: Haiti and the Geography of Blame*. Berkeley, CA: University of California Press, 1992.

Karenga, Maulana. "Black Religion." In *African American Religious Studies: An Interdisciplinary Anthology*, ed. Gayraud S. Wilmore Durham, NC: Duke University Press, 1989, 271–300.

Kowalewski, Mark R. "Religious Constructions of the AIDS Crisis." *Sociological Analysis* 51 (1990):91–94.

Murray, Gerald Francis. "The Evolution of Haitian Peasant Land Tenure: A Case Study in Agrarian Adaptation to Population Growth." Ph.D. diss., Columbia University, 1977.

National Council of Churches of Christ in the United States. *Resolution on the Churches' Response to the AIDS Crisis*. 22 May 1986.

Sabatier, Renee. *Blaming Others: Prejudice, Race, and Worldwide AIDS*. Philadelphia: New Society Publishers, 1988.

West, Cornell. "Nihilism in Black America: A Danger that Corrodes from Within." *Dissent* 3 (1991):221–26.

Glossary

Abbasids—the dynasty of **caliphs** based in Baghdad who ruled the Islamic empire from 700–1258 and claimed descent from the prophet **Muhammad's** uncle, Abbas.

Abraham—father of the Jewish people and first of the three patriarchs of the nation of Israel found in the book of **Genesis**.

Abu Bakr—(573–634 CE) first **caliph**, or successor to **Muhammad**.

Abu Hanifah—(d.767 CE) Muslim theologian whose teachings were developed into the Hanafi school of **fiqh**.

Afghani—native of Afghanistan.

Aflaq, Michael—founding father of the **Ba'ath party**.

Agunah—bound one; refers specifically to Jewish women whose husbands will not grant them a divorce; adj. **agunot**—bound.

Ahimsa—nonviolence, one of the leading principles of Buddhist ethics.

Alim—Arabic: "a learned or knowledgeable person"; one of the *ulema* (pl.) or Islamic religious scholars.

Allah—the Arabic word for "God."

Altiplano—high plateau or plain.

Amah—a female servant.

Analects—selections from a literary work/s.

Ancillary—auxiliary, supplementary.

Annulment—official declaration by a Roman Catholic church tribunal that there was never, at any time, a valid marriage between a particular couple.

Anti-Semitism—hatred of Jews.

Anti-Taurus—mountain range in south-central Turkey.

Aquinas, Thomas—(c. 1225–74 CE) greatly influential Roman Catholic theologian and saint.

Archdiocese—territorial jurisdiction of an archbishop.

Artificial defloration—see **hymenotomy**.

Asabiyya—term used by Ibn Khaldun, a fourteenth-century Muslim philosopher-historian, to refer to the sense of solidarity and obligation that united and inspired a **patrilineal** kin group.

Ashkenazi Jews—Jews of middle and northern Europe who trace their ancestry from the Jews who settled there in the Middle Ages; adj. **Ashkenazic**.

Ataturk, Kemal—(1881–1938 CE) first president of Turkey; led the Turkish war for independence and the secularization movement.

Athra Kadisha—Jerusalem-based Orthodox Jewish group dedicated to preserving holy places.

Augustine—(354–430 CE) highly influential theologian and early Father of the Christian Church; bishop of Hippo in North Africa; author of numerous writings including the autobiographical *Confessions*.

Autochthonous pacha—cosmic and historic space and time in Aymaran society.

Aymara—a South American Indian people living mainly in Bolivia and Peru.

AZT—azidothymidine; a drug used to treat AIDS.

Ba'ath party—Arab political party which advocates the formation of a single Arab socialist nation; founded in 1943 by Michael **Aflaq.**

Bahrain—country on a group of islands in the Persian Gulf.

Baptism—one of the **sacraments** of initiation into the Christian church.

Barrio—community, ward, or district.

Bayeux Tapestry—embroidered length of linen (231 ft. x 19.5 in.) depicting **William of Normandy**'s conquest of England and the events leading up to it.

Bet Din—three-judge tribunal which has religious authority as well as civil authority in some areas of Jewish law.

Bodhicitta—in Buddhism, the spirit of awakening.

Bodhisattva—an enlightened person who has achieved the state of **Buddha** but who chooses to postpone entry into **nirvana** in order to stay on earth and assist suffering humankind.

Bodhisattva Dharmakara—"spiritual hero" who vowed to forgo supreme enlightenment until all beings enter the **Pure Land.**

Brendale v. Confederated Tribes and Bands of Yakima—case in which the Supreme Court ruled that tribal authorities could regulate small non-Indian lands, if the majority of the land area was tribally owned.

Brit milah—Jewish covenant of circumcision.

B.S.—Bachelor of Science.

Buddha—a perfectly enlightened one, existing in the state of **nirvana.** *The* Buddha was Siddhartha Guatama of India, who founded Buddhism in the sixth century BCE.

Caliph—English rendering of the Arabic: **khalifa** (delegate, deputy, or vicegerent); the title taken by **Muhammad**'s successors.

Calvados—local apple liqueur of Normandy, France.

Campesinos—peasants or farm workers.

Canonical—in accordance with scripture or religious tradition or law.

Carabao—water buffalo.

Caritas—Roman Catholic agency serving the poor in various regions of the world, including Latin America.

Casuistry—the application of ethical principles to solve specific problems of right and wrong.

Chalcedon—ancient city in Asia Minor which was the site of the Fourth Ecumenical Council.

Chancery—a court of equity.

Chavurah—a purposeful informal gathering of Jews.

Chrysostom—(c. 347–407 CE) theologian and Archbishop of Constantinople; famous preacher (the name means "Golden Mouth") and prolific writer; removed from office after conflict with the imperial family; died in exile.

Classic of Filial Piety—important text of Confucianism that stresses filial piety or honor of one's ancestors, which is one of the major principles on which **Confucian** teaching is based.

Clitoridectomy—complete removal of the clitoris.

Clomid—a fertility drug.

Comedore—women's group kitchens that collectively buy, prepare, and serve meals to all the families that contribute to them, usually referred to as *comedores populares.*

Commandments—term used to refer to the Ten Commandments which are part of the **Mosaic Law** given by **Yahweh** to Moses. The first three commandments concern relation to and honor of Yahweh, and the last seven concern the manner in which human beings should conduct their dealings with one another. Sometimes used to refer to the two-fold gospel commandment given by **Jesus** instructing Christians to love God and to love their neighbor as their self.

Communion, sacrament of—see **eucharist**.

Confucian—one who follows the way of life taught by Confucius (551–479 BCE) and followed by the Chinese for more than 2,000 years. Confucius believed in the perfectibility of all persons, concentrating his teachings on the concept of *jen* (love or virtue), which itself was made up of the principles of loyalty to nature, of reciprocity, of righteousness, and of filial piety.

Conscience—the faculty of recognizing right and wrong and a desire to act in accordance with what is judged to be right.

Conservative Jews—Jews who try to preserve the essential elements of traditional Judaism, but who allow for some adaptation of tradition to modern life, in a less radical way than do **Reform Jews**.

Cystic fibrosis—a congenital disease characterized by malfunctioning of the pancreas and frequent respiratory infections.

Dakar—capital of Senegal in West Africa.

Dalai Lama—head of the dominant order of Tibetan Buddhists and, until 1959, both spiritual and temporal ruler of Tibet.

Dana—in Buddhism, the virtue of generosity.

D&C—dilation and curettage; surgical procedure in which the cervix is dilated and the uterus is scraped to remove layers of cellular accumulation.

Desideratum—something needed and wanted; pl. **desiderata**.

Deuterocanonical Septuagint—the Greek (Septuagint) version of the Old Testament that includes the Apocrypha, books not found in the Hebrew version of the Old Testament.

Dharma—in Buddhism, *dharma* is the universal truth, proclaimed by **Buddha**, that is common to all individuals at all times. In Buddhist metaphysics, the word in its plural form (*dharmas*) is used to describe the interrelated elements of the physical world.

Dharmadhatu—realm of **dharmas**.

Diaspora—dispersion of a people; the dispersion of the Jews beginning with the Babylonian exile and eventually resulting in their settling all over the world.

Disconnected capital—ownership structures in which the human development of the workers in their organizations is not considered important.

Doctrinal—according to the principles and creeds or doctrines of a religion.

Dyarbekir—a city in southeastern Turkey.

Ecclesiastical—pertaining to the church.

Ecumenical—concerning or intending to foster unity of the Christian churches.

Ecumenical Council—assembly representing all of Christianity at which matters of dogma, doctrine, and disciplines are decided.

Emirates—United Arab Emirates, a union of seven nations on the east coast of the Arabian Peninsula on the Persian Gulf.

Enlightenment—a European intellectual movement of the seventeenth and eighteenth centuries celebrating the power of human reason.

EPA—Environmental Protection Agency, United States.

ESL—English as a Second Language.

Ethnocentricity—focus on a particular culture or ethnic group.

EU/European Union—organization in which most Western European countries are members and that works toward the economic and political integration of those member states.

Eucharist—a **sacrament** of initiation into the Christian church wherein Christians partake of bread and wine, in which they believe dwells the presence of the body and blood of **Jesus** Christ; also called the sacrament of **communion**.

Eurobond—a bond issued in an international (usually European) market and repayable in the currency of issue.

Euthanasia—the practice of causing death painlessly, usually in order to end the life of one who is suffering.

Evangelical—that which is according to the Gospels or the **New Testament**, or which engages in a ministry to bring people to belief in **Jesus'** message; can also be used to apply to those Protestant churches that emphasize salvation by faith.

Excommunication—exclusion, by **ecclesiastical** authority, from membership in a church and participation in its **sacraments**.

Exegetes—those who do explanation, analysis, or interpretation of literature, especially Scripture.

External forum—courts, laws (particularly religious ones), and other such methods of solving dilemmas by the mediation of outer institutions.

Fascist—one who practices fascism which is a system of government characterized by rigid one-party dictatorship, forcible suppression of opposition, militarism, nationalism, and racism.

Fa-Tsang—(643–712 CE) Chinese Buddhist monk who first systematized the doctrines of the **Hua yen** school of Buddhism.

Fatwa—in Islam, a legal opinion or decision based on the **shari'a** and given by an **alim** or **mufti**.

Federal Reserve Board—board of governors of the Federal Reserve System, the central banking authority of the United States.

Fee lands—private land that non-Indians own within a reservation.

Fiqh—Arabic: "understanding"; refers to the process of jurisprudence, the techniques for determining the scope of rulings of Islamic law.

Fornication—unlawful sexual intercourse, usually pre- or extramarital sex.

Four beginnings/ four sprouts/ four seedlings—the four aspects of human nature determined by **Mencius**: (1) tendencies to feel compassion; (2) sense of shame; (3) deference to parents; (4) preferences for one thing over another; if cultivated, they will develop into the four virtues of benevolence, righteousness, propriety, and wisdom.

Fuqaha—plural of *faqih*, jurists in the early schools of **fiqh** or Islamic legal interpretation.

Gallup—city in northwestern New Mexico.

Gambia, The—republic in West Africa.

Genesis, book of—Greek: "birth" or "origin"; the first book of the Hebrew Bible/Old Testament; it opens with the creation of the world and goes on to narrate the establishment of the nation of Israel and the early history of the Israelite people.

Genital infibulation—the most drastic form of female circumcision in which the inner lips of the vulva are cut off, then the outer lips, then the clitoris, and then the sides of the crotch are sewn up.

Genkan—Japanese: "entryway"; the entrance to a Japanese home where both family members and guests remove their street shoes before proceeding farther into the house.

Genocide—the destruction of an entire race.

Gentile—anyone who is not a Jew.

Get—Jewish divorce decree.

GIFT—gamete intrafallopian transfer.

Gospels—the four books (Matthew, Mark, Luke, and John) of the Christian **New Testament** which narrate the earthly ministry, teaching, death, and resurrection of **Jesus** Christ.

Grace—for Christians, a gift of God, given through the Holy **Spirit**, which allows human beings to participate more fully in God's presence.

Greek Orthodox—the Church of Greece; part of the Orthodox Catholic or Eastern Orthodox Church which is one of the three major branches of Christianity.

Guardian ad litem—individual appointed by the court to look after the best interest of a minor or person deemed legally incompetent.

Guernica—a 1937 painting by Pablo Picasso inspired by the bombing of Guernica, Spain in that same year.

Hacienda—a large estate or plantation.

Hadith—reports of the sayings and actions attributed to the prophet **Muhammad.**

Halakhah—the Judaic legal code.

Hanafi school of fiqh—one of the four **Sunni** schools of Islamic law. The founder of this school was **Abu Hanifah** d. 767 CE.

Hanbali school of fiqh—the school of legal thought developed by Ahmad ibn al-Hanbal d. 855 CE.

Hastings, battle of—(1066) battle in Hastings, England, in which the English were defeated by **William of Normandy** and the course of English history was changed.

Hausa—people found chiefly in northwestern Nigeria and southern Niger; the largest ethnic group in the area.

Hebrew Bible—a collection of books, traditionally called **Tanakh** by Jews and the Old Testament by Christians, which are held sacred by both religions. The term is often used today by Christians in preference to "Old Testament" because the latter term seems to imply that the Old Testament has been replaced by the **New Testament**. It begins with the **Torah** (the first book of which is **Genesis**), which is followed by the books of the prophets and concluded by The Writings.

Hectares—10,000 meters or 2.47 acres.

Hinoki—Japanese cypress tree.

HMO—Health Maintenance Organization.

Hokkaido—northernmost of the four islands making up Japan.

"Hola, Juanito, como estas? Y su familia?"—Spanish: "Hello, Juanito, how are you? And your family?"

Homo faber—tool-making man.

Homo laborans—working man.

Hosea—first of the twelve "minor prophets" in the books of the Hebrew Bible/Old Testament.

Hua yen—school of Buddhism founded in China in the late sixth or early seventh century by Fa- Shun and systematized in the seventh century by **Fa-Tsang**; it taught that all phenomena are related and that every being possesses the "**buddha**-nature" within.

Hymenotomy—the membrane rupturing of the hymen that occurs at the time of a woman's first intercourse; also **artificial defloration**.

Hypertension—abnormally high blood pressure.

Ibadan—capital city of Oyo state, Nigeria; second-largest city in Nigeria.

ICPD—International Conference on Population and Development.

ICU—Intensive Care Unit.

'illa—the reason or rationale behind a pronouncement of the Qur'an or the *sunna*.

Imam—Arabic: "leader"; in Islam this may refer to a leader of prayers, the founder of a legal school, or a political chief.

Indirect employers—states, unions, international agencies, financial institutions, etc., who make decisions regarding levels and conditions of employment.

INS—Immigration and Naturalization Service, United States.

Integral human development—cornerstone principle to Roman Catholic tradition which insists that development is not merely economic but affects all aspects of the human.

Internal forum solution—settling moral questions not in the legal or institutional **external forums** but in the internal forum of good **conscience** and good faith.

In vitro fertilization—fertilization of the human ovum outside the womb by mechanical means.

Iquitos—Amazon River port in northeastern Peru.

Isaac—in the book of **Genesis**, the son of **Abraham**, given by **Yahweh** to Abraham and his wife Sarah although Sarah was past the age of childbearing; Isaac is the second patriarch of the nation of Israel.

Ishmael—in the book of **Genesis**, the son of **Abraham** by his concubine Hagar; Ishmael was later banished to wander the desert with his mother and is traditionally regarded as the ancestor of certain tribes of desert peoples.

IUD—intrauterine device; an object implanted in the uterus to prevent conception.

IVF—**in vitro fertilization.**

Jacob—in the book of **Genesis**, the son of **Isaac**; Jacob was given the name "Israel" after wrestling with an angel; he is the third patriarch and the traditional ancestor of the people of Israel.

Jeepney—in the Philippines, a small bus, or jitney, that has been converted from a jeep.

Jesus—Jesus Christ, the focal point of the Christian faith. Christians believe that he is the Son of God and the second person of the Trinity, which includes Father, Son, and Holy **Spirit**, that he was crucified, died, and was buried, and then rose on the third day after his death. The story of Jesus is described in the **Gospels.**

Jihad—Arabic: "struggle in the path of God"; may be an individual's spiritual struggle against ego or negative traits, material or personal sacrifice for religious causes, or Islamically justified war.

John the Baptist—in the **Gospels**, the prophet who prepared the way for the coming of **Jesus.**

Juku—Japanese: "cram school"; where Japanese students prepare for the national exams.

Kaolack—town in west-central Senegal.

Karakami—paper-paneled sliding door common in traditional Japanese architecture.

Karet—Hebrew: "cut off"; to be excised from the covenant community.

Karma—Sanskrit: "deed"; in Hinduism and Buddhism, a principle which holds that individuals determine their own being through the actions of their past and present lives.

Karo, Joseph—(1488–1575 CE) Spanish-born author of the last great code of Jewish law, the *Bet Josef* which in condensed form is known as the **Shulhan 'aruch.**

Karuna—compassion, one of the leading principles of Buddhist ethics.

Ketubah—in Judaism, a marriage contract.

Khafid—in Islam, term for female circumcision.

Khalifa—Arabic: "delegate, deputy, or vicegerent"; may refer to a Muslim political leader or more generally to God's designation of all humans as representatives or vicegerents of **Allah.**

Khitan—Arabic term for circumcision, whether male or female.

Kirkuk—city in northeastern Iraq.

Klal-yisrael—Jewish unity, community unity.

Kristallnacht—German: "night of glass"; the night of November 9–10, 1938, a night of German violence against Jewish persons and property, called *Kristallnacht* because of the large-scale smashing of windows in Jewish-owned shops.

Kurdish Front—a group fighting for an independent **Kurdistan**.

Kurdistan—land of the **Kurds**; contiguous areas of Iraq, Iran, and Turkey where the Kurdish population is concentrated.

Kurds—an ethnic group of people concentrated in **Kurdistan** who speak a distinct language, are **Sunni** Muslims, have a strong clan structure, and have their own costume, music, and dance; supposed to be the fourth largest ethnic and linguistic group in the Middle East.

Kyoiku mama—Japanese: "education mother"; a mother who devotes her time to seeing her children through the Japanese national exams.

Laissez-faire policy—French: "allow to do"; policy of minimal government interference in the economic affairs of individuals and of society.

Laity—collective term for those who are not members of the clergy.

Lakota Sioux—one of the three main divisions of the Sioux, a North American Plains Indian confederation of peoples; the Lakota, or *Teton*, were the "Western Sioux."

Landless movement—in Brazil, the struggle of poor migrants, to be allowed access to some of the vast tracts of land which lie, often unused, in the hands of only a few owners.

Laodicea—ancient city in Asia Minor which was the site of one of the **ecumenical councils**.

Le bon Dieu—French: "the good God."

Levirate marriage—biblical obligation for a Jewish widow to marry her brother-in-law if her husband dies without leaving children.

Madhabs—Arabic: an Islamic legal school. These schools, which tend to be dispersed in regional patterns, follow slightly different interpretations of Islamic law, especially in matters of ritual practice.

Maghrib—the northwest of Africa from Libya west through Morocco.

Mahayana—one of the major Buddhist traditions, the one most widely adhered to in China, Korea, Japan, and Tibet.

Maitri—loving kindness, considered by Buddhists to be one of the most virtuous attitudes toward sentient beings.

Maliki school of fiqh—the school of Islamic legal thought developed by Malik bin Anas (712–795 CE).

Marxist—follower of Marxism, a doctrine developed by Karl Marx and Friedrich Engels in the mid-nineteenth century that called for the end of class divisions so that all people, including workers, could share equally in the product of labor.

Menarche—the beginning of the menstrual function; the first menstrual period of a female.

Mencius—(c. 371–289 BCE) revered as the "second sage" of the **Confucian** heritage, Mencius said that all people are innately good and should cultivate themselves for the service of heaven.

Michelangelo's David—marble sculpture in Florence, Italy, of the biblical figure David which was sculpted from 1501–1504 by Italian Renaissance artist Michelangelo.

Microenterprises—small-scale economic organizations seldom having more than a few workers.

Migratory resource—air, water, and animals that move from one geographical location to another.

Montana vs. The United States—1981 United States Supreme Court case in which the court decided that under some specific conditions tribes may retain inherent power to exercise civil authority over the conduct of non-Indians on **fee lands**.

Moredet—Hebrew: "rebellious woman."

Mosaic Law—moral and ritual prescriptions for the nation of Israel which were given by **Yahweh** to Moses. These commandments—traditionally 613 in number—form the bulk of the **Torah**. Among them the Ten **Commandments** have pride of place.

Mosul—city in northwestern Iraq.

Motility—quality of being capable of spontaneous movement.

MST—Movement of the Landless; Brazilian land reform movement of the late 1980s and 1990s.

Mudita—empathetic joy, considered by Buddhists to be one of the most virtuous attitudes toward sentient beings.

Mufti—Arabic: a scholar qualified to give a **fatwa** or Islamic legal opinion.

Muhammad—prophet or messenger of **Allah** and founder of Islam. In the early seventh century Muhammad received a vision telling him he was Allah's messenger, and for the rest of his life he received revelations from Allah, which were later gathered into the **Qur'an**.

Mullahs—Muslims trained in traditional religious law and doctrine and usually holding an official post.

MVA—Manual Vacuum Aspiration; the most common method of induced abortion.

New Testament—the second part of the Christian Bible, comprised of the **Gospels,** the letters of **Paul,** and other books written by the followers of **Jesus.**

NGO—Nongovernmental Organization, often privately funded social service agencies.

Nicea—ancient city in Asia Minor which was the site of the first **ecumenical council,** Nicea I.

Nikkei—the stock exchange of Japan.

Nirvana—the Buddhist term for the state of enlightenment that transcends the limitations of this world through complete awakening to the nature of reality

Nürnberg trials—series of trials held in 1945–1946 in Nürnberg, Germany, in which former Nazi leaders were tried as war criminals by an international military tribunal.

Objective morality—the view that the morality of an action can be determined by external, objective criterion/a.

Old Testament—a collection of books held sacred by both Jews and Christians, this is the name traditionally given to the first part of the Christian Bible, now sometimes referred to as the **Hebrew Bible**; it begins with the **Torah** (the first book of which is **Genesis**), which is followed by the books of the Prophets and concluded by The Writings.

Ombudsman—impartial official who investigates reported complaints and helps to achieve settlements.

Open-pit mining—one of the most common types of surface mining in which a large pit is formed in the process of extracting a mineral.

Operation Provide Comfort—United States proposed response to securing **Kurds** against future attacks and persecution from Iraq.

Orthodox Jews—those Jews who adhere most strictly to traditional beliefs and practices.

Ottoman Empire, Ottoman Turks—(c. 1300–1918) empire of the Turks, which at its peak in the sixteenth century included much of southeastern Europe, southwestern Asia, and northeastern Africa.

Pakoras—a dish of vegetables fried in chickpea batter common in South Asia.

Para—a northern state in Brazil.

Paschal Mystery—the mystery of the suffering, death, and resurrection of **Jesus** Christ.

Pastoralists—those who raise livestock, especially nomadic herders.

Patriarchy—social organization based on the supremacy of the father in a family, and the calculation of descent and inheritance through the father's side; adj. **patriarchal**; also **patriarchalism**, the act of being patriarchal.

Patriline(al)—tracing descent and kinship connections through the father's side instead of the mother's side.

Paul, Saint or **Apostle**—(born c. 20 CE) Paul was converted from Judaism to Christianity a few years after the resurrection of **Jesus** Christ by an appearance of Christ himself, and later became a great missionary, helping to make Christianity into a worldwide religion. His letters make up a great portion of the **New Testament** and have been tremendously important in developing Christian theology.

Pergonal—a fertility drug.

Pharisees—members of a Jewish sect of the biblical period, noted for their strict observance of the rites and ceremonies of **Mosaic Law** and their insistence on the validity of their own tradition.

PID—pelvic inflammatory disease; a general, acute inflammation of the pelvic cavity in women, caused by bacterial infection of the cervix, uterus, ovaries, or fallopian tubes.

Pikuach nefesh—in Judaism, principle calling for care of the body.

Polygamy—practice of having a number of wives at the same time; adj. **polygamous**.

Potsherd—a piece of broken pottery.

PPO—Preferred Provider Organization; a form of health insurance which allows the insured to choose his or her own healthcare provider.

Pratityasamutpada—in Buddhism, doctrine of interdependence.

Pre-op—procedures done on a patient to prepare him or her for an operation.

Primitive streak—earliest period of life in the womb with neural differentiation.

Prodigal son—prodigal: recklessly extravagant; parable told by **Jesus** in the **Gospel** of Luke about a son who leaves home, squanders his inheritance, and returns, impoverished, to his father's house. He is prepared to re-enter as a servant, but his father welcomes him back with joy.

Promotores—term often used to refer to health promoters who teach basic disease prevention and detection in local communities of Latin America.

Protease inhibitor drugs—drugs that help in combating HIV by preventing the final processing of a number of important HIV proteins carried out by the enzyme protease.

Ptolemy—ancient astronomer whose astronomical system placed the earth at the center of the universe.

Publican—a Jewish tax collector for the ancient Romans.

Pure Land Buddhism—one of the more familiar schools of **Mahayana** Buddhism; pure land refers to a celestial land of spiritual ease.

Quilombo—originally a fortified settlement of fugitive slaves in Brazil.

Qur'an—the holy book of Islam, accepted as the true word of **Allah** as it was revealed to the prophet **Muhammad**; alternate spelling: Koran; adj. **Quranic**.

Rabbi—Hebrew: "master" or "teacher"; a Jew trained and ordained as a religious leader, especially the official leader of a Jewish congregation.

Rabbi Hillel—in the first century BCE, the compiler of "seven norms" for explicating the meaning of biblical passages in ways that will address the needs of new situations.

Rabbinical courts—courts presided over by **rabbis** and governed by Jewish law.

Reform Jews—those who have modified traditional Jewish beliefs, laws, and practices to adapt Judaism to a modern, changing world.

Relativism—the view that ethical truths depend on the individual or group who holds those truths.

Rerum novarum—papal encyclical issued by Pope Leo XIII in 1891, explaining the Roman Catholic position on worker rights and economic justice.

Roe v. Wade—1973 United States Supreme Court decision which legalized abortion.

Rostock—city in northeastern Germany.

RU 486—drug taken orally to induce abortion; named for "Roussel-UCLAF" the drug's French manufacturer and the laboratory serial number 486.

Sabbath—the seventh day of the week, observed from Friday evening to Saturday evening as a day of rest and worship by Jews and some Christians.

Sabi ghair mumayyiz—in Islam, a child who lacks the capacity to distinguish between good and bad.

Sabimumayyiz—in Islam, a child who can easily distinguish between legal and illegal, benevolent and detrimental.

Sabras—native-born Israelis.

Sacrament—a symbolic process through which the members of the Christian church participate in the presence of God by receiving the gift of **grace**. There are seven possible sacraments, including **baptism, eucharist** or **communion**, and marriage.

Samosa—a flaky, stuffed, deep-fried pastry common in South Asia.

Samuel—religious hero in the history of Israel, who was seer, priest, judge, and prophet and whose life is related in the **Hebrew Bible** in the First Book of Samuel.

Sarariiman—Japanese: "salary man"; term for white-collar worker.

Sari—woman's garment of lightweight cloth, draped so that one end forms a skirt and the other a head or shoulder covering commonly worn by South Asian women.

Seljuk sultanates—the reign of the Seljuk Dynasty sultans who were **Sunni** Muslims of Turkish origin who ruled in Mesopotamia and Persia in the eleventh to thirteenth century.

Semitic—relating to those speaking a Semitic language, such as Hebrews and Arabs; sometimes loosely used to apply only to Jews.

Sensus fidei—Latin: "the sense of the faithful."

Serer—a people of western Senegal who speak a language called Serer.

Shabbat—the Jewish **Sabbath**.

Shafi'i school of fiqh—the school of legal thought developed by Muhammad ibn Idris al-Shafi'i (d. 719 CE). Followers of the Shafi'i school are primarily found in Egypt, other parts of the Arab Middle East, and South East Asia (Malaysia and Indonesia).

Shah—title for the currently exiled hereditary ruler of Iran.

Shakyamuni, Buddha—name applied to Siddhartha Guatama, founder of Buddhism.

Shaliakh liqabalah—Hebrew: "messenger of receipt"; one who serves legal notice.

Shari'a—Islamic law.

Shi'i—sect of Islam whose followers assert that the descendants of Ali, cousin and son-in-law of **Muhammad**, should have been his immediate successor, followed by Ali's descendents, the **Imams**, who alone had authority to be political and spiritual leaders.

Shinjuku—the largest district of Tokyo and the city's main retail and entertainment district.

Sh'lom bayit—in Judaism, the principle of household harmony, peace within the family.

Shop steward—a person elected by coworkers in a union shop to represent them in dealing with employers.

Shulhan 'aruch—the condensed form of the code of Jewish Law written by **Joseph Karo**. It is still authoritative for **Orthodox Jews**.

Sitar—an Indian lute with a long neck and a varying number of strings.

Slag—refuse left over from melting down metals.

Smriti—Sanskrit: "newer literature"; in Hinduism, the secondary revelation that includes the great epics of the people of ancient India and of Rama as well as the law books which include explanations of ritual and meditative practices.

Soteriological—having to do with redemption or salvation; in Christianity, that which relates to the doctrine of salvation of humanity through **Jesus** Christ.

Southern Song Dynasty—(960–1279) dynasty that ruled China during one of its most brilliant cultural epochs; only in the South after 1127 .

Spina bifida—an inborn cleft of the vertebral column in which the membranes that surround the spinal cord, and sometimes the spinal cord itself, protrude from the back.

Spirit—the Holy Spirit, the third person of the Christian Trinity (the God of three persons, Father, Son, and Spirit, in one essence).

Sruti—Sanskrit: "scripture"; in Hinduism, refers to the Vedas first composed in the twelfth century BCE.

SSI—Supplemental Security Income; United States government program providing income for the disabled.

Statism—concentration of economic control in the hands of a centralized government.

Stewardship—careful, responsible management of something entrusted to one's care.

Structures of sin—particular conditions, particularly systemic ones, that prevent people from flourishing.

Sublunary world—the earth.

Subsidiarity, principle of—the principle, central to Roman Catholic thought, that it is an injustice, a grave evil, and a disturbance of right order to transfer to a larger collectivity those functions that lesser and/or subordinate bodies are able and capable of undertaking.

Sunna—Arabic: "the way" or "the customary practice"; practices and traditions of the prophet **Muhammad** and the early Muslim community which believers follow. By extension, *sunna* may refer to the practice of male or female circumcision. *Sunna* denotes genital infibulation in certain parts of Africa such as Sudan, while in other parts of the continent such as Egypt it refers to the more moderate forms, such as a **clitoridectomy** or the removal of the clitoral hood.

Sunni Muslims—sect of Islam whose followers make up the majority of Muslims and accept the first four **caliphs** as being the rightful successors of the prophet **Muhammad**; also Sunnite.

Sutra—in Buddhism, texts or scriptures, particularly those regarded as discourses of the **Buddha** or collections of his teachings; also sutta.

Sweat lodge—a hut or lodge heated by steam from water poured on hot stones and used by Native Americans for ritual sweating.

Synagogue—the house of worship for a Jewish congregation.

Syncretic—characterized by the combination of different forms of belief or practice.

Synoptic Gospels—the three **Gospels** (Matthew, Mark, and Luke) which, because of their similarities in content, are thought to have been written from the same basic sources.

T-cell count—T-cells are one of the types of white blood cells which are necessary in helping defend the body against disease. A normal adult human has between 5,000 and 10,000 T-cells, but the count can fall during illness or stress. Getting a T-cell count is a regular process for a person with AIDS.

Tailings pond—pond that is created on a mining site as a place to deposit waste, or "tailings," created by the mining process.

Talaq—divorce pronounced by the husband.

Talmud—collection of ancient rabbinic writings composed of two collections of Jewish oral laws, the Mishnah and the Gemara.

Tanakh—the term traditionally used by Jews to refer to the collection of books which are held to be sacred. It begins with the **Torah** (the first book of which is **Genesis**), which is followed by the books of the prophets and concluded by The Writings.

T'ang Dynasty—(618–907) dynasty that stimulated a cultural and artistic "golden age" in China.

Torah—the first five books of the **Hebrew Bible/Old Testament**. The word means "law, teaching, and instruction." According to tradition, they were given by Israel's God to the prophet Moses. They contain narratives of the early history of humanity and Israel and **commandments** God revealed for the guidance of humankind. These books are also known as "The Pentateuch" or "The Law of Moses."

Treaty lands—lands legally acquired through treaty by both the United States government and Native Americans.

Treblinka, Dachau, Auschwitz, Mauthausen, Maidenek—Nazi concentration camps.

UDR—Rural Democratic Union, a landowner association in Brazil.

Ulama—Islamic religious scholars.

Umayyads—an Islamic Arabic dynasty based in Damascus in 660 CE whose army extended the frontiers of Islam into Asia Minor, India, North Africa, and Spain until their elimination by the **Abbasids** in 750.

Umma—in Islam, the community of believers.

UN, United Nations—international organization, founded in 1945, whose purpose is to maintain peace and security among nations.

Upeksa—equanimity, considered by Buddhists to be one of the most virtuous attitudes toward sentient beings.

Vaso de Leche—Spanish: "glass of milk"; program in Latin America for children and nursing mothers, funded by Social Democratic parties in Europe.

Vatican II—the second Vatican council of the Roman Catholic Church, which took place from 1962–65 and brought reforms including a re-evaluation of many church practices, such as greater participation of the **laity**, renewal of the liturgy, and greater acceptance of other religious traditions.

Vietnamese boat people—refugees who emigrate from Vietnam by boat and land illegally in neighboring countries, seeking asylum.

William of Normandy—(c. 1028–1087 CE) duke of Normandy who conquered the English at the Battle of **Hastings** in 1066 and became king of England; also known as William the Conqueror.

Winters v. United States—1908 United States Supreme Court case in which the court decided that when tribes entered into treaties to create reservations, they implicitly reserved for themselves enough water to fulfill the purposes for which the reservation was created.

Wolof—a Muslim people of Senegal and The Gambia.

Xenophobia—fear or hatred of foreigners.

Yahweh—the God of Israel.

Yarmulke—skullcap worn especially by Orthodox and Conservative Jewish males.

Yoff—airport to the north of **Dakar**, Senegal.

Yoruba(n)—one of the largest ethnic groups of Nigeria, concentrated in the southwest of that country.

Yuan—monetary unit of China.

Yuan Dynasty—(1206–1341) dynasty established in China by Ghengis Khan; first dynasty to make Beijing its capital.

Zagros—mountain range of western Iran.

Contributors

Ismail H. Abdalla is an associate professor in the Department of History at The College of William and Mary. He specializes in Islam in Africa and Islamic medicine and is the author of *Islam, Medicine and Practitioners in Northern Nigeria*. He has written over forty articles that have appeared in the *International Journal of Middle Eastern Studies, The Middle East Journal, Orient, African Studies Review*, and others. He received his Ph.D. from the University of Wisconsin at Madison.

Frances S. Adeney is the Brooks Professor of Religion at University of Southern California School of Religion. Prior to that appointment she was an associate professor of social ethics at Satya Wacana Christian University in Central Java, Indonesia. She holds a Ph.D. in social ethics and sociology of religion from the Graduate Theological Union, Berkeley. Recent publications include "Seeking the Self in a Post-modern Age" in *Insights* and "Citizenship Ethics and Classical Virtue Theory: A Test Case for a Hermeneutical Method" in *Penuntun: Jurnal Teologi dan Gereja*.

Leke Adeofe, a Yoruba, graduated from the University of Ife (now Obafemi Awolowo University) in Ile-Ife, Nigeria, and the University of California, Los Angeles. He is an assistant professor in the Philosophy Department at Howard University. His primary research interests are African and African-American philosophy and philosophy of the mind. He is neither a Christian nor a Muslim.

Ehud Ben-or is an associate professor in the Department of Religion at Dartmouth College. He is trained in both traditional Jewish law and modern philosophy. He is the author of *Worship of the Heart: A Study of Maimonides' Philosophy of Religion*.

Christopher Key Chapple is a professor of theological studies at Loyola Marymount University in Los Angeles. A specialist in the religions of India, he has published several books, including *Karma and Creativity: Nonviolence to Animals, Earth, and Self in Asian Traditions*, and a co-translation of *Patanjali's Yoga*. He is also the editor of *Ecological Prospects: Scientific, Religious, and Aesthetic Perspectives* and of two forthcoming volumes: *Hinduism and Ecology* and *Jainism and Ecology*.

Mitchell Chefitz is rabbi of the Havurah of South Florida, an independent fellowship that creates opportunities for Jewish prayer and learning. He has edited a nationally syndicated Torah column, served as president of the Rabbinical Association of Greater Miami, chairperson of the National Havurah Committee, and serves as adjunct faculty in Jewish studies at Florida International University and the University of Miami.

David Cotter, OSB, is a Benedictine monk at Saint John's Abbey in Collegeville, Minnesota, where he works as an editor for Liturgical Press and teaches at Saint John's University. His doctorate is in Old Testament.

Bahar Davary was born in Tehran, Iran, in 1964. She studied Islamic theology at the University of Tehran and since 1995 has been an adjunct professor of Islam at Catholic University in Washington, DC, where she is completing a Ph.D. in comparative religion in the Department of Religion and Religious Education.

Mohamed Adam El-Sheikh, an American citizen, was born in Sudan in 1945. He has an L.L.B. degree with honors from the faculty of Shari'ah and Law at Umdurman Islamic University and worked as a judge in the Shari'ah Courts in Sudan. He has a master's in Comparative Jurisprudence (M.J.C.) from Howard University, an L.L.M. degree from George Washington University, and a Ph.D. in comparative jurisprudence from Temple University. Currently, he is head of the Islamic Judiciary and Arbitration Council of the Shari'ah Scholars' Association in North America & Canada (SSANA), member of the Fiqh Council of the Islamic Society of North America (ISNA), and Imam and Director of the Islamic Center of Baltimore, Maryland.

Evaz Fanaian was born in Sanghesahr, Iran, where he was trained in the Baha'i faith. He later spent some years in Venezuela as a Baha'i missionary. Having earned B.S. and M.S. degrees in engineering at the University of Missouri, Rolla and Columbia, he has worked as an engineer in Florida and currently lives in Georgia with his wife and three sons. He has traveled extensively for business and religion. His primary interest continues to be teaching and promoting the principles of the Baha'i faith.

Ludger Gaillard, who was born in 1944 and grew up in a family of Protestant and Catholic mixture (his father had emigrated from Belgium), is a Protestant minister in the university town of Göttingen, Germany. He is engaged in ecumenical and intercultural reconciliation efforts and is the regional director of the Evangelical Lutheran Church's Islamic dialogue. He is married and has two adopted children from India.

The Rev. Carol J. Gallagher was ordained an Episcopal priest in 1990 and holds a Master of Divinity degree from Episcopal Divinity School (EDS) and a Master of Theology degree from Princeton Seminary. She currently serves as the Rector of Saint Anne's Church, Middletown, Delaware. She is married to Mark Gallagher and they have three daughters, ages twenty, fifteen, and ten. A member of the Cherokee nation, she serves on the Episcopal Council of Indian Ministries, co-convened the 1997 Jamestown Covenant Event, and was liturgist for the Celebration of Survival in 1992. She presently serves as Ecumenical Officer on the Executive Committee of Diocesan Council, is a member of the Pilot Congregation in Delaware, and is a member of the alumni board at EDS. Carol commits her time and ministry to anti-racism work, cross-cultural dialogue, women's issues, and Christian education.

Dr. Mary Gendler, a psychologist, photographer, and world traveler, wrote her first article about Jewish feminism in 1970. Her articles have appeared in Jewish journals such as *Response* magazine and *Jewish Heritage* and ORT as well as in several anthologies of Jewish feminist writing. She lives in Andover, Massachusetts, with her husband and has two married daughters and a grandson.

William P. George is an assistant professor of religious studies at Dominican University, River Forest, Illinois. He holds a Ph.D. in ethics and society from the University of Chicago Divinity School, where he wrote his dissertation on the law of the sea. His articles on such topics as gun violence, concern for future generations, and religion and international law have appeared in the *Annual of the Society of Christian Ethics*, the *Heythrop Journal*, the *Christian Century*, and elsewhere. His current research and writing centers on Christian theology and international law.

Ronald M. Green is the Cohen Professor of Ethics and Director of the Ethics Institute at Dartmouth College. He has published in many fields of applied ethics, including business ethics and bioethics. His most recent book is *The Ethical Manager*.

Christine E. Gudorf is professor of religious ethics in the Religious Studies Department of Florida International University, following fifteen years at Xavier University in Cincinnati. She has written books and articles in religious ethics, feminism, and development ethics. Her last book was *Body, Sex, and Pleasure: Reconstructing Christian Sexual Ethics*. She is working on a volume on postmodernity's challenge to religious social ethics.

Stanley Samuel Harakas is the Archbishop Iakovos Professor of Orthodox Theology, Emeritus at Holy Cross Greek Orthodox School of Theology in Brookline, Massachusetts. Among his publications are *Living the Faith: The Praxis of Eastern Orthodox Ethics, Toward Transfigured Life: The Theoria of Eastern Orthodox Ethics, Health and Medicine in the Eastern Orthodox Tradition: Faith, Liturgy, and Wholeness*, and *Contemporary Moral Issues Facing the Orthodox Christian*.

Edeltraud Harzer Clear teaches Sanskrit and Hindi as well as religious traditions and liituratures of India. At present, she is a visiting scholar in the Department of Asian Studies, University of Texas at Austin. Her articles have appeared in scholarly journals and encyclopedias. Her first book on Indian philosophy is forthcoming.

Marcia K. Hermansen is a professor of Islamic Studies at Loyola University Chicago. She graduated from the University of Chicago and lived and studied for extended periods in Egypt, Iran, India, and Pakistan. Her research interests are Islamic thought, Islam in South Asia, women in Islam, Islamic mysticism (Sufism), and Islam in North America. She is an active member of the Chicago Islamic community.

Diego Irarrázaval has been the Director of the Instituto de Estudios Aymaras in Chucuito, Peru, since 1981. He is the author of *Religion del pobre liberación* (1978), *Rito y pensar cristiano* (1993), and *Cultura y fe latinoamericanas* (1994). Involved in justice and peace issues since the 1960s, he understands himself as a collaborator with indigenous peoples in their theological agenda.

Charles B. Jones is an assistant professor of religion and religious studies at The Catholic University of America. He holds the Master of Theological Studies degree from Duke University Divinity School and has a Ph.D. from the University of Virginia. His dissertation, "Buddhism in Taiwan: A Historical Survey," is forthcoming. He spent three years in Taiwan doing research and studying Chinese.

Rebecca J. Manring is a visiting assistant professor in religious studies at Indiana University. She teaches Sanskrit, Hindi, and literatures of India in the new India Studies program there and also teaches Introduction to Religions of the East. She holds a Ph.D. from the University of Washington. She has published articles on Gaudiya Vaisnava hagiography in the *International Journal of Hindu Studies and the Journal of Vaishnava Studies*.

David McMahan is a visiting assistant professor in the Department of Religion at the University of Vermont in Burlington. He holds a Ph.D. in religious studies from the University of California, Santa Barbara, and specializes in Buddhism and South Asian religions.

Diane M. Millis received her Ph.D. in family studies and human development from the University of Minnesota. She currently teaches spirituality of marriage and the family at the College of Saint Benedict/St. John's University in Collegeville, Minnesota. In addition to writing and teaching, she leads retreats on family spirituality.

The Rev. Dr. Ronald Y. Nakasone, an ordained priest in the Honpa Honganji Sect of Pure Land Buddhism, was born and raised in Hawaii. He holds an M.A. degree in Buddhist studies from Ryukoku University, Kyoto, Japan, and a Ph.D. in Buddhist studies from University of Wisconsin-Madison. He is a member of the core doctoral faculty at the Graduate Theological Union. He is author of *Ethics of Enlightenment: Sermons and Essays in Search of a Buddhist Ethic* and edited *Reflections on the Okinawan Experience: Essays Commemorating 100 Years of Okinawan Immigration.* He has also ministered at the San Jose Buddhist Church and the Southern Alameda County Buddhist Temple, Union City, California.

Michael J. Naughton is an associate professor at the University of St. Thomas, where he holds a joint appointment in the theology and management departments and is the director of the Institute for Christian Social Thought and Management which explores the relevance of the Christian social tradition to management practices and theories. He is currently working on a book entitled *The Integrity of Work: Overcoming the Privatization of Faith in the Modern Corporation.* He received a Ph.D. in theology and society from Marquette University and an M.B.A. from the University of St. Thomas. He is author of *The Good Stewards: Practical Applications of the Papal Vision of Work* and co-editor of *The Dignity of Work: Pope John Paul II Speaks to Managers and Workers.*

Richard K. Payne is dean and associate professor of Japanese Buddhism and religion at the Institute of Buddhist Studies and a member of the core doctoral faculty of the Graduate Theological Union, Berkeley. He is author of *The Tantric Ritual of Japan,* editor of *Re-Visioning "Kamakura" Buddhism,* and co-editor together with James Foard and Michael Solomon of *The Pure Land Tradition: History and Development.* His research is currently directed toward the creation of a genealogy of the *homa* and the development of a cognitive theory of ritual. He has a Ph.D. in history and phenomenology of religion from Graduate Theological Union, Berkeley.

Gregory Pope has been a pastor in the Bethel Baptist Church in Ft. Lauderdale, Florida, for almost twenty years. He is also the assistant dean of the Congress of Christian Education of Seaboard Baptist Association of the National Baptist Convention. Rev. Pope earned both a B.A. degree and an M.A. degree in religious studies from Florida International University. His interests are in liberation theology and the intersection of black theology with the social needs and situation of the black community.

Terry Rey has studied in universities in Australia, Germany, and Zaire, where he also worked as a Peace Corps volunteer. He holds a Ph.D. in religion from Temple University. A former professor of sociology of religion at l'Université d'Etat d'Haiti in Port-au-Prince where he also served as director of the Human Rights Fund, he is now assistant professor of African and Caribbean religions at Florida International University in Miami.

Adam Silverman is a Conservative Jew, fluent in Hebrew and Arabic, who has studied Judaism in the United States and Israel. He holds an American master's degree in comparative religion, a British master's degree in religion and politics, and is a Ph.D. candidate in religion and terrorism at the University of Florida. His chief interest is in the impact of religion on social and political behavior, on which topic he has published and delivered papers at professional academic conferences in various social science disciplines.

Vesna A. Wallace is a lecturer in the Department of Religious Studies at the University of California, Santa Barbara. She teaches the Sanskrit language and courses in Buddhism. Her current research focuses on Indian Tantric Buddhism. Her forthcoming book is *The Inner Kalachakratantra: A Buddhist Tantric View of the Individual.*

Regina Wentzel Wolfe is an assistant professor of theology and holds a joint appointment in the Department of Theology at the College of Saint Benedict and in the School of Theology/Seminary, St. John's University, Collegeville, Minnesota. Born in the United States, she has lived out of the country for twenty-three years, primarily in Europe and Asia. She has a B.S.B.A. from the School of Business, Georgetown University, an M.T.S from Loyola University Chicago, and a Ph.D. from King's College, University of London. Her interests are in the areas of economic justice and organizational ethics.

Of Related Interest

Christan Ethics
A Case Method Approach (2nd edition)
Robert L. Stivers, Christine E. Gudorf,
Alice Frazer Evans, Robert A. Evans
ISBN 0-88344-608-1

A widely used textbook that includes 16 cases in timely
and sensitive areas such as human sexuality, assisted
suicide, land reform, and business practices. Each case
includes a commentary and suggested resources for
further reading.

"An outstanding educational tool [for] undergraduates to
seminary ethics courses."
— *Lisa Sowle Cahill, Boston College*

Justice and Peace
A Christian Primer
J. Milburn Thompson
ISBN 1-57075-141-2

An introductory college text that reviews the complex
challenges of the world today, and the role of ethics in the
face of rapid globalization.

Please support your local bookstore, or call 1-800-258-5838.
For a free catalogue, please write us at
Orbis Books, Box 308
Maryknoll NY 10545-0308
or visit our website at www.orbisbooks.com

Thank you for reading *Ethics and World Religions*.
We hope you enjoyed it.